Thunder in the Mountains

This Large Print Book carries the
Seal of Approval of N.A.V.H.

THUNDER IN THE MOUNTAINS

CHIEF JOSEPH, OLIVER OTIS HOWARD, AND THE NEZ PERCE WAR

DANIEL J. SHARFSTEIN

THORNDIKE PRESS

A part of Gale, a Cengage Company

Farmington Hills, Mich • San Francisco • New York • Waterville, Maine
Meriden, Conn • Mason, Ohio • Chicago

Copyright © 2017 by Daniel J. Sharfstein.
Maps by Bill Keegan.
Thorndike Press, a part of Gale, a Cengage Company.

**LIBRARY OF CONGRESS CIP DATA ON FILE.
CATALOGUING IN PUBLICATION FOR THIS BOOK
IS AVAILABLE FROM THE LIBRARY OF CONGRESS**

ISBN-13: 978-1-4328-6382-1 (hardcover alk. paper)

Published in 2019 by arrangement with W. W. Norton & Company, Inc.

Printed in the United States of America
1 2 3 4 5 6 7 23 22 21 20 19

For Ann, Saul, and Abe

CONTENTS

It is natural . . . to wish to fight. We have always fought our enemies. We now engage in the biggest fight of all — the fight for our survival. If we must do it without weapons, so be it.

— JAMES WELCH,
Fools Crow

The new men of Empire are the ones who believe in fresh starts, new chapters, clean pages; I struggle on with the old story, hoping that before it is finished it will reveal to me why it was that I thought it worth the trouble.

— J. M. COETZEE,
Waiting for the Barbarians

AUTHOR'S NOTE

In 1865, the United States was a beacon of liberty and equality to the world. It had fought a war to abolish human bondage, and Congress was committing to a reconstruction of the South that would enable millions of people who had been held as slaves to claim the rights and privileges of citizenship. The values that constituted the nation had new strength and clarity, animated by a government with an unprecedented capacity to make those values meaningful for every American.

Just thirty-five years later, in 1900, the possibilities of the prior generation had given way to an entirely different consensus. The government at every level was engaged in a vast project of sifting and sorting, of guarding the boundaries of unyielding hereditary privilege. Much of the country was consumed with separating the races — black, white, yellow, red, brown. This segregation was not simply physical or geographical. Citizenship itself was divided and tiered. Being an American had no unified meaning. The very course of a life — whether one could expect to survive infancy, go to school, learn to read, earn a living, and avoid arbitrary arrest, coerced labor, and sudden and violent death — depended on whether one was white or of color, man or woman, rich or poor, native or foreign born. The country's physical borders had become less places of entry than of exclusion, where the nation's integrity — often explicitly defined as its white purity — was guarded, secured, and maintained. At the same time, the United States transformed itself into an imperial power conquering territories from San Juan to Manila, driven by ideas of the white man's burden and a hard, racialized sense of manifest destiny.

The nation's pivot from emancipation to Jim Crow and empire set the terms for more than a century of conflict over the contours and substance of citizenship and the proper size, scope, and purpose of government. Like other stories central to the American experience, it can be told in many ways. We can conceive of it as the defeat of Reconstruction and the triumph of the forces opposing it, the promise of the 1860s curdling in the economic depression of the 1870s, the North's commitment to liberty and equality eclipsed by its own fears and hatreds, as immigrants remade the cities and workers engaged in increasingly bitter struggles against newly mechanized industries controlled by vast corporations. Or we can imagine the transformation occurring at the end of the nineteenth century as less a rejection than an extension of Reconstruction, a national project that above all succeeded in expanding the size and reach of the federal government.

One path from emancipation to empire went through the West. While the Union Army was crushing the Confederacy, soldiers in blue uniforms were massacring Native Americans from Colorado to California and developing elaborate

12

justifications for the bloodshed. In the decades that followed, the West became a proving ground for conquest, the site of a massive exercise of state power to benefit one group at the expense of others. Understanding how a nation forged by Civil War and Reconstruction came to see the West — and how some of the same people who fought for one vision of America became the architects of a seemingly antithetical vision — is crucial to understanding the divisions that define modern America.

Thunder in the Mountains tells a story of the turn in American values and the clash over the nature of government through the lives and battles of two people, a general named Oliver Otis Howard and Chief Joseph, a leader of a band of Nez Perce Indians in the Far Northwest. It explores their continuing legacy through the stories of two men who were intent on remembering them both, a lieutenant named Charles Erskine Scott Wood and a Nez Perce warrior named Yellow Wolf. General Howard and Chief Joseph came from opposite sides of the country, worshipped competing gods, and saw the world — time, space, and history — through different eyes. But after their paths intersected in the mid-1870s, together they came to embody some of the defining struggles of the American experience. Their ideas and actions inspired generations of people to consider who belongs in America, what belonging should mean, and how liberty, equality, and citizenship can assume meaningful forms alongside a government capable of exerting total control over individuals. Their story plumbs the nature of political struggle in the United States and the ability of outsiders and dissenting voices to speak to and move

13

sources of power that can seem remote and impossibly large, omnipresent yet invisible. In many ways we continue to live in their world.

General Howard emerged from the Civil War to play a key role in Reconstruction. As head of the Freedmen's Bureau, the first big federal social welfare agency in American history, he led the government's efforts to support and protect millions of newly freed people; Howard University was named for him. As Reconstruction collapsed, he rejoined the active duty military and was sent to command army forces in the Northwest. Although the nation's values were changing, Howard was determined to stay in government and represent its shifting interests. He did not see his actions in the West as a betrayal of Reconstruction, but he was marked by Reconstruction's failures as much as its successes.

Out west, Howard's most formidable adversary was Joseph, a young leader who took it upon himself to convince the government to let his people keep their ancestral land. In the 1870s, very few Native Americans were regarded as citizens of the United States. They could neither vote nor bring suits in court. While most Americans were governed primarily by the laws of the individual states in which they lived, most Indians were subject to the plenary power — the full, unadulterated might — of the federal government. As a result, when Joseph argued for his land, he had to figure out how his arguments about liberty and equality and property rights — in essence, his people's capacity for citizenship — could reach a government thousands of miles away.

In the summer of 1877, Howard commanded US forces in a small, brutal war against several

14

Nez Perce bands, including Joseph's, that had resisted moving onto a reservation. From the canyon country of north-central Idaho through the peaks and valleys of Montana and Wyoming and up to the Canadian border, Howard led a column of infantry and cavalry and sent orders to other columns of soldiers by telegraph. The people he called the "hostiles" were not simply an enemy military force. Rather, the vast majority of his foes were full families, men, women, children, and the elderly. Joseph was not a war chief; he spent most of his time among noncombatants. Through murders, massacres, and harrowing battles fought across some of the roughest and most remote terrain in the nation, Joseph's war was less a series of military tactics than a cruel lesson on what the government could do to Americans as they tried to live the lives they wanted.

In the years to come, Howard wrote hundreds of pages about the Nez Perce War, and Joseph was widely celebrated, his words recited by schoolchildren, his speeches adapted into poetry. As the nineteenth century gave way to the twentieth, Joseph's critique of what America had become worked its way into a new set of ideas that tried to resurrect government's role as a force for equality while at the same time recognizing civil rights and civil liberties as sharp limits on its power and glorifying personal freedom over any single public morality. From one generation to the next, Joseph's people kept his memory and the memory of the Nez Perce War alive, recognizing the sustaining power of words, how the stories we tell constitute the ways we live and how others let us live.

Thunder in the Mountains attempts to tell Joseph

and Howard's story — the story of their world — through the eyes of the people living in it. It recognizes that even as politics, ideas, economics, and law may transcend any one individual or place, the currents of history are filtered through personal experience, through the routines of everyday life and the rituals of home, family, group, and nation. The people in this book posed questions they did not know the answers to. Most of the time they had little idea how their stories would end. Only by living their lives did they figure out what battles they could win and which wars they would keep fighting.

Nez Perce Country

Columbia River

Walla Walla

Lewiston

Lapwai

Kamiah

Weippe Prairie

Camas Prairie

Clearwater River

Grande

Traditional Nez Perce territory
Post-1855 treaty
Nez Perce Indian Reservation (1863)
Valleys
Bitterroot Mountains

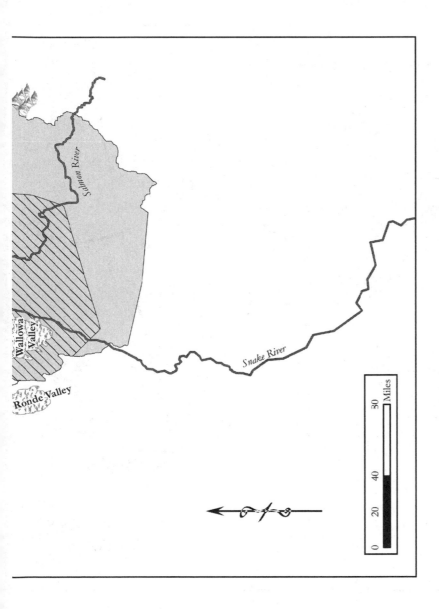

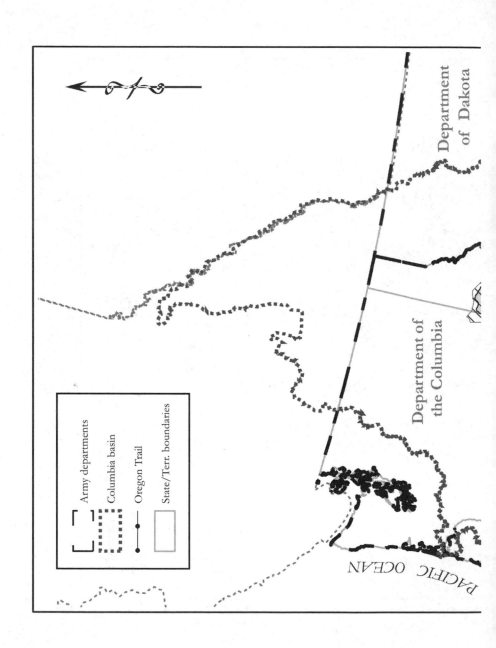

Department of Dakota

Department of the Columbia

PACIFIC OCEAN

Army departments

Columbia basin

Oregon Trail

State/Terr. boundaries

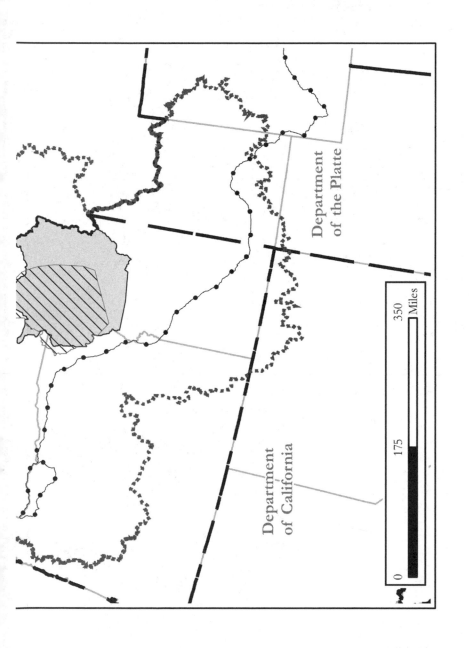

Department of California

Department of the Platte

0   175   350
Miles

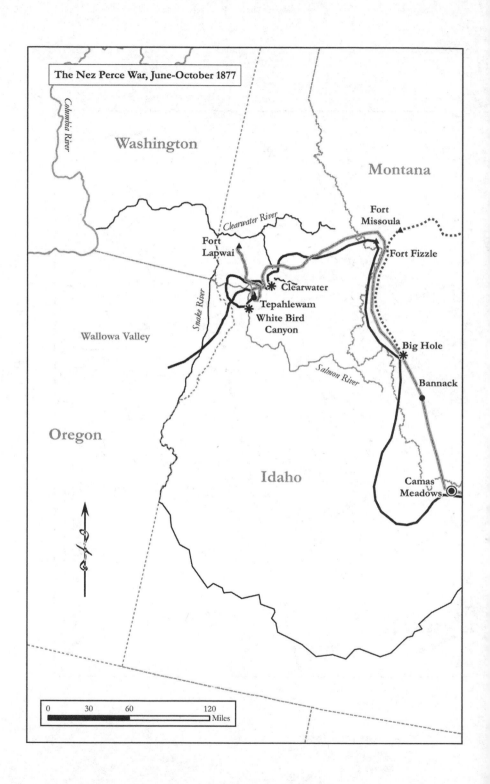

The Nez Perce War, June-October 1877

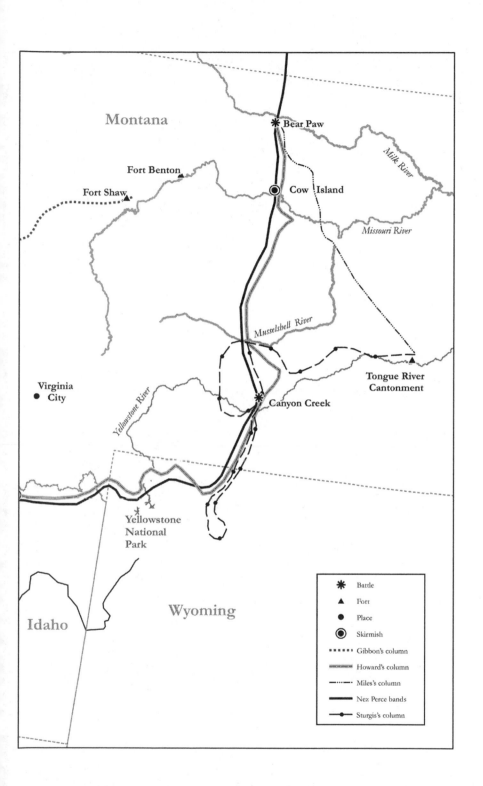

Montana

Fort Benton

Fort Shaw

Bear Paw

Cow Island

Milk River

Missouri River

Musselshell River

Virginia
City

Yellowstone River

Canyon Creek

Tongue River
Cantonment

Yellowstone
National
Park

Idaho

Wyoming

✳	Battle
▲	Fort
●	Place
◉	Skirmish
▪▪▪▪▪▪	Gibbon's column
═══	Howard's column
▪–▪–▪	Miles's column
━━━	Nez Perce bands
●—●—	Sturgis's column

PROLOGUE:
THE DREAMERS

Battle of Fair Oaks —
Seven Pines, Virginia,
June 1, 1862

Bullets cracked and splintered the trees overhead as Oliver Otis Howard readied his men to fight. They gathered along railroad tracks that crossed their position, a rare straight line cutting through dense forest and deep mud ten miles east of Richmond. Howard's New York volunteers — two regiments, about three thousand men — had never been under fire, so he resolved that he and his younger brother and aide-de-camp Charles would take the lead on horseback. The brigadier general mounted his brown horse, only to have it shot from under him within seconds. To keep the soldiers from running away, he screamed for them to drop to the ground. A few minutes later, he rose atop his second animal, large and gray, and shouted, "Forward! March!" Howard was short and thin, his fine features and sharp blue eyes blunted by a long black beard. His voice was high and reedy. But his command gained power as every officer down the long line shouted it in turn. Two words from him, and his men were roaring for battle.

The first advance was easy, straight to the

25

forward Union lines. Even so, rebel fire reached them. A ball punched through Howard's right wrist, leaving a small hole and a blood-soaked cuff. His brother's horse was killed. Charles ran over and tied a handkerchief tight round Howard's wound. Howard could no longer hold his sword, but he and the men kept moving. When they reached the front, he saw no point in stopping. On his say, they scattered an enemy position, saw soldiers in gray fleeing into the woods, then made for the crossroads called Seven Pines. A Union Army campsite the day before, it had been abandoned so quickly under overwhelming attack that the tents were still standing. It was midmorning. The air was already thick and hot. Howard and his men pushed through the tidy array of canvas straight into a waiting rebel line.

Howard could see the enemy kneeling thirty yards away. In their first concussive volley, his gray horse staggered, left leg broken. As each side opened fire, Howard did not notice he had been wounded again. It was hard to see and hard to breathe for all the smoke. Strong hands were pulling him from his mount. A New York lieutenant, barely old enough to shave, was leading him to cover. The junior officer called through the fight, "General, you shall not be killed," then fell dead, in Howard's words, "giving his life for mine." Howard looked at his right elbow. It had been burst into tiny shards of bone.

On the battlefield by a large tree stump, a surgeon bound Howard's shattered arm. Charles came limping over, his thigh mangled, an empty scabbard now a crutch. While his brother lay on a stretcher, draped with a fox-fur robe to prevent shock, Howard insisted on walking to the hospital

26

that had been set up next to his corps commander's headquarters. He fell in with a ragged troop of what he called the "wounded wanderers," and after an excruciating half mile they approached a grand home ringed by large tents and berms of dirt piled over felled trees.

The army surgeons were overwhelmed. Their two field hospitals, with capacities of forty or fifty, each had five hundred patients. Most of the wounded had been hit low, in the abdomen, leg, or thigh, but dozens more had been shot in the head, chest, or face. A doctor recognized Howard, examined his wound, and guided the general to a tiny hut behind the house. Instead of a door, a blanket was hanging over the entrance. Eyes adjusting to the gloom inside, Howard saw an elderly black couple staring back at him, and he understood that he would live or die on a slave's bed. Several more surgeons filed in and examined Howard's elbow, until it was agreed: when the worst of the day's heat passed, the arm would have to be amputated. It was eleven in the morning. He had six hours to wait.

The first time Howard had faced muskets and cannon, a year earlier at Bull Run, he had experienced a jolt of fear, immediately followed by feelings of shame for being weak and afraid. He prayed — "I lifted my soul and my heart," he later wrote — and cried, "Oh God! enable me to do my duty." From that point on, men would speak of Howard's unsettling calm in a fight. Even so, enduring the slow hours leading up to his amputation was far worse than battle. The air inside the hut was humid and musty. It had poured rain two days before, and nothing was completely dry. Doctors were performing minor surgeries outside. Occasionally, someone would remark to a passerby that General Howard was inside the hut, soon to be relieved of his right arm.

Otis Howard knew from long experience that he could overcome any manner of affliction. His beloved father had died in 1840 when he was ten. At twelve he left his mother and brothers to live with an uncle and eventually board at a school forty miles from the family home in Leeds, Maine. Through constant study, he made it to Bowdoin College at age sixteen. After graduating near the top of his class in 1850, he was offered a commission to West Point. From the very first cannon blast that roused him out of bed at five in the morning, the academy's hazing and harsh discipline and seeming celebration of what Howard called "the coarse & profane" were a constant affront. Ostracized and tormented by pedigreed classmates such as Custis Lee, son of the post superintendent Robert E. Lee, Howard worked — and sometimes fought — until he demanded their respect, eventually graduating fourth out of forty-six.

As a junior officer, he had to start over once more, posted at the end of 1856 to bleak and febrile Tampa, Florida. What he experienced there, radical and profound, would define the rest of his life. More than a thousand miles from his pregnant wife Lizzie and his baby boy Guy, with loneliness and melancholy "tugging & burning" in his heart, he went to a Methodist meeting and abruptly experienced a spiritual awakening that left him "trembl[ing] like a leaf." "The choking sensation was gone," he wrote his wife, "& for once I enjoyed present happiness. . . . I was saved through the goodness & mercy of Christ." Barely able to sleep, feeling what he called "a new well spring within me, a joy, a peace & a trusting spirit," Howard became convinced that God "pluck[ed] my feet from the mire & place[d] them on the rock" for a reason. Out of a life of struggle and redemption, he now knew that a greater purpose awaited him. "While, I am humiliated in view of a Being so great, so just & good," he wrote home, "I cannot help rejoicing that He has so honored me, that He has granted me such a big boon." It was like a waking dream.

When the southern states seceded in 1861, the thirty-year-old Howard had been planning to leave the army and go to seminary. Again his path revealed itself: the national call to arms would be his higher calling, blessed by God and nurtured by his constant prayer. He saw the transcendent possibilities of government service. Now he would help realize God's kingdom on earth by devoting himself to the noble cause of Union. Elected colonel of a Maine regiment a month after the bombardment of Fort Sumter, Howard introduced himself to the volunteers and immediately started talking about the Ten Commandments. One of his soldiers wrote in a diary that Howard had "the tone and manner of an itinerant preacher."

Showing a singular, meticulous, and even cheerful devotion to executing his orders, Howard was given command of a brigade before ever facing the enemy. During the war's first year, he spent far more time out of battle than in. At his camp three miles west of Alexandria, Virginia, the struggle for the souls and sobriety of his men came to eclipse the remote military objectives of army command. Moreover, the whole nature of the war seemed to change as men, women, and children appeared in his camp, seeking to escape lives of bondage.

Although a decade earlier Howard's southern rivals at West Point had accused him of being an abolitionist, initially he did not equate the Union cause with slavery's demise. If "slave property" passed through his pickets, Howard assumed that he would follow orders, in his brother Charles's words, "to have nothing to do with such cases." But the reality proved more difficult. In August 1861, as Howard was finishing lunch with a few visitors from Waterville, Maine, a terrified woman ran into his camp. Charles wrote the next day that she was clutching "her babe & a boy about 10"; they admitted they were slaves and begged for freedom. On their heels, however, was a sallow woman, poorly dressed — by Charles's description, "lowlived, ugly tempered, & revolting in appearance" — who demanded her property returned.

At first, Howard reflexively told her "she could have them," but the mother "declared they would not go back." She "cried & besought," Charles wrote. "The slave woman said she would drown herself before she would go back." Howard never forgot the way she "kept pressing her child to her breast and with her large eyes filled with tears continued to look toward me, repeating, 'Oh! my child, my child!' " In the abstract, his orders were, he wrote, "most stringent," but "in the fact of this actuality I was greatly puzzled with the case before me." On the cusp of ordering them returned to slavery, he paused. Overwhelmed by feeling, he looked at the mother and her children and did not see property.

Howard's visitors from Maine, "unqualified abolitionists," urged him to "pay no attention whatever" to his superiors' orders, he wrote. Such insubordination, however, was anathema to him. His entire success in the army — his rise from lieutenant to colonel to brigadier general in a year — had hinged on his being a stickler for the rules. His calling seemed to demand that he serve and embody the great national cause, not stand apart from it. He would not risk his success by converting to abolitionism.

But as he watched the mother weeping with her children, he experienced a smaller revelation — a bureaucrat's awakening: that even the clearest rules had a certain amount of give. A general in Washington might issue an order that seemed unambiguous, but it only gained meaning as enforced, or not, by officers far in the field. Turning to the slave owner, Howard announced "he did not wish to act upon it without further orders." When the white woman grew "exasperated & talked very harshly with coarse language," Howard sent her away. By the next day, he had found a way to follow his orders without betraying his conscience. He said she could claim her slaves but refused her demand of an armed escort, leaving her unable to force them to return to bondage. "I had reluctantly complied with the letter of the law and fancied that to be enough," he wrote. That night, the mother and her children crossed the Potomac and found freedom in Washington.

In the months that followed, people running from slavery kept confronting Howard. They argued with him, jolted him, and gave him a new way of seeing the war. Two weeks before the battle at Seven Pines, he wrote his wife that the army should "arm & train the negroes under intelligent sergeants and corporals" and "encourage fugitives from 'secession.' " Such a policy was not simply an expedient measure "to weaken the enemy," he wrote. It would also "encourage & elevate the black men." Howard was coming to believe that eradicating slavery — turning slaves into citizens — was not only part of God's plan "to humble, disenthral & purify the nation" but also part of the path that had been laid out for him.

Lying in the slave hut, faint from pain and loss of blood, Howard was forced to reckon with another impending moment of transformation. When he stumbled, one of his first reflexes was to reach out with his right hand, yet now he could not steady himself. In the late afternoon, a tall officer limped through the doorway to visit the general — a friendly sight. At twenty-one, Nelson Miles was less than a year removed from a job as a clerk at a crockery store in Boston. After proving himself a devoted student of military tactics, the lieutenant was now one of Howard's trusted aides. Under fire for the first time at Fair Oaks, Miles had been nicked in the heel. The battle was over, and neither side could claim a great victory. Many of the survivors were busy digging mass graves, big enough for ten, twenty, even a hundred bodies.

Miles was at Howard's side at five o'clock when the brigade surgeon came for the general with four large soldiers. They moved him from bed to stretcher. The doctor tied a tourniquet just below his shoulder, then twisted the cloth tighter and tighter. The general never forgot the agony. He was carried to an outdoor area, part operating theater and part abattoir, strewn with amputated arms, legs, hands, and feet. Howard gazed at the pile of gray limbs, useless, leaking, drained. Surgical instruments were soaking in cold, bloody water. He would remember other wounded soldiers, "poor fellows with anxious eyes" waiting their turn for the scalpel and bone saw. He was lifted onto a long table, cushioned and surprisingly comfortable. Miles was holding his right arm, keeping him still. The doctor loosened the tourniquet, soaked a rag with chloroform, and sent Howard into darkness.

La Grande, Oregon, July 4, 1872

Drumrolls trilled and fifes whistled high as the settlers of Oregon's Grande Ronde Valley marched through the dusty streets of La Grande, the Union County seat. After quickly covering the town's few blocks, the celebrants — young and old, country and town — arranged themselves around a platform shaded with willow branches. One man stood under the arbor and delivered a patriotic oration, followed by another who recited the Declaration of Independence. Then it was time for a feast that the ladies of La Grande had spent days preparing. "The tables groaned beneath the loads of viands, spread by gentle women's hands," one visitor remembered of these gatherings. "The reader and the orator of the day would take positions at either end, and the meek chaplain in between, while the bashful country boys would lead up their girls, until the table had been filled."

La Grande had stood for only a decade. Its frame houses, shops, and stables looked fragile and exposed on the prairie. It was still so small that it had no churches; the Methodist and Episcopal congregations and various charismatic itinerants had to pray in a vacant commercial building that bore the sign of a bygone tenant, the O.K. Grocery. Despite the transient feel of the place, its citizens wanted their festivities to be more than a rote observance. They aspired to create a civic tradition, according to the local *Mountain Sentinel,* "to make glorious the natal day of the Republic."

Many of the settlers lived on remote farms and ranches, isolated and alone, some coming from as far as fifty miles away. For them July 4 was an occasion to think about collective enterprise — the nation but also the valley — and for seeing old friends, trading partners, and the people they told stories about. They could shake hands with James Slater, until recently the local prosecutor, known as "solid rather than brilliant," now home on recess while serving as a Democrat in Congress. Just about everyone recognized Alfred Meacham, bald and heavy-browed, who owned the toll road that ran north through the Blue Mountains toward Walla Walla. A prominent local Republican, he had just spent three years as the federal superintendent of Indian affairs in Oregon. Anderson Corden Smith, slight with a lavish beard and a taste for white canvas pants and moccasins, was known as "the man of the mountains," someone who could scale the steepest slopes that surrounded the valley, "cut off a grouse's head with his Henry rifle, or kill a grizzly first shot," the *Mountain Sentinel* boasted. "Superior in all respects to Kit Carson."

If Smith was a local legend, even he was overshadowed by his two guests that day, large men

34

near thirty, both over six feet, broad-shouldered and strong. They were draped in bright blankets and wore shirts and leggings adorned with intricate beadwork. Their hair was combed up from their foreheads. Long side braids, banded and feathered, dropped from shoulder to chest, and between their braids they wore clusters of necklaces. Unlike just about every other man at the picnic, they had smooth faces. Their skin was darker — more coppery, a local might say — than that of the tannest of the farmers. Smith introduced them as brothers, Joseph and Ollokot, leaders of a band of Nez Perce Indians living in the Wallowa, a high valley just over the mountains to the east.

Since the first years of La Grande's existence, chiefs in beaded regalia had been guests at the town's Fourth of July gatherings and occasionally addressed the crowd. Eight years earlier, Joseph and Ollokot's father Tuekakas had joined the Umatilla chief Cut Mouth John at the celebration. While chiefs typically talked of peace and friendship, Tuekakas had bluntly stated to the assembled folk that "he thought it was an injustice for the White men to fence in" areas of the Grande Ronde Valley where Nez Perce women came every year to dig for camas roots. A year after Tuekakas's death, his sons were in La Grande on a different errand.

Joseph and Ollokot stayed mostly quiet during the celebration. But when the meal was finished and the crowd dispersed, they stayed behind for an audience with Congressman Slater and former superintendent Meacham. Smith, who knew several native languages, interpreted. The *Mountain Sentinel* dubbed the impromptu council an "interesting wow wow." Like most of the other chiefs who had spoken at La Grande, Joseph and Ollokot declared they "did not contemplate hostilities" and had always been loyal to the United States — "ever true to the whites," the newspaper reported. But they declared that their father "had never signed away his right to the Wallowa Valley and charged his sons to keep it as a home for them and their people."

Recent events had compelled their presence in La Grande. Smith had been spending the summer bridging the Wallowa River and building a toll road up and down the mountains just beyond it. There was big money in easing the way for settlers to try their luck with new farms in the Wallowa Valley. In early 1872, homesteaders were just starting to make the eastward trek with their herds along Indian trails, piling belongings onto mules or hacking paths through the forests that were wide enough for wagons. Without Smith's road, the mountains forced travelers to take their wagons apart, carry the pieces up thousands of feet, and put them together again.

From the hilltops, the pioneer families — men, women, and children — had what the *Mountain Sentinel* called "one of the grandest sights imaginable." Thick forests and meandering streams, rolling meadows covered in bunchgrass or swaying with more wild hay than anyone could possibly cut — it was what the Grande Ronde Valley had looked like ten years earlier, when the grass was so tall that entire herds of horses and cattle could get lost in it. One man recalled that "as soon as I came to the top of [the] mountain and looked out into the valley I said to myself 'This is where I want to live.' " The settlers felled trees and tied them to the wagons to serve as anchors for the steep ride down. As they entered the Wallowa country, the trees dragged behind them, scoring the earth with coarse wandering lines.

In the spring of 1872, the valley appeared pristine and unoccupied. But as the weather warmed, Joseph and Ollokot's band emerged from the canyons that plunged from the eastern edge of the Wallowa country, where they spent winters with their large horse and cattle herds. Seeing homesteaders on their ancestral land, they realized that what they had long feared was coming to pass. Years before, their father had been one of the first Nez Perce converts to Christianity, described by one admirer as an Indian who "prayed with his heart." Tuekakas initially believed he would raise his family in "the bosom of the visible church on earth," as Presbyterian minister Henry Spalding called the Indians' new faith, and prepare them for lives as farmers near Spalding's mission on Nez Perce land in Idaho. But as settlers began streaming into Nez Perce country, Tuekakas broke from Spalding, renounced his new faith, and retreated with his band back to the Wallowa Valley and the old ways of living — "back to Egypt," one missionary lamented. "My father was the first to see through the schemes of the white men, and he warned his tribe to be careful about trading with them," Joseph would say. "He had sharper eyes than the rest of our people."

Tuekakas, his sons, and their people rejected Christ and committed instead to the sacred power of dream. For decades among the Nez Perce and neighboring tribes, prophets had predicted the arrival of white people and the physical and spiritual catastrophe they would bring. "You ask me to

37

plough the ground! Shall I take a knife and tear my mother's bosom?" one of the holy men would say. "You ask me to dig for stone! Shall I dig under her skin for her bones? . . . You ask me to cut grass and make hay and sell it and be rich like white men! But how dare I cut off my mother's hair?" If all Indians lived according to tradition, the Dreamers preached, the invasion and calamity of the whites would not last. In time, the Indians would once again find themselves alone on the land, and the land would be restored and redeemed, all traces of white destruction swept clean.

When settlers finally appeared in 1872, Joseph and Ollokot's band could have retreated into the hills or gathered their rifles and war clubs, summoned help from other bands, and wiped out the newcomers. Instead, Joseph introduced himself to them. He greeted them warmly and took their hands in his. He bent his head to clear the low doors of their rough cabins. Standing inside, he could fill a small room before folding himself back down to sit in a hard chair. He accepted the food the settlers offered him and smiled and laughed and played games with their children. He offered horses for trade and took turns at a favorite pastime for whites and Nez Perce alike: shooting at targets. All the while, he talked to them, quietly — politely, the settlers thought — in the regional trade language that some of them understood, Chinook Jargon. Charmed by him, many came to describe Joseph as a friend. Yet he never welcomed them to the Wallowa Valley. Instead, he told them calmly, assuredly, and face-to-face that they were trespassing. Joseph was determined that they would see their presence for what it was — an invasion — and he wanted them to know the people who rightfully claimed the land.

When Joseph rode into Smith's camp that June, the mountain man insisted that he had every right to build his road, citing an 1863 treaty that had put the Wallowa Valley in the public domain. As a consequence, the United States General Land Office had surveyed the land and divided it into eleven townships, and homesteaders could formally register claims at a federal office in La Grande before crossing the mountains. Undaunted, Joseph countered that the government had made a mistake and lacked the authority to give away his land. The Nez Perce chiefs who had signed the 1863 treaty did not represent his band, he asserted, and his people had rights that were being violated. Listening to him speak, Smith recognized that Joseph was making more than a moral argument, and it could not be addressed as Indian claims so often were, ignored or bargained away one conversation at a time. Rather, Joseph's case was different: he was casting doubt on the legal basis for all white settlement in the Wallowa Valley, using language and logic that left Smith decidedly uneasy.

Joseph well knew that he was raising questions of law that demanded some formal resolution. He said Smith should stop building the road — and whites should stop settling on his people's land altogether — "until the authorities at Washington could be heard from." But the capital was an impossible distance from Nez Perce country. The Wallowa Valley's new settlers could look at the mountains and canyons and rivers all around them and be forgiven for thinking that even La Grande was dauntingly far. On the edge of the familiar world, the idea of American power — the mechanics of government — blurred. It was hard to tell what Joseph meant when he asked for intervention from "the authorities."

Without any idea about who could weigh the merits of Joseph's claim, Smith invited him and his younger brother Ollokot to La Grande on July 4 because there, at least, they would find some approximation of government power: Congressman Slater and former superintendent Meacham. But on their own Slater and Meacham had no authority to pronounce the brothers' arguments right or wrong and did not pretend to be anything other than the most attenuated agents of the federal government. They declined to issue any formal statement about what they believed would properly resolve the Wallowa dispute; there was no point in doing so. Even if they could reach some consensus about the competing claims to the valley, no one, settler or Indian, had any reason to consider their opinions binding.

Joseph had once spent his days mostly in silence — tending to his herds, tracking prey in the forests, descending into the canyons, crossing rivers and mountains — but the invasion of white settlers had forced him to live a talking life. When he spoke out loud, his words no longer recounted the kinds of stories his people had passed on for thousands of years: about the beginning of time, or the struggles of everyday life, or friendships and conflicts with neighboring tribes. Instead, Joseph voiced his people's responses to the white settlers and the threat that they posed to his band's way of life. And as he forced himself to communicate with people who did not speak his language, he had to develop new perspectives on

40

history, tradition, and justice. It required him to focus on a particular version of the past, one that began in 1805 when Nez Perce Indians first encountered Lewis and Clark on their transcontinental journey, continued through long years of friendship with the United States, but concluded with the warnings Tuekakas had given that "we will never give up [the graves of our fathers] to any man."

Joseph was not the sole authority in his band. Leadership was shared with his brother and among any number of elders, hunters, fishermen, warriors, and Dreamers. In matters that required a collective decision, individuals often remained free to follow their conscience. But Joseph presumed to "speak for his people." The strength of his words, he believed, could keep the peace. With words, he could clarify and redeem his band's claim to the Wallowa Valley. His conversations, eye to eye, would put him in a position of equality with the settlers and show them that his people's rights were deserving of respect. His ideas would reach the heart of American power, transform the whites, and create a new dream for his people. They did not need another warrior. In Joseph's mind, they needed an advocate. "Some of you think an Indian is like a wild animal. This is a great mistake," Joseph would say. "I will tell you all about our people, and then you can judge whether an Indian is a man or not."

41

PART I

PREVIOUS PAGE: The Wallowa Valley, the traditional summer territory of Chief Joseph's band, the place he called "that beautiful valley of winding waters."

CHAPTER 1
A WILLING EXILE

August 1874

It was late afternoon when Otis and Lizzie Howard and their seven children took one last ride through Washington, DC. They went two and a half miles straight south, a short and steady descent from their hilltop house to the Baltimore & Potomac Railroad depot in the heart of the city. Crossing wood-planked Pennsylvania Avenue, they had a strained glimpse at the White House. The Capitol dome, visible through the trees close to their left, was blushing in the low sun. The choking summer heat — the dust, the thick smell of waste and rot — was starting to loosen its grip for the night.

The B&P station was in its final stages of construction, rising in the middle of the National Mall. To some, it was an atrocity, cutting the Capitol building adrift from the rest of the District's public spaces and turning the people's great park into a sooty crisscross of iron track. Others regarded the depot as a beacon of industry and progress, a fitting companion to the Smithsonian Castle nearby. The Gothic clock tower, solid brick trimmed with locally quarried stone, had just been completed. It was an instant monument, flying the flag that had covered President Lincoln's coffin nine years earlier on its slow journey by rail from Washington to Springfield, Illinois.

Railmen and porters, passengers and their friends were all busy preparing for the 5:40 train, voices cutting through the huff and roar of engines, brakes, whistles, and steam. The Howards needed help with their baggage. They were going away for a long time, maybe never to return. And while Otis at forty-two was, according to one observer, "apparently constructed of steel wire," he could only carry so much with his left arm. His right sleeve was rolled up and pinned almost to his shoulder. Otis, Lizzie, and their five youngest children, ages three to fourteen, were heading west. If their sleeping berths were not already prepared on their through-car to Chicago, they would be soon. As the Howards boarded, they bid goodbye to their oldest children Guy and Grace, who were staying behind. After searching the family house one last time, they would journey north to a cousin's shorefront cottage at Marblehead, Massachusetts, then on to Yale and Vassar in September.

The Howards started out of Washington along a path that covered over what had been Tiber Creek and an old canal, soft swampland known in earlier days for being unbearably foul — a competing railroad derided the Baltimore & Potomac as the "Sewer Route." Clear of the city, the train could punch through the night at forty miles per hour. A good night's sleep, and the Howards would be past Pittsburgh and into Ohio. By the next evening, Chicago would be in sight.

On board it was easy to forget that nearly eight hundred miles — mountains, plateau, and plains — separated Washington and Chicago. Many passengers only experienced the cities at each end of their journey as well as the train itself, a long quaking village of strangers. The places in between were a blur filtered through a grimy window, forgotten as passengers slept or read. One could imagine that the space between Chicago and Washington was inconsequential, that one city was merely an extension of the other.

The Howards, by contrast, celebrated the distance. By many measures it should have been difficult to leave. They had spent nine years in Washington. Their children had grown up there, and the three little ones had known it as their only home. A large crowd of friends had attended a farewell supper a couple of nights earlier. They could not imagine life in Washington without General Oliver Otis Howard and his family. Otis had built their community; it was what he had been called to the capital to do in the spring of 1865. After commanding Sherman's right flank in the March to the Sea and Carolinas Campaign, he had been appointed head of the Bureau of Refugees, Freedmen, and Abandoned Lands, a new government agency responsible for making citizens out of some four million people who had been held as slaves. At the same time that he managed the bureau, he helped found the politically powerful First Congregational Church, a bastion of New England radicals, and opened its doors to people of color. He had also been the guiding force in creating a university in Washington that would train a new generation of doctors, lawyers, teachers, and ministers — black and white, women and men — for a new, more hopeful nation. The institution had been named in his honor: Howard University. Thousands of people owed their jobs to General Howard, and thousands more credited him with something even greater — their health, education, spiritual well-being, sobriety, the very contours of their lives as free people.

Yet if Howard's friends and neighbors celebrated his role in Reconstruction, many more vilified him for it. From the beginning his political enemies had accused him of mismanaging the Freedmen's Bureau, and Howard spent years defending himself from increasingly fraught and embarrassing corruption inquiries. By 1874, the bureau no longer existed, and the promise of Reconstruction was all but dead. The District of Columbia, the first slave territory to grant people of color the right to vote, had just become the first to take it away. In the upcoming congressional election, the Democrats — the party of slavery and secession — were poised to take control of the House of Representatives for the first time since before the war. Despite their deep ties to the place, when the Howards were presented with the opportunity to leave Washington, they took it.

The Howards held tickets to ride more than twenty-eight hundred miles to San Francisco. From there they still would have another seven hundred to go — north by steamer from San Francisco Bay through the Golden Gate to the Pacific, up the California and Oregon coast to the mouth of the Columbia, across the treacherous bar where the river swells and buckles into the ocean, and then upstream to the Willamette River. Oliver Otis Howard was carrying orders to proceed to tiny Portland and assume command of the army's Department of the Columbia, with responsibility for Oregon, Washington Territory,

Idaho Territory, and the newly acquired Alaska. After nearly a decade leading and answering for the Freedmen's Bureau, Howard had rejoined the active-duty military in early July 1874 and been immediately posted to the Northwest. He was not just leaving Washington. He was going about as far as a traveler could go without crossing an international boundary. Howard recognized the assignment for what it was — a friend described it as an "exile."

Once they learned of their destination, the Howards had barely a month to sort through their possessions and pack. What books would make the journey, and what would stay behind? Which piano would they ship, and which would they sell? What would it cost to put a horse or two on the train? They considered how to pack the velocipede that fourteen-year-old Jamie enjoyed pedaling around town. They decided they could keep their puppy but had to give away eleven-year-old Chauncey's pet rabbit. Otis crammed two decades of official papers into four large boxes. "There is plenty to do & talk about," he wrote as the family closed house and business "into as compact shape as possible"; "it has already brightened us all." They left town so quickly that they nearly forgot to take an inventory of their freight. It was less a departure than an escape. Even their closest friends admitted it was for the best.

Few travelers found the train to Chicago — the first leg of the journey west — relaxing or enjoyable. One writer promoting western travel described the route as "tedium and weariness, dust and inconvenience." The destination was hardly any better. Much of Chicago was still in ruins three years after the "Great Fire" had destroyed the city's center. Nevertheless, its unyielding efforts to rebuild generated an optimistic energy. The sense that something great was rising from the ashes would have appealed to Otis Howard. It prompted at least one new arrival at the time to proclaim right on the train platform, "This is the place for me!"

Chicago was more than a thousand miles from where Otis and Lizzie had grown up in Maine, but the few days the family spent in the area felt like a homecoming. Otis's three younger brothers had gone west for faith and fortune. The first stop was Glencoe, just north of Chicago, where Otis's brother Charles had built a mansion for his wife and their three children, all under the age of six. With a total of eight boys and girls shouting through the house, Otis and Charles may have had neither time nor inclination to contemplate the terrible things they had seen together. But the memory of the war was never fully erased from their lives. Charles's mansion was named Fair Oaks not for the towering trees outside but for the 1862 battle where he took a bullet in the thigh and Otis lost his right arm. After serving as his brother's aide in war and at the Freedman's Bureau, he moved to Chicago in 1868 to oversee projects across the South for one of the bureau's most important partners, the American Missionary Association, an abolitionist society that had established hundreds of schools for the freedpeople after the war. Then Charles entered the world of business, buying a controlling stake in a Congregationalist newspaper in 1872.

There was plenty for the brothers and their wives to talk about. Together after years of corresponding, they could marvel and despair at the human frailty of their heroes. Otis had written Charles regularly with accounts of his ill treatment in President Grant's Washington. And Charles could not stop printing stories in his paper about the great abolitionist minister Henry Ward Beecher's "supreme indiscretion" with his congregant Mrs. Elizabeth Tilton, a scandal so deliciously appalling that the *Chicago Tribune* devoted five entire columns of its front page to it while the Howards were visiting. The Howards had been living in a world of disappointment and failure, yet seeing Uncle Charlie, Aunt Katie, and the cousins transported them from their troubles.

After a couple of days, it was time to move on: a hundred miles west to Princeton, Illinois, where Otis's brother Rowland had been preaching at the First Congregational Church since 1870. In his short time in Princeton, Rowland had lost one wife to illness and married another. Otis's family would finally meet her. They could also see Otis's mother, Eliza Gilmore, who was staying with Rowland and his family for the time being. The Howards' visit would have to be a short one. Perhaps it would be Eliza's last glimpse of her grandchildren, given her age and how far the family still had to go. They left her with a collection of photographs to remember them by.

The Howards kept traveling west, but managed to remain within the comforting embrace of family. A few hours outside Princeton, they crossed the Mississippi River into Iowa on a narrow mile-long bridge. In 1874, enormous log rafts — the last of the great northern forests — were always floating below. It was several hours more to Cedar Rapids, where Howard's half-brother Dellie —

short for Rodelphus — had one of the city's leading law practices. An insistent advocate, he wrote
Otis that he had to stop for a proper visit, not "20
minutes at the depot while you are hurriedly eating your supper at 8 o'clock in the evening when
you both and your children are tired and hungry
and the children getting sleepy and ready to go to
bed." Dellie wanted his "little people" — Eliza,
Ralph, and Deane — to have something more
than just a "vague and unsatisfactory" memory of
their famous uncle. "My children are nothing
wonderful perhaps but they are mine," he wrote,
"and I want them to know yours so you must plan
some way to . . . spend some time with us." The
Howards stayed long enough to receive a call from
a large delegation of the city's black residents.

From Cedar Rapids, the Chicago & Northwestern — damned with faint praise by a travel guide
as "the best of the Iowa railroads" — spent most
of a day roaring through acres of farmland. At
Council Bluffs, where the Missouri River cut a
muddy gash through the flatlands, the train
reached a vast steaming rail yard. There the
Howards walked to a small "Dummy Train" that
took them across an enormous iron span. The
Union Pacific Railroad Bridge was, according to
one guide, a "mechanical wonder [that] fills every
traveler with a sense of awe and majesty." Just two
years old, it was not graceful so much as relentless — a square trestled cage, a matter-of-fact
statement that nothing was impossible anymore.
With the city of Omaha rising up from the Missouri's west bank like so much factory smoke, the
bridge seemed to mark the end of one world and
the beginning of another. Now the Howards' real
travels could begin.

■ ■ ■ ■

The stout brick Union Pacific depot in Omaha had its own gravitational pull. From all over the country — all over the world — people gathered here for the great journey west. It was a scene of stark chaos. Passengers begged for clerks to attach brass claim checks to their trunks and portmanteaus before the railroad's infamous "baggage-smashers" hurled them on board. People demanded spots on the Pullman sleeping cars and wept upon hearing there was no room until the next day's train. Men and women wandered in the crowd — drunk, sober, hopeful, desperate, cursing and praying, flush with poker winnings, fleeced by confidence men. Travelers from the East Coast commented on how strange the people waiting for the train in Omaha seemed compared to everyone they had encountered in the thousand-plus miles along the way. "Here the phases of human life are indeed spread out with a lavish hand," one reporter wrote. "Women, children, aged grandfathers, border ruffians, dogs, gambling sharps, peripatetic vendors of unconsidered trifles, soldiers, thieves and pickpockets, are jumbled together in a heterogeneous mass." Even the air felt different in Omaha, insistently dry — a hint of what was to come.

The crush and confusion did little to shake Otis Howard's abiding sense that God's Providence was sending him in the right direction. At Omaha his family was joined for the journey west by the general's two aides and a civilian clerk, their wives, and their children: a party of nineteen sprawled across plush divans, in "quite complete possession of a railway car," Howard wrote. Their home for the next five days was a familiar world — close, warm, joyful — within the more attenuated collection of strangers on the train. During the day the car was a wood-paneled parlor, brightened with stripes of sunlight, softened with the slack drape of heavy tapestry. At night it was a bedroom that slept twenty-four, with the upper berths folding down from the ceiling and lower berths made up over the seating. The passengers could say their evening prayers by the glow of gas chandeliers overhead. After all the effort it had taken to get to this point — dozens of stops, multiple transfers, hours endured in boredom or in conversation with strangers, the struggle required just to get on board in Omaha — it could be hard to believe that the Union Pacific's transcontinental journey began like any other train's. A guide described it simply: "The bell rings, the whistle shrieks, and off you go."

Five years earlier, on May 10, 1869, former California governor turned railroad baron Leland Stanford wielded a silver hammer at Promontory Summit, Utah, and drove the rail spike that signified the joining of the Union Pacific and Central Pacific Railroads in the desert north of the Great Salt Lake. News of America's first transcontinental railroad was telegraphed east with the simple word "Done." Across the nation brass bands played, fireworks crackled, church bells pealed, ministers intoned prayers of thanks, and hat-waving crowds paraded by the hundreds of thousands. By 1874, however, few were celebrating the "iron way." Some of the gripes were old, and some were new. The trains were oppressive, forcing people to conform to rigid timetables, passively follow a set route, and sit and sleep next to strangers. Trains were dangerous to body and mind, leaving behind a legion of workers and passengers maimed and broken by accidents. Trains were polarizing, as workers felt compelled to organize and make unsettling new demands. Railroads were greedy: While would-be pioneers had long been able to count on the government for free land in the West, now they had to buy at a steep markup from railroads that had been granted millions of acres of public holdings. And with monopolies over freight routes, railroads were forever gouging western farmers and ranchers, who in turn were forced to raise prices for consumers in the East.

Toward the end of 1872, Congress began to investigate the construction practices and financing of the transcontinental railroad. The Union Pacific's directors, it turned out, awarded construction contracts to a company that they had formed themselves, which they called the Crédit Mobilier. Flush with cash from bonds that Congress authorized the UP to issue, the railroad could accept bids from Crédit Mobilier that were far higher than its actual costs. As railroad executives siphoned away millions of dollars of construction profits right off the top, they decided to share the wealth with their many allies in Congress, giving them stock in Crédit Mobilier. Yet by the time 1872 turned to 1873, corrupting the political process was the least of the railroad's wrongs. If the railroad titans — Stanford of the Central Pacific, Collis Huntington of the Union Pacific — became some of the richest people in the world, the railroads themselves were piling debt upon debt to construct tens of thousands of miles of track with no prospect of any return on the investment. By September 1873, banking institutions had loaned so much money to ever-riskier railroad ventures that they could not cover seasonal withdrawals to finance the fall harvest. Jay Cooke & Co., the biggest investment bank in the United States, collapsed, and the economy collapsed with it. In the year that followed, dozens of railroads defaulted on their loans. Hundreds of banks suffered runs on deposits and failed. Property values plummeted. Foundries and factories closed, and unemployment reached 25 percent in big cities. Tramps became a common sight even in remote rural areas, and all over the country workers demonstrated for public employment. By January 1874, police were fighting pitched battles with seven thousand unemployed rioters in Tompkins Square Park in New York.

The depression the railroads had triggered was disastrous for Oliver Otis Howard. Much of what he had tried to build during Reconstruction at the Freedmen's Bureau collapsed, seemingly in an instant. The Panic signaled the end of Reconstruction, as northerners began to regard the effort, and "moral politics" more generally, as a failure, something subversive or at the very least a luxury. The economic collapse became the occasion for the final political triumph of Reconstruction's enemies, aided by concerted paramilitary efforts to terrorize black voters throughout the South. Outside of politics, thousands of freedpeople lost everything they had saved since emancipation. Henry Cooke, a partner in his brother's bank and its chief lobbyist in Washington, was in charge of investments for the Freedman's Bank, which held the deposits of tens of thousands of freedpeople. A friend of President Grant's and after 1870 the territorial governor of the District of Columbia, Cooke had funneled the bank's money to Jay Cooke & Co. and its ultimately ruinous stake in an uncompleted railroad that promised to connect Minneapolis to Tacoma. A month before the Howards left Washington, the Freedman's Bank failed, with more than a million dollars of Henry Cooke's bad loans on the books.

On a personal level, the depression almost ruined Howard as well. He had invested what little fortune he had in Washington real estate — seemingly a sure bet, as the city spent millions to grade and pave its treacherous streets and contain and channel its endless flow of sewage. Within months, however, his holdings were worth little more than the mortgages he had on them. To move his family to Oregon and pay his children's tuition at Vassar and Yale, he had to borrow seven thousand dollars from a friend.

If Howard felt disgusted with the railroads and their leaders, he did not share this sentiment with anyone. As he traveled west with his family, he radiated good cheer. The abstract politics of the railroads were something wholly apart from the immediate experience of riding the train. And it was difficult to articulate a major criticism of the railroads that had not been leveled at the Freedmen's Bureau too. The bureau had closed its doors in 1872. For three years following the war, it had coordinated a massive relief effort for millions of destitute southerners, white and black, built hospitals and asylums and orphanages for the freedpeople, found paying jobs for thousands of people who had suffered in bondage, opened schools across the South, and established entire court systems to resolve the inevitable disputes of

57

a new free labor system. At the end of 1868, however, the Freedmen's Bureau ceased all activities outside of promoting schools for freedpeople and paying government bounties to veterans of the colored regiments in the Civil War. By 1870 it had lost its funding for education.

Despite its disappearance from the world of policy, the bureau remained a political battleground. While Congress was probing the railroads, it turned simultaneously toward the Freedmen's Bureau, and Howard was constantly testifying in its defense. Months-long congressional inquiries uncovered no criminal conduct but did unveil a wealth of uncomfortable details about how Howard ran the bureau. Given enormous discretion over how the bureau spent its budget, Howard generously funded Howard University, which in turn gave his family a large home on an acre of land. The mansion — like all of the university buildings — was built with bricks molded out of sand and lime by a building-block company that Howard and several other Freedmen's Bureau officials had formed. Although Howard defended the scheme as a business that would employ university students, and no one profited from it, under congressional scrutiny it appeared like an especially poor exercise of judgment after two walls of an unfinished hospital building cracked and collapsed during a warm spell in December 1868. To make matters worse, when the bureau was winding down its operations between 1870 and 1872, the financial officer whom Howard had tasked with directing the bounty payments diverted the money to private accounts. It was ostensibly a way to get a good return on bureau funds, but tens of thousands of dollars went missing on Howard's watch.

In early 1874, as congressional Democrats called on Howard to pay back the missing funds himself, Howard was tried before seven army officers convened in a special Court of Inquiry by President Grant. The secretary of war drew up corruption charges against Howard, and for much of the spring, a judge advocate argued relentlessly for his personal liability. Ultimately the court exonerated Howard, finding that he "did his whole duty . . . and deserves well of his country." President Grant approved the verdict on July 2, and within days Howard had accepted command of the Department of the Columbia. But a favorable verdict was not enough. Howard had been humiliated, "crippled & broken," he wrote, nearly bankrupted by the cost of lawyers. As his moment of escape drew closer, Howard remained haunted by the recent past. "I risk everything for the President's policy and am rewarded . . . with charges," he wrote after the trial. "I say this without bitterness, but yet think it is true."

After years of suffering, Howard knew that the army post offered the prospect of redemption. "Now that the Chapter has come to an end, you will, perhaps, not altogether regret what has occurred," a friend counseled, "for gold does not become pure gold until after passing through the fire, and it is true, whether fortunate or unfortunate that continued sunshine does not develop genuine manhood either Christian or otherwise." Yet the prospect of redemption was not the same as actual redemption. During the four years before he went west, Howard had been transformed in the public eye. No longer was he the "Christian general" who had devoted himself to the health, prosperity, and rights of the freedpeople. Instead, he was painted as the head of the "Freedmen's Ring," a feast of graft that differed from the Crédit Mobilier scandal only in magnitude. When Mark Twain and Charles Dudley Warner satirized Washington's culture of greed in their 1873 novel *The Gilded Age,* they described two pieces of legislation that epitomized the venality of the day: one concerned railroads; the other, the freedpeople.

Far more devastating, as Howard's reputation was tarnished, so was the entire idea that the government could take an active role in addressing jobs, education, health, hunger, and political participation: issues directly related to whether the freedpeople in their new capacity as citizens could expect equal footing with whites, and more broadly to what extent equality would be a defining value in American life after hundreds of thousands of men had died to eradicate slavery. Not ten years past war's end, the government seemed capable only of benefiting one group at the expense of everyone else. For much of the public, at some level every government action was graft — something to bemoan, mock, and repudiate. Years too late and unconvincing in the particulars, Howard's exoneration did not change how most people would remember his bureau. After the Court of Inquiry's verdict in Howard's case, the judge advocate general issued a pointed and lengthy critique. Across the country, newspapers were still debating his guilt as he fled the capital.

Aboard the train, Otis delighted in his newfound anonymity. When other passengers came through the car where the Howards and the rest of their party were sitting, they seldom noticed the general. Instead, they fixated on the children. "People would come along and take a look at the car filled with children," he wrote, "and if they liked children would come in and enjoy their gayety, and play with them; but others would say: 'Don't go in there, that car is full of young ones.' Those who did come in were happy and helpful, and I hardly think that a more jovial company ever made the journey."

The Nebraska plains seemed endless. Travelers likened the ride to an ocean crossing, with empty landscape under cloudless sky, prairie grass to the horizons north and south, and green turning to yellow and brown in the summer sun. Very occasionally, the train would pass a wood cabin, usually so new it was "still sweating from the axe," as Robert Louis Stevenson would write. From the top of a train car, the novelist remembered, one could see the track stretch for miles to the east and to the west, "like a cue across a billiardboard." Travelers might see an animal grazing in the prairie, but gone were the days when passengers could shoot buffalo from the Union Pacific train as it rolled along the Platte River Valley. By 1874 the herd that roamed the southern plains, once hundreds of thousands strong, had been almost completely slaughtered, hides stacked in freight cars and transported east to be sewn into shoe soles, carcasses left rotting in the field. At night the plains glowed dimly under the stars, the monotony broken only by prairie fires, which transformed the gray void into what one traveler described as a majestic furnace, flames twenty feet high, whipping with the wind as fast as the train. Although the fires may have appeared to be a humbling display of nature's power, they were usually caused by rail sparks.

As comfortable as a Pullman car could be, the plains had a way of getting inside. The locomotive's roar was no match for the rushing hum of grasshoppers, day and night. The dust was incessant, in one's clothes and sheets, hair, mouth, eyes, and nose. "No brushing, no shaking removes it," a well-heeled woman from New Haven wrote after traveling to San Francisco in 1872. "It sifts, it penetrates, it pervades everywhere. After two or three days you grow to hate yourself." The landscape could be hypnotic. In its thrall some passengers felt tiny and defenseless, a speck in a vast wilderness; others experienced a sensation of hugeness and mastery. Many more found the plains maddeningly boring — better to focus on a book, take a long nap, or lose oneself in thought.

Otis Howard insisted that he was not inclined to brood. He had known and weathered hard times before. His faith was a constant support. "No depression sticks to me long," Howard wrote his brother Rowland. "God in his mercy has given me much recuperative energy and I am apt to be light hearted, and I know better than to quarrel with his dealings with me."

When Howard did reflect on his experience in Washington, he considered how he had "not always done right even in Bureau matters." "In many things," he wrote, "I ought to have been more careful." In his view, the trouble lay in the fact that as head of the Freedmen's Bureau, he was the primary person interpreting the scope of his agency's powers. The statute that created the bureau gave it "the control of all subjects relating to refugees and freedmen from rebel states." As Howard read it, Congress had given him the discretion to do just about anything that promoted the education, health, and political rights of the freedpeople. But his enemies offered a competing vision of the agency's authority that plausibly defined many of Howard's actions as illegal. Howard wished he had anticipated the counterarguments and proceeded on a more conservative course. He never would have been defamed and debased, he wrote, "had I been more rigid & exacting & stuck to the literal rendering of the law, . . . but then there would have been no schools &c. &c. . . . I was working with my might & energy for the interest of my charge & gave the most sanguine & liberal interpretation to every law."

Pondering the roots of his undoing, he lingered also on another long journey, one that had occurred nine years before he would travel across the continent with his family. In October 1865, six months after the Civil War's end, Howard left Washington for an extended tour of the South. It was painfully slow: first a ferry down the Potomac to Aquia Creek, then a coach to Fredericksburg and then Richmond. There the general could catch a train, but it was little improvement, rickety cars running ten miles an hour on worn-out rails. On the other side of the state line, the bridge at the Roanoke River had not been rebuilt. Howard's traveling party had to cross by boat before continuing on to Raleigh. "Let no man come into the Carolinas this fall or winter for a so-called pleasure-trip," a journalist warned. The simple act of moving forward was an ordeal.

Howard proceeded south that fall surrounded by reminders of past and present struggles. His aide, Harry Stinson, was twenty-two but gasped for breath like an old man. Howard had watched him get shot through the lungs in battle near Atlanta, and for more than a year he had been slowly dying, a "mere boy," a traveler wrote, coughing all night. Joining them in Richmond was John W. Alvord, a Congregational minister who had met the general in 1864 while distributing religious tracts to the Union troops during Sherman's March to the Sea. Now Alvord preached a gospel of education and thrift. He led the Freedmen's Bureau's efforts to establish schools while also actively promoting the privately run Freedman's Bank, which he had founded earlier that year to give freedpeople the same opportunities to save and accumulate wealth that savings banks were affording the "working men of the north." Rounding out the group was another minister, Howard's brother Rowland, who had been visiting Washington from Maine when the general was ordered south. When Otis asked if he would like to come along as his secretary, Rowland bought a straw hat and linen coat and proclaimed himself ready for what he called the "hot country."

Howard's traveling party had left town as the late summer heat suddenly broke. At the general's large brick home high on a bank above the dusty street, his children were past a bout of whooping cough but still covered in mosquito bites. Government workers sat at their desks shivering. There was a run on overcoats. The cold weather did not slow the constant stream of visitors from the South. Willard's Hotel was packed with former rebels. When Otis took his brother to the White

House to attempt an audience with President Johnson, they passed rooms full of southern planters. Rowland looked in and saw scoundrels and traitors, "a hard faced 'rich-looking' set" who "might wait there a long time," he wrote his wife, "before I'd pardon them."

But the president saw something else. He had spent the past several months restoring thousands to their rights, men who over the course of the summer came to believe that the terrible war had, in fact, not changed their world as much as Howard and his allies had hoped and presumed.

The day before Rowland's arrival in Washington, a man had entered the Freedmen's Bureau to demand an audience with the general. Barnwell Rhett was no ordinary southern pardon-seeker. Described as an "arch Rebel — original dyed in the wool," he was a Charleston newspaper editor who had led the calls for secession before the war. When Sherman took Savannah, Rhett moved his four hundred slaves to a family plantation in Alabama where he could keep them in bondage. Now, after meeting with President Johnson, he was emboldened to ask Howard for an order transporting them back to South Carolina at government expense. "Sir," said Howard, "would you have asked this of the confederate government?" Rhett replied, "Most certainly not." "Then," Howard screamed, "I regard it as the height of impudence for you to do as you do in reiterating it to me!" Howard ordered a guard to eject him.

The newspapers celebrated Howard's response — a rare moment when the Christian general lost his temper — but he well knew that people like Rhett now had the upper hand in Washington.

When Howard first set up the Bureau of Refugees, Freedmen, and Abandoned Lands in a town house that had belonged to a Southern senator, he had what General Sherman called "Hercules' task": "the future of 4,000,000 souls." The responsibility did not just flatter Howard — it felt providential. As the war drew to a close, Howard had been "pondering[,] . . . What as a young man of thirty-four had I better do?" Lincoln himself, he was told, had identified him as the man to lead the bureau. It was not simply a big job. He had been called to create a new kind of governing.

Before the war, the federal government played important roles in people's lives — delivering mail, allotting homesteads and selling land — but it was often hidden from view, relying instead on volunteers, state and local officials, and contracts with private groups and businesses to do most of the work on the ground. The bureau, by contrast, would be an agency that employed thousands of agents across the entire South, distributing food and medicine and coordinating work and schooling for millions of people. In its contours and capacity, the bureau would be an experiment, an unknown quantity in much the same way that freedom went undefined in the Emancipation Proclamation and the Thirteenth Amendment. Howard envisioned the bureau playing a crucial role in giving freedom concrete meaning and determining how former slaves would assume new roles as citizens.

Almost immediately, it was clear to Howard that land would be an essential link from freedom to citizenship. The bureau had jurisdiction over almost a million acres of confiscated property. While not nearly enough for every former slave, the land promised to give millions of people the ability to support themselves independently and without having to seek employment from — without having to depend upon — the people who had once claimed them as property. When pardon-seekers began to find a receptive audience in the president, Howard tried to accelerate the property distribution. At the end of July, he ordered bureau offices across the South to set aside and rent or sell as much abandoned land as possible.

But Howard did not anticipate how quickly President Johnson would repudiate the bureau's mission. While the general was spending the month of August at home with his family in Maine, the president blocked Howard's order distributing the confiscated land. When the general returned to Washington, Johnson called him to the White House and forced him to instruct Freedmen's Bureau officials to return nearly all land belonging to people who had been pardoned. Instead of becoming small farmers, the new citizens would wind up landless laborers dependent on their former masters and at the mercy of abstract forces such as labor markets and the international demand for cash crops. By September, Howard was besieged by planters. "Otis is the hardest worked man I ever saw," Rowland wrote. "His office is full all the time. . . . He is very busy now giving up their houses & land to them — the rebels."

Most of the land under the bureau's control had not been distributed to freedpeople, so returning it to pardoned rebels was a simple, if distasteful, set of transactions. But the Sea Islands south of Charleston presented a far greater challenge. Early in the war, Union forces had occupied the Sea

Islands and given liberated slaves control over their former masters' plantations. In January 1865, with thousands of people fleeing for Union lines during the March to the Sea, General Sherman designated a broad swath of confiscated cotton and rice plantations in the Carolina low country, from the Sea Islands inland thirty miles, as a reserve for freedpeople. With plots of "not more than forty acres of tillable ground," the former slaves remade themselves as subsistence farmers. Their successes were precisely the reason that Howard had ordered the rest of the confiscated lands given to freedpeople as quickly as possible. He recognized that unlike most other former slaves, the Sea Island homesteaders had, in his words, "passed happily from a state of bondage to the condition of freemen." "Those interesting people," he said, "are comparatively happy; they work diligently, they raise good crops, and they are more prosperous than they ever dared to hope for in their wildest dreams." Millions of others across the South shared the expectation that their liberty, too, would be rooted in the land.

But by the fall of 1865 President Johnson had pardoned the Sea Island plantation owners, and this small group of families — some of the earliest leaders of the rebellion, Barnwell Rhett among them — was demanding their property back. In October the president ordered Howard to travel south to "endeavor to effect an agreement mutually satisfactory to the freedmen and the land owners." For once, the president found it useful to have a champion of the rights of freedpeople working for him. It was widely feared that former slaves would take up arms to hold onto their land. Howard was uniquely positioned to deliver the bad news — dashing the hopes of millions — while convincing them not to resist. "The President sends him down because he thinks he can persuade the Freedmen not to make a row about it," wrote Rowland. Howard saw Johnson's order as a profound betrayal of his mission, and of the trust that so many people had invested in him and the bureau. The prospect of brokering the surrender of the Sea Islands sickened him. It was almost too much for him to express. While he would say that the turn of events made his heart "sad" and "chagrined," his brother had a blunter assessment. "He dreads it like death!" wrote Rowland. "How can he do it!" Yet Howard prepared for the journey. "Why did I not resign?" he asked himself years later. "Because I even yet strongly hoped in some way to befriend the freed people."

During his trip through the South, the general was constantly at work. Everywhere he stopped, freed men and women crowded churches and homes to see him speak. Their applause rattled the windows. They stood to praise the work of the bureau. They delighted him with hymns such as "On Jordan's Stormy Banks," declaring "I am bound for the promised land, / I am bound for the promised land; / Oh who will come and go with me?" In once-grand homes now occupied by Union officers, Howard met with bureau officials and learned how they expected the freedpeople to suffer in the coming winter — not enough warm clothes, or medicine, or food. All the while Howard was also meeting with former rebels who were back in control in North and South Carolina, people who, Rowland reported, were "whipped, but . . . proud again, with the idea that Pres.

Johnson is on their side." Newspapers raged against the bureau. Women — "well-dressed ladies," Rowland wrote — "utter[ed] in low hissing tones those hated words 'these Yankees.' " In filthy rooms smeared with tobacco juice, southern politicians received General Howard "dead & cold," demanding the withdrawal of "your troops — your Bureau, your School, & everything else," unrepentantly insisting, to Rowland's disgust, that slave owners were "the purest, most benevolent, holiest people in the whole world!" Their goal was obvious, according to Otis and Rowland's brother Charles, who was working in the Freedmen's Bureau in South Carolina: "to put the foot again upon the neck of the black man." Still, Howard kept heading south, from Richmond to Raleigh, from Raleigh to Wilmington, and at last, on October 17, to Charleston.

There the weeklong journey — bitter, gray, dusty — seemed to soften. In the depths of autumn, the weather was, Rowland marveled, like Maine in June. Charleston was in bloom, oleanders pink and white, roses in shades of tea and cinnamon. The general and Rowland had a warm reunion with their brother. They woke up every morning in a confiscated home with a view of the desolate ruin of Fort Sumter. Still, Otis remained focused on pressing business. At the bureau's office he received a delegation of Sea Island planters who railed against Reconstruction — only now Howard could not order them out as he had Barnwell Rhett. Instead, he invited their lawyer to go with him on October 19 out to Edisto Island.

The steamer to Edisto was piloted by Robert Smalls, who had escaped slavery in 1862 by putting on a captain's uniform, stealing a Confederate military transport from Charleston harbor, and steering it to the Union blockade. Howard was joined by his brother Charles, John Alvord, and William Whaley, the planters' lawyer. Rowland could not make the journey because he had "the diarrhea," and the bureau's assistant commissioner for South Carolina, Rufus Saxton — who had directed land distribution efforts in the Sea Islands during the war — did not have the heart to come along.

At the steamboat landing they saw a welcome party in the hundreds. A procession of men riding horses and mules saluted as Howard climbed into a carriage and escorted him past swamps and abandoned fields on the way to an Episcopal church. The homesteaders on Edisto received Howard "with gladness," Alvord reported. But some of the riders recognized Whaley, whom they had not seen in four years. The very sight of him, wrote a teacher on the island, "awakened terrible misgivings in the minds of the escort" and seemed to confirm rumors of what was to come. Thousands of freedpeople were waiting at the church. Howard saw that they knew what he would say. The audience was visibly in pain. No one could speak over the welter of "noise and confusion," he would remember, until one woman — and slowly the entire church — began singing, "Nobody knows the trouble I feel — Nobody knows but Jesus." As the song ended, Howard stood and explained, "kindly and gently," that the president had ordered the lands on Edisto Island returned to their former masters. He urged them to make contracts with their old masters, prompting "murmurs of 'No, never.' 'Can't do it.' " "They did not hiss," Howard wrote, "but their eyes flashed unpleasantly, and with one voice they cried, *"No, no!"* People in the audience "did not weep," according to Alvord, "but seemed overwhelmed!" From the gallery, a man stood — "very black . . . thick set and strong" — and shouted, "Why, General Howard, why do you take away our lands? You take them from us who are true, always true to the Government! You give them to our all-time enemies! That is not right!" Another man said that "he had lived all his life with a basket over his head, and now that it had been taken off and air and sunlight had come to him, he could not consent to have the basket over him again." A teacher in the audience thought that without Howard's presence, Whaley's "neck would [not] have been safe." Howard asked, "How many will work for their former masters?" A New England woman working with the freedpeople on Edisto reported, "None, or almost none raised their hands."

It was a heartbreaking moment. "I am ashamed of the vacillating and weak course of the Government," wrote a teacher who was in the audience. "One woman said to me, 'The rebels will laugh at the Yankees now.' " Hearing about the meeting from Alvord, Rowland Howard wrote to his mother, "The old Masters are getting their people again & treat them just like slaves." To his wife, he admitted, "I am glad I was not there."

Still, General Howard managed to return to Charleston in much better spirits than when he had left for Edisto. As humiliating as the meeting with the Edisto homesteaders had been, he took heart from the fact that ultimately he was able to command their goodwill. Howard pledged to help them secure good terms from the plantation owners — let them keep the existing crop, stay in their homes. He would appeal to Congress for property. He asked the group to appoint three men to represent the freedpeople in negotiations with the planters. He hoped that they would be able to lease or eventually purchase the land. Finally, he asked "how many would trust the question to him, feeling that he would do all he could that justice should be done to them." "All raised their hands," said a teacher, "and now another man stands in their minds with our dear President Lincoln, General Sherman, and General Saxton — General Howard." Howard could regard that vote as a success. Even as President Johnson was crippling the bureau's mission, Howard still felt that he could help the freedpeople, that he was more useful to them leading the bureau than he would be out of government.

In the days after General Howard left Edisto, the freedpeople on the island vowed to move rather than submit to contracts to work for their former masters. For them, property, a homestead, was the difference between slavery and freedom. "What troubles them most," wrote a teacher, "is that if the owners do come back, they, the colored people, will not be allowed to purchase one foot of land." "We wish to have A home if It be but A few acres," a committee of Edisto freedmen would write. "Without some provision is Made our future is sad to look upon. yess our Situation is dangerous."

Before the month was out, the Edisto committee — men who had secretly learned to read as slaves — told Howard that they refused to forgive their former masters. "*You* only lost your right arm. In war and might forgive them," they wrote.

"The man who tied me to a tree & gave me 39 lashes & who stripped and flogged my mother & sister & who will not let me stay In His empty Hut except I will do His planting & be Satisfied with His price & who combines with others to keep away land from me well knowing I would not Have any thing to do with Him If I Had land of my own. — that man, I cannot well forgive." They had been loyal to the Union. They were "A free people and good citizens of these United States." It represented the height of unfairness to put their rights behind the rights of traitors and rebels, especially when all they wanted was "land enough to lay our Fathers bones upon."

Before his trip south, such words might have led General Howard to resign in protest. But back in Charleston, he seemed "cheerful & well." It was a typical reaction for him. He was, an aide wrote, "noted for his amiability, and neither that nor his equanimity is easily disturbed." He had been the same way in the thick of battle. Even among hardened veterans, it seemed strange. Howard's supporters regarded his good cheer as a sign of strength, bravery, leadership, and faith; he was determined to keep his soldiers' morale high and refused to waste his energy looking back when there were battles that remained to be fought. General Sherman joked that nothing fazed Howard in combat because he was convinced he was going to heaven. But others saw something cold and detached in his affect. Some of his soldiers were enraged by Howard's "hardihood" and "unfailing cheerfulness" — his "unctuous smile," one wrote — as hundreds of Union corpses were still warm on the battlefield. Howard could seem like "a downright hypocrite," as General Joseph

Hooker would describe his onetime junior officer, "no more a Christian than my boy James. . . . He is a bad man, Sir, a bad man."

After Edisto, Howard was quickly reconciled with the new order of things and determined to find the next best course for the freedpeople. With "very little time to rest or reflect," it always seemed he was accomplishing something, as if he still had more to do. After a few final days in South Carolina, he, along with Alvord, Stinson, and his brothers, headed for Savannah, then Jacksonville, Tallahassee, and New Orleans. There was no quick route home. They traveled by steamer and omnibus, even in a boxcar on a freight train, where they "thumped & thumped away all night" like tramps. They found what Charles called "the various surrounding disagreeables" — filth, poverty, revolting breakfasts — something to laugh about, a reminder of their days as soldiers. They nibbled on sugarcane, plucked oranges off trees, and enjoyed a concert of "five Negro minstrels, a guitar, banjo, two violins & a bass viol." All along the way, they spoke with what Rowland called "the colored brethren" — at enormous church meetings, in small well-heeled gatherings, and in huts of split cypress wood built into the ruins of brick buildings. Their testimony — their dreams for the future, their support for and belief in the bureau, in General Howard himself — was profoundly affecting. "You couldn't help tears, I know," Rowland wrote, "when you should hear them speak freely of their wrongs & their hopes for themselves & their children."

At the same time, the travelers kept encountering defiant former rebels with their "talk, talk, talk" — "morning noon & night" — "about the negro & his rights & oppressions." Rowland tired of southerners, ugly deep down, who "worked hard with their 'niggars' 9 mos in a year in order to play the gentleman . . . for the other three." At Mobile, the general sat in astonishment as Josiah Nott, a physician who had written multiple books theorizing the races of mankind, declared in a private audience that "Niggars are an inferior race & must be kept down or exterminated." "He would prefer the latter," Rowland wrote.

But constant reminders of the need for profound and radical change — the need for a bureau that did not bow to the demands of former rebels — failed to shake Howard from his conviction that the best course was to keep working, regardless of the odious parameters fixed by the president. In time, he became convinced that there was no point in resisting Johnson, and even that acts of protest over their lesser set of rights would destroy the legitimacy of the freedpeople's claims to citizenship. By the time he reached New Orleans, Howard could declare to a theater full of his most ardent supporters that it was "necessary to define" freedom, "for it is most apt to be misunderstood, misapplied, and its meaning, extended beyond what's right." Freedom, in his telling, now had no connection to property. "Many amongst the freedmen . . . think that freedom must bring forth a change in their material condition," he said. "But it is not so. They must work as heretofore; they must work more than before." Asking for anything else would court disaster. Howard closed his speech with a cautionary tale. "There is an Island whose inhabitants introduced political agitation among themselves, and were ruined in consequence," he said. "And to-day, the example of that Island is instanced to prove that freedom is a curse for the black man. So much for indulging in political agitation; for it is only that agitation which ruined that Island, and not emancipation." The island Howard was describing was Haiti. It was a reference that many in the audience, descended from refugees of the revolution there, were sure to understand. But as Howard traveled through the South, as he committed to stay in government and work for Reconstruction in whatever form it would take, his words became a lens for viewing Edisto as well. The Edisto Islanders pressed for their right to be treated as equal citizens on the ground that their claims deserved "to be considered before the rights of those who were Found in rebellion against this good and just Government." But it was all too easy for Howard, their former champion, to see their exercise of citizenship as something illegitimate — "agitation," or worse — that had to be controlled.

From New Orleans, Charles returned to South Carolina, and Otis and Rowland went north, up the Mississippi to Vicksburg, by train to Memphis, and again on the water to Cairo, Illinois. They were a thousand miles from Washington, which they had left more than a month before. But in Cairo they knew they would have reliable train service, and it took only three days to go east: a sleeper car to Columbus — Rowland's first — connecting to the "Lightening Express." As they made their way home, Rowland reported that Otis and he had relished a good bath, a comfortable bed, and clean clothes. To pass their final hours traveling together, he wrote, "we sung patriotic songs with a gusto."

■ ■ ■

Years later, the Howard family's journey west was not much faster than the journey south had been. The Union Pacific train seldom reached more than twenty miles an hour. In 1869, four years after the rebel surrender, the transcontinental railroad was described as the iron binding that held the Union together, turning the nation's axis from north-south to east-west. But it was a loose binding — a light track, hastily built, engineered for little traffic. Trains had to proceed slowly, a luxury for some, "insufferable tedium" for others. Even at its deliberate pace, the rails were exponentially faster than any other mode of travel. Where impassable mountains gave way to endless deserts — for countless pioneers, sites of misery, starvation, and death — the train kept moving. After two days going through Nebraska and Wyoming, the Howards had seen towering mountains to the south, climbed startling grades and descended into deep canyons, plunged blind through mountain tunnels, and rolled through landscapes that were blistered and bleached of life. They reached altitudes that left many easterners gasping, aching, and parched. They passed a lone tree up a steep canyon that marked the thousandth mile from Omaha and after another hour or two reached Ogden, Utah, on the eastern shore of the Great Salt Lake.

At Ogden the Howards unloaded and traded their Pullman sleeper for a Silver Palace car on the Central Pacific line, the railroad that would take them the rest of the way to California. A traveler in 1874 sniffed that she "met with *no silver whatever* in these cars," but the Howards and their friends did not mind the rigid schedule for raising and lowering the beds, the shared lavatory with no lock, or the communal towel and bar of soap. They had only three more days until they reached San Francisco Bay. By then the rails were a familiar world. Their fellow passengers were no longer strangers. They were a community, with its own newspaper published on board each morning by the railroad, and its own distinct rhythms of morning, afternoon, and evening.

It was natural to think of the stark landscape surrounding them as simply a sight to be seen, bearing no connection to the orderly, if dusty, world inside the train. At stops for meals, usually the passengers had only twenty or thirty minutes, too little time to stray from the station and see what lay beyond. They might get some hint of another world out there — a helping of antelope steaks or prairie dog stew, served by Chinese waiters who had remained along the railroad route after building it the previous decade. Passengers might stretch their legs outside and encounter people uncomfortable in conversation, people who had chosen to live outside society, spending most of their days alone hunting and trapping or panning for gold.

On occasion, the passengers might even see the people who had lived in the area before it was bound by rail — a glimpse of Indians riding in the distance or approaching the train station to trade or beg. These brief encounters suggested a parallel reality that most easterners would have found hard to imagine. As the Howards made their way to California, newspapers ran short dispatches about trouble just beyond the railroad:

mail stages captured in Texas, their drivers scalped; Cheyenne and Arapaho getting "ready for war" near Fort Laramie, Wyoming; Winnebago, Chippewa, and Sioux returning to "old haunts" in Minnesota and Wisconsin after exile in Nebraska, where there were "no berries nor game, and they were so homesick that they could not stay there." Meanwhile, a young lieutenant colonel, George Armstrong Custer, was reporting back from an expedition through South Dakota's Black Hills that the uncharted land was "beautiful beyond description" and had "gold in paying quantities." His men were armed for attack but had not encountered the Sioux. In New York or Chicago, such stories read like foreign dispatches, utterly detached from daily life. Riding in a Silver Palace car, however, a passenger might begin to understand how the corridors of civilization were, in fact, indelibly connected to the world beyond — how the violence along the edges of society made it possible for modern life to exist.

The Central Pacific rattled through Nevada into California, past collapsing shacks that once sheltered railroad construction crews, past mining towns shabby with dreams of silver wealth and overrun with saloons, past alkali flats and more desert, past cattle ranches and irrigated farms and an occasional Indian village. The train clung to mountainsides in the Sierras, with drops of two thousand feet to the rivers below, and through passes that in winter were snowbound for weeks. Half a day from their destination, the Howards felt the air thicken as they descended from the heights past the gold settlements of the '40s and '50s. A short stop in Sacramento, through a tunnel that cast the train into darkness for two minutes, past miles of farms and pastures and tidy villages — it was finally possible to imagine the train's destination. In gentle summer heat, the Central Pacific rolled through Oakland's proud suburbs, past stately homes on wide streets paved with macadam. Otis Howard and his family and entourage stepped off the train at a wharf in Oakland, surrounded by more than a hundred acres of rail yards and engine shops.

On the boat crossing the bay, the air grew cooler, and San Francisco emerged in the distance. At the ferry landing, a carriage was waiting to take the Howards half a mile up Market Street to the Occidental, a grand hotel that took up an entire city block and was the favorite of visiting army officers. Along San Francisco's wide, orderly streets, Otis Howard could have imagined that after weeks of travel, he had not gone any distance at all. San Francisco could have been a city on the East Coast. It was bigger, and much more impressive, than Washington. But within minutes of arriving, he was reminded how truly far he had come. The Occidental's carriage charged its passengers in gold. Greenbacks were no good in San Francisco. Howard would have to exchange his paper money for coin at sixty cents to the dollar.

CHAPTER 2
NEW BEGINNINGS

Portland, Oregon,
Fall 1874

Day after day the letters arrived at General Howard's office. They were postmarked New York City, Philadelphia, San Francisco, small towns in Maine, and army posts from Alaska to Georgia. They came several at a time, outnumbering the official correspondence of the army's Department of the Columbia. Just about every entry in this slow-rising mountain of stationery began with the usual pleasantries: congratulating Howard on his new appointment, wishing his family comfort and good health in Portland. But the tone inevitably shifted. The writers all wanted something from the general, and there was neither the time nor space for subtlety. In one scratch of ink, glad tidings gave way to blunt requests. A paragraph might begin with a fond reminiscence of attending a Sunday school session taught by General Howard before the war, only to end with "& now General I will come to the point & tell you what I should be pleased to have you do for me."

The entreaties were insistent and often sad. Did the general need another orderly on his staff? Could he help the wife of a veteran get a position at the San Francisco Mint? Could he provide a reference for a New Englander willing to do "anything honorable" in Oregon after losing his wife back east? Could he recommend a former army colonel — "now in some ordinary business in St. Louis," married to "pious, excellent wife" — for work as an Indian agent in Arizona or Oregon? Could he order a chaplain transferred to Washington Territory from Atlanta, where "the climate has caused a return of the dysentery which he contracted during the war"? Could he find a job for a man hoping to move west because his persistent cough was "getting worse every day"?

During reconstruction Howard declared in speech after speech that the "aid given the freedmen by the Government could only be partial and temporary." Freedom, in his view, was not just a legal status or state of being — the absence of slavery, or the ability to move, marry, own land, and make contracts. Rather, freedom was a moral test, a righteous struggle from the bottom of society upward that produced ideal and deserving citizens. It necessarily forced people to fend for themselves and their families, to display what Howard called "manly individuality and self-reliance." Those who made it through were fit to be regarded as equals, "purified and strengthened" by their tribulations, Howard believed, "just as the children of Israel were by the experiences they encountered in passing from Egypt to the promised land." But too much government interference would only foster dependency, the general worried. Its beneficiaries would never have the opportunity to rise to the challenges of life, attain the true dignity of self-ownership, and deserve to be treated as equals. They would experience the opposite of true freedom, a spiritual poverty, slavery in all but name.

Exiled at the far edge of the continent, his years at the Freedmen's Bureau remembered mainly by government officials who periodically sent him nasty letters about unaccounted-for sums, Howard began learning a different lesson. He discovered the extent to which his talk of self-reliance and dependency, a great commonplace of Reconstruction, was only half right. Government aid might foster dependency, but so did the absence of government assistance. As the Panic of 1873 deepened into what became known as the "Great Depression," many Americans did not show their self-reliant mettle. Instead, by the thousands they sought out patrons — the richest, most powerful, and best-connected people they could find — and begged for help: a job, a reference, a few dollars. Afflicted by poverty and failure, they did not want independence. They devoted every effort to becoming someone's protégé or hireling. The difference between a world in which the government provided relief to the needy and a society that left them without any support was not the difference between dependency and self-reliance. Rather, the difference centered only on the nature of the dependency: Would Americans look to the government for help, or to their social and economic superiors? Almost everyone was dependent on somebody.

Though distressing, the daily litany of want reminded Howard that despite his personal ordeal of Reconstruction, he remained a powerful man. He had some measure of influence with religious charities, the government and the military, and the university named for him. At the same time, the constant stories of woe — of good people brought low, often people who had once achieved something — suggested how fragile the boundary was between pauper and patron, and how easily he might find himself on the other side of the line. Howard well knew what it was like to write those letters. He had written many throughout his life. And though he assumed a position of command with an entire army of men obeying his orders, he could not forget that he had barely avoided bankruptcy in Washington and still owed thousands of dollars for his move west. Asked for money from a man who had worked for the state of New York during the Civil War only to go "insane [leaving] a very destitute family," Howard wrote from Portland, "I wish I could make some suggestion for your personal relief but I cannot. I am struggling to get clear of debts. . . . I simply can say that I sympathize with you."

Howard did what he could to help the men and women who begged for his aid. He recommended them for jobs, sent cash when he had it, and urged them to keep their spirits up — to keep faith, in his words, that "the light sometimes breaks suddenly." Their degradation, the suffering of their children, could bring Howard to tears. He was inspired to write page after page of poetry about hungry families in a cold world, proclaiming "The human soul doth ever seek / A genuine Sympathy!" And every day he worked to turn his capacity to feel and sympathize into palpable action.

For Howard, the idea that everyone deserved a second chance was more than fond sentiment. It was an article of faith, a defining principle of his new life in Oregon. He surrounded himself with second chances. When he looked across his desk at William Cudlipp, the clerk who logged the hard-luck stories sent to Howard and transcribed many of his replies, the general saw someone he had saved from the street in Washington, DC. In the summer of 1865 Cudlipp had been, Howard remembered, a "straight, slender" young man with a handkerchief on his head to block the sun — too poor to afford a hat. Howard hired him as a clerk in the Freedmen's Bureau, then found him a position in the Interior Department when the bureau folded in 1872. But in July 1874, with a wife and baby daughter to support, the clerk lost his new job when it was discovered that as a twelve-year-old boy he had stabbed a man in the heart and spent a decade in the Virginia penitentiary. Cudlipp came to Howard pale and despairing. Howard asked him one question: "Cudlipp, look at me. Who am I?" And with that, the general hired the clerk again and brought him and his family to Portland. "There he became," Howard wrote, "in my office, as he had been before, an energetic, hard-working, faithful clerk."

When Howard stepped out of his office, he could see second chances in the buildings all around him, along the wood-planked sidewalks that drummed under his boot heels, and among the men and women — dressed in finery or for the frontier — walking past under cloudy skies. Portland was a monument to new beginnings. Just thirty years earlier, the settlement did not have a name. Now it was the richest city in the Northwest, its population somewhere north of eight thousand, pronounced by one visitor to be "juvenile but audacious." The army's headquarters could easily have passed for a public building in

Washington — an ornate white façade, gabled and corniced, with classical symmetry. Yet it represented a different order of power. The building was six years old, a dressed-up commercial block fronting the Willamette River. The army shared its space with a grocery wholesaler, advertising bacon, hams, lard, butter, brine, eggs, dried apples, plums, and chickens; an importer of crockery, glassware, china, clocks, and lamps; and a partnership that imported and sold stoves and metals. In Washington, DC, the shifting currents of politics had made Howard's life a misery, but in Portland, they seemed irrelevant. Power and politics bowed to money and trade.

The building's owner was the Oregon Steam Navigation Company, known as OSN. It was the essential reason why Portland was swollen with cash. OSN had a monopoly on boat traffic the length of the Columbia River, a waterway surpassed in volume in the United States only by the Mississippi, Ohio, and St. Lawrence. Incorporated in 1860 by a small group of local merchants and bankers, the company profited from every passenger and every item going up and down the river. As tens of thousands of people moved into Oregon — it doubled its population from 1860 to 1870 and was on course to double again by 1880 — and tens of thousands more followed rumors of gold east into Idaho Territory, an OSN steamboat ticket was the price of entry for nearly everyone. As the Willamette Valley and points east emerged as major farming areas, with "golden harvests" of wheat and oats shipping as far as Liverpool, England, the company exacted its toll on every grain, as well as every apple, pear, quince, gooseberry, or plum going to market. Even the army's ability to secure the interior depended on OSN, and it, too, was constantly paying the company — rent for Howard's headquarters, but also passage for all the people and equipment heading upriver to forts in eastern Oregon and Washington and in Idaho. In essence, the company had the power to tax the government.

OSN's profits, endless and limitless, stayed largely in Portland. Because people kept moving to the Northwest after the national economy collapsed, the company had one of its best years following the Panic of 1873. Figuring that its unchallenged run would end once the transcontinental railroad was built, the company's principals had sold a large stake to the financier Jay Cooke in 1870, earning ten times their investment, but in 1874, after the Panic ruined Cooke, they bought their shares back for pennies on the dollar. The steamship company was the reason why Howard could look out from his headquarters onto a lively choreography of boat traffic on the Willamette, why Portland's docks were piled high with freight, why stonemasons and iron workers were lavishing new commercial buildings throughout the downtown with intricate decoration. Even the most jaded visitor in 1874 — a seasoned political journalist sent west by German railroad investors to investigate why a local entrepreneur was defaulting on bond payments — could look at the bustling streets and river, take in distant glimpses of Mount Hood, Mount St. Helens, and Mount Adams, and declare that Portland was "surpassed in few respects by any other city in the United States."

Nearly all who made their fortunes in Portland had come from somewhere else. The city was named by a man from Maine. OSN's founders had moved west from Ohio, Massachusetts, and New Hampshire, among other places. William Wadhams, the grocer in the offices next to Howard's, was born along the banks of Lake Champlain in upstate New York. The stove and metal dealers in the building, Julius Loewenberg and Phillip Goldsmith, were German Jews. Regardless of where they had come from and why they had left, they started anew in Portland. Goldsmith's brother Bernard had come to town in 1861 after peddling dry goods to miners in California, eastern Oregon, and Idaho from the back of a mule. In Portland in the 1860s, he set himself up as a jeweler, currency trader, wheat merchant, and shipping investor. Eight years after arriving, he was one of the city's richest men. It did not matter that he was a foreigner and a Jew. In 1869, he was elected mayor. After two years in office, he was succeeded by another German Jew. New beginnings and second chances bloomed in Portland like thickets of flowers.

Howard admired what he called Portland's "good sense": its wealth and energy, its thoughtful layout, its big beautiful parks. At the same time, he needed little reminder that it was, at root, a frontier outpost. From any distance it looked like it had been hacked out of the surrounding forests, its edges bounded by burnt stumps and swirling dust. It was impossible for a lady to keep her dress from bearing the imprint of city streets, slick and reeking with manure. Miners from upriver hauling fifty-pound sacks of gold could celebrate in dozens of saloons — there was one for just about every hundred residents. At the end of the day,

Howard left his office, turned his back on the river, and faced the setting sun. His path from army headquarters to home crossed ten downtown blocks. Drunks sitting in doorways, even sprawled on the sidewalk, were familiar obstacles along the way.

As Howard walked past the semiconscious men, he looked to see if he recognized anyone. If his official duties required him to manage army affairs in Oregon, Washington and Idaho Territories, and Alaska, he expected to fight his most important battles on Portland's streets. Long before he became a general, an evangelical, and an abolitionist, he was a temperance man. As a teenager prepping for Bowdoin, he had pledged to his mother that he would not touch a drop of strong drink. In the twenty-five years that followed, people doubted that a teetotaler could lead men to victory in battle, and Howard's worst critics considered his refusal to imbibe stuffy, womanish, and even sinister. He endured ribbing from old friends, West Point classmates, fellow officers, and soldiers serving under him. Yet Howard was unapologetic. When his admirers toasted him during the war, he held up a glass of what he called "the only beverage fit for a soldier," cold water.

During Reconstruction, he picked up the temperance banner alongside the cause of liberty and equality for all. He asked Freedmen's Bureau agents to encourage the freedpeople to sign pledges to abstain from intoxicating spirits, and as head of the Young Men's Christian Association in Washington, DC, he sought to save one drunk at a time. Howard saw the temperance crusade as another struggle for liberation and redemption. His work would free people from yet another

90

relentless and uncompromising form of bondage. He would nurse young men back to health, put them in touch with their families and their God, and give them a new start in life.

Out west, Howard knew he was taking charge of soldiers at remote outposts who were bored, lonely, and sun-starved. From Fort Stevens to Walla Walla, the temptations of the bottle were constant. Soldiers on furlough from Sitka could be as wild as any sailor on shore leave. Even Howard's officers in Portland were not above tippling. A couple of months after Howard assumed his post, his adjutant general Major Henry Clay Wood — the chief administrator for the Department of the Columbia and a fellow Bowdoin graduate from Maine — reached a state of "at least partial intoxication" at a local hotel and insulted a lower-ranked officer. Howard took Major Wood to task for "offensive language" and for "some other things too painful to speak of," only to shield him from further punishment after he apologized and pledged "to abstain altogether from alcoholic drinks." Wood continued working for Howard and used his second chance to become one of the general's principal advisers in the Northwest.

Quickly assuming leadership of Portland's YMCA, Howard was determined to turn the group into what one of his aides called "the cavalry of the Church — the Church of Christ on horseback." If Portland was a drinker's town, it was also a place where souls could be saved. Indeed, Howard was not alone in his struggle. Five months before he arrived in town, dozens of women declared "war" on Portland's saloons, bursting into various establishments — the Web-

Foot, the Cornucopia, the Diana, the Mount Hood, the Oregon Exchange, the Cosmopolitan — to "pray, sing, read the Scriptures, or exhort," according to one observer, or "bandy words with degraded sots," according to another. The scenes, a journalist wrote, "rivalled Pandemonium." Women knelt in the streets while saloon owners and assorted "street idlers . . . roughs and blackguards" called them whores, blew whistles and beat gongs, threw glasses at them, and drew pistols and knives. Women kneeling in loud prayer — urging *"Death to the fiend that lurks within the cup!"* — became fixtures of the city's saloons. The temperance crusade that began in the spring of 1874 caused some bars to close and prompted a few men to dry out. One of them would later tell Howard, "God bless them women!" But the struggle augured less of a new beginning for the saloon's denizens than for the crusaders themselves, described by local suffragist Abigail Scott Duniway as women "of wealth, of position . . . the young ladies who sit in the parlor entertaining idle callers, or dawdling over novels." Once they experienced such "excitement" and "fanaticism," Duniway wondered hopefully, would they begin to feel "the desire to have an *actual existence:* the desire to be a concrete number in the sum-total of humanity"?

Howard supported Portland's women activists and found enthusiastic allies in his aide-de-camp Melville Wilkinson as well as in William Wadhams, the grocer who shared the OSN building with the army headquarters. After work, the three of them would journey into areas where city boosters and travel writers seldom ventured, places, in Howard's words, of "much wickedness." They might invite themselves into a drunkard's verminous home and, amid filthy children and a "slatternly dressed" wife, force him to swear on the Bible and sign a temperance pledge. Or they might walk together along the river to the storefront — once a saloon — where Howard rented space for the YMCA. At their prayer meetings Howard stood surrounded by familiar faces, men he worked with and men he had saved.

On first impression, Howard was mild and pleasant. But when he testified about God's redemptive love, a journalist wrote, his passion and resolve flashed through, "the veins in his face and neck standing out like tight-drawn cords" for an instant, only to retreat again to sympathetic calm. The effect was "like a gunshot after nightfall." Drunks wandered in and out of the YMCA meetings, some seeking a second chance, others just a warm room on a cold, drizzly night. Howard sat, talked, and sang hymns with them. Usually they were young, the same age as his soldiers, alone and away from home. After these encounters, Howard wondered if they were too far gone to remember their conversations with him. Days later, as he walked the streets, Howard kept an eye out for the men he had counseled.

One night, as Howard was leaving work, he saw a young man who had approached him at a YMCA meeting a couple of days earlier. Sitting in front of a shuttered storefront, the man was barely able to remain upright. Too drunk to walk, he told Howard, "I am ashamed." Howard got him to his feet and hailed a cab, and together they made their way out of downtown. Three-quarters of a mile away, they reached a quiet residential block. In the early 1870s, Portland's merchants, bankers, and shipping magnates were beginning to trade their whitewashed saltboxes for three-story mansard-roof estates surrounded by lush gardens. But the southwest corner of Tenth and Washington still could have passed for New England. Until the spring, when they would add a towering addition to a home two blocks south on Morrison, the Howards were living in a simple cottage. Inside, the general and his drunk companion found Lizzie Howard. The general had loved her since he was a sixteen-year-old boy. Her hair pulled back into a severe topknot, she was still young by firelight. Although the cottage was crowded with small children — including a five-year-old who spent part of the fall of 1874 suffering from what the general called "whooping cough minus the whoop" — Lizzie always kept it fit to receive visitors. At home the Howards were "plain decent people with a large spice of Puritannic [*sic*] precision and energy," a visitor noted in the fall of 1874. And on the evening when the general showed up with a drunkard off the street, the family put that energy to work. They stripped the young man of his filthy rags and sent him straight to bed. Lest he "give us the slip," Howard remembered, they hid his clothes and kept him several days until he dried out completely. He became a regular at YMCA prayer meetings, was "restored to his parents, and . . . soon married." He was "a new man," Howard wrote — a common label in Portland.

Working alongside Lizzie Howard in the family cottage was another new man. Moy Ling, the Howards' house servant, was slender and still baby-faced in his early twenties. He may have kept the family's cottage tidy, or helped the general button his uniform in the morning. Some of Portland's richest families were beginning to appreciate a good Chinese cook. The general found him to be a calm presence in the house — "very dignified," he wrote.

Just two years removed from a seventy-day voyage across the Pacific, Moy had spent his entire life surviving war, famine, and flood in a small village in the Pearl River Delta near Canton. His parents were dead. In Portland he found a few hundred Chinese men — almost no women — clustered in two-story brick buildings among the saloons and brothels in the blocks south of Howard's army headquarters. It would be several years before the railroads and salmon canneries attracted thousands of Moy's countrymen to Oregon. By 1874, most of the Chinese in the state had found their way east to the gold mines, where they dug ditches, or south to the Willamette Valley, where they cleared thousands of acres for the wheat crop. Many had fled California, which was becoming an impossible place for the newcomers. But the hostility had begun to follow them north by the time Moy arrived in Portland. During his first year in town, twenty-two blocks along the waterfront went to ashes in a fire deliberately set outside a laundry that the city's federal judge, among many others, attributed to "wicked anti-Chinese fanatics." That same year, as local newspapers warned of the "dirt, filth, stench and horrible smells" of the "Chinese nuisance," the city council voted to ban public works projects from hiring Chinese laborers. The measure did not survive a veto from the mayor, who was a wealthy merchant who wanted to keep labor costs low. He declared that the measure violated the Fourteenth Amendment's guarantee of equal protection under law as well as America's treaty obligations with China.

Such discrimination disgusted General Howard. He viewed his servant through the same lens of redemption and rebirth that he applied to any number of young men whom he came across in the course of a day. In the fall of 1874, the general found a Bible printed in Chinese and placed it in Moy's hands. Although Moy had had seven years of traditional education in China, and his mother had taught him to burn incense at the altar of his ancestors, he silently read the book and, according to one of his admirers, "a light . . . dawned on his mind." He began attending church services, and Howard had the pleasure of seeing a new life take hold over the next few years. Moy became a missionary, an English teacher, and a shop owner — a reverend in a three-piece suit, as devoted as Howard to a gospel of rebirth and redemption, second chances and starting over.

In the warm glow of a gas-lit chandelier, the general looked out onto a full room. He had spoken at countless prayer meetings, testified before Congress, and rallied his troops, but seldom had he seen such a fashionable crowd. The town's best people — "a larger, more intelligent and refined audience one does not often see gathered in Portland," reported the *Oregonian* — had paid for the privilege of watching Howard on a cold November night. With two large maps as his backdrop, he spoke without notes. The audience sat transfixed as he described the Battle of

Gettysburg as he saw it.

Eleven years earlier in 1863, Howard's conduct at Gettysburg had been much disputed. Three thousand men in his 11th Corps were killed, wounded, or captured on the battle's first day. In the heat of battle, General Meade placed an officer junior in rank over Howard, leaving him feeling "mortified and . . . disgrace[d]." His soldiers — many suspicious of their evangelical, teetotaling Yankee general — took to calling him, in a play on his initials, "Uh Oh Howard." Although Howard ardently defended himself, and his men held their position at Cemetery Hill on the battle's second day, he would have to wait until the Chattanooga and Atlanta campaigns in 1864 before he found success on the battlefield. At that time William Tecumseh Sherman promoted Howard to command the Army of the Tennessee and praised him in exactly the way he had wanted to be known, as "one who mingled so gracefully and perfectly the polished Christian gentleman and the prompt, zealous, and gallant soldier." Yet critics such as Ambrose Bierce, who served under Howard in Georgia, would persist in branding the general a "consummate master of the art of needless defeat."

By contrast, in Oregon in 1874, Howard recounted a story of pathos and personal fortitude that his audience readily accepted. He recalled the moment early on the first day when he learned that his immediate superior, Major General John Reynolds, had been killed, leaving Howard — just thirty-two years old — the senior commander on the field until General Meade could arrive. Howard said he felt "an emotion never experienced before or since": hopelessness, as scattered

Union forces faced the full weight of Lee's army. And still, he kept faith. "God helping us," he thought, "we will stay here till the army comes."

The audience was rapt as Howard remembered riding through town, which was eerily silent, his men tearing up at the sight of a lone woman standing on a porch waving her handkerchief. He described the battle on Cemetery Hill, dwelling on the stories of those who died around him in "a sheet of fire" — dear friends and fellow officers, good men mourned by their families. At Howard's position in the Evergreen Cemetery, bombs exploded to his left and right and up in the air. Tombstones toppled as the living joined the dead. "Men fell while eating, or while the food was in their hands, and some with cigars in their mouths," Howard remembered. In an instant a young boy holding the officers' horses "had his left arm clipt off with a fragment of a shell." When Howard saw a Union artilleryman, "cheerful and hearty, singing and whistling at his work," admiration quickly turned to horror. "He is struck," Howard said, "gives one cry and is no more!" The general and his audience relived the ordeal for an hour, at which point prolonged applause shook the lecture hall.

A gifted storyteller, Howard could craft a narrative full of suspense and brimming with sentiment. His audience laughed at the light moments and let their tears flow as he recounted one noble death after another. "Very interesting and in excellent taste," pronounced the town's federal judge, a notoriously tough critic to please. Howard's performance presented an entirely different level of excitement from Portland's usual evening fare — lectures on pioneer life, the Transit of Venus, the "Chinese Question," or "Why are not all Marriages happy ones?"; revues by self-styled "artistes" from California that promised "all the late novelties . . . in rapid succession"; or the small circuit of chamber concerts, minuets, and other fancy-dress events that passed for society. The general was invited to give the lecture again and again in the fall of 1874 — as well as a second lecture on Sherman's March — until he was obliged to turn down invitations. His success as a lecturer made it seem possible that he could one day pay down his debts, and it cemented his reputation as one of Portland's leading lights.

Howard had arrived in Portland determined to live without bitterness. "Let it all go — I shall try," he wrote his brother Rowland, "am trying to let go the past & give the present to duty." But in countless ways he could not leave the past behind. Treasury auditors were still regularly questioning him about expenses relating to the Freedmen's Bureau. His left big toe had ached since 1861, when his heavy saber accidentally fell on his foot and crushed his toenail. And most saliently, every time he dressed in the morning or picked up a pen, he was reminded of charging the rebel lines at Seven Pines.

In Portland, Howard began to see how a long memory could be valuable. His acts of remembering — at a comfortable distance — allowed him to create a happier past. When he spoke of the Civil War, he did not have to waste his time arguing his case against people who thought he was a bumbler. He had the respect of his audiences the moment he took the lectern. And when nearly every black citizen of Portland decided impromptu to march to Howard's house one September evening and serenade him with a brass band, Howard did not have to defend his record in Reconstruction. The leader of the group paid tribute to Howard's "moral integrity and Christian character" and tireless "services in behalf of their liberties." They welcomed him to Oregon and wished that his stay would "be fraught with blessings and prosperity to you and yours." Howard, in turn, could trumpet the accomplishments of Reconstruction and the great successes of "the colored people," their progress in education and industry and in "the art of self-government." Howard said a prayer for his serenaders.

From Portland, Howard could fashion a new role for himself in history. In his retelling, he would be humble, a man of modest New England origins who by God's grace was able to overcome daunting odds time and again. He would be magnanimous, describing his critics and enemies among the Union officer corps as "conscientious, brave and devoted" and offering praise even for the rebels, "their prowess, their spirit of devotion, their sacrifice." He would be a gentleman and a man of feeling, a sympathetic patron and an occasional poet. He was a hero, and also something more. He was an authority.

A month after he arrived in Portland, Howard stepped from his headquarters with his aide-de-camp Joseph Sladen, walked a short distance out onto the OSN dock, and boarded a steamer. It was one of the first of what would be regular trips — every month or two — to inspect his far-flung command. Sometimes he went 250 miles upriver, beyond the Dalles to Fort Walla Walla; other times he steamed all the way downriver from Portland to the two forts guarding the mouth of the Columbia. The OSN fleet could reach only a fraction of Howard's territory. To get to Fort Klamath near Crater Lake in southern Oregon, or Fort Lapwai near the Clearwater River in northern Idaho, or the Indian reservation across Commencement Bay from Tacoma, the general and his retinue traveled by rail, ferry, mule-drawn springwagon, and horseback. "You will never know the roughness of this country," Howard wrote his half-brother back in Cedar Rapids, "the difficulty of crossing a single acre of land."

Through forests and mountains and prairie, down rapids "roaring frightfully, — enough to disturb our nerves," Howard saw new frontiers, where soldiers, functionaries, farmers, traders, miners, churchmen, and chiefs were slowly working out how to live together, make a crop, get rich, serve God, or just survive. Howard breathed smoke and damp and rotting fish, salt sea air and the sharp perfume of desert sagebrush. He rode through rough pioneer settlements where the sounds of drunken revelry percussed through tavern walls. He reached newly created reservations far from anything resembling a town. He slept fitfully as "wild and frightful" songs abraded the deep endless night. He struggled to calibrate his sense of danger, to separate real alarm from what he called "superstition based on ignorance!"

In the light of day, Howard stood among wigwams and clusters of canvas teepees, smoke rising from each in small clouds. With "half-starved" horses grazing nearby, or yellow dogs roaming like "young wolves or fierce coyotes," Howard spoke with all types of Indians, from the shores of Puget

Sound to the plateau country east of the Cascade Mountains. Puyallup, Muckleshoot, Nisqually, Yakama, Spokane, Nez Perce, Cayuse, Umatilla, Walla Walla, Paiute, Bannock: although Howard thought of the tribes as a singular presence and set of interests and concerns in his department, he also took note of their infinite variety. They were tall and short, fat and starving, meticulous and "forlorn." Their hair was shorn, or long and uncombed, or tightly braided with scalps daubed in red paint. They wore wool trade blankets — stripes, tartans, solid — or old army uniforms buttoned to the neck, or buckskin coats and breeches, or the ordinary homespun that any white farmer might wear. On their heads were ruined stovepipes, soft tasseled caps, wide-brimmed straw hats, maybe a feather or two — sometimes they removed their hats when they spoke to Howard. They had long knives on their belts, pipe tomahawks, pistols with ivory handles.

The farthest reaches of Howard's command could seem worlds away from Portland, but the cultural distance was never insurmountable. Whether on a steamboat landing or in a windowless one-room lodge, someone might greet the general with a little English, or the regional pidgin called Chinook Jargon that Howard regarded as "miserable," full of "queer words" like "muckymuk" for food. Everywhere he went, he could rely on finding a white man married to a local Indian who could interpret. Howard called them "squaw men" and never lost his fascination with their living habits. Although they reflexively brought to mind the disasters that befell Samson when he married the Philistine Delilah, Howard concluded that "they compare favorably to our own citizens who have cl[u]stered around the many Indian reservations simply for greed."

Through interpreters or on their own, the Indians pledged their friendship to Howard. They spoke of their new lives as farmers on reservations, or wished that they could still hunt and drive herds. They praised the federal Indian agents who worked with them, or registered complaints. They sought the blessings of Christ, or attempted to explain the power of dream and prophecy. Time and again, they gave Howard names in their own languages, usually identifying him by his most prominent feature. He was the One-Armed Soldier Chief, Arm-Cut-Off, or — most simply — Cut Arm.

It was not the first time Howard had left the world he knew in search of Indians. When he had been stationed in Florida in 1857, the army was trying to root out the last of the Seminoles — reduced to mere dozens after forty-plus years of war — from the interior swamps. In smothering June heat, Howard left Tampa and led a small group of soldiers as well as three Indians — a man, woman, and child — on a "peace expedition" through the Everglades to Lake Okeechobee. He was ordered to find Chief Billy Bowlegs and convince him to surrender, but whether it was Howard's good fortune or bad, Bowlegs and his tribe never revealed themselves.

Fifteen years later in 1872, just as the Freedmen's Bureau was shutting down, President Grant twice sent Howard to Arizona as a special envoy to the Apaches. After negotiating a treaty with one group, Howard set out to convince the Apache chief Cochise to end his decades-long war against American ranchers, soldiers, stage drivers, and mail riders. To the chagrin of officers who had spent months pursuing and battling Cochise's band, the Chiricahua, Howard rode into the chief's mountain stronghold with only his aide Sladen plus a civilian guide and two Apache interpreters, chosen by Howard because they were Cochise's old friend and two nephews. Aside from their revolvers, they were unarmed.

In Arizona, Howard relished traveling into the unknown. The southwestern landscapes were eerie, magnificent, and unforgettable: narrow canyons blasted with heat, steep mountains twisting impossibly toward the clearest skies, parched lakebeds in constant shimmering mirage. The place names were something out of a novel for boys: Silver City, Ojo Caliente, the Dragoon Mountains, Middle-march Pass. At night Howard and his men would wrap themselves in blankets and sleep on hard ground, saddles for pillows, a profligate wash of stars above. Before dawn they crouched by a smoldering fire, eating the soldier's breakfast of coffee and bacon.

It was grand adventure, and Howard was once again the hero. On a more profound level, he saw his journey as an expression of faith — in the president, in Providence, and in his own power to persuade. After the brutal Indian wars of the 1860s — from Minnesota to Texas to California, against the Cheyenne, Kiowa, Comanche, Sioux, Paiute, and Shoshone, among others — President Grant had pivoted to what was known as a "Peace Policy" with the Indians. Favoring treaties over armed conquest, Grant sought to establish reservations in close consultation with the Christian groups — the Society of Friends, the American Missionary Association — that had played such a big role in coordinating relief efforts and schooling for the freedpeople in the South. Howard believed in the Peace Policy. On reservations the Indians would have the resources to learn "just the right way to plow and harrow, furrow and plant," he wrote, and they would be shown the path to Christ. They would have the opportunity to live tranquil, productive lives as Americans. Howard suspected that the policy had many enemies in the War Department and in Congress, which had previously staffed Indian reservations with patronage hacks. But he was determined to show that it could work.

At any moment as Howard's party approached the chief's stronghold, Cochise could have had them killed. Yet he spared Howard and his men and met them face-to-face. With Cochise's camp in sight, Howard flew a white flag and greeted his enemy with a resounding "How, amigo?" He sat on Cochise's buckskins, distributed crackers and sugar lumps to the Chiricahua children, and invited the chief to eat venison at his side. At night Howard danced in a long line by drumbeat and firelight, one woman holding his left hand, another his empty right sleeve. He slept under an oak tree thirty yards from Cochise's lean-to. Day after day, Howard suggested possible sites for a reservation. When the chief rejected one place, Howard proposed another. Finally, at a tribal council, after the women sang what sounded to Howard an approximation of "the low moaning of the wind," Cochise — nearly seventy, exhausted by life as an outlaw — declared that the spirits wanted peace. At the end of ten days, Howard left the Chiricahua with the guarantee of a large reservation in eastern Arizona and an Indian agent of Cochise's choosing. The regular killings in southern Arizona stopped, and Cochise never waged another war on Americans.

When Cochise died two years later in June 1874, a cavalry lieutenant wrote Howard that the chief was "on the Reservation that he promised you he would remain in. He remained true to his promises." Among settlers who had sought to exterminate the Chiricahua people, there was near-universal agreement that Howard had saved their lives and property. Word reached Howard just as he was arriving in Portland. It was, for him, a rare bit of good press after the Freedmen's Bureau inquiry and offered a specific pathway to redemption. As the general set out again to meet with Indian tribes in the Northwest, he was ready to be an instrument for peace. Everywhere he went, he was heartened by what he saw. Among the Yakama at the Simcoe reservation in eastern Washington, Howard found nearly everyone dressed as farmers. At the newly formed Malheur reservation in southeastern Oregon, the Paiute described their surprise and delight as their fields grew rich with "corn, potatoes, squashes, onions, and turnips," Howard wrote, "and all this product was to be their own." There might be a few holdouts for the old life, people whom Howard called "restless roamers," but he came away from his visits thinking that they held little sway over their tribes or, better yet, that many wanted to change their ways. When a Makah chief left his reservation at Neah Bay on the tip of the Olympic Peninsula, got drunk, and wound up in irons at Port Townsend, Howard went to his jail cell. Upon hearing "great contrition" and "the most solemn promises," he ordered the man released back to his tribe.

Howard's faith and experience led him to believe that the chief would make the most of his second chance.

Although Howard saw nothing to alarm him in his frontier travels, his encounters with tribal leaders in the Northwest were not free of the shadows of war. A year before his arrival, the Modoc tribe had engaged in a series of protracted battles with the army among the lava beds of far northern California after refusing to move to a reservation across the Oregon line near Fort Klamath. When the commanding general met with the Modoc chief Captain Jack at a peace parley in April 1873, Captain Jack shot the general and cut his throat. But within two months the tribe had surrendered, and in October 1873 Captain Jack and three other Modoc leaders were hanged. The rest of the tribe was exiled nearly two thousand miles away to the northeast corner of Indian Territory, bordering Kansas and Missouri. Coincidentally, while working as an aide to Howard at the Freedmen's Bureau, Melville Wilkinson had been specially deployed from Washington, DC, to supervise the resettlement of the Modoc. When Howard reached Portland in 1874, he ordered Wilkinson to continue his work with the tribe and supervise the journey east of one last group remaining in Oregon. Although Wilkinson initially put his exiles in handcuffs, he relented upon discovering that they were "obedient and well disposed," Howard wrote. He took heart from their cooperation; it was, he thought, "another instance where kindness conquers and wins." The Modoc proved to Howard that they were capable of learning their lesson, and they provided a useful and instructive example for every other tribe in the region. In the fall of 1874, Howard counted more than two dozen tribes in his department, and not one seemed close to the warpath.

Despite the recent violence, Howard persisted in his belief that he would preside over an era of peace. In the towns Howard passed through while touring his command — from Astoria to Walla Walla — and back in Portland, he told crowds eager for news from the frontier that he believed that soon there would be a strong and abiding peace with the Indians. He assured audiences that he would do everything in his considerable power to preserve that peace. And in the process, Howard might have imagined, he and the tribes alike would remake themselves, turning failure to success, and rejection to acceptance. It did not seem impossible. It appeared, in Howard's view, almost inevitable. To his daughter Grace he confided, "My work is not very hard."

CHAPTER 3
QUITE GOOD FRIENDS

April 1875

General Howard woke at four in the morning. Riding on streets lined with trees beginning to bud, he passed homes that were dark but warm with life, chimneys still smoldering from the previous night's fires. When he reached downtown Portland, he crossed lonely blocks under the blank stare of shuttered storefronts and empty commercial buildings; even the drunks were asleep. Howard could tell he was nearing the Willamette River when he saw his destination start to glow with gaslight in the east.

At the docks near Howard's army headquarters, preparations for the five o'clock eastbound steamer were well underway. The general was expected and knew where to go once on board. Settling into a long bench in his cabin, he tried to nap but kept jolting awake. Steamboats were never quiet. Howard had to contend with what he called "the music of the tread of the walkers and the talkers, the monotonous sounds from the engine, and the dripping drive-wheel always rolling and splashing, half in and half out of the water." By the time the steamer reached the Columbia River and Fort Vancouver passed on the port side, Howard had given up any prospect of slumber.

109

He would enjoy breakfast instead, which he knew from previous trips meant "good coffee, good salmon, always good steak and potatoes." Back in Portland, his children Chauncey, Harry, and Bessie were sick, with sores on their hands and feet. The general had left Lizzie to administer regular doses of quinine and sulfur. Already it was a distant memory, something that was happening in a separate world.

On the boat Howard could count on some friendly conversation. His aide Sladen was at his side, and the steamer captain joined them for meals. Howard commended his "unfailing good company" and "manly manners and voice." For much of the trip, Howard was like any tourist on an excursion, looking out the window, his mind wandering. He was a religious man, yet his thoughts did not turn to God. "How can any one go from western Oregon to the Dalles without thinking of the unsurpassed scenery?" he asked. He was mesmerized by the banks and bends of the river, always changing, always on the verge of becoming something new. The boat steamed upriver past flowering meadows, ancient woods still untouched, and waterfalls wild with spring rain. There were mountains so high that he could not see their peaks from his window — he had to walk to the boat's rear platform "to take in their lofty heads."

Every so often the steamer would hit a patch of the Columbia's fabled rapids, and as the boat twisted and rocked and pounded the water, Howard took a moment to admire the river pilot's "quick eye and steady nerves." One series of cascades was too rugged for any boat. The first leg of the journey ended, and all the luggage was unloaded. The passengers walked the gangway to a small train that ran five miles along the falls. Howard savored the slow upward procession of the portage, the constant rushing water, mist and mirage, light splitting into rainbows. Another steamboat was waiting at the top of the falls, "cheery," the general thought, with white cloth on the dining room table and a friendly captain at its head.

On Howard's travels around the Department of the Columbia, the reminders that he was conducting army business were infrequent, but jarring. The sharp 4 a.m. knock on the door of his hotel room at the Dalles, waking him for another day of travel east. The concussive blast of a steamship boiler breaking down — "more sudden and terror-inspiring," Howard thought, than "a clap of thunder in a clear sky; an earthquake at midnight; . . . the sudden and awful collision of two sleeper trains in the darkness." A mountain in the distance that looked, he thought, like nothing so much as "a pictorial wild Indian's head in battle." After a day, a night, and another day of travel, Howard reached the Columbia River port of Wallula, the gateway to Walla Walla.

Howard loved saying the word "Wallula," but "its sweetness," he noted, "stops with its name." The grass and flowers were withered — "forlorn," the general thought. An old Hudson's Bay Company fort lay in ruins, a reminder of the years when the only whites in the area were trappers and traders. The wind blew sand in his face. The stage road inland to Walla Walla was as rough and dusty as any he had traveled. "You ate, drank, and breathed *in,* but not *out,* the finest and most abundant of dry alkaline dirt," he wrote.

The end of the road was no better. As picturesque as the journey had been, Walla Walla was its opposite. Between wilderness and civilization there seemed to be an unavoidable intermediate step, a chaos of ruin that preceded the coming of true and effective order. At the beginning of April 1875, the town's streets and alleys were unusually squalid. It was more than the predictable winter accumulation of mud and horse manure. Walla Walla was "the filthiest place on the coast," a local paper pronounced. Riding up high on a horse provided no relief from the nauseating rot. "Dead cats and putrifying litter salute the olfactories at every turn," the *Walla Walla Statesman* complained. "The wonder is, not that so much sicknes[s] prevails, but that the population of the town is not decimated."

It was Howard's good fortune not to be staying there for long. At the local garrison, there was a horse waiting for him, as well as a cavalry captain to serve as his escort. Just a few minutes of riding took him back into glorious country. South and west from Walla Walla, the land folded and swelled like waves along a lakeshore. From the rises it was possible to look across the prairie all the way to the Blue Mountains, hazy in the east. But down each hill the horizon closed until there was nothing beyond the next ridge, just swirling grassy slopes. Wind muffled the sound of birdsong. Saddles groaned alongside the steady thump of hooves hitting dirt. Grasshoppers fluttered and clicked. The horses snorted and huffed, and snuck mouthfuls of bunchgrass when they slowed down to water in creeks clotted with flowering weeds and stunted trees. It required a feat of imagination to look ahead, to appreciate how far one had come, or how much longer one still had to go. As the horses strained into each successive climb, the sun and sky looked small, within reach. In spring-time the light was still gentle, but come summer, it would be blistering. That there was a world beyond the hills became an article of faith.

It was still cold outside, but General Howard was pleased to be in the field, his latest effort, as one newspaper reported, "to see the country for its own sake, and to thoroughly understand it in case any military necessity should arise to require it." The previous month he had braved the spring mud, which he noted was "deep & sticky," to reach a reservation outside Salem, Oregon's capital. Despite the challenges of traveling just after the thaw, Howard found these visits invari-ably pleasant, and he often paired them with lectures and church services in the nearest towns. In Salem he had addressed audiences of more than a thousand. Although one Democratic news-paper complained that the "great 'Christian soldier' " was demanding too much money — "one half of the receipts from each and every lecture," including charity benefits — Howard had scheduled sermons as well as his talk on Gettys-burg in Walla Walla.

Out on the prairie, Howard and his escort rode from ridge to valley and up again, across the line from Washington Territory to Oregon, mile after rolling mile. This was coveted country, the point at which pioneers on the Oregon Trail emerged from the mountains and realized that all the risk and sacrifice had not been in vain. Many of them stopped their trips short and bought property right here. It was ideal rangeland, and in the 1870s the settlers were learning that this was one of the best places on earth to grow wheat. Past the farms and ranches, Howard crossed a seemingly arbitrary divide into what the settlers considered to be hundreds of thousands of acres of empty land. Forty or so miles from Walla Walla, Howard and his escort cleared a final set of hilltops and reached an austere collection of log and frame buildings rising from the mud, surrounded in the distance by small farms, rail fences, and clusters of teepees.

The Indian agent for the Umatilla reservation, a tall man with short white hair and a full white beard, greeted the general warmly. The people who worked on reservations — administrators, teachers, doctors — were by and large a congenial group, Howard had found. Although on occasion he crossed paths with gruff characters with names like One Arm Brown — a "singular little man," in Howard's estimation — one of the general's favorite words to describe the government personnel he met in Indian country was "sprightly." At the Grand Ronde reservation near Salem, he had been impressed by the agent's "sprightly Irish wife." And at the Umatilla reservation, Howard was pleased that the agent himself, Narcisse Cornoyer, appeared at a glance to be a "sprightly Frenchman."

The reservation that Cornoyer administered had been formed for the Umatilla, Cayuse, and Walla Walla tribes during the great June 1855 council that also yielded treaties with the Yakama and Nez Perce nations. Back then Cornoyer, a recent arrival from Illinois by way of the California Gold Rush, had been fighting in the battles among the tribes and encroaching settlers that flared over the course of a decade in the Northwest. By 1855 the young man was known as Captain — soon Major — Cornoyer, leading a militia company composed of French Canadians in the fur trade.

In his early years in the West, Cornoyer had seen firsthand how peace could be harder than war. Immediately after the 1855 treaties were signed, Governor Isaac Stevens declared much of eastern Washington to be "open for settlement." As a result, the agreements had the perverse effect of attracting throngs of squatters to tribal territory, people who threatened and insulted the Indians they encountered, taunting them that their land was lost. By September, a federal Indian agent was traveling through Yakama country to investigate reports that white miners and travelers were being murdered. A young warrior tracked the agent down, cut his throat, and burned his body.

Cornoyer and his volunteers went back on the march, joined by other militiamen and companies of army regulars. Across eastern Washington, they fought against an alliance of Yakama, Umatilla, Walla Walla, Palouse, Cayuse, Spokane, and Coeur d'Alene. At the Battle of Walla Walla in December 1855, Cornoyer personally parleyed with the Walla Walla chief Peopeo Moxmox, a longtime advocate for peace. Although the chief had waved a white handkerchief, and Cornoyer attested to his good faith, a commander of the Oregon volunteers ordered Peopeo Moxmox taken hostage. Within a day, his guards had crushed his skull with their rifle butts, then scalped him, cut off his ears, and distributed his flesh as trophies.

The battles would continue for three more years, but after 1858 the region appeared to be at peace. If Cornoyer saw himself as someone who had helped to create that peace, he was also continually reminded of its cost. As members of defeated tribes settled onto reservations, Cornoyer moved with his family from western Oregon to a 160-acre claim — horses, cattle, and grain — just a few miles south of where Peopeo Moxmox had been murdered. In 1871, President Grant appointed Cornoyer Indian agent to the nearby reservation, on the recommendation of Oregon's Catholic bishop.

At the Umatilla reservation, Cornoyer invited Howard into his home, crowded but comfortable, suffused with the warm smells of pipe tobacco and wood smoke. As the general recovered from the long ride, the Indian agent introduced three of his five daughters, ages six to twenty-one — all beautiful, Howard would remember. He caught a few glimpses of their mother, who had Indian and Canadian ancestry — a métis — but she mostly stayed out of sight. Cornoyer was fifty-four, with a challenging set of responsibilities, but he showed unfailing good humor in conversation with Howard. "I was royally entertained," the general wrote.

Cornoyer was proud of his reservation. It was a beautiful site, twenty-five miles square, prairie yielding to forested foothills, described by one report as "embrac[ing] a large body of the most valuable land in Eastern Oregon." Its streams were full of trout, and salmon during the spawn. He could point Howard to men and women tilling the soil, most of them wearing what the agent called "the dress of the whites." They showed their "well-marked religious and devotional character" every Sunday at the Catholic chapel, forming "a more orderly and attentive congregation," according to one official, than most white Christians. A

116

couple of dozen children in uniform, hair shorn, sat in the reservation's school with the resident priest, reciting lessons in English, a language new to them all. Because it was only a day school, the students left in late summer to accompany their parents east into the mountains to hunt and fish. Cornoyer hoped he could find funding for a manual-labor boarding school, to keep the children year-round.

After devoting much of his tenure to arresting and punishing settlers who sold liquor to the tribes, Cornoyer also happily reported that "it is now extremely rare to see a drunken Indian." As a result, the agent thought the Indians were devoting themselves with special vigor to their wheat and oat farms while steadily enlarging their traditional herds of horses and cattle. Their work ethic and morale did not break after clouds of grasshoppers destroyed their crop the year before, nor did they give up their inclination to peace and industry after the measles killed "a good many" children despite the best efforts of the resident physician. The reservation's resilience was no small achievement. The wars of a generation earlier had begun when a similar measles outbreak in the spring of 1847 turned the Cayuse against missionaries who had settled near Walla Walla. The Whitman Massacre, named for the murders of Marcus and Narcissa Whitman and a dozen others at their Presbyterian outpost, suggested to many that whites and Indians could never coexist. But by 1875 Cornoyer could believe that he was working toward a new age of peace and prosperity, helping the Indians "morally and intellectually, so that they may become law-abiding and self-supporting citizens."

The peace was holding, but Cornoyer knew it was fragile. Settlers were crowding the land along the reservation boundaries — north, south, east, and west — and demanded that the Umatilla property be opened up for settlement. Local whites described the reservation as a colossal waste, its value lost on "a few worthless Indians." Cornoyer used the same adjective for the whites: they were "persons of a worthless character," benighted by their greed for land. Every day the settlers tested the reservation's borders by running their cattle into Indian country. They repeatedly sounded false alarms about impending Indian attack, drawing troops into the area.

Although the settlers wanted a fight, the Umatilla reservation tribes were refusing to give it to them. Faced with threats on all sides, the Indians used their treaty as a shield. They had an exacting knowledge of what it entitled them to — the borders that it delineated and the money and services that the federal government had guaranteed them. Indeed, because the tribe believed in the security of their agreement, they exempted themselves from the typical battles over land boundaries and water claims that defined the early days of frontier life, those moments before strangers became neighbors. The treaty protected them, at least temporarily, from the imperatives of the markets for real estate and cattle and grain. The settlers might be "universal and ardent" in their desire to take the reservation, but as long as the federal government stayed on the Indians' side, the treaty gave the tribes something that they regarded as more powerful. They had rights. There was no need to go to war. With their treaty in hand, the reservation Indians were, as one official wrote, "in all things ready to obey the law; . . . they are great sticklers for their rights (and they are pretty well posted on this head)."

Yet in Cornoyer's view, the threats to the reservation were not limited to "rapacious" white settlers. Equally troubling were the Indians who remained off the reservation, still approximating a traditional way of life on the Columbia River, hunting and fishing and migrating with the seasons. The agent could talk at length about the problem of "nontreaty" Indians: how they "all believe[d] in and practice[d] polygamy" and, more troubling still, how they rejected Christianity for the teachings of a radical false prophet — a "self-constituted chief" whom Cornoyer knew as Smo-hol-ler, an old Wanapam man from near Wallula who was attracting followers from many of the neighboring tribes. He was "constantly preach-ing," Cornoyer wrote, "that the day is coming when they will again be a great and powerful people, and will be strong enough to drive the whites from the country."

The danger that these roving Indians posed was arguably minimal. The agent guessed that there were only two thousand of them, including women and children, all different tribes, in small bands scattered across a vast distance. More than any real commitment to violence, their religion reflected how much their world was changing and how thoroughly beaten they had been. But Cornoyer had reason to worry. From his perspective it mattered little if the nontreaty Indians clashed with whites. Rather, his main concern was that they kept the men and women living on the Umatilla reservation from fully embracing their new lives as farmers. The holdout groups "h[e]ld a

119

control" on the reservation Indians, Cornoyer feared, taunting them as "whites and half-breeds," "appealing to [their] passions and pride," suggesting that there was a better life on the outside. "Until these Indians are placed under proper control," the agent reported, "there will be no material improvement among the Indians on the several reservations in Eastern Oregon and Washington."

As Cornoyer briefed Howard, two men walked into the agent's home. One, a Cayuse man, spoke no English. The other man was Cornoyer's interpreter, John McBean, the son of an Indian woman and a Hudson Bay Company officer, who had been raised at Fort Walla Walla to speak the local languages. Without McBean, the best Cornoyer could do was struggle through a conversation in Chinook Jargon. Although the interpreter wore western clothes, it was thought that he "could pass at any time for an Indian" and rumored that on occasion he had donned traditional dress and snuck into tribal councils.

McBean announced that he was accompanying a messenger from a chief named Joseph, who was staying at a camp nearby with the Cayuse leader Young Chief and hoped to meet the new army commander. This was unexpected news. Howard had heard enough about Joseph to know that he did not live on this reservation. He led a band of Nez Perce Indians a hundred miles east, in Oregon's Wallowa Valley. The very fact that he had reached the Umatilla reservation was an impressive feat. Joseph would have had to cross two mountain ranges as well as the Wallowa and Grande Ronde Rivers. Even in the best weather it would have been difficult, but in April 1875, eastern Oregon was emerging from one of the worst winters in memory. La Grande, a settlement midway between Nez Perce country and the Umatilla reservation, had registered temperatures of eighteen degrees below zero. In the Wallowa Valley, thermometers froze. Bottles of kerosene froze. Four feet of snow fell in one day. By the time Joseph forded the rivers, they were swollen from the thaw.

Howard told McBean and the Cayuse messenger that he welcomed the chance to speak with Joseph. While the messenger delivered word from Howard, Cornoyer stood with the general and walked with him to inspect the reservation's buildings. A half hour later, outside in clear daylight, eleven Indians approached the general and the agent in single file. They were big men, "noticeably tall and stout for Indians," Howard thought, "particularly fond of ornament and display." The general regarded the party as "quite carefully dressed in Indian costume."

One by one, the men greeted Cornoyer, then shook Howard's hand. It was not the sprightly salutation that Howard received from the Indian agent upon arriving at the reservation. Nor did it compare to Howard's cheerful hello, which had famously put the Apache chief Cochise at ease. The Indians were quiet. The sounds of the outside — breeze, insects, birds — remained vivid. There were no pleasantries or smiles. The procession assumed a careful rhythm, in Howard's opinion "most solemn."

Then Joseph walked to Howard. The chief was more than six feet tall. He had high broad cheekbones and large eyes, a square jaw and strong chin. At thirty-five years old, he was a decade younger than the general, his face just beginning to crease — at the mouth, his brow, the corners of his eyes — despite a lifetime in the sun, snow, and wind. He stepped close and looked down at Howard, black eyes to blue. Howard looked back at Joseph. They stood still, hand in hand, until the time began to stretch. Though Joseph towered over Howard, the general did not feel threatened or intimidated. The chief's gaze did not strike Howard as "an audacious stare." Instead, the general felt something else. It was hard to define. Joseph was showing strength, Howard thought, but also vulnerability. "He was trying to open the windows of his heart to me," Howard later wrote of that moment, "and at the same time endeavoring to read my disposition and character."

Joseph broke the silence — just a few words in a deep voice — and the moment passed. "I heard that Washington had some message for me," the chief said through McBean the interpreter. "I came to visit my friends among the Cayuses. Young Chief told me to speak to the agent. That is all."

"There is no word from Washington," the general replied. "We are glad to see you and shake you by the hand."

Within minutes, Joseph and his party were filing back to their camp. In the rolling country, they disappeared quickly from Howard's view. The general was alone again with the Indian agent, and their pleasant visit resumed as if it had never been interrupted.

Soon Howard would try to make sense of what had just happened. He thought it had been a good meeting, like so many others he was having with chiefs throughout his command. The previous commander of the Department of the Columbia had identified Joseph's homeland in the Wallowa Valley as a site for potential trouble, where ranchers and gold miners were starting to move onto traditional Nez Perce land. Not long after arriving in the Northwest, Howard had met with the tribe's Indian agent, and now he resolved to learn more about the Wallowa situation. Having met Joseph face-to-face, Howard felt he had little to fear from the chief. His encounter with Joseph had moved him. As the memory receded, the general reduced it to a story he could tell and even laugh about — that warm moment when the chief's calloused hand wrapped around his, that steady gaze, the feeling that Joseph was trying to read his thoughts. Perhaps, Howard imagined, Joseph had succeeded. "An Indian is usually a shrewd physiognomist," the general wrote. "I think Joseph and I became then quite good friends."

General Howard left the reservation late on Friday, April 16. He and his companion the cavalry captain headed back to the army's fort at Walla Walla the way they had come. As they rode, the sun at their backs cast the Blue Mountains in red before disappearing below the hills to the west. Even in the dark, they expected an easy journey. The moon, just a few days from full, silvered the rolling country. Howard had hours on his horse to think about the lectures he would be giving in town. From Walla Walla, he would then be riding out to the Colville Indian Reservation, which had been formed along the upper Columbia River by executive order in 1872 to accommodate an assortment of small tribes that had never made treaties with the United States. It was two hundred miles to the north, five days each way, never an easy trip, but one that he could make in good cheer. When he finally returned home to Portland, sometime in early May, the whole Howard family, save the two eldest children, would steam to Alaska. There would be army outposts to inspect and native chiefs to greet, and he planned to deliver yet another lecture on Gettysburg. But he would have many days — and many bright nights — to spend with his wife and children. It would surely be a glorious summer, the beginning of another happy year in the West.

By midnight, Howard and his escort were ten miles short of Walla Walla, on the banks of a river just below the Washington line that the locals knew as the Tum-a-Lum. The moonlight was proving to be deceptive. The men could not find the one spot where riders could easily ford. They tried going along the water's edge, but nothing seemed familiar. The water looked too deep to cross.

That disoriented feeling — the sense of dislocation — was a shock in the night. After hours of progress on a settled path, it had been easy to forget that he and the cavalry captain were, in fact, alone in the dark. Splashing in the Tum-a-Lum, Howard had a glimpse of a profound truth: very little was certain on the frontier. One could know the land — one could be sure of the route — yet never reach the destination.

That unmoored moment did not last long. After a little while, Howard and his escort spotted a farmhouse and pounded on the door until they woke the farmer, a Scotsman about Howard's age. To the general's relief, the man recognized him by sight — perhaps had read the most recent edition of the *Walla Walla Statesman,* announcing his arrival in the area — and immediately offered to help. The farmer saddled his horse, led the way to the ford, and escorted the officers across. Once they reached the far bank of the Tum-a-Lum, Howard asked the farmer if he wanted payment for his valuable service. According to a published report, the farmer replied, "Not one cent; I owe you for more than that for fighting for my country!" Laughing, Howard shook the man's hand and thanked him.

CHAPTER 4
WINDING WATERS

The moment Joseph left Howard and Cornoyer at the Umatilla reservation, he was no longer a figure of mysterious power. To Howard he may have been the very picture of an Indian chief, with his striking touch and deep black gaze, but Joseph's Cayuse cousins had known him as a boy and young man, once overshadowed by his father Tuekakas and charismatic younger brother Ollokot. Back among kin and tribesmen, changed out of his ceremonial clothes, Joseph could shed the very names by which Howard and other whites knew him. First, his tribe was not Nez Perce — that was what the French had called them after seeing them make a sign for the tribe that suggested a nose being pierced. Instead, he considered himself one of the Nimi'ipuu, "the real people." Just as important, he was no longer Joseph. The men who walked with him to meet General Howard and the Indian agent knew him as Heinmot Tooyalakekt. Years later, when he explained his name to a little girl who spoke only English, they said the words together several times. Then he translated the words as "T-under (thunder)," the girl remembered, " 'tunder in mts.' and with his arm he described the course of thunder which reached from the base, to the very summit of the mts. His voice, too, was deep and full." He was Thunder Rolling in the Mountains, or Thunder Rising to Loftier Mountain Heights. "Joseph" was what his father had been christened in November 1839 by Henry Spalding, who had recently come from New York to preach the gospel to the Nez Perce people.

In the spring of 1840, when Tuekakas asked Spalding to baptize his infant son, the boy was called Ephraim. But after his father left the church and returned to the Wallowa Valley, the child lost his Christian name. When whites saw his father at the treaty negotiations in 1855 and beyond, they continued to call Tuekakas Joseph. And when they met his son, they forgot he had been baptized Ephraim and called him Joseph, too. They were Old Joseph and Young Joseph, the past and present leaders of one of the largest and most important of the Nez Perce bands, consisting of several hundred men, women, and children and vast horse and cattle herds.

On the Umatilla reservation, Heinmot Tooyalakekt — Young Joseph — could walk where his father had spent part of his youth. Riding homeward through the Grande Ronde Valley, he went through the country where his mother, a Nez Perce woman, had been born. But if the visit connected the chief to his ancestral past, it also presented a startling vision of the future. West of the Blue Mountains, he saw reservation Indians dressing and praying like whites, their land fenced and plowed. These new ways of living echoed what was happening on the east side of the mountains. Over the past fifteen years, the lush landscapes of the Grande Ronde Valley had been transformed, the roll and swell of bunchgrass uprooted for fields of wheat, oats, and barley, dairy pastures, and apple and pear orchards. Gold miners blasted the mountains, dug trenches and pits, and fouled the streams. A steam-powered flour mill turned skies black, and four other grain mills and three sawmills fed on the rivers and creeks. Forests were felled, and frame homes and commercial buildings rose in clusters.

Hundreds of people were now living in towns — La Grande and Union, Oro Dell and Summerville — buying the produce of the farmers and ranchers and selling goods and services to, in one local's phrasing, "the miners, packers, stage owners and other migratory classes" who constantly circulated through the valley. There were hotels for the weary traveler, taverns for the thirsty ones, tobacconists and bootmakers, butchers and smiths, lawyers, land dealers, and shipping agents. In the early 1870s, a man could make his fortune in La Grande by sweeping out the town's businesses, carting piles of dirt to the river, and filtering out stray bits of gold dust, the lost by-products of innumerable transactions. Locals could argue about editorials in competing newspapers, Democratic and Republican.

Over one more seam of mountains, and the chief was home in the Wallowa Valley, more than three thousand square miles of rich high country. When Joseph's nephew Hemene Moxmox (Yellow Wolf) dreamed of this place, he said that four images came to his mind: mountains, streams, prairies, and the lake. Almost everyone in Joseph's band could remember when there were no others besides themselves; it had been only four years, the spring of 1871, since the whites started venturing in from the Grande Ronde Valley. Joseph and his band had spent most days alone, their lives constantly adjusting to the seasons, the herds, the bloom and wither of the land, and the needs and obligations that defined family and extended family, from teepee to village to band of villages.

Mountains, streams, prairies, and the lake. The colors were simple: black, gray and white, deep enveloping blue, the green of spring fading through summer to yellow and brown. Most days Joseph and the men, women, and children of his band could turn from east to south to west and see sharp peaks silhouetted by sun. Mountains surrounded the valley, shadowed it, protected the valley from the surrounding world, and watched the lives within. The ancient basalts, granites, slate, and marble were a silent record of massive lava flows, advancing glaciers, and a sea floor raised thousands of feet. White in winter, the mountains ran wet with the spring thaw and echoed and amplified the melting rush that gave the land below its name: Wallowa, translated by Joseph as "that beautiful valley of winding waters."

As the weather grew warm, the Wallowa River and a tangle of creeks — all tributaries of the Grande Ronde — ran thick and silver with salmon. At protected holes along the river, Nez Perce men and women worked their spears and nets night and day from spring to fall, as one species of salmon, then another and another still made their spawning runs. In the dark the torchlight split and swayed in the water. People waded in the cold streams, swam, splashed through on horseback, and paddled dugout canoes and rafts lashed together from driftwood. They caught hundreds of salmon at a time. In the days that followed a great catch, the sun moved across the sky to the flat thump of women pounding fish with mortar and pestle. Salmon was dried in the wind, cooked over fire, and cured with smoke. The fragrance scented the air, a hint of the sea hundreds of miles from the Pacific.

If the bounty of the Wallowa's waters sustained Joseph's band, every day they appreciated the plenty of the hunt. Nez Perce men and women wore shirts, breeches, leggings, and dresses made from animals they had taken from the valley's towering forests — whitetail deer, mule deer, pronghorn antelope, bighorn sheep. With tools fashioned from bone and horn, they skinned their kills and stretched the hides tight, scraped them clean from fat and flesh, and tanned them with brains. The women took special care to leave the tails intact, to place at the nape of the neck when they cut and sewed the hides into dresses, showing which animal had given its skin and announcing the skill and success of the hunter. When a hunter killed a bear, his family wore necklaces that rattled with its claws. When he had the good fortune to slay an elk, the women in his family celebrated by decorating their dresses with its teeth. After many years, a great hunter's wives might wear dresses covered entirely in molars.

In the forest groves where the animals ran, the ponderosa pines stood tall and brown, bleaching red in the sun, bark cracked like weathered faces. Though the profound quiet suggested a world before people, the trees bore hundreds of years of slashes and scars. In the starving times of early spring, Nez Perce families would eat the inner layers of the bark so they could live to the next season.

Across the prairies and meadows, the band's herds of horses and cattle grazed and slept. From a distance they looked still, a pattern of dots on a hillside, but up close the animals were in constant motion, rooting and walking and trotting, down to the creeks, along beaten paths, through the blanket of grass and clover. In the heat of summer, the prairies bloomed blue with camas lilies. The women, who often fed their families with berries and roots, pulled up camas bulbs by the bushel, piled the sweet roots high, peeled their black skins, steamed and baked them in great pits, and pounded them for soup and bread for the coming year.

After long days of quiet toil, the men and women of Joseph's band could rest at night and talk about their collective life, a history of births and deaths, storms and accidents, extending season by season from the eternal present to a remembered past, to the past of their parents and grandparents and great-grandparents, and back further still. Nez Perce people had lived in this part of the world for thousands of years. The signs of ancient life that they found scattered throughout the area — ancient rock shelters, paintings on cliffsides, footprints frozen in basalt — had been left by their ancestors.

The stories parents told their children went back to the dawn of existence: before the animals assumed their present shapes and roles, when there was no hierarchy of man and beast, and when the ancestors of everything living shared the world with other beings, called monsters. The animals — coyote, bear, magpie, skunk, rattlesnake, wolf,

131

eagle, goose — had walked and talked like humans. They told jokes to and about each other. They forged friendships, made promises, and warmed each other at night by urinating in their beds. They married and went hunting together. They found victims to trick and murder and cook over fires. In these stories — warm, violent, quietly funny — men and women explained how the world had come to be while also acknowledging that it could have taken another path. Long ago, they knew, life had been very different. Animals were not created to serve humans. Humans had not always thought of themselves as separate, above, and apart from the rest of nature. Nez Perce stories revealed a sensibility that was both ironic and deeply engaged, open to the imperfections of existence, the messiness of living, and the smallness of one's life amid the vast scale of the world.

In the middle of the Wallowa Valley, a herder could look in every direction and imagine the prairies stretching onward forever. But a quick ride east, even a few steps up a rise, revealed that the unchanging landscape was an illusion. After rippling gently for miles, the valley abruptly fell away into a series of canyons thousands of feet deep. They were too deep to see the rivers — Imnaha, Snake, Salmon — that pushed and sliced their way through the rock, but the men, women, and children in Joseph's band could hear the waters rush, a sound deeper than the constant whisper of the wind. Across this great rift in the earth, the far canyon walls were shadowed in the afternoon sun by the cliffs on which the people stood, a perfect dark reflection of the place where the Wallowa

Valley ended.

In the warm seasons, it could seem that Joseph and his people's lives extended only as far as the cliff's edge, that the other side was another world. But Nez Perce country rolled on for more than a hundred miles beyond the canyons, east all the way to the snow-capped Bitterroot Mountains. Joseph, his band, and their herds were constantly climbing up and down hills and cliffs, passing from one side of the steep canyons to another. Their journeys were dictated in part by necessity. At four thousand feet above sea level, the Wallowa Valley was too cold in the winter to support Joseph's band and their horses and cattle. In the canyons the weather was warmer, and the animals were protected. From the upper limits of the valley, Joseph could wind his way down a steep dirt path, switching back again and again until he reached water rushing northeast toward the Grande Ronde River. Down at the bottom, his band often spent the winter at the confluence of the creek and river. Just south along the canyon, the cave where Joseph had been born in early 1840 lay hidden in the rock.

Settlers, explorers, and travelers in the Northwest were constantly describing the mountains' impossible heights, their majesty and cruelty, the inspiration they gave to the lives lived on the flat land down below. For them, the mountains were a miracle. But for Joseph's band the peaks, cliffs, and canyons signified instead the constant struggle of every day. The chief understood that he lived in a world of steep ascents and sharp drops. Mountains were no barrier. Nez Perce lives were defined by confronting them.

Every season — sun, wind, rain, and ice —

proved the essential truth that life was harder than rock. The mountains surrounding the Wallowa Valley were shaped like animals or human figures or benches or tools — even white people could see that — but up close Nez Perce men, women, and children could read the shapes within the ridge-lines. The hills each told their own stories, each suggested a way up and across: dull paths where people and animals had walked for centuries, stretches of grass rising through rock, shrubs and small trees revealing tiny creeks. Every hill, no matter how stark, asked to be climbed and crossed.

The mountains turned boys and girls into adults. After studying with their parents, an elder, or a spiritual leader, the children traveled alone into the hills for a day, even a week, with no food, no weapons, just a little water. Fasting until they reached a trance state, they searched the world around and within them for their *wey-ya-kin,* a guiding spirit that defined their talents as individuals — for hunting, war, speed, cunning — and their role in their band. The *wey-ya-kin* could be a bird, a beast, the wind, lightning, a rainbow. In the mountains the thunder revealed itself to Joseph. It was where a vision of a yellow wolf appeared before his nephew. "You may think I am nothing!" it told him. "You may think I am only bones! But I am alive! You can see me! I am talking to you!"

The *wey-ya-kin* instructed the children on the objects they needed to carry with them in daily life to ensure health and success: whistles and clubs to make war, paint to apply before battle, the songs they needed to sing as they faced death. With their spirit's powers, the children assumed a new, deeper place in their family, village, band, and tribe, a set of tasks, functions, and obligations — a set of stories that they could tell — that had been generations in the making. The encounter with an outside spirit made them more fully human. Emerging from seclusion, they announced how they had changed. In search of their *wey-ya-kin*, often they went into the mountains with one name and returned with another.

Nez Perce families and fortunes spanned mountain ranges. One of Joseph's wives, Heyoom Yoyikt, was the sister of a Nez Perce leader in Lapwai, the "place of the butterflies" east of the Snake and Salmon Rivers, near where Henry Spalding had built his first mission. Joseph's band included many husbands and wives from other Nez Perce bands and nearby tribes, Cayuse, Palouse, Umatilla, and Walla Walla. For centuries kinship fostered commerce, and vice versa. Across the mountains the Wallowa Valley band had traded for horses since the early eighteenth century, the root of their great herds. In the outside world they found the glass beads and cowries that replaced dyed porcupine quills as decoration for clothing, saddles, shoes, and bags. On horseback, Nez Perce hunting parties ventured hundreds of miles east over the Bitterroots to vast plains that trembled with bison. They learned to kill buffalo alongside the Flatheads, who became connected to them in countless ways through marriage, and learned to communicate through elaborate signs to all the Plains tribes.

When Nez Perce people considered their history, they were never alone. They could tell stories of great friends across the mountains and of great enemies as well. Some of the stories extended

135

back decades, to fathers, grandfathers, and great-grandfathers, achieving the power of myth. Never, though, was war an abstraction. Within living memory, Nez Perce warriors had fought the Snake tribes close to the Wallowa Valley — Bannock, Shoshone, and Paiute — and with Blackfeet, Crow, Sioux, and Cheyenne far away. The battles were intimate, fought face-to-face by knife and war club, arrow and rifle. Warriors could describe the eyes of their foes, sharp with fury, resigned to their fate, unseeing in death. After generations of conflict, Nez Perce leaders made peace with the Plains tribes in the early 1870s. But on their bodies they continued to carry the scars of their journeys and encounters across the mountains. The scalps of their onetime enemies remained among their possessions, shriveled and dry. The stories of cutting them — "over the eyebrows," one remembered, "above the ears and on around the head[, t]hen a jerk of the hair" — stayed fresh.

In Nez Perce country, the mountains were not a miracle — the miracle was level ground. The valleys were places of plenty, safety, and rest, where cattle grew fat over long warm days, where children rode and raced and learned to hunt and shoot. For Joseph's people, within one miracle, the Wallowa Valley, was another: a deep finger lake four miles long hidden in the hills at the valley's southern edge, so blue that even brilliant summer skies looked wan in comparison. Sparkling in sunlight, the lake was bounded to the south by towering mountains, and to the north by the giant, gently sloping glacial moraines that had dammed it thousands of years earlier. After the spring thaw, while rivers raged at flood stage, the lake sat quiet and still, sustaining life without constantly threatening to wash it away. When Joseph approached, he could see teepees clustered along its shores.

About twenty miles northwest of the lake, where the Lostine River met the Wallowa, Joseph's father was buried in a fenced plot at the foot of a hill. In his final days in the summer of 1871, Tuekakas had called for his son. Eyes cloudy and dim, too feeble to ride a horse by himself — he rode double, holding on to a boy — the old man told Joseph, "My body is returning to my mother earth, and my spirit is going very soon to see the Great Spirit Chief." He then pronounced Joseph the leader of their people. "They look to you to guide them," he said.

At the center of Tuekakas's burial ground stood a red pole topped with a bell. For three years it rang as the wind blew. Then in 1874 a white man stole it. Tuekakas died just weeks after the first ranchers had ventured with their herds from the Grande Ronde country into the Wallowa Valley. From one spring to the next, as Joseph's band returned to the valley after winter in the canyons, they found an increasing number of intruders, spread from the valley's upper reaches to the lake — log cabins, furniture, wagons, bales of hay, cattle and sheep wandering the bunchgrass.

Joseph had never known a world without whites. Some people in his band were old enough to remember the first time the missionary Henry Spalding set foot in the Wallowa Valley in July 1839 and pronounced it beautiful — the first time any white man had seen their land. Very few could remember the world before September 1805, when Meriwether Lewis, William Clark, and their

137

Corps of Discovery appeared on the Weippe Prairie above the Clearwater River. After crossing the Bitterroot Mountains through deep snow at the Lolo Pass, the explorers were starving, frozen, near death. When Nez Perce elders told stories of this encounter, they described how tribal leaders first debated whether to kill the outsiders. But one woman spoke for them: Wat-ku-weis (Returning After Being Captured), who had been taken as a girl by the Blackfeet and sold to the French in Canada, only to make her way home years later. Wat-ku-weis convinced the group to spare Lewis and Clark's lives because long ago the whites had treated her as one of their own. "These are the people who helped me!" she said. "Do them no hurt!"

Lewis and Clark's party was taken to a large village, fed, and nursed back to health. When they were strong again, they paddled Nez Perce canoes to the mouth of the Columbia River. The Corps of Discovery returned in May 1806 to go east back through the Lolo Pass, staying with their Nez Perce friends for a month until the snow finally melted and then relying on Nez Perce guides to get them across the mountains. Lewis and Clark left behind peace medals and American flags, hair ribbons and beads, and a handkerchief, as well as guns, powder, and hundreds of balls — the Nez Perce people's first firearms, a major source of advantage over enemy tribes. In 1875, Joseph's band had ample occasion to remember this moment. They knew one of their oldest members, Halahtookit (Daytime Smoke) as the son William Clark fathered during that spring with the sister of Hohots Ilppilp (Red Grizzly Bear), a chief on the Clearwater.

Nez Perce men and women explained and made natural the daily rhythms and routines of their lives with stories of animals, mountains, and winding waters. They established their place in a larger world with tales of friendship and war among the constellations of tribes that surrounded them near and far. When Joseph's band tried to make sense of their encounters with the white people who had come onto their land, however, their stories often centered around law.

Life in the Wallowa Valley and among the many Northwest tribes required law. To manage the pasturelands for great herds, to divide fishing grounds, to trade for goods near and far, to hunt and fight honorably, to make lasting peace — Joseph and his people nurtured a set of ways to live properly as well as a strong sense of right and wrong. "Our fathers gave us many laws, which they had learned from their fathers. These laws were good," Joseph would write. "They told us to treat all men as they treated us; that we should never be the first to break a bargain; that it was a disgrace to tell a lie; that we should speak only the truth; that it was a shame for one man to take from another his wife, or his property without paying for it." The punishments for breaking the rules were felt in this world and the next. "We were taught to believe that the Great Spirit sees and hears everything, and that he never forgets," Joseph recalled, "that hereafter he will give every man a spirit-home according to his deserts: if he has been a good man, he will have a good home; if he has been a bad man, he will have a bad home."

With Lewis and Clark, Nez Perce leaders declared their friendship with the United States.

That sense of connection survived the rough army of fur trappers and traders who came in the 1820s and became regular buyers of Nez Perce horses as they scoured the Northwest for beaver pelts. But from the 1830s onward, nearly every encounter with whites was mediated by new sets of rules. Henry Spalding preached the Ten Commandments and a version of Christ's teachings that left little room for the old ways of living. Those in his charge who disobeyed him would be flogged, he said. When Tuekakas left the church and returned to the Wallowa Valley, he was choosing between one set of laws and another.

In 1842, with England and the United States each claiming the Northwest, a New Yorker named Elijah White visited Nez Perce country as the American government's first Indian agent, embracing the task of establishing federal authority over the tribe. Instead of the Ten Commandments, he went one better and demanded that the Nez Perce accept a code of eleven laws. Some of the laws enumerated punishments and offenses — hanging for murders and arson, the lash for theft. At the same time, he sought to clarify the process of making and enforcing the law. His rules specified that the chiefs would punish Indian wrongdoers, while white criminals would face justice from the Indian agent. Furthermore, White insisted that the tribe create a new title for one of their leaders: head chief. It initially appeared to be a meaningless formality to the far-flung bands, which remained completely autonomous, each with its own sets of chiefs, elders, village leaders, spirit men, warriors, hunters, and fisherman. Still, the leaders accepted White's terms. They had little reason to consider the agent as anything but a friend. As a practical matter they understood that the head chief could serve as a liaison between the US government and the bands.

Thirteen years later the treaty of 1855 was made, during a time when the Nez Perce bands' commitment to peace and law had withstood the fighting that gripped nearby tribes. When Cayuse warriors murdered the missionaries Marcus and Narcissa Whitman in 1847, Spalding found sanctuary among his Nez Perce neighbors. In the conflicts that followed, the tribe sided with the US Army and local settler militias. When one member of Joseph's band recalled the greatest battle of that time — the battle during which the peace emissary Peopeo Moxmox was murdered — he did not decry the perfidy of the Oregon volunteers. Instead, he remembered fighting side by side with white soldiers besieged by swiftly circling Yakama warriors. At night, after the bullets and arrows stopped flying, he guided the soldiers to safety through the enemy's cordon.

Joseph's people had strong memories of the June 1855 treaty council, which guaranteed the Wallowa Valley for them. They were equally certain that the 1863 treaty ceding the valley, which Tuekakas never signed, amounted to theft. The second treaty had been negotiated soon after gold was discovered in 1860 on Nez Perce land along the Clearwater River in Idaho Territory. In one year fifteen thousand whites poured in, as fast as the Oregon Steam Navigation Company could ferry them. The gold rush that made Portland rich turned the country east across the canyons from the Wallowa Valley into a hash of mining settlements and squatters' farms. Whites far outnumbered Indians. They chiseled boulders into dust.

141

Their horses picked the prairies bare. Their axes turned forests into scrubland.

Although the intruders were all on Nez Perce land illegally, removing them seemed far beyond the power of the civilians in charge of Indian affairs. On the other side of the continent, the army was fighting for the life of the Union. It was not about to go to war against tens of thousands of nominally loyal Americans in the Northwest. Instead, the government offered the Nez Perce a smaller reservation with boundaries that a federal Indian agent would be capable of policing. The treaty delegation met only with leaders from bands near Lapwai, including the man who held the title of "head chief," a Christian who spoke so well that he was known as Lawyer. The proposed new reservation took almost none of their territory but ceded nearly everything else, more than five million acres — 90 percent of the 1855 reservation, including the Wallowa Valley as well as land claimed by several other bands.

When Tuekakas first considered the 1855 treaty, he disputed whether humans could own any part of the earth. But when he learned of the new treaty, he behaved in a way that whites would have recognized. He claimed his land. He marked the boundaries of his band's territory — poles set in stone mounds, "in order," Joseph wrote, "to have all people understand how much land we owned." "Inside is the home of my people — the white man may take the land outside," Tuekakas announced. "Inside this boundary all our people were born. It circles around the graves of our fathers, and we will never give up these graves to any man."

As Tuekakas prepared to join the ancestors — as

142

his band watched government surveyors explore the valley to site townships and then as the first ranchers worked their way past his boundary markers — the dying chief prepared a final message to his son. "Always remember that your father never sold his country," he told Joseph in the summer of 1871. "You must stop your ears whenever you are asked to sign a treaty selling your home." With sightless eyes, Tuekakas envisioned what the Wallowa Valley would look like in just a few years' time. "White men will be all around you. They have their eyes on this land," he said. "My son, never forget my dying words. This country holds your father's body. Never sell the bones of your father and mother."

Watching his father die, Joseph made him a promise. "I pressed my father's hand," he wrote, "and told him I would protect his grave with my life."

CHAPTER 5
THE WILDERNESS OF
AMERICAN POWER

Wallowa Valley,
1872–1875

The ride from Lapwai to the Wallowa Valley in the dead of August 1872 taxed John Monteith's strength to the utmost. "105 miles distant," he practically panted in a letter to his boss in the Office of Indian Affairs, "over a very bad trail across the mountains." It took the gaunt Presbyterian two days, with another reservation employee and two Indian guides riding at his side. Pale and hollow-eyed, his beard wilted and large balding head shiny and slick in the heat, he looked older than his thirty-five years. Arriving at Joseph's camp on August 22, he announced his presence, only to hear that the chief was not ready to see him.

When Joseph and Ollokot spent the Fourth of July in 1872 meeting with an Oregon congressman and a former federal Indian superintendent, the results gave little comfort. The Nez Perce leaders' argument for why the Wallowa Valley should remain in Nez Perce hands had impressed James Slater and Alfred Meacham enough for them to pass along word to other officials who, they believed, might have more power to act. Slater wrote a letter to the Office of Indian Affairs, asking for the "appointment of some person to visit [Nez Perce] country and settle differences between Indians and settlers in regard to certain lands."

In Washington, the letter was logged by a clerk in a registry book and directed to someone in the office to read. It was soon determined that Slater's request should be forwarded to Thomas B. Odeneal, the newly appointed superintendent of Indian affairs for Oregon. Without any instructions the letter was sent back across the country again. Joseph and Ollokot's words in La Grande had yielded an exercise of government power that amounted to a shuffling of papers, so slight as to be imperceptible. Reflecting on the July 4 meeting in La Grande, the *Mountain Sentinel* believed nothing would change, predicting that "it is in the nature of things that this beautiful [Wallowa] Valley will be settled immediately."

But relationships between the United States and the Nez Perce and other tribes were not simply the province of a single office with the definitive power to resolve claims by ignoring them. Nothing was ever so neat. Indian affairs were administered by a rough agglomeration of politicians and functionaries, multiple layers of bureaucracy that consisted of thousands of people in Washington, DC, and spread thin across the West. Closest to the Wallowa Valley — across the Snake River in Lapwai, Idaho — was Monteith, the Indian agent assigned to the Nez Perce reservation. His duties included encouraging the tribe to embrace agriculture and logging, managing a mill that processed the grain that the Indians were growing, and providing a school for Nez Perce boys and girls. Appointed to the position the year before, Monteith had brought along his father, a minister, to run the local mission. Monteith supervised any number of skilled support staff, from teachers, interpreters, and doctors to farmers, blacksmiths, and carpenters. In 1872, the federal government was paying more than twenty different kinds of specialists and tradesmen on reservations. On issues relating to the Wallowa Valley, Monteith worked with a federal superintendent of Indian affairs for Oregon, and they, in turn, reported to the staff of the Office of Indian Affairs in Washington, DC. The head of the office, the commissioner of Indian affairs, served under the secretary of the interior, who ultimately answered to President Grant.

As big as the Indian affairs bureaucracy was, from the capital into the field, it still did not have a monopoly on administering native life. Congress set, funded, and continually revised many of the policies directed at Indians. President Grant sought independent advice on civilizing the Indians humanely from the Board of Indian Commissioners he appointed, a voluntary panel of Protestant ministers and philanthropists with its own staff and authority to inspect reservations. And all the while, the army retained a critical role in engaging with native tribes, regardless of whether relations with them were peaceful or hostile. Army policy relating to Nez Perce Indians went up the chain of command from local garrisons in Lapwai and Walla Walla to the Department of the Columbia, the Division of the Pacific, the commanding general of the army, the secretary of war, and finally, President Grant, the commander in chief.

Great power and administrative capacity did not yield clear, iron-clad policy. Different departments of the bureaucracy overlapped, sometimes working in tandem but often following parallel tracks or even competing with each other. And all the while, individual agents and superintendents exercised an enormous amount of discretion that affected thousands of Indians' lives — where they lived, how they supported themselves, whether they went to school, and how they prayed. This friction and inconsistency created vast gaps between policy and practice. In the remote wilderness and far on the frontier, where the government's grip was weakest, the extent and meaning of Indian rights were hashed out and improvised every day.

After a couple of visits from Wallowa Valley settlers that summer, Monteith had resolved to "fix up matters" with the Indians himself. He did not expect it to take long. "I was in a hurry . . . as I had plenty to attend to at home," he wrote. But Joseph was determined to impress upon the Indian agent that he was a guest on someone else's land. He kept Monteith waiting an hour while members of his band dressed and gathered in a lodge house they had built for meeting with the settlers. It was a temporary structure, wood and hides, more a tent than a building. But it was impressive for its size, about 240 feet long, far bigger than anything the settlers had constructed in the valley. It represented a level of planning and enterprise that made it a monument to the Nez Perce claim on the valley. When Joseph finally summoned the agent, Monteith found about fifty Nez Perce men waiting for him "in their finery," he wrote, "faces painted, &c."

When Monteith pressed Joseph for "what he

had to say," the chief put him off again. Joseph repeated his claim that "his father never traded off that country and on his dying bed about a year ago bequeathed the whole valley to him for his band." But he would not talk any further until the settlers could be invited to join them the next day. Joseph's tactic was a shrewd one. Making the federal government's representative in Nez Perce country stay the night was an exercise of power and will, but it also showed responsibility: Joseph wanted all the interested parties together to create a legitimate result. Monteith had to agree that it made sense to wait.

The message went out that day, and thirty settlers answered the call and came to Joseph's camp by morning. Eighty Nez Perce were there, "painted up &c.," Monteith wrote, "ready for a talk." Only then, with the stage set, did Joseph begin to speak. His words were directed to the present yet had the allusive texture of myth. He referred to the line of cairns that Tuekakas had constructed along the western boundary of the valley — what the settlers had taken to calling "Old Joseph's Dead Line." "His father planted a stick on the Mountains between the Grand Rond Valley and the Wallowwa," he said, "that now that stick had grown to a large tree, that the whites derived subsistence from one side and the red people from the other." This careful balance was now at risk. "Whites were trying to get on their side and drive them away from their food," Joseph said. It violated his band's ancient claim. "His father bequeathed to him that country for subsistence of himself and band and wanted all the whites to leave the Valley," he told the Indian agent.

After listening to Joseph's account, Monteith

had a quick and seemingly obvious retort: the Nez Perce people had given up their land by the treaties of 1855 and 1863. Although Joseph's band would be allowed to hunt and fish in the valley, they had to accept that "the Country was sold to the Govt. [and] had been surveyed and brot. into market." Monteith said that he "had come to them as a friend to keep them out of trouble" but "that the Govt. had acted in good faith with them and expected the same on their part."

Monteith's officious pronouncement did not end their dialogue. Joseph pushed back. As to the notion that his band was bound by the 1863 treaty, Joseph said, " 'it was a lie', that his father never traded off that country and never received anything for it." "I know you are my friend and you are a good Agent and I do not like to talk to you so," he told Monteith, "but these [settlers] you see here are the cause of the trouble. All I want is for them to go away and leave us our country."

Monteith, in turn, responded with what sounded like a riddle. If Joseph's band attacked the whites, the agent warned, he would return to the valley "with force enough to bring the Indians on the reservation where I could take care of them." Yet he had no power to remove the settlers. "I told him it was useless for them to talk about sending the whites away," Monteith wrote, "that they were there by higher authority than I."

Joseph weighed Monteith's words. Apparently, this agent could call in the army and, in essence, start a war if, in his discretionary opinion, it would serve the president's commitment to moving Indians to reservations and turning them into Christian farmers. Yet Monteith claimed that

149

resolving the simple question of who owned the Wallowa Valley was beyond his capacity. He could not make or adjust policies that he had a seemingly limitless ability to interpret and enforce. So what would it take to change the substantive direction underlying these vast enforcement powers and convince the government to remove the settlers? Joseph defused the agent's threat of force, assuring him that his band would not "do anything that would cause trouble, but would have the matter settled peaceably." At the same time, the chief stayed committed to his position that the valley belonged to his people and that the government should, as Monteith remembered his words, "order the whites out of the valley."

If the council had reached an impasse, it seemed to be a genial one. Monteith had come to the Wallowa Valley worried about bloodshed, but talking with Joseph had a calming effect. After spending the previous year in charge of the reservation, the agent had come to view "those who term themselves 'Non-Treaties' " as an enormous impediment to what he called "progress towards civilization among these Indians." His ultimate goal was citizenship for Indians, which meant equality before the law but left no room for traditional life, or what he called "wild habits," within a tribal structure. But from the moment he rode into Joseph's camp, Monteith saw a chief who, though painted and beaded, wrapped in hides, and draped with a blanket, was not wild. He spoke through an interpreter but was conversant in American values. Joseph adamantly opposed what Monteith regarded as "civilization," yet the chief seemed curiously modern, the administrator's worthy foil. Committed to following a meticulous set of procedures and protocols, Joseph recognized the importance of including the settlers in the council. In advocating his position as forcefully as he could, he welcomed and recognized the authority of the national government. Joseph had "wild habits," no doubt — he told the agent that his father, upon learning the details of the Treaty of 1863, had destroyed the Bible that Reverend Spalding had given him during the time they spent together in the 1830s. However, in the conflict over the Wallowa Valley, Monteith recognized that Joseph was behaving as responsibly as any American citizen.

The council disbanded quickly. Monteith took the settlers aside and advised them to "keep away from the Indians and not interfere with their hunting and fishing." Then he saddled his horse, "left bidding all a good bye," and began the long journey from the prairie down into the canyons, across the Snake and the Salmon, and over the mountains back to Lapwai. If he could maintain a quick pace, he would get back to the reservation in time to observe the Sabbath.

Every one of Joseph's conversations with government officials seemed to end in the same way: with a vague reference to "higher authorities" — the only people who could definitively settle the Wallowa question — yet no sense of who they were or how to reach them. Joseph stated and restated his position to anyone who would listen, but he had no way of knowing whether his words would find a way out of far northeastern Oregon, whether they had the strength to climb mountains and cross canyons and ford rivers to find an audience able to grant him relief. As the Wallowa Valley's settlers encountered the strange world around them, they had cast Joseph and his people into a different kind of wilderness, the wilderness of American power, opaque and inscrutable, everywhere and nowhere.

Still, Joseph kept speaking his mind, and his words began to assume a life of their own. The chief had impressed Monteith in August 1872, as he had Slater and Meacham the previous month. Within a couple of days of returning to Lapwai, the agent reported to the commissioner of Indian affairs, Francis A. Walker, that "it is a great pity that the Valley was ever opened for settlement." With its high altitude and winters too harsh for farming, it was only fit for horses and cattle and would never attract large numbers of settlers. Riding to and from Lapwai, Monteith had not seen a single structure built by whites; ordering them to leave, it seemed, would take nothing away from them. "If there is any way by which the Wallowwa [sic] Valley could be kept for the Indians," Monteith wrote, "I would recommend that it be done."

At first, Monteith's recommendation was barely acknowledged. By early 1873, A. C. Smith had finished his bridge across the Wallowa River, large enough for wagons and herds. As new settlers crossed, they took to calling the mountain on the far side of the river — the last obstacle before the Wallowa Valley opened up to them — Smith Mountain. But then Monteith wrote a second letter in January 1873. Although Monteith was far less invested in the Wallowa Valley situation than Joseph was, the Indian agent, like any other ambitious bureaucrat, wanted to attract the attention of his superiors. His first letter was ignored, so he knew he had to find some new way to character-

152

ize the Wallowa dispute so that it would become a priority in Washington. Astutely, Monteith related the Wallowa Valley to the single most pressing issue for the Office of Indian Affairs, the war with the Modoc tribe then raging in the Lava Beds along the Oregon-California border. He singled out the Wallowa Valley as a potential site for a second, simultaneous war in the Northwest — perhaps the start of a broad regional conflict, something the commissioner of Indian affairs could not ignore. When Joseph's band returned from the canyons that spring, Monteith warned, there was bound to be trouble. "I had no fears of any difficulty with the 'non treaty' bands of the Nez Perces," he wrote, but "if the Indians in question are to be kept out of the valley in order to avert difficulties force will have to be used." Almost immediately, the secretary of the interior ordered Monteith and Thomas B. Odeneal, Oregon's superintendent of Indian affairs, to arrange another meeting with Joseph.

Joseph's claims had found a powerful audience. In March, he rode to Lapwai to see Monteith and Odeneal and again argued at length why the Treaty of 1863 did not bind his people. He described how the Nez Perce lived in independent bands, and how Chief Lawyer did not — could not — represent Joseph's band when he signed away the Wallowa Valley. Forceful and sincere, Joseph had little trouble convincing the two officials that he was right. "If any respect is to be paid to the laws and customs of the Indians," they concluded to Washington, "then the treaty of 1863 is not binding upon Joseph and his band." Monteith and Odeneal were inclined to pay such respect in large part because "the laws and

153

customs of the Indians," in Joseph's telling, also tracked common sense and core democratic values. Joseph explained the treaty as the equivalent of a white man approaching him and saying, "Joseph, I like your horses, and I want to buy them," and then upon being told, "No my horses suit me, I will not sell them," turning to the chief's neighbor and paying *him* for Joseph's horses. "The white man returns to me and says, 'Joseph, I have bought your horses, and you must let me have them,' " the chief would say. "If we sold our lands to the Government, this is the way they were bought."

Following Monteith and Odeneal's assessment, the secretary of the interior in April 1873 gave Joseph's band permission "to remain in said valley and occupy it during the summer and autumn, or for such time as the weather is suitable, according to their previous custom" and indicated that the government would take further action "setting apart this valley for the exclusive use of said Indians." That May, the General Land Office stopped registering homesteads in the Wallowa Valley, and Odeneal announced in the *Oregonian* that he would be appraising "the claims and improvements of settlers" in the Wallowa Valley "with a view to paying therefor."

The government's actions were a stunning validation of Joseph's advocacy. Just a year after attending the Fourth of July picnic in La Grande, Joseph had prompted the government 2,500 miles away to do the impossible: remove land from the public domain and give it back to the Indians. In doing so, the chief gained a first glimpse at the nature of American power: fluid and unfixed, changeable but not predictable. The nation had mobilized millions of men and women over thousands of miles to fight the Civil War, followed by years more of reconstructing the economic and social structure of the South. The transcontinental railroad and the telegraph had made the country both bigger and smaller, opening huge tracts of land to settlement while tethering these once inconceivably remote places with coasts and cities. In little more than a decade, the government had developed a tremendous new capacity — peaceful and violent — to shape people's lives, for better and worse. Yet this modern state was often neither coherent nor singular when it came to setting the direction of its vast administrative machinery.

Alongside the freedpeople in the South, Indian tribes were among the first to experience the contradictions of this new system of American government. Unable to vote in elections and outside the jurisdiction of courts, Indians affiliated with tribes lived entirely in a realm of federal power, where it seemed there was no specific center of authority, only sprawling bureaucracies, diffuse to the point of invisibility, resisting efforts to locate, speak to, or influence them. Despite his frustration with the government's opacity, Joseph's experience revealed that diffuse administration was flexible administration; it was possible to alter policies, even flip them completely. Where power was split among thousands of individual officials, in the capital and in the field, there were countless occasions to explain why the government's positions were wrong and why another course was better. Opportunities regularly presented themselves to convince low-level bureaucrats to adjust how they exercised their discretion. Each small gain, in turn, created leverage to change how officials in the capital — who depended upon the observations and opinions of agents in the field — understood an issue. Joseph saw how he could get a hearing — how his positions could gain traction, even when his audiences repeatedly claimed that they had no authority to make policy.

On the other hand, as new policies were announced, there was little reason for anyone disadvantaged by them to acquiesce. Government initiatives that reached into people's daily lives thousands of miles from the capital were bound to need revision, and there would always be occasion to argue for reversing them, to try to convince some set of the government's agents to change direction once again. The structure of American power — hard to identify, yet responsive to outside voices — encouraged struggle over what the law should be and how the bureaucracy should interpret it.

It was only natural, then, that as the government prepared to buy out the Wallowa homesteads, the settlers began to make their own case. In April 1873, they gathered at the courthouse in La Grande and enlisted James Slater, who had quit Congress after one term, to their cause. Although the previous July he had passed along Chief Joseph's concerns to the Office of Indian Affairs, he now prepared a memorial to the secretary of the interior pleading that the "renegade Indians, known as 'Joseph's band' . . . be restrained from going into Wallowa Valley, or interfering with the settlers there."

With the bureaucrats in the Interior Department favoring the Nez Perce side, the settlers also sought other sources of power and authority. They

156

found ready allies in Oregon's congressional delegation. That May, James K. Kelly, a prominent attorney serving a term in the Senate, and Joseph Gardner Wilson, a former state supreme court justice who succeeded Slater in the House of Representatives, submitted to the commissioner of Indian affairs what amounted to a legal brief countering Joseph's arguments. The Oregon legislators argued that it defied all common sense to allow "the sub-chief of [a] small band of disaffected Indians" to opt out of one treaty and, in effect, make a new compact with the government. There would be no end of groups that would splinter from a tribe whenever they found something "displeasing" with a chief's conduct, they wrote. "It is true that Joseph did not sign the treaty, but surely it cannot be seriously contended that the simple refusal or neglect of one Indian to make his mark to a treaty . . . will make the act invalid."

To make matters worse, Kelly and Wilson argued, the government would end up supporting the nomadic lifestyle of Joseph's band because they only lived in the Wallowa Valley during the summer. Preserving the valley for seasonal use was wasteful; "extensive tracts of fertile land" would be left "merely for hunting and fishing purposes." Far more importantly, it would set a precedent that would cripple the government's attempts "to wean these wandering tribes from their nomadic life, and to teach them how to labor and cultivate the soil." The very existence of nomadic bands impeded the operation and success of the reservations, the congressmen pointed out. Few Indians wanted to abandon their tradition in favor of small farming plots when the old ways of living

157

were still available. Joseph's victory would ripple outward from the Wallowa Valley, undermining the primary purpose of American Indian policy.

Finally, Kelly and Wilson suggested that it was undemocratic for Joseph to dispute Lawyer's authority to sign the 1863 treaty. Joseph's right to the Wallowa Valley, they wrote, hinged on a claim to royalty — to having inherited a chiefdom from his father. While the "will of the majority, the vast, overwhelming majority of the Nez Perces" recognized Lawyer as their leader, they wrote, Joseph viewed him as an "upstart . . . not as royally born as he." Surely, they contended, the treaty was "entitled to a little respect from a Government which recognizes the right of the majority to rule." Indian tribes, it appeared to them, were incompatible with American popular sovereignty, elevating tyranny and hierarchy over democracy and equality, collective will over individual rights. "The two races," they concluded, "cannot live together in peace while the Indians maintain their tribal relations."

While Joseph could have disputed all of these points if they had been presented to him at a meeting, they made obvious sense to the officials in the Office of Indian Affairs, who, despite the announced policy of the Interior Department to restore the Wallowa Valley to Joseph's band, began to shift back toward the settlers' favor. On June 16 President Grant signed an executive order designating only half the valley — 912,000 acres — as a "reservation for the roaming Nez Perce Indians." By giving just part of the area to Joseph's band, the government tried to strike a compromise that would also satisfy the settlers. But nearly three thousand miles away in the capital, the officials drawing up the executive order made a crucial mistake. The order gave the Indians the northern section of the valley, where most of the homesteads were, while the most important tribal areas — where Wallowa Lake, Tuekakas's grave, and the largest summer camping grounds were located — remained open to settlement.

Though some ranchers welcomed the prospect of the government buying out their claims, others raged at the executive order — nothing less than a crime, the *Mountain Sentinel* declared, "robbing the settlers of the Wallowa of their homes, their everything." "Citizens of the Wallowa!" one headline demanded. "Awake and drive Joseph and his band from the face of the Earth." As homesteaders formed a militia company and built a stockade — promising "WAR TO THE KNIFE," if necessary — others packed their wagons and headed back to the Grande Ronde Valley. "The other day I looked up the valley," one rancher wrote that spring, "and lo! I saw seven or eight wagons, men women and children, stock, dogs and all, running I don't know from what, but I suppose it was from the Indians." In his telling, he heard the families singing over the creak and groan of their wagons and the weary clop of hooves on a dirt path: "Run nigger, run nigger and try to get away / For it is high time for it is almost day. / Come along, get out of the Wallowa, / Before old Joseph kicks up a row."

In reviving a song from a generation earlier about a slave outrunning a night patrol, the settlers were not just passing the time. They were making a blunt political statement, taking the ideological battles of the Civil War and Reconstruction into new territory. Years removed and a continent away from the battlefields of the Civil War, abolition and Reconstruction continued to supply the moral valences for debates over policy — remembered and refracted, faded and distorted into a new vocabulary of liberty and oppression. Rightly or not, the settlers of the Wallowa saw themselves as slaves, denied a precious liberty — their right to property — and the sure path to wealth that the valley promised. Yet as they compared their lot to slavery, they also claimed kinship to the former rebels. The federal intrusion was no better than Reconstruction, oppressive and corrupt, designed to enrich the Indian agents and their bosses, all traitors to the white race. Their decision to cede the Wallowa Valley, the *Mountain Sentinel*'s editor wrote, "stinks in the nostrils of every decent man east of the Cascades." "Pray how has this miserable government of ours treated the people of Oregon?" he asked. "Much as the poor and down trodden Southerner has been treated."

The sense of injustice only grew as the government appeared to be unable, or unwilling, to return the Wallowa Valley to the Indians. Although Joseph had won an executive order, nothing seemed to change. In the months that followed, a team of appraisers traveled through the area to value the homesteaders' property, but the government never paid the settlers. With the future uncertain, most stayed on their land and continued to tend their gardens, run their stock, and cut hay for the winter. They opened a post office and began receiving mail. In July 1873, the first baby — a girl — was born to settlers in the valley. A few months later, the settlers gathered to celebrate their first wedding. They set up their own local precinct where they could vote in the 1874 elections.

When Joseph visited Lapwai in the fall of 1873, Monteith surprised him by demanding that the band either settle year-round in the Wallowa Valley as farmers or move inside the reservation boundaries set in 1863. Although it had been the Indian agent's letters that led to the executive order, months of protest and pressure and counterargument had brought Monteith back to his civilizing mission. He was consumed with doing everything possible to make the Nez Perce people "worthy of becoming citizens," whether that meant forcing nontreaty Indians to accept twenty-acre allotments on the reservation or calling in the military to prevent the Nez Perce already at Lapwai from leaving their farms and crossing the Bitterroot Mountains for their summer buffalo hunt. "The only thing that can be done with these Indians," he now wrote the commissioner of Indian affairs, "is to compel them to remain in one place or the other and to accomplish this force will be necessary." Monteith's sudden turn from sympathy to disregard shocked Joseph. He urged the Indian agent to stop speaking with a "forked tongue."

If Joseph's disbelief and disappointment were only natural, he quickly surprised Monteith: he told the agent that he wanted to meet with President Grant. "At first I let the matter pass," Monteith wrote, "supposing it was a mere jest of his but two days after, he came to bid me good-by . . . and renewed his request that I be sure and write to the Great Chief, saying he wished very much to go to Washington and have a talk with

161

him, in regards to their affairs." The request may have seemed grandiose to Monteith, but it made perfect sense to Joseph. Without Monteith's support, he needed another way to speak to the government. Despite his skepticism, Monteith passed along the request in his next report to the commissioner of Indian affairs.

Joseph's request, just months after the executive order, was already too late. By the following spring, the commissioner of Indian affairs was personally meeting with Senator Kelly to assure him that "nothing more would be done toward establishing a reservation . . . and that settlers in the Wallowa Valley would not be molested in any way by the Indian department." The valley was "open for settlement," the *Oregonian* reported on its front page, "and . . . the former order of the Commissioner of Indian Affairs has, in effect, been rescinded."

As federal policy trembled and gave way, Joseph's band tried to preserve the fabric of their traditional life. Spring ripened into summer, and they emerged from the canyons as they had always done. The landscape was what they remembered and dreamed about, but the world had changed. When their horses and cattle roamed, they mixed with settlers' herds that had survived the deep snows of the previous winter. Separating the animals, once easily accomplished, now caused fights. When Nez Perce ponies began grazing on one settler's claim, he roped the stallions and castrated them. "He done this," it was reported, "to prevent his mares from breeding from such inferior stock." In the washes and creek valleys, far from anyone else, small groups of young men, homesteaders and Nez Perce, clashed. Their threats, incomprehensible to each other, popped through the silence like the grasshoppers in the surrounding brush. Their guns grew warm and heavy in the summer light, level as their horses shifted beneath them, but they stopped short of firing. The settlers knew that a war would leave no one alive, and the Nez Perce men, though free to follow their conscience, refused to shoot the first blast.

When stories of "saucy" Indians and heavily armed settlers reached Lapwai, Monteith finally asked the army to intervene. Two cavalry companies rode into the Wallowa Valley from Walla Walla at the end of June 1874. It was one of the last orders given by Oliver Otis Howard's predecessor commanding the Department of the Columbia. While the army's arrival led some nontreaty Nez Perce leaders to call for war, Joseph once again saw an opportunity. He quickly realized that he had a new way to make his case to the government: the officers represented the United States just as Monteith did and were equally capable of passing along word to Washington that Joseph's band was peaceful and had a strong claim to the valley.

Joseph's band was engaged in the annual salmon catch when Captain Stephen G. Whipple entered their camp and rode among their lodges. Stout and thick-browed, beard streaked gray, the forty-year-old from northern California was unlikely to have sympathy for Indians. He had come to Fort Walla Walla after spending the early 1870s fighting the Apaches in Arizona. A decade before that, he had commanded a volunteer company, the 1st Battalion of Mountaineers, that killed nearly every

Indian man, woman, and child in the hills around his home in Humboldt County — a campaign of "heavy chastisements" and "vengeance and extermination" that, according to one report, stopped just short of "hunt[ing] the redskins for a pastime."

Despite Captain Whipple's predispositions, Joseph and his people could confound even a hardened Indian hater. After spending the summer in the valley, Whipple described Joseph's band as "giving no intentional cause of offence, but quietly and industriously . . . preparing food for future use." He left that September impressed with the idea that the Wallowa country was land "they highly value and apparently consider as justly theirs."

August 1875

When a young cavalry lieutenant named Frederick Ward entered Joseph's camp by the Wallowa River on August 23, 1875, the word that came readily to mind was "perfect." It was a perfect summer morning, near eleven o'clock. The people he encountered in the village showed him "perfect good will," welcoming him as they prepared for feasting and performances to mark the end of a council with neighboring bands and tribes.

Though he saw warriors on horseback rehearsing a grand procession and noted that they were well armed with "Henry rifles, carbines of various patterns, and some few Colt's pistols," Ward was at ease. In his experience, Indians on the warpath did not travel, as Joseph's band did, with women, children, and what the lieutenant called "the old decrepit." Men of fighting age were a distinct minority in this settlement of five hundred or so

164

Indians. Enormous amounts of salmon were hanging out to dry. By every appearance, Ward thought, the band had come to the Wallowa Valley at midsummer as they always had, "solely to hunt and fish."

As the lieutenant walked around the village, he saw several local settlers happily circulating. One had even brought a son and two daughters to watch the festivities. They had heard that an "Indian Dreamer," a local shaman, had envisioned harmony in the Wallowa country. The pageantry suggested a festival to celebrate peace and the bounty of the season: the large graceful circle of the parade, ceremonial robes so heavily beaded that their wearers could barely move, a horse painted white with red human footprints across its body, another painted black with red stripes. A cow from the Indian herd had been slaughtered, and it crackled in the fire. Everywhere, Ward wrote, there was "a feeling of perfect safety."

For the Nez Perce celebrants, the tranquility of the event was hardly a given, nor was it the outcome of a Dreamer's prophecy. A few weeks earlier, Joseph had visited John Monteith at Lapwai and heard the crushing news that President Grant had formally rescinded his 1873 executive order and reopened the entire Wallowa Valley to white settlers. The chief "was inclined to be ugly and returned to his camp very much dissatisfied with the action of the Government," the Indian agent reported. But over the course of a few days, Joseph regained his equanimity and "came back and talked more reasonably." It was as if nothing had changed from the time the settlers had first invaded the valley three years earlier. Joseph continued to assert his band's claim.

Monteith urged Joseph to move immediately to the reservation, but the chief insisted on riding home to the valley. Waiting for him there he found about a hundred recruits under Captain Whipple, two companies ordered in from Walla Walla. The Indian agent had reported that Joseph's band and the settlers were bound to fight. The soldiers pitched their tents and pastured their horses just a couple miles from Joseph's village at the confluence of the Wallowa and Lostine Rivers. Despite the army presence, Joseph decided to host a council with other nontreaty bands from across Nez Perce country.

As the air cooled on an August night, Joseph and his guests sat around an open fire. While Joseph was known among the settlers for his physical presence, penetrating gaze, and thoughtful voice, here he was one among many, obscured by the play of flame and smoke, humbled by the endless sky above. He was surrounded by large men, chiefs and warriors who stood six feet tall, with strong shoulders, thick necks, and broad chests that swelled with beads, feathers, and leather fringe.

Although Joseph's band was the biggest and most prosperous nontreaty group, he was the youngest of the chiefs. He had no reputation for fighting other tribes, unlike Alalimya Takanin (Looking Glass), who had once stood his ground as a Blackfeet warrior shot at him point-blank and then tried to charge. Recently returned from across the Bitterroots, where he had joined the Crows in bringing death to the Sioux, Looking Glass crowned himself with a top hat wound with fur tails.

Joseph did not make his name going east to hunt

buffalo like Peopeo Kiskiok Hihih (White Goose, but commonly known among settlers as White Bird), who in his seventies was the oldest of the chiefs, descended from generations of warriors, and distinguished in battle himself. Nor did the Nez Perce bands hold Joseph in awe for raw strength or spiritual purity as they did Toohoolhoolzote, a Dreamer who alone among his band could carry two blacktail bucks, one under each arm, through steep mountains. It once took eight men to restrain him when he was angry.

Although Joseph and Ollokot had championed peaceful advocacy, each leader, with his own claim to greatness, had a vision of what the nontreaty bands should do. At various councils over the previous year, the chiefs had considered the possibility of going to war against the settlers and their government. The reasons were clear. Many of the nontreaty Indians were experiencing the invasion of settlers as an ongoing catastrophe. When White Bird spoke, quiet and deliberate, everyone listening knew that his band, who lived along the eastern bank of the Salmon River, had suffered some of the worst trespasses during and after the gold rush. White Bird's people grew to expect that miners and merchants would cheat them. They bore scars from dogs that the settlers had set on them. Settlers had shot several men in White Bird's band, and none had faced justice. The Indians crossed paths constantly with these cold-blooded killers, who remained unrepentant, even proud of their crimes.

For Toohoolhoolzote, moving to the Lapwai reservation offended the natural order of the world. His people did not simply claim their land, which was far from the settlers in the rugged

167

mountains between the Snake and Salmon Rivers. Rather, the land claimed them. In a "heavy, guttural voice" that fit his name, Toohoolhoolzote declared that "he who lives above set me down where the rivers flow, where the mountains stand. I must not make him angry by going elsewhere." It was now time, he thought, for the people to defend themselves from outsiders. "When I was . . . a boy," he told the other nontreaty chiefs, "I learned to use the arrow and bow. . . . When I shot any kind of bird, when I killed, I saw that its life went out with its blood. This taught me for what purpose I am here." The chief's vision was stark. "I came into this world to die," he said. "My body is only to hold a spirit life. Should my blood be sprinkled, I want no wounds from behind. Death must come fronting me."

Despite obvious reasons for showing the rifle, peace held sway at the August council. Everyone understood that the bands risked everything, land and lives, if they waged a war with the United States. Looking Glass lived within the 1863 treaty boundaries along the Clearwater River. His people gained nothing from a fight; they would have to leave their gardens, their herds, their place in the world. Although he was known for his bravery in battle, he spoke words of compromise and reconciliation.

War held little allure for the nontreaty bands, and Joseph continued to believe that he could convince the American government to shift course once again. Early one morning, he rode into Whipple's camp accompanied by seventy-five of his men. The chief greeted the captain, his friend from the previous summer, and explained that he had just returned from Lapwai and was "tired and sore from a hard ride." Whipple explained to Joseph that the soldiers regarded both settlers and Indians as "friends . . . as long as each tried to do right." Joseph assured him that his band would "do no violence to person or property."

It could have been a short meeting, an exchange of goodwill gestures. Instead, Joseph asked if Whipple had anything more to say. When the captain said no, the chief was silent for a moment and then admitted, Whipple wrote, that "he hoped I could tell something of a possible doubt of their being obliged to relinquish this valley to the settlers. I told him the case was decided against the Indians by higher authority than that of an Army officer."

Although Whipple reported that his words "did not make the countenances of the Indians more cheerful," Joseph pressed on. He had heard such disclaimers for years, yet rather than return to his camp and prepare for his council, Joseph sat and parleyed with Whipple for three hours. The chief, along with members of his retinue, "spoke of the bitter disappointment to them," Whipple wrote, "that this Valley was thrown open to settlement after it had been for so long a time understood that it should be reserved to them." But Joseph also conveyed to the captain that his band was looking ahead. Given the current state of affairs, he told Whipple that "the Indians desired to share [the Valley] with the white people and hoped they might do so in peace and harmony."

Never before had Joseph advocated sharing the valley. As a proposal for the future, it seemed implausible. White settlers had never been able to share the land that they had taken from the public domain. Although the Wallowa country at the moment could sustain the horses and cattle of both the Nez Perce families and the homesteaders, once the herds grew, Joseph's band and the settlers would be competing for the same pastureland. Even if they could share the valley, Joseph's vision differed from the ideas of just about everyone else at the time who thought the Indians and whites could coexist. Rather than adopt Christianity and the farming life, Joseph retained the traditional ways. He did not want to assimilate into citizenship, as Indian agents sought to help their charges to do. Equality did not mean becoming just like everyone else. Rather, Joseph envisioned two sovereignties coexisting in the same space. It required a new understanding of equality, perhaps a new definition of citizenship.

Sharing the valley struck Whipple as a step too far; he had long believed that "the two races may not dwell together in a friendly way." Joseph himself admitted that he preferred that the valley be reserved for his band alone. But the chief's willingness to compromise gave moral strength to his argument that the valley in fact belonged to his band, discrediting the alarming rhetoric of impending war that drove the effort to remove Joseph's people to the reservation. While the captain had felt some measure of sympathy for Joseph the previous summer, now he and his men were wholly won over.

Marching from Walla Walla to the valley, several of Whipple's recruits had deserted rather than risk their scalps in an Indian war. But as soon as the cavalry encountered Joseph, they knew that they would have no trouble. Rather, they savored the prospect of a lovely summer in a beautiful place, of days spent exploring and swimming, and nights eating salmon and trout and trading yarns around their campfires about bear sightings. For such blessings, they felt they had Joseph to thank, and their gratitude gained substance as they considered the Wallowa situation. "The stories of the hostile attitude of the Indians are entirely without foundation, and the white men of the country are perfectly safe as far as the Indians are concerned," one soldier wrote the *Oregonian.* "They (the whites) don't seem to understand the principle of living and let live, but would appropriate to their own use even the air the poor Indians breath[e]."

Ten years after massacring Indian women and children to keep the tribes — in his view, barely human — away from white settlers in California, Whipple saw Joseph as an equal negotiating partner, someone who was fit for citizenship, had rights, and deserved a hearing. "This band of Indians is by no means a vagabond set," the captain wrote. "They are proud-spirited, self-supporting, and intelligent; and if it be possible that Indians can rise in the social scale, I know of none who give better promise of rewarding an effort in that direction."

Although Whipple told Joseph that he could not reverse President Grant's order, the captain reported to his superior officers that the chief was right about the Wallowa situation. Joseph's band had formed a "separate and independent community" from the rest of the Nez Perce tribe, Whipple wrote, and "had never surrendered claim to this valley." The valley was too high to support farming and would be of little use to white settlers, many of whom wanted to "sell out at first opportunity, and settle in a more promising locality," he wrote. The Indians, by contrast, "desire[d] ardently to make it their abiding place." Whipple concluded that the Wallowa Valley should belong to Joseph's band. "I can think it a pity that [the valley was again thrown open to settlement]," the captain wrote, "nor can I think the case was fully understood by the gentlemen who influenced the legislation."

Unlike just about every other report of the Wallowa situation, Whipple based his conclusions on actual experience in the valley. He exposed as self-serving fictions the accounts of hostile Indians that some Wallowa settlers and their friends in the Grande Ronde Valley were peddling and that Monteith so readily accepted at his post in Lapwai. Whipple's superiors recognized that the captain was providing invaluable intelligence. At the Department of the Columbia headquarters, General Howard read Whipple's words closely. In the fall of 1875, when it was time to write his annual report to the secretary of war, Howard attached a lengthy excerpt of one of the captain's letters.

Knowing that the secretary had a critical role in governing the Indians, Howard added his own pointed assessment of who should get the Wallowa Valley. "I think it a great mistake to take from Joseph and his band of Nez Perces Indians that valley," he wrote. "The white people really do not want it. They wished to be bought out. . . . I indorse Captain Whipple's opinions herein expressed." By making his case to Whipple, Chief Joseph had found another path to Washington. Once again the capital was considering the rights of his band. "Possibly Congress," Howard wrote the secretary of war, "can be induced to let these really peaceable Indians have this poor valley for their own."

CHAPTER 6
ADONIS IN BLUE

Vancouver,
Washington Territory,
January 1876

On the coldest days of January 1876, the Columbia River froze. Upstream from Portland the ice was solid. For once, the ferryboats — their churning sidewheels and towers of smoke — were not a constant, almost natural, part of the landscape. The steamer fleet went out of service, put to dock until the thaw save for the few hulls that could be reinforced with wood planks. Oregon and Washington Territory were no longer separated by water. Settlers in the towns and homesteads along the river enjoyed the novelty of walking from bank to bank. The trails across the Cascades were impassable in winter, and without the steamboats, the distance to the big city stretched. For a short time eastern Oregon experienced the isolation of pioneer days. Still, commerce never stopped. Where the freeze was thickest, bundled crews of men spent every daylight moment, seven days a week, staking, grooving, sawing, and gaffing, harvesting blocks of ice by the ton for the summer months ahead.

The river still flowed past Portland, but it was choked with ice. When a young second lieutenant

174

named Charles Erskine Scott Wood wrapped himself in a wool overcoat and began his journey from his post at Fort Vancouver, Washington, to an engagement in town — eighteen miles away — he was left standing at the ferry landing. Although steamers to East Portland usually ran every half hour, it was too dangerous to cross that day, the boatmen told him. Gazing at the treacherous gray water, Lieutenant Wood could have returned to his post. His business in Portland was not urgent. Canceling the visit would have caused a few people some minor inconvenience, nothing more. But instead of giving up, he walked along the frosted shore until he saw an unclaimed rowboat. And then he, in his own words, "appropriated it."

Wood pushed off from shore and dragged his oars through the water until the boat was surrounded by ice and he could go no further. He waited for the river to open up, then shoved off and rowed until he was trapped again. Once more, he awaited an opening. During Wood's thirteen months with the 21st Infantry, he refused to let the power of nature, which inspired awe and fear even in the most settled parts of the West, control his life. It was almost as if he insisted that he was living somewhere else, nearer the tamed places where he had grown up. In his first assignment after graduating from West Point, back in December 1874, Wood had gone to join his regiment at a fort in the far northeastern corner of California. Above Reno the snow was too deep for stagecoaches to travel, so Wood, who had never been west of Terre Haute, Indiana, took an old horse and set out through the mountains on his own. Coyotes were soon following closely. Again, he refused to turn around. Insulted by their pres-

175

ence, Wood aimed his revolver and picked off the leader of the pack. Upon reaching the next stage station, he coaxed a recalcitrant driver to take him through a snowy pass by sticking his weapon in the man's side. "I'm going to obey my Government if I have to kill you," Wood remembered telling him. "You pick up those reins and your whip and start and if you want help on the way I'll help you but if you try to stop me I'll kill you. Now do you understand that?"

Thirteen months later, crossing the Columbia presented itself as an easier endeavor, a welcome break from a junior officer's routine. The river gave the illusion of being completely still. Pushing from floe to floe, Wood could imagine he was always just leaving shore. Yet the current under the surface was moving, causing the ice to break up and re-form, slowly dragging him downstream. He was well on his way before he realized that his skiff was, like the river, less solid than it appeared. The seams along the boat's flat bottom had not been caulked. They had been sealed by ice, but on the river and in daylight, it was melting. As Wood pushed and rowed, the boat started taking on water. When he was a young boy in Pennsylvania, he had nearly drowned trying to punt a homemade raft down the Erie Canal. Wood never forgot the shock of clawing at the water and then breathing it in, what he called "the agony for air," before losing consciousness. In the Columbia River, on the other side of America, he kept shoving through the ice until he neared Hayden Island, a narrow spit midway between Vancouver and Portland. He jumped into the shallows, let go of the boat, and waded ashore as it slipped under.

On solid ground again, Wood crossed the island

and walked toward the pounding of axes on trees — as steady a sound in Portland as one's heartbeat. Hayden was close enough to the far shore that Wood could hail a group of lumberjacks, who rowed over to the island and collected him. Once on the mainland, they sent him down a muddy road gashed and rutted through thick fir forest. After walking a couple of hours, he reached a ferry that would take him the quick distance west across the Willamette River to downtown Portland. He landed at Stark Street, a block south of army headquarters. Within minutes he was greeting General Oliver Otis Howard.

That evening at the YMCA, after a tasteful selection of organ music, Howard introduced Wood to the sizable crowd that had turned out for the winter lecture series. The audience could immediately see why the night's featured speaker had stood out among dozens of officers and attracted the general's favor. Wood commanded people's attention. Towering over the slightly built general, the lieutenant was twenty-three years old, big and strong, with green-gray eyes, black hair in curls, and a flush of rose in his cheeks — an Adonis, thought at least one of the young ladies he had squired along Flirtation Walk back at West Point. His many admirers relished his gentle familiarity, his delight in an amusing story, his large hands — paws, he said — holding theirs.

Wood first came to Howard's notice in the late summer of 1875. On August 31, Philip Sheridan, one of the most powerful generals in the army, visited Portland, newly married to a woman half his age. Howard was waiting for the Sheridans as they walked across a gangplank from their ocean steamer to a Willamette River ferry, and he served as their host through several days of public and private receptions. Based in Chicago, General Sheridan was known for burning the Shenandoah Valley in 1864 and in the years since had commanded the army in wars against the great tribes of the Plains: Comanche, Kiowa, Cheyenne, Arapaho, Ute. He was months away from planning a campaign to take South Dakota's Black Hills from the Sioux. In Portland on an extended honeymoon, his twenty-two-year-old wife Irene wore pale pink silk to one reception, a purple gown with a lace overskirt to another. Howard watched at a large celebration as she, the belle of every ball, chose to dance the first waltz with Lieutenant Wood. Although Wood had arrived at Fort Vancouver with his regiment only days earlier after riding hundreds of miles through Oregon's Harney Desert in the dead of summer, he could dance with a smart step. He loved a Strauss waltz more than just about anything in the world.

Upon meeting Wood — and certainly after learning that he never drank anything stronger than the occasional glass of mulled ale — Howard figured that the young man would be an ideal friend for his eldest son Guy, who had just graduated from Yale and was working at a bank in Portland. He also saw the lieutenant as a worthy social companion, perhaps something more, to his daughter Grace, who had moved west after two years in the preparatory program at Vassar. By New Year's Day 1876, Wood was taking the ferry to Portland and making social calls and attending fetes as the Howard family's guest. It was an easy trip when the river flowed fast.

At the YMCA three weeks later, Howard explained the "many difficulties" Wood had faced on the icy Columbia, all so he could make his engagement. Prepared by Howard's gracious words, the audience could appreciate that Wood was not just a beautiful man but rather a beautiful *soldier,* brave and determined and bound by duty. Wood knew from long experience how to look and act the part. Beyond his silhouette and West Point diploma, beyond his stately name — "too many initials," one Portlander groused upon meeting him — he had pedigree. His family was not rich, but because of the military, they were significant. His father, William Maxwell Wood, had joined the navy as an assistant surgeon in 1829, days before his twentieth birthday. It was the best way, he had thought, to support his widowed mother and five younger siblings who were scraping by in their home town of Baltimore. Four decades later, he was the navy's first surgeon general, the author of two lively books on his travels around the world, a man who had smoked a pipe with the king of Siam, shared bowls of "delicious bean soup" with Andrew Jackson at the White House, and taken Zachary Taylor into his home when the president, never a healthy man in the year he served before dying in office, was stricken nearby with vomiting, diarrhea, and the "shakes." Enterprising and fearless, the elder Wood had risked the firing squad in the late spring of 1846 by crossing Mexico, from Mazatlán to Veracruz, as a spy in civilian clothes. Pretending to be an Englishman and speaking fluent Spanish, he inspected the country's military defenses and dispatched crucial intelligence reports to the commodore of the navy's Pacific Squadron. California, Erskine was repeatedly told, belonged to the United States as an immediate result of his father's valor.

Wood experienced a navy childhood, shaped and shadowed by a man he feared more than loved. The warship on Lake Erie where his father was stationed in the late 1850s became young Erskine's playground, where he stuffed himself with sailors' hardtack and learned swordplay with hickory rods from an old marine. William Maxwell Wood's tours of duty — from St. Petersburg to Shanghai — could last years, but when he was home, he subjected his six sons to what Erskine called "fine remorseless Naval discipline." Even the slightest infraction and his father would send him "to the calaboose," locking the boy in his room with a slice of bread and glass of milk for dinner. Keeping his distance, Erskine watched his father sit in his study and read Cervantes in the original Spanish while puffing on a seemingly endless supply of Havana cigars. Decanters of Madeira, bourbon, and brandy were within reach on a mahogany sideboard.

A practiced observer and born performer, Wood began to speak in a resonant baritone. While the general continued to draw acclaim as a lecturer throughout the Northwest for his unsparing chronicles of battle, the lieutenant sought to serve lighter fare. Instead of war, his topic was "Children." Although he did not have any of his own, some of his happiest hours in the West had been spent singing and telling stories with his fellow officers' families. With four younger siblings — his sister Roberta was seven years old when he left for California — Wood found that the presence of children put him at ease and could turn even a dull gathering with uncultured colleagues into "a grand romp." Describing a holiday party in 1874 that he spent mostly among youngsters, he wrote, "I laughed till I brought on a headache."

Wood's talk, the *Oregonian* reported, "was replete with witty and humorous anecdotes, narrated in a pleasing manner and fitting language." The audience was rapt, and at General Howard's prompting, they gave Wood a standing ovation. No one minded that the lieutenant was not speaking on a more serious subject. Ready to be charmed, they hardly could have expected Wood to present something more adventurous. As a new officer who had only served in peacetime, he had few exploits to recount. The Civil War was not even a decade past, but for Wood and his rising generation, it was a remote memory.

At Wood's graduation in June 1874, forty-one newly commissioned second lieutenants gathered on the lawn in front of West Point's turreted stone library for a few informal remarks from William Tecumseh Sherman, the commanding general of the United States Army. Immortalized in the scowling photographs he had posed for as he burned Georgia and the Carolinas, Sherman's face had softened with age. On a day of high celebration, he offered words of reassurance and consolation. Reminding the graduates that "he had been in every war since the Mexican War" — thirty years of a fighting life — he told the class not to feel "too downhearted at the idea that there would be no more promotions, no more wars, no more soldiers and armies." Wood listened to the general carefully and never forgot his words: "He said he had never known 25 years had passed without one or more very sizable armies and we should look forward with hope."

While the Civil War had given a generation of West Point men — Sherman and Oliver Otis Howard among them — the causes and struggles and opportunities of a lifetime, the Class of 1874 was a few years too young to have been able to enlist and fight. When Wood sat for his entrance exam, there was one aspiring cadet who had gained fame as a twelve-year-old drummer boy at Chickamauga in 1863, but he did not pass the test. Wood and his classmates quickly discovered that they stood on the wrong side of a stark divide. War had defined the lives of every senior officer and thousands of enlisted men. Wood's professors had been tried by war; they remembered dozens of promising cadets who had not survived the ordeal. Wood and his classmates could not share this experience, however, and the army that they were preparing to join seemed no longer central to American society. As the Civil War receded in Americans' memories, it was unclear what a life devoted to military service would signify. After Sherman's remarks, Wood recalled, the graduates broke ranks and scattered. Wood knew exactly where he had to go. He headed straight to the barracks, where a tailor from New York was waiting to fit him for a fine suit of civilian clothes, the better to enjoy what he termed the "hurly-burly" of celebration amid the beauty of late spring in the Hudson River Valley.

Wood could not help that he belonged to an untested generation. Although William Maxwell Wood had what Erskine called "a fine American democratic contempt for ancestry," his children — two girls by his first wife, and six boys and a

182

girl by his second — were, in essence, aristocrats, with the promise, destiny, and power of America as their birthright. Erskine wore that mantle casually. He never quite understood the conflict between the North and South that marked his childhood years. Days before his ninth birthday, he stood with his father for a glimpse of Abraham Lincoln, en route to Washington for his inauguration in 1861. Erskine saw a tall man in a black frock coat and remembered the crowd all around him, so crushing that an officer traveling with the president-elect dislocated his shoulder. The words Lincoln spoke that day — his affirmation of "the Constitution, the Union, and the perpetuity of the liberties of this country" — were lost on the boy.

When Fort Sumter was attacked a few months later, Erskine had only the vaguest sense of the struggles ahead. He felt his mother's disquiet — "as if the sky had fallen," he later wrote — and watched her weep as his father left to serve as fleet surgeon for the naval blockade of Norfolk. But while his mother tried to raise six boys on her own during the dark early days of the war, while his father sawed away at the wounded after the ironclads the *Monitor* and the *Merrimac* battled at Hampton Roads in March 1862, while his half-sister Hannah vowed to grieve to the end of her days for a fiancé who fell at Gettysburg the following year, Erskine led something approaching a carefree boyhood. Sent to live with an uncle in Baltimore, Erskine devoted his idle hours to the local sport of egg-picking, in which boys knocked eggs against each other, butt to butt, and won the ones they broke. He played marbles "for keeps," despite warnings from his elders that such games were, in his words, "a riotous progress on the highway to destruction." He sorted through his devout Presbyterian uncle's books — "theology, theology, theology" — until he found an anti-Catholic tract on the depravity of nunneries. Decades later he remembered that "this illicit and sexual reading was a great delight."

As the war progressed, it remained a sideshow to Erskine's youth. Visiting his father at the blockade while on vacation from school one year, Erskine rowed through the site where the ironclads had fought, cutting pieces of rope from the exposed masts of the *Cumberland* and the *Congress,* two ships that had been sunk by the *Merrimac.* He ate dinner with his father and Lieutenant John Worden, the *Monitor*'s captain, face freckled with gunpowder from a rebel shell, and watched them sweep aside the dishes and reenact the battle with saltshakers. But the visit did not inspire Erskine to reflect on the northern cause. His most enduring memory was the painful sunburn he suffered from swimming naked in the Chesapeake.

The war's end was similarly opaque to Wood. When Richmond fell, Baltimore celebrated quietly, with candles in windows. Erskine could not understand why his uncle and aunt were angry with neighbors — known simply as "Sympathizers" — who kept their home dark. Not two weeks later, Erskine's teacher broke the news to his class that the president had been shot. "I am sure we knew that every American had lost his best friend," he wrote. But at the same time, he felt glad that school was let out for two weeks. He was, he would later realize, a "small irresponsible boy."

By the time Erskine was old enough to understand the ideas and commitments of Union and abolition, there was little occasion to do so. The world had changed, and so had Erskine's life. Ashore after years of blockade duty, his father found what seemed to be an excellent price on hundreds of rolling acres northwest of Baltimore. He built a grand addition onto a plantation house and called the estate Rosewood Glen after Erskine's mother, Rose Wood. Thirteen years old in 1865, Erskine was at last reunited with his parents and younger siblings. Although he took the train into town to go to school, he lived the next four years at Rosewood completely sheltered from the politics of Reconstruction. While the nation fought over the contours and direction of American democracy, Erskine spent day after day exploring the forests, fields, and creeks that surrounded his house. He learned how to hunt possum and rabbits and sat and watched flying squirrels leap from the treetops. He rode bushels of the family's wheat, corn, and rye to nearby Owings' Mills for grinding. He delighted in the constant covered-wagon traffic running along the Reisterstown Pike to and from the city — "picturesque, jingling, happy," he wrote. He called on young heiresses who lived in mansions an easy ride away.

His parents abhorred slavery, yet in their country life the Wood family experienced what Erskine called "the taint of slavery." Previous owners of their plantation had held people as their property, and many of these men, women, and children stayed on the land after emancipation. The world was changing, but Rosewood Glen stood, at least in the Woods' view, outside of time. The family barely paid the longtime residents, who survived by trapping rabbits, possums, and raccoons and foraging for chestnuts and wild grapes. But the freedpeople still served the Wood family. They cooked corncakes in the kitchen and tended the rose gardens, berry patches, and tomato vines that surrounded the big house. They planted and harvested Rosewood Glen's fields. Erskine called them "Aunt" and "Uncle." They called him "Massa Ernie." Frequently complaining that her servants were like children, Erskine's mother "was continually trying to make her women folks in the house understand why she couldn't buy them back for herself as slaves," Erskine remembered without irony. "It was almost hopeless to make them understand it was against the law and a great war had been fought to free the slaves and abolish slavery." Despite their politics, the Woods lived like slave owners, and Erskine did not question it.

As he grew older and followed a path that was smoothed by his father's renown, he never felt challenged to think more seriously about his place in the world. At age seventeen, the boy visited Ulysses Grant in his private office at the White House. Erskine's father had arranged the audience, after which the president personally gave Erskine an at-large commission to West Point. The boy remembered little of his conversation with the hero of the Union cause. What impressed him was the way that Grant smoked a cigar down to the stump and then used it to light a new one.

The West Point Class of 1874 included James Webster Smith, the first man of color admitted as a cadet. Though Wood noted the curiosity of his presence as they took the entrance exam together, he felt no stirrings of conscience as Smith was ostracized, tormented, and ultimately dismissed from the academy. After a miserable plebe year,

Wood spent the remaining three peacocking his way through a brisk whirl of waltzes and cotillions and hops. A swooning romantic and determined flirt, he went deeply into debt for uniforms, gauntlets, boots, and buttons — "plumes, sash, gold shoulder knots, gold sword belt etc. etc." — thousands of dollars for wool, leather, silk, porcelain, gold, and mother of pearl. The diary he kept during his cadet years did not focus on his daily life, aspirations, or training in engineering, philosophy, or fencing. Instead, he called it his "journal of feelings," in which he documented a fevered desire for one society belle. His feelings for young ladies were often requited. Walking through the trees on the Hudson's west bank, he might offer a female companion a keepsake, the brass button just over his heart on his meticulously tailored cadet's uniform. After returning to the barracks, he would sew on another one, only to clip it for his next guest. One woman — "beautiful Minnie Buckmaster," he remembered — asked him to close his eyes so that she could better gaze at his long curling lashes. The temptation was too great. She let him kiss her lips.

Erskine Wood's heart beat for the prospect of writing his name on a beautiful woman's dance card. Years later, he would remember the warmth of close contact, of bodies moving together, an alchemy of adrenaline and deep calm that was as close to complete joy as Wood had ever known. Occasionally he would step outside the ballroom, walk until the music was as faint as a trail of perfume, lie down in the cool grass, and look up at the stars. In that moment, he was blessedly free of thoughts of soldiering, of leading men into battle, of honoring and upholding army tradition.

The past was the last dance, the future the next one.

Aside from courses on drawing and on ethics and law, Wood showed little interest in his schoolwork, and even less in following West Point's rigid codes. Graduating twenty-fourth in his class of forty-one, he ranked thirty-eighth in discipline, with 566 demerits over four years. It was not easy for him to figure out what he was working toward. As the Civil War became history, the army's mission blurred. To Wood, committing to the officer corps often seemed equivalent to taking a vow of poverty that served no higher cause. His mind wandered. He mused to his father that he might prefer to leave West Point to write novels or fight abroad as a mercenary. William Maxwell Wood grew ashamed of his shiftless son. Although Erskine decided to stay and finish, he never developed a true sense of purpose. After drawing infantry duty, he tried to transfer into Custer's cavalry because he enjoyed riding horses. The army denied his request.

On the other side of the continent, Erskine Wood would recline in a caned chaise in his quarters and listen to Fort Vancouver's band practice its repertoire each evening. While the lamplight flickered, the music took him back to long nights of dancing at West Point. "It rises and falls on the air," he wrote soon after arriving at the post, "now low and voluptuous and then swelling into a perfect ecstasy of sound — There! It has stopped." Wood still buttoned his cuffs for balls. At his first posting in northeastern California, he waltzed and square-danced with girls from the local Mexican families at parties thrown in large barns. Once his regiment was posted to Fort Vancouver, invitations to events in Portland came fast and insistent. On many evenings, Wood found himself at parties making earnest conversation over plates of apple pie a la mode, watching other men take discreet pulls from their hip flasks. The world of high army society was small enough that oftentimes his dance partners knew friends of his from his life at West Point. They had even heard stories about him months or even years before. He was "*that* Mr. Wood.*"

Although Wood never spoke of it, some of them knew he had a special attachment to a debutante in the capital named Nanny Moale Smith. He had called on her in Washington, saw her at West Point, and fell in love with her over two summers on long rides and rambles at her aunt's graceful mansion, Atamasco, which neighbored the Wood estate near Owings' Mills. Orphaned as a girl and raised by a doting stepfather, she dressed in the finest gowns, drove a phaeton made of woven willow branches, and was attended to by a young servant — she called him her "tiger" — dressed in full silver-buttoned livery.

Unlike Wood, Nanny Smith had experienced the Civil War up close. In 1860, she had gone to Fort Sumter to live with an aunt married to an army officer posted there. The five-year-old girl was evacuated with other women and children shortly before the rebels began bombarding it in April 1861. At age seven, while living with a Union garrison occupying New Bern, North Carolina, she was on board a reconnaissance trip up the Neuse River when rebels on shore raked the boat with a lethal volley. As survivors on board returned fire with rifle and cannon, the girl hid on deck, ears ringing, eyes dotted by the flash of gun muzzles, throat burning from gunpowder.

Ten years later, all was forgotten, as Nanny Smith embraced a life of pleasure. The bustled socialite entertained crowds of suitors past midnight at hops and cotillions. Her dark hair endlessly braided and layered high on her head — combed out, it went down to her ankles — she danced and laughed and showed a gift for making her male companions laugh, too. When Erskine Wood met her — when she picked him from a crowd — he was struck in much the same way that other women had been dazzled by him. A mutual friend described the couple as "diamond cut diamond," Wood remembered. "We were both such outrageous flirts."

By the time Wood left for California, he had shared kisses and exchanged promises of marriage with Nanny Smith, but her stepfather refused to bless the union until the young lieutenant showed that he could support her. They embraced, wept, and parted. She wore a ring he gave her, but not on her left hand. He carried a lock of her hair. Separated from her by thousands of miles, he continued to play the role of the gentleman in society. But at the end of a night out, he would return to quarters and gaze at tintypes of his "best girl" that he had framed in walnut and velvet, so many that his fellow officers joked that his rooms were a gallery. He would stay up until reveille composing endless reams of passionate declarations signed "Your loving lover, Ern." He wondered if he took any pleasure from his countless social engagements. "I am sick and tired of all nonsense," he wrote. "Parties are positively bores and I think all the time, Oh if I only had a sweet pretty little home with Nan there waiting for me."

If many people went west to seek a second chance, Wood was living a life that had yet to begin. Every day he encountered alien worlds, but he saw it all from a distracted remove. Pining for Nanny Smith, imagining a cozy home with her, curating obsessive displays of souvenirs of their courtship — "things that you probably never remembered having given me an hour after you did so," he wrote her, "bits of ribbon, cards, . . . flowers, everything your sweet fingers have touched" — it all had the effect of distancing him from his new life as an army officer in the West. While in wartime he would have depended on his fellow soldiers and valued them accordingly, in peace he could filter his friendships through how he imagined Nanny would see them. When officers invited him to dinners of canned salmon and corn and chicken salad without celery, when they made conversation that, in his words, "murdered the King's English," when their jokes mostly centered on the antics of drunken men, he was already composing his letter home. "You might perhaps call them vulgar in the sense of being rather common and below us," he wrote, "but they are not morally bad by any means."

Wood's superior officer, Captain Robert Pollock, had risen through the ranks during the Civil War by the point of his bayonet. To him, the regiment's initial posting in California was an idyll of hunting and fishing and exploring. He was delighted to have a lieutenant better educated than he was. He "slapped me on the back royally," Wood wrote, and "made me do all his clerical work." While Wood was fond of the man he called his "good old captain," he could not follow

Pollock's lead and embrace their surroundings. Instead, Wood shuddered when the captain called him "Charley," not Erskine. He fixated on how Pollock tippled his morning dram, "swears like a trooper and is idle, worthless and happy all day long."

Sent into the field to collect new recruits from Reno, protect their payroll from highwaymen, or map new routes to the marshlands across the Oregon line, Wood was unmoved by the adventure — it was all an inconvenience. He grew a beard to fit in with everyone else on the frontier but shaved it off after Nanny Smith wrote him that she could not stand to kiss a bristly man. Sleepless, isolated, and alone, he wondered how the woman he loved, who back in the capital continued to maintain an enthusiastic social calendar, would know enough to have such firm preferences about kissing. "You say 'I hate 'em' just as though you had a vast experience," he wrote.

Not even the most novel experiences of the West could stem Wood's obsession. With little urgent business in California, Wood began hunting swans with a local Paiute man named Debe. Debe kept the meat, while the feathers went to Wood, who sent some to Nanny Smith for stuffing the pillows she embroidered, and distributed the rest among the women at the fort. Despite the hours he spent visiting with Debe's family, breakfasting on their dried huckleberries, the lieutenant kept his intellectual and emotional distance. In letters to Smith, they were "those poor devils the Pi-Utes." "I was at one of their wik-ee-ups yesterday it is nothing in the world but a semicircle of brush to keep the wind off," he wrote. "And the little papooses keep as fat as butter. . . . Now Nan if we could live like

192

those Pi-Utes there would be not a bit of trouble in going to housekeeping."

In the summer of 1875, Wood's regiment was ordered to Fort Vancouver. The prospect of being a short ferry trip across the Columbia from Portland was almost beyond comprehension. "What could be better than that?" he remembered. "Nothing." The only real upside to California, Wood thought, was that he had had nothing to spend his money on. After six months in the army, he had managed to retire about eight hundred dollars of his debts; soon, he thought, he would be able to save enough money to get married. Still, when an English master tailor transferred into the resident cavalry company at his fort, Wood could not resist the extravagance of a pair of hand-sewn buckskin breeches. He wrote home for skeins of black silk and for smoked pearl buttons — "don't want em with eyelets," he specified, "want holes." "With a pair of riding boots and my white gauntlets," he wrote Nanny, "I'll be the swellest beau you ever had ride with you in your life."

In July the 21st Infantry marched straight through eastern Oregon. Captain Pollock and Wood led the column on horseback, while the officers' wives rode in canvas wagons. The soldiers hunted for their dinner — antelope and sage hen — and drank water that they pumped from volcanic crevasses. Wood followed the silhouettes of buzzards and birds of prey in the bright high desert sky. At night under the stars, he could not sleep for all the birdsong. Decades later, Wood described the Harney Desert as deeply inspiring, "tremendously beautiful, breathtaking . . . enough to impress the most calloused heart in the world." But when he was finally able to post a letter to

Smith in September 1875, he did not describe a meditative odyssey through the wilderness. In his scant telling, it was a "tedious, hot dusty trip."

Halfway through their march, the 21st Infantry stopped at Camp Harney, an army outpost along the banks of the inauspiciously named Rattlesnake Creek. There Wood befriended Charles Bendire, a German-born captain who was spending every moment of peacetime amassing one of the world's great collections of birds' eggs. Bendire admired two dried and cured birds that Wood had shot along the way, "wonderful blue birds," Wood remembered, "blue as a blue humming bird's throat — glistening, metallic, wonderful." The naturalist asked for them, having never seen those birds before. Although Wood knew that the captain was "celebrated as a bird expert in two continents" — and never forgot how Bendire declared that the specimens were "worth more than any fortune to me and to the world of science" — Wood hesitated at the request. Astonishingly, he said aloud that he wanted to send the birds back to Nanny Smith so she could decorate her summer hats.

Emerging from the desert at the Columbia River port the Dalles, the enlisted men got drunk seemingly all at once. Wood had the unenviable task of following the mob as they wandered through town. The lieutenant caught up with a crowd of soldiers in a saloon and ordered them back to their tents. When one of the men sassed him — "impudent and disobedient," he reported — Wood knocked the soldier to the floor and left his ear a bloody mess. As the sun rose, and the regiment boarded a steamer for the final eighty miles to Fort Vancouver, the lieutenant began to shed his affect of aggrieved melancholy. In a moment of supreme understatement, he wrote, "The scenery coming down the Columbia River surpasses that on the Hudson." For the first time, it seemed, he knew that he was experiencing something that Nanny Smith would enjoy.

But the malaise of peacetime persisted at Fort Vancouver. Wood was immediately put to work recording the proceedings of the post's court-martial. It could seem as if an army officer existed to do little else besides generate, circulate, and file records of every sort. Processing disciplinary cases took up most of Wood's waking hours; the soldiers were idle, and there was no shortage of establishments nearby where they could swallow shots of whiskey and roll ivory balls across felt. It was meticulous and exacting work to reduce all the resulting fistfights, stabbings, shootings, and occasional out-and-out riots into piles of paper.

Though he did not express his discontent with the usual army pastimes of drinking, smoking, gambling, and fighting, the drift of days affected Wood. Every so often, a big gun would boom in the distance — not the sound of war, just a signal that another ocean steamer had arrived in Portland — and the lieutenant would reflexively wonder if it was bringing mail from his love. As his time apart from Smith extended into its second year, Wood could not escape the notion that being an army officer was not enough. The move to a more expensive and cosmopolitan post made it difficult to pay down his debts, let alone save enough money to satisfy Smith's stepfather. Even worse, he learned that his family back in Baltimore was struggling. The Rosewood estate looked lovely, but its soil was exhausted to an extent that no amount of manure, guano, or oyster-shell lime could remedy. Retired from the navy, Erskine's father spent his days in an angry fog, dosing himself with opium until he could collect his monthly pension and drink it away with his old mates. Erskine could expect no support from his family in his bid for Nanny Smith. To the contrary, he faced the prospect that he might have to support them; it was far from certain that his parents would have enough to send his younger siblings to school. "I spend nothing on myself or I should hate myself," Erskine wrote. "Oh how I curse and curse that farm."

Wood cast about for ways to augment his income. After talking with an old housepainter who once got twenty dollars for a small rendering of Mount Shasta, Wood decided that he could make money in the picture trade. He had shown potential in his drawing classes at West Point and quickly did a pastel still life of peaches and pears; "they really look very tempting," he wrote, but "it rubs off if you touch it." Then he made a couple of watercolor landscapes. Pleased with the results, he was determined to get hold of canvas and oils. "Then I will paint some worth a fortune," he wrote.

In their months apart, Nanny Smith's letters remained encouraging. She cried herself to sleep over Wood, she wrote, and could not wait to stand barefoot on a lynx pelt that he had bought for her. "I won't ever want to put on my stockings & slippers," she added suggestively. As much a realist as a romantic, she was pleased that Wood was now near Portland. From her aunts who had married army men, she knew that being close to a department headquarters was good for a young officer's long-term prospects, with more interesting work, more cultured and ambitious colleagues, and better opportunities for promotion. "Ern," she wrote him, "I would honestly like to know how far into the future you look sometimes & what you think of the prospects. Sweetheart you are only planning for one thing — the wedding — do you ever go farther?" Wood admitted that he could not. "I look . . . just far enough to hope to be out of debt and let all my dreams end with the day I marry you," he replied. That day seemed forever beyond his grasp, just on the other side of the horizon.

As Nanny had anticipated, Wood soon benefited from leaving the California wilderness for what he described as "the very midst of civilization." Even he would agree that General Howard was an important friend to have. Though the connection did not tangibly affect Wood's day-to-day work at Fort Vancouver, where he remained at the bottom of a baroque hierarchy of officers, what Howard gave him was something else entirely. Wood may have written Nanny Smith that he preferred to spend all his spare time alone in his quarters contemplating her picture, but the Howards provided him with his first joyful family relationships since he had left home for West Point at age eighteen.

Dining with the Howards, Wood looked out at an improved version of his own family. The children were the same ages as Wood's younger brothers and sister. He soon counted the two oldest as close friends; they called him "Wood." In Guy Howard, he found someone who was also having trouble getting started with life. Guy was frustrated to find that a recent Yale degree meant little as a banker in Portland. He chafed as young men with few qualifications were promoted above him. Like the lieutenant, he was convinced that he needed something more. Guy's younger sister Grace was more serious than Wood's typical waltzing partner. She kept tickets to Andrew Johnson's impeachment in her scrapbook. An accomplished horsewoman, she rode with her father on several of his forays into Indian country. She wore black dresses, even though her mother felt that she looked prettier in dark greens, blues, and browns. Her dark hair was parted severely down the middle and pulled into a tight simple bun, accentuating her large eyes and full lips. Home for a year or two before starting college at Vassar, she relished being able to help her mother care for her youngest siblings, jotting in her diary the funniest things that they said. Wood came to appreciate that Grace wrote "chatty" letters; reading them after a meal, he thought, was like having a second dessert. He decided that she was "one among many, a womanly woman with rare qualities."

Among the Howards, Wood kept quiet about his own skeptical views about religion. "How I hated Sunday," he later wrote, "the Church service, the tedious nonunderstandable sermon and the sense of awful grewsome superstition." Nevertheless, the Howards' piety — grace at the table, bedside devotionals, sermons and Sunday school lessons, YMCA meetings — was deeply familiar to Wood, whose mother was such a devout Presbyterian that she would not allow Erskine to whistle on the Sabbath. Wood might have taken heart from the fact that little Bessie Howard shut her eyes tight instead of saying her prayers and that Harry

Howard got into fights at Sunday school when other boys pulled on his long curls. But the lieutenant also saw that the Howards' religion was warmer and more welcoming than what he had known as a child. It was rooted in love, not fear and control.

As the Howard children gave Wood their friendship, so did their parents. Lizzie Howard was plainer than Wood's mother but more content. Wood described himself as "tortured" by the fact that his mother had to engage in what Erskine called "a bare and bitter economy" to support the family while suffering abuse from a husband who on the best of days was "moody, and changeable [, n]ervous, peevish, irritable &c &c." By contrast, Mrs. Howard's most difficult days in Washington, DC, were behind her. Although his hair had grayed and thinned since leaving the capital, by 1876 General Howard looked back on their first year in the Northwest as the easiest of his previous twenty. In contrast to Erskine's father, once fearsome and now debased, General Howard presented another model of career officer. Unlike William Maxwell Wood, Howard was sober. He worked constantly, traveling the department and evangelizing in Portland and everywhere else he went. The lieutenant had never met a man in Howard's position who seemed so unselfish. "He has such a sweet gentle disposition," Wood wrote Nanny Smith.

Howard shared and supported Wood's desire to make more money. If Wood was determined to be a painter, Howard was on his way to being a writer. The general's lectures were generating requests for articles; toward the end of 1875, the *Atlantic Monthly* offered him two hundred dollars for essays about his Civil War experiences. That winter, when a local newspaper editor took a three-month leave, Howard filled in and wrote all the editorials. The column inches came easily to him — mostly "sketches of our public men of the past," he remembered, "of Presidents and other statesmen, comparing and contrasting them with the statesmen of that day who were well known to the country." Quietly pleased when he heard discerning local citizens comment on how the paper had "new life," Howard was inspired to wonder if he could find even more success writing books — about the war, perhaps, or something based on his Sunday school lessons that drew on his Maine childhood. Grace was helping him make some notes.

Unlike Wood's father, who berated Erskine for failing to embrace army life more fully, General Howard could understand and sympathize with the young man's anguished search for something better out of life. Howard had himself experienced just such a crisis after leaving West Point. Back in 1857, ten years after the Mexican War and four years before the next great conflict, there was little sense to army service. Howard was a bored and depressed junior officer questioning his place in the world. He found solace in serving the Lord and the less fortunate, and it carried him through war and peace, through good years and bad. Wood was living in similar times, feeling similar emotions and asking similar questions. What would give meaning to his days? What was he destined to do? He had yet to find any answers but was determined to remain close to the general. Having Howard as a friend and mentor gave him hope that one day his true calling would announce itself.

The ferry from Portland back to Fort Vancouver was a fight against the current where the Willamette emptied into the Columbia. Wood could look back at the city lights and know from the days he spent with the Howards that life could be enjoyed. But as the lights grew distant, as the steamer pushed ahead, Wood was left facing darkness, the incessant Northwest drizzle pricking his face, damp seeping into his clothes. Try as he might to imagine a happy future, the dreams receded like the tides. He walked up from the ferry landing to his quarters and lit a candle in a special room he had decorated to wait out the night. He called it his "blue room": "blue curtains . . . blue table covers, blue mantelpiece, a number of blue velvet picture frames and sometimes a decidedly blue boy in the Canton chair at this table."

CHAPTER 7
WIND BLOWING

Wallowa Valley,
June 1876

"Shoot the son of a bitch!" Wells McNall was screaming as he struggled in the dirt. Although his neighbor Alexander Findley was just a few yards away, McNall had trouble seeing him. When McNall's eyes were open, he could see only the Indian man on top of him. He could smell him, feel his rough grip, hear his angry breaths. Why hadn't Findley fired already?

"Shoot, you damn fool, shoot!" McNall shouted. The Indian was slightly built, an even match for McNall, whom people described as "wiry." Once he was down, it was hard to find the leverage to get back up. There was not much level ground where they were fighting. Slender lengths of aspen trees blotted the sky, leaves still new, trembling in the breeze. All around them were freshly killed deer, some hanging high from pine branches, some dropped in the dirt, still warm, seeping blood. Down the slope was Whiskey Creek, named for the barrels poured into the stream four summers earlier, after the first Wallowa settlers caught a group of men who had followed them into the valley to sell spirits to Joseph's band.

The Indian had the advantage over McNall, but

Findley hesitated to raise his weapon. He knew who McNall's foe was, who the man's people were, and he liked them. The land that Findley tilled was directly across the Wallowa River from Joseph's main camp. Although it was still too early in the season for Joseph's band to reach the southwestern corner of the valley — they had just emerged from a winter in the canyons and were digging kouse roots fifty or sixty miles away — Findley and his family had grown to expect their return each summer. Over the course of a few years, Findley became a familiar sight, a friendly face staring through a thicket of hair and beard. Joseph was a regular visitor to his cabin. He had joined the Findleys for dinner. He had kind words for the farmer's wife. Findley's six children sat on the chief's lap. They invited him to play with them, and he taught them the games that children played in his village. He brought trinkets for them to keep.

"God damn you," McNall cried, "why in hell don't you shoot?"

Findley should have been home plowing his fields. When he woke that morning, however, four of the horses that he had been using were gone from the pasture behind his farm. McNall, who lived just upriver from him, was helping with the spring planting. The two men saddled up. McNall pulled his soft hat low over his eyes, and they rode into the hills that shadowed their land. For a few miles of broken country and thick woods, they saw little sign of the animals or of anyone who might have taken them. Then they found the deer carcasses strung high, ringing a campsite. Ash from an old fire, piles of horse manure: a small Nez Perce hunting party had been staying there, probably no more than a few days, sent ahead by the main group of Joseph's band, which often ran low on meat at the start of summer. The camp was empty. The hunters were out in the hills, stalking more prey.

McNall was convinced that these Indians had stolen Findley's horses. He had never liked the Indians. Although he had fenced his property, their ponies always had a way of getting through and eating his grain. He was convinced that someone was helping them over the fence. Whenever he saw members of Joseph's band, he accosted them with a catalog of escalating grievances. He had gained a reputation among them as "bad" or "quarrelsome," a man whose hatred and hot temper defined him.

After a short while, several Nez Perce hunters rode into the camp. They dropped the morning's kill, turned their horses loose, and approached on foot. By McNall's account, "a parley ensued and the talk was friendly, the Indians denying any knowledge of the lost horses." But when McNall reached for a gun — maybe his, maybe a hunter's — one of the Nez Perce men grabbed back. Their struggle blurred against the stillness of the forest. McNall's screams grew increasingly strident.

Although Findley later said that he was "resolved not to shoot until I saw our lives were in danger," he finally raised his rifle. It was a breech-loading needle gun, a modern gun for the West, what hunters were using to slaughter the buffalo herds and what soldiers were carrying in the field. For one moment, the world around him, trees and animals, hills and creek, fell away. The people standing close, McNall and his foe, disappeared. All he saw was one point on a man's body. He felt the trigger and then heard nothing but the blast and the ringing in his ears. Smells of pine, dirt, horse, and man surrendered to the mineral burn of gun smoke. Findley saw McNall standing again. But Wilhautyah, also known as Wind Blowing, lay dead alongside the deer he had helped kill.

As Wilhautyah's companions grieved over his body, Findley and McNall fled to the homesteads along the Wallowa River. By the time Findley's plow horses turned up near his land a few days later — they had been lost, not stolen — McNall was gone, riding to the Grande Ronde Valley to report the incident to a county judge. The judge, in turn, notified the commander at Fort Walla Walla, who passed the news up the chain of command to the Department of Columbia's headquarters. When a group of settlers went back to the hunting camp, they found it deserted. The hunters had already tied Wilhautyah to a horse, collected their venison from a number of camps in the area, and made the long ride home to Joseph's spring village.

With one shot in the forest, Findley had cast the lives of the settlers as well as of Joseph's people into deep uncertainty. A praying man, he did not need the censure of nearly all his neighbors to know that he had done something disastrous. Would Joseph's band demand his life for Wilhautyah's? Were they going to attack all the homesteaders in the area?

North and east across the Wallowa Valley, Joseph, Ollokot, and their band had questions of their own as they made sense of the killing and consoled Wilhautyah's widow. They wondered how the murder would upset the uneasy accommodation that they had reached with the settlers the previous summer. Would the killers face justice, or did settlers have free rein to kill Indians, just as they seemed to have across the Snake River in Idaho? If the killers faced justice, whose justice would it be? For countless generations Joseph's band had handled vengeance and redress for the occasional deaths that were inevitable in a nomadic, tribal life — fights and accidents within the band, deaths in horse raids and battles with outsiders. But did a death at the hands of a white man constitute a new kind of event, something outside their history and experience, that compelled a different response?

In the alternative, Joseph and Ollokot also considered whether the killing would become proof that whites and Indians could not live together. If so, Wilhautyah's death could become a pretext for forcing the band onto the reservation. Still, Joseph counseled peace, and the band stayed where they were, far from the late summer village. They continued to dig roots and then followed their traditional summer course, slow and deliberate, through the valley. Their use of the land, their connection to it, was unshaken by the tragedy of a single day. Perhaps, Joseph thought, the killing could even strengthen their claim on the Wallowa country.

The man Joseph greeted as "my friend" was sallow, with stringy thinning hair, a wispy mustache, and a tangle of whiskers cascading from his chin. Officer's stripes graced his uniform, but he did not look like a warrior. Major Henry Clay Wood more resembled the lawyer he had trained to be after graduating from Bowdoin College in 1854. Although he had chosen a soldier's life and bore the scars of Civil War battles, he was now the adjutant general, the chief administrator, of the Department of the Columbia. He was not normally called upon to conduct sensitive missions, but in the past year he had become the army's resident authority on Nez Perce affairs. After Howard asked him to evaluate Joseph's claim on the Wallowa Valley, the major analyzed the relevant treaties and executive orders, pored over official reports and correspondence, and attempted to master the decentralized system of Nez Perce bands. In January 1876, he published a pamphlet concluding that "the non-treaty Nez-Perce cannot in law be regarded as bound by the treaty of 1863," taking care to note that "the Nez-Perces are distinguished . . . for their superior intelligence, their power, and wealth of cattle and horses, their fine physical development, freedom from disease, and comparative virtue, . . . [and] unshaken fidelity to the pale-faces."

When word of the killing in the Wallowa Valley reached Portland, General Howard ordered his adjutant to go east to investigate and keep the peace. The major was pleased to make the journey to Lapwai. Studying the Indians had left him feeling, in his words, "a strong desire for further information of this remarkable tribe . . . and their country." Inspired by Joseph's strong sense of justice and convinced that the settlers did not have a proper claim to the valley, he already thought of Wilhautyah's death as an "unjustifiable killing" — a "murder."

As the major steamed up the Columbia River in mid-July, the rhythms and rituals of the journey were exactly what he would have expected. The landscape remained unchanged. The sublime progression of hills and cliffs was beyond time. The rapids still battered the boat and unsettled passengers. The china and silver settings at meals, the noises at bedtime, the strong morning coffee — all were the same as on any number of journeys.

But in the six weeks it took for him to put his affairs in order and travel to Lapwai, the world had changed. Across the Bitterroot Mountains some six hundred miles east in Montana Territory, the army was battling the Lakota and Cheyenne. All spring and summer, soldiers had been campaigning in the valleys of the Powder River, the Yellowstone, Rosebud Creek, and the Bighorn. Leading the 7th Cavalry was George Armstrong Custer, who two years earlier had started the chain of events that resulted in this war when he reported finding gold while surveying the Lakota's sacred Black Hills. As in Nez Perce country, would-be miners flooded the area, after which the government determined that the Lakota would have to cede the land. When thousands of Lakota and Cheyenne refused to give up the Black Hills or comply with an impossible ultimatum to move onto reservations at the height of winter, the War Department took jurisdiction over the matter from the Interior Department, and the army went on the offensive. At the end of June, Custer's scouts reported an enormous Lakota village on the Little Bighorn River. Rather than wait for reinforcements that were days away, Custer charged the village on June 25, 1876, with 210 troops, only to discover that Lakota and Cheyenne warriors outnumbered them eight to one. Within an hour, Custer and his men had been overwhelmed and slaughtered.

When news of the debacle reached the cities to

the east, the nation was celebrating its century of independence. After barely surviving the fight over slavery and freedom, Americans now saw another threat to their existence. Although the government had taken a conciliatory approach during the Modoc crisis of 1873 in order to keep the western tribes peaceful — the executive order reserving part of the Wallowa Valley to the Nez Perce was, in part, a wartime measure — Custer's Last Stand made compromise with nontreaty Indians seem anathema to the national project. President Grant's Peace Policy was quickly giving way to a bloody endgame.

If American opinion roughly divided between those who wanted to annihilate the Indians outright and others who supported peaceful methods to force them onto reservations, Joseph and Ollokot tried to imagine another option. Through their words and deeds, they were showing how their people were equal to settlers and fit for citizenship. In doing so, they pushed at the very definitions of citizenship and equality. As Joseph and Ollokot fashioned them, these concepts would no longer require Indians to live as whites. Rather, equality and citizenship gave people in tribes the right to be different, to lead different lives and see the land — their world — differently. Although the nation recoiled from such ideas after Little Bighorn, the Nez Perce position remained compelling. By choosing as his envoy an officer who had publicly supported the Indians over the settlers in the Wallowa Valley, General Howard hoped to establish the government's good faith in its negotiations with the nontreaty Nez Perce bands. The choice of his adjutant also may have suggested that he was still willing to consider Joseph and Ollokot's arguments.

Major Wood met Chief Joseph and Ollokot in a crowded council room at the Lapwai reservation on July 22, 1876. Three dozen men had gathered at the officer's invitation. After the journey through the mountains into Idaho, Joseph and his retinue were dressed simply, in what one observer called "the ordinary covering of the Indian — leggings, moccasins, and blankets." A delegation of treaty Indians who lived on the reservation also joined the meeting, distinguished by the fact that they had, as the major reported, "adopted the dress, habits, and occupations of civilized life." Chief Reuben, Joseph's father-in-law, had succeeded Lawyer as head chief on the reservation. Reuben's son James Reuben, a devout Presbyterian in his twenties, knew English well enough to interpret for the chiefs and officers.

Flanking the major were officers from the Lapwai garrison: the post commander, David Perry, a cavalry captain with a nose that looked broken, his wavy hair parted tightly along his scalp; his first lieutenant, William Parnell, a heavy-browed Irishman with a grand mustache and carefully tended beard; and the army surgeon, Jenkins FitzGerald, dark with a muscular build, newly arrived from a posting in Sitka, Alaska. Together they had nearly half a century of military experience; each had joined the Union cause early in the Civil War, surviving dozens of battles in the south and afterward in the west. Also in attendance was the Indian agent John Monteith, who sat fuming because the army was taking such an active interest in negotiating with the nontreaties; managing the various Nez Perce bands was supposed to be his job, not the adjutant's.

Although Joseph and Ollokot had been summoned to Lapwai, they quickly took control of the meeting. For the adjutant the greetings treaded a line between the mundane and the mystical, dozens of handshakes giving way to what he described as "a period of silence, during which each part was apparently studying the countenances and physical characteristics, and estimating the mental calibre, of individuals in the other." The formal introduction impressed upon the major how far he had traveled, and how important he had become. After hearing his name in English and Nez Perce, being touched and gazed upon, feeling examined and judged, the adjutant began to speak. With Lieutenant Parnell taking notes, he explained that he was "the writer of the little pamphlet concerning the Nez Perce nation." Joseph knew the publication and immediately began peppering the major with questions about it. The chief, according to Parnell's notes, "wanted to know how Major Wood came to write the pamphlet; was he induced to write it by some one else, and if so, who; or did he write it of his own motion, and for what purpose. Who told Major Wood about the tribe?" The major might have been flattered by such close interest in his research and writing process, but the questions revealed Chief Joseph to be more interested in the mechanics of American power. How could his words find their way to someone far from the Wallowa Valley, someone who had never seen him or his people? And how could such a person render an opinion with far-reaching consequences for them all?

After discussion of the pamphlet, the conversation began in earnest. Rather than impose a preordained structure on the meeting, the major began by welcoming Joseph's thoughts "concerning the recent killing of one of his band by whites in the Wallowa Valley." The chief, in turn, seized the chance to leverage a eulogy for a man he called "quiet, peaceable, well-disposed" and "much respected by the tribe" into a two-day conversation about the Nez Perce claim to the valley and the obligations of the American government to respect Indian rights. For weeks Joseph had kept his band from avenging Wilhautyah. Now he tried to use the tragedy to convince the government to rethink the valley's ownership. Wilhautyah's life, Joseph explained, "was of great value; . . . worth more than the Wallowa Valley; . . . more than all this country; . . . more than all the world; . . . the value of his life could not be estimated." Just as his father's bones had sanctified the valley, so did Wilhautyah's. "His . . . life had been taken in Wallowa Valley, his body buried there, and the earth there had drank up his blood," Joseph said. "The valley was more sacred to him than ever before, and he would and did claim it now as a recompense for the life taken; that he should hold it for himself and his people from this time forward forever; and that all the whites must be removed from the valley."

The major demurred, deflecting Joseph's words with the meandering assurance that Findley and McNall would be "tried for their crime by the court having jurisdiction in the vicinity of the locality where the crime was committed — probably the town of Union." But Joseph and Ollokot were unfazed by the officer's legalistic talk. For four years, the question of their rights had been foremost on their minds. They welcomed the op-

212

portunity to talk with a trained lawyer who had devoted considerable time and thought to the same issues and who had experience with how the government worked. Though James Reuben had to interpret, the chiefs and the adjutant spoke the same language.

Joseph questioned whether the government was doing its job when it could not keep the settlers from committing atrocities. "Among the Indians the chiefs controlled the members of their bands," Joseph said, "and had power to prevent bad Indians from doing wicked things, and in case of their so doing to punish them." Without that power — without the broad ability to regulate individual conduct — there could be no justice. "If the chiefs did not restrain or punish bad Indians," he added, "they themselves were responsible for their bad acts." It followed, then, to Joseph's mind, that "those in authority over the whites had, or should have, the same control over their men; and hence the white authorities in the vicinity of Wallowa Valley and elsewhere were directly responsible for" Wilhautyah's murder.

In effect, Joseph was questioning American government as it assumed a truly national scope. It was ambitious enough to declare liberty, equality, and the right to vote for millions of new citizens in the South. It had the might to make treaties with the great western tribes and exchange vast surrenders of land for other bundles of rights, among them sovereignty and self-rule, property allotments on reservations, and entitlement to payments and other services from Washington. Yet in the South and the West, the American government was too weak to protect these rights when even the humblest individuals sought to take them away, whether by donning a white hood or building a split-rail fence.

Howard's adjutant had no satisfactory response to Joseph. The major explained that "among the whites those in authority did not have immediate control over the persons of individual members of society to prevent, or arbitrarily punish for, misdeeds; that each individual was personally responsible for his acts; that offenders were reached and punished by the law." His explanation was an admission. The structure of American liberty — marked by individual rights and policies that were made and enforced by different areas of government — produced a nation that might not be able to protect the liberty of all. Not everyone could be equally free. All the major could do was hope that long after the fact, the courts in the Grande Ronde Valley would do right by the Nez Perce people.

Ollokot continued to press Joseph's point, questioning whether the government had any capacity to treat Indians fairly and whether it had ever done so. "I want you to tell me what the whites did when they first came to this country," he said to the adjutant. "Did they make treaties with Indians, and then afterwards remove them to other lands?" He added that he also wanted to know "all about the different tribes and treaties since then." His questions flummoxed the major. Although he professed to find the Nez Perce people "remarkable," he and other outside admirers of Indians often did little more than romanticize their supposed simplicity and purity, primitive qualities that could not survive the settling of the frontier. But as their keen questioning of American policy revealed, the Nez Perce Indians were not obviously doomed. Ollokot, for one, was neither primitive nor naïve. "He seemed to desire an accurate and full account of the different treaties with the various tribes," the adjutant wrote, "and of the action taken by the Government regarding those tribes and in reference to the stipulation of the different treaties."

To his chagrin, the major admitted "that he was not familiar with all the various tribes and treaties and the action of the Government concerning them . . . [and] that he would have to talk a week to give . . . a full answer to his question." Then, like every other official with whom Joseph and Ollokot had met, he questioned his own ability to sway anyone in a position to reverse the disposition of the Wallowa Valley, "doubt[ing] if anything has ever been reported at Washington, as they never hear anything from any reports ever made." But Joseph knew better — he had seen how routine reports could swim upstream to the capital — and the adjutant gave him some reason to think that his arguments could find a powerful audience again.

Even as the major made it clear to Joseph that "the settlers and local authorities had no authority to give up this land to the Indians," he informed the chief that his pamphlet had been sent to Washington. General Howard was requesting "a commission of five distinguished men appointed, at an early day to confer with Joseph and his band and hear all they had to say upon the subject of Wallowa Valley and their differences with the Government, and if possible effect a settlement." To Joseph, this was welcome news. It seemed to suggest that the United States — which had opened the Wallowa Valley to homesteaders, closed it, and then reopened it in the short time frame of four years — was now admitting that it had not resolved the dispute with any finality. The major then wondered aloud what Joseph would think if jurisdiction over his band were transferred from the Interior Department to "the control of the War Department," whose officers had repeatedly taken Joseph's side in their evaluations of Nez Perce claims. As he spoke, he reinforced the possibility that the government could be poised to change direction once again. Although Joseph shrewdly asserted that "not being a treaty Indian and upon any reservation he was not under the control of the Interior Department or any other Department of the Government," the chief signaled that he would participate in the new regime. "If *good honest men* were sent as members of the commission," Joseph said, "[I] would be glad to meet them."

The adjutant found Joseph's conduct at the meeting pitch-perfect — dignified, well informed, and constructive. "His face, manners, and general appearance are calculated to impress one favorably," the major wrote. "He wears no smile, but seems thoroughly absorbed in the business under consideration. His speech is fluent and impressive: his action energetic, yet graceful." The major regarded Joseph as a partner and ally, someone whose ideas were essential as the Wallowa Valley situation was revisited and finally resolved. "With proper and just treatment, uniformly maintained by a strong, yet kindly hand," he wrote, "I am of opinion Joseph would prove a powerful agent for peace and friendship as between the whites and Indians."

If the major's suggestion that the War Department take over from Interior promised the dawn of yet another new day for Joseph's band, he encouraged Joseph and Ollokot even more by asking them to specify for him the boundaries of their claim to the Wallowa Valley. On the second day of their council, Ollokot produced a map he had drawn himself. By this point the meeting had moved from the council building at the reservation to the small army fort at Lapwai, perhaps an additional sign that a new set of officials had taken over from the Office of Indian Affairs and would reconsider Joseph's argument. Ollokot had sketched his map with pencil on a piece of paper — "crude but quite accurate," the major recognized. At a glance he could tell that the area Ollokot had drawn — "embracing the Grande Ronde, Wallowa and Im-na-ha rivers . . . together with additional land not shown on the map" — was far bigger than the territory reserved for the Nez Perce in 1873 by President Grant. Rather than dwell on the boldness or practicality of such an expansive claim, the major was transfixed by figures Ollokot had drawn that covered the page. They showed "whites, Indians, an Indian woman, animals, guns, &c., intended to depict the scene and actors in the killing of the Indian, and other matters," the adjutant wrote. They were "the usual Indian pictures," he thought, but also "a kind of historical painting of that event." It was as if the claim to the Wallowa Valley were inseparable from the experiences Joseph's band had shared there. It was that history that inspired them to identify themselves so completely with the valley, a history that belonged to them and no one else. When the major asked if he could have a copy of the map made, Ollokot refused and took it back.

At the end of two days of meetings, the major announced that he had "nothing further to speak of." Ollokot said he would make some closing remarks. He stood up, and all of the Nez Perce men in the room stood with him. James Reuben, the young interpreter, looked at the adjutant and said that everyone had been asked to rise. The adjutant and the garrison officers left their chairs. It was a bald assertion of control and gave Ollokot's words the power of sermon. With his command, Ollokot intended to bridge the gap between words and deed, the council's end and the important work that had to follow. "In strong language," the major wrote, Ollokot "asserted their right to, and determination to possess and hold, the Wallowa Valley country."

Ollokot spoke, he said, "as one having wisdom" and signaled that he keenly understood the role the officers played in making Indian policy. Even though he was speaking to just a few dozen men in one room, he hoped that his words "through them might be known everywhere as his true expressions and the feelings of his heart." As the major stood and listened, Ollokot cast his eye to history. "The whites in early times had cheated the Indians then on account of their ignorance," he said, "and had continued to cheat them since in the belief that the Indian was still ignorant." Such treatment was no longer acceptable. Ollokot impressed upon the adjutant why his people deserved to be respected as equals. The whites had to acknowledge, he said, "that the Indian has learned something." Namely, he suggested, his people had learned something about law and power. They knew their rights and were capable of protecting them. They could make their voices

218

heard, thousands of miles away and up to the highest levels of authority. From its humblest bureaucrats to the president, the government had to rethink who the Indians were and why their claims mattered. The United States "must . . . now consider the Indians not as ignorant men," Ollokot said. It was a simple notion, clearly stated, a point sharp enough to keep the crowded room silent. It did not need elaboration. When Ollokot was finished, he took a breath and said, "I am done."

CHAPTER 8
A SHARP-SIGHTED HEART

Fall 1876

Two years after going into exile, General Oliver Otis Howard was back in Washington, hailed as a powerful man on business of the highest importance to the Republic. With the crisis in the Wallowa Valley threatening to become a "war that might exceed in magnitude the war with the Sioux," one daily reported, Howard had come to the capital in September 1876 with a plan to save the nation from another perilous Indian campaign. He would press the Interior Department to appoint a commission to negotiate with Chief Joseph and convince him to accept a generous payment for the Wallowa Valley and settle on the Nez Perce reservation in Idaho. He had the full support of General Sherman and the new secretary of war, J. Donald Cameron.

If Howard had suggested just the year before that the valley be reserved for Joseph's band, by the time he reached Washington, his thinking had turned. Though convinced that Joseph's band had a valid legal claim to the Wallowa country, he had never had much sympathy for the idea that any group of Indians should remain Dreamers who moved with the seasons. Howard had gone west as an earnest believer in Grant's Peace Policy, which envisioned the government coming to fair terms with tribes for their land and then providing ample services to help Indians adopt new lives as Christian farmers on reservations. For Howard, the policy seemed to achieve for the Indians what he had tried and failed to do for the freedpeople during the early months of Reconstruction: create fit, moral citizens through land ownership, supported by a government that could protect them from grasping white settlers until they had earned and achieved an unimpeachable equality. Because the alternative all too often seemed to be war, the Peace Policy, to Howard's mind, was the surest way to save Indians from annihilation. In supporting Chief Joseph's position, Howard was, if anything, making an exception to his usual and strongly held sentiment.

During the months that followed his 1875 recommendation that Congress be "induced" to restore the valley to Joseph's band, Howard found every reason to reverse course and stick to the Peace Policy. As a matter of politics, it seemed apparent that Congress would never act in the Indians' favor and against the fervent wishes of Oregon's delegation in the capital. The outcry that President Grant had sparked when he gave part of the valley back in 1873 had lasted for two solid years — until he formally overruled himself. The settlers would never abandon their farms and ranches without a fight.

Moreover, in the unlikely event that Congress was inclined to court such controversy again, clearing the valley for the Indians would be disastrous to Howard's attempt to restore his status, power, and reputation. Allowing Joseph to keep his land was a decision Howard had no power to make, so at best, the general would be a bit player in the ensuing events — carrying out policies crafted by civilian authorities. At worst, he would be a villain, obligated to use force to dispossess white settlers. In 1873, the settlers had almost reflexively made the link between losing their homesteads in the Wallowa Valley and federal Reconstruction policies. If Howard took it upon himself to champion and then enforce a policy that favored Joseph, he would be committing what he once perceived to be his true sin as head of the Freedmen's Bureau: testing the law to its limits in order to achieve something unpopular but just. He would risk becoming once again a national object of hatred and derision, all the more so after Custer's Last Stand.

By contrast, if Howard could manage to reopen consideration of the Wallowa question and then take a leading role in moving the seven hundred or so nontreaty Indians to the reservation, he would be cast as the hero — a shrewd steward of his territory, the man who could solve a pressing "Indian Problem." The proposal he was bringing to Washington struck him as humane but also had the added advantage of neutralizing what many perceived to be his key failings during Reconstruction. After leaving the Freedmen's Bureau under a cloud that he had either wasted or stolen tens of thousands of dollars in government funds, now he purported to save the government "at least ten million dollars" by taking steps to avert war with the nontreaty Nez Perce bands. Even the papers with Democratic sympathies recognized that this was an eminently sensible proposal and that Howard, the man who had convinced Cochise to surrender and move onto a reservation, was perfectly suited to the task. In resolving the Wallowa crisis, Howard was engineering his own redemption.

By September 1876, most of Howard's old enemies were out of power. In a suggestion of divine justice at work, the previous secretary of war, William Belknap, who had spearheaded the corruption investigations that nearly ruined Howard, had himself been obliged to resign the previous spring after it came to light that he had been receiving quarterly kickbacks from a concession he had granted for a lucrative trading post at Fort Sill in Indian Territory. Although Howard still faced lawsuits over missing Freedmen's Bureau funds, Sherman assured Howard that the legal actions would amount to nothing. Earlier in the summer, Howard had received two additional items of correspondence attesting to the resilience of his connections to the highest levels of power. First, a kind letter from the Republican presidential candidate Rutherford B. Hayes gave Howard hopes that his star would rise again after the 1876 election. Second, General Sherman sent a telegraph informing Howard that his son Guy would be commissioned an army officer. While Custer's Last Stand occasioned a national outpouring of grief, among military folk it had meant something entirely different: vacancies in the officer corps, opportunities for commissions and promotions that rarely arose in peacetime. Infantry officers pressed for cavalry assignments, and for Guy Howard, a perennially thwarted junior banker in Portland, it became possible to dream of the army as a more adventurous and rewarding life. That Howard could get his son a coveted commission when so many others were trying to do the same spoke to the general's newly favored status.

With few reminders of the dark days, Howard could spend his three weeks in Washington focused on, and even reliving, his happiest times. By late September, the worst of the summer — sweat, dust, mosquitoes, and stink — had given way to the sweet days of early fall. The institutions he had helped build were thriving. When he addressed afternoon and evening gatherings of the YMCA, they sang the hymn, "Blest Be the Tie That Binds," a reminder of his deep connection with the place as well as the debt of gratitude that everyone there owed him for years of tireless work. When the medical school at Howard University invited the general to speak at its ninth opening exercises, he stood before a faculty and student body that bridged the color line, promising a new brotherhood that transcended race. Howard's visit, "though so brief," one newspaper wrote, "made it seem quite like the times a few years ago when he was . . . working earnestly for the colored people."

While Howard was in Washington, newspapers advertised two articles he had written in the August and October issues of the *Atlantic Monthly* on the Battles of Chattanooga and Atlanta. The articles not only reminded the *Atlantic*'s wide readership of Howard's finest moments during the Civil War but also enabled the general to defend the legacy of abolition and Reconstruction at a time when it was being questioned and undermined. "Gradually the work done by our great soldiers, Grant, Sherman, . . . and other helpers, is passing into history. Just now it seems almost a shame to have lived to mingle in these times," Howard wrote. "Those who sought the nation's life are becoming its rulers, but our Union heroes have a proud satisfaction in knowing that they were the direct means of killing secession, state supremacy, and slavery in America, and that it is only the enlarged generosity of the victors that has lifted up the vanquished into the higher position of power." While laying claim to the nation's past, Howard was using history to speak to the present. If the struggles of the 1860s remained relevant to the struggles of the 1870s, then he and others like him could continue to claim a central moral role in directing the course of the nation.

At the Office of Indian Affairs, Howard found an audience that quickly recognized his authority in assessing the situation in the Wallowa Valley. Within a couple of weeks, Interior Secretary Zachariah Chandler — a new appointee to Grant's cabinet whose predecessor had also resigned under a raft of corruption charges — had approved a commission to negotiate with Joseph's band. On October 13, the members of the commission, Howard included, received instructions by telegraph to rendezvous in Chicago. Preparations for the journey were made in haste. The next day, Howard left Washington on the train west.

Two years earlier, Howard had traveled with his family in relative anonymity. Now he made the journey in the company of leading men. At the opulent Palmer House in Chicago, where silver dollars were embedded in the tiles of the lobby barbershop, the general met three of his fellow peace commissioners. David Howell Jerome, a merchant from Saginaw, Michigan, was a former state senator with designs on the governorship. Amos Chafee Barstow, who made his fortune manufacturing stoves, had served as speaker of the Rhode Island House of Representatives and mayor of Providence. William Stickney, a Washington banker, had married into one of the capital's most powerful families. His wife Jeannie, who accompanied him on the journey, had recently inherited the fortune of her father Amos Kendall, a fixture of Andrew Jackson's kitchen cabinet and one of the earliest investors in Samuel Morse's telegraph. On land that he owned, Kendall had established the Columbia Institution for the Instruction of the Deaf and Dumb and Blind, and now Stickney helped run the innovative school, working closely with its first superintendent, Edward Miner Gallaudet. All three of Howard's traveling companions — Jerome, Barstow, and Stickney — were prominent enough in the national Republican Party to be asked by President Grant to volunteer on the Board of Indian Commissioners, the group of missionaries and philanthropists who advised him on providing compassionate and effective government services on Indian reservations. Now they were key members of Howard's commission.

Howard enjoyed the company of his new colleagues. They deferred to the general's experience in negotiating with tribes and shared his belief that the commission would resolve the difficulties in the Wallowa Valley. Just as important, they admired Howard's commitment to Christian service, which seemed essential to integrating the many peoples of the West with the rest of the nation. Their admiration only deepened when their steamer, the *George W. Elder,* docked in Portland. That night, Howard took them to visit a Chinese school run by Baptist missionaries. When they arrived, the *Oregonian* reported, "the school was a busy hum of voices," but soon after the school's superintendent called the students to order, the room was silent. Howard and his guests watched the students perform what the newspaper described as "a short session of the usual exercises." The order that the students were able to maintain, the "evident diligence and interest of the scholars," suggested to the commissioners that the problem of Chinese immigration had obvious solutions: education and religious conversion.

Each commissioner took the podium and addressed the students, "urg[ing] upon them the importance of knowledge and good morals to all." One of the commissioners implored his audience to embrace "the acceptance of our civilization, because of the fear which many of our people have of Chinese habits and contact." Only by making themselves indistinguishable from the white American majority would the Chinese be able to make a plausible claim to belong in the United States. Becoming true Americans — becoming entitled to American liberty and equality — required schooling and routine and habit, but the commissioners believed just as strongly that it was a question of religion. When another commissioner lectured the students about the spread of Western values in Japan — where there was "as large a number of schools as Massachusetts in proportion to its population" — he predicted that the Japanese would continue to make progress in one crucial way: soon they would all be Christians.

In Portland, Howard and his companions were joined by the fifth and final commissioner, his adjutant Major Henry Clay Wood. Though he had sided with the Nez Perce claim to the valley before, he would assuredly defer to the general when working side by side with him. Together, the commissioners steamed east, 350 miles up the Columbia to the Snake and into Idaho Territory. Where the Clearwater joined the Snake, they stopped at Lewiston, the gateway to Nez Perce country, a town that seemingly sprang up overnight on reservation land during the gold rush of the early 1860s. While not entirely past its rough early days as a miners' settlement, the town had remade itself as a port for area farmers who were bringing wheat, potatoes, apples, and flax to market. The commissioners did not stay long in Lewiston, where even the hint of revisiting the 1863 treaty was anathema to its existence. They went straightaway to the stage station and were soon rumbling swiftly along the Clearwater and through the canyons. It was fifteen miles to Lapwai.

With each phase of the journey, from long-settled areas to frontier to wilderness, the commissioners' progress slowed: a week on the train going 1,700 miles from Nebraska to California, then four days steaming 600 miles up the coast, followed by yet another four days for the final 370 miles inland and upriver. If the commissioners experienced the usual frustrations of a long and arduous trip — boredom, nausea — such obstacles only heightened the satisfaction that they would take in bringing peace to the Wallowa Valley and doing the nation an invaluable service. General Howard, the commission's driving force and guiding light, knew that he was on the cusp of a signature achievement, a return to grace.

On the night of the presidential election, November 7, the men were saluted by the guards of the Lapwai garrison as they arrived. Deep in the interior, they were too far removed from the rest of the country to know that the election — a final battle over Reconstruction — was casting the country into crisis. Across the South, white supremacist paramilitary groups had organized a massive terror campaign against black voters that succeeded in tilting the results to the Democratic candidate, New York governor Samuel Tilden. In response, Republican officials in three southern states threw out ballots in the bloodiest areas and certified Hayes as the winner. In the races for governor of Louisiana and South Carolina, no one would concede defeat, and in the weeks that followed, Republicans and Democrats set up competing administrations. The supposedly civilized parts of the United States were mired in unresolved, if not unresolvable, conflict. But on the other side of the continent, in the heart of Nez Perce country, nothing disrupted the peace of a cold night. The world was as still as the stars. At least in matters relating to the Wallowa Valley, the commissioners had no doubt that they could find a solution to every problem.

On November 8, the sun rose bright but cold, a sign of hope, perhaps, at the start of six months of winter. Yet on waking, the commissioners made a painful discovery: Chief Joseph, the man they had come thousands of miles to see — the man on whom Howard had pinned so many of his hopes — was nowhere to be found. To make matters worse, the commission reported, "no reliable tidings had been received from Joseph." Weeks earlier, Howard had wired a message to the Indian agent Monteith, informing him that the commission would be in Lapwai around November 8 and instructing him "to lose no time in sending for the non-treaty Nez Perce Indians, and especially for Joseph and his band, to be there at that time." Now, it may have been difficult to find Joseph, to travel fifty rugged miles after the first snows through the mountains to the canyons northeast of the Wallowa Valley. Or perhaps Monteith had purposely dawdled in getting the word out; the Indian agent did not want the military meddling in what he saw as his negotiations with the non-treaties. Or Joseph himself may have taken a slow path to the reservation. Then again, perhaps it was bad luck — he had run into foul weather or impassible trails. It was also possible that he wanted to show, as he had suggested in July, that his band was not subject to the commission's jurisdiction. Or maybe he had heard that the commission was coming to extinguish his claim to the valley once and for all. Whatever the reason, Howard found the absence of Joseph and Ollokot, the interruption and delay of his triumph, galling.

By ten that morning, the commissioners gathered in Monteith's office. The Interior Department had designated David Howell Jerome, the Michigan merchant, as the panel's chairman, but from the start he deferred to Howard. At the general's suggestion, Jerome began by inviting Howard's adjutant Major Wood to update the group on the situation in the Wallowa Valley. The major then relayed a series of alarming reports from officers in the field during the late summer and fall.

After meeting with the major in July, Joseph and Ollokot had returned to the valley, back to their traditional late-summer camp on the Wallowa

River, near the site of the murder. Three times Joseph crossed the river to visit and dine with Alexander Findley and his family, trying to understand how and why Wilhautyah was killed. Racked with guilt, Findley told Joseph everything he could remember about the shooting.

Despite the farmer's openness, the courts in the Grande Ronde Valley had done nothing to indict, try, or punish Wilhautyah's killers. After months without justice, members of Joseph's band invited almost every settler in the valley to a council near their camp on September 2. They specifically requested Findley and McNall's presence. When a mere dozen or so settlers turned up at the council — McNall and Findley stayed clear — the Nez Perce attendees seemed offended and declared, according to one man present, that "the Wallowa was their own country and they were going to have it and that the white settlers must move out."

Yet even at their angriest, Joseph's people had spoken not of war or vengeance but of law. "When I saw all the settlers take the murderer's part," Joseph remembered, "I told them there was no law in favor of murder. I could see they were all in favor of the murderer, so I told them to leave the country." Various speakers from Joseph's band demanded that Wilhautyah's killers be handed over for trial. They presented claims not for blood but to sovereignty over their land and full equality with the whites. "As it was their country they had jurisdiction over it," the attendee remembered. "They argued that if an Indian killed a white man he would be tried by the whites therefore, when the whites killed an Indian they had a right to try the white man according to their laws."

In the days that followed, Nez Perce drums pulsed from the campsite, sharp and unyielding. A messenger rode to Walla Walla to summon the cavalry as groups of families huddled together for safety, holing up in the most secure cabins and stockpiling weapons and ammunition. At McNall's cabin, where the Findleys had gone, dozens of Nez Perce riders circled slowly. Looking out through narrow windows, the settlers waited for the end.

It never came. The monotony of the siege broke not with a charge of warriors but with the approach of a single grieving woman. Wilhautyah's daughter walked up to the cabin and called out to Findley, asking him to surrender himself. Facing the woman, hearing her request — humble, dignified — Findley told his family and others in the cabin that he was going to walk outside and turn himself in, but the men held him down. Wilhautyah's daughter departed without him, and the rest of her people rode away soon after.

By this point the settlers were convinced that war was inevitable, but Joseph's band was following its own logic. When Lieutenant Albert Gallatin Forse rode into the Wallowa Valley the next week with his cavalry, he heard that the settlers there and in the Grande Ronde Valley were preparing to attack Joseph's band. Instead of putting his troops in danger and confronting the Indians immediately, Forse went to the settlers instead and found forty armed men. Hearing their complaints that "the Indians of late had been very impudent, letting down their fences, and allowing their stallions . . . to run at large with the settlers' . . . mares," Forse worried that the settlers would provoke violence and left his troops with them, in part to protect them and in part to keep them away from the Indians. The lieutenant then rode on with a local guide and an interpreter to Joseph's camp, only to find a long line of men on horseback waiting for them high on a ridge, painted and stripped to their breechcloths for battle.

Seeking to prevent imminent bloodshed, Lieutenant Forse asked to parley with their chief. When he spoke with Ollokot, even on the brink of battle, he found him to be more of a diplomat than a warrior. Joseph's brother claimed that the band had prepared to fight only after hearing rumors that soldiers and settlers were preparing to attack them. The lieutenant assured him, in turn, that the cavalry were there to keep the peace. He told Ollokot that he would urge Wilhautyah's killers, Findley and McNall, to turn themselves in to authorities in the Grande Ronde Valley and that he would arrange for two of the Nez Perce hunters who witnessed the killing to go, too, protected by an armed escort. Ollokot, in response, vowed that there would be no fighting, and the lieutenant was inclined to trust his word. "I feel satisfied," Forse wrote, "that the cause of the trouble originated from the killing of the Indian, and that if McNall and Finley had been arrested, tried, and punished, there would have been no trouble."

Once again, a potential disaster for Joseph's band had turned into another opportunity to register their claim to the Wallowa Valley with a representative of the government. "I earnestly recommend that the question of right to this valley should be settled now," Forse wrote to Major Wood. "If it belongs to the whites the Indians

233

should leave and vice versa, for they cannot get along peaceably together, and sooner or later there will be trouble." Shortly before Forse and his cavalry returned to Fort Walla Walla at the end of September, he received a telegram from General Howard that he had gone to the capital seeking to create a commission to revisit the competing claims to the Wallowa Valley. The lieutenant passed along word to Joseph. The news "seemed to give him satisfaction," Forse wrote.

As Howard's adjutant reported it to the peace commission two months later at Lapwai, Lieutenant Forse's recommendation might have offered some benefit for Joseph's band. But whether by design or accident, no one from the band was there to argue their claim to the Wallowa Valley during Wood's presentation. In Joseph's absence, the commissioners began their council sitting alone at a table, convinced, as Howard had become, that as long as the settlers and Indians shared the same territory, there could be war at any moment. The two groups had to be separated, and forcing Joseph's band onto the reservation appeared to be the only plausible option.

With nothing scheduled for days, the commission attempted to salvage its mission and do what fact-finding it could as it awaited Joseph and Ollokot's arrival. John Monteith stepped forward to brief the group on whether and how the reservation could absorb Joseph's band and the other nontreaties. The Indian agent looked drawn and sickly, an ominous way to start the long and unpitying winter. On the subject of relocating Joseph's band, however, he grew animated. Speaking, the commissioners thought, with "intelligence, sagacity, and tact," Monteith quickly convinced them that the nontreaties would be able to thrive on the reservation, but he also revealed the enormity of the dislocation they would experience. Joseph's band had horse and cattle herds that numbered in the thousands, yet Monteith envisioned them becoming wheat farmers on tiny and difficult plots. Though there was only enough flat valley land to divide into five- or ten-acre farms, he said, "the low hills and table-lands produce as fine crops of wheat as can be grown in the valleys." All the Indians had to do was "adopt the same mode of cultivation in use by the whites." With the support services the government was willing to provide as part of its Peace Policy — millers, carpenters, blacksmiths, doctors, teachers — the commission was content to regard the Lapwai reservation as Joseph and his people's future home.

Joseph's absence was filled in other ways, too. The commission next decided to hear from Nez Perce men who lived on the reservation. Seventy-five treaty Indians had come to see them, some from as far away as Kamiah, sixty miles east up the Clearwater River. To accommodate everyone, the commission moved on Friday, November 10, from the Indian agent's office to the nearby Presbyterian church. Dressed in Western clothes, singing hymns and reciting prayers in Nez Perce, the treaty Indians welcomed the commissioners. Those who testified regarded the treaties of 1855 and 1863 as, in one man's words, "a father and a mother to us," providing them with new land and entirely new lives. They spoke proudly of their farms and the value of hard work and their deep love of "the Son who was sent and the Father who sent him." Such testimony confirmed much of

what General Howard and the other commissioners hoped and believed that the Indian reservations would accomplish. These Nez Perce men
held the same values and priorities as any other
American. "In all dealings we wish to be equal to
the whites," the teacher and interpreter James
Reuben told the commission.

Even so, the treaty Indians' comments also suggested that there was no easy path to equality.
The people testifying at Lapwai were not becoming an indistinguishable part of American society,
but rather analogous to the nation's most vulnerable populations. Like the freedpeople in the
South, these children of law still needed the
government to protect their rights every day.
White settlers continued to encroach on their
land, they said. Whites and Indians alike could
commit crimes on the reservation with little fear
of punishment. The government was not providing adequate services — the sawmill was in
disrepair, and the teacher at Lapwai had died six
months earlier with no replacement. "We know
something of law," said Chief Timothy. "By what
law will we be enabled to recognize each other as
we should? (whites and Indians.) . . . The Bible
gives to us friendship toward the whites; still,
beyond that, you can help us lift the load."

Though the treaty Indians identified great challenges ahead, their testimony filled General
Howard with pride. And — equally satisfying —
in response, he could tell the Indians something
that he was never quite able to say to the freedpeople during Reconstruction: that the federal
government, civilian and military, was fully on
their side. The army would make every effort to
protect their land from trespassers, and the Indian

236

agent would get more resources to help them prosper. The Indians would be able to get everything the Edisto Islanders had sought from him in 1865, the land, security, and ability to make a living and improve themselves that so many freedpeople had dreamed of. He was confident that the Nez Perce people could become fully integrated into American life. They would be citizens like everyone else, and at the same time they would also represent a new kind of citizenship — a citizenship constructed by the power of the modern American state.

While Howard pushed the rosy consensus that the 1855 and 1863 treaties had enriched the material and spiritual lives of the Nez Perce tribe, he refused to listen to dissenting voices. Billy, who as chief of a band in the Grande Ronde Valley had agreed to take his people to Lapwai, told the commission, "We are poor and want you to notice it." They had been guaranteed warm homes, only to be told that the government would not help build them. The wagons and tools that had been given them as payment for his land had broken long ago. "When he was off the reservation," he was reported as saying, "he was much better off." In the meantime, "he had traded a country from which millions of dollars in gold had been taken, and of which he had got none." Howard responded coldly, reading verbatim from a statute detailing the government's obligation to the Nez Perce people. It was a dispiriting council for Billy. "Have you come to us honestly?" he wondered aloud. "As you are in a hurry to go away, I am afraid there is some flaw." Even though Billy's ancestral country was right next to the Wallowa Valley, and his band presented an intuitive anal-

237

ogy to what Joseph's band might face on the reservation, the commission found it easy to ignore him. Billy was a lone shrill voice drowned out by what the commission regarded as a "full and warm" chorus of "gratitude to the whites for civilizing and christianizing influences extended towards them."

That Sunday, the commissioners returned to the church to share the Sabbath with the treaty Nez Perce. The church was a simple wood structure, comforting to Howard, who had prayed in dozens of places like this, in New England, across the South, and in the Northwest. On a sharp cold day, the congregation generated its own heat, "densely packed," the commission found, with people who were "attentive, serious, and devout." Howard recognized the hymns. Some were sung in English, and he could even sing along to the ones in Nez Perce — they all had familiar settings.

The general then stood before the church, as he had done countless times, and spoke of scripture, of the place of Christ in his life, and of the many joys that came from following the word and example of the Lord. As Howard educated and exhorted the congregation, a Nez Perce interpreter repeated his words line by line. The repetition slowed his talk. It would have been reminiscent of a call-and-response sermon — which Howard knew well from his days during Reconstruction praying among the freedpeople — except the response merely translated his words. In truth, it was more of a lecture, to an audience he found entirely receptive to his message.

The commissioners stayed all day with the congregation, listening in the afternoon to a sermon by a Nez Perce man in his early thirties, Archie Lawyer, one of Chief Lawyer's sons. The visiting dignitaries found Lawyer — dressed in a clean black suit, his thick hair cut short and combed — "earnest, serious, and graceful." Afterward, they returned to their quarters convinced that life on the reservation had succeeded in civilizing the treaty Nez Perce and making them fit to be Americans. How wonderful it would be when every band in the tribe was similarly blessed.

The next day, the commissioners returned to the church. Without its congregation, it provided just the barest amount of shelter from the soaking rain outside. Some of the treaty Indians had gathered again, and the commissioners knew that soon the building would fill even more. That weekend, word had finally come that Joseph was setting up camp eight miles away. David Jerome, John Monteith, and James Reuben rode out to meet the chief and learned that "he had come with a considerable portion of his band, by easy stages, and that his business, even now, did not demand haste." While the general saw the council as a climactic moment in his narrative of redemption, the chief appeared to be taking a more casual view of their meeting. It was immaterial whether Joseph was asserting his power, disputing the commission's jurisdiction, or attempting to undercut the assertion that its word on the Wallowa Valley would be final. The effect was infuriating. Howard was insulted and embarrassed in front of men he had hoped to impress. After he had assured the most powerful officials in multiple departments of government that he could negotiate with Joseph, Joseph had left him waiting for almost a week.

Early in the afternoon, Joseph was seen approaching the church on horseback, leading a column of sixty or seventy men, eight abreast on animals that were elaborately dressed and beaded. The group "amassed itself in front of, but at a considerable distance from, the church," the commission later reported, and paraded with "military precision and order." Although such exhibitions before official meetings had never failed to impress the agents of the United States government, Howard took little pleasure from the horsemanship of Joseph's band. Forced to linger day after day in remote and miserable Lapwai, Howard had trouble distinguishing whether the display showed "dignity and reserve," as a local newspaper phrased it, or insolence and disregard — whether Joseph was the "chief of some great nation" or "a leader of a small band of outlaws."

Joseph did little to restore Howard's favor when he and his retinue entered the church. The setting gave the chief no comfort. Churches, to him, were monuments of disruption, places where Indians were exhorted to see the world in new and damaging ways. Asked by a fact-finding commission in 1873 if he would like the government to build a schoolhouse for his people in the Wallowa Valley, Joseph declined the offer because a school "will teach us to have churches." When the panel asked, "Why do you not want churches?" the chief replied, "They will teach us to quarrel about God, as the Catholics and Protestants do. . . . We may quarrel with men about things on this earth, but we never quarrel about God. We do not want to learn that."

Walking into the church at Lapwai with Ollokot at his side, Joseph saw the commission sitting on the raised dais straight ahead. The kind of intimate, tactile greeting that he had given Howard the year before, and Howard's adjutant earlier that summer — tight grip, close stare, meaningful silence — would not be possible. To speak to them, he would have to stand below them and look up, a supplicant's pose. Joseph's delegation, the commissioners were advised, included "prominent non-treaty Indians" from outside his band, as well as "some malcontents among those who acknowledge themselves bound by the treaties." Asked to take a seat in one part of the congregation, Joseph refused and sat instead in a different section, at the commission's left across the aisle from the treaty Indians. The commissioners did not see his move as stately. It was just more delay.

The commissioner Amos Barstow began the meeting with a prayer. General Howard introduced the commissioners and spoke plainly about their mission, which David Jerome, as chairman, then amplified. "The President had heard of the troubles between the whites and Indians in Wallowa Valley, and deeply deplored it," the chairman said. "He wished them to live peacefully and improved in their condition as regards civilization; to place themselves under the protection of the Government."

At the outset it became apparent to Joseph that the commission had been designed to force his people onto the reservation. Joseph began by explaining that his band was not party to the 1863 treaty because the 1855 treaty split the Nez Perce tribe — essential background to understanding their claim to the Wallowa Valley. But Jerome cut him off, immediately rejecting the underlying premise of Joseph's claim. "The President understands that all the lands of the Nez Perces, but the

241

reservation, had been given up to the Government by them," he said. Jerome cited the treaty. A majority of Nez Perce leaders had signed it, he asserted, "and the law among the whites [was] that the majority in all cases rule the minority."

Denying the legality of Joseph's claim, Jerome pressed him to talk about his land claim — perhaps with an eye toward offering him money for it. But Joseph asked the chairman to explain his position further, specifically what he envisioned as the band's future. According to a transcript of the meeting, "Mr. Jerome informed the Indians that the only protection they could get from the United States would be found on the reservation. He urged them to abandon their roaming life and settle down and begin to learn how to take care of themselves, as the whites do."

Rather than placate Joseph, as Jerome likely intended, the idea that Joseph and his band were not taking care of themselves — let alone that they had to go to the reservation — put the chief on the defensive. From that point onward, he refused to negotiate with the commission. "My heart is a sharp-sighted heart and not easily cheated," he said.

Joseph's response baffled Howard and the other commissioners, who saw themselves as doing his band a great favor. "Do you think the commission wishes to cheat you?" Jerome asked. "I do not care to talk about settling down," Joseph replied. "What do you wish to talk about?" Jerome said.

Joseph disagreed so fundamentally with every one of Jerome's points — about the treaty, the reservation, whether the band could take care of themselves — that he retreated from the legalisms he had previously used to great effect. Instead, he chose to make a plea for his traditional way of living, of moving with the seasons and the herds. His words dramatically departed from the arguments he had been perfecting for the past four years. Instead of reaching out to his negotiating partners, he spoke about a world without white people. His language was so abstract that it struck the commissioners as absurd: "The country was made without lines of demarcation, and it is no man's business to divide it," he said. "It is in no person's power to make a boundary. That which has no limits has no right to be divided."

With that, Joseph ended the meeting, saying he would return to the council the next day only if the weather cleared. "My mind it is for you to hear and listen to and understand," he said. "I will show you my thoughts." The commissioners scoffed at such rhetoric. Joseph, they believed, was just stalling for time. "Never was the policy of masterly inactivity more fully inaugurated," they wrote. Joseph sounded just like the Dreamers they had been warned about, people who would never accept the sovereignty of the United States government, who threatened to reverse all the progress the government had made in civilizing the Indians and turn every Christian farmer humbly tilling a reservation plot into a roaming troublemaker.

The next day, Joseph's band stayed in their camp, and the commission composed a written statement to deliver to the chief about how it expected to resolve the Wallowa Valley situation. The statement was labeled a set of "propositions." The United States government — "we," in the commission's words — would provide enough "tillable

243

and pasture lands," tools and farming implements, and help with building housing and fences to enable Joseph and his band to be "self-supporting during the life of the Nez Perces treaties." The president, they promised, would also secure fishing and hunting grounds for the band. If the government's obligations were negotiable, what was expected of Joseph was not. "Under any arrangement," the propositions read, "said Joseph and band are to assent to become subject to the laws and control of the United States." The commission formally "advised Joseph and his band to abandon their roaming lives, and accept the friendly offers of the Government to provide them homes and protection." Otherwise, the Indians "while roaming about [were] liable to collision with the whites," and in the Wallowa Valley would be governed by the laws of Oregon, where "the Indian does not get along with the State courts as well as the white man." The commission presented its position as the last word on the matter, with no other path — no appeal to another governmental department or person in power — that could possibly create a different result.

After delivering their message, the commissioners adjourned and dispersed to different parts of the reservation. As the sky darkened, Joseph's band finally appeared in Lapwai. They were able to find two of the commissioners, Jerome and Barstow, who said they would listen to the chief "if he had anything to say." Joseph could only express his frustration. All of the discussions he had been having with government officials were coming to naught. "I have talked so many years about lands," he said; "still we have not understood each other rightly. . . . I did not expect to be talked to again about my country by the whites."

Joseph desperately tried to start the conversation over again. Unable the previous day to express his argument for keeping the Wallowa Valley, now he began to focus his words and thoughts by returning to the moment of the early encounters in 1872 between white settlers and Joseph's band. "When we heard the whites say that they came to settle there by authority of a Government officer, our hearts were sick," he said. "I think a great deal of my country. I cannot part with it. At that the whites became angry, and told me it was not my country. . . . I asked the whites if I ever called them to my country. For what purpose did you come to my home?"

It was an emotional appeal that Joseph paired with a legal one. He had always found listeners who sympathized with his account of his band's right to the Wallowa country. "The right to the land was ours before the whites came among us; white men set such authority aside," he said. These rights, he suggested, were the foundation of any lasting peace between Indians and whites. Disregarding them, Joseph said, "ought to fill you with fear." Lest Jerome take his words as a threat, he assured the commission's chairman that he had no interest in war. Joseph insisted there had to be a way to resolve the situation peacefully in his band's favor. "Perhaps a law will be found applicable to the case," he said. "Law is not without eyes; hence, friends, listen; we will hold to our chieftainship."

But Joseph's arguments went unreceived for a second time. Jerome barely registered his words. He gave Joseph and Ollokot until morning to decide whether to leave the valley and move to the reservation.

That night, Joseph's band was gripped by fear. They saw that the commission was indifferent to their leader's words. Many of the elders "have accused me of talking like a child," the chief said. Several had their own opinions about what they should do next, but they were too afraid to express them to the commission. When the band returned to Lapwai for another day of council, Joseph found himself standing alone, looking up at the commissioners.

It was Joseph's third attempt to reach and connect with the commissioners. Running out of chances, he was determined to be heard. The men on the dais tried to put Joseph and his people at ease, saying that they were "here in the interest of the Indians as much as in the interest of the whites" and "did not blame them for wishing to keep the Wallowa Valley." At the same time, they emphatically warned Joseph that the life he imagined for his people was no longer possible. "If all the white people who are in the Wallowa Valley were driven away, others would come who would act the same toward the Indian," Jerome said. They were unwilling to recommend that the president take the valley out of the public domain once again. "It was opened to settlement. It cannot now be recovered," Howard said, bristling with vexation. "The object now is to get you to come on the reservation and get a good home."

Joseph looked at the five men in front of him and assessed their conversation — hours of talk with barely a step forward, like climbing a steep mountain. Rather than continue straight up the daunting slope, the chief, as any accomplished climber would, now decided to change course completely, to switchback his way toward his goal. He began by asking the commission where on the reservation they would like him to settle.

His question disarmed the commissioners. Finally the chief appeared to be someone they could work with. After an excruciating week in Lapwai, they saw the possibility of a breakthrough, of reaching the kind of accord that would be celebrated in the east. Howard became cheerful again. He suggested one possible location, but was quick to add that he would "tak[e] Joseph's advice as to the best land." Jerome suggested that soon Joseph would be able to sell "large quantities of produce," as other Indians were now able to do.

Instead of guiding Joseph to their position, their response gave the chief just the opening he needed to change course once again. "When did I ever ask anything from the Government that you should speak to me in that way?" he asked. "The way you have spoken is not the way my heart has been on the subject of lands. I see the whites all over the country gaining wealth, and see their desire to give us lands which are worthless. . . . Do you think me a man who has neither eyes nor ears?"

Joseph was trying to turn the commission's focus from the reservation to his ancestral territory. Jerome challenged Joseph. "What did you expect the commission to do when it came?" But the pointed question only strengthened Joseph's hand. "We expected you to talk about the lands," Joseph said. "The whites in the Wallowa . . . acknowledged if the commission decided against them they would have to leave the valley."

"Is there any other place where you would like to go?" Jerome asked. Joseph answered, "I see no place but the Wallowa Valley. It is my home." It was a simple statement but undeniably powerful. After all but ignoring Joseph the day before, Jerome felt compelled to consider the chief's commitment to his home. "Haven't you a stronger affection for peace than you have for the land?" the commissioner said. "What will we say to the President when we go back?"

Tantalizingly, Jerome's question suggested that despite their words to the contrary, the commissioners were not the final arbiters of the Wallowa situation. Perhaps they could advise Ulysses Grant, and he would change the government's course. After years of trying, and occasionally succeeding, to reach the president's ear, Joseph could see the opening.

"All I have to say is that I love my country," the chief said.

Joseph's remarks were sentimental, patriotic, and open to multiple meanings. He loved the Wallowa Valley, to be sure. But his people had also been a steadfast ally of the United States government. He was making a statement of his rights, and also of how unfair it would be to take them away. It reflected a noble and civilized sensibility. He was someone any gentleman of feeling would understand and sympathize with.

Yet the one self-described gentleman of feeling in the room was unmoved. Impatient to reach the resolution he had touted in Washington and pinned his hopes on, General Howard interrupted the colloquy between Joseph and Jerome: "Suppose several thousand men should come from

248

Oregon with arms, what would you do?"

Joseph sidestepped the question, talking instead about Wilhautyah's murder: how it "caused [him] to feel that darkness pervaded [his] heart," yet he was still able to decide that he would "not take [the murderer's] life for the one he took." It was a decision the commission felt obliged to acknowledge was "very generous." But then Joseph continued, again linking his noble sentiment to a statement of rights. "I spoke to the murderer and told him I thought a great deal of the land on which he had shed the blood of one of my people," he said. "You see one of our bodies lying dead. I am not talking idly to you. I cannot leave that country and go elsewhere." Once again he countered their argument with his own logic. The commission had been warning Joseph that unless he and his people moved to the reservation, they would be vulnerable again and again to white settlers. Yet Joseph insisted that such bloodshed only strengthened his connection to his land.

After days of speaking past each other, it finally seemed that Joseph was engaging the commissioners, earning their trust and admiration. After staying silent for most of the council, Howard's adjutant felt moved to interject, "Joseph speaks well. He speaks with straight tongue. . . . Joseph speaks as he did to me in July last."

Turning away from his insistence that Joseph move to the reservation, Jerome broached the possibility that Joseph's band would be able to stay in the Wallowa Valley. "The commission wants to know, if authorized, if Joseph will go into the Wallowa Valley and remain there," the chairman said. "If he does, he will be under the laws of Oregon." Would Joseph be content to keep the valley, yet forswear his traditional way of life?

Joseph did not immediately answer yes or no, but rather invoked one of the most important American values: equality. "This one place of living is the same as you whites have among yourselves," he said. "When you were born, you looked around and found you lived in houses. You grew up to be large men. At any time you wished to go from any point to another, you went. After making such a journey, perhaps you came back to a father. I grew up the same way." A rooted life was not the marker of civilization, he was suggesting. It was simply tradition, how life among whites had long been experienced. If Chief Joseph followed a competing tradition — if he viewed the world another way — he was nonetheless an equal, and in the end more similar to the commissioners than different. "Whenever my mind was made up for travel, I went," he said. "I was clothed with wisdom. My eyes were opened. I did see. I saw tracks going in all directions. . . . I saw in what kind of houses you lived. I approve of them for your use. Whenever I see houses, I know whites have been there; but it is not for me to demolish them." If he respected how the whites lived, he implied, the whites should allow him to tend to his herds.

Appealing to sentiment and asserting his equality, Joseph could not have developed an argument that, in theory, was more attuned to General Howard's sensibility. During Reconstruction, no one had been more committed to the idea of equality than Howard. As head of the Freedmen's Bureau, he had been among the very first people to define and apply the Fourteenth Amendment's promise of "the equal protection of the laws."

Monuments had been built to celebrate his devotion to the equality and brotherhood of man. When Joseph spoke of his equality, of deserving fair treatment from the government — when Joseph spoke of his connection to the land that Wilhautyah's blood had soaked, the land where his father was buried — Howard was not hearing such words for the first time. Back in 1865, the freedpeople of Edisto Island had pleaded with him for homesteads that the government had offered them but then snatched away. In South Carolina they had asked him for "land enough to lay our Fathers bones upon." And to Howard's regret, he had presided over their dispossession. More than a decade later, on the other side of the continent, Howard found himself with a second chance to give concrete meaning to the principle of equality and to recalibrate the question of whose rights the federal government would protect.

But Howard did not see Joseph's rhetoric as presenting any kind of opportunity for redemption. Instead, he only saw opportunities slipping away. Fleeing Reconstruction for the West, he had staked his reputation on being able to convince the Indians to join the American nation as small farmers, settled and Christian. Howard believed that until the moment, perhaps a generation away, when the Indians would be indistinguishable from everyone else claiming the rights of American citizenship, it was his role to keep them separate on reservations. During Reconstruction he had created institutions — schools and universities, employment agencies, courts — that brought whites and blacks together. Now he told Joseph, "The Government has to make boundaries to keep us from interfering with each other." If Joseph dissented from that view, then he was not just denying Howard a signature accomplishment. He was turning Howard into a failure once again.

Just as Joseph's skillful plea to live on the land as his ancestors had before him appeared to move the commission, the general responded with cool fury. "I have been here in command of this department for two years. I have always been called the friend of the Indian," he said. "I was sent twenty years ago to the Seminoles; they are now in the Indian country, doing well. I was sent to the Apaches to make peace with them. One band had been at war twelve years. I made peace with them, and they went on a reservation. I visited the Indians on the coast, five tribes in Alaska, Indians at Fort Simpson, at Tulalip, Lummi, S'Kokomish, Puyallup, and other Indians down the coast; also those at Malheur, Colville, and the Spokanes and others, and we are at peace with them all." After cataloging all of his achievements, Howard became pointed and clipped. "The only place of trouble has been the Wallowa Valley," he said. "Colonel Wood came to investigate. I read his report. He recommended a commission. I go to Washington and get the commission. The President sent it. Here it is. But Joseph won't have what it offers. We ask, 'What do you want?' You say, 'The Wallowa Valley.' We ask if you will stay there if it is given you. You say you want to go where you please. If you do want the valley, now is the time to take the offer made you."

Whatever momentum Joseph had built for his position, whatever understanding and common ground he had created with the commissioners, Howard's comments wiped them away. If Jerome had suggested the possibility of giving Joseph's

252

band the Wallowa Valley, now he once again "explained to them the treaties of 1855 and 1863, and urged Joseph to comply with its requirements (treaty of '63) by abandoning the valley in question." Monteith chimed in, urging them once again to come onto the reservation.

Joseph could only refuse. "Why do you persist in talking about it?" he asked. "You know my mind."

The commissioners adjourned, "with no favorable result." They would leave for Portland the next morning. There would be no more meetings. General Howard stayed with the Indians after the panel disbanded, hoping to salvage something from the council, "endeavoring to urge them to comply with the propositions of the board but without success." He could report to the newspapers in the east that he was confident that peace would reign in the Wallowa Valley, yet the commissioners had failed in their fundamental mission. Few in the capital might have recognized the magnitude of the failure, but it did not escape the local settlers. "Their coming was announced . . . with a great flourish of trumpets touching what they were to do," crowed the weekly *Teller* in nearby Lewiston. " 'The mountain has brought forth a mouse' would be too strong an expression of that which they have accomplished." The commission not only failed to convince Joseph's band to move to the reservation, the paper suggested, but by revisiting the Wallowa question — by "appeasing an outlaw" with "the defiant wanton and independent spirit of Joseph" — the commissioners might have emboldened nontreaty bands across the Northwest to hold out and resist the government.

Howard keenly felt he had taken a risk for Joseph, and now he was being punished for it. At the end of their final day of council, Joseph told the commissioners, "As for the Wallowa valley, I will settle there *in my own* way and *at my own* pleasure." At those words Howard looked down at Joseph and saw an enemy. "If that was his final decision," the general told the chief, "he must not complain if evil happens to him."

PART II

CHAPTER 9
ALOFT

Spring 1877

Charles Erskine Scott Wood had filled countless nights scribbling ardent, obsessive letters to Nanny Smith, but as 1876 turned to 1877 their correspondence trailed off to nothing. The cannon fire from arriving steamboats no longer signified a letter from his love. Wood was earning barely enough to survive in Fort Vancouver, let alone pay down his debts and amass enough of a fortune to win Smith's stepfather's blessing. All the while, Smith had never quit her busy social life in the nation's capital, and when it seemed clear that their engagement was an impossibility — a youthful fantasy — she began entertaining four serious suitors, including a West Point classmate of Wood's who had had the good fortune to be posted to Fort Monroe in Virginia.

On the other side of the continent, Wood remained close to General Howard and continued to pay social calls to his family, but the lieutenant's best friends in the Howard household were far away. Grace was back at Vassar. Guy had passed his officer's examination and was now serving in an infantry regiment in California. Wood's work tending to disciplinary cases as a judge advocate kept him busy but left him with little sense of how

257

he could advance in life or what would relieve his abiding loneliness. The general remained fond of Wood; he respected his ability and sympathized with his desire, however vague, for something more.

In early April 1877, Wood had no reason to believe that he was on the cusp of a new life. The column inches of the local papers were dominated by news from points east, as the disputed presidential election of 1876 neared its final resolution. Although the Republican candidate, Rutherford B. Hayes, had been given the White House, Democrats were retaking state governments in South Carolina and Louisiana, a final triumph for white supremacy. But the death of Reconstruction was hardly felt in the Northwest. Spring had come quietly to Portland and Fort Vancouver. The fruit trees were budding. Salmon fishing was under way. The baseball season was about to begin.

When the steamer *Ajax* reached Portland from San Francisco, it marked no break from the endless comings and goings on the Columbia and Willamette. On board was Charles Henry Taylor, a commission merchant on the Chicago Board of Trade who sold grain futures and derivatives, bets on whether prices of the commodity would rise or fall. He had planned a brief stop in Portland on his way to Alaska, arguably the largest wager on future value in American history. Ten years earlier, the United States had purchased the vast northern territory from Russia. Although the purchase, at more than seven million dollars, was derided as Secretary of State William Seward's "folly," American officials and travelers were beginning to appreciate the wealth of their new empire of fur, fish, and precious ores.

Taylor was not on a mission from the Chicago Board of Trade. He had no interest in getting rich in the north. His journey would be for knowledge and pleasure. When asked his hobbies, he listed music and literature and gazing through telescopes at the stars, but his true passion was mountaineering. Two years earlier, he had set a speed record for climbing up and down Mont Blanc in eighteen hours. Musing on how the children of Chicago loved to "pursue the eagle to its nest, and chase the prairie-hen to its mountain fastnesses, hazarding their lives for the eggs," the *Tribune* claimed Taylor's feat as the city's: "The chief wonder is that it took Mr. Taylor so long to take a flake from the snowy crown of the monarch of mountains."

Now, Taylor was turning his attention to another great peak, Mount St. Elias, which in his mind made Mont Blanc and even the Matterhorn look like "child's play." At the base of the Alaska's thin southern tail, straddling the border with the Yukon, St. Elias rose impossibly steep from sea to sky, reaching an altitude of 11,250 feet. It had never been climbed, or "at least there is no account on record of any person succeeding or even attempting to reach its summit," the *Oregonian* reported. Determined to be the first to scale it and measure its height, Taylor traveled with "all the necessary instruments, scientific apparatus, etc." But the mountain was too remote to plan the entire expedition in advance. Taylor would have to assemble a team — guides, porters, interpreters — and arrange for boats and food along the way.

From the steamboat landing in Portland, it was a short walk to the Department of the Columbia headquarters. Taylor had stopped in Oregon because he needed an army escort. With the department commander's blessing, Taylor could expect additional aid from the garrison in Sitka, his final staging ground before attempting his climb. General Howard had fond memories of summering in Alaska in 1875. Although Mount St. Elias was uncharted territory, Taylor was confident that, "well provided with every requisite," he would succeed. Howard was delighted to oblige the distinguished mountaineer.

Howard then considered the kind of man Taylor would need to accompany him north. The army escort had to be strong and reliable, physically and morally. At the same time, he had to be unessential to the everyday business of the Department of the Columbia if he were to be away from active duty for months. Given the manifest peril of traveling through remote wilderness to climb a mountain that had never been climbed before, the escort had to be someone who would embrace what to many would seem a dangerous lark — someone engaged with science and ideas, attracted to the idea of discovery and exploration and breaking new ground, or at the very least bored with peacetime service and hungry for adventure. On reflection, it seemed to Howard that his choice was clear, and making it offered the same satisfactions to the general as any of the countless other times he had opened a new path to a fellow in need. He dashed off a note and marked it for immediate dispatch on the next ferry to Fort Vancouver.

The envelope that Erskine Wood received was small, his name slanted left in Howard's humble hand. The lieutenant had received similar packets from the general before on all manner of subjects.

He opened the letter and studied its three sentences — an astonishing gift from his friend and mentor. Each word seemed heaven sent. "If you would like to go with Mr. C. H. Taylor Scientist on a trip to Alaska starting Saturday morning from Portland, come on with such hasty preparations as you can make by the Vancouver tomorrow (Friday) — or by the Dalles boat Friday evening," Howard wrote. "You would probably be gone two months."

In an instant Wood had sprung free of the unending routines of army life. He collected a few things — including a leather-bound journal that fit in his vest pocket — but otherwise left his quarters just as they were. He informed his captain to assign another lieutenant to his company and then willingly surrendered his place on solid ground. The prospect of climbing Mount St. Elias gave him a purpose that went beyond quietly doing his duty. His name would find its way into the pages of newspapers across the country, and if he could write his own stories about his adventures in Alaska — as his father had written about his exotic ports of call decades ago — he could realize the yearnings that he had felt back at West Point, for fame and fortune and a literary life. By Saturday, April 7, he was walking the decks of the *California,* steaming toward the bar where the Columbia opens onto the Pacific, turning from river to sea, north from west.

When a customs agent in the 1870s went steaming in the Sitka Sound, he described the scene as "equal to the Bay of Naples," "beautiful in the extreme," "a Grecian archipelago." When Lieutenant Wood arrived on April 15, 1877, he imagined

261

he was entering a tropical port. To the west, on Kruzof Island, was the round snow-covered dome of a massive extinct volcano, Mount Edgecumbe. On Baranof Island to the east, just behind the town, was "the sharp peak of Vostovia — a triangular patch of white against the sky." Below the snow line, the mountains seemed impossibly lush, thick with firs and pines and cedars. The humidity made the forty-degree temperature feel warm to Wood as the steamer *California* cut through a scrim of fog and found the narrow channel that led to the harbor. Turning his gaze down from the mountains, Wood saw an Indian village on the beach, with "a fleet of very graceful canoes." Above it on a great rock, the American flag flew from a large log building encircled by palisades — the old Russian castle. From Wood's vantage, the trees along the waterfront, stunted and wind-bent, resembled palms.

Officials in the various government departments who counted Alaska as their charge were always regarding the territory at a remove. Distance turned Alaska into a series of administrative challenges. As a physical matter, it was an abstraction, a wash of blank space on the map still waiting to be surveyed, an untried and unsecure border with Canada. Although they were gaining some sense of Alaska's fishing, fur, and mining wealth, officials assigning rights to these resources continually struggled to figure out the contours and boundaries of the land, how to keep poachers and trespassers out and how to keep people from taking more than what they had been granted.

Administering the new territory raised the question of the scope of the government's presence up north — the proper size and distribution of army garrisons, the routes of the Treasury Department's revenue cutters, the frequency of mail delivery, the effectiveness of efforts to stop the importation of whiskey, and the availability of courts and clear laws laying the groundwork for civil society. In 1877 Alaska remained, by and large, lawless, with no clear set of practices for buying land or securing mining or timber rights, a "singular embarrassment" on American soil that was hard to believe, a treasury agent reported, yet was "the frozen truth." Without any mechanism to allow creditors to collect what was owed them, he wrote, theft and fraud were, in essence, legal in Alaska, "the paradise of the dishonest debtor." And with no orderly process to disburse the estates of settlers who died, the territory could well have been a haven for something far worse. "A man may be murdered in Alaska," he wrote, "his will forged, and his estate scattered to the four corners of the earth, and there is no power . . . to redress it."

Yet settlers kept coming to Alaska, forcing General Howard and others to take pains to preserve peace with the natives. In doing so, they had to reach an understanding of who the natives were: whether their lives and societies were completely alien to the American experience, or whether they were more properly regarded and classified as Indians. If they were Indians, Howard wondered, should they be treated like tribes in the West and resettled onto reservations? Independent of classification, officials considered the importance of civilizing the natives. The experience of empire inevitably put Americans in contact with foreign peoples. If the government did not turn them into something recognizably American, by fostering trade or education or missionary work, would the natives taint the settlers and make them something other than American?

As Wood steamed into Sitka Harbor, the abstract questions that Alaska inspired gave way to immediate sensation. The dock was choked with people waiting for the *California.* Wood had never encountered such a strange mix — "Indians, Russians, half-breeds, Jews, and soldiers" — but he felt a certain kinship to them. They viewed the steamer's "monthly arrival [as] life itself," Wood believed, their one link to the outside world, their true selves: hometowns, family and friends, all the lives going on without them. At Fort Vancouver, Wood had been part of that crowd, perpetually waiting for something that never quite arrived, or was never quite enough. Now he pushed his way through the choke and jostle, and then past the "drunkenness, squalor, debauchery, prostitution, stagnation, filth and all uncleanness" that he saw all around the port.

Normally the lieutenant's first stop would have been the local garrison, to call on the officer in charge and trade information. They would have had much to discuss. The steamer had brought an abundance of important news: as a matter of economy, the army would be pulling out of Sitka at some point in the summer, probably July or August. All of its soldiers, famously desperate to head back south, would at last gain their wish. But Wood did not stop at the fort, because he was no longer on active duty. He was living a different life now and had other places to go. With Charles Taylor he walked a few blocks into the heart of town.

Sitka was mud-spattered, saturated with cold

rain, like any number of rough frontier towns Wood had passed through during his army duty, yet unfamiliar at the same time. Near the center of town, the green domes and spires of a Russian church gestured toward cloudy gray skies, rising above houses and shacks that Wood judged to be "rambling, dilapidated." Down the main street was Wood and Taylor's destination, a frame building that was as much a communal gathering place as the church, William Phillipson's trading post.

Phillipson was a man in his thirties, the town postmaster, occasional shipping inspector, and custodian of the navy's local stockpile of coal. He had lived in Sitka long enough to have two children by a first wife being raised by a second, long enough to remember when the town was called New Archangel, or Novo Arkhangelsk, when the Russians had been in charge. "They was the most happiest people I ever see," he told Wood. His trading post was a crossroads, where local Tlingit men and women sold things they had caught or made and where new settlers went to buy these exotic items and send letters and packages home. On a soaked day, not quite winter and not quite spring, Wood learned that there was bound to be "a group of loungers standing around the trader's stove."

The exchanges that Phillipson brokered helped settlers make sense of the natives, who far outnumbered the Russians and Americans. The Tlingit village had been walled off from the main town, but the stockade was rotting in the rain, easily broken off for firewood. Settlers feared the worst for when the army abandoned the garrison. At the trading post, however, the native presence was domesticated, reduced to a display of pelts

265

and curios for sale, though never quite erased. As the wife of an army doctor described a rival Sitka trading post in a letter home to Pennsylvania in 1875, "the store was full of Indians, always is, with things they bring in to trade." "If you could have stood the awful Indian smell," she wrote her mother, "you would have been interested in the medley of things — furs, skins, feather, Indian dollies, Indian rattles, wooden carvings of all sorts and painted all colors (hideous things), little dollie hats (about the neatest thing there), and lots of table mats made like the baskets."

Wood and Taylor sought out Phillipson because in addition to bringing settlers and local natives into regular contact, his trading post connected Sitka to the rest of Alaska. He owned a small wooden sailing ship, the twenty-five-ton schooner *Nellie Edes,* which plied the waters south to Wrangell and as far west as Kodiak, returning to port after cruises of a month or two laden with fur: beaver, seal, sea otter, land otter, silver fox, bear, mink, muskrat, ermine, and, best of all, Russian sable. On occasion the *Nellie Edes* took passengers to the remote reaches of the territory, and before traveling north, Taylor had determined that the schooner was the one boat capable of transporting his expedition to Mount St. Elias. He wrote Phillipson in advance to hire her and, upon landing in Sitka, was eager to finalize the arrangements before assembling the group who would accompany him to the mountain.

When Taylor and his army escort appeared in the damp gloom of his trading post, Phillipson delivered some disappointing news. His ship had already set sail for points north and would not be back for at least a month. It was a stroke of fortune that launched Wood even further out of the world that he knew. Now the only people who could take him and Taylor through the treacherous spring waters to Mount St. Elias were the local Tlingit.

The two men left straightaway for the Indian village, with Phillipson's advice to tell the Tlingit leaders what the expedition needed — probably a *yaakw,* a large war canoe that could carry several dozen men — and then "let'm alone" and wait for them to quote a reasonable price. The beach was lined with fishing canoes, busy in April with the halibut and herring catches. Just beyond high tide, the local native clans lived in rows of large, gracefully gabled rectangular houses, constructed of thick cedar planks fitted watertight. Some villages were studded with totems that told clan histories, stored the ashes of the dead, and shamed wrongdoers, the outsides of homes streaked with images of ravens, bears, wolves, and other animals that shaped Tlingit lore and life. The native settlement at Sitka, however, was comparatively austere. Shadowed by pine forest, it resembled a New England fishing village from a distance. Up close, the homes were windowless with a hole in the bark roof for a chimney and a circular door draped shut with a curtain of fur. To go inside, Wood had to get on his hands and knees and crawl through.

Seeking out the families who owned the largest canoes, Wood found himself in cavernous rooms lit by cooking fires in the middle, with plank floors covered in robes and woven blankets. He immediately understood how little he mattered in these spaces, how inconsequential an American officer was in this world. Wood was a large man, but many of the Tlingit were bigger. He was greeted with "stolid indifference," he wrote, as people simply "reclined and squatted as usual," boiling halibut and "scooping up handfuls of raw herring-roe, which they munched with great gusto." His eyes adjusting to the dim light, he tried to make sense of the people around him. In one house he supposed that the women he saw were the wives of a great man. The men who served them must be slaves, he imagined. The notion of slavery continuing on land claimed by the United States might have bothered someone who had fought to eradicate human bondage in the Civil War, but it was exotic local color to the young lieutenant. "This slavery does not seem to be very arduous," he later wrote. "A stranger would not notice it — all the same they are slaves and may be killed by the master or mistress."

The Tlingit, Wood discovered, drove hard bargains. Confident of their advantage and of their place in society, the men and women who negotiated with Taylor struck Wood as haughty, cold, "grasping, shrewd, and unscrupulous," he wrote. Making deals could mean days of parley and palaver. It took Taylor about a week to come to terms with one man for a four-ton canoe. He retained the owner as its pilot, hired two more native men as crew, and found an interpreter whom Wood nicknamed Sam and described as a "Russian half-breed" with a fondness for the home-brewed molasses liquor called hoochinoo. Rounding out the expedition were two privates and a corporal from the local army regiment, as well as a Canadian prospector who, Wood reported, was looking for "coal, silver, lead, copper, &c." along the coast above Sitka.

With their plans set, Taylor and Wood momentarily returned to a world they understood, the polite society of high-ranking military officers, customs officials, agents for large fur companies, and their wives and daughters. The mountaineer and his army escort celebrated their success in organizing their expedition the best way they knew how: by waltzing. On the night of April 23, two and a half weeks after departing Portland, they hosted a ball. No matter that it was held on a Monday night, the local paper reported: "The *beau monde* of Sitka enjoyed themselves till a late hour."

The next day, mild and dry, the ten men in Taylor's Mount St. Elias expedition shoved off from shore. The canoe was loaded so fully that they could barely move. With every awkward stroke Wood worried that they would capsize in the frigid water. They paddled through an intricate archipelago of islands, big and small, that shielded them from the Pacific's swells, traveling what was known as the "inside passage." Looking straight over the high prow, there was never a clear path forward. It always seemed that there was land ahead, until at the last minute the coastline seemingly broke apart into islands and the water revealed itself. Straits and narrows opened onto generous bays, only to close up again. Towering snow-capped mountains on the mainland appeared and disappeared "like a shadowy host of snowy domes and pinnacles," Wood wrote, constantly framed and reframed by the ragged shifting coastlines.

The islands the expedition passed rose steeply from shore, completely covered in trees. On many there was barely a place to beach a canoe, just a tiny strip of black sand or not even that, just trees growing all the way to the edge, clinging to rock, hanging out over the water. Clouds rippled overhead and seeped down the hills. They turned to fog, then mist, then steady diagonal rain, gentle but soaking. When the sun broke through, the water warmed from stone gray to sparkling green-blue. From cloud to sun, travelers could taste salt from the sea, their running noses, their sweat. It crusted their beards and stung their lips and eyes.

The journey north developed its own cycles of toil and leisure. Navigating the inside passage was "as safe as river travel," Wood reported. After long days in the canoe, the men found landings from which they could watch the sun set on the mountains. They prepared dinners from enormous clams and mussels, herring and cod and salmon, "halibut — eternally halibut," Wood wrote, seal and porpoise, and occasionally the "warm-blooded meats" he craved — duck, geese, venison, goat, and bear. For something sweet, they chewed dried cedar bark.

Resting at the end of a long day, the crew puffed away on the expedition's supply of tobacco. Wood sat apart and took out paper and ink. He sketched a portrait of Sam the interpreter from behind, lavishing detail on his misshapen hat, a spread of thin hair reaching past his collar, a baggy coat and trousers sagged at the knee, large hands loosely clasped. Sam's face was an abstraction, a glimpse of shaded skin impossible to decipher, directed who-knows-where into a blank beyond.

While the prospector nosed around for promising sites for mines — at one camp he claimed to find lead with silver — Wood explored the islands. On the water the wind blew constantly, almost singing, but in the forests and swamps it huffed and sighed as if it were whispering secrets. The islands appeared to be a wasteland yet were thickly layered with life — moss, lichen, bramble, grass, and stunted trees. Pumice stones floated in stagnant pools of different colors, dun to red, glossed with white scum. Mudflats surrounding the pools were stamped with the tracks of birds and bears.

After threading between Baranof and Kruzof Islands, the expedition followed the Peril Strait, which separated Baranof from Chichagof to the north. The men then paddled up the east coast of Chichagof and rounded it into the Cross Sound. Their canoe shared the sound with enormous icebergs. North across the water from Chichagof, the mainland appeared to be a blinding wash of glaciers. At Cape Spencer, which sheltered one last bay before open sea, the crew gestured at a large peak that dominated the northern horizon and indicated that their journey was complete. But they were mistaken, Taylor and Wood explained. That peak was Mount Fairweather, formidable but known. Mount St. Elias was at least another hundred miles up unprotected Pacific coast, just beyond Yakutat Bay.

Once they understood Taylor's true destination, the crew dropped their oars. "One mountain is as good as another," Wood remembered the canoe's owner saying in view of Fairweather. "There is a very big one. Go climb that if you want to." Although the Tlingit were acclaimed for their skill in piloting canoes through rough water, pushing off high waves with their oars as if "they are pushing the sea down," as one geographer wrote after visiting southeastern Alaska in 1881, the idea that they would take the canoe onto the ocean struck the crew as absurd. "The Indians made a stand and refused to go farther," Wood wrote back to General Howard, "saying no canoe could live in the open sea through a voyage of five or seven days; that no canoe ever had done it and plainly intimating that that particular canoe never would." If at the outset their negotiations with Taylor had been rushed and allusive, shrouded in the ubiquitous Sitka fog, now they made themselves excruciatingly clear. "Threats and bribes were alike useless," Wood wrote. "Pay or no pay, our crew would not put to sea."

When Taylor determined that there was nothing to negotiate, he ended the expedition on the spot. The deliberate pace of the first part of the journey gave way to a frantic rush to get back to Sitka in time for Taylor to catch the May steamer back to Portland. They reached Sitka on May 10, a day ahead of the steamer, "a weary, disappointed, and crest-fallen set of individuals," according to the local paper.

Wood found himself with a choice to make. The reason for his leave was over, and he easily could have joined Taylor on the *California* and returned to active duty. But Wood had been counting on two months of freedom. He had long hoped for the kind of attention and acclaim that would come with climbing Mount St. Elias and making a contribution to scientific knowledge. Since leaving his post at Fort Vancouver, however, he had only experienced sixteen days in the field, none of which, he thought, was groundbreaking for him or anyone else. "Owing to our hasty travel both ways," he complained, "I could see nothing and do nothing."

A generation earlier, Wood's father had made the most of his opportunities traveling around the world with the navy, performing feats of wartime daring and writing two acclaimed books about his adventures. For Lieutenant Wood, to return home with nothing to show for the freedom General Howard had given him was deeply distasteful, all the more so because the expedition's failure invited speculation, of the type the *Sitka Post* immediately engaged in, that Taylor and his crew "were quite willing to abandon the enterprise" once they "began to realize the peril and difficulty of their undertaking."

"Storm bound" for several days in "wet and disagree-able" Sitka, Wood reflected on his lot. Because part of his role as Taylor's escort was to collect "information of value" to the Department of the Columbia, he convinced himself that he could stay behind and explore on his own for at least another month and remain faithful to his orders. When the steamer *California* left Sitka a week after its arrival, Wood was not on board. In his place the boat carried a letter he had scratched to Howard, explaining his intentions. He would return to Cape Spencer and "take a look at the country, its resources and inhabitants." After that, he considered a more ambitious destination: the mainland northeast of Sitka where the Chilkat River wandered steep into the mountains. The interior had never been seen by American eyes. If he could follow the river up to its source, Wood theorized, he could then cross into Canada and make an even more significant discovery nearby: the source of the Yukon River. Taylor's expedition had set him aloft, but he was determined to go higher. "I would like to do a little something," he wrote, "before I come down."

In later years, Wood had trouble untangling his Alaska idyll. Journeys, people, and places never quite emerged from the fog that veiled them. While he was there, what he saw always seemed filtered through what he imagined. In time, some memories eroded, like the glaciers he watched shedding icebergs into cold Cross Sound. Others he consciously let go, embellished, or remade. The lieutenant liked to tell a good story, and there were things that he wanted to forget.

On his own in the middle of May, Wood knew that he had about three weeks before the steamer from Portland returned with orders from General Howard either to remain in the north or come home. In the event that Howard let him stay, Wood planned to mount a June expedition to discover the source of the Chilkat River. He thought less of the prospect of advancing science than of the sheer thrill of the journey. His mind rushing, he became convinced that he would be traversing taboo ground — territory forbidden to whites. After talking with local merchants and with the Tlingit leader known as Sitka Jack, Wood identified a clan house leader in a village at the mouth of the Chilkat River as the man who controlled access to the entire region: Danawaq, or Silver Eye. Although Danawaq supposedly got his name because years earlier the Russians had given him a pair of spectacles, Wood took the name to mean that Danawaq had only one eye, an obvious sign of violent and tyrannical rule. Although Howard had met him two years earlier without incident, and Sitka Jack assured Wood that Danawaq, a kinsman, would be welcoming — that he "wanted his country explored, wanted the mines opened, wanted maps made" — Wood chose to picture Danawaq as the "barbarian Chilcat monarch," a "one-eyed despot of sanguinary principles," an "old pock marked tyrant who held in feudal baron fashion the Chilkaht river." Embracing the liberty that his imagination afforded him, Wood prepared to experience the height of adventure.

In the time he had until word from Howard arrived in June, Wood decided to retrace his journey with Taylor's expedition. He used much of the money he had taken with him to Alaska to hire another canoe, and with two prospectors as well as the oarsmen and interpreter from the previous outing, he set out for Cape Spencer. The rain tapered off, and the weather warmed to summer mild, almost sixty degrees.

Wood's first journey through the inside passage had been defined by its haste, the imperative of the ever-efficient if misguided mountaineer Taylor, going north toward Mount St. Elias and then back to Sitka as quickly as possible. As Wood glided among the thickly forested islands, not a trace of humanity to be seen, it had been easy to feel alone out on the water. But on his second trip, when his destination mattered less, Wood could spend more time chasing experience. While he was able to explore some of the glacier-bound inlets on the coast above Cross Sound, his most enduring experiences involved the people he met along the way. Between Sitka and the Chilkat was country that belonged to the Hoonah — one of several Kwáans, or groupings of clans and villages among which Tlingit land and water were divided — and Wood's expedition repeatedly encountered Tlingits of the Hoonah K̲wáan in their summer villages.

In Alaska, Wood had been set loose from the rules, social roles, and expectations that defined who he was supposed to be. Despite what he imagined, however, he was traveling in an inhabited world. The places here had names, even if Wood did not know them or was unable to pronounce the Tlingit consonants or tones. Over time, these names had grown synonymous with the origins and guiding mythologies of entire peoples or commemorated events that had happened within living memory. These places solidified the bonds of clan and K̲wáan, the rules for living. The landscape could look empty, but it was crossed with subtle and enduring threads that connected individuals and families, ideas and ways of seeing the world, across vast and forbidding distances.

Villagers could see Wood's canoe coming from far away. In early June, the lieutenant arrived in places of plenty, the rows of plank homes marking where abundant sea met lush forest. The beaches were arbored with halibut, salmon, and herring roe drying on great wooden racks. Seaweed, pressed into cakes or rolled into bundles, cured on boards in the sun. Baskets so large they had to be carried by two people overflowed with berries: strawberries, raspberries, blueberries, gooseberries, currants, cranberries, huckleberries, cloudberries, and more. Potatoes, bought from the Russians decades ago, grew in small plots.

The lieutenant crouched around fires with Hoonah families, ate their food, smoked their pipes, and shot guns with them. He watched women weave baskets from spruce roots that had been stripped and soaked until soft, then pulled into threads. He asked the men and women he met to recite Tlingit legends, stories of the world made by Raven, the animal they "held peculiarly sacred." At his prompting, they explained their systems of kinship and governance and religious belief. Through his interpreter, Wood tried to listen to the people he met, and perhaps he understood them. His transcriptions were imperfect, and later he would pad what he remembered with other travelers' accounts of the area. Yet even as he listened, even as he tried to immerse himself in this new world, he could never stop seeing it through the one he had left behind. He knew that the stories the Hoonah were telling him were souvenirs, objects that he could now claim for himself, every bit as valuable as the rattles and amulets and carved horn spoons he was actively bargaining for. They would find a ready audience back home.

As Wood's days among the Hoonah stretched, often what he saw was himself reflected in their eyes. At one settlement, he found, children "were greatly frightened of me, and would not let me approach them." At another, it seemed that no one could stay away. Everyone stood and pointed at the crotch of his pants, "the buckskin reën-forcement of my riding trowsers" — appliqued onto his pants like a pale leather codpiece — "excit[ing] childish wonder" and prompting him to explain what horses were and how people in the southern lands rode them. "Their astonishment over the wonderful animal was greater than their delight at comprehending the utility of the trowsers," he wrote. He told other stories of home, "of a wonderland where the *yahks* were as large as islands and moved against the wind without the help of hands; of great horned animals giving milk; . . . of thousands of great stone-houses; of the vast multitude of white people." Wood judged their reaction to be one of "courteous deference."

After a couple of weeks, Wood and his traveling companions turned back toward Sitka, well aware of the June steamer's impending arrival. On the way, they stopped at one last village, where a man approached them with a boy who was sick with fever. When Wood recounted the story in years to come, he gave the man a gauzy title — "the old head chief of the Hoonáhs" — but no one could claim that position in clan-based Tlingit society. The lieutenant opened his kit and found quinine and an effervescing seidlitz powder, an antacid and laxative. Wood was trying to help the boy, but also performing for a crowd. The seidlitz powder "foam[ed] magically," he wrote, as he mixed it with water using two horn cups, and he was pleased that he had made an impressive display of "big medicine." As the boy recovered from Wood's dosing, the lieutenant and his crew pitched camp next to the village.

The evening began like many others Wood had spent among the Hoonahs. Soon it would be solstice, and the sky remained light deep into the night. He had supper, the day's large meal, with his hosts, whom he found to be "disinterested kindness itself." It was a "bountiful board," he recalled, one of "ease and luxury." He ate seal flipper dressed with wild celery.

But after dinner, when Wood normally attempted conversation with ethnographic value, something out of the ordinary happened. A woman invited him to sleep in her house. The overture was not a complete shock to Wood. In the journal he had taken with him on his northern travels, he did not shy away from observing that prostitution had become a necessity of frontier life, or describing women as "fit for no man's wife" or "filthy dirty slovenly sluts." But he would remember this woman differently. She was "young, plump, good looking," he observed, "(as the round faced Thlinkit women are — goodlooking after their fashion)." She had status, claimed kinship to the clan house leader Danawaq in Chilkat country, and owned "plenty of slaves and canoes." In his telling, "she had really princessly, autocratic, executive ways about her." "She preferred no other soldiers," he wrote. "Just me."

Wood had turned twenty-five in February. Much of his adult life had been devoted to cooing and crying over Nanny Moale Smith and inking hundreds of declarations of love — heated, playful, pained, and all for naught. Though he still wore the sky blue trousers of his uniform, he had sprung free of army discipline, and it could not have escaped his mind that his time aloft might only last until the June steamer arrived in Sitka. Over the past weeks, Wood had defined his freedom in various ways: by traveling where he wanted, fashioning himself an explorer and adventurer, a man of science and of letters. But his freedom, he discovered, meant more than just aspiration and opportunity, more than his livelihood. Freedom could define how he lived his life. That night in Alaska, the lieutenant followed the woman home and became, in his words, "her lover," warm in the night's chill, "very comfortable with bear, seal and fox furs." "The 'princess,' " he wrote, "after the simple frank fashion of her sex among her people made love to me."

For his entire life, Wood had been bound by strictures of honor, morality, and gentlemanly conduct that almost required him to be, in his words, a "bashful Scotch Presbyterian lad . . . as confused and awkward and blushing as any girl ever was." Yet for all his "utmost Puritan modesty and . . . religious reverence for a girl's virtue," for all the naïve treacle that had filled his love letters to Smith, he was no stranger to what he called "the irrepressible sex power and passion which Nature has made so overwhelming." His father, "a very sensible man and physician . . . gave us early talks on . . . masturbation and venereal diseases," Wood recalled, and at school there had always been rumors about "the very decided partiality" between certain teachers and students. Back in Maryland, a decade or more before his travels in Alaska, the nanny who minded his younger brothers and sister came to his room one night, and as he remembered it, "locked the door on the inside and lay on the bed with me and under the pretence of a game she called 'Bridge' . . . irritated me into a juvenile erection and used me for her sexual gratification."

For years after that experience, Wood seemed content to be pursued. As he reached his teenage years, he wrote, "sexual advances and suggestions were made to me by girls older than I, which I did not understand at the time, or later if I did understand I pretended not to from bashfulness." One neighborhood girl lifted her skirt, then leapt from a swing and straddled him. As he remembered it, she "kissed me violently, but I struggled to be free." On a separate occasion, another neighbor "seized my wrist," he wrote, "pulled up her petticoat and jerked my hand up between her thighs. When I felt the hair . . . I thought it was some animal, a chipmunk perhaps." In retrospect, Wood was struck by the desire that had always accompanied the restraint. "From my experience," he concluded, "I would say where the girls or women felt themselves safe they were quite apt to be the wooers and pursuers as any men."

Wood never wrote down the name of his Hoonah lover. Like so many other women memorialized in the writings of American sailors and soldiers who traveled to the far reaches of the American domain, she was always the princess, or the "young Indian woman" who was "one of the comeliest of her race" and "mended my clothes and my sealskin boots," or the "niece of old I forget his name the Chilkaht chief." Although Wood could be very specific in pinpointing the places where he traveled in Alaska, he never quite identified where his encounter with her had taken place. Had it been on an island? "I'm not sure it *was* an island," he later wrote. "Come to think of it I think it was the mainland at the foot of icy bay near the face wall of a great glacier — feeding icebergs into the bay." As the years passed, he took to saying that he had been marooned in the village by a "furious storm." It became hard to tell what he had experienced and what he had imagined.

Wood insisted that his intentions had been honorable, that he had shared with his "princess" his aspiration to trace the Chilkat River to its source and that she, in turn, "proposed that . . . she would fit out two appropriate canoes, manned

281

by slaves, and she would go with me up the river as far as canoes could go — then the slaves would be packed and we would go over the divide to the Yukon." He claimed that he sought a one-year leave from the army — later tellings stretched it to three — to travel with her. His memories almost formed a brief arguing that Alaska had become something more than a backdrop for his personal drama of self-discovery, that it changed him, that with freedom came insight, even revelation. But in truth, he still saw the world with the same eyes. He never requested a long leave from General Howard and, while staying among the Hoonah, never lost track of the need to return to Sitka in time for the June steamer. His sojourn in the summer village could not have lasted more than a few days. His expedition took at most a week longer than his brisk first outing had after covering much of the same distance.

Wood maintained that he rowed to Sitka "fully expecting to return to her." When he pulled to shore, the "stagnation" and "loafing" that had formed his initial impressions of the town had given way to frenzied activity fueled by panic. Under the orders that had arrived on the May steamer, the army was busy evacuating its posts at Sitka and Fort Wrangell, selling its stores and mules. All the Americans, it seemed, were trying to leave. The *Sitka Post* had ceased printing, declaring in its June 5 issue that "the town of Sitka will receive a blow from the crushing effect of which it is not likely to recover for some time to come, if ever." The local prostitutes were "wretched" with fear. Wood observed moments of heartbreak all around him: "The leave taking. Mistresses and sweethearts. Soldier's parting with his child. The old Russian woman praying to be taken to Portland."

The June steamer arrived on the eleventh, a Monday. In years to come, Wood would describe how it carried the news that compelled him to head south. It was necessity, he would explain, "sudden and unexpected," that "made me break my word to this girl and add one more example of man's — and white man's perfidy." After weeks aloft, he was crashing to earth.

But Wood's account was a trick of memory, if not outright deception. The *California* carried a letter from General Howard asking Wood to stay north. The general had received the note Wood had posted on the May steamer and pronounced it "excellent, not too long." Once again, Howard offered Wood an extraordinary opportunity. "I propose to give you temporary command of Alaska," he wrote. "Any information of value to the service and to the government that you may obtain without too much peril will be gladly welcome." The appointment gave Wood power without responsibility. He would have free rein to travel and explore — no one higher in rank to answer to, and after the steamer left with Sitka's army companies, no one lower in rank to keep in line.

Yet Wood made arrangements to board the *California* all the same. As Sitka was coming apart, the talk of the town fixated on the inevitable reprisals that the Tlingit would exact on the settlers who remained. Seventy years after the Russians had besieged the local natives, the Kiks.ádi clan still kept the raven helmet worn in battle by the great leader Katlian. They were just biding their time, it was said, waiting for the right moment to strike.

As soon as the army had gone, the settlers — Americans, Russians — would surely be shot, clubbed, gutted, burned to ash. Listening to the Russian priest's wife, Madame Mitropolsky, prophesy "attack and murder," Wood must have wondered what cruel fate would await him as the only soldier left in Alaska. He determined that there was some freedom he could stand to forsake.

On Thursday, June 14, a "tearful group on the wharf" gathered to send the *California* on its way, disappearing from sight as the steamer turned south. "Farewell to Sitka," Wood scrawled in his journal. Those three words, terse and final, left no room for anyone or anything he had left behind. Instead of dwelling on the people and places he had encountered over the previous two months, Wood focused his attention on the boat ride, the brief stop in Wrangell, the foggy rain and hard winds, the passengers laid low with seasickness. Five days later, on June 19, the steamer reached Port Townsend in Washington Territory, at the tip of the Olympic Peninsula.

While one of the artillery companies from Sitka rotated for another company that was moving from Townsend to Fort Vancouver, Wood heard something unsettling. He may have fled Sitka to avoid Tlingit attacks, but Alaska, it turned out, was a picture of calm. Elsewhere in the Department of the Columbia, he recorded in his journal, there were "rumors of war." In his haste to leave Sitka, he had fallen into a far worse situation.

The rumors were confirmed as soon as the *California* crossed the bar and reached Fort Canby at the mouth of the Columbia. "The telegram," Wood jotted. "Stirring news. No companies to disembark. All under orders for the front." In the

284

time that Wood had been steaming south, the Wallowa situation had become a crisis. In far-off Idaho, Nez Perce bands were on the warpath.

CHAPTER 10
SPLIT ROCKS

June 1877

They were easy to kill — more scattered than the bison of the plains far to the east, harder to see at a distance as they foraged in the creek valleys that rippled the land between the Salmon River and the Snake, but not wild. Unlike bison, cattle did not bound away at the sight of men on horseback. By the 1870s Nez Perce families had been building their herds for a generation, from the time tribesmen showed their goodwill to the wagon trains on the Oregon Trail by trading for stock too weak to continue the journey west.

Joseph, his brother Ollokot, and the other men in their small party — Half Moon, John Wilson — could ride close to their herd, take deliberate aim, and drop a cow with a shot. A blast in the hills, a final heavy step, then collapse to the ground, blood flowing like a creek in summer, silent but swift, soaking dust into mud, coloring the grass, slicking rock. An easy kill, and then the work began for the women who had accompanied the hunters: Joseph's daughter Hophop Onmi (Sound of Running Feet), twelve years old and nearing adulthood; Ollokot's wife Wetatonmi; and Welweyas, who had been born male but dressed as a woman and was regarded by the band as "half-man-and-half-woman." With sharp blades they sliced through skin, fat, and sinew, cut bone from bone: familiar, quick work.

Chief Joseph's party took a dozen or so cattle from the herd, killed them one after the other, cut them down, and loaded them onto pack horses. Then they filed north and east, slow, careful, for about twenty miles, a couple days of riding. Their procession defied powerful forces: gravity's heavy pull, the chaos of a strong current, the sun's focused rays. They descended a twisting path to the Salmon River, furious in spring flood. Crossing the river was agonizing; it was the third time they had done it in the past weeks, each one fraught with the danger of people drowning, animals washed away, food and possessions lost to the water. On the other side, they rode up through the canyons, the heat receding as they rose, the sky growing big and clear.

Up on the prairie, rock and dust, peaks and drops, gave way to gentle rolling country, blossoming with pale blue camas flowers. Soon the riders could anticipate seeing their band's teepees clustered near a small sparkling pond. For generations Nez Perce families had gathered for the long days and brilliant nights of early summer at this place, called Tepahlewam (Split Rocks). While the men gambled and raced horses, paraded and told stories, the women pulled and cured a mountain of camas roots.

In a small teepee set apart from the others, Joseph's younger wife Toma Alwawinmi (Springtime) was preparing for labor and birth. Attended by midwives, she did not step outside. She cooked and ate her meals in the brown muffled shade of buffalo skins and woven reed mats. In the previous weeks, she might have found the time to decorate a buckskin cradleboard. When the band journeyed out of the Wallowa Valley, across the great canyons of the Snake and Salmon Rivers, and up to their campground, she could have beaded as she rode, hide stretched across her saddle's horn. But in the scramble to round up the herds and strike and pack their villages, there may have been no time. Any day now, Joseph's band would welcome a new life. The baby had been conceived as summer ended and would be born as it began again, blood and afterbirth raked hot into the ground. Renewed in warmth and sunlight, Joseph's band was moving with the seasons, following the cycles of life, giving to and taking from the world around them.

Perhaps in those weeks there was comfort in the knowledge that so much could be the same even as everything was changing. Joseph's people had endured waves of despair. From moment to moment, it only seemed that their lives were ending, not beginning again. After Joseph had met with General Howard's commission in November 1876, his band spent the winter in the canyons below the Wallowa Valley as they had always done. But in the cold, dark days a messenger came from Lapwai, telling them that the government in Washington, DC — the Department of the Interior — had decided to follow the commission's recommendations and force Joseph's band from their ancestral lands.

In the middle of March 1877, Ollokot rode to Lapwai to clarify what Monteith intended to do and argue once more that the government's policy should change. In long conversations with Monteith over two days, Ollokot affirmed his peaceful intentions. "The same being created both the white and red man and created the earth for them. They are to get their living and money from the earth and by laboring both grow happy," Ollokot told Monteith. "I have a wife, children, cattle and horses. I have eyes and a heart and can see and understand for myself that if we fight, we would have to leave all and go into the mountains. I love my wife and children and could not leave them. I have always been a friend of the whites and will not fight them."

As before, Ollokot's words pulsed with an assertion of fundamental equality, a deep human connection, and once again suggested that the Nez Perce people could follow their traditional life alongside the white settlers. The Indian agent replied with what he thought were words of assurance, but he did not recognize Ollokot's brand of equality. Monteith saw an equality between the two peoples, but it was one that assumed that Indians could and should live as whites. "I told Ollicut," the agent wrote at the time, "that the Govt wanted him and his people to come on the reserve where they could be furnished with houses, land, agricultural implements, and get a good start in agricultural pursuits, after which they could do for themselves and eventually get rich, by being industrious." Unaware that Joseph's band already considered themselves rich, Monteith missed entirely the impact of Ollokot's words. The agent reported instead, "I told him, I knew he was a good worker, could plow as well as any Indian, could cradle grain and do all kinds of farm work."

After talking in vain to Monteith, Ollokot struggled to find someone else to reconsider his band's claim to the Wallowa country. He rode 150 miles south and west to the Umatilla reservation to see the local Indian agent, Narcisse Cornoyer, and William Henry Boyle, an army lieutenant stationed there. Reluctant to resign himself to a life behind a plow, Ollokot now proposed that Joseph's band could move onto the Umatilla reservation, nearer to the Wallowa Valley and populated with a closely allied group of Indians who continued to live traditional lives. Although for five years officials of every stripe had responded sympathetically and often pressed the band's case to higher authorities, Ollokot's reception at Umatilla that March was chilling. According to one account of the meeting, Lieutenant Boyle "very curtly said . . . 'General Howard's orders are that you are to pack up and go to the Nez Perces.' No explanation, no softening of the blow."

The nontreaty Nez Perce bands appeared to have finally run out of audiences, options, and time. Whenever Ollokot met with American officials, he spoke of how the Nez Perce had helped Lewis and Clark, had saved the missionary Spalding after the Whitman massacre, had given crucial aid to Governor Stevens during the Indian wars of the 1850s — "had never shed white man's blood." But in the spring of 1877, he began to despair that the tribe's alliance with the United States would be its undoing, that years of negotiation, assurances, and goodwill had been for naught. At Umatilla, after the interpreter spoke Lieutenant Boyle's words to him, Ollokot's face flushed. He pointed at the officer, a witness remembered, walked toward him, then "spread his fore finger and middle finger forming a Y, which . . . symbolized a snake's forked tongue."

"General Howard talks with two tongues," Ollokot said. "I have talked straight. Why does not General Howard talk straight?"

Frustrated with Boyle, Ollokot requested an audience with Howard, and Monteith and Cornoyer both agreed that the general should come east, confident that he could put an end to any lingering sense by Ollokot and Joseph that they still had room to maneuver. "I think if you could spare the time to come here and see Joseph," Monteith wrote, "and impress upon his mind that it is the unalterable purpose of the Government, that he and his people shall be removed to and located upon this reserve, or some other one, the desired result would follow in a short time." Hearing word that Howard was on his way, Ollokot rode from the Umatilla agency to Fort Walla Walla in April 1877.

Horses crowded the fort's hitching posts as he arrived. Ollokot and his retinue — several members of his band, the Cayuse leader Young Chief — were led to a room in a barracks to meet with General Howard. The building was full of onlookers — the Indian agent Cornoyer and his interpreter McBean, Howard's aide Melville Wilkinson, officers from the garrison, and a number of curious Walla Walla residents. Ollokot had come, however, only to be abased and humiliated. Many people were present, but few would listen. When he spoke, the room bristled, impatient with his oratory. "Alli-cott . . . done most of the talking, and occupied much of the time in the usual stereotyped phrases of 'I talk with a good heart,' 'I want to show you my heart,' &c. &c.," reported the *Walla Walla Statesman*. "Who wants to see his heart? Indeed, if somebody had made a hole there

291

for inspection some time ago, it might have saved a heap of trouble."

Howard's response to Ollokot was spare and shattering. The army was preparing to occupy the Wallowa Valley and would soon drive Joseph's band to Lapwai, the general said. "The Indians would be required to go on the reservation," with an annual right to hunt and fish in the Wallowa country, "but always with a pass from the agent." Howard left no room for conversation, let alone compromise, promising "the guard-house" for "any . . . dreamer leader for non-compliance with government instructions." He requested that Joseph and the other nontreaty leaders meet him at the garrison at Lapwai in early May to plan the final move.

On hearing Howard's ultimatum, Ollokot was stunned, "afraid to promise anything" about leaving the Wallowa Valley, Howard thought. Keenly aware of his people's delicate situation, Ollokot was not trying to destroy the world around him or pretend that the forces of commerce, industry, and migration did not exist. His band had long benefited from its place in the United States. Nez Perce herds had grown strong because of the settlers passing through. Rather, Ollokot's plea for his people was a plea to coexist with American ranchers and farmers and miners without having to become them. At various points in the previous five years, Monteith and Cornoyer and Howard had all listened to him, sympathized with his position, and taken great efforts to support it. Now, however, they ignored him and viewed his plea as impossible, a nuisance, a threat. For five years there had always been another official to appeal to, another who could be convinced of the justice of Joseph and Ollokot's position. Now the band was trapped. Although Howard had asked for one more meeting, in two weeks at Lapwai, Ollokot had little reason to think that the general would see with new eyes.

Afterward, the chief walked through downtown Walla Walla, its streets soft and yielding, deep with spring mud. Decades later, someone who had been there remembered how "Indians and white men [were] thronging the sidewalk by the old wooden courthouse of Walla Walla." All eyes, sympathetic and not, were on Ollokot, described by a journalist as "the observed of all observers." Although the local newspaper suggested that the chief had been "strutting around Main Street" in an aimless display of primitive vanity, the chief had a destination in mind. Not long after the meeting, he found his way past the courthouse to a photographer's studio.

The studio's proprietor, Charles Phillips, just twenty-one years old, posed Ollokot on a bench in front of a plain drop cloth, flanked by two of his tribesmen. Ollokot sat tall and straight. Perhaps the photographer braced him to keep still through the long exposure. In the Dreamer fashion, Ollokot's thick hair was combed high from his smooth forehead. Long white feathers cascaded from a wavy sidelock down to his left shoulder. His plaid shirt was open to the middle of his chest, displaying the gentle arc of eight beaded necklaces. He wore a trade blanket wrapped around his leggings and draped a white fur down his left leg, perhaps a wolf, its tail lying across his moccasins. A wide-brim felt hat, lushly adorned with feathers, lay on his lap.

Phillips was taking a picture of a man at the

height of his powers, physically imposing, strikingly handsome. But even as the photograph recorded his strength, his pose, his clothing, and the very fact that he was posing for a photographer all suggested that Ollokot had reconciled himself to a place in the settlers' world. He was the picture of a traditional warrior, but his shirt, hat, and blanket had been made in distant mills, workshops, and factories. His very image, in turn, would be pasted onto card stock and sold to white people near and far.

While Ollokot and his companions posed for the picture, a crowd from the street, Indian and white, filled the studio, gathering round the photographer while Phillips opened his shutter and captured his image. Later in his darkroom, the young man watched it appear crisp and knew he would profit from it. In the portrait, Ollokot's arms seemed pinned to his sides, hidden from view behind the men sitting to his left and right. With most of his body obscured by his hat, blanket, and fur, he appeared diminished, just a torso, a whole man reduced to a bust. Ollokot had looked sharply at the camera, expression pained and eyes tired, defined by the dark lines underneath.

Riding east from Walla Walla, Ollokot found Joseph and their band in a late-winter camp north of the Wallowa Valley, along a creek by the Snake River where generations of Nez Perce had fished at night for eels. Eating and smoking in his brother's teepee, Ollokot reported bad news from Walla Walla: "Government wants all Indians put in one place." The meeting that Howard had called with all the nontreaty chiefs in May was an easy ride from their campground. As they set out, fifty men, women, and children joined Joseph and Ollokot, aware that momentous decisions were about to be made.

Joseph's band reached Lapwai on May 3, ahead of the other nontreaty bands, who had to travel slick and snowbound trails out of the mountains. Setting up camp just out of sight from the fort, they prepared themselves for the council. They painted their faces red and drew the color back into the parts of their hair. They braided and tied ornamental strings into their sidelocks, wore their best beadwork, wrapped themselves in bright blankets and shawls.

The fort was a sparse set of clapboard structures built around a parade ground, designed not to repel invaders but to house the small force of soldiers who policed the Nez Perce reservation's boundaries. Approaching on their ponies, Joseph's band could see General Howard waiting with his aides, alongside several treaty Indians in Western clothes, Agent Monteith and an interpreter, the reservation's Catholic priest, the garrison's officers, and the officers' wives. On the green a large hospital tent had been pitched for the council, its sides tied up and open to the spring air, reminiscent of the council hall that Joseph's band had built for their first discussions with Wallowa settlers five years before. The closest building was the guardhouse. The rank-and-file soldiers waited inside their barracks, perhaps watching from the windows.

Joseph's band rode in a long column, men first, then women, then children, slowly circling the entire perimeter of the fort, then stopping in front of Howard and his party. As they approached, they sang a song that echoed and broke among the buildings. Taking their time, Joseph, Ollokot, and several other leaders of their band dismounted, walked to the tent, and insisted on long formal greetings with Howard and his retinue. For many of the people who had come with Joseph and Ollokot, it was the first time they had set eyes on Howard. He did not appear powerful. "A soldier was there with only one good arm," Joseph's nephew Yellow Wolf remembered. "Right arm mostly gone. Left arm sound. This soldier was General Howard."

After the priest said a prayer in Nez Perce, Howard announced, "I am here to listen to what you have to say." Joseph told the general there was no hurry, that it would be better to wait for the other nontreaty chiefs — Toohoolhoolzote, White Bird — to arrive. "We want to talk a long time . . . about our land," one of the elders added. But Ollokot could not hold his tongue, appealing to Howard's sense of equality under law, arguing that Indians should not be treated differently from whites. "There should be *one law* for all," he said. "If I commit murder I shall be hung; but if I do well I should not be punished." Joseph's band had always done well. Why were they being punished?

Howard's response unnerved the members of Joseph's band who watched from outside the tent. While the general agreed that the council could wait, he signaled that there would be no compromises, and no other authority to which Joseph could turn. "You may as well know at the outset that in any event the Indians must obey the orders of the government of the United States," Howard declared. Equality, he suggested, did not mean that the law had to treat everyone equally or give

296

everyone the same set of rights. Rather, being "under the same government" meant only that everyone, regardless of race, had the same obligation to submit to what the law required. "What it commands us to do, that we must do," he said. In their case Joseph's people were obligated to accept the Interior Department's decision that they had to move to Lapwai. They could have their pick of open land, but "if the Indians hesitate to come to the reservation," the general warned, "the government directs that soldiers be used to bring them hither."

If Joseph's band had ridden to the fort with proud ceremony, the ride back to camp that night was a demoralizing retreat. They were unsure how to respond to General Howard, unsure what words could do. Abruptly, speaking without respect or compassion, Cut Arm had announced the end of their way of life. "This hurt the Indians," Joseph's nephew Yellow Wolf would remember. "They said no more in that sun's council. But there was talk in camp that night. Many wondered what would happen."

The next day, a Friday, brought no comfort. The Salmon River bands — White Bird and Toohoolhoolzote's people — had arrived. But if the nontreaties' procession around the fort was reinvigorated — as Howard would remember it, their songs "louder and stronger" — they made no progress in the council that followed. Joseph and Ollokot sat mostly silent, while White Bird kept his large ceremonial hat on and obscured his face with an eagle's wing. By agreement, Toohoolhoolzote spoke for them all. "I belong to the land out of which I came," he said. "The Earth is my mother." Spoken outside, under a brilliant cloudless sky, his words made intuitive sense. Emphatic, impassioned, his voice was carried on a wind that washed over the chiefs, the officers, the Indian agent, and the dozens of Indian witnesses looking on from the parade grounds. Howard would later comment on how the breeze "caus[ed] the abundant grasses and flowers to ripple and sparkle in long noiseless waves," from the valley where they stood all the way to the soft hills that surrounded them. All the world around them was swirling, fluid and alive. It made a gathering of great men appear small, a dot on an infinite landscape, their pretensions of ownership absurd. But Howard's mind was unswayed. He found the chief's rhetoric tiresome — it was nothing he had not heard before. In response, the general could only recite what he called "the old answer": that "we are all subjects, children of a common government, and must obey its requirements." Still, he agreed to continue the conversation the following Monday.

When Joseph and Ollokot sat with Howard once again, they were joined by additional nontreaty leaders, including Husishusis Kute from near the Palouse River and Looking Glass from reservation land along the Clearwater. At one point Howard and Monteith appeared to make a conciliatory, or at least sympathetic gesture: the agent assured the gathering that the government would not interfere with their religious beliefs. But when Toohoolhoolzote again spoke with what Howard would call "the usual words concerning the earth being his mother," the general could not hide his exasperation. "I don't want to offend your religion, but you must talk about practicable things," he said. "Twenty times over I hear that the earth is your mother and about chieftainship from the

298

earth. I want to hear it no more, but come to business at once."

Once more, Agent Monteith repeated the demand that all the Nez Perce move onto the Lapwai reserve. "The law is, you must come to the reservation," he said. "The law is made in Washington; we don't make it." And once again, as Joseph and Ollokot had done for years, Toohoolhoolzote responded by asserting that the 1863 treaty *"wasn't true law* at all." But instead of emphasizing that Lawyer had not signed the treaty for the entire tribe — a point about representation that American officials were bound to take seriously — Toohoolhoolzote fell back on a more traditional argument. "The earth is part of my body," he said, "and I never gave up the earth . . . What person pretended to divide the land and put me on it?"

"I am the man," Howard said. He had heard enough; his exasperation was becoming contempt. "I stand here for the president, and there is no spirit, good or bad, that will hinder me. My orders are plain, and will be executed. I hoped the Indians had good sense enough to make me their friend and not their enemy."

Aware that the council was taking a dangerous turn, White Bird tried to calm the gathering, but the hostility between Howard and Toohoolhoolzote only escalated. Dozens of Nez Perce watching from the parade grounds could see that the general was "showing mad," as Yellow Wolf remembered, "strong mad." "You are trifling with the law of the earth," Toohoolhoolzote warned. "So long as the earth keeps me," he declared, "I want to be left alone."

"Joseph and White Bird seem to have good

hearts," Howard replied, "but yours is bad. . . . The Indians can see no good while you are along; you advise them to resist, to lose all their horses and cattle, and have unending trouble." Howard threatened to exile the chief 1,700 miles away to the Indian Territory. "I will send you there," he said, "if it takes years and years." Howard ended the council, ordering a soldier to seize Toohoolhoolzote and throw him into the guardhouse. When the chief refused to go, the soldier pushed him, and the old man stumbled over people sitting outside the tent.

The Nez Perce witnesses were aghast, their "restlessness," as one warrior called it, palpable. Howard's exercise of power was at once terrifying and insulting. "In peace councils, force must not be talked. It was the same as showing us the rifle," Yellow Wolf later said. "General Howard was just pricking with needles." The general pressed forward, unfazed by the gasps of the crowd. "The question is," he said to the chiefs, "will the Indians come peaceably . . . or do they want me to put them there by force?"

With Toohoolhoolzote jailed, Howard asked the other chiefs to spend the next several days riding with him around the reservation. After a week, the nontreaty leaders, including Joseph and Ollokot, finally agreed to take bottom land and hills along the Clearwater, about a hundred miles northeast of the Wallowa Valley, near Looking Glass and at a healthy distance from Lapwai. Compared to their ancestral territories, the reservation allotments were minuscule, almost certainly not big enough for the bands' herds. But after years of resisting the loss of the only life they knew, they appeared to accept the government's authority and the finality of its latest decision. Eager to complete the transition as soon as possible, Howard gave them a month, until mid-June, to abandon their home territories for the reservation.

For five years Joseph and Ollokot had held on to the Wallowa Valley, but in the months following their meeting with the commission in November 1876, they came to the crushing realization that they had no more outlet for their advocacy. The council with Howard in May 1877 marked not only the end of their life on their land but also the end of a particular understanding of their place in the United States. For years it had seemed that there was no reason to surrender their position. Joseph and Ollokot saw how the government, remote yet responsive, sprawling and fluid, could continue to hear their voices and shift course. They believed that refusing to leave land that they claimed as rightly their own was not lawlessness or resistance — it was what any American would fight for, what anyone with a stake in American society would do. It was what the settlers had done, too. Yet at Lapwai, Howard crushed Joseph and Ollokot's experience of American government. The general treated them not as people who were participating in a new way of making policy, but rather as outsiders who were showing disrespect for it, who could never be governed without brute force.

The general backed his words with provocative action. When Joseph's band returned to the Wallowa Valley, the cavalry was waiting for them, ordered by Howard to occupy the area while the final council was taking place. Still, Joseph and Ollokot felt they had one path to follow. "None of the chiefs wanted war," remembered Peopeo

Tholekt (Bird Alighting), then a young man in Looking Glass's band. "They knew they could never win." Instead, they prepared for their move to the reservation.

Howard had given Joseph's people only one month to leave the Wallowa Valley, to abandon where their ancestors had lived and were buried. They would no longer spend their days among hills, canyons, and rolling meadows that defined their present while also continually reminding them of their past. Leaving their land for the reservation was a move from the known to the unknown. The break was all the more profound because the physical ordeal of traveling from the Wallowa country to Lapwai in early summer stretched the boundary between the possible and the impossible — more the stuff of myth than anything they had experienced in their remembered past.

The women had four weeks to pack everything they owned, everything the band had been gathering and preparing to sustain themselves for the summer and beyond. The band's stores of roots and other food were far too much for their horses to carry, so they preserved, wrapped, and buried enormous amounts, hundreds of loads, in the hope that someone would be able to return to the valley later. In that same time the men had to do the work of months, to round up horses and cattle that were spread across vast distances, from the Wallowa country down into the creek valleys and canyons of the Imnaha and Grande Ronde.

Their packing complete, the band set out with their herds, with their food and possessions, with young children and old men and women. Joseph's band had to cross two great rivers, the Snake and the Salmon, rushing high with ice cold floodwaters. The path into the Snake River's gorge wound tight along the mountainside, a steep descent of several thousand feet. When untraveled, the trail was imperceptible from the water. But as Joseph's band filed slowly from the top of the canyon down to the river landing known as Dug Bar, the entire length of the trail appeared as a dark wrinkle on the rock face, like a vein of ore. The screams of children, the distress of the horses and cattle, were lost in the river's livid rush. The people crossed on rafts made of buffalo hide, a fragile skin separating air from water, life from death, horses tied to each corner, riders on each horse. None of Joseph's people drowned, but they watched dozens of animals succumb to the currents and disappear downstream. It was excruciating work, two days of struggle almost beyond comprehension. At the Salmon River, which General Howard knew as "a torrent with mountain shores," Joseph's band decided to cross without their animals, leaving them with herders in the rough country between the two rivers. They reached Tepahlewam, their traditional resting place, on June 2, ahead of the general's deadline.

The campground, just outside the reservation boundaries, was an oasis of normalcy. After experiencing an arduous journey and the loss of their land, Joseph's people had reached a place they knew well. They had often traveled here. Despite the catastrophic change in their lives, the blue-flowered prairie was as it had always been. It was almost as if the previous month had not happened. Here their days passed in familiar work, familiar play, and the familiar company of the other nontreaty bands led by White Bird, Toohool-

303

hoolzote, and Looking Glass. After Joseph's band had raised their teepees and settled in, the chief, his brother, and their small party made their journey back across the Salmon to slaughter cattle. They left their people just as they were beginning to find comfort in the resilience of the old ways.

On June 15, Joseph and his party drove their packhorses back to camp from the Salmon River country, loaded with hundreds of pounds of meat. They were waiting to hear of the birth of the chief's child, to learn of the bands' preparations to pack up again for their final journey to the reservation lands that they had been allotted. As the group approached the prairie campground, however, they saw something unexpected: most of the teepees had already been taken down. From a distance, they could see a man riding out from Tepahlewam to meet them; soon they could tell he was Two Moons, from Joseph's band. He brought grave news. The previous day, Two Moons reported, three young men had left before dawn for the white settlements that had encroached on White Bird's territory along the Salmon River, about twenty miles south. That night, they had returned with horses they had stolen from white men they said they had killed. Upon hearing this news, Looking Glass's people left for their traditional lands on the reservation. White Bird and Toohoolhoolzote's people were preparing to flee north and east across the prairie to a campground in the canyons where Cottonwood Creek emptied into the south fork of the Clearwater River. Instead of an end to their travels, Joseph and Ollokot learned there would be war.

Joseph and Ollokot galloped to camp while the women tended the packhorses. Amid the confusion, they learned more about what had happened. Two days earlier, on June 13, White Bird's band had staged a *tel-lik-leen,* a ceremonial circle that commemorated past battles. For a people scarred by the loss of their land, it was an opportunity to remember and affirm a collective strength that had overcome every challenge. But in the middle of the ceremony, someone taunted one of the riders, a young warrior named Wahlitits (Shore Crossing), son of Tipyahlahnah Siskan (Eagle Robe). Why was he taking part in the event, he was asked, when he had failed to avenge his own father's murder at the hands of a white man?

The barb touched on an open wound. For three years White Bird's people had lived alongside Eagle Robe's killer, a Salmon River settler named Larry Ott, after a grand jury refused to indict him for the crime. But Wahlitits, who was married and had a place of prominence in the *tel-lik-leen,* had not appeared to suffer a loss of status or honor for leaving Ott alive. As he lay dying, Eagle Robe himself had warned his son not to kill his murderer. "Do nothing to the white man for what he has done to me," he was remembered saying. "Let him live his life!" Wahlitits knew why — if he killed a settler, his people would lose everything.

Performed for generations, the *tel-lik-leen* celebrated decades of raids and reprisals, chronicling a deep history of individual and collective acts of bravery, honor, and revenge — a history without white people. Wahlitits had long understood that the settlers were not simply another rival tribe. Life among them did not belong on the same historical tapestry. After being humiliated in front

305

of his people, however, Wahlitits resolved to pretend that he and his tribesmen were still living the old life and following the old rules. He decided to treat his father's killer no differently than he would have treated an Indian — according to the harsh yet comforting logic of the *tel-lik-leen*. "You will be sorry for your words," he told the assembly.

After the *tel-lik-leen,* the warrior wept at his public rebuke, then painted his face and dressed for war. As his tribesmen slept, he set off to Ott's cabin, joined by his close friend Sarpsis Ilppilp (Red Moccasin Tops) and a young cousin, just seventeen years old, Wetyetmas Wahyakt (Swan Necklace). They rode south and west, down from the prairie into the canyons for fifteen miles until they reached the Salmon. Then they followed the river's horseshoe bends, turning south, upriver, against the unyielding spring current. It was familiar country — their homeland — and it was enemy territory.

Ott's place was deserted, but the three young warriors refused to return unavenged. They did not have to look far to find another settler who had murdered an Indian with impunity. Richard Devine, an English prospector, lived alone thirteen miles farther upriver. Whenever Indians had approached his land, Devine would set his dogs on them. White Bird's people remembered him as someone quick to aim his rifle at them, and he had pulled the trigger once, killing Dakoopin (Wounded Leg), a tribesman who could barely walk.

Devine's cabin was shambling and small, hidden among the trees bending out of Carver Creek. In the darkness on June 14, Wahlitits and Sarpsis Ilppilp pushed open his door while Swan Necklace

306

tended to their horses. In the end Devine had only enough time to register his surprise — no Indian had set foot inside his cabin before. He was easy to kill: one shot, dead in a beat. The killers' ears rang from the blast. But Devine's death appeared to change very little in the world. It was still dark outside. They felt the same chill in the air. The cabin was still standing. Their people were asleep at Tepahlewam, dreaming, perhaps, of what they had left behind, or of new lives to come. The settlers slept, too, behind the fences they had built across Indian land. The warriors took Devine's rifle and ammunition and rode six miles back north along the Salmon, looking for the next settler who deserved to die.

After sunrise the warriors reached land on John Day Creek now claimed by Jurden Henry Elfers, who had left Germany for California to prospect for gold in 1849 and then settled the Salmon River area during the 1862 gold rush. A wealthy rancher, he had opposed bringing Ott to justice for the murder of Wahlitits's father. White Bird's people remembered hearing the rancher say, "He should not be prosecuted for killing a dog." In recent months, Elfers had served on a council of arbitration that refused to punish another settler for whipping two Indians.

Elfers's land was tucked between steep hills. In late spring, the only sound was the water's relentless rush — hard to talk over it, let along hear footsteps or hoof beats. A rough-hewn barn stood on the south bank, running alongside the creek. To the southwest, a path climbed two hundred feet up a hill to a plateau where Elfers pastured his stock. The warriors left their horses in the middle of Elfers's field and hid in the brush. When the rancher walked up to tend to his herd, the warriors watched him examine their horses, his puzzlement quickly turning to panic. They tackled Elfers as he ran for home, then shot him point-blank. Within a few minutes, as Elfers's nephew and hired man came up the path to the pasture, the warriors killed them, too. On their way back down the creek toward the Salmon, they saw Elfers's wife churning milk and minding her three children, all under the age of six. She watched the Indians pass, suspecting nothing; the roar of the creek had swallowed the sound of gunshots.

The war party kept riding north along the Salmon River, back toward Tepahlewam. Halfway there, at the mouth of White Bird Creek, they passed a cabin belonging to Samuel Benedict, a shopkeeper who was hated for killing a Nez Perce man, cheating his Indian customers, and selling whiskey. They shot him in both legs and left him for dead. Turning up into the canyons, they began their final climb before reaching home.

After sunset on June 14, Swan Necklace rode into camp on one of Elfers's horses, telling of the day's exploits. The elders had gathered to discuss their move across the reservation boundary in the next day or two when they heard someone shouting, "You poor people are holding council for nothing! . . . It will have to be war!" As the news of the killings spread throughout the camp, hundreds of people prepared to flee. But seventeen warriors, almost all young men who had been calling for war, rode out to join Wahlitits and Sarpsis Ilppilp for a second raid on the Salmon River settlements.

When Joseph and Ollokot heard what had happened, they walked through the campsite, pleading with people not to flee. "Let us stay here till the army comes!" Ollokot's wife Wetatonmi remembered them calling out. "We will then make some kind of peace with them." After years of negotiating with army officers, Joseph and Ollokot were convinced that they could avoid collective punishment for the deeds of a few young men. But outside their own band, no one believed them. For five years, Joseph and Ollokot had emerged as essential leaders of the nontreaty bands because of their ability to speak to the government. But as the May council with Howard had proved, their ideas and strategy, their sense of American power, no longer mattered. The young warriors who remained at Tepahlewam scoffed at Joseph and Ollokot's vision of a peaceful resolution, predicting that the chiefs would soon betray the other nontreaty bands and join the reservation Indians at Lapwai or Kamiah. "They were watched closely by the warriors," Wetatonmi later said. Instead, the young men would follow other leaders. Soon everyone finished packing and started to leave. Joseph found his wife Springtime and met their baby girl. By nightfall, Joseph's band was alone at Tepahlewam — familiar ground, but a new world.

Before midnight, Joseph's nephew Yellow Wolf woke from sleep inside the chief's teepee. He heard hoof beats drumming the ground, closer, louder, stopping just shy of camp. Voices in the darkness, words Yellow Wolf could not understand. It was a group of whites. They kept their distance, but Joseph's band knew they were there. For a while the riders did nothing — why had they come? Then the crack of a rifle pierced the night. A bullet ripped through Joseph's teepee. Yellow

Wolf grabbed his rifle and forced himself from the warmth of the teepee into the cold air outside. He fired as the horses galloped away. Again and again, all night long, the riders kept coming back, only to retreat when Joseph's men tried to engage them. At sunrise, exhausted, Yellow Wolf heard Joseph resignedly say, "We must pack and go . . . where the other chiefs are." If white vengeance would be inevitable and indiscriminate — if war was unavoidable — then Joseph would cast his lot with White Bird and Toohoolhoolzote. "From that time," the chief's nephew would recall, "the Nez Perces had no more rest. No more soft pillows for the head."

The next day, Joseph's people headed across the Camas Prairie to find the other bands at their campground twenty-five miles northeast. In the past the rolling plain had always been a place of leisure, peace, and sustenance. Now it was clouded by signs of war. The travelers heard gunshots in the distance. When a Nez Perce rider crossed paths with their column, he passed along word that warriors had killed a white man nearby and taken two wagons.

In clear daylight Joseph's band found White Bird and Toohoolhoolzote at Sapachesap, like Tepahlewam a well-known camping site. It was located between water and rock, where a large cave hollowed the hills. Had the bands held a *tel-lik-leen* there, they could have told the story of how Sapachesap (Drive In) got its name. Around the time of Lewis and Clark some seventy years earlier, Nez Perce warriors had chased a large war party of Bannock or Shoshone, perhaps two hundred or more. After their enemies took shelter in the cave,

310

the warriors built a big fire at the entrance and killed them all. They died unseen, suffocated by smoke, or slaughtered by arrow, knife, and war club as they fled into the light. It was one of many events Nez Perce families passed on across generations, a reminder of the old world that the warriors seeking vengeance on the settlers were trying to replicate. But now the vision from Sapachesap was decidedly bleak. Joseph, Ollokot, and the other chiefs could see that a merciless foe would soon be pursuing them.

Not long after Joseph's band arrived, two more men reached Sapachesap with news of one of the many skirmishes — random, face-to-face — breaking the quiet of the prairie. After a night of travel, they had spent part of the morning sleeping at an abandoned ranch. As they were leaving, a group of settlers attacked. The two men watched as a third companion, Jyeloo, was cornered, riddled with bullets, his skull crushed. They had managed to escape but left Jyeloo's bloody body in the tall grass. Hearing of the first Nez Perce man killed in the violence of the previous days, thirty warriors, Yellow Wolf among them, rode out to the prairie.

Already the violence was overtaking the Nez Perce bands. Instead of setting up their teepees, Joseph and Ollokot decided with the other leaders that they all had to keep moving. They would head back south, past the rolling fields of camas flowers, to a sheltered winter village site down toward the Salmon River. The settlers called the area White Bird Canyon. The Indians called it Lahmotta. They would reach it by nightfall. Perhaps there, away from the gunplay on the prairie, they could find a moment of respite and plan their next step.

CHAPTER 11
FAIT ACCOMPLI

Oliver Otis Howard recited bible verses one after another to the relentless pounding of his own boot heels. Back and forth he paced across a broad wooden porch spanning two houses at Fort Lapwai. While he often quoted from the scripture, this verbal stream, quick and mumbled, was fundamentally different from his careful sermons and earnest Sunday school talks. Instead of interpreting and unlocking the text, Howard was turning God's word into a mechanical chant, sound divorced from meaning, something primitive, enveloping, hypnotic. From a short distance, a four-year-old girl, daughter of the post's surgeon, watched the general "with awe," she later wrote, puzzled by the quiet spectacle, transfixed by his empty, rolled-up right sleeve. Her mother thought that the general looked anxious — endearing but "awfully queer" as he "promenad[ed]."

Howard's exercise, pacing and reciting, gave him deep comfort in times of uncertainty. Everything had been going exactly according to his plan. To be sure, the general had walked the same porch a month earlier during his council with the non-treaty bands, nervous as anyone would have been when, in his words, "what next is yet to appear." But once he jailed Toohoolhoolzote, he thought the council had gone rather well. Joseph, White Bird, and the other nontreaty leaders "spoke pleasantly," Howard wrote, showing "a far different spirit" from that of the defiant "Old Dreamer." "Their tones changed," the general observed, and it was only a matter of days before they agreed to move onto the reservation land that he showed them. Joseph, as far as Howard was concerned, was once again "our Indian friend." As the council dispersed, Howard was confident that the chiefs would comply by mid-June. *"Fait accompli,"* he noted. "So seemed the closing interview at Lapwai an accomplished work. We felt almost sure that there would be no difficulties with the Nez Perce." In a gesture of magnanimity, he granted the chiefs' petition to release Toohoolhoolzote.

The negotiation confirmed everything that Howard had come to believe about handling nontreaties, Dreamers, and malcontents of all sort. Given a hard line and the threat of force, they would back down from any talk of resistance. "In dealing with Indians," he would write, "my conviction is strong that the true policy is to demand obedience to the requirements of the government of the United States." Otherwise, "these wild Indians" would presume "all the latitude and leisure that their hearts desired."

Howard was certain that, at a basic level, he was saving the Indians from themselves. Maintaining their old roaming lifestyle was a war they simply could not win as the United States expanded west. Instead of losing everything, they could get good land and relative freedom from grasping and encroaching settlers. As property owners and

314

diligent farmers, they could claim the same rights as everyone who had been trying to steal their land. Only as equals, indistinguishable from the settlers, could the Nez Perce persist as a nation. The freedpeople in the South had seen how land, freedom, and equality were linked, and back in 1865 had asked for much of what Howard was allowing the nontreaty Indians. Ultimately, Howard's distaste for the Dreamers was less about the Indians' prospects for salvation in heaven than about their survival on earth. If Nez Perce leaders in the thrall of their religion were so benighted as to deny good Indians the one path to survival, then Howard felt no qualms about bulldozing them into submission. To his mind, the hard line was really a kindness.

Once Joseph, White Bird, and the other non-treaty chiefs had agreed to their allotments on the Nez Perce reservation, Howard steamed west down the Columbia "with the feeling," he wrote, "that a difficult task had been done." By the time he reached home, the Portland newspapers had reported his triumph in resolving the Wallowa crisis. "Settlers in the Wallowa valley . . . will now be rid of annoyance and danger," the *Oregonian* predicted. "The promptitude with which Gen. Howard and Agent Monteith settled this matter . . . is creditable to them, and they will receive the thanks of all the people of that region."

The city's delight in springtime seemed to match Howard's mood. At the end of May, residents awoke to the morning serenade of swallows newly returned from points south. Houses were decked with festive bunting. Fresh strawberries sold on the street at two pounds for a quarter. The air was sweet with flowers, an unusually lush crop, and every man in the street, it seemed, was wearing what the *Oregonian* called "a button-hole bouquet."

After a week with his family, Howard crossed the river to observe Decoration Day at Fort Vancouver. It was the tenth year of official remembrance of the Union war dead. Reviewing a grand parade of the soldiers, he saw the bulk of the forces under his command. Placing flowers on the graves at the fort's cemetery, he saw once again the costs of war. If the occasion was somber, bringing to mind the dozens of people — friends, comrades — he had seen perish in front of him, it also suggested the magnitude of his achievement at Lapwai. By convincing the nontreaty bands to move onto the Nez Perce reservation, he had avoided more bloodshed and loss, more rows of tombstones.

Returning to Portland that afternoon, Howard packed a small valise that he could easily carry with his one hand. It was time for him to travel east once again, so before dawn the next morning, he "bade adieu" to his "drowsy family." Accompanied by an aide and an Interior Department inspector, the general wanted to ensure that as the deadline approached for the nontreaty bands to move onto the reservation, it would not provide any occasion for unrest among the many Columbia River tribes. Not particularly worried, Howard took pleasure in every aspect of the journey — the comforts of a "palatial steamer," enjoyable conversation with his traveling companions. They spoke of Joseph and his allies, but about their various Civil War experiences and many lighter topics as well. "What books would be written to fill the world," Howard wrote, "if what is said and done on transport steamers and other vehicles were only jotted down!" Even after many similar journeys, the "Hudson-like scenery," the "twice ten thousand hills and the old mountains beyond them," never failed to strike Howard as simply miraculous.

Within a few days, Howard began to see his journey as more of a valedictory tour than a military necessity. The general first stopped at Fort Simcoe, sixty miles north of the Dalles in Yakama Indian country, to meet with various Columbia River tribes. There he had every reason to feel that he was among friends. The Yakama tribesmen appeared "remarkably contented," Howard thought, as they smoked the tobacco that he had brought for them. A couple of days later, on the first Sunday in June, the general prayed at a Methodist church "overflowing with Indians, . . . the fences lined with their waiting saddle-horses." "That church was without a speck of dirt," Howard would marvel, "even a tobacco stain!"

The picture of reservation life only grew rosier for Howard. The next day, he watched the Yakama brand calves from their herds. It was an elaborate, even exhausting process "to catch, to throw, to fasten, to hold, to brand," but it gratified Howard to see the Yakama make such progress as ranchers. Although he described the work as "almost like a battle in its excitements," in truth it signified the opposite. The Indians were at peace, on the lands that had been allotted them, embracing their new lives.

Over the next few days, every newspaper report and every field dispatch that reached Fort Simcoe confirmed what Howard had been sure would happen: the nontreaty Nez Perce were keeping the promises they had made to him, rounding up their herds and getting ready to move to the reservation. The news "gladdened the hearts of the Yakimas," the general wrote, and surely would dissuade anyone inclined to make trouble. When the Columbia River chiefs whom the general described as "renegades" met with him at the fort, they swore their fealty to the United States and vowed to move onto reservations within a few months. Even the Wanapam leader Smohalla, thought by Howard to be "the author of the 'dreamer religion' . . . and the cause of the restlessness of the Columbia River tribes," said exactly what Howard had hoped he would say. "Your law is my law," Smohalla proclaimed at a public gathering. "I say to you, Yes. I will be on a reservation by September."

After about a week with the Yakama, Howard and his two traveling companions went by wagon and canoe one hundred miles to Wallula. Pushing through summer heat and deep sand, they arrived after midnight on June 12, just in time to catch a night steamer up the Snake River to Lewiston, Idaho Territory. For two days the boat struggled against the strong current. Howard did not mind. The delay allowed him to catch up on his sleep.

The steamer reached port shortly after dawn on the morning of June 14. The Lapwai post commander Captain David Perry, two other officers, and Monteith's clerk — his brother Charles — were waiting at the dock and jumped on board to brief the general. All the news was good. The nontreaties were camping right on the reservation's boundary and gave every indication that they would move onto their land before the next day's deadline. Various townspeople affirmed the glad tidings. Local settlers had long expressed loathing for the Nez Perce people, but on this occasion, they were in agreement: "The Indians are all right."

The reports seemed so favorable that Howard was inclined to wait in Lewiston and let the Interior Department inspector go on to Lapwai. As far as the general was concerned, the Nez Perce troubles had become primarily a civil affair, and the local garrison could provide ample support as the reservation accommodated its newest residents. But Captain Perry asked Howard to accompany him back to the fort, and it was hard to say no. The sun was warm, and it gave the general great pleasure to ride one of Perry's "spirited and handsome" horses for twelve miles on excellent roads. As he made the long "whirling" descent from stark rocky plateau to valley, he looked forward to seeing old friends.

The general had gotten to know Lapwai's officers and their families on multiple visits over the previous years. They were all about Howard's age, and he found them to be pleasant company, if not "altogether sunshiny." Perry looked the part of a commanding officer, a tall, strapping man with "a clear Saxon eye" who enjoyed taking target practice on the range beside the fort. While he had distinguished himself in the South during the Civil War, the fighting had never stopped for him. He moved west to battle Snake Indians in 1866, then Modoc warriors in 1873.

The other cavalry captain at Lapwai, Joel Trimble, had come with his company from Walla Walla toward the end of May. Trimble was quiet but genial, tall and thin as a late-afternoon shadow. Although his eyes were clouded from a wound he had received at Gettysburg, his Civil War service — from the 1862 Peninsula Campaign, when Howard lost his arm, to Appomattox — was less a defining moment than a brief interruption of twenty-five years of fighting in the West. Trimble had received his first battle scars as a teenager too young to enlist in the army, along the Rogue River in Oregon in the early 1850s. Twenty years later, in the Modoc War, he personally captured the renegade leader Captain Jack.

The two cavalry lieutenants were just as familiar to Howard. Perry's lieutenant, Edward Theller, had made himself a colorful presence in the pages of multiple disciplinary reports — he could not stop gambling. But he had gained useful experience fighting Apaches in Arizona, and, more important, was a warm man with a friendly wife, Delia. At their house on Lapwai Creek, with their Maltese cat and bird dog, the Thellers were known and admired for the "cheery hospitality" they always showed visiting officers. When not playing the horses in Lewiston, Theller preferred nothing more than to gallop as fast as he could around a track next to the fort.

Trimble's lieutenant, William Parnell, was impossible to forget. He had joined the Union Army a year after emigrating from Ireland in 1860. With every breath he remembered the Civil War: an infected saber wound had left him with a large hole in the roof of his mouth that army doctors managed to keep covered with a fragile metal plate so he could talk and eat. A man of hulking size with a grand mustache, he could only speak with a high voice after his injury but had many stories to tell, not only of dozens of cavalry actions during the Civil War and out in the West but also of an earlier life in the British military. As a teenager in Dublin, he joined the 17th Lancers during the Crimean War, shortly before its doomed Charge of the Light Brigade at the Battle of Balaclava in 1854. Though Parnell never left Great Britain for the Crimea, he "claimed a high degree of skill in [Her British Majesty's] service," according to one of his men, and it was long supposed that he was one of the Light Brigade's few survivors.

General Howard arrived at the fort mid-afternoon on June 14. If he was celebrating his impending triumph, he did it quietly. The garrison did not notice. A sergeant described the day simply as "monotony" — "nothing to do but lie down in the shade . . . and read." But Trimble's company, at least, shared Howard's keen anticipation of the morrow. As soon as the Indians were settled on their new lands, the soldiers could return to their families and a clean set of clothes in Walla Walla. They thrilled at reports that, in the sergeant's words, "Joseph ha[d] put his pride in his pocket" and that the nontreaties were co-operating. For the general, seeing the Indians onto the reservation would be the signature achievement of three years in the Department of the Columbia. Securing peace in the Northwest — saving lives and money, opening land to unchallenged settlement — was sure to bring Howard notice and an outpouring of acclaim in the capital and across the country.

As the sun set and the mosquitoes came out to feed — "a chorus of them sang me to sleep last evening but the music is too 'touching,' " a sergeant wrote in his diary — a courier delivered a letter to Captain Perry. While every other report had confirmed Howard's hopes for an easy resolution, this dispatch — from a man whom Perry trusted in Mount Idaho, a mining settlement about eight miles from the Indian campground on the Camas Prairie — sounded a discordant note. According to the letter, the Indians were stockpiling guns, powder, and ammunition and had mounted a two-hour "grand parade" the day before that was "well armed, and went through the maneuvers of a fight" — the *tel-lik-leen* at Tepahlewam. Despite the worrisome events, the letter writer was careful to note, "I do not feel any alarm," and Howard and Perry regarded the account as a mere "ripple" in their plans, a "slight warning" at best.

Howard awoke the next morning ready to welcome the nontreaty bands to the reservation. Instead, by nine o'clock, he was hearing the first frantic accounts of the killings along the Salmon River that had taken place the previous day — right around the same time that Howard and his party were steaming into Lewiston, flush with success. When Swan Necklace rode through Tepahlewam on Henry Elfers's stallion, spreading word of the murders, three young men — reservation Indians who had been camping with their nontreaty friends — started for Fort Lapwai to warn the army. As they spoke through an interpreter, Howard listened in shock. The news was almost beyond comprehension. He had the men repeat their story to the Indian agent and Joseph's father-in-law, a chief whose band lived at Lapwai. They, too, were flummoxed, as was the interpreter James Reuben. They understood the killings as isolated acts of revenge — a crime and not an act of war, capable of being resolved through ordinary justice.

"Insist[ing] that Joseph would not fight," Howard wrote, they volunteered to ride out to the non-treaties, speak reason to them, and bring them onto the reservation.

The bloodshed beggared belief because even though Joseph's people and the other bands had rejected the 1863 treaty, they were hardly renegades. For years they had been participating in a long and protracted process; if they were called "nontreaty" Indians, it was not because they rejected any possibility of a productive accord with the United States. Rather, they had regarded themselves as allies of the American government for seventy years and were "nontreaty" only because they felt that they deserved different terms — a different treaty. After dozens of meetings and councils, Howard, his officers, and a number of civilian officials had gained a ready familiarity with Joseph and Ollokot and had often felt respect and sympathy for their cause. When White Bird had appeared at Lapwai the week before and watched the soldiers drill, at least one soldier regarded him not as a nuisance but as a "grand looking Indian," admired for the eagle's wing in his headdress. As tensions and grievances with the settlers grew in recent years, the officials had come to rely on the chiefs as partners in keeping the peace. They felt fondness for the Indians, even imagined that they were friends.

As the news rippled through Fort Lapwai, the officers' wives sought each other out. Desolate with worry for their husbands, even they found it hard to contemplate war with the nontreaty Nez Perce bands. "It is dreadful to think what might happen," the post surgeon's wife wrote in a letter home on June 15, "but I can't think these Indians, those we have seen so often, are going to fight the troops."

The women gathered on Captain Perry's front porch, where Howard was talking with the garrison's officers. Reservation Indians were sitting on the steps. "The most intense feeling now existed at the fort and at the agency," Howard would remember. The general made a special effort "to preserve his equipoise, . . . to be perfectly cool and self-possessed," when the reservation Indians who had ridden out to find Joseph returned after just a few hours with a courier, another Indian, bearing two more letters from Mount Idaho. Howard read the messages to himself before sharing them with his officers, trying not "to be moved by" what he called "the contagion of others' excitement."

The violence was spreading to the Camas Prairie. Nez Perce warriors were intercepting settlers as they fled their isolated farms and ranches for the comparative safety of Mount Idaho. The dispatches that Howard read were spare: one man mortally wounded, another "killed and left in the road," a third shot in the hip, a woman with broken legs. The letters did not convey the full horror of the previous night on the prairie. The woman with broken legs had been found crawling through the brush, shot through the calves and so slick with blood that she was mistaken for an Indian. Settlers found another woman crazed and inconsolable, gored with an arrow and raped; her three-year-old daughter was hiding behind her slain father, bleeding from her neck, the end of her tongue bitten off. But even without those details, and with only a hint of a second, more widespread killing spree along the Salmon River,

Howard understood the gravity of the crisis he was facing. "Don't delay a moment . . . send to Lewiston and hasten up," the first letter implored. An hour later, the same writer begged, "Hurry up; hurry!"

Howard had two cavalry companies on hand — one commanded by Perry and the other by Trimble, with fewer than a hundred men in total. It would be impossible for the infantry companies at Lapwai to cover the sixty miles to Mount Idaho quickly enough to respond to the emergency, and regardless, given how widespread the violence was, Howard needed them to keep the fort secure. Two more cavalry companies were a hundred miles south in the Wallowa Valley, sent under Whipple's command to keep the peace while Joseph's band gathered their herds and left. To deliver a message to Whipple and get his men to Lapwai would take days. Howard could send orders by telegraph to the rest of his forces, most of them spread thin along the length of the Columbia, but the nearest telegraph station was at Fort Walla Walla, about 115 miles away.

With little time for decision, Howard quickly scrawled a note for the settlers blockading themselves at Mount Idaho. He had resolved to send the two cavalry companies at Lapwai to their aid. "Help shall be prompt and complete," he wrote. As one courier rode southeast with the message, Howard's aide-de-camp headed west with another set of messages to deliver to Walla Walla and wire to Portland and to division headquarters in San Francisco — it would be a journey of sixteen hours by horse and stage. While the infantry at Walla Walla and Whipple's cavalry companies in the Wallowa Valley would head directly to Lapwai,

Howard wanted as many troops in the Department of the Columbia as possible to steam for Lewiston.

It was late afternoon on June 15 when Howard issued his orders and a bugler blew the clarion notes of "Boots and Saddles" — the call for the cavalry companies to mount and assemble — but the general knew it would be hours before Perry and Trimble's cavalry companies could ride into the field. Preparing them for battle was not merely a matter of rounding up from pasture and saddling a hundred army horses. After a decade of Indian wars in the West, the army had come to realize that the success of soldiers on horseback depended on another animal entirely: the mule. Behind every cavalry column was a ragged mule train, laden with hundreds of pounds of food, ammunition, and medical supplies. An army at war needed mules by the dozen, as well as a legion of packers who could load them — an art as much as a science, crucial to the mules' ability to carry the most supplies for the longest distances. Though civilians, packers were often heavily armed and well aware of the dangers they faced alongside the cavalry. At the same time, they had to have a special temperament to deal day after day with the nasty, ornery, uncooperative beasts.

At Lapwai, Howard had only five mules at hand to accompany the cavalry. He ordered the post's quartermaster to Lewiston to hire thirty more, but they would arrive too late. The companies had to leave with a small train and just a few days of supplies, many of them in the soldiers' saddlebags, enough to allow them to relieve the settlers at Mount Idaho, but little more. As officers, soldiers, and packers prepared for the journey, the fort was a hive of activity — "constant motion," Howard wrote. At the same time, after hours of trading gossip and opinions about the outrages of the previous day, everyone worked mostly in silence. It reminded the general of the time "before a battle, when men are often pale and thoughtful."

At 8 p.m. the cavalry left the fort, riding toward the darkness spreading east to west across the sky. Countless times during the Civil War, Howard had been at the head of columns of men. Now he had to stay at Lapwai and organize his fighting force as it came together from across the Northwest. Captain Perry was in charge of the expedition, with Trimble leading his company. Eight Nez Perce men from the reservation joined them as scouts, in the hope that they could convince the nontreaties to stop fighting. Howard imagined that the Indians would put down their weapons at first sight of the army. "Think we will make short work of it," he telegraphed his commanding officer in the Division of the Pacific, General Irvin McDowell. But after the bitter surprise of the previous day, Howard could not know for sure. Perhaps he would have to send more troops forward. Or if other tribes west along the Columbia joined the uprising, he would have to deploy his soldiers elsewhere.

As he watched the cavalry ride away, Howard was not alone — the infantry companies and their officers remained. But he took special notice that the women of the fort were watching, too. Trimble's and Parnell's wives lived in Walla Walla, and Perry's wife was on her way to Portland. Only Lieutenant Theller's wife was there to say goodbye. "To remain behind and wait," Howard would later write, "it awakened in my heart unusual sympathy for other watchers, nay, a painful feeling hard to bear. . . . Who but woman is equal to the task?"

For a month, Howard believed that Joseph and the other nontreaty leaders had listened to him and reconciled themselves to moving onto the reservation. Even if they had initially resisted, they appreciated that they had no other option and would make the best of their new lives. But over the course of one day, Howard's plans for the Nez Perce and for his own redemption had come to ruin. A sense of serene confidence gave way to the churn of deep anxiety. He had to keep busy. He tried to read. He pored over maps of the area — impossibly rippled with rivers, mountains, and canyons — and calculated how long it would take for cavalry to ride and infantry to march from one point to the next. He paced back and forth, for hours.

Chapter 12
A Perfect Panic

The moon was a wan smile, a thin crescent overwhelmed by night, shedding little light on the path ahead. The road from Fort Lapwai to Mount Idaho sixty miles to the southeast would be excruciating for Companies F and H of the 1st Cavalry, steep for miles through hills and canyons before it reached the prairie. Thickets of tree branches reached for horses and riders along the way, and roots cracked and knobbed the ground. The mules were unsettled, as they always were on the first day of a long journey, and frequently fell behind, forcing the entire column to stop again and again through the night. The road was soft after a rain-soaked early June. The darkest spots, shaded by rock or forest, were thick mires of mud — ripe for an ambush. Wrapped in their overcoats against the cold night, the soldiers stayed awake, certain that they were being watched by Nez Perce scouts hiding behind every ridgeline and tangle of brush.

For most of Perry and Trimble's men, riding slowly through the dark on a treacherous road was an apt metaphor for their lives in the army. While their officers had decades of military experi-ence — one sergeant had fought in the Mexican

War thirty years before — almost all of the privates were in their first enlistment. Only about twenty of the hundred or so men had experienced battle. An equal number had been in the cavalry less than a year. Mostly in their twenties and mostly born overseas — Ireland, England, and Scotland, Germany, Austria, France, and Denmark — they could well remember their attempts to succeed in civilian life. In the towns and cities of the eastern United States, they had plastered walls and painted them, cobbled shoes and shoed horses, built boats, laid bricks, made jewelry, cut hair, butchered meat, and worked in factories. But in the years following the Panic of 1873, it was hard enough to prosper. All many could hope for was mere survival, and it was separated from starvation by the thinnest of lines. For various reasons, good and bad — "reverses in business," a ruinous thirst for strong drink — the 1st Cavalry's recruits had run out of options in the world they knew, so they traded their failures for something entirely unknown. Thousands of miles from home, they learned to wake up, get dressed, eat their meals, go to bed, and mount and dismount to a bugle's call. On the alien landscapes of the West — mountains, desert — they practiced riding their horses in formation and at a gallop and took cursory instruction on how to shoot their Springfield carbines and Colt .45 pistols. The idea of fighting Indians was more than terrifying — it was the latest curse in their already afflicted lives. In prior years, when the cavalry rode from Walla Walla to the Wallowa Valley to keep the peace, a few recruits deserted rather than face Nez Perce warriors. But in June 1877, in the darkness, in the mountains, in the mud, there was no place to go.

The next morning the cavalry approached a ranch house in the gentle hills of the Camas Prairie, near the town of Cottonwood, forty miles from Lapwai. The place was deserted but serene. Near a shed the soldiers found that in the past couple of days someone had rifled through a few wagons that were full of supplies. Otherwise, a sergeant wrote, the house "looked so homelike and peaceful that it was hard to realize there was anything wrong or that the owner was lying dead in the road a few miles beyond." Stopping for breakfast and setting their horses loose in an enclosed field, many of the soldiers were capable only of lying on the ground to sleep. After a few hours, around noon, the exhausted men were back in their saddles.

They rode slowly, with advance riders on all sides to guard against attack. At various distances along the horizon, they saw columns of smoke marking the big sky. Piles of hay, mainly — the soldiers were not quite sure what to make of them, perhaps signals of some sort. After a few hours, they encountered the first unambiguous evidence that the Camas Prairie was a large rolling battlefield. They found an abandoned wagon, attacked two nights earlier when the owners of the ranch tried to flee for Mount Idaho, a tableau of misery and terror — boxes thrown across the path, slain horses at roadside, the smell of rot, the stillness of death beneath the industry of insects on carrion. Indian attackers had emptied a barrel of whiskey but scattered dozens of cigars. The bodies were gone.

A short distance up the road, the cavalry saw other people for the first time since leaving Fort Lapwai — a mounted patrol of settlers waiting for

331

them in a line. Together they rode until sunset, when they reached Grangeville, a farming hamlet just a couple of miles from Mount Idaho. Preparing to stay the night, the soldiers let their horses loose in an enclosed pasture, but the animals lay down to sleep, too exhausted to stand after twenty-four hours of walking. Sergeant Michael McCarthy, a ruddy thirty-two-year-old — born in Canada, ten years of army service in the West — was so tired that he felt he could sleep "even if there were Indians around," but the cooks riding with the cavalry gave him a reason to stay awake: "bean soup, my great favorite on a march."

As soldiers foraged for wood and built their fires, settlers streamed into their camp. Much of their talk was what McCarthy described as "ghastly gossip": who was dead, who was dying, who was missing, who had been outraged. But the mounted patrol of settlers who had accompanied the cavalry to Grangeville had another story to tell. They urged Captain Perry not to spend the night on the Camas Prairie. The Indians had left the area before noon, they said, and were headed back toward the Salmon River at White Bird Canyon, the place the Indians called Lahmotta. In their view, there was no need to defend Grangeville and Mount Idaho — it was far more important to capture the nontreaty bands before they crossed over the Salmon back toward Oregon and the Wallowa Valley and would, in Perry's words, "be comparatively safe from pursuit." Perry called his officers together to hear out the settlers.

The leader of the mounted patrol, Ad — short for Arthur — Chapman, was a gaunt, lank-mustached Iowan with a wide-brimmed white hat. He was a talker, and the officers felt compelled to listen. Having raised horses for fifteen years along White Bird Creek, he had unsurpassed knowledge of the place where the nontreaty bands had fled. And he claimed to know the Indians as no one else did, married to an Umatilla woman and fluent in Nez Perce after living with a tribesman, according to the man's nephew, "in the same house, just as brothers." Unless the cavalry deployed now, Chapman said, they would lose any opportunity to capture the rogue Nez Perce families. And if the officers did choose to fight rather than let the Indians escape, Chapman added, he was confident that they would catch the Indians at a vulnerable moment, right as they were crossing the Salmon River. Chapman's words suggested shame if the cavalry stayed in Grangeville, and glory if they rode for White Bird Canyon. Although their soldiers were desperate for rest, Perry, Trimble, and Lieutenants Theller and Parnell had no qualms about another long night. Before the beans on the fire had softened, before the horses had finished their feed, a bugler blew Boots and Saddles once again. The men were ordered to leave everything behind save their rifles and revolvers, ammunition and long coats. Going on the offensive "was the best, in fact the only thing to do," Perry later wrote.

Past midnight, after three or four hours of riding in the dark, the cavalry, guided by a small group of armed settlers, including Chapman, and accompanied by the Nez Perce scouts, crossed the ridge separating the Camas Prairie from the Salmon River Valley. They had reached the top of White Bird Canyon. The column halted, and soldiers swung down from their horses. They would wait until light to attack. For several hours,

Sergeant McCarthy walked among his men in Company H, trying to keep everyone awake but often finding soldiers and horses lying next to each other, fast asleep. As darkness softened to dawn, the orders came whispered from front to back: "Mount without noise or loud commands and move forward."

No one could see the destination. The canyon below was steep, narrow, still cloaked in night. The valley bottomed out maybe four miles away at White Bird Creek and the Salmon River. There was no sign of the Indians. But as they prepared to descend two by two into darkness, many of the soldiers heard a coyote howl — just one, just once — "a long howling cry," according to Lieutenant Parnell. It received no answer. "Not quite natural," McCarthy judged. "That cry was an Indian signal," a private in Company F was certain, "enough to make one's hair stand straight up."

At the bottom of the canyon, shielded from sight behind a series of rolling buttes and hidden among the trees that grew along White Bird Creek, the Nez Perce camp at Lahmotta looked like any other summer settlement. The women had raised about thirty teepees for a few hundred people — members of Joseph's, White Bird's, and Toohoolhoolzote's bands — as they had at this very place many times before. But in the darkness of June 16, the normal routines of a summer camping ground, the meals and preparations, the games and stories dictated by the season and its bounty, the social occasion of disparate bands coming together, warped into something else, known and unknown.

For a time there was something resembling a

celebration, but without joy. Many of the men, young and old, made themselves sick with drink, from barrels they had taken from the homes and stores and wagons they had attacked. They had avenged trespasses, insults, cheatings, beatings, and unpunished murders. They had raided and warred, acted in ways that for generations had turned boys into men and men into great men. Some of the warriors had shed their first blood. But as familiar as the experiences of the past two days had been, so similar to the stories they told and retold, these men knew that they had stepped outside their history. They had not attacked the Snake or Blackfeet or Crow or Lakota. Their victims were whites. Instead of strengthening and perpetuating their sense of self and band and tribe, instead of creating new stories with new heroes that their children and grandchildren would tell, they knew they had started a fight that would be their undoing. The army would come. Everything would be lost. So they burned their throats with whiskey — and then felt nothing, colder and blacker than night.

Hours before dawn, a sentinel rode into camp from high up in the canyon. Having heard the dull pounding of a hundred horses, he knew the soldiers were coming. For the Nez Perce men who were sober, or at least sober enough to awaken — there was no rousing about half of the 130 or so men of fighting age — the rest of the night was a rush of collective enterprise and intensely indi-vidual reckoning. Joseph, Ollokot, White Bird, and Toohoolhoolzote met and asked their bands to work together to round up the herds. With their horses close, and the fastest and surest ones tied up, they could fight, and they could escape.

The sky lightened, and two more scouts rode into camp to report that the army was moving toward them: "Big bunch of them!" In dawn's chill, maybe five or six dozen men began stripping for battle, the only ones able to wake up. Some had never experienced war — had never had the occasion to conceive of themselves as warriors — and had to be convinced that they were warriors now, that now was a time to fight. Many only had bows and arrows or hunting pieces like what one warrior described as "an old-time musket loaded from the muzzle," probably traded for fur pelts decades earlier. While the cavalry slowly descended into the canyon, each man performed his own ritual that had been revealed to him alone in conversation with his *wey-ya-kin* — paint and medicine to wear that would inspire valor or keep bullets away, a song to sing that would bring focus and purpose to the coming battle, that would help one cross the boundary from life to death.

One by one, the men gathered behind a series of buttes and knolls, a ridgeline that separated the campgrounds from the canyon. In some of these rolling swells lay the remains of chiefs of earlier generations. Over the previous month, the non-treaty bands had reconciled themselves to leaving their traditional lands. Joseph had anguished over breaking the pledge he had made to his dying father never to abandon the place where his ancestors were buried. Now the warriors were taking a stand on hallowed ground.

While the warriors waited, the leaders of the three bands remained hopeful that they could avoid war. Joseph's commitment to peace, however suspect to many of the young men, continued to make sense to White Bird and Toohoolhoolzote.

The cavalry had never been their enemy. In previous years, when the settlers had armed themselves for war and committed acts that cried for revenge, Joseph and Ollokot had worked with the army to cool any tension and advance their cause. The officers had listened to their concerns. Perhaps they would do so again. Until bullets started flying, the chiefs could imagine that there was no war, just another occasion to negotiate; the cavalry column was not a fighting force but another group of government officials. The chiefs appointed six tribesmen who would approach the cavalry under a flag of truce, and Joseph and Ollokot joined the men behind the buttes — Ollokot as a leader, Joseph as one of the many. Joseph's influence would be limited in the event that fighting broke out. He would never be a war chief. Many other leaders had far more extensive battle experience. He would defer to them, knowing that if he went against their decisions, few others would follow him. The warriors received a final instruction: they must not fire the first shot.

After years of insult, days of fury and dread, and one night of frantic preparation, the wait for a final confrontation felt interminable. Some, like Joseph's nephew Yellow Wolf, climbed to the top of the buttes and peered over, trying to spot the army in the early light. The canyon ran steep downhill from north to south, bounded east and west by imposing ridges. Long and narrow up high, then widening toward the bottom, the canyon floor knolled and buckled. From Yellow Wolf's perspective, it was not easy to find a path to the top, where the soldiers supposedly were. The rolling terrain created a myriad of draws that seemingly climbed the canyon but led nowhere —

dead ends at sheer walls impossible to climb. With the sun rising, the young warrior was finally able to discern more than just rock. "Something seemed moving away up country," he said. "Yes, there came the soldiers a good distance off. We all lay flat and watched."

The soldiers leaned back in their saddles, cold, hungry, and exhausted, as the horses walked an old wagon road on the eastern edge of the canyon. As the path meandered up onto the bluffs and then back down among the willows in a dry creek bed, the soldiers were convinced they were being watched. To their left and right, sharp rocky rises provided innumerable places for attack; someone could walk along the far side of the ridge completely undetected, shoot down at the cavalry, and escape with no way to give chase. The soldiers would never know that their enemies were coming. Even in silence, it would have been hard to hear over the step of the horses, the creak of their saddles, and the wind in their ears.

The men took no comfort when early in their descent they heard a woman's voice shouting, "My God! My God! Soldiers!" Thick shadows emerged from the underbrush: a woman and two daughters, in rags, shivering, starved — one of the girls, four years old, with a broken arm. Three days they had been hiding, since fleeing their house at the bottom of the canyon in the initial waves of violence on June 14. That morning, the woman's husband and girls' father — the storekeeper Samuel Benedict — had been shot through the thighs by the first group of attackers. He survived, but a second group returned and killed him as he climbed out a window and tried to

338

escape. The officers and men felt sympathy for Bell Benedict and her children, but their appearance seemed to dash any hope for a peaceful resolution. The woman said that Indians had been passing into the canyon all night. The Nez Perce scouts remained with the soldiers, ready to negotiate, but the riders knew they were going up against, in Lieutenant Parnell's phrasing, "Indian deviltry and Indian warfare," wicked and relentless. They passed the Benedicts as much food as they could but kept going, deeper into the canyon.

In the full light of morning, the cavalry approached the bottom of the canyon, their path opening onto a rolling valley maybe five hundred yards wide. Straight ahead of them was the succession of ridgelines and knolls that they would have to cross to reach the Indians at White Bird Creek and the Salmon River. Captain Perry sent Lieutenant Theller ahead to lead an advance guard of eight soldiers, including a trumpeter to relay messages, along with the settlers and Nez Perce scouts. Perry's company would ride behind them, followed by Trimble's company. The soldiers took off their overcoats and loaded their rifles.

The Nez Perce warriors watched their peace delegation climb the ridge, white flag in hand, and then vanish. After a quiet moment, a single shot cracked. The peace party rode back over the hill to take cover, and soldiers appeared at the ridgetop — about twenty men, some in uniform and some, as Yellow Wolf observed from his knoll to the east, "dressed more like a citizen." The young warrior realized that the people in civilian clothes were local settlers when he recognized Ad Chapman's big white hat and white horse, unmistakable against the roll of pale green grass. Chapman turned toward Yellow Wolf and a dozen or so other warriors and might have recognized them, too. Yellow Wolf had counted Chapman as a friend. Now the settler raised his rifle and fired at them. The soldiers followed suit, but it was impossible to shoot straight while sitting atop spent, skittish horses. From his mount, a few yards apart from the rest of the advance guard, the trumpeter began to play.

The warriors well knew what the trumpeter was doing — "calling orders . . . to [the] fighting soldiers," judged Two Moons, who was standing by Yellow Wolf. Even if they had never fought against the cavalry before, the men had seen the riders maneuver and drill at Fort Lapwai and in the Wallowa Valley. Hundreds of yards away and downhill, armed only with a bow and arrow, Yellow Wolf knew he could do nothing to stop the trumpeter. But Otstotpoo (Fire Body), an older man, had a rifle. He turned to Two Moons and said, "You now watch! I will make a good shot and kill that bugler!" He took aim and picked the man from his horse before he could finish playing.

As the rest of the cavalry raced toward the advance guard's position, Captain Perry tried to order his men to drop their rifles, draw their pistols, and charge the Indians, only to learn that his trumpeter had dropped his instrument in the rush forward. With one bugler dead and the other with nothing to play, Perry had a sickening feeling. "A Cavalry command on a battlefield without a trumpet is like a ship at sea without a helm perfectly unmanageable," he would say. His voice could not carry over any distance in a canyon crackling with gunfire. Reaching the ridge, Perry's company took a position at the center, with Trimble's company deploying to his right — toward the west of the canyon — and the settlers taking the knolls to the east. The soldiers dismounted and sent their horses back down the hill. Together the cavalry and settlers had formed a long, thin battle line — secure on the high ground, Perry thought.

Just below the settlers, Two Moons led the warriors around him — maybe fifteen other men — to their horses. They galloped up a crease hidden in the hills to the east of the settlers and attacked from the side. If the cavalry had little training or experience in warfare, the settlers, aside from one Confederate veteran, had none. The air around them whipping with bullets, they ran away so quickly — after about five minutes — that it was difficult for their foes to believe that anyone had been fighting from the knoll. Two Moons said that he "hardly saw them at all." A settler remembered an Indian running after him, calling out, " 'Stop, stop' (so he could get a shot at me), but I did not stop."

From their position — protected high ground to the left and even behind the army lines — the warriors with Two Moons had a complete view of the battle. As they poured fire on Perry's company, they watched as a group of Nez Perce fighters across the canyon to the west, under Ollokot's lead, charged Trimble's company. While many of the riders were hanging off their horses and shooting under cover, three men rode tall, side by side, wearing long red blanket coats. Two Moons recognized them: Wahlitits and Sarpsis Ilppilp, who had shed the first blood along the Salmon

341

River three days earlier, as well as a third warrior, Tipyahlahnah Kapskaps (Strong Eagle). They rode as if they were daring the soldiers to shoot them, the kind of bold action that was immortalized in story and song. "Those three warriors came through that wild charge . . . untouched," Two Moons marveled. "They did not pay attention to enemy bullets that must have been as hail about them."

As the settlers fled from their position at Perry's left, the captain realized that his men had been flanked and soon would be surrounded. To his right, the warriors' charge had left Trimble's company shocked and disoriented, gasping in a cloud of dirt, barely able to fire their weapons. Soldiers fled for their horses, but the animals were just as panicked, bucking and scattering, falling from gunfire seemingly on all sides. After marching for thirty-six hours, the troops had been routed in just as many minutes.

The soldiers who survived White Bird Canyon would remember almost nothing of their foes. They heard the air whistle with lead, saw their comrades and horses wounded and dying, but barely laid eyes on Indians before running away. The enemy's power was an anonymous fury, shrouded in dust and smoke. When the Indians charged, the soldiers could not see who was shooting at them; it looked and felt like they were in the middle of a horse stampede. Racked with thirst, ears ringing, the soldiers imagined they were outnumbered two or three times over, by warriors who had studied the latest in cavalry tactics. But the warriors remained out of sight. What the soldiers saw instead — what imprinted itself on their minds — was the grassy roll of the canyon as they turned away from the field of battle, impossibly long, dauntingly steep, with no clear route to safety. To escape annihilation, the soldiers found themselves with two choices: they could run on foot or try to ride their exhausted and terrified horses. With the enemy shooting close behind them and to their left and right, they took any path they could find.

After the cavalry broke and ran, the Nez Perce warriors experienced the battle in a completely different way than their enemies. It was intensely personal. The canyon became an intimate killing ground. Running uphill was nothing extraordinary for Nez Perce men and their horses. Again and again, they cornered, surrounded, and overwhelmed soldiers. In the folds of the canyon, there were no long distances. It was impossible to fight a faceless foe. The warriors encountered men, flesh, bone, and blood. They were so near — and the experience of battle so novel — that some warriors remembered being surprised that the soldiers tried to take a stand instead of, in one Nez Perce man's words, "receiving [them] and asking [them] questions." Encountering the unarmed Nez Perce scouts, the warriors did not shoot them. Instead, they taunted the reservation Indians, yelling at them to return to their homes and abandon the fight.

Up canyon, the shooting was so close and thick that the warriors giving chase with Joseph and Ollokot had to caution, "Be careful! Don't shoot each other!" The soldiers frantically tried to stay alive. They stripped off their blue shirts, hoping their gray undershirts would blend into the rock. They burrowed into the brush that grew thick in the hollows. They fired their guns until they had no more bullets. Killing them was close work, resembling fights with other tribes, where bludgeoning an opponent face-to-face with a war club — counting coup — was the height of honor and courage. Yellow Wolf, whose arrows had been useless at long distance, now shot one foe in the chest, another in the shoulder, and minutes later used his bow as a club. From a dead soldier, still warm, he picked up a carbine and ammunition belt. Husis Owyeen (Wounded Head) remembered chasing the soldiers armed only with "an old-time pistol with one bullet and the last powder and cap in place." When he encountered a soldier who had been thrown from his horse, the rest of the battle faded for a moment as the warrior found himself in a duel. The soldier raised his gun, but at point-blank distance, one bullet was all Wounded Head needed. He shot the man "between the eyebrows," took his dead foe's gun and cartridges, and left his own old one behind "as a present," the warrior would later say. "Laid it on his breast."

As he watched his men retreat in what he called "a perfect panic," Captain Perry tried to organize the soldiers around him. If they could make any kind of a stand, they could slow their pursuers and allow more to escape unharmed. But few were inspired by his calls, which he shouted to anyone close enough to listen, that they should take a stand and "die right here." "It was impossible for me to exercise any control over the men," Perry later complained, "as they did not pay the slightest attention."

Soldiers found two primary paths to escape, over the steep rise to the west of the canyon or back up the old wagon road to the east. Horses stumbled and collapsed on the terrain, ran wounded until they died. One threw its rider, killing him. Perry and Trimble escaped west, the commanding officer on foot, his horse too tired to run, forced to watch Trimble race ahead of him out of sight. Their lieutenants, Parnell and Theller, retreated along the old eastern path. Parnell, veteran of the English cavalry and dozens of Civil War battles, kept his men fighting all the way up the canyon, for miles, "from knoll to knoll," he wrote, "waiting at every halt until the Indians came near enough to receive the contents of our carbines" — even if they never hit anyone. With his sergeant Michael McCarthy, they "scolded, swore, and abjured" the men to stay in their deliberate formation "if for no other reason," McCarthy wrote, "than to breathe themselves." Haunted by the faces of the wounded men they were leaving behind, the sergeant had one horse fall under him, then another. Trying to climb on foot up a steep rise as pursuers fired at him, McCarthy fell off the side of the road, then watched the warriors gallop past. He cocked his pistol, considered shooting himself, and then made a different resolution: he would crawl into the bushes and wait out the Indians.

Parnell and his surviving men reached the top of the canyon at the same time Perry and many of the settlers made it there from the west — a moment of relief after hours of terror, even if the fighting seemed far from over. They found Bell Benedict, passed her children to two riders, and gave her a horse. But soon after they began riding, the woman was thrown from her mount. She crawled back, once again, into the brush.

Captain Trimble was long gone, riding to Mount Idaho, and so, Perry presumed, was Lieutenant Theller. Within minutes of leading the advance guard that fired the first bullets, Theller had no horse and, clutching his carbine, struck Parnell as "somewhat confused and excited." "He seemed to have lost all control of himself," Parnell later said, and it appeared to Perry that Theller "did not seem to know what he was doing." As the retreat began, Parnell caught a horse for Theller, and Perry appealed to his lieutenant to try to organize the soldiers to fight. One settler remembered Theller regaining his sense, rallying a dozen or so men to make a stand, then leading them farther up the old wagon road.

Theller loved racing horses. He relished a game of chance. Now, riding bareback through White Bird Canyon, he gambled with his life. Halfway to the canyon's head, he and seven men rode off the road — perhaps they came under fire, or someone saw a shortcut. They may have lost the path, or Theller's wits escaped him again. After a short distance, he and his men slid to the bottom of a steep ravine, where they found themselves snarled in thorns. With Nez Perce warriors galloping close, then surrounding them, Theller and his soldiers drew their weapons. They were low on bullets and out of luck.

CHAPTER 13
DEATH IN GHASTLY FORMS

On June 27, Charles Erskine Scott Wood walked through White Bird Canyon and was staggered by the pall of death. Thirty-four soldiers, more than a third of Captain Perry's cavalry, had fallen over ten miles of country. Coming from the Camas Prairie to the head of the canyon and then down, Wood saw the battle's effects in reverse — the dead scattered far apart toward the end of the desperate retreat, clustered more tightly at the initial firing lines. If the tall grass, rippling hills, and brush-clotted hollows did not reveal the corpses easily, the intense smell gave them away.

In his years as a judge advocate traveling around the Department of the Columbia, Wood had gotten to know dozens of soldiers in the fullness of their idiosyncrasies and imperfections. But deep in the canyon, the air tight with summer heat, the dead all looked the same. Exposed ten days to intense sun and afternoon thunderstorms, they barely resembled humans. "Arms and cheeks gone, bellies swollen," Wood recorded in his diary, "blackened faces, mutilations, heads gone." Stripped of their weapons and ammunition by Nez Perce warriors and the women following in their wake, the bodies had been trampled by horses, picked over by the birds and beasts of the canyon, and ravaged by insects. They had "changed into awful shapes, too dreadful for our eyes," a young lieutenant named Harry Bailey recalled. A private described the carnage as simply "the most sickening sight I ever seen."

Finding a body was not a momentary horror. It marked the beginning of a prolonged ordeal. The dead had decomposed too much to be moved, so the infantry searching the canyon could not dig one burial trench for all the bodies. Instead, they had to stand by each foul, bloated mass and go to work with their wide trowel bayonets, first scratching shallow graves out of the rocky soil and then using their spades to roll the bodies in. Sweat, thirst, sickening rot: the task was too much for anyone to do for long. "We had to run a distance every little while," Lieutenant Bailey admitted. With each body that was buried, the soldiers placed large stones atop the loose soil. Otherwise, their fallen comrades would find no peace in White Bird Canyon. Coyotes were waiting to unearth the remains.

Most of the bodies had been rolled into graves the day before Wood rejoined his company, but a good number of the dead, including Lieutenant Theller, remained missing. Not being able to find them unsettled General Howard and the eight army companies — two cavalry companies that had come from the Wallowa Valley, five infantry companies, and one artillery, more than two hundred men — that had set out from Fort Lapwai on June 22 under his personal command. The experience of informing Delia Theller of her husband's death was still raw for Howard. "It is easier to go into a battle than to do this," he would later write. "I endeavored to control myself, and break the tidings gently. But Mrs. Theller read them in my face before I could speak, and words had no place."

The officers could still picture the grieving wife pacing the fort's grounds wraithlike, "no tears, . . . in a half-dazed fashion," wrote Wood's commanding officer, Captain Robert Pollock. At times she bemoaned her husband's fate. "Oh, my poor Ned," she would say, "lying there with his face blackening in the sun." Soon after the news arrived of the debacle at White Bird Canyon, rumors of an impending Indian attack cast the fort into a panic. Delia Theller wore Lieutenant Theller's cartridge belt and brandished his gun "as if she were ready to avenge her husband," the post surgeon's daughter remembered.

Mostly, though, Delia Theller placed her hopes in the stories of several people who had been presumed killed by the Indians but days later emerged from White Bird Canyon unharmed. Sergeant McCarthy, after hiding in brush and forest and casting aside his heavy riding boots, walked fifteen or so miles until a group of settlers near Grangeville found him, his sore feet in makeshift wraps that he had fashioned from the legs of his drawers. Bell Benedict reached Mount Idaho after the Nez Perce warrior Wounded Head found her wandering, not long after he had killed his first soldier of the war. To her surprise and eternal gratitude, he "instructed her to escape with her life" and, as he would remember, "shook hands with her." Perhaps, Delia Theller imagined, her husband would also find his way back to the living world. Before Howard's column left the fort, she asked Captain Pollock "to try to find him sleeping or a captive," the captain wrote. "She refused to believe him dead. . . . Made me feel squeamish."

Back with his company for the first time since early April, Charles Erskine Scott Wood was struck by the grim mood. In his diary he recorded no pleasant social calls with General Howard. "Gentlemanly officers looking like herders," Wood wrote, "rough aspect of everyone, business and not holiday costumes." It was a jarring contrast to the freedom from army discipline, the explorer's sense of possibility, that he had embraced in Alaska. Only a week earlier his steamer from the north had crossed the Columbia River Bar, and he first learned that he would be heading to war. The news was cruel, just what he thought he had avoided by leaving Sitka. When the steamer made its first stop on the Columbia at Astoria, the lieutenant was greeted by an excited crowd that urged the soldiers, in his rendering, "Go in and kill 'em all boys. Don't spare the bloody savages." Wood was taken aback. "Confound these cusses," he wrote in his diary. "Wish they were going to fight them instead of standing on a wharf and pat-[ting] us on the back."

After docking in Portland and visiting General Howard's wife, then stopping at Fort Vancouver just long enough to "say howdy do and goodbye in a breath," Wood steamed east on the *California*. The boat was crowded with five anxious army companies and laden with "the munitions of war, field pieces and gatlings and howitzers." Weathering the rapids, Wood was uncomfortable, with no personal supplies for the campaign ahead. His blankets and clothes — "everything I own," he wrote — had been in the ship's hold since it had left Sitka, and he needed a hat. But the journey could have been worse. At the first word of trouble, Wood's infantry company, waiting in a dusty camp near Wallula for Joseph to move onto the reservation, had steamed to Lewiston in a small boat with twenty-five cavalry. "Men all over the superstructure, squealing, winnying, neighing horses, full of fear as were some of the men," Captain Pollock wrote home. "It was an odoriferous trip as we huffed and puffed up the Snake River. It looked as if some of these horses had not evacuated their bowels and bladders for six months. This also goes for some of the command who are strictly landlubbers."

Along the way, Wood kept watching the people who had gathered to watch him. The well-wishers did not spark any desire to fight. At the Columbia River Cascades, after observing a "party of damsels gaze on the defenders of the Country," Wood felt "very much like staying in Dalles and keeping some of the pretty girls that look so favorably upon us from any sadness or anxiety on *my* account." East of the Dalles, he noticed a "poor Indian" standing on the rocks to "wave encouraging signals to us to go on and kill and be killed. Hard to tell," Wood jotted, "which they prefer."

At every stop on the river, dire rumors circulated: sixty men missing, Lapwai abandoned. "Don't believe it," Wood wrote. Still, as the boat neared Lewiston, the lieutenant was gripped by what he called a "peculiar nervous feeling of going to death." Immune to the scenery from the Columbia River to the Snake, Wood passed the hours deep in "the desire to investigate immortality, thoughts on death, inability to change the mode and tenor of life and thoughts." Surrounded by other soldiers, he could only consider "each ones expectation that *he* will escape" the coming campaign with his life.

After days of airy reflection, landing in Lewiston on June 24 awakened Wood to the protean realities of campaigning. Lapwai was abustle, having already sent Howard's column off and now preparing to dispatch many more companies of soldiers in search of the renegade Nez Perce bands. The amount of hardtack, bacon, tobacco, coffee, tea, and sugar to sustain hundreds of soldiers for any length of time was immense. But if Wood felt bound for tragedy, he saw only comedy in the packers' attempts to load the dozens of braying mules that Fort Lapwai's adjutant had managed to hire from outfitters in Lewiston. No matter how disciplined a column of soldiers might be, the mule trains followed them in rough parody, "an irregular body," General Howard would write, "going backward and forward, hither and thither, unstable as water."

Even the troops that set out with Wood on June 25 were, in the Lapwai adjutant's delicate phrasing, "fresh from garrison life and not hardened to marching." Through driving rain, "pouring rain," Wood wrote, "cold drenching rain — hail," they made slow progress to the Camas Prairie, then passed through a ghostly sequence of deserted ranches the next day. Everywhere he looked, the lieutenant noted signs of sudden terror and lives interrupted — "flowers and chickens uncared for, milk pails left on the fence" — and later, graves lining the trail.

Finally catching up with his company on June 27, Wood found soldiers who all seemed convinced that at any moment they could be attacked, that they, too, could wind up rotting in the sun. Every coyote howl, they feared, was a war cry. More than once, skittish night pickets mistook other soldiers for Indians and fired. There were times when the noises of the dark convinced the soldiers that "we were actually surrounded by a thousand warriors," Lieutenant Bailey wrote. "My young mind imagined every kind of disaster, such as a sudden silent rush upon the tired soldiers, and every throat cut!" Searching White Bird Canyon the day before, they saw someone who appeared to be upright. Guns cocked, they approached in force, only to find it was yet another dead soldier, his body wedged tight into a small tree, "swollen beyond recognition," according to Bailey, "torn and torn with bullets." When afternoon storms rolled through the canyon, the first thunderclaps caused panic. "I thought we were fired upon by a line of Indians along the crest," Bailey wrote. "It was most realistic!"

At the heart of the soldiers' fears was one man: Joseph. After years of negotiating with him, years of being moved in equal measure by his words and powerful physical presence, Howard, his army, and the settlers assumed that it was Joseph who had masterminded all the events of the past two weeks. The deceptive move to Idaho that made it appear as if the nontreaty bands were going onto the reservation, followed by the attacks on settlers when everyone's guard was down — both must have been the product of Joseph's dark genius. The efficient slaughter at White Bird Canyon must have come on Joseph's instructions, according to Howard. "Joseph had managed to conceal in the hollows, and behind the buttes and rocks . . . every sign of his force," the general would later write. Having set the trap, Howard thought, Joseph had surely ordered the charges that smashed Perry's battle lines.

No one else among the Nez Perce leadership seemed remotely as formidable. Soldiers and settlers could joke about Toohoolhoolzote being rough and obstinate and White Bird as unknowably primitive with his face hidden behind an eagle's wing, but Joseph had often commanded their respect. He was, in Howard's reckoning, a remarkable leader, "keen-eyed and active." There was no doubt that he could lead a rebellion, and that the rebellion could spread beyond Nez Perce country. At Fort Lapwai, rumors circulated that "the Non-Treaty Nez Percés, to a man, joined Joseph's forces," as the post surgeon's wife wrote home, "and he is being constantly reinforced by bands from other tribes that are encouraged by the success he has already met with."

As they marched to find and fight the nontreaty Indians, the soldiers tried to learn more about their adversary. Along the way, they sought out settlers who said they knew Joseph. Those who did painted a picture of the chief that gave the troops little comfort. "They tell me he is . . . shrewd," Captain Pollock wrote his wife, "cunning (which we have found), has a fierce affection for his people, blames the government for his woes and will kill anyone who gets in his way without any more qualms than bending a blade of grass."

On the day Wood reached White Bird Canyon, the soldiers finally found Lieutenant Theller's body, along with the others who died beside him. They buried him as they had the others. That night, a

354

downpour mired their camp in what Captain Pollock called "mud till you can't rest." In the midst of the chaos, Wood saw how quickly the horrors of war — "mutilated corpses and death in ghastly forms" — were starting to seem normal, something a fighting man could come to live with. Now that they were done burying the dead, the soldiers prepared for battle the next day. The nontreaty bands had been sighted just on the other side of the Salmon River, waiting, it was supposed, to attack while the soldiers were trying to cross. Many composed their last messages and set aside treasured possessions for their loved ones. At the same time, Wood listened to them joke about dying. The camp grew rowdy, in his description, with "singing story telling and swearing, profanity, carelessness." Wood may have joined in the grim festivities. "Everybody seems very cheerful," judged his commanding officer, Captain Pollock, in a letter home. "While I write, all the young officers are singing . . . in my tent." They could have been singing spirituals or the nostalgic paeans to slave life on a plantation — "The Dear Old Home We Loved So Well" — that touring minstrel shows were making popular. Pollock, writing to his wife and children, did not specify. He called them "nigger songs."

After a sleepless night "for fear of Indian habits of attack," according to Wood, Howard's column assembled at daybreak on June 28. They were now more than five hundred strong, comprised of the companies that had marched with Howard, the additional companies with whom Wood had traveled, and a hundred local volunteers. The cavalry that fought at White Bird Canyon had been reorganized and reinforced. Perry's company had guided Howard through the battlefield, while Trimble's was scouting upriver near Slate Creek, one of the first sites of Nez Perce attacks on settlers.

General Howard knew that his soldiers had been whipped two weeks earlier and that burying the dead had been a demoralizing task. He understood the fear that untried soldiers felt before facing a vicious foe, the dread that veterans had in returning to a fight. In the Civil War, he had suffered defeat, been humiliated by superior officers, and been publicly derided in the press. But he ended the war at General Sherman's side, promoted and celebrated, largely because he was able to distance himself from the immediate trauma of battle, learn from his mistakes, and follow defeat with victory. So much of a fight was out of his hands. It depended on the competence, courage, and sustained attention of his subordinate officers, the discipline and toughness and physical condition of men and horses, the flow of supplies and the availability of reinforcements. The difference between success and failure on the battlefield also hinged on terrain and weather and sheer luck. Howard held to a simple truth: "In a combat," he coolly observed, "both parties cannot be equally successful." Triumph was not the only experience of war. "Every eminent commander has had his lessons of defeat," he wrote. "They are often the essential stepping-stones to subsequent victories."

Upon getting word of Perry's debacle days earlier, Howard began searching for the lessons of White Bird Canyon. The battle soon revealed to him important truths: the "hostiles," as the general called them, knew the country far better than the army did, and the broken, plunging landscape

356

favored them strongly. To prevail, Howard would need something aside from an advantage in numbers and weaponry — he needed a set of tactics that would leave the nontreaty Nez Perce no escape. But until he could figure out those elusive keys to victory, he would take every measure to ensure that his forces would not be routed again. Much as the Union Army had learned to fight during the course of the Civil War, he would proceed with superior force, protected flanks, and strong supply lines — all missing at White Bird Canyon. Although the settlers were crucial partners in helping the army find its way across the land, Howard had to resist the local pressure for immediate action and wait for the right set of circumstances to align before committing his troops.

Over the previous couple of days, army scouts had seen the nontreaty bands on the other side of the Salmon River. After so much bloodshed, Howard knew he could not let them escape. As long as the bands roamed, they posed a grave danger to settlers and threatened to provoke a more general uprising among neighboring bands and tribes. Already the general was receiving reports that Looking Glass, whose nontreaty band had returned to their land on the reservation at the first sign of violence, would soon join the warpath, emboldened by the events at White Bird Canyon. Before preparing to cross the Salmon, he sent Perry's company back to Lapwai for more supplies and ordered the cavalry that had come from the Wallowa Valley — Captain Whipple's companies — to ride on Looking Glass's village, about forty miles northeast through the Camas

Prairie and down the South Fork of the Clearwater River to the Middle Fork, and seize the chief.

On Howard's orders, the infantry and artillery companies approached the Salmon River in the rain. Peering across the water, Wood glimpsed the enemy for the first time. They were far away, he wrote, "Indians speckling the hills like ants," their taunts and occasional gunfire muffled by rain and river. Safe on his side, Wood felt his courage swell. "Nervous eagerness for the fight," he later scratched in his diary, "desire to be at the front. All thoughts of the future vanishing, only want a crack at an Indian and feel no disposition to show any quarter."

The Nez Perce warriors disappeared into the hills almost as soon as Howard's soldiers began shooting back at them. Far more imposing than the Indians, however, was the river itself. From the ridgelines above, the Salmon had looked to Howard like a "little silvery thread." The general knew that Joseph had crossed it twice with all of his people in the month of June — in fact, he had gone across four times — so Howard figured that the river "could really be no obstacle." But up close, at the bottom of the Salmon's deep canyon, the river was revealed to be hundreds of yards wide, flowing fast and angry. The brutal crossing that the general had forced upon Joseph's band to reach the reservation was now Howard's to make. "Torrent," how he repeatedly described the Salmon, was too gentle a word for Captain Pollock. To the captain, the river was "vicious," a "God feared boiling caldron."

While the Nez Perce families had been able to cross on buffalo-skin rafts tethered to horses with riders, it took days for Howard's column to cross, some clinging to a fragile rope they had spent hours stretching across the water, others waiting for boats from Lewiston. Many of the soldiers did not know how to swim. The river ravaged the pack train, and mules "whirled over and over in the awful current as they were swept down," wrote Lieutenant Bailey, but in the end no man or animal drowned. By July 1, Howard's column was on the other side of the Salmon, ready to continue the pursuit.

The trail that the Nez Perce bands and their herds — thousands of horses and cattle — had taken was unmistakable, in places "as broad as a city street," one soldier wrote. Almost immediately above the Salmon River, the path was a muddy gash switchbacking sharp for miles up a steep treacherous rise — the trail ascending, in Wood's estimate, at forty-five degrees. As they climbed, thick rain soaked the soldiers' hats, clothes, blankets, packs, and shoes, uncomfortable even on the best days. It matted hair and beards and made marching slow, heavy, and cold. Already their supplies were running low — just enough for mean breakfasts and dinners of hardtack, bacon, and coffee, and on at least one occasion some "*horse* beef," according to one officer who put a brave face on it, "admired by the Parisians." Camp that night was "misery," Wood wrote, "sleeping in water." Few had tent canvas. Most lay outside, wrapped in their overcoats, pressed tight around large pine campfires.

Up the mountain, rain turned to sleet. Horses and mules scrabbled and slid in washes of mud. Again and again, pack animals lost their balance and were carried by their loads over the side, so many that in his diary Wood named the army's route "Dead Mule Trail." The troops watched with amazement at how quickly the mules tumbled thousands of feet. The falls were so shocking, tail over mane, that some soldiers had to laugh. With plumes of flour spurting from their packs with each impact, the mules' sad fate was "no doubt breaking the Packers' hearts," Lieutenant Bailey dryly remembered. Another officer recalled each sudden horror by exclaiming, "Overboard!" "Of course," he wrote, "there was not much pack and very little serviceable mule left when the bottom was reached."

After two days of struggle, the soldiers reached the ridgetop. But the trail remained dauntingly rugged, all the more so because no one was sure when it would end. One of the Idaho volunteers thought their progress aimless, a mere ten or twelve miles a day, "trusting that Providence would deliver the enemy into our hands without special effort on our part." In camp, enlistees, officers, and civilians alike speculated freely about where the families were headed. Would they cut across the mountains, descend the depths of Hell's Canyon, cross the Snake River, and return to the Wallowa Valley? Where else could they go? Exactly a year after the Battle of Little Bighorn, the soldiers saw unmistakable parallels in their pursuit of Joseph, whom they regarded as a charismatic leader of skilled fighters, the next Sitting Bull. Perhaps, one lieutenant wrote at the time, the Indians were planning to "escape and join the Sioux."

On July 3, the men awoke wet and exhausted, but the clouds were gone. The trail that had bedeviled them now afforded "the most beautiful mountain scenery the eyes ever beheld," Captain Pollock wrote, with long rolling meadows that a reporter accompanying Howard described as being "literally covered with the finest grasses and bespangled with wild flowers of every hue." After braving sleet the day before, now they watched their uniforms "steam and smoke" in strong summer sun — a "sweat bath," a lieutenant wrote. Dry by late afternoon, the column began to get its bearings.

Just as the soldiers began to make good progress, however, they faced another daunting challenge. The trail led them not to the Snake River and Wallowa Valley but down once more to the Salmon. By July 4, Howard was left contemplating a galling turn of events: the hostile bands had led him over the river and through the mountains only to cross back again. He had fallen for an elaborate ruse. Well ahead of his column, the Indians had returned to the Camas Prairie, which was defended only by Perry and Whipple's remnant force, a little more than a hundred men.

Now, the general had to get his men, horses, mules, and artillery across the Salmon River a second time. But the river would not let them pass. Undaunted, a recent West Point graduate, new to one of the artillery companies, became convinced he could construct a raft out of cavalry lariats and the long timbers from a nearby settler's cabin. At his urging, the soldiers tore down the cabin and lashed rope to log. After a day's work, the lieutenant floated the raft — and earned the nickname "Crusoe" when the raging water promptly washed him miles downstream.

Seeing no alternative, Howard ordered everyone to march back to the army's original crossing point, a "long weary dragging march," by Wood's description, that took two days. There they found a couple of boats that they could row across with horses and mules in tow. They began crossing on July 8, and it was not until the ninth that everyone had made it across.

While Howard, his staff, and a cavalry company rode ahead to Grangeville on the first day, the infantry and artillery companies climbed through White Bird Canyon on July 9, finding it still accursed, one soldier remembered, with "the smell from half-buried bodies." They reached the top after dark. Rations were low. "No food. No anything," wrote Wood, who tried foraging for berries. The troops were indignant. It was bad enough that the Indians had fooled them, but even worse to consider the army's inability to cross a river. Was the army too hidebound and bureaucratic to maneuver effectively in the broken terrain of Nez Perce country? "To get [Joseph] quick, we should think Indian and play Indian," Captain Pollock complained on the banks of the Salmon. "All the little command does is follow staff orders and march, march and march."

On July 10, a fleet of wagons driven by local settlers came early to camp to ferry the army across the Camas Prairie. A full week after the Nez Perce families had passed through, the soldiers were rumbling along the countryside, most too hot, filthy, famished, bored, or exhausted to comprehend the terror that had seized the area while they were on the other side of the Salmon River. Riding a couple of hours straight northeast, they never got closer than fifteen miles from the ridge where eleven soldiers and two local scouts had been chased, trapped, and slaughtered in quick running gunfights on July 3, the very day Howard's column began thinking its fortunes had finally turned for the better.

At breakfast in Grangeville, Wood listened as his hostess, the wife of one of the area's pioneers and leading men, talked on and on. Two of her eight children had fought and fled with the Idaho volunteers at White Bird Canyon. As she spoke, Wood may have heard some of the settlers' widely held outrage at the army's conduct on July 5, when a hundred soldiers had looked on from a safe position — in trenches, with a Gatling gun — while seventeen Idaho volunteers fought for their lives in full view a mile and a half away. The cavalry commander — Captain Perry, routed two weeks earlier in the canyon — had not wanted to risk another massacre against a foe that could seemingly kill at will. By the time sixty soldiers rode to the volunteers' aid a full hour later, two were dead, one more dying. Within a few days, Joseph's, White Bird's, and Toohoolhoolzote's bands and their herds had disappeared from the prairie, leaving a trail of burning farms, fields, and fences. Convinced the army was too slow and timid to engage the Nez Perce bands, a battalion of volunteers had set out on its own to find them.

After breakfast, Wood and the rest of his company spent hours more in wagons, going another twenty miles clear across the prairie until the land broke and fell away into canyons descending to the South Fork of the Clearwater River. For the first time since they had left Lapwai, they were back on the Nez Perce reservation, at its southeastern corner. Beyond the river, the foothills of the Bitterroot Mountains began their long rise over dozens of miles to a row of snowy peaks, sharp in the distance like bayonets at attention. Wood appreciated the "wild flowers, tulips, &c." blooming along the way. Winding down to the bottom of the canyon, the soldiers were finally able to cross a river on a bridge.

On the east side of the Clearwater, up steep bluffs and through thick trees to the ridgetop, Wood saw the ruins of a burned ranch, then pickets guarding the nearby bivouac where Howard's command had slept the night before. After riding ahead with part of his force from White Bird Canyon to Grangeville on July 8, the general had consolidated his troops with the cavalry that had stayed behind on the Camas Prairie. Yet even as he chased the Indians, he found himself on a defensive footing. He was derided in the newspapers as well as by the settlers whose help he desperately needed. Locals approached him and bluntly accused Captain Perry of cowardice for his timid conduct during the previous week. While Captain Whipple had acquitted himself more admirably on the Camas Prairie, he had failed in his central mission: to capture Looking Glass. The chief and his band had fled the troops, presumably to swell the ranks of the renegades.

In his bid to settle the Wallowa situation, Howard had sought a new chapter as a public man. Instead, with the situation tumbling out of control, he was cast back into the acid whirl of vituperation and shame that had marked the end of Reconstruction. Negotiating with Joseph had required Howard to consider the interests of the Nez Perce bands, treaty and nontreaty, neighboring tribes, settlers and local and state politicians, the Indian agent and other Interior officials, as well as General Sherman and the War Department. Fighting Joseph, it seemed, would require a similarly delicate balance. Howard's campaign for redemption was running out of time.

The next day, Howard finally heard some good news. The Idaho volunteer battalion sent word that they had spotted a large Indian village at the bottom of a canyon, where Cottonwood Creek emptied into the South Fork of the Clearwater. The settlers had dug in on a ridge near the canyon's entrance. After one fired his rifle, a small group of warriors promptly besieged the group, stole their horses, and kept them in a churning panic with their taunts and gunfire. Although the settlers pleaded to Howard for help, he stayed focused on the larger imperative. Rather than relieve the volunteers, the general resolved to strike the enemy and rode with all the forces in his command straight to the Clearwater.

Although the nontreaty bands were camping primarily on the west bank of the river, Howard made the counterintuitive decision to cross to the far side. Given how badly the fight had gone in White Bird Canyon, the prospect of using the normal approach from the west — leading his army down another steep canyon that was heavily watched and guarded — might have struck Howard as an invitation to another massacre. Perhaps he doubted he could reach the village at all and, as one soldier later suggested, was anticipating a next move "so as to head them off." The Indians' progress seemed to be steadily north and east, and settlers and the press speculated that they were going toward Looking Glass's camp on the Middle Fork of the Clearwater and from there trying to escape through the Bitterroot Mountains to Montana.

The troops were following the path to Looking Glass's territory, but Howard would describe a more immediate aim: "taking the enemy in reverse." He wanted to find the Indians before they moved again. Attacking the Nez Perce village from the east presented obvious challenges. It required going down the bluffs and across another difficult river; deep and still fast with spring flood, it was, a reporter wrote, "now not worthy the name of 'Clearwater.'" But Howard's soldiers could surprise the village while holding crucial high ground with howitzers and Gatling guns. Perhaps these tactics would finally break the advantage the Nez Perce bands had claimed since the bloodletting began.

Early on the morning of July 11, Howard and his column — 180 cavalry, two hundred infantry, two hundred artillery, and civilian guides and scouts — broke camp and began marching north in a course parallel to the river. A thousand feet up in the hills, river valley out of sight, Howard's latest attempt to find the Indians struck some of the soldiers who had followed the general across the Salmon as yet another "blind man's bluff," in Lieutenant Bailey's words. The grinding tedium of the campaign had resumed, the army advancing slowly along hilltops that opened onto a broad plateau, with rolls of tall grass punctuated by large rocks and occasional stands of trees. The column extended for more than a mile — men on horses, men on foot, dozens of mules. The trail was far from the edge of the cliffs, which were cut with deep ravines plunging to the water. As the infantry marched, scouts and officers rode out along the bluffs, searching over the side for signs of Indians.

"We were . . . hoping for anything," Bailey remembered, "if only we might some day finish the hard, hard forced marching, on two meals a day."

Toward noon, as the day grew hot and shadows no longer veiled the canyon floor, one of Howard's aides looked south from the bluffs and finally saw the Nez Perce village. The column had gone two miles too far. Scouts and other officers gathered to get a better look and then sent for the general. "I rode to the bluff," Howard later reported, "and saw plainly the hostiles, who, judging from their motions, had just discovered our approach." He had the element of surprise, which was deeply gratifying. After so much mystification of their fighting prowess and command of the terrain, it was a relief to know that he was capable of surprising these Indians. As he watched their initial reaction upon seeing the army — driving their horses and cattle out of harm's way — he realized that it would not take long for them to slip his grasp once again. He ordered his column to reverse course and head south again, to two ravines that the soldiers could follow down to the river.

At the same time, the general called for one of the howitzers to be set up at his position. In the mountains artillery was broken into special packs that three mules could carry — the barrel, smooth iron, which weighed two hundred pounds; the limber that held it at the proper angle, set on large wheels that could move and turn the cannon in the heat of battle; and gunpowder and exploding shells. Over the course of an hour, a team of artillerymen placed and assembled the piece and rammed it with powder and shell. On Howard's orders, they began firing.

The howitzer was light, with a range far too small to hit a distant camp from high bluffs. No matter to Howard — the cannon served other purposes. With every shot its thunder ripped the canyon twice, first at the sharp pull of the discharge, and again a few moments later, when the shells exploded midair. The steady booming would pace his soldiers as they maneuvered to take the Nez Perce village, rousing them from the waking slumber of the march as effectively as any drumroll or trumpet call. With criticism mounting that the army was not acting aggressively enough, the artillery signaled to the reporters, civilian scouts, and the people they reached from the Camas Prairie to the capital that Howard was, at heart, a fighter, determined to close an unfortunate episode with lethal dispatch. Most of all, he was sending a message to the Indians — a message to Joseph — that their marauding days, their games of cat and mouse, were over. There would be no escaping the army, no escaping its overwhelming might.

CHAPTER 14
BULLETS SINGING LIKE BEES

By noontime, when she walked into the Clearwater, Wetatonmi had likely been working for hours. Nez Perce women rose early. They parted and braided their hair, front to back, saving every strand pulled out by their leather-wrapped wooden combs, to be buried with them or burned at their death. They brought water to their camp in tight woven baskets, gathered wood for cooking fires, cleaned their teepees, and prepared food for their families, with the men and older children served first. As the day brightened, they foraged for berries and spent hours pounding roots into meal, meat and fish into dry sheets. They scraped, cured, cut, and sewed leather; wove baskets, mats, and bags from grasses and husks; crafted tools and sharpened blades. The child Wetatonmi had had with her husband Ollokot was dead, but perhaps she helped other women care for their babies, such as Joseph's younger wife Springtime, who had given birth a month earlier at Tepahlewam, their band's last birth before the war.

After lunch, the midday heat trilled through the village, which had been raised on a traditional campsite called Pettahyewahwei — in Nez Perce, Mouth of the Canyon — where Cottonwood

Creek opened onto the Clearwater. Wetatonmi, sweating and uncomfortable, decided to take a short break from the daily routine. She walked away from camp — Nez Perce women were expected to show modesty, avoiding eye contact with men who were not their husbands, covering their bodies even when breastfeeding — until she found a place to swim. The sturdy percussion of the day's chores gave way to the languorous click of grasshoppers, the river's long exhale.

Wetatonmi had not been shielded from battle. After White Bird Canyon, the women had knelt over and handled the dead, pulling guns from their hands and holsters, gathering ammunition, and peeling shirts and coats off some of the corpses. Within the past week while crossing the Camas Prairie, Wetatonmi had watched from a short distance as her husband rode out against the cavalry. Told that Ollokot's horse had been shot in the fighting, she braved thick fire to lead a new one out to him. "I heard bullets passing me on both sides," she later said. As he changed his saddle to his new mount, Ollokot gave his wife advice that she had never needed before and would never forget. "Line your horses with the soldiers' firing!" he warned. "Do not stand broadside to them." On their way to the Clearwater, the Nez Perce bands buried their first warrior to die in battle, a man of middle age, shot three times by an Idaho volunteer whom several fighters recognized as the son of a settler they had always regarded as a friend.

The village on the Clearwater was bigger than the camp at White Bird Canyon. The ranks of the nontreaty bands began to swell immediately after the fight, when two of the great warriors of their day arrived at Lahmotta straight from a buffalo hunt east of the Bitterroot Mountains, along with several other respected hunters. People told stories of the valor and fighting skill that Wahchumyus (Rainbow) and Pahkatos Owyeen (Five Wounds) had shown in many battles with rival tribes. Five Wounds could kill men with bow and arrow when others missed with their guns. Rainbow's enormous physical size corresponded with a deeper strength. In one telling, he claimed "that he got his power from the air, the rainbow too giving him fighting strength, wherein, while seen, it could not be grasped. Thus his name was one of might and power." The men, who had pledged that they would fight and die together, immediately assumed positions of leadership, devising the strategy — "counseled the trick," in Yellow Wolf's words — of crossing the Salmon River and then quickly crossing back, leaving the pursuing army stranded on the far side.

Soon after the nontreaty bands erected their teepees, Looking Glass's people streamed into camp, raising the number of men, women, and children to about 750. They told shocking stories of the end of their world, the destruction of their ancestral village and plentiful gardens on the Middle Fork of the Clearwater, only six or seven miles north and east of Mouth of the Canyon. Captain Whipple and his cavalry had appeared on a hill above the village on July 1 — a Sunday, which even Dreamers on the reservation had adopted as a day of worship and rest — and demanded to meet with Looking Glass. The chief sent Peopeo Tholekt, a young warrior whose wife had recently given birth, to explain that at the

371

first sign of war, the entire band had rejected violence and returned to their land within the reservation boundaries.

Peopeo Tholekt approached the soldiers waving a white flag, relaying the message that Looking Glass "does not want war! He came here to escape war. . . . We do not want trouble with you whatever!" In the summers of 1875 and 1876, Whipple had worked closely with Chief Joseph in keeping the peace with the settlers, sympathetic to his claim to the Wallowa Valley and ready and open to negotiate even when many thought that war was inevitable. Now, the captain shed his role as a peaceful emissary; as he had been in California in the 1860s, he was an Indian killer once again. After delivering his message, Peopeo Tholekt felt a gun muzzle cold in his ribs and had what he imagined would be his final thoughts: "I said to my heart, 'Now I am to die as a brave man!' " An interpreter urged the soldiers to let him go, but as Peopeo Tholekt rode back to the village, they opened fire and charged. Looking Glass and his band made a desperate flight to rugged ground, unable to get more than a few shots off. With bullets hissing from behind, injury and death came by surprise. Riding a panicky horse just ahead of the cavalry, Peopeo Tholekt suddenly had trouble seeing. One of his moccasins was filling with blood. "Everything looked yellow," he would remember. "Then all color, all light went from me." A woman bound his wounded leg tightly, and another fleeing man rode him to safety, two in the saddle.

The band returned afterward to find their teepees destroyed, gardens trampled, and herds entirely plundered. They remembered a teenager, bleeding out of his thigh, feeling for his pistol, dying with the words "Tired, tired! Now I sleep." They remembered a mother, her baby on her back, swept away with her horse by the Clearwater. "Of course that settled it," Peopeo Tholekt would later reflect on the army's determined violence. "We had to have a war."

The nontreaty bands had experienced battle and dislocation, crossed rivers and traveled hundreds of miles over the past six weeks. Yet it was still possible from moment to moment to feel as if nothing had changed. Along the trail to the Clearwater, as the warriors fought, the women kept digging for camas and cous roots. At Mouth of the Canyon, the women dug large holes in the ground and buried baskets and parfleche bags filled with food, supplies, and items too heavy to carry a long distance. These traditional caches were what all bands left behind in the course of their seasonal migrations. It was as if this campsite were a normal stop in a year like every other. They buried supplies because they expected to return to them. Outside of camp, men and boys raced horses along the river. Wetatonmi found a quiet spot to swim. The river ran cold and fast, a strong force pushing and pulling her, but she was unbothered, wading in waist deep.

Alone in the river, Wetatonmi felt the water's restorative jolt, the release from the heat and grime of daily toil, and the moment of privacy, precious in a communal life. But she had barely begun to swim when a voice from the bank interrupted, calling her back to the world. A man was yelling, "We are under a big body of soldiers! An army is approaching on us! Probably a fight will start any minute!" Looking north, Wetatonmi could see soldiers on the distant bluffs. She saw a cannon, then a silent puff of smoke. A heartbeat later, she heard the boom.

If the cannon fire prompted Wetatonmi to get dressed and return to the village, it signaled the opposite for the warriors. She watched them strip for battle, down to moccasins and breechcloths. The chiefs said that they would not move the village unless it became impossible to defend. After so much wandering they were determined to stay, and perhaps a military victory would prompt a parley with Howard and a negotiated end to the conflict. About a hundred warriors gathered to consider their options. A scout reported that there were a thousand troops in the hills, a "long string" of fighting men that extended for miles.

Just minutes earlier, Yellow Wolf had been racing horses along the river, sun strong on his back, wind fast in his face, the picture of a young Nez Perce man at leisure. But in an instant, among his fellow warriors, the twenty-one-year-old was forced to confront the possibility of dying. In the three and a half weeks that had passed since White Bird Canyon, he had only known victory fighting the cavalry. But he knew his enemies possessed their own sources of strength. On the Camas Prairie a week before, he had stood over a soldier shot once in the forehead and twice in the chest. Instead of dying, the man sat against a rock, "washed his face with his own blood," Yellow Wolf said, "looked around" with blank eyes, and "made a clucking noise, a sound like that of a chicken." Another warrior shot the man twice more in the chest, but he sat upright again, still rubbing his streaming blood into his face, making the same noise. To Yellow Wolf's mind, the man was "calling to his Power." "The Indians, hearing, wondered!" Yellow Wolf would say. "They asked one another, 'What about him? He must be more like us!' "

With cannon blasts whistling through the sky, the warriors split into two groups. Twenty-five men would climb the bluffs and immediately start to fight, while eighty or so would stay behind to guard the village and their herds in case the soldiers broke through. Despite the daunting odds, Yellow Wolf joined the warriors galloping to battle. "We had to stop those soldiers going to our camp!" he would later say. Led by Toohoolhoolzote, the men forded the Clearwater and climbed a large ravine just opposite the village, the trail they presumed the soldiers would follow from the bluffs to the river. Going through thick trees, the chief sent Yellow Wolf ahead to scout. At the top of the ravine — what he called "the mountain's brow" — he looked north and saw "many soldiers . . . getting ready for the war." The warriors tied their horses and ran up to the open flats to block the army's path.

As they piled stones to create cover, Yellow Wolf watched Toohoolhoolzote crawl up a small rise, aim and fire his front-loading rifle, carefully pack another shot, and fire again. Smoke curled from the muzzle, and soldiers started showering the warriors with bullets. Yellow Wolf felt the impact through the stones of his rifle pit. He heard the warriors' horses straining at their ropes, crazed with fear. When Toohoolhoolzote crawled back from his sniper's perch unharmed, the young warrior marveled at the power of the chief's *wey-ya-kin* to keep him safe.

At White Bird Canyon and on the Camas Prairie, every soldier Yellow Wolf encountered had been outnumbered and surrounded. Fighting alongside his fellow warriors was a social experience, an exercise of brotherhood. The gunfire of trapped enemies did not make him afraid. Rather, their last attempts to survive felt inviting, he thought, as if they were "calling, 'Come on! Come on! Come on!' A calling to death." Now, however, it was Yellow Wolf and his comrades who were trying to hold off hundreds of infantry, cavalry, and artillery. He could glimpse the soldiers, even thought he saw some of them fall. But as he huddled behind his pile of rocks, the intimacy of war as he had known it gave way to an experience that was colder, lonelier, and far more terrifying.

Safe behind rocks and accurate with their fire, Toohoolhoolzote's men kept the enemy from advancing to the ravines long enough to convince the rest of the warriors that the battle would not come down to the village. Behind Rainbow and Ollokot they rode up to join the fight. They could hold the army back but were too few to crack the battle line, a long arc stretching two miles north to south opposite the ravines. These warriors, who included Joseph in their rank and file, found themselves pinned down in a bitter firefight, with little room to maneuver or even consider the full sweep of the battlefield. "I did not look around while fighting, I had no time to see!" Peopeo Tholekt recalled. "I was aiming to do all harm to the soldiers in front of me; all the time watching myself."

The afternoon hours passed slow and hot. The battleground was too open and flat to allow the warriors to race around the ends of the line, the kind of flanking action that had routed the army at White Bird Canyon. As vicious as the warriors' fire could be, these soldiers did not run away but left their dead on the ground and kept fighting. After a time, they brought howitzers and a Gatling to the line and opened up a steady, pounding cascade. Warriors charged the artillery in small groups, riding, sliding off their horses to shoot, mounting again. They briefly overtook some of the big guns before a ferocious infantry charge forced them to retreat. "The Indian way of fighting is not to get killed," one of the warriors said while remembering the battle. "Killed today, there can be no fighting tomorrow." Women and boys rode up and down the bluffs, bringing water from the river to the rifle pits.

In the middle of the afternoon, the soldiers tried taking the offensive. It seemed as if they were running right at Yellow Wolf, too many for him to count. "Bullets came thicker and thicker," he would say. "Bullets were singing like bees." Quickly surrounded on three sides, Toohoolhoolzote's warriors ran for their lives, abandoning their horses. Heart pounding, Yellow Wolf was "thinking only for escape." But then he stopped. He remembered his fast black bay, a companion in war and peace. Leaving him behind would be a betrayal, even an act of cowardice. "I grew hot with mad!" he recalled. "I made myself brave!" Bullets beat earth into dust all around Yellow Wolf as he ran for his horse, then galloped down through the trees, whipping the animal until it strained and huffed at every step.

Tying his horse at a safe distance from the fight, Yellow Wolf gathered his composure and resigned himself to dying that day without tears or regret.

From the time he was young, he knew he had the "warrior power," what he thought of as "a Power to be strong in battle, in war, where life is against life. It was a power derived "from the fowls that fly, from the creatures that creep or leap through the wilds," and nurtured through his lifelong study of "how I should go to war against different tribes and fight from horseback."

Even stripped to his breechcloth, he was bound in this warrior power. Looped around his wrist, he carried a war club that he had crafted and painted years ago as a small boy. Instructed by his Spirit, he had found a river rock that he could not break, then tied it to a long stick wrapped in elk rawhide and otter fur. Holding the club, Yellow Wolf felt the deadly force of thunder, the power "to kill as it strikes and rolls along." On a buckskin string around his neck and left shoulder, a war whistle dangled under his left arm. Guided again by his Spirit, he had fashioned it from the wing bone of a crane and decorated it with two small eagle-down feathers that fluttered in "good prayer" when he rode or ran. When he sounded its one piercing note in battle, he knew that "the soldiers then could not hit me."

Yellow Wolf also wore two cartridge belts, around his waist and across his left shoulder and under his right arm. In his hands he held his treasured Winchester repeating rifle, sixteen shots, which his mother had taken care to save as she fled Looking Glass's camp, then brought to him at Mouth of the Canyon. His parents had given it to him, trading it for "one good horse" — a sign of their wealth and love and devotion to him. With this rifle he had shot bear and buffalo, from the Wallowa Valley to the geyser lands east of the Bitterroot Mountains.

Yellow Wolf's sense of himself as a warrior had defined his life — his daily routines, seasonal journeys, family relationships, and religious beliefs, his understanding of the past and aspirations for the future. In the woods below the battlefield, he saw there was only one path he could follow. He ran uphill again, back toward the gunfire. "If we die in battle, it is good," he would later say. "It is good, dying for your rights, for your country."

The young man soon encountered several older men behind a rifle pit. Many warriors wore war paint as dictated by their *wey-ya-kin,* but the faces of these men also ran red with blood, wounded by rock splinters propelled by the bullets pounding their position. Yellow Wolf joined the group and fired at the soldiers. Like many of his comrades, he searched the army lines to find an officer to kill; he looked especially for the only one he had ever seen before, General Howard. But he found no easy target and crouched again behind the rocks. Late in the afternoon, as the enemy's gunfire poured thick, cannons thundered, and the air rolled black with smoke — like "grass on fire," one of the boys carrying water later said — Yellow Wolf stopped shooting. He stretched flat on the ground, eyes clenched, "seeing nothing, hearing only the battle."

Lying on hot ground, needled by dry grass, Charles Erskine Scott Wood pictured himself thousands of miles away. To his left and right, bullets were "zee-zipping" past him, as he described it, the air above "filled with invisible humming birds bearing mortal stings." "I was thinking," he wrote, "that if I pulled through this, I would try and . . . see . . . the old familiar scenes at my home once more." All around him, "the wounded were writhing and groaning and cursing" — no cover, no shade, canteens empty, no hardtack to eat. His commanding officer, Captain Pollock, moved along the line, bareheaded and stripped to his red flannel shirtsleeves, focused and composed. Having enlisted as a private before the Mexican War thirty years earlier, Pollock was well acquainted with western battlefields. Wood, by contrast, struggled to imagine the exact opposite, the lush peach orchard at his childhood home Rosewood Glen and the quiet days he had spent there "listening to the peaceful hum of bees."

The soldiers had tried digging trenches, but much of the ground was too hard for their bayonets to pierce and turn quickly. So they lay down flat behind whatever rocks they could gather into piles. While the soldiers were exposed on a broad treeless plateau, the enemy was hard to see among the boulders and pines that marked the canyons down to the river. Those who looked too intently became targets. Over the course of the afternoon, soldiers were shot through the heel, thigh, buttock, wrist, chest, arm, shoulder, ear, scalp, and head. Occasionally, small groups of Indians charged boldly, picking off soldiers or packers, as one sergeant wrote, "in less time than it takes to tell it" before disappearing back toward the ravines.

If the rhythms of battle were jagged and unpredictable, the noise was relentless. Hour after hour, over roaring howitzers and steadily hammering Gatlings, rifle fire popped in "one continual peal," a soldier wrote. Officers shouted orders. Men cried and begged for water. And the Indians were close enough that Wood could hear the "red devils . . . yow-yowing and war-whooping." Behind the soldiers, toward the center of their semicircular line, dozens of mules squealed and honked and snorted, a chorus of braying fright.

Among the animals, inside a flimsy circle of packsaddles, General Howard established his headquarters. Despite his long-standing reputation for calm under fire, he kept his distance from the front on the bluffs above the Clearwater. In the battle's early stages, he dispatched his aides through heavy fire to organize the lines and make sure the army's flanks and supply trains were secure. Amid the cacophony, Howard developed a clear course of action: he would array his troops in a fundamentally defensive posture. The deep arc of the battle line, impossible to get around, effectively contained the Nez Perce warriors; "the whole bluff was enveloped," he wrote. Within the semicircle, he could keep soldiers and cavalry horses in reserve and set up a hospital for the wounded. Their food supplies were running low, but pack trains would be coming from Lapwai.

Howard knew the hot afternoon would be agonizing for his troops — "a ticklish business," as one private said during the battle. The only nearby spring was at the top of a large ravine. Even though his men had pushed the Indians back behind it, it quickly became clear that the warriors could pick off anyone who approached, leaving each soldier with one canteen for the entire day's fighting. But the general also knew that his soldiers had little choice but to stand their ground and fight. Unlike White Bird Canyon, they had nowhere to run.

Howard had not chosen the battlefield. It was not the surprise attack that he had envisioned. But in certain ways, the vicious stalemate on the bluffs suited his fighting force. Howard knew from bitter experience — debacles at Chancellorsville and Gettysburg — that an untrained and untested army could fail spectacularly in battle. Howard was fighting Nez Perce warriors with an army consisting largely of raw recruits. They had never had target practice and could not shoot straight at any distance. Most of them had single-shot guns — not because of any bureaucratic failing or parsimonious or corrupt provisioning, but because at the first sign of trouble, one officer explained, enlisted men with repeating rifles would immediately exhaust their ammunition. They were at their worst while on the offensive. In the deep afternoon, when Howard ordered parts of the line to charge the Indians, the army could not sustain its advances; in the tumult, the sun and smoke, the troops were shooting at each other within minutes. By holding their line, his men would not conquer the renegade Nez Perce. But the longer they lasted, the more they came to resemble soldiers.

A crucial part of making Howard's army an effective fighting force was reducing the Nez Perce warriors from figures of myth into a humbler, more comprehensible enemy. After a cascade of military and tactical humiliations, and through the exhausting tedium of weeks of forced marches across a broken, alien landscape, the soldiers could not help but inflate the power and genius of their foes — tireless legions following the great warrior and master strategist Joseph, who himself was Achilles and Odysseus in one. The soldiers'

382

sense that these Indians were impossible to beat did not waver in the initial hours of the fight above the Clearwater. Pressing themselves against the earth, breathing the dust kicked up by Nez Perce bullets, officers estimated an opposing force in the hundreds, a force that "manifested extraordinary quickness and boldness," Howard wrote.

Even though most of the casualties occurred during just twenty minutes when warriors had tried to capture the howitzer and Gatling gun, as the hours stretched soldiers imagined their enemies were crack sharpshooters, perched high in the treetops, blasting down. At the same time, a wounded officer, shot through the lungs, described the Indians as "black snakes." They would "creep and crawl and twist through the grass until within range," another officer wrote. "It is hard to tell which bunch of grass does not conceal an Indian." The occasional brazen attacks on their line — what Howard called the warriors' "savage demonstrations" — impressed the soldiers with the fluid ease with which they rode and moved, and the gentle calm of their horses under fire. When one artillery captain rallied his men to charge, he inspired them to valor by crystallizing their collective fear. "Men," he shouted, "get up and go for them; if we don't do something they will kill us all."

Only nighttime brought relief from the heat and endless gunfire. A squeezing panic slackened into what Wood described merely as a series of occasional "anxious times." Indian voices — a woman wailing, a man "haranguing the warriors" — carried across the battlefield, but few shots cracked in the night. Stars bright overhead, Howard left his headquarters and walked along the line, from company to company. Restocked with a full complement of ammunition, the soldiers would spend the night following Howard's orders to collect rocks and hack at the soil with their trowel bayonets until they had fashioned proper breastworks. The general went with his surgeon, hospital attendants, and several officers to the spring and brought buckets of water to the men.

With rumors flying "that we were in a bad fix," as one soldier would write — some estimating upwards of eighty dead and wounded — Howard set about dispelling myths and boosting morale. According to one sergeant, the general did the troops an invaluable service by speaking plainly about "how many we had lost" — forty casualties, but only twelve killed and one missing. He praised the steadfast courage — the fighting spirit — of the soldiers on the line. He spoke calmly and confidently about "our prospect of a victory next day." And he ordered flapjacks cooked behind lines and delivered to all of the men at dawn, their first meal since the previous morning. As light striped the sky, rifles started blasting again near the spring. Cooks getting water for coffee dashed back to the lines. Straightaway, Howard ordered infantry and cavalry to charge the spring and clear the snipers; howitzers fired shells into the trees just beyond. Soon the soldiers were eating their breakfast, ready to finish their task. "We kn[e]w how things stood," one wrote.

Yellow Wolf woke up in his rifle pit still stripped for battle, the sharp night air cold in his bones. Many of the warriors had retired to the village after sunset, or to a protected rock formation down the ravine where men who were too old to fight had ensconced themselves during the previous afternoon, puffing on pipes and discussing the war while it raged above them. Yellow Wolf considered joining the rest, considered sleeping in relative comfort under a warm blanket, but then decided that he preferred to stay on the battlefield. The Spirit, the source of his warrior power, wanted him to be alone. Yellow Wolf's visions — the animals who approached and spoke, disembodied voices in the darkness — came to him when he was by himself, when he was hungry and cold and searching for their guidance. On freezing nights in buffalo country in Montana, when he slept in the saddle, the voices had kept him from getting lost, or worse, from crossing paths with enemy tribes. They tethered him to life in this world, and he would continue to take their counsel.

In the early light, Yellow Wolf peered out from behind the rocks. He took measure of the soldiers' solid barricades and wondered if the army had come closer to the ravines in the night. When the shooting started, three men joined him, the same who had fought there before, but in his mind Yellow Wolf remained alone in battle. "I paid attention to myself only, what I was doing," he would say. "I thought nothing about the warriors with me." The soldiers' fire, formidable on the first day of fighting, felt far heavier now. "Shots from the soldiers were not scattering," it seemed to Yellow Wolf. "Their volleys became one continued roar."

Hour after hour, well past noon, Yellow Wolf crouched behind the rocks, shooting at the soldiers, hiding again. A bullet hit him below his left wrist, bulging under the skin without hitting bone. He rolled on the ground in agony but soon returned to the fight, pleased that he had not cried out. Then a rock fragment slashed under his left eye, slicking his face with blood. Yellow Wolf kept firing.

Perhaps because his sight had dimmed, Yellow Wolf stood his ground in the midafternoon heat as soldiers rose from their barricades and charged. Only a strained voice behind him brought him back into the moment. Wottolen (Hair Combed over Eyes), an esteemed warrior whose childhood memories preceded the coming of the first missionaries in the 1830s, was out of breath. He had heard Yellow Wolf's rifle and run to tell him that they were the only two warriors left in battle. The previous night and through the day, the others had been debating whether to abandon the fight. Wahlitits and Sarpsis Ilppilp, the young men who had started the war with their revenge killings along the Salmon River, advocated finishing it. They wanted the warriors to organize for a great charge, a final attempt to smash Howard's line. "Make it the last fight," Yellow Wolf was told of their position. "Whichever side whipped, to be the last fight." Rainbow, too, advocated a mass rush for the soldiers' lines — they could decide the war in close combat. But others hesitated, asking, "Why all this war up here? Our camp is not attacked! All can escape without fighting. Why die without cause?" After eight hours of heavy fighting, only four warriors had been killed. A final stand would only invite death.

The warriors neither reached a resolution nor made plans to hold out while giving the camp time to evacuate. Instead, over the course of the day, as Howard's army showed its strength, men began abandoning their rifle pits. Without enough men to go on the offensive, leading warriors — including Rainbow and Five Wounds, Wahlitits, Sarpsis Ilppilp, and Strong Eagle — left for the village. Even more followed them down. Soon, it seemed, "everybody was running," Peopeo Tholekt would recall, "some catching up — some getting behind. All running, skipping for their lives for the camp."

Watching their lines thin, Joseph knew that it was only a matter of time before they broke, and once the soldiers had access to the ravines, the entire camp at Mouth of the Canyon would be within range of the army's big guns. The chief, no leader in battle, assumed responsibility for the village, riding down from the bluffs to warn everyone that they had to flee. Within fifteen minutes, they could see soldiers standing on the bluffs, and bullets started landing in camp, hitting some of the horses. Women, children, and the elderly grabbed what they could carry and hurried up Cottonwood Creek with the herds, deep into the canyons. "The cannon boomed, and the Gatling gun rattled out shots after the flying families," Peopeo Tholekt wrote. The warriors took their place after them, prepared to fight again if the soldiers followed.

By the time Yellow Wolf fled his rifle pit, bugles were calling, and soldiers were cheering. Bullets hummed all around him. He ran for his horse while Wottolen walked at his own deliberate pace, trusting a promise of survival that his *wey-ya-kin* had given him. The younger warrior barreled straight downhill, grateful that his horse could keep its footing at a gallop. Entering the village, he saw that it looked just the way he had left it the day before. The teepees were still standing, with food, clothing, cooking pots, and tools still inside, a ghostly tableau of lives left behind. Shells from howitzers whistled through the village, toppling trees, blasting rock into gravel.

Over the din, over the sound of his breathing, the huffing of his horse, and the wind in his ears, Yellow Wolf heard a voice, a woman crying. Among the abandoned teepees, he was shocked to find Springtime, Chief Joseph's younger wife. In the rush to the canyons, she and her daughter, born a month earlier at Tepahlewam, had been left behind. Now the cannon fire was making her horse leap and stomp, impossible for her to mount while holding her baby. With the soldiers firing down, she swung into the saddle but had to leave the infant girl on the ground, wrapped in her cradleboard. Still, she could not abandon her daughter.

When Springtime saw Yellow Wolf, she shouted, "I am troubled about my baby!" He galloped over, leaned off his saddle, and reached down, a move he could have practiced as a boy pretending to fight rival horsemen. Yellow Wolf had just spent two days crouching behind rocks. Only as he fled his enemies could he ride again like a warrior. He plucked the cradleboard from the ground and handed the baby to her mother. They rode into the canyons as fast as their horses would run.

In low sun, Lieutenant Wood walked along the battlefield. The din of war had given way to more enduring sounds — wind and river, the tidal drone of insects. Most of the soldiers were down the ravine, preparing to cross the Clearwater or guarding a beachhead on the other side — to the chagrin of some of the officers. Chasing the Indians into the canyons was deemed too risky. Wood's infantry company had been ordered to stay up on the bluffs and collect the dead. They spotted eight bodies, blue uniforms easy to see against rock and yellowing grass. A private who had left the line to fill four canteens at the spring was never found. Although the faces of the dead were already blackening after a day in the field, the bodies were intact. Wood's company could carry them to a wagon and then bury them in a single trench behind the field hospital.

That night, Wood camped with the wounded. He knew many of the twenty-seven men lying in the field hospital. With the cavalry guarding the ends of the battle line, the infantry — all in Wood's regiment — saw some of the heaviest fighting and suffered accordingly. Nearly half of the wounded were officers, a small fraternity in the Northwest, many of whom Wood had met in his travels as the Department of the Columbia's judge advocate. Their injuries reflected the hodge-podge of weapons and ammunition the Indians were using. Round musket balls tended to pass clean through the body. Conical bullets went flat upon impact, shredding and shattering everything in their path and leaving gaping holes on exit. Come morning, pack mules would drag the injured men on canvas litters twenty-five miles to Grangeville and eventually back to Lapwai. Some of them were unlikely to survive the ordeal. A corporal shot in the femoral artery was barely alive after losing almost all of his blood on the battle-field. A drummer's abdominal wound was leaking urine.

The next day, Wood crossed the river and

explored the village. Although it had been erected within the previous week, it was a stunning contrast from the soldiers' rough bivouac. "The Indian camp appeared to have been their home for a long long time," a lieutenant wrote. Wood was struck by how confident the Indians must have been to stay in their village while the battle raged across the river. "Many had evidently believed they would wipe us out as they had in every encounter . . . with the whites," he later wrote.

If the army regarded the nontreaty bands as marauding savages, they lived with infinitely more wealth and civilization than the soldiers did. After starving on the battlefield, nearly everyone not on picket duty lit fires under the Indians' copper pots and cooked their enemies' food. "We got flour, bacon, coffee, dried beef and camas," one soldier wrote. "I got some potatoes, fresh bacon, boiled beef, a cup of tea from one & coffee from somebody else, and had a hearty meal; it was breakfast, dinner, and supper all in one." The soldiers, filthy after weeks of campaigning, washed in the river. And after what felt like a resounding victory after a hard battle — a decisive charge, enemy warriors in full flight — they slept easy, "sound as a top," one wrote.

Orders circulated to burn the camp, but the soldiers helped themselves first to buffalo robes, clothing, and tools. Packers and civilian scouts from the Camas Prairie wandered the camp, piercing the ground every few feet with stakes or ramrods. They told the soldiers that Nez Perce women dug caches at their campsites, and soon soldiers and civilians were excavating what amounted to a record of seventy years of prosperous commerce with whites: silver spoons that one lieutenant "judged dated from an early Hudson's Bay period," jewelry, gold dust, bronze bells. Some of the soldiers viewed the goods as pure trophies of war; taking them was an act of dominance. One sergeant watched his comrades "putting on style rigged out in captured buckskin shirts, leggings, and moccasins," parodying their enemies, cutting them down to size, in a dizzy pageant of plunder.

But many others recognized that the objects abandoned by the Nez Perce families had a different kind of value. Pack mules returning from the battlefield to Lapwai carried hardtack boxes that soldiers had stuffed with fringed buckskin shirts and dresses, beaded sheaths, and leggings. "They are made of beautifully tanned skin, soft as chamois skin," a woman at the fort wrote in a letter to her mother in Pennsylvania. "You never saw such bead work." Even as they pursued the non-treaty bands, the settlers and soldiers admired the things they had made.

Breathtaking as it was, this artistry had never caused the settlers or government to regard the Nez Perce people as civilized or deserving of their land or way of life, partly because the beadwork was not made for or traded with outsiders. But on the Clearwater, in the absence of actual Indians, the artifacts of their daily life immediately became a valuable commodity. Destroying the culture that framed them and gave them meaning made them all the more precious and coveted. Looking inside a teepee, Wood saw a drinking cup carved from buffalo horn and pocketed it. In time, General Howard would amass a large collection of Indian artifacts. And when the battlefield surgeon returned with the wounded to Lapwai a week later, he spread the word that he would pay good money for beaded outfits for horses. "Doctor Sternberg is an enthusiast on the subject of collecting curiosities, and he purchased from men who had gotten them, four or five of these garments," wrote the wife of another army surgeon. "For one, he gave ten dollars in coin, and for another with a horse fixing, 25 dollars. So you see, they must be handsome."

CHAPTER 15
HEART OF THE MONSTER

The Nez Perce families rode north through the hills, up, over, and down again, and the Clearwater curved to meet them. Only twelve miles from the village they had abandoned at Mouth of the Canyon, this part of the valley — Kamiah — did not resemble a traditional camping ground. A cluster of frame buildings overlooked the river: church, boarding school, saw and grist mills. On each bank, farmhouses — "real houses," as General Howard once described them — echoed the official reservation architecture, crowning tidy plots, fenced and cultivated.

Had Joseph's band moved peacefully onto the reservation a month earlier in June, one history of his people would have ended quietly, and a new one would have begun. The land that Howard had promised them was nearby. The people who would have been their neighbors were successful farmers, complimented by the general as "well dressed and well behaved." Missionaries had tended to them for forty years. They were carefully taught in school. The Indian agent managed them, Howard thought, with skill and sympathy. In time, Joseph's band could have become indistinguishable from the other residents of Kamiah, and ultimately from the settlers outside the reservation, too.

But after weeks of battles, the nontreaty bands set up camp outside the sunbaked settlement, prepared to move on the next day ahead of the soldiers who were surely coming. They rejected the future Howard had envisioned for them, yet war did not allow them to hold on to their old lives. The initial victories at White Bird Canyon and on the Camas Prairie may have felt familiar, like fighting the Blackfeet and Sioux, but the stalemate on the bluffs above the Clearwater and the headlong flight from the village were different from anything anyone had experienced. The days that followed were steps in the dark, the bands traveling on well trod ground but drawing ever farther away from their ancestral lands. With the army in pursuit, they had been pulled from the world they knew, and there was no sure path home.

Just upstream from Kamiah, past the reservation buildings, past the farms, a modest rock formation fringed with grass rose from the valley floor. Though dwarfed by grander and more graceful hills in every direction, the small mound signified the oldest and most enduring connections that the Nez Perce people had with their land. It was a physical object, a fact of their world, but its power — what they saw when they looked at it, what they felt when they rode past — came from stories they had always told. When elders pointed it out to children, they called it the Heart of the Monster.

Before there were people, the stories went, when animals shared the world with creatures beyond explanation, a great monster had come to Kamiah and swallowed everything around it. It swallowed eagles, crows, and owls, deer and elk, buffalo, salmon, bears, wolves, rattlesnakes, rabbits, and foxes. Hearing of the monster and of the destruction it had brought to his world, Coyote sought it out, traveling from the Wallowa Valley through the Salmon River country. From miles away he saw it. Coyote could not believe that something so big could exist. With grass ropes he tethered himself to the mountains. He tied bunchgrass to his head and painted his body with clay to blend with the earth.

Ready to take on the vast creature, Coyote called out and challenged the monster to swallow him. The monster responded by turning toward Coyote and inhaling — dominance came with the very act of breathing. As he was pulled toward the monster, Coyote's ropes almost cut through him, then snapped. Sucked across the prairie, casting camas seeds along the way, Coyote was drawn into the monster's mouth. Among the bones of its victims, he found a world of animals living inside the monster. But rather than take his place with them, Coyote devised still another plan. He walked to the monster's heart and lit a fire under it. Writhing in pain, the monster called on him to leave. Instead, Coyote began cutting at the heart with sharp flint knives, slowly slicing it from the monster's body. When he finally tugged the heart free, the monster fell dead, slain from the inside. Escaping from the monster's various orifices, Coyote and the other captive animals found themselves back in their home country. But it would never be the same. Even dead, the monster had the power to remake the world. Coyote butchered the monster and everywhere he threw its parts, north, south, east, and west, the peoples of the world — Cayuse, Shoshone, Flathead, Crow, Blackfeet, Pend Oreille, Sioux — arose. At Kamiah, Coyote washed his filthy hands and sprinkled the ground. Out of this mixture of blood and water, the Nez Perce people, the "real people," were born, destined to live in sight of the monster's heart, now turned to stone.

Crossing the Clearwater on buffalo hide rafts and climbing into the hills on the other side, the nontreaty bands traveled with the Heart of the Monster at their backs. But as they rode on, away from the settlement at Kamiah, the rock formation well out of sight, the monster of their deepest past was following them. In breaking from their recent history, in departing from all that could be remembered, the Nez Perce families were experiencing something more recognizable as myth. They had traced the same route that Coyote had — from the Wallowa Valley to the Salmon River country and across the Camas Prairie to Kamiah. They had tried to anchor themselves to the land. They had fought with Coyote's stealth, hiding in the grass, in the folds of rock. But their foe was too immense. Just by existing, it had swallowed everything in their world. Whether they knew it or not, it had swallowed them, too. Inside the monster, they could search for an exit. They could slash at it from the inside. But if they found a way back to their homes, what kind of new world would be waiting for them?

The path ahead was both familiar and treacherous. With everyone safely on the far side of the Clearwater, a scout brought word that Howard's column was nearing Kamiah. Warriors hid along the banks and watched the cavalry descending down a broad hill, their rumbling gallop growing to thunder. As the soldiers neared the ford, the warriors opened fire; after just a few minutes, they knew they had nothing to worry about. "We laughed at those soldiers," Yellow Wolf would remember. Although a swollen river separated them from the warriors, the cavalry and their horses panicked as if the ambush had come point-blank, men diving into a wheat field along the river, horses stampeding away. The warriors caught up with the rest, confident that Howard's column would be stymied for days by yet another river to cross.

North of Kamiah, the abrupt climb from the Clearwater Valley eased into broad plateau. As with every bit of flat land in Nez Perce country, the people knew this area, Weippe, well. In other years many would have come there earlier in the summer to dig camas root. Like the Wallowa Valley, the gentle roll of the earth gave no hint that the prairie just fell away to the south and west at the Clearwater. To the east, the Bitterroot Mountains loomed close enough to slow the sunrise. Twenty miles from where they had left the army behind, the nontreaty bands pitched camp.

The Nez Perce friendship with the United States had begun at this very place. It was at Weippe where William Clark and seven members of his Corps of Discovery emerged after nearly starving and freezing to death in the seemingly endless steeps of the Bitterroots. Clark appreciated the miracle of a plain among mountains with two words in his diary, "butifull Countrey," and called the people he found there "Pierced Noses." They accepted colorful ribbons from Clark as tokens of friendship and fed the men dried salmon, berries, buffalo meat, and camas bread and soup.

Seventy-two years later, this history was well known to the Nez Perce bands riding across the Weippe Prairie. Wottolen, who had survived his slow retreat from the battle at the Clearwater when a cousin rode back and pulled the old man onto his horse, could talk at length about Lewis and Clark. His grandfather Red Bear was the chief at Weippe who had chosen to befriend the expedition rather than kill them all. Halahtookit, known by all to be William Clark's son, was traveling with his daughter and baby granddaughter.

As familiar as Weippe was as a historical site, as much as it signified the start of the best season of the year, a sense of finality palled the nontreaty bands' time on the prairie. The warriors saw scattered reminders of Lewis and Clark's legacy — a few ranch buildings — and promptly torched them. After leaving enormous amounts of food behind at Mouth of the Canyon, the women busied themselves slaughtering the cattle they found. They had to dry enough beef to sustain 750 people for what everyone knew would be a long journey ahead. They found several Nez Perce families — forty or so men, women, and children — already camping on the land: Red Heart's people, friends of theirs who wanted nothing to do with the war. As the small band prepared to descend from Weippe back to Kamiah, their goodbyes were fraught with sorrow, "a farewell," Yellow Wolf remembered, "that we would never return to our homes again!" An old man, Hatya Takonnin (Accompanying Cyclone), rode from the reservation into their camp to beg his son the warrior Heinmot Too-tsi-kin (Speaking Thunder) to put down his rifle and return home. "Death awaits

398

you on the trail you are taking," Yellow Wolf heard the old man say. "I see the future. It is dark with blood!" His son refused, telling his father, "I want to go with my brothers and sisters. If I am killed, it will be all right." Wiping away tears, Hatya Takonnin spoke once more. "I am willing that you go," he said. "It is all right for you to go help fight. But soldiers are too many."

In council on July 15, the chiefs and leading warriors considered their next move. From the Weippe Prairie, they could try heading west, back toward the Salmon River country and the Wallowa, or they could go east through the Bitterroot Mountains. And if they decided to cross into Montana, they still had important choices to work out. They could go north through the mountains to Canada; south back into Idaho and then west toward the Snake, Salmon, and Wallowa; or east to the Yellowstone country and the plains where Nez Perce hunters chased buffalo.

Initially, Joseph and Ollokot may have argued against abandoning their lands, as some remembered them doing, but they quickly deferred to a plan to go east, advocated by Looking Glass. Appearing to be the ablest leader among them, Looking Glass was younger and more active than White Bird and Toohoolhoolzote and a more experienced hunter and warrior than Joseph or Ollokot. With the support of most of the people at the council, Looking Glass urged the bands to travel over the mountains on the familiar course of the great Nez Perce hunters: down through the Bitterroot Valley, east to the Yellowstone country, and finally to the buffalo plains. In the Bitterroot Valley, Looking Glass argued, they would find sanctuary and could claim a large herd of horses from the Flatheads, with whom Nez Perce men and women had long lived, traded, and intermarried. Past Yellowstone, the chief was confident that the Crow, allies of a more recent vintage, would either take them in or join the struggle. Rainbow and Five Wounds, who had just returned from months of buffalo hunting, confirmed Looking Glass's sense of the tribes on the far side of the mountains.

The next day, July 16, the nontreaty bands rode east from Weippe into the Bitterroots. Tracing Lewis and Clark's steps in reverse, they were embarking on a journey of undoing. The route, called the Lolo Trail or "the path to a different country," snaked along the mountainsides, up and down thousands of feet, again and again, for a hundred miles. The travelers rode through perpetual dusk, rayed with thin sun. The forest never stopped reaching for the riders and their horses, scratching, poking, snagging, and holding. Except for occasional clearings, there was no grass for the herds to eat. Hundreds of fallen trees blocked the narrow path the entire distance, so in addition to steep climbs, the horses were constantly jumping over obstacles. In the gloom, paths stayed wet and slippery. At its heights, the trail came close to the snow line. One false step could lame a horse, or cast it over the side, to depths that could only be judged by the stray sunlight sparkling in the creeks that rushed along the hollows.

The Bitterroots could seem insurmountable, the great boundary between nations, the spine of the world. But the Nez Perce people lived their lives crossing over mountains, and from the time they first mounted horses in the early eighteenth century, the buffalo plains had been within their reach. Although Joseph and Ollokot did not know the eastern country, many others had ridden the Lolo Trail. For some it was an annual migration. Only the timing of the journey and the size of the traveling party were unusual. The mountains barely slowed the group — men, women, children, the elderly, a herd of thousands of horses, strung out over miles. They emerged on the other side, at the high flowery meadows and hot springs that marked the Lolo Pass, in less than a week. Apart from their first day on the trail, when warriors guarding the rear of the column encountered three Nez Perce scouts working for the army — they killed one and wounded another — no one had followed them through the mountains. Perhaps Looking Glass's plan for them had already worked, and the war was something that they could escape. They could continue to live free, turn their conflict with the United States back into a negotiation, and even return home someday. They rested and bathed and turned their horses loose in the rustling grass.

When John Martens's neighbors relayed the news that "Joseph's band of Indians" had showed themselves near the Lolo hot springs, the forty-five-year-old farmer felt the light leach from the sky and the air grow heavy and tight. After weeks of reports of the slaughter in Idaho accompanied by speculation over whether the Indians would take their rampage eastward into Montana Territory, his worst fears were coming true. Martens owned 150 acres in the Bitterroot Valley, a thin gap of flat land that ran for ninety-five miles down from the Lolo Pass. The Nez Perce families were surely coming through, as they had often done on their way to buffalo country, and the settlers who had carved up the valley were doomed. With mountains towering to the east and west, there was no escape.

Even as his neighbors spoke, the world around Martens punctuated his dread. "While they were talking," he wrote in his journal, "a storm came on it was moore than a storm it was a Tornado acompanied by Hail." The soldiers and Nez Perce warriors repeatedly described their battles as deluges of violence, the gunfire pouring like rain or hail. Now, with stunning power, a true storm foreshadowed what appeared to be an inevitable human catastrophe. In ten or fifteen minutes, much of what Martens had been working for since spring was wiped away. His days had long been preoccupied by the struggle to "arigate" his land, but now, he wrote, "the water came in torents down the gully and hallows." "The destruction of Property was tirreble," he scrawled, his phonetic spelling betraying his immigration to the United States two decades earlier from Denmark. "Fences were blown down und the crops were beat into the Ground Everything was destroied aperently." What little was left would be eaten by the hogs that were now free to roam across the area's farms.

Although the clouds parted and everything was soon "warm as usiall," Martens and his neighbors feared that their troubles had only begun. After the storm, it was impossible to travel the ten or so miles to the nearest town, Stevensville. No one knew if the renegade Nez Perce bands had already begun killing settlers. Several hundred Flatheads and many Nez Perce lived within walking distance. They had always been friendly, working with and sometimes employing the local settlers — Martens had rented his first farm in the area from an

Indian. Just a few weeks earlier, settlers and Indians had celebrated July 4 together with a feast of hams, chicken, and turkey, a summer's bounty of berries with cream, and what a reporter described as "pies, great piles of them." Yet Martens and his neighbors could not be certain if the local Indians would join their allies and kinsmen on the warpath.

The neighbors — six or seven families and several unmarried men who, like Martens, farmed alone — gathered at one house and spent the entire night trying to "fortefy ourself . . . to widstand a considerable atack." Though signal fires flashed in the darkness, the sun rose on a quiet valley. Over the next several days, Martens spent hours "watch[ing] for Indians," but in the absence of any sinister activity, he also found time to go out on his own, feed the mules, begin fixing his fences, and try to round up the livestock running in the fields. Even with the world about to end, the work of the farm — what Martens described as the struggle to "regulate" nature — never stopped.

On Thursday, July 26, a longtime settler who worked for a rich Indian rancher in the area rode by with some good news: the Flatheads were not joining forces with the Nez Perce. But the man also brought a warning from the local chief, Charlo, that the Nez Perce bands would be coming into the valley the next day. Charlo urged the settlers to go to Stevensville and barricade themselves inside Fort Owen, a small adobe trading post surrounded by high walls built in the days of Blackfeet raids a generation earlier. Over the past six years, it had gone to ruin after John Owen, the fort's namesake and pioneer owner, went insane and had to be sent east to relatives in Philadelphia, but when Martens and his neighbors reached the fort, they found it a place where already, he wrote, "exitement prevailed," newly reinforced with fresh-cut blocks of sod and crammed with about 250 jittery settlers. Yet even as people were arriving, many were preparing to leave: the territorial governor had issued an order for all men to arm themselves and report to the Lolo Trail to block the invaders' path.

Martens had lived a hard life. Born on a remote Baltic island, he was an infant when his mother died, and by age eight he was herding sheep. By the time he crossed the Atlantic and became an American at age twenty-four, he had worked six years as a shepherd, four as a sailor, and then six more as a carpenter. Soon after arriving at Castle Garden, he went west. In 1858, he walked across the Kansas plains to Pikes Peak during a gold rush in Colorado, pushing his tools in a wheelbarrow. After farming and milling flour in Colorado and New Mexico, he set out for Montana in 1864. The past decade had been the steadiest, happiest, and most prosperous he had ever known. The land was fertile, the weather comparatively mild. Farmers could do good business selling to mining settlements and boomtowns like Bannack, about fifty miles south of the valley. Now all he had accomplished was under threat. Although hardly thrilled at the prospect, Martens was ready to fight for his life. Early on Friday, July 27, he rode out with two neighbors to what he called "the Seat of War."

At the eastern extreme of the Lolo Trail, in a narrow stretch of woods between two steep hills, the Bitterroot farmers found hundreds of men —

three dozen regular troops from the Missoula garrison thirty miles away, volunteers from Missoula and the valley, and even twenty or so Flatheads, white handkerchiefs on their heads to mark them as friendly. They were gathered behind a barricade and breastworks that they had been constructing for two days out of dirt and felled trees. "Everything was live and bustle," Martens wrote.

Around the time Martens arrived, the commanding officer, an infantry captain named Charles Rawn, rode several miles up the trail toward the Nez Perce camp with a white handkerchief tied to a gun barrel. While Rawn sought a parley with the chiefs to convince them to surrender, the men at the barricades were left wondering if the Indians would take the white flag as an opportunity to kill Rawn, as the Modoc renegades had killed General Edward Canby during their peace conference in 1873. After a short time, though, the captain and his Flathead interpreter appeared again on the trail, unharmed but unsuccessful in pressing the demand that the Nez Perce bands "disarm and dismount, surrendering all stock." Looking Glass, joined by Joseph and White Bird, had scoffed at Rawn's terms. The chiefs countered that "if allowed to pass unmolested," they would "march peaceably through the Bitter Root Valley." But Rawn had no authority to negotiate for anything other than total capitulation. Back behind the barricades, the captain told his soldiers and volunteers that come morning, hundreds of Nez Perce warriors would attempt to smash through their lines. After recalling the Modoc treachery, the men unsettled themselves with more recent memories, resigned to a fight that would undoubtedly be, in one volunteer's words, "another 'Custer massacre.'"

On Saturday, July 28, Martens still had the farmer's presence of mind to note, war or no war, that the weather was "clear and bright." With that information recorded in his journal, he then scrawled, "Exspected an atack from the Indians." The soldiers and volunteers had woken in darkness, loaded their rifles, and assumed positions behind the barricades. Soldiers and volunteers alike may have sought courage from a demijohn of whiskey that a saloonkeeper had brought down from Missoula. Captain Rawn's interpreter instructed the men to "shoot low and kill horse then shoot Injun." They waited, watching for warriors, listening for the thunder of their horses.

After a few hours, around nine o'clock, a Bitterroot farmer who had gone with a lieutenant's field glasses to observe the Nez Perce camp sent back word that the Indians were on the move, heading down toward the barricades. As he followed them, however, he saw that the entire camp was turning off the trail a quarter mile above the fortified camp and climbing a high ridge. Captain Rawn refused to believe it. "He replied that it was impossible for them to go around on that steep hillside and that it was only a scout or so that I saw," the farmer would remember, "and when I said I saw squaws and children with camp stuff going up he turned back into his tent with [an] insulting remark."

By two o'clock it became clear to Martens, certainly to his relief, that there would be no last stand. "The Indians . . . like sinscible falows found a way aroun us and let us alone," he wrote. Rawn ordered the group to pack up, abandoning the barricades that immediately became known by the derisive nickname "Fort Fizzle." At the bottom of the trail, the soldiers and volunteers from Missoula turned north toward home. The Nez Perce bands had entered the Bitterroot Valley, and the settlers were entirely on their own. As Martens saw it, the only chance the farmers had to survive was if the offer Looking Glass had extended to Rawn was still on the table. "No choise," the farmer wrote, "but to make pease widt the Indians."

The women rode into town first. For close to three weeks, after they had left almost everything behind at Mouth of the Canyon, their lives had been an uninterrupted struggle. It required constant improvisation and invention — new camps every night, food for 750 people without ready access to staples, the exhausting journey through mountains and the constant challenge to keep the herd healthy and intact. But now they were back on level ground. No one was chasing them anymore. Chief Charlo had shocked the Nez Perce families by refusing them sanctuary, but he allowed them to settle on good land just above his village. While the leaders continued to argue about whether to head north straight to Canada, or south and east toward buffalo country, the women set about restoring normalcy once again.

Although they had dressed to make an impressive public display, the women found little audience as they forded the Bitterroot River and rode into Stevensville. They were escorted by a small group of warriors who had been instructed by Looking Glass, "Don't shoot, don't shoot. Let the white men shoot first." Soon after arriving in the valley, Looking Glass had personally assured forty men returning from Fort Fizzle that no harm would come to the settlers, but few seemed to be taking him at his word. The town looked largely deserted — shops locked, salons shuttered. But in the middle of the main commercial blocks, the riders saw signs of life in one small frame building. Buck Brothers, general mercantile, was open for business.

The women walked into the store, a single room twenty feet across and twice as deep. Henry, Amos, and Fred Buck, all in their thirties, were busy arranging items on the shelves. Boots, shoes, and clothing, tools, canned groceries, local fruits and vegetables and milk — the brothers stocked dry goods from Salt Lake, let farmers pay for them with produce, and sold wagonloads of food and supplies to mining communities all over the territory. Established just a year and a half earlier, the business had already begun earning the brothers the fortune — fifty thousand dollars a year, they said — that they had been searching for from the time they caught gold fever and left their parents and ten siblings behind in Michigan in the 1860s. When they thought the Indians were on the attack, they carted their entire inventory to Fort Owen, but as soon as they sensed there was money to be made, they filled a wagon and rolled it back to the store.

The women recited a long list of items that they hoped to buy: fruits, vegetables, coffee, sugar, tobacco, various articles of clothing, and calico by the yard. In later days, the brothers insisted that they had hesitated to engage in commerce with the enemy but knew that if they refused to sell to them, the Nez Perce bands would just take what they needed. "We held a consultation over the

408

matter and decided that 'Prudence was the better part of valor,' " Henry Buck wrote, "so decided to trade with them." More likely, the brothers restocked their shelves in the first place because, in Henry Buck's words, "we had always considered the Nez Perces as a wealthy tribe." In their "apparently new showy blankets," the Indians did not disappoint. Even though most of their possessions had been looted and burned, the women had held on to their money — thousands of dollars in greenbacks, sacks of gold dust, silver. In advertisements the Buck brothers offered nice discounts for cash purchases. The Nez Perce women paid with gold coins.

The very act of doing business with whites held certain deep comforts. Despite complaints about shopkeepers and peddlers on the Salmon River who cheated their Nez Perce neighbors or, worse, ruined them with whiskey, trade had been a fixture of life for half a century or more. The elders could remember the origins of their thriving herds in the cattle bought from pioneers on the Oregon Trail. The bands' horses were an enormous source of wealth in part because many settlers prized Nez Perce breeds, so much so that several Bitterroot farmers and ranchers decided to take the risk and emerge from hiding to buy them from the nontreaty bands. Indeed, trade gave the Nez Perce people rights that extended far beyond the terms of treaties. In trade they could meet whites in a position of equality. They could drive hard bargains and demand fair and honest treatment without being seen as "saucy" or subversive. Despite what General Howard and their Indian agent believed, the traditional ways of life — the horses they raised, the buffalo they hunted — had undeniable value in the market-place. With every purchase from the Buck brothers, the women showed once again that their people could coexist peacefully with settlers. The supplies that the women were buying would help make any journey that followed feel less like a wartime retreat and more like a regular seasonal migration. On a warm Tuesday morning, the last day in July, the practice and ceremony of commerce suggested that the Nez Perce families could travel back to happier times, far from the horrors of the previous months.

If the Buck brothers had any regrets about the day, it was that they had not stocked any flour. The women asked for a lot of it. So, like good businessmen cultivating loyal customers, the Bucks directed them to a mill just north of town. It was no matter that the mill was right next to Fort Owen, where most of the settlers in the area had hidden themselves away. As they rode by and negotiated for their flour and had their horses weighed down with the sacks — a Catholic priest who tended to the Flatheads near Stevensville estimated that the visitors bought $1,200 worth of goods in town — the Nez Perce women finally had their audience.

Inside the trading post's walls, the settlers tried keeping a close eye for Indians. After riding down from the Lolo Pass, John Martens spent the last days of July looking out from the safety of Fort Owen. As word spread of "a number of Indians in town trading paying for what they got," the settlers' emotions began to shift from cold fear to something more curious. At least once Martens felt confident enough to venture into Stevensville "to see how things look." He saw Nez Perce men carrying an intimidating arsenal of repeating rifles, and as more warriors started streaming into town, he, like other settlers, fretted over the fragile peace, fearing that an ill word or barrel of whiskey could tilt the balance from amity to massacre. But the settlers also heard that Looking Glass was demanding good behavior and sending undisciplined warriors back to camp. Martens's anxiety about the Indians blurred into a hope that his friends who were bold enough to "trade widt them . . . will do well." "People somewhat pusled as to whaht the Indians will do," he wrote in his journal, "wheather they will keep Pease or make war."

For days to follow, the people inside Fort Owen remained convinced that, in Martens's words, "the Nes Perces will go to murder and plunder." But they were scanning the horizon for something that would never come. By August 1, the Nez Perce families had moved twenty-five miles south, to land near the town of Corvallis, where settlers had holed up in another compound, walled twelve feet high with sod, that they called "Fort Skedaddle." Over the next week, they slowly traveled another sixty-five miles, until they climbed into the hills that bounded the south of the Bitterroot Valley and crossed the Continental Divide.

While several leaders — White Bird, Toohoolhoolzote, and Wottolen — had argued strenuously in favor of heading north beyond the Medicine Line that separated the United States from Canada, Looking Glass, asserting that he had been given "the whole command" as war chief, convinced the group that they should cast their lot with the Crow nation in the buffalo country.

411

After three weeks without a battle, and after all the trade that had taken place in Stevensville, it was tempting to think, as Yellow Wolf would remember, "No more fighting! We had left General Howard and his war in Idaho." At the same time, the Nez Perce families were painfully aware that the conflict did not end upon crossing the mountains from Idaho to Montana and from Nez Perce to Flathead territory.

To be Nez Perce, continually moving from Oregon to Idaho to Montana and back, almost required an awareness of the continuity of American power across boundaries. Decades of negotiating, signing, rejecting, and protesting treaties bred deep familiarity with the federal government. Its many agents often found themselves explaining the far-flung scope of federal jurisdiction as well as the separate and distinct powers of state and local authorities. The Nez Perce people knew that the army was actively fighting Indians in Montana. At the Lolo Pass, three men joined the nontreaty bands after deserting as army scouts along the Yellowstone River searching for renegade Sioux a year after the battle on the Little Bighorn. Upon riding into camp, one of the men — called Ugly Grizzly Bear Boy — reportedly told the chiefs "they were a band of fools, that it was folly for a handful of Indians to think of fighting the United States government." He urged them to turn north and set out for "the British Possessions." If his warnings were not sharp or specific enough, the enormity of the enemy's reach came into exacting focus when Nez Perce warriors saw Flatheads among the settlers at Fort Fizzle, and when their chief Charlo bluntly refused to take their side in the conflict. "Why should I shake hands with men whose hands are bloody?" he reportedly told Looking Glass. The killings in Idaho had followed the Nez Perce to Montana.

Despite the objections, Looking Glass still favored taking the familiar route to the buffalo plains. The war might not be over, but General Howard's complete failure to give chase, coupled with Captain Rawn's impotent display at the Lolo Pass, gave the chief confidence that the bands could cross Montana's vastness without a fight. Looking Glass could easily have imagined that once they reached the Crow, they would be impossible to defeat on the battlefield. Sixty men had slaughtered the cavalry at White Bird Canyon. Just two dozen warriors had held Howard's entire force at bay above the Clearwater. If they could expand their force many times over, who could conquer them? With every peaceful interaction with white settlers, the Nez Perce families would make local civilians think twice about volunteering to fight, depriving the army of a crucial source of support in rough and remote country. At the same time, the goodwill that the bands were gaining would earn them leverage for an eventual negotiation that might allow them to head home. Even if they ultimately had to flee to Canada, it still made sense to go through the buffalo plains. By hunting along the way, they could restore at least some of the wealth they had lost in Idaho — fur and skin for clothing and teepees, bone and horn and hoofs for tools, a winter's worth of meat — and approach Sitting Bull from a position of strength.

As the Nez Perce bands rambled south through the valley, breaking camp late and stopping before sunset, many remained convinced that the war would catch up with them. Yellow Wolf enjoyed the easy August days, the beautiful country, and interactions with settlers that struck him as friendly, yet something nagged at him, he later said, "a feeling some of us could not understand." Wahlitits, who had shed the first blood along the Salmon River and wanted to finish the war with a grand charge above the Clearwater, began dreaming of his impending death — a significant vision for a people who believed in the power of prophecy. "My brothers, my sisters, I am telling you! I will be killed soon!" he proclaimed. "I do not care. I am willing to die. But first, I will kill some soldiers. I shall not turn back from the death. We are all going to die!"

Another warrior, Peopeo Ipsewaht (Lone Bird), announced, "My shaking heart tells me trouble and death will overtake us if we make no hurry through this land!" The vision that had been revealed to him was so compelling that he felt it necessary to interrupt the chiefs as they sat in a circle smoking. "Maybe our enemies are now overtaking us, and we get whipped!" he said. "Be ready for fighting any time! Keep going! Move fast! Death may now be following us on our trail." Wottolen, respected for his spiritual power, dreamed of soldiers. White Bird openly questioned Looking Glass about their pace. "By the way you are acting you seem to anticipate no danger," the older chief said. "How do we know but that some of these days or nights we shall be attacked by the whites?"

"Who is going to trouble us?" Looking Glass countered. "The little bunch of soldiers from Missoula are not fools enough to attack us. We had best take the world as easily as possible." Everything the Nez Perce bands saw confirmed the chief's sense of their situation. When about ten Nez Perce families living in the Bitterroot — strong hunters led by Wahwookya Wasaaw (Lean Elk, known to local settlers as Poker Joe) — decided to accompany the bands to buffalo country, the journey felt all the more like a normal, joyous summer migration.

On the far side of the Continental Divide, the bands set up camp alongside a lush creek in a high grassy valley ringed by steep hills thick with pine. Yellow Wolf knew the place well from his journeys to and from buffalo country. Nez Perce travelers had long camped at Iskumtselalik Pah — Place of the Ground Squirrels, known to settlers as the Big Hole. They put their horses out to pasture — "good feed for horses," Yellow Wolf recalled — and the women went to work, chopping down and peeling the bark off trees to make lodgepoles. They had left hundreds of them back at Mouth of the Canyon.

At night, the chill in the air already hinting at summer's end, the nontreaty bands celebrated as they had not since gathering at Tepahlewam seven weeks earlier to prepare to move onto the reservation. Once again, the warriors paraded. There was no shame in their procession, no one to insult after the valor and victories of June and July. Everyone sang, laughed, and told stories. They imagined the plenty that awaited them in buffalo country. "Everybody with good feeling," Yellow Wolf said. "No more fighting after Lolo Pass. War was quit. All Montana citizens our friends. . . . It was past midnight when we went to bed."

After the battle above the Clearwater ended on

July 12, the land became Erskine Wood's enemy. One night march followed by twenty excruciating miles in the mid-July sun, dry grass up to his knees — no sleep, no breakfast, shoes worn through, no water, "no nothin' now," the lieutenant wrote in his diary — and the "killing, stifling" heat ripped through his company, dropping enough men that "we had to dump our packs from the mules to carry the sick." When the sun set, Wood could not read books or write letters even if he wanted to. With rumors flying that the Indians would turn back toward the Idaho settlements, light of any kind — campfires, pipes and cigars, even a stray match — was forbidden. In dark and often muddy camps, Wood unrolled his rubber tarp and ate hardtack cold with sardines, currant jelly, and tomatoes that he had bought from his captain with an IOU. His skin was layered in grime, his two pairs of drawers and three pairs of socks unspeakably filthy. "We are living like pigs and look like them," one officer wrote from the field. War was boring, and it was agony. Wood craved what he called "rest for the weary sole."

On Saturday, July 21, Howard's army camped beside one of the creeks that cut through the prairie and prepared to stay for a few days. Wood's prayers — "trout, ease, and comfort" — were answered. At leisure, Wood could let his mind wander freely, to, in his words, "Joseph, and sickness, the World, the Flesh, and the Devil." He could think back on the marches, tedious but also romantic in their way, "hillsides speckled with herd and pack train," reminiscent "of an Oriental camp in some desert, or steppe," the kind of exotic scene he had pictured when he toyed with leaving West Point to join the French Foreign Legion.

Wood could also contemplate the enemy. Even in close fighting, the Indians had appeared to him only in quick, blurry glimpses, dark forms scrambling through the smoke, brush, and rock. After the Clearwater battle, Wood might have held his plunder from the abandoned village — sipped water from the drinking horn — and fancied himself a Nez Perce warrior, but it would have been an act of pure imagination. Only when the army reached Kamiah did Wood see Nez Perce men, women, and children up close. On July 16, Red Heart's band presented themselves to General Howard, the chief announcing that his people had been in Montana at the start of the violence and never wavered in their commitment to peace. But Howard confiscated their horses and ordered the families jailed as prisoners of war.

Assigned to oversee their initial confinement — his captain serving on a commission that tried and failed to determine their guilt or innocence — Wood listened to the "woes and troubles of the innocent captives," mulling "the unhappy people and the fate before them." It was the first time since leaving Alaska that he had talked with Indians. He tried to be objective and scientific, noting the "difference in physical characteristics between these Indians and the Alaskans" and how impressed he was that the Nez Perce captives were more of "the Roman type. Alaskans purely Asiatic." Ultimately, though, the conversations forced Wood to consider "the Indian as . . . a man and brother" — borrowing a phrase that the abolitionists had famously deployed in proclaiming their sympathy with slaves. He wanted to be lenient, to "read them a lecture for general effect and say, 'go and sin no more,' " but he had no authority to decide their fate. Red Heart's people were sent away from Howard's column, marched under guard to Lapwai, and, lamenting the people, land, and lives they were leaving behind, put on a boat to Fort Vancouver.

On Sunday, July 22, while Wood rested, reinforcements from as far away as Fort Yuma in Arizona Territory began streaming into camp, with hundreds more expected from Atlanta, Boise, and Washington Territory. Amid the bustle, the lieutenant's leisure was interrupted by orders to appear before the general. Despite their personal relationship, Wood had not seen much of Howard during his month in the field. But now he was informed that the general, seeking to replace two aides who had fallen sick, would be adding Wood to his staff. Joining him would be the general's son Guy, Wood's dear friend, an artillery lieutenant newly arrived with his company from San Francisco. Once again, General Howard had changed Wood's life.

Up on a horse, Erskine Wood could finally see the Camas Prairie's easy roll. Just a few feet from the ground, the air was lighter, the breeze more constant. The view was broader. Wearing the buckskin-patched riding pants he had brought to Alaska, using a saddle and spurs borrowed from the general, the lieutenant immediately began to experience a different war from what he had known. No longer defined by the drift and drudgery of endless marching, his days were packed with purpose. Fifteen, twenty, twenty-five miles of riding — no easy task — but then his real work would begin. Waiting for the mule train and assessing the state of the column's supplies might require three more hours of work in the sun.

Afterward, he would open a wooden traveling desk and begin climbing the general's mountain of correspondence. There was no rest — "I hardly have time to wash my hands," another aide complained — but it never quite settled into a routine that bored Wood. New tasks had a way of "burst[ing] forth with the most startling unexpectedness," he described in one the few letters he managed to write as an aide-de-camp. "A ragged courier or a naked Indian dashing madly into camp at any hour of the day or night may bring to me work enough to last a month." Although he would drolly describe himself as "an overworked and much abused individual," it was plain to everyone that Wood relished his new role — it was the most meaningful work he had ever done in the army. He stopped imagining what awaited him elsewhere. "I like Wood much better in camp than I did in garrison," another officer wrote. "He has plenty of pluck and energy and is doing his duty."

At night Wood dined with the general, the chief of staff, a few other aides-de-camp, the quartermaster, the army surgeon, and a reporter who sold stories to papers in Portland and New York. The men in Howard's mess ate with silver spoons. Instead of sleeping under the stars, Wood now shared a tent with the general and his son. Up close, Wood saw a man who needed the comfort of familiar faces. Everyone else, it seemed, was against him. Settlers had been openly disrespectful as Howard rode through the Camas Prairie. Local papers portrayed him as a blunderer and a coward. Rumors trickled into camp that his effigy was burning at Lewiston. His immediate superior, General Irvin McDowell, sent an aide from Division of the Pacific headquarters in San Francisco to investigate the conduct of the war, amid press dispatches from the east that President Hayes was exploring "the advisability of superseding General Howard, under consideration by Cabinet."

To work for Howard was to fight on many fronts. In war, lives were occasionally lost, but reputations were always on the line. With each battle's end came the beginning of new struggles over whether the results signaled Howard's strength or weakness as a commander. As the campaign's second month began, the general found himself the butt of what an aide called "the most unjust and wicked attack," a "stream of vile slander," all the more galling because "men who know nothing of warfare presume to take to task men who have spent their lives in it." Howard's worst days at the Freedmen's Bureau had not thickened his skin. Once again, he felt the abuse "keenly." Most demoralizing was the talk in the capital of relieving the general of his command. The very idea of it — being summoned to Washington for a public humiliation — sickened Howard. "He says he would rather die than be thus disgraced," his chief of staff wrote on July 23.

At the Clearwater, fortune finally smiled on the general. McDowell's aide arrived just in time to see the army's final charge and the Indians in headlong flight and pronounced that "nothing can surpass the vigor of . . . Howard's movements and action." The general seized on the ringing endorsement and began waging a campaign to sway public opinion. Leapfrogging protocol, Howard ordered the aide's report sent directly to the president, and saved his job. But with the renegade Nez Perce bands still at large, Howard knew it was only a temporary reprieve. For a moment after the battle, he had thought that Joseph would surrender and even discussed terms with a Nez Perce man claiming to be the chief's messenger. It turned out to be a false hope — a cruel trick, Howard thought, designed by Joseph to stall the army while the Indians took to the Lolo Trail. Driving the hostile Nez Perce bands out of Idaho had silenced some of his harshest critics in the territory, yet as soon as the Indians emerged from the Bitterroot Mountains, a new round of vituperation from a different group of settlers would surely begin.

Howard realized there was no stopping the Indians before they reached Montana. Joseph had an enormous head start. And if Howard's major failing in waging this war so far had been his complete — perhaps inexcusable — inability to move his army across rivers, now he had to traverse the kind of terrain that an aide had called "a perfect sea of mountains." Howard well knew that along the trail, the army would have to proceed at a snail's pace in a thin line that extended for miles, practically inviting an attack. Already, when his scouts tried to ride into the mountains after the Nez Perce, they had been quickly spotted and turned back under heavy fire, leaving one man dead, another shot in the chest. As the events of the past month had proven, it would court disaster to rush after the bands without everything in place. Howard was determined to be patient and prepare carefully.

Outfitting the army was an arduous process. The general needed more troops. He wanted fresh mounts for the cavalry; after a month in the field, the old horses were bone thin and could barely reach a trot. The quartermaster at Lewiston was trying to collect and distribute enough food, medicine, supplies, and ammunition to support a thousand men for weeks in the wilderness, not to mention an extraordinary moving infrastructure to carry everything — hundreds of mules, wagons pulled by two- and four-horse teams, packers, teamsters, blacksmiths, wheelwrights, saddlers, and corral masters. Nothing — people, animals, equipment — came easy. The Oregon Steam Navigation Company had hiked its government rates by 10 percent, and civilians were demanding high wages in coin. The wagons called in from all the forts and army depots within steamer's reach were often old, rotten from disuse — unlikely to last a day in the mountains. Most of the local mules were scattered among isolated farming communities that needed them to survive. It would take upwards of two weeks before the army could begin its march to Montana.

With every day that passed, Joseph was slipping Howard's grasp. But the general still had one weapon that could stop the nontreaty bands: the telegraph. As soon as it became clear that the Indians were heading east, he wired messages to the army garrisons at Missoula and Fort Shaw, both an easy distance from the eastern end of the Lolo Trail. If they could delay the Nez Perce bands, Howard's column could close in and trap them.

Until that moment, until the army could, in one aide's words, "over take Joseph . . . [and] whip him out of his boots," Howard would have no sway over the course of the war in the coming days and weeks. He kept despair at bay by work-ing relentlessly on what he could control: amassing and maneuvering his fighting force. In the quiet moments, in his tent and under starry skies, Howard calmed himself by asking his aides to sing hymns to him. He specifically requested that they sing "What Shall the Harvest Be?" It was a favorite of the temperance movement, a hymn that drew its power from uncertainty. Paul's epistle to the Galatians taught that whatever a man sows, he shall also reap. The hymn moved men to quit strong drink by forcing them to reflect on what they had done with their lives, whether they had "sown in the darkness or sown in the light, sown in our weakness or sown in our might." The third verse in particular was known to cause temperance meetings to erupt into sobs: "Sowing the seed of a lingering pain, / Sowing the seed of a maddened brain, / Sowing the seed of a tarnished name, / Sowing the seed of eternal shame; / Oh, what shall the harvest be?" As Howard felt the lingering pain of Reconstruction, brooded over his reputation, and considered the shame of failing to capture Joseph, he was asking the same question of himself.

CHAPTER 16
LIGHTNING ALL AROUND

Riding through the Bitterroot Valley, Lieutenant James Bradley saw things differently from the rest of the 7th Infantry. At Fort Owen and in Stevensville, the soldiers spent most of their time gathering intelligence from the settlers about the Nez Perce bands, shaming the people who had done business with the Indians, and recruiting volunteers for the fight ahead. Bradley understood and was focused on the task at hand. But it could not have escaped him that they were passing one of the oldest trading posts in the territory, a place he had written about in an old journal — "built as a Catholic Mission, called St. Mary's and sold to Major Owen who renamed it after himself." An amateur historian, he had spent many months trying to imagine what life had been like for the first traders forty years earlier — eating dogs and raw buffalo flesh to survive, forging delicate alliances with local chiefs, battling hostile tribes, raising families with Indian wives. As the lead scout for a force of 160 soldiers under Colonel John Gibbon's command, the lieutenant was continually obliged to imagine what was about to happen — what was over the ridge, around the bend, through the thicket. From the moment his company had set out from Fort Shaw, he had been mapping in his mind where the Indians would go — surely, he thought, south along the Bitterroot Valley to the Big Hole. But even as he busied himself predicting the future, he knew, better than anyone around him, that everything he saw had a past. There was always another story that could be told.

Bradley was built like a teenage boy — slight, drawn, with big dark eyes and sharp cheeks. Only a black mustache, carefully trimmed, suggested his true age and experience. At thirty-three, he had spent nearly half his years in uniform, since April 1861, when he enlisted in an Ohio regiment at a month shy of seventeen. After dozens of battles and six months imprisoned at Andersonville, the lieutenant had learned that what defined a life in the army was not how one fought, but rather how one spent the time between fights. The only reason he was pursuing Chief Joseph in the first place was because of a decision he had made off the battlefield. While serving with the garrison occupying Atlanta in 1871, he had devoted his idle hours to wooing the post surgeon's fifteen-year-old daughter. After they eloped, his enraged father-in-law demanded that he request a transfer, and in 1872, Bradley and his young bride went west. There, on the frontier, the lieutenant saw how some of his fellow officers spent their days hunting and fishing. Some were keen on exploring and surveying the great wild spaces that surrounded them. Some lost themselves in poker games and love affairs. Bradley soon found another way to pass the hours: he would write a great history of Montana.

Bradley's interest caught flame when he was sent to Fort Benton, a hundred miles below the

Canadian border, on the ruins of the last and most remote of the fur trading posts on the Upper Missouri River. On freezing nights the young soldier listened to the old traders huddled around the chimney. Faces glowing red "by the rude hearth embers," they told "tales of rare adventures, . . . scenes of strife and carnage," Bradley wrote. "Where danger is, there is fascination, and heroes of the fur trade needed not the embellishments of fancy to put this charm to their recitals."

Intrigued, Bradley interviewed the men, and soon he was seeking out anyone who could share details of the old life, from the first priests who served Montana to the children of some of the original trading hands. He tasked himself with collecting "all obtainable books belonging to the bibliography of Montana," and in the home he shared with his wife and baby daughter, he amassed a library of a hundred volumes. In letters to the founder of the Montana Historical Society at Helena, he announced plans to write a book he would call *Land of the Blackfeet.* Drafting in earnest, he contributed pieces to local papers and showed himself to be, in the judgment of the *Bozeman Times,* a "writer of ability."

Montana's history was within Bradley's grasp — dating to the early 1830s, the fur trade in Blackfeet country was only about a decade older than he was — but it could feel strange and remote, irretrievably gone. By the mid-1870s, almost everywhere he traveled in the territory had been tamed, rendered safe and secure, girded with rail ties, plowed by farmers, befouled by miners. "Even the Indian character that one may study," Bradley surmised, "is a character distorted from the proud and haughty original, ere fear of the

426

white man had put its seal upon it."

The wild past, in Bradley's telling, was a story of incredible men — "strong, brave, hardy, generous trappers," indomitable, shrewd, and eloquent chiefs, and, on occasion, eccentric naturalists and artists, including one honest-to-goodness German nobleman who appeared at a trading fort in 1832 wearing "a white slouch hat, a black velvet coat, . . . and probably the greasiest pair of trousers that ever encased princely legs." They lived by rough codes of honor. They died desperately — in ambushes and mass slaughters, from infected wounds, in mires of mud and quicksand, in churning river rapids, from cholera and scurvy and "severe colic." In the throes of strong drink, they killed each other over slights, real and imagined. Some committed murders cold sober, for no reason at all, "as if infatuated with a relish for blood."

As he studied the history of Montana, Bradley could not help but consider the native tribes — Blackfeet, Blood and Piegan, Gros Ventre, Assiniboine, and Crow. Bradley began talking with the Indian scouts who worked under his supervision, learning what he could about Indian myth and religion, as well as great early chiefs like the Crow leader Rotten Belly. For much of the first decade of fur trading, whites were a trivial presence in the wilderness, little more than an audience for the real drama of war and peace among the Indians. As the interlopers made alliances with the Blackfeet, the Crow treated them as they would any other enemy tribe, stealing the traders' horses and besieging their forts. Still, the presence of white men exerted a certain gravitational force — Indians began hunting beavers to scarcity, then buffalo as fashions in the East changed, trading thousands of pelts for arsenals of modern weapons — but the basic logic of tribal life remained unchanged.

Over time, in sudden shocks, the tribes were pulled apart. In 1837, smallpox all but destroyed the local tribes. In village after village, the loss defied comprehension — twelve hundred warriors reduced to eighty, six hundred to thirty. A trader Bradley interviewed described riding through one settlement of sixty lodges that had appeared normal from a distance, if eerily silent. Up close, the air grew suddenly thick. "Hundreds of decaying forms of human beings, horses and dogs lay scattered everywhere among the lodges," Bradley wrote. "It was like another Assyrian host that the Angel of Death had overwhelmed in a night." From then on, the white forts became central to a decimated Indian population. After the great dying season, the traders noticed a great increase in their buffalo trade, with tens of thousands more pelts than any prior year. Puzzled at first because so many hunters had perished, they soon realized that the remnant tribes were surviving by selling the robes of the dead. The great cities of the United States, Bradley imagined, were clothed and upholstered in "thousands of robes taken from the decomposing bodies of these victims."

A generation later, in 1862, the discovery of gold was similarly catastrophic. Within months, thousands of whites were turning the wilderness into mass excavations or, just as devastating, into towns, farms, and ranches. In much of Montana the Indians had no place and no way to live, except on reservations. When Bradley began his research a decade later, he considered the Indians

428

as historical subjects above all, firmly part of Montana's past. Indian unrest — the Sioux crisis of 1876, now the Nez Perce — was a mere death spasm, a sign of things, in Bradley's words, "that were but are not."

Bradley knew that it remained possible to experience what life had been like in old Montana. It was a lesson that he had learned in his first moments in the territory, when he arrived at the Helena railroad station sick with what turned out to be smallpox. His first two months in the West, the worst of winter, he spent quarantined with his wife in a small miner's cabin on the far outskirts of town. In the years that followed, as he marched through mud, deep drifts, and freezing wind, as he blacked his eyes with lamp soot to ward off snow blindness, it required no leaps of imagination to understand what the early trappers had endured.

The lieutenant was also aware that he, too, was living in historic times. For much of 1877, he had put down his drafts of *Land of the Blackfeet* to focus on more recent events — various army campaigns over the past several years that culminated in 1876 with what he called "our Centennial Indian War." For once, he did not have to rely on informants. His field notes were brimming with firsthand observations. While Custer had gone east from the Dakota Territory, Colonel Gibbon had led a column of infantry and cavalry west from Montana, with Bradley as his commandant of scouts. Everywhere the column went, the lieutenant found occasion to reflect on what had happened there in the past; their route took them by an old Missouri Fur Company trading fort, ancient Indian rock glyphs, the scene of an 1872 battle with the Sioux. But as the soldiers neared Sitting Bull's village on the Little Bighorn River in late June 1876, Bradley considered the ways in which the campaign would be unprecedented, "one of the biggest Indian battles ever fought on this continent, and the most decisive in its results." "There is not much glory in Indian wars," he wrote on June 24, "but it will be worth while to have been present at such an affair as this."

A few days later, when Crow scouts came into camp weeping so hard that they could barely tell their story — a disastrous defeat, "the corpses of Custer's men . . . strewn all over the country" — many refused to believe them. "Such a catastrophe it was asserted was wholly improbable, nay, impossible," Bradley wrote. "If a battle had been fought, which was condescendingly admitted might have happened, then Custer was victorious." The lieutenant, however, believed the scouts. On June 27, 1876, Bradley rode ahead into the Little Bighorn Valley. There the scouts found a dead horse — a cavalry horse — and upon investigating, the lieutenant climbed a ridge, looked down, and became the first soldier to see Custer's cavalry lying in the field. He counted the dead — most stripped, some scalped, some bludgeoned with war clubs — and then led several officers back to the scene of the Last Stand, watching as they identified Custer.

Upon his return to Montana, Bradley began giving interviews about the Last Stand and published a letter about his experience among the dead. Determined to portray the soldiers as heroes, he recounted the scene as appalling, yet ennobling. Custer's body had been stripped naked and left to rot in the sun, yet in Bradley's telling, it remained capable of inspiring the living. It moved the lieutenant to picture scenes of incredible courage, the men of the 7th Cavalry rallying around their charismatic leader, refusing to surrender, never giving up even when surrounded by an overwhelming and terrifying foe. Bradley's blend of hard testimony and gauzy myth was irresistible to readers. It established him as a public man, someone whose fifth wedding anniversary and routine comings and goings to and from Fort Shaw were now found worthy of mention in the Helena papers. When he advertised that he would be writing about the Sioux campaigns, he was so encouraged by the number of advance subscriptions that were sent to him that he resolved to make the book bigger — an octavo instead of a duodecimo — and a hundred pages longer. "With thanks for the hearty encouragement," he wrote, "I will do my best to produce a book worthy of it."

Polishing his rough notes into something worthy of publication, Bradley had reached his diary entry for June 26, 1876 — the eve of his grisly discovery — when he was called into the field to follow the Nez Perce bands. The 1877 campaign, too, was shaping up to be fodder for another book. The lieutenant had left Fort Shaw with little expectation that Colonel Gibbon's column would catch Joseph, who had an enormous head start. For Bradley, the real drama was taking place thousands of miles away in Georgia: his wife had gone home for the summer with their young daughter, a second child on the way. But in the Bitterroot Valley, it became apparent that the army was gaining rapidly, covering twice as much ground as the Indians. Riding in wagons most of the way, the infantry was well rested. There just might be a battle after all.

Along the way, three dozen settlers joined Colonel Gibbon's column, including some who had lived in the valley long enough to be fruitful sources for Bradley's research. Carrying rifles, their belts heavy with cartridges, they loudly proclaimed their hatred for the Indians. At least one, Amos Buck, was making up for the fact that they had spent the previous week trading with the Indians, although he was loath to admit it. In his words, "there was too much of the good red blood of the revolutionary forefathers running through our veins to permit these ruthless savages to get off scot free." Others, like the young man who ducked into Bradley's tent one night and volunteered to fight, were looking for easy adventure, plus horses from the Nez Perce herd. With an old pistol and a needle gun, twenty-three year-old Tom Sherrill and his brother Bunch, pasty and lank, were ready for a bit of glory and "that bunch of ponies." "I was nothing but a boy," Tom would remember. "I thought it would be a snap." They had butcher's knives from home, sharpened just before they left. "We would take our knives out of the scabbard," Bunch recalled, "and run a thumb over the edge to see if they were in good shape to raise a scalp with."

By sunset on August 7, Gibbon's column was looking up at the Continental Divide. That night, the colonel sent Bradley ahead with sixty men, including most of the volunteers, to find the Nez Perce camp. The next day, as the main column struggled to get wagons up the steep trail — pulling them with dragropes, hacking at large rocks and fallen trees that blocked the way, abandoning

432

worn-out mules by the trailside — Bradley rode toward the Big Hole. Then, leaving his men at a safe distance, he crawled with another lieutenant through the pine slopes bounding the valley. After a while, they heard a dull rhythm — axes pounding. Inching forward, they got close enough to see women chopping lodgepoles, then closer still, until the men were listening to conversations in a language they did not understand. They climbed a tree and looked down at the Nez Perce camp. Past the herd roaming the hillsides, just on the other side of the willow-veiled stream that meandered through the Big Hole, about ninety teepees ran north and south by the water, the prairie stretching wide beyond. Bradley sent word of his discovery back to Gibbon, who left his wagons and field howitzer under a small guard and marched his men quickly forward. They reached Bradley's bivouac, about five miles from the Indian camp, at sundown on August 8.

After a cold dinner — hardtack, raw bacon, and water — and naps on beds of pine branches, Gibbon's army of 180 men set out before midnight, no overcoats, no canteens, each carrying only weapons and a hundred rounds of ammunition. Bradley had briefed the colonel on the camp, the herds — maybe two or three thousand horses — and surrounding terrain. It was the kind of description the lieutenant had perfected, as a scout and as a historian. His manuscripts were filled with accounts of settlements — how big they were, how close to the water, what they traded, where the herds grazed, where the whiskey was stored, how they were built to survive raids and sieges by hostile tribes. These places were static points, momentarily fixed amid the constant cycles of seasons, booms and busts, weakness and power, war and peace, life and death. Gibbon listened to Bradley and devised his attack.

By two o'clock, the soldiers could see fires across the stream, teepees glowing in flickering light. They heard voices — "none of us understood their lingo," a volunteer remembered — and babies crying. Silence ebbed and flowed as dogs bayed in call and response with coyotes. Gibbon whispered his orders. They would strike at dawn. Bradley would lead the volunteers and some soldiers in attacking the north end of the camp. Two companies would hit the center, and a third would come from the south. Three more companies would lay back in reserve. The soldiers would get as close as they could to the Indians, blast low into the teepees — three volleys — then charge. One officer described the plan as a "reveille of blood."

After waiting two cold, anxious hours — "few men go rejoicing to a bloody conflict," one of the lieutenants wrote of that moment, "but anything is preferable to the suspense" — the soldiers moved toward their positions. Bradley walked his men downhill, slipping past the Nez Perce horses — they would take the herd later — then trudging through tangles of brush to the bogs at streamside. But before they could reach the water, a single unsuspecting Nez Perce man rode slowly out of the willows. Too old to be a warrior, most likely he had woken early and crossed the stream to check on his horses. He never reached them. Under a sky streaking red, the volunteers blasted him three or four times. Up and down the line Gibbon's soldiers began shooting across the water into the teepees.

Told by the colonel's aide to "go in and strike

them hard," Bradley shouted for his men to charge through the stream and into the camp. He had been picturing this moment from the time he first saw the Nez Perce teepees the previous day — before Gibbon's column arrived, he weighed the possibility of attacking just with his scouts, one of them remembered, "to charge through the camp, each man for himself, then charge back again, and in that way hold them until Gibbon came up or whip them before he came." Bradley's notebooks were stuffed with forty years of ambushes, attacks, and pitched battles, a welter of gore that provided the most enduring connection between Montana's past and present. He had devoted considerable thought and imagination to the moment when "silent rifles began to speak," that "sudden roar [when] the storm of bullets is hurled into the unsuspecting throng." He had written about the "wild commotion" of a charge, about hearing wails of fear "mingled with some notes of agony from the wounded."

As shattering as the first volleys had to have been — as he heard the Nez Perce families shouting and weeping — Bradley knew that the enemy would find a way to fight back, that a hum would soon rise from the camp "like that of a swarm of angry bees." In his writing about Indians, he could confidently generalize that "when the safety of their villages, with their wives, children, and all that they possess is involved . . . , they prove themselves able to fight with something of the courage and resolution of civilized men." From the other side of the stream, Nez Perce warriors started firing their rifles.

Charging a determined foe is a test. In one notebook, the lieutenant quoted what the great

435

Crow chief Rotten Belly was heard to say before his final battle, a decade before Bradley was born. "Now we shall see who are brave men," the chief declared, just before rushing at twelve Gros Ventre warriors. "I shall lead the attack though I feel that I am to fall in it." Bradley would be creating a new chapter for the West, and at the same time would be reenacting an old story. He and his men would show no mercy. They would humble the Nez Perce hostiles, end a war, and avenge the Idaho settlers. They would do what Montanans had always done. With one of the volunteers by his side, the lieutenant ran at the willows that lined the stream. He took just a few steps before he fell, dead from a bullet to the face.

In Nez Perce myths, death is constant and strange. Creatures drown in freezing water, are poisoned by droplets of urine, pierced by arrows, spears, and sharp stubbled grass, and crushed by clubs, stone axes, and powerful jaws. They are killed by uncles, grandmothers, and lovers. Coyote feeds Bear a searing hot stone hidden in delicious lacy caul fat, burning him to death from the inside. Salmon, wearing Rattlesnake's teeth, bites Wolf as he drinks from a stream — "Oh, he just writhed away in mortal agony," a storyteller recounted, "and suddenly fell dead." Raccoon Boy, chased up a tree, shoves a thorn needle deep inside a pursuing She-Bear's ear. Weasel buries himself in a nest of voracious ants, which pick his bones clean. Death is rooted in reality, yet is beyond reality. Nez Perce men, women, and children could nod at the fates of these creatures, situate the deaths among the steep canyons and churning rivers, even as they could never experience death in the same way.

Waking in darkness to a thick deafening roar, hundreds of bullets riddling their teepees, lodgepoles splintering, many Nez Perce wondered if they were trapped in a dream. For most of the people in the camp, weeks of fighting and fleeing — of dislocation, of dispossession — had finally given way to an enduring sense that their lives could go on as in times past. When they had gone to sleep late the night before, they could envision the months and even years ahead, staying among friends, hunting buffalo on the plains, living happy lives, lives of plenty. But they woke before dawn, and their resilient world, the world that they knew, was bursting apart.

Nez Perce families crawled from their teepees out among slaughtered horses and dead dogs. Their faces and eyes were showered with dirt and twigs, their ears ripped and ringing. What was happening to them they found hard to describe. It felt like a summer hailstorm, survivors would say, or acorns falling in a hard autumn wind. The guns barked like beasts. The air sang with bullets. "It was like spurts of fire," remembered Red Elk, ten at a time, "lightning all around." It was, the warrior Two Moons said, "raining lead."

The people saw and heard things that none of them had ever imagined. They died in ways that they never conceived possible. By the teepees, they crawled past a wailing baby on a dead woman's breast. Sixty years later, a woman had never forgotten the sight, the lifeless mother, the baby "swinging one arm shattered by a bullet," she said. "The hand, all bloody, hanging by a string of flesh and skin, dropped back and forth with the moving arm." Farther along, a fifteen-year-old boy crawled beside an old woman until a bullet ripped through her chest. "You better not stay here," she told him. "Be going, I'm shot." "I heard the bullet strike," he remembered. "Then she died."

Women and children sought cover in the willows by the stream, only to run straight into soldiers charging the village. A five-year-old watched his mother and baby sister drop silently as they fled, a single bullet killing them both. Reaching the brush, a woman tried to curl herself around a little girl, only to feel the child go slack and die — "killed," she would say. "Killed under my arm." In freezing water up to his shoulders, a ten-year-old boy watched a girl raise her wounded arm up in the air, dazed with pain, the bullet hole so big he could see through it. In the smoky twilight, Ollokot's wife Wetatonmi recognized the body of a beautiful boy, "nearly half-grown," by the water. "Everybody liked that boy," she said. It did not seem possible that he was gone. "I thought maybe he had been dreaming and, hearing shots, ran out and was killed," she later said. "I was hardly awake myself when I ran from the tepee." She kept running, not knowing where her husband was.

The soldiers rampaged through the south end of the camp, torching teepees, shooting everyone they saw. The smell of burning hides and canvas filled the air. Parents who had left their children hiding inside under blankets and buffalo robes listened to them scream and choke and burn.

The shooting was so thick that many warriors could not reach for the guns they kept tied to lodgepoles, but Wahlitits held his rifle as he and his pregnant wife fled their teepee. They were barely outside when she was wounded and could go no farther. Wahlitits lay flat behind a thin log, almost completely exposed, and began firing as soldiers streamed through the willows. Wahlitits had caused the war almost two months earlier when he sought revenge along the Salmon River. He had pleaded with his fellow warriors to finish it with a grand charge on the bluffs above the Clearwater. His war ended in the Big Hole as he had dreamed it. He shot one soldier before he was hit, then lay on his back and died facing the dawning sky. His wife took his gun, killed another soldier, then was shot dead lying across her husband.

The great warrior Rainbow dashed into the cold air resolved to face death — it was what his guiding spirit, his *wey-ya-kin,* had always told him. During the day bullets could not touch him. "I can . . . walk among my enemies," he often said. "I can face the point of the gun. My body no thicker than a hair, the enemies can never hit me." It was a power — a promise — that came with an equally certain truth. "If I have any battle or fighting before the sunrise," he knew, "I shall be killed." Although some people were running north, where the initial volleys did not materialize into a charge, Rainbow took his rifle and headed straight at the soldiers. His gun misfired, and he fell in the willows, shot in the heart.

Joseph held his baby girl in his arms. With his wife Springtime wounded in the first volleys, the chief left her in their teepee toward the north of camp, ran with their child to the tall grass by the stream, and hid while the soldiers charged through. Soon after, the warrior Two Moons came running past. The camp was starting to burn, and Joseph was powerless to stop the carnage. "I have no gun for defending myself," he told Two Moons. He was barefoot, with no leggings — he wore just a shirt and had wrapped a blanket around his legs. "Skip for your life," Two Moons urged. "Without the gun you can do nothing. Save the child!"

From the willows, from the fires, from the north end of camp, voices screamed out, urging the warriors to regroup and attack. "My brothers!" the warrior Kowtoliks shouted. "Our tepees are on fire! Get ready your arms! Make resistance! You are here for that purpose!" War whoops began to sound amid the roaring gunfire. "Now is our time; fight!" White Bird called. "These soldiers cannot fight harder than the ones we defeated on Salmon River and in White Bird Canyon. Fight! Shoot them down."

Heeding such calls, Yellow Wolf ran south through the camp toward the battle armed only with his war club. Past two warriors — one bleeding from the head, one dying from a bullet in the stomach — he saw a wounded soldier, "crawling like a drunken man." Yellow Wolf bludgeoned his enemy with such force that the man's false teeth fell out of his mouth. Now the warrior had an army rifle and a belt full of cartridges. He ran on and saw the burning teepees. He knew there were people inside. "I grew hot with anger," he later said. "It was for the lives of women and children we were fighting. If whipped better to die than go in bondage with freedom gone."

As the sun rose, Yellow Wolf crouched and darted among smoldering fires and the dead and dying. He preferred to fight alone. Other warriors, maybe ten, scattered through the southern part of camp. From teepee to teepee, the killing was so close that warriors recognized settlers with whom they had amicably traded in the Bitterroot Valley the week before. Yellow Wolf was near enough to his enemies to know that every blast of his gun would bring death. He shot one soldier, then a second, then a third. With each kill Yellow Wolf collected another rifle, another cartridge belt, to hand out to any warrior who needed one.

While the battle raged, Joseph devoted himself to what needed to be saved. At the north of the camp, where the soldiers had never charged, women and children could survive the fight. Handing off his baby girl, he went for the herd. Without it, the Nez Perce families had nothing — no wealth, no way to outrun the army. On foot, it would be impossible to carry large stores of food. They would have to leave children and the elderly behind. They would be destroyed. Taking a young man with him, Joseph crossed the stream and ran uphill. Others, mostly too small to fight, were following them. They found the herd huddled in panic. Mounting two horses, they drove the rest up the slope, far from the soldiers.

Across an hour, then another, the Nez Perce warriors grew stronger — more men fighting, with more and better weapons. The soldiers' lethal grip on the camp went limp. A man on horseback — obviously their commander — rode in, but instead of rallying his troops, he drew immediate fire. Soon his pants were soaking with blood, and his horse was dying. Warriors hiding by and across the stream were pouring bullets back into the camp. The soldiers had no easy targets, and they were being picked off one by one. They began running back across the stream, wading past bodies floating in the water.

South and uphill, through the willows, on the

441

open slopes below the trees, the warriors gave chase, near enough to their foes that they could reach out and touch them. In the tight struggle, one Nez Perce warrior fired a bullet clean through a soldier and hit another Nez Perce warrior. Yellow Wolf shot one fleeing man through the heart, bludgeoned another with his war club. His nose was grazed by a desperate swing of an army knife.

The soldiers who made it to the woods dug holes and rifle pits, hid behind fallen logs. Warriors surrounded the position and shot at anything moving in the shadows. From their trenches, the soldiers could return deadly fire, but they were trapped, pinned down in the dirt. The chase giving way to a siege, Yellow Wolf left the battle line to gather more guns and cartridges from corpses. Fresh wounds steamed in the sharp morning air. He ate a dead soldier's hardtack and bacon.

When it seemed that the worst of the fighting was over, the hillsides concussed. After the battle along the Clearwater, the warriors could recognize a howitzer's toll, whistle, and boom. Higher along the ridge, a plume of smoke revealed the gun, still hitched to a mule team that had just arrived at the Big Hole. Several warriors, including Peopeo Tholekt, raced uphill. They killed the soldier loading the cannon, wounded two others, and slaughtered one of the pack animals. The rest of the gun crew ran off. The warriors debated what to do with the cannon, silent but still hot. Peopeo Tholekt argued that they should reposition the gun and turn it on the soldiers — warriors who had scouted for the army claimed to be able to fire it — but the others set the mules free and ran back to the battle. Left alone with the big gun, Peopeo Tholekt could follow its barrel north and east and see the camp in the distance. When the soldiers had attacked, he had fled in the dark across the stream and then joined several others in shooting back into the village. Now he could see the devastation down below, plumes of smoke, dead bodies. In the distance, past the scattered gunfire, the soldiers keening and swearing, perhaps he could hear his people, a chorus of indescribable loss. Peopeo Tholekt tried to drag the cannon to the siege by himself, but could not wheel it over a rock. He lifted the gun from its mount and rolled it down a steep drop.

Warriors began filing back into the camp, and others came out of hiding. "They had to see what had been done," Wetatonmi remembered. They found a scorched field of bodies, clusters of women and children, soldiers and warriors tangled together. Some teepees were still standing in the ruins. Yellow Wolf peered into the southernmost teepee, where a woman had spent the previous night in seclusion giving birth. He saw the new mother and her midwife lying inside, shot point blank — the baby, too, skull crushed by a boot or rifle butt. Just yards away inside another teepee, Yellow Wolf recognized her two other small children, both dead.

All the survivors, it seemed — men and women — were wailing. Wounded children were screaming. "The air was heavy with sorrow," Yellow Wolf would later say. "I would not want to hear, I would not want to see, again." A prisoner was marched into the camp and promptly shot. His killer, Yellow Wolf's cousin Otskai, called out, "Look around! These babies, these children killed! Were *they* warriors? These young girls, these young women you see dead! Were *they* warriors? These

443

young boys, these old men! Were *they* warriors?"
People recognized the dead man from the Bitterroot Valley — it made their calamity even harder
to comprehend. "These citizen soldiers!" Otskai
said. "Traded with us for our gold! . . . Our words
were good. They had two tongues. Why should we
waste time saving his life?"

Warriors debated whether to avenge their losses
on the hillside or stay back and tend to their
families, living and dead. They visited the bodies
of their fallen comrades. They wept over Rainbow,
shocked at the loss of such a powerful man.
Rainbow's fighting partner Five Wounds "cried
over his friend," Wetatonmi recalled, "cried long."
From childhood, the two men had never been
apart. Five Wounds remembered the vow they had
taken, to live together and die together. "This sun,
this time, I am going to die," he announced. "My
brother is killed, and I shall go with him." Five
Wounds walked out of camp, up the hill to the
battle line. He disappeared into the trees, heading
right up to the trenches. The soldiers heard his
death song, drowned it in gunfire, and watched
him fall. Also attacking the trenches was Sarpsis
Ilppilp, one of the first Salmon River killers, who
had charged the cavalry at White Bird Canyon in
his red blanket coat. Like his partner in both
endeavors, Wahlitits, Sarpsis Ilppilp died in a
storm of bullets. He was still wearing red.

As the living buried the dead — they found
maybe thirty fighting men, and twice as many
women, children, and people too old to fight —
Joseph rode the herd down into the valley. Women
began packing what was left of their camp, the
only work they did that could bear any resemblance to their normal routines. They tied some of

the wounded into their saddles. For the others, they tied lodge-poles to the horses and stretched hides and canvas between them. The day before, the women had harvested the wood so they could live well in buffalo country. Now the lodgepoles would be used for travois, dragging the dying on the hard, steep trails ahead. By afternoon, most of the warriors had returned to the hillside, working with Ollokot to hold off the army while everyone else rode east. Joseph, along with White Bird, would lead the women, children, and elders. With guns popping in the distance, they rode across the Big Hole, still moving toward buffalo country, but unable to imagine the lives that awaited them.

CHAPTER 17
FURY

From the hilltops above Kamiah, the Nez Perce reservation looked idyllic: tidy farms, plunging canyons, and gentle prairie. "I was astonished and delighted with the prospect spread out, as it were, at our feet," the army surgeon Jenkins FitzGerald described to his wife upon joining General Howard's column at the end of July. But down in the valley of the Clearwater, the doctor found it a completely different place. "Of course, it looked better at a distance," he wrote, "for . . . here on the scene, you come in contact with the more repulsive features of the still savage inhabitants." It was all a matter of perspective.

Along the Lolo Trail through the first week of August, whenever Howard's soldiers climbed a ridge, they gazed awestruck at the snowy peaks, blooming meadows, and thick, wooly forest. It was the most beautiful place on earth; the men clipped flowers and pressed them into letters home. But there was nothing sublime in the grueling miles from one height to the next. Steep, muddy, and doused with rain, it was "slip, slip, all the day," Howard wrote. The way was clotted with trees and fallen logs, littered with dead and dying animals abandoned by the fleeing Indians. The soldiers woke in the dark, roused from warmth into piercing cold, their washbasins and buckets clotted with ice. They marched twelve hours a day. They missed their families. Their horses and mules were slowly starving for want of grass. When a supply train from Lapwai reached the column with a few live cattle, FitzGerald did not savor the prospect of a beef dinner. Instead he wrote, "Poor things."

General Howard knew that the morale of his men turned on how they understood the hours and days and weeks that they would spend on the campaign. If Chief Joseph's escape to Montana was their shame — a mark of their failure to capture him and his people in Idaho — then they would focus on every physical hardship and indignity of the trail. But if they believed that Joseph was fleeing because the army had defeated him in the battle above the Clearwater, then their journey would feel entirely different. Part of Howard's job as a general was to ensure that his men saw their mission through the right lens.

For the most part, the soldiers and officers managed to behave just how Howard hoped they would: "cheery, hearty, happy," by his description, full of "lively stories to the circle around the campfire." The rain could not be anything except miserable, but even a glimmer of sunlight and "presto, everybody is changed, and a generally cheerful aspect prevails," the surgeon FitzGerald observed. "The life we lead . . . is very rough, and it would puzzle many to account for the fact that it is, to some extent, enjoyable." At times Howard's chief of staff fretted that his hand trunk "was in a sad state of smash" or that rain showers would ruin the "nice Bible" he had packed in an inexplicable lapse of judgment, but more often he could honestly admit, "I am well, comfortable, and dirty."

After a couple of days in the mountains, General Howard produced something few of the men had seen since the start of the war — a newspaper. The local dailies, with scathing commentary on the army's conduct, were conspicuously absent from the supply trains sent from Lapwai. Instead, Howard unfolded the more favorably inclined *Oregonian* and began reading aloud to his officers. The front page was dominated by news of massive railroad strikes that were paralyzing the East: rioting in Reading, Pennsylvania; martial law in Pittsburgh; battles between vigilantes and strikers in Chicago; mounted police charging the mob in Buffalo; tracks torn up in Brooklyn and Binghamton; people shooting at trains in Hoboken; mighty rail hubs — Cincinnati, Kansas City, St. Louis — rendered idle. The nation's great industries, its richest cities, seemed to be collapsing, their inequitable, morally hollow foundations laid bare. It was shocking news, yet had the paradoxical effect of boosting the officers' morale. To the extent that they had already botched the fight against the Nez Perce, it was almost a relief to realize that "the dreadful riots in the East," in one officer's words, "quite throws *our war* into the shade."

While the men envisioned themselves catching the hostile Nez Perce and thrashing them, bringing ponies from the Indian herd home for their children, it was never far from their minds that the enemy could already be out of reach. Initially, some predicted the Indians would head straight for the British territories, and that "our mountain climbing this week and next will not accomplish any substantial result." But even when a messenger brought word that the nontreaty bands were riding slowly through the Bitterroot Valley with Gibbon in hot pursuit, it was hard to believe that any kind of decisive battle would follow. "If the Indians want to get away I don't see what is to prevent them from doing so," Howard's chief of staff wrote. "They certainly can travel as fast as we can." The worst that could happen, it seemed, was that Howard's column would never have the chance to fight. However galling or humiliating the possibility, most of the officers could see that in the grand scheme of the nation, in the summer of 1877, whatever might happen in Montana would pale in relative significance to the upheavals occurring elsewhere. With so little at stake, they could focus on enjoying the journey, the camaraderie, and the strange sights.

After a week in the mountains, Howard's column emerged from the Lolo Trail on August 6 to good roads, grassy meadows, and a pleasantly sulfurous soak in the local hot springs. But after a messenger brought word that Gibbon was nearing the Indians on the other end of the Bitterroot Valley, Howard left his infantry behind and rode ahead with only his staff officers, surgeons, and two hundred cavalry. Covering seventy-five miles in three days, the general was "feeling very anxious to form junction with Gibbon or communicate with him," he wrote. With his Bannock scouts and twenty cavalry on the healthiest horses, Howard raced ahead before dawn on August 10. They made fifty-three miles at a trot and reached the Continental Divide by sunset. Along the way, they met seven civilian volunteers who had deserted from Gibbon's fight. Howard thought their stories were too grim to be believed — "men escaping from the field invariably exaggerate the horrors of a battle," he wrote — but he dreaded what he would find. Sending his Bannock scouts ahead in the night, Howard climbed over the pass and reached the Big Hole the next morning.

Howard discovered that for once, the deserters had not been stretching the truth. Sixty-nine men, fully half of Gibbon's force, had been killed or wounded. After running into the woods on August 9, they had spent a freezing night in wet clothes with no blankets, no food, and little ammunition, struggling to remember last messages that dying comrades had whispered for their families, resorting to prayer when at one point Nez Perce warriors tried to set the woods ablaze. Pinned down in rifle pits, tasting dirt and gravel kicked up by Indian bullets, the soldiers and volunteers were stuck with men who moaned for hours or, worse yet, predicted dark and violent fates for them all. "Every once in a while a fellow . . . would say 'Another Custer massacre,' " the volunteer Tom Sherrill remembered. "Darned talk like that did not make a fellow feel very happy you can well believe. And especially in such a close place where his prophesy might come true any minute."

Despite their ordeal, Howard found the men "cheerful and confident." Though they had to admit, in one volunteer's words, that "the Indians gave us a nice dressing," they found other things to celebrate. The last Nez Perce warriors had abandoned the siege the previous morning. Soon after, a supply train reached the soldiers with food; they had never before realized how hardtack,

450

bacon, and coffee could be a feast, infinitely better than the raw flesh they had carved from an officer's dead horse, bloating in the sun. They walked to the stream below, tasted cold water, bathed and washed their clothes. They buried and honored their dead, taking pride in the fact that they had held their position. It was not going to be another Little Bighorn after all.

On the creek banks and beyond, in the scorched remains of the Indian camp, the men found it more difficult to tell a happy story about the last few days. When Howard's Bannock scouts had reached the Big Hole, they went down to the camp, pried Nez Perce bodies from their shallow graves, and scalped the corpses. There was nothing abstract about the dead. Their bodies, at least five or six small children and a dozen or so women scattered across the ground, resisted attempts to justify what had happened to them. One woman, half unearthed and then yanked up for scalping, appeared to be sitting, gone but joltingly present. An infantry sergeant stared at the mutilated bodies and at the Bannocks rinsing scalps in the stream, and vomited. "You could not help but see them," he later wrote.

Wandering the camp, the soldiers and volunteers realized that they knew some of the Indian dead. "I . . . think I recognized those two large squaws who sat in the Council tent last April in Lapwai," the surgeon FitzGerald wrote home, "one of whom you questioned about her bead work leggings and who refused to answer you. Also I saw the body of the large Indian who wore that robe trimmed with ermine skins." The merchant Henry Buck, who had driven a wagon to the battlefield to find his brother Amos, remembered seeing a

451

woman "who used to come to our store in Stevensville to trade. . . . The calico dress that she wore [was] made from cloth that I had sold her only a few days before." While some men swore that the women had fought just as fiercely as the warriors, other soldiers and volunteers knew that these deaths were inexcusable. "Why should I shoot an Indian woman, one who had never injured me a bit in the world?" Tom Sherrill would later ask. "I heard a fellow bragging that he had killed . . . two women. I could never have forgiven myself if I had been that man." Howard's chief of staff described the scene as a "dreadful sight." "I have never been in a fight where women were killed and I hope never to be," he wrote.

General Howard was appalled by the carnage. Sitting with Gibbon on the hillside, he said as much. "I heard Gen. Howard remark," wrote a sergeant who stood nearby, "that if he had got there sooner, General Gibbon would not have attacked the camp. Howard . . . believed in capturing, and not killing." Although he had not personally led the attack on the Nez Perce camp and would not have chosen to do so, Howard had been responsible for deploying Gibbon's column and urging him to engage the Indians in battle. At the Big Hole, he walked among the bodies of people who had sat around him at Lapwai, who had greeted him and sung for him. This was his war, and these were his deaths.

But as stunned as he was by those "poor, harmless forms" — he described himself as "deeply disgusted, horror-stricken" — Howard never forgot that he was fighting more than just the Nez Perce bands. He was always being judged by his superior officers, politicians and bureaucrats in

452

the capital, local settlers, and the public at large. Encircled by atrocity, Howard willed himself to look past the killings, to see the battle through different eyes. He turned the fight into an abstraction and characterized the military defeat as a victory in an almost reflexive pivot that he had mastered in his Union Army days. Gibbon's forces had inflicted stunning losses on the renegade Indians, Howard reported to his superiors and to the public — no matter that most of the dead were women and children. And despite being outnumbered, he could write, the soldiers had fought gallantly — an assertion that could be applied to just about every battle.

From those generalities, Howard dove into the details, singling out by name some of the men who had died at the Big Hole. "Heroic devotion to duty in Indian warfare saves lives by interposing one's own," he would write. "Lieutenant James H. Bradley fell in action, to rise no more. . . . In order to punish guilt, to secure peace, and serve faithfully his country, he gave the full measure, — his life."

From abstraction to specificity, Howard left little room for anything in between. As for the women and children, Howard found a way to think of their loss in relative terms. Seventy, eighty, ninety dead — it was nothing compared to what he had witnessed at Gettysburg. Every day in the United States was wrought with violence, as the copy of the *Oregonian* that he had read on the Lolo Trail well attested. To be American was to live with that central truth, to understand the bloodshed and loss as progress and civilization. Terrible as the deaths at the Big Hole were, Howard would write, and as disturbing as it had been to walk through the Indian camp, "it is the same with railway accidents, and with fire and pestilence."

The general ordered his men to dig new graves by the remains of the Indian camp. Reburying the enemy dead would not only allow his men to look past what had just happened, but it would also inspire them to keep fighting. Howard marbled his anguish over the Nez Perce dead with distaste for his "ferocious" Bannock scouts. By his calculation, the sympathy that he and his men could not help but show was no liability to the campaign. Rather, he imagined, their sympathy was what distinguished them from Indians. It was why their cause was just. It was why they had to see this war to the end. As long as they were stirred by the sight of a dead woman, the fact that their bullets had killed her was irrelevant. What mattered to Howard was that one of his Indian scouts could say in the days that followed, "My chief is kind. I saw him and his staff officers . . . tenderly bury the women and children with their own hands." Their sentiment obviated any need to take responsibility for what had happened. In a relative sense, a civilization that could retain its capacity for sympathy would always be better than the alternative. Reflecting on the Big Hole, Howard was able to declare that "Indian warfare is horrid; but Indian massacres, outrages, and brutality, and Indian rule, which is war, are a thousand times worse."

Riding far behind the rest, Yellow Wolf could watch the dust from the herd rise like smoke into the sky. Scouting alone, as his *wey-ya-kin* had instructed, he looked for signs that the army was following the Nez Perce families south through

454

the mountains out of the Big Hole and into the next valley, the Horse Prairie. After the massacre, everything that moved was cause for alarm. "If antelope acted curious, it might be danger," he later said. "If prairie birds flew up . . . , it might be buffaloes stampeding, getting away from something — maybe soldiers!" He followed a strange shadow bending along a rock in the distance. As he drew closer, slowing his horse to a trot, the shadow rose and materialized into one man — no, Yellow Wolf realized, there were eight of them, probably local ranchers, waiting in ambush. The warrior galloped away laughing while their gunfire cracked in the distance. His *wey-ya-kin* had promised that no rifle could kill him. "I thought I might die in a war somehow," he said, "but not by the bullet."

Ahead of Yellow Wolf were more warriors, then the herd and packhorses, and finally the women, children, and elderly riding under Joseph's watch. They were dying with every step. At each new camp, the warriors dug rifle pits while the wounded were lifted from saddles and travois and put onto warm buffalo robes. There were people to bury and mourn, mothers and fathers and grandparents. There were orphaned children to feed and comfort. The wounded moaned through the night. In the mornings, some never awoke. Early on, an old woman asked to be left behind, to die alone.

Every day, the ordeal began anew. The Nez Perce families rose in darkness, traveled until midmorning, ate and let the herd graze for a few hours, and then went another eight or so hours until it was dark. Though they were too hurt to do anything but inch across the landscape, they were

making good progress toward buffalo country —
a small solace. Alongside the pain, sadness,
misery, and thirst, they were charged with fury.
Fury at the army and at the civilians who had
agreed to let them pass, did business with them,
and then betrayed them. Fury at each other, for
disregarding the voices of caution and fear, for
refusing to listen to dreams, for believing they had
escaped the war in Idaho and could live as before.
Looking Glass took the most blame for leaving
them exposed and allowing the massacre to happen. Dropping him as their leader, the people
sought guidance instead from Lean Elk — called
Poker Joe by the whites — who had joined them
in the Bitterroot Valley. While the warriors revered
Ollokot and Toohoolhoolzote for leading the siege
at the Big Hole — just as they had showed their
heroism above the Clearwater and at White Bird
Canyon — no one knew the route to Crow
country as well as Lean Elk. He planned their
long days so they would always stay out of the
army's reach.

Without any pretense that the journey eastward
to Crow country was a normal migration, the warriors fanned out across the prairie. Every horse
they could find — maybe two hundred — they
took, to strengthen the herd, but more importantly
to deprive the army of fresh mounts. While most
of the ranches were deserted, the Indians found
several men who had stayed behind. There would
be no negotiation or trade, as in the Bitterroot
Valley. Rather, the encounters were swift and
lethal, like the revenge killings on the Salmon
River. Inside cabins, the warriors went straight for
the mattresses and emptied them, covering the
dead with feathers and carrying away the cloth

ticking. Of all the supplies they could have taken from their victims — weapons, greenbacks — what they needed most was fabric that could be torn into bandages.

The families kept moving, from the Horse Prairie back across the Continental Divide into Idaho Territory. Five days from the Big Hole, on August 13, they reached the Lemhi Valley, long and narrow, surrounded by snowy peaks. Channeled south and east, past stockades where hundreds of settlers were hiding, past a local Shoshone tribe that offered them no sanctuary and eyed their herd, the Nez Perce bands rode across bleak prairie, gnarled sagebrush reaching for them like beggars' hands.

After two days, the hills leaned closer, stark rock with wind-worn hollows, like skulls stacked into towers. Warriors scouting in shadowless noon reached a wandering wash of green, a creek cutting through the valley. They saw wagons and trailers, forty horses and mules grazing, and charged. Eight men — four teamsters, two passengers, and two cooks — crawled out from underneath the wagon train and surrendered. Carting freight into Idaho from a railhead in Utah, they had stopped at Birch Creek for lunch and a nap. The warriors ate their food, made them hitch the animals, and escorted the train toward the rest of the Nez Perce families. While the prisoners took heart that they were still alive, an Indian took one of the teamsters aside and told him to hide in the brush by the creek — the warriors had no interest in sparing them. By the time Yellow Wolf rode into camp after a day of scouting, the other three teamsters and their passengers had been riddled with bullets. The two cooks, recent Chinese immigrants, sat weeping by the wagons; when Yellow Wolf thought back to the odd sight of them, their inconsolable fear, he laughed.

Taking the horses and mules for the herd, the warriors began ransacking the wagons. Glass panes, window sashes, cans of food, crockery — useless. Barrels of whiskey, on the other hand — as the sun set, some of the warriors began drinking themselves mad. Worried that the soldiers would catch up to them, the chiefs asked Yellow Wolf, Peopeo Tholekt, and other sober warriors to pour the liquor out into the dirt. The drunk warriors drew guns and knives and turned on their own. By the end of the melee, a warrior who had distinguished himself at the Big Hole was slowly dying. The cooks escaped in the night. The Nez Perce bands left the next morning, August 16, wagons and cargo burning behind them.

East and north, after two days' climb through lava rock and across a plunging creek canyon, the world opened again into a wide stretch of pastureland dotted with ancient volcanic formations. Known as the Camas Meadows, the area may have resembled the Camas Prairie back home when it bloomed blue every spring, but by August 19, the flowers were gone. The Nez Perce families could feel the coming winter in the chill before dawn. Ten days from the Big Hole, the wounded were still dying. The living were still burying the dead. As the women and children moved slowly east with the herd, Peopeo Tholekt ranged behind them, scouting with two boys not quite old enough to be warriors. Miles from the rest, they left their horses in a shallow gulch and climbed a hill that afforded a sweeping view. At the top, Peopeo Tholekt scanned the horizon, then looked through a field glass. He found the dull swath that the Nez Perce families had worn through the grass and followed it west. There, right on their trail, he finally saw what they all knew and feared would be coming. Soldiers — "not far," he would recall. He watched the dust swirling in the army's wake, high and thick, evidence that there were a lot of soldiers, "a big bunch of them."

Sending one of the boys ahead with the news, Peopeo Tholekt stayed to watch the army's progress. They were gaining fast. The warrior told the second boy, "Go hurry! Get your horse and notify the people the soldiers are now right up with us. In a few minutes there will be an engagement." Now alone, Peopeo Tholekt sat perfectly still as the sun peaked in the sky. He saw the soldiers riding past. Some stopped and looked his way, then turned right at him and began climbing the hill. Spotted by the enemy, he raced out of sight, reached his horse, and galloped toward his people. By the time he reached them, they had already heard from the two boys. While the women and children and the packhorses and herd kept moving, the warriors had stopped. Peopeo Tholekt expected them to be stripped for battle, singing their death songs. But "they were smoking their pipes, . . . silent, keeping quiet," he recalled. "They only asked me, 'Tell us the news, what the next news?' " Peopeo Tholekt urged them to ride west to the soldiers and fight. They told him they had a different plan.

Howard knew he was within striking distance — so close that his scouts were finding manure from Nez Perce horses still steaming in the cold air. As the Indians headed south from the Big Hole, the general had anticipated that the hostiles would eventually turn toward buffalo country. Cheered on by settlers in the Horse Prairie — a rare show of local support — he tacked east through barren alkali country on the Montana side of the Beaverhead Mountains, paralleling the Indians' course through the Lemhi Valley over in Idaho. One hundred fifty miles away, they were bound to follow Henry's Fork of the Snake River north and east through the mountains to its headwaters at Henry's Lake, and then turn sharp east over the steep Continental Divide at the Targhee Pass, near where Montana, Idaho, and Wyoming meet. If the Indians made it over the mountains, they would enter country where they would be very difficult to catch: the great basin of the Yellowstone River, more mountains, and then the buffalo plains. Although Howard was confident he could beat the Indians to Henry's Lake and force a final confrontation, he hoped to cut them off even sooner, along a stage road that passed from Montana south through the mountains toward the western edge of the Camas Meadows.

Leaving the Big Hole on August 13, Howard's column reached the stage junction in five days. But before Howard could turn south and spring his trap, a courier brought disheartening news: the hostile Indians had already crossed the stage road — they were still ahead of the army, if barely. Though the general could have stayed in Montana and moved on to Henry's Lake, he deviated from his plan to overtake and surprise the enemy. He sent just a token force of forty cavalry ahead, to "harass enemy if found," but ordered everyone else down into Idaho and back into direct pursuit, following the Indians' trail.

Howard knew this strategy carried the scent of failure. As he started from the Big Hole, he had quickly rejected "a stern-chase" as "hopeless." Through June and July in Nez Perce country in Idaho, he had never succeeded in catching the enemy. Perhaps now, he thought, he could get within striking distance on flat open terrain. More likely, he worried that if he kept going on the Montana side of the mountains, the hostile bands would have free rein to slaughter any settlers they encountered. Two months earlier, he had been stranded on the far side of the Salmon River while the Indians terrorized the farmers and ranchers on the Camas Prairie. The Idaho settlers had complained so loudly he had almost been relieved of his command. A stern-chase would demonstrate the general's concern for the locals.

Or perhaps Howard no longer felt he could defeat the Nez Perce in battle. The general rode with his mounted force, about two hundred men, plus his Bannock scouts and a few civilian volunteers who had come all the way from Nez Perce country. Another cavalry company based in Montana, fifty strong, had ridden all day, all night, and all the next day to meet them at the stage junction. A hundred more soldiers and local volunteers were marching, with most of the infantry still a couple days behind. The horses were worn out, many of them beyond recovery. The mule train was limping and stricken. Wagons were laden with men too "leg-weary" to march, the brass screws in their boot soles digging into their feet, their blisters impossible to bear — "as big as four-year-old watermelons," one scout wrote — or their rheumatism flaring up, a consequence, according to Howard's surgeons, of "deficient . . . overcoats, blankets, socks, and shoes" and "privation of rest." Even with troops and mounts healthy and strong, and even if they managed to overtake the Indians at Henry's Lake, the fact remained that Nez Perce warriors never fought to the end. They always fled, Howard complained. If confronted at Henry's Lake, they could turn around and head back through Idaho, or bypass the troops altogether as they had at the end of the Lolo Trail, climbing mountains that no one thought possible to climb.

By this point, Howard had begun to believe that he would eventually turn the chase over to another army force. Montana was in the Department of Dakota, outside Howard's command, and Wyoming was in a third jurisdiction, the Department of the Platte. Even as Howard's column gave chase from the west, it seemed impossible to trap the hostile Nez Perce without soldiers from the other departments closing in from the north, south, and east. If only Gibbon had had more men at the Big Hole, Howard thought, everyone would be heading home by now. "Surely he might have had from all this Territory three times as many," he telegrammed his superiors in San Francisco. The longer his troops marched from home — and the less they resembled a capable fighting force — the more it appeared inevitable that there would have to be a changing of the guard. It was a comforting thought, one that Howard shared with his officers. From the Big Hole and the Horse Prairie, they started writing their families that they would be home within a couple of weeks, regardless of whether they caught Joseph. It helped them bear, even enjoy, the agonies of the march.

Howard knew that the war was his responsibility. After the Indians fled from the Clearwater battle in July, General Sherman had ordered Howard by telegram "to follow them up, no matter where they go . . . regardless of boundary lines. If the Indians can find food, the troops can also." Before cutting east from the Horse Prairie, however, Howard wired division headquarters to ask, "Is it worth while for me to pursue them further from my department? . . . Please advise me, that I may not wear out our troops to no purpose." As the column neared the junction with the stage road, an adjutant in San Francisco issued a blunt reply. "The division commander thinks you need no further instructions on this subject," the telegram read. "You, it seems to him, will certainly be expected — by the General of the Army, the War Department, and the country — to [carry] on the most active and persistent operations practicable to the very end." The notion that his column would be relieved shortly was fantasy. "In all kindness," the adjutant wrote Howard, the division commander, General McDowell, "asks me to suggest to you to be less dependent on what others, at a distance, may or may not do, and rely more on your own forces and your own plans."

Crossing into Idaho, Howard's soldiers finally found telltale signs of their quarry: the hazy waft of dust ahead, a wide trampled trail extending east, and fresh graves lining the way. The Nez Perce bands were only fifteen or twenty miles ahead — one night march away from a decisive engagement. But in the Camas Meadows, early in the afternoon on August 19, Howard halted his column and made camp between two willowed creeks. Although much of the area was trampled and worn — the Indians had slept there the night before — there was good grazing land punctuated by knolls of lava rock. It was a Sunday. Perhaps the general was trying to rest his men and their horses after covering nearly fifty miles over the past two days. He still had a few days to strike before the Indians reached Henry's Lake and the terrain bent skyward again — better to wait and attack at his strongest. But he may have pulled up short rather than force a confrontation that he doubted he could win.

The men reported seeing individual Indians nearby — scouts, most assuredly, marking the army's position. The general doubled the usual guards all around the camp, ordered the cavalry herd inside the picket lines, and had the mares that led the mule train hobbled to keep them from straying too far. In as good a position as he had ever been to confront the enemy, he instead sent off another plaintive telegram to San Francisco. "Have driven the hostile Indians from the Clearwater to the Yellowstone, without regard to the department or division lines," he wrote as he settled in for the night. "Shall I rest, resupply, and pursue further, or return?"

An hour before dawn, all light had been skimmed from the sky. Peopeo Tholekt started crawling with a group of warriors, but when he reached the first of the soldiers' tents, he looked back and saw no one behind him. In thick black night, what was familiar one moment could be strange the next. He knew this part of the Camas Meadows. He had woken right here the day before. But now it was another place. The army was camping here. It was enemy land.

Twenty-eight warriors had ridden all night, slowly and silently, no smoking, no talking, together but alone. The moon, three days from full, had set by the time they neared the camp. Out of the soldiers' earshot, they stopped and held a brief council. Two Moons and Wottolen suggested that the warriors leave their horses back and sneak into the camp on foot. They would first kill Howard and his officers, then slaughter and scatter the rest of the soldiers. Although Two Moons drew on his experience fighting the Shoshone, the Sioux, and the Blackfeet when he proposed an attack without horses, his plan would mark a new way of making war. From White Bird Canyon to the Big Hole, the warriors had trained their sights on every officer they could find, an effective tactic in the heat of battle. But this would be a colder strike, a deliberate assassination under cover of darkness.

Looking Glass heard the elders out, then insisted that most of their party stay mounted. Rather than break with the past, he advocated one of the most traditional actions a Nez Perce warrior could make: instead of targeting Howard and attacking the soldiers, they would steal their horses. A horse raid was how countless warriors gained status in Nez Perce country and beyond. It was so familiar that a wounded man back in their camp had found comfort in his agony by dreaming about just such a scenario. Once again, they seemed to be adhering to tradition at the moment they faced its certain demise. It was as if they were still fighting rival tribes and not the US Army. The plan was simple: the young men would sneak into the camp on foot and untie the cavalry horses, and then the rest would charge through on horseback and stampede the herd.

The war party reached consensus around Looking Glass's plan. "An Indian does not like to be far from his horse in any fighting," Wottolen would later say. Ollokot, who after leading the siege at the Big Hole commanded the loyalty of many of the young warriors, called for action. Daylight was coming, he said. It was time to move.

The warriors split into groups and rode toward different parts of the camp, walking their horses so slowly that their hoof beats did not sound on rock. A few younger men, Peopeo Tholekt and Yellow Wolf among them, slipped off their mounts and crawled toward the soldiers. Out of the dark they heard a voice call out in English — "Who are you there?" — but they managed to inch past the guard.

Peopeo Tholekt walked among the tents. He had been in a soldier camp before, back in June, when he had tried to convince the cavalry not to attack Looking Glass's village. After speaking a message of peace from his chief, he thought the soldiers were going to shoot him. That day, his world had changed forever. But that night in the Camas Meadows, a thought from his old life came back to him — he wanted good horses. And through the darkness, he saw one, a gray horse, "fine-looking," he later recalled. He approached and felt a jolt of recognition. He knew this animal from before the war, when he had admired its swift stride. The horse belonged to a settler in Nez Perce country in Idaho. A friend to the Indians in earlier days, he had been seen fighting with the army at White Bird Canyon — so many months later, still riding with Howard's army, it seemed. "I laughed to myself as I untied this gray horse,"

Peopeo Tholekt would remember.

The other young men were working quietly, cutting tethers, taking bells off the pack mules and mares. In an instant — too soon — a gunshot burst through the silence. "Who in hell do shooting?" wondered Wottolen, who was guarding a point just outside the camp. It had come from well behind his position, far from the soldiers. Otskai, a warrior with a reputation for "crazy actions," Wottolen said — in Yellow Wolf's estimation, "at times his head did not act right" — had discharged his weapon. The warriors would be sure to tease him after sunrise.

At the gunshot, guards started shouting, running in every direction. A bugle screamed in the night. Abruptly, the warriors on horse-back charged through the camp, and panicked horses and mules began kicking up dust as they ran. At the same time, the first light punched through the thick black — muzzle flashes. The warriors were spraying bullets through the camp, while the soldiers tried to shoot back but only wound up "firing like crazy people in the darkness," Wottolen recalled. "Nothing they can hit."

Within minutes, the raid was over. The warriors raced out of the camp as quickly as they had swept in. The young men on foot "skipped away in the darkness," Peopeo Tholekt said, sending occasional shots back toward the flashes from their enemies' guns. Yellow Wolf cut three more horses loose before sprinting to his own mount. Outside camp, he could hear the soldiers behind him, still shooting, shooting at nothing. He let out a yell, flicked his lash, then fired his six-shooter in the air, sending the three horses galloping toward the larger herd stampeding ahead. In quieter moments, he would think about the sensation of standing in the camp, alone in the blackness with chaos twisting around him. Through the din, a strange sound reached his ears. The soldiers were not just shouting. They were crying. "I heard them cry like babies," he said. "They were bad scared."

At Henry's Lake the wind was cold and constant — "blowing a gale," Howard's chief of staff Edwin Mason wrote, "which I am informed it does up in this country 365 in the year." Tents quaked and jumped, flaps whipping open and shut. The men in Howard's column walked naked for the first time since bathing in the hot springs at the end of the Lolo Trail on August 6. They finally washed their blue uniforms and foul red flannels — rags, really. They picked the lice out of their scalps. They plunged into the clear frigid water of the glacial lake and scrubbed off weeks of grime.

The rank-and-file troops appreciated the rare moment of leisure. Huddled together, drinking coffee, chewing their mingy ration of fried dough, they entertained each other by telling "whoppers," reported one officer who eavesdropped from inside his tent. A soldier kept his comrades rapt by describing a dream he had had, "that the rivers were running full of whiskey and a virgin awaited at every bend." "He is either the damdest liar I ever heard or has the best imagination," the officer wrote. "At least it takes their minds off their feet."

The officers found little escape from their painful situation. Although the Indians had hoped to steal their horses at the Camas Meadows, they wound up with an equally important bounty — 150 mules, almost the entire pack train. After giving halfhearted chase, during which a bugler fell dead from his horse, a bullet through the heart, Howard ordered a retreat to camp rather than attack the main Nez Perce column, only ten miles away. That night, the rest of the infantry arrived. Howard now had six hundred men, but not enough animals and less than a week of rations. Loading what they could on the horses and mules that remained, the soldiers broke camp on August 21 and forged onward in a wide phalanx, animals and wagons in the middle, for three days, sixty miles along Henry's Fork of the Snake River, up through the mountains past ten thousand feet.

By the time Howard's troops reached Henry's Lake, the Indians were easily forty miles east, through the Targhee Pass, crossing the new national park that had been established in the Yellowstone basin in 1872. The Bannock scouts were disgusted that the army was not pursuing the Nez Perce more aggressively. One cavalry officer grumbled that they could have vanquished the enemy after the mule raid if only he had had more support. An infantry officer who wanted to push vigorously ahead could not believe the cautious pace. Mocking the notion that the army could overtake the Nez Perce bands, he wrote home, "They were to be caught at this place for sure, ha! . . . As usual the Indians have vanished."

The officers blamed their predicament entirely on their general. For weeks they had been writing letters home promising that their campaign would end in a matter of days; Howard had all but assured them of relief. Now, at their lowest point, when it seemed to make the most sense for them to stop the chase, Howard suddenly changed his mind: they would keep going. The officers now

469

realized they would not see their families for months. They ached to see their wives and children; "I want to go home as any schoolboy ever did," one wrote. With winter firmly in the air — frost and freeze every night — there would be no finding a way to enjoy the march. It would be "fruitless," the officers complained, "a game of hide and seek," "mighty monotonous." "The Hostiles . . . are traveling like the wind toward the great buffalo country," one wrote. "By the time we are ready to start after them they will be two or three hundred miles away."

To many, the general's equivocations revealed not just weakness but vanity. Explaining to his wife and mother why the column would not be coming home, Howard's usually loyal chief of staff Mason pointed to his commander. "The General is disappointed at not reaching a brilliant end before this," he wrote. "The craving after newspaper applause overrides every other consideration." Respect for Howard curdled into disdain. "Poor man," the surgeon FitzGerald wrote home, "and yet I do not think he deserves pity. Not many officers are in sympathy with him, and a great many think he is guilty of folly of the gravest kind to follow on at the expense of loss in men and animals in a hopeless pursuit."

Just about the only officer who kept his spirits high was Erskine Wood. With no one at home to miss — neither wife nor, in his words, "some 'flesh pot' " waiting for him — Wood wrote that he reveled in the privations of the trail, his long beard and matted hair, his riding pants "out at the knees and fringed at the bottoms . . . the wreck of a white slouch wilted on my head and a tattered blouse fluttering on my back." He was "naked and careless as becomes banditti of the frontier," he enthused, "more artistically and picturesquely ragged than any other officer." He felt less like an aide to a brigadier general than a lieutenant to the Italian guerrilla leader — and hero of a popular opera — "Fra Diavolo." He expected, hoped even, that the campaign would last through Christmas.

Despite having loyal tent mates, Howard knew his officers had turned on him. The knowledge only made him less sympathetic. "One minute he is a happy man; the next he is worried, cross or pouty," an officer wrote. "Ought to see our doctor about his frequent gutaches, too proud I guess. . . . He says that nobody likes him and this is truer than he thinks." Feeling "quite wrathy," he left his troops at Henry's Lake and rode sixty-five miles north to the mining town of Virginia City, the nearest place where he could resupply the expedition with food and mules. The officers appreciated his absence.

Reaching Virginia City on August 24, Howard stopped at the telegraph office to share his bad news with Division of the Pacific headquarters in San Francisco — a nest of smug critics. To make matters worse, he received a message from General Sherman. The commanding general of the army happened to be visiting Montana this very moment and was training his full attention on Howard's conduct of the war. "Telegraph me some account of affairs that I can understand," Sherman wired. "What is your force? What are your plans? Spare nothing to insure success."

For once, Howard had no optimistic story to tell about capturing the Nez Perce bands. He could only ask Sherman to order "an eastern force" — perhaps the 7th Cavalry, Custer's old regiment, based on the other side of the national park — to head off the hostile Indians "before they disaffect the Crows or unite with the Sioux." Assuming fresh troops were available to intercept the Indians from the east, Howard wrote, "I think I may stop near where I am and in a few days work my way back to Fort Boise slowly, and distribute my troops before snow falls in the mountains." Despite telling his officers that he wanted to continue the pursuit, he practically begged Sherman to let him end it. "My command is so much worn by overfatigue and jaded animals that I cannot push it much farther."

It was humiliating to admit to Sherman that he could not catch Joseph. Howard had seen his greatest successes as an officer serving under Sherman in the last year of the Civil War. Now he was disappointing the man who had always supported him when others attacked his military record. But Sherman's quick reply added new depths to Howard's abasement. "That force of yours should pursue the Nez Perces to the death, lead where they may," Sherman wired. "If you are tired, give the command to some young energetic officer, and let him follow them, go where they may, holding his men well in hand, subsisting them on beef gathered in the country, with coffee, sugar, and salt on packs." Sherman was suggesting that instead of giving up the chase, Howard go home alone while his men marched on.

For the next three days, Howard contemplated the kind of failure that could mark him for the rest of his life. Virginia City was surrounded in every direction by high mountains covered in snow. Fifteen years ago, it did not exist. For ten years until 1875, it had been Montana's territorial capital. Its sprawl of frame buildings and houses had erupted from the valley with the gold rush of the 1860s, and now it was set on a slow journey back to mud. Beyond the mountains, under the same sky, Joseph was riding ever eastward. If there were no soldiers to cut the Indians off, then someone had to keep them moving.

The general found food for his men — they would have rice rations instead of flour — and negotiated for pack animals. With everything arranged, he returned to camp on August 25. Two days later, he sent a courier to Virginia City with a message for Sherman. "You misunderstood me," Howard's wire read. "I never flag. It was the command, including the most energetic young officers, that were worn out and weary by a most extraordinary march." He could envision victory again. His Bannock scouts were riding "on the heels of the enemy." His men were rested and resupplied. "You need not fear for the campaign," he wrote. "Neither you nor General McDowell can doubt my pluck and energy. . . . We move in the morning and will continue to the end."

CHAPTER 18
A WORLD OF OUR OWN

Two men stood in front of the roaring bonfire, faces shadowed by broad sombreros. Strapped with pistols, rifles, and knives, they menaced the seven people standing in front of them while their audience roared with delight. Back in Helena, Frank Carpenter and Al Oldham were respectable young men, but on August 23, determined to mount "a grand jollification" on their last night in Wonderland, they made perfect brigands.

For nearly three weeks, the group had been making a 170-mile merry escape from a parched, oppressively hot Montana summer that swarmed with grasshoppers. When Frank mentioned his plan to go to the new national park and see the geysers, his sister Emma and her husband George Cowan promptly shuttered their house in Radersburg, a mining boomtown halfway between Helena and Bozeman, and joined the expedition. It seemed that everyone who heard of their plans wanted to come along: Frank and Emma's thirteen-year-old sister Ida, and three of Frank's friends from Helena, Al Oldham, William Dingee, and A. J. Arnold. If George had any worries about closing his law practice for a month, he could soon rest easy; Charles Mann, Radersburg's clerk of court, also joined their party, sketchbook in hand. After hiring eighteen-year-old Henry Myers to handle the horses and cook, they set out in a double-seated carriage, with a separate wagon for baggage.

Emma Cowan had long wanted to see the geysers. As a ten-year-old girl just arrived from Black Earth, Wisconsin, in 1864, she was captivated by the "rough and uncultured" stories of an old trapper, tales that she figured could only be "the phantasy of his imagination": "fountains of boiling water," she wrote, "crystal clear, thrown hundreds of feet in the air, only to fall into cups of their own forming." She soon learned that in the endless spaces of the West, the truth could defy fantasy. Despite the drudgery of her daily life — she went from working on her father's dairy ranch to keeping house for her husband, a thick-whiskered Union Army veteran twelve years her senior — she was never far from a landscape of boundless dreams.

Every day of the journey south to Yellowstone was an idyll of joy and plenty. The traveling party gorged themselves on the trout, sage hens, grouse, ducks, and geese they caught along the way. They gathered eagle feathers and swansdown. They softened their camp beds with "fragrant pine boughs" chopped from the trees around them. Reaching Henry's Lake on August 10, Emma Cowan watched "innumerable flocks of wild fowl" circling and swirling overhead. That night, under a thin crescent moon, she and the rest rowed out onto the lake, set pine-knot torches afire, and watched dozens of trout rise to the light. During the day, they might split up and explore, but they could always look forward to "a rousing fire, good supper, comparing notes, telling stories, singing songs." Dark-haired and prim, taking excursions sidesaddle on her favorite horse Bird, Emma was experiencing the West as she had imagined it since she was a little girl. "My fancy had run riot," she wrote, "and I fully expected to see the Old Man of the tales of my childhood."

The travelers cut their names into a grove of cottonwood trees as they crossed the Targhee Pass on August 13, then descended through pine woods to the Madison River. At its western boundary, Emma admired the park's "picturesque scenery," but it looked like much of what they had already seen on their journey: pine-cloaked hills, flowering meadows, meandering streams rich with trout, all framed by immense peaks studding the far eastern horizon. Emma's husband and some of the other men rode ahead, scouting for easy places to ford and looking for deer and antelope — Emma had been craving venison steaks for supper.

As the rest of the group in the carriage approached thick forest, they heard hoof beats pounding ahead. The advance riders sprang out of the woods, gasping two words — "Indians coming" — then waiting expectantly for Emma and her sister to scream and faint. No one fell for the joke. Along the way to Yellowstone, they had heard what Emma described as "rumors of Indian trouble," but she felt no cause for worry. Her sense of the wilderness — her imagined West — simply did not include people. She saw wide open places, she wrote, "fresh from the Maker's hand." Everything about their journey to the park confirmed the "intense solitude [that] pervaded this land," she wrote. "We seemed to be in a world of our own." Since leaving behind the more settled areas of Montana, "not a soul had we seen save our own party, and neither mail nor news of any sort had reached us."

Emma was hardly alone in her vision of an empty West. Even Montana was now a place of modern life, law, agriculture, and industry. The national park — pure, primordial — would not simply enrich and ennoble its visitors with sublime vistas but would take them back in time to a shared past, rooting them in the same ostensibly untamed, empty land that had proven the pioneers' mettle and made the country strong. If alongside Emma Cowan's sense of the West, there had always been a competing mythology — that it was savage, not Edenic, that the pioneer experience was defined less by exploration and discovery than by killing and being killed — the native threat was remote to her, easily forgotten, even quaint. When her family had arrived in Montana during the gold rush years of the 1860s, bandits and outlaws, not Indians, posed the most tangible dangers to civilized life. An Indian might appear every now and then on the streets of Helena, but by August 1877, it could be an article of faith that his day had passed, that the world had left his people behind. Emma Cowan would not be fazed by what she called "an old time Indian scare."

After camping one night on the banks of the Madison, the tourists worked their way upstream, then south along the Firehole River, through canyons and mountain passes, grabbing fistfuls of wild raspberries and strawberries along the way. "The poetry of nature seems to have collected here," Frank Carpenter wrote. But in the afternoon of August 15, the intense but familiar beauties of their journey gave way to a tableau almost impossible to conceive. Up one rise, the view to the south opened, and they saw in the distance a jet of steam pluming hundreds of feet into the air. They had arrived in Wonderland.

At the lower geyser basin, with its countless attractions, the group scattered, calling to each other with amazing finds, "simply wild with the eagerness of seeing all things at once," Emma Cowan wrote. Every sight was new — bubbling mud pots "as thick as hasty pudding," steaming vents, and pools showing a startling rainbow of colors, chalk, rust, orange, moss green, mold, and deep frozen blues, ever-changing as the sun moved through the day. Walking with her young sister, Emma regaled Ida with the stories that had fascinated her as a little girl. "How vividly they came to mind!" she wrote. When she paused, they heard alien sounds — rumbling, thudding, spluttering, hissing, groaning, rushing. The ground was cracked, solid enough to support them, but churning just inches below. The party gathered around a geyser and watched a placid pool begin to bubble, then boil, then rumble, and finally burst to the sky. Showered with mist, "we salute[d] it with a demoniacal yell," Frank Carpenter wrote, "enthusiastic with the wild grandeur of the scene."

With every breath, the ecstasy of discovery gave way to what Emma described as "a somewhat creepy feeling." The world beneath them was alive. Emma began imagining how easily it could consume them. She smelled sulfur, brimstone, "the smell of the Inferno." "One involuntarily reverts to the story of Satan and his imps," her brother wrote. Setting up camp in a clearing by the woods near the lower geyser basin, over the

478

coming days they ventured nine miles south to the upper geyser basin. Soon, wonderment gave way to a certain restlessness.

While Charles Mann sketched the landscapes, others carved their names into the stone around the geysers, adding to graffiti left by a decade of visitors. They threw their laundry into Old Faithful and after it erupted pronounced the clothes "as nice and clean as a Chinaman could wash it with a week's scrubbing." No longer fazed by the grandeur of the scene, they were soon dumping all of their garbage into the geyser and watching it shoot eighty feet in the air — "an entertainment of unusual magnitude and duration," Frank Carpenter enthused. Yet the real dangers of the site remained. When Henry Myers stepped into a hot spring by accident and rolled down his stocking, "the skin and flesh adhered to it," Carpenter wrote. "His limb was literally cooked."

After about a week among the geysers, the tourists were hailed by a guide who had been leading General Sherman on a twelve-day trip through Yellowstone. Finally hearing news of the battle at the Big Hole, the group "received the very unpleasant impression that we might meet the Indians before we reached home," Emma Cowan wrote. "No one seemed to know just where they were going."

Rather than fret, however, Cowan's brother and friends persisted in making light of the situation. They decked themselves and their horses in eagle feathers "in true Indian style" and charged into camp while giving "the Indian war whoop." The others played along "in excellent spirits," greeting them "how, how." As worrisome as the news had been, they still felt little danger. It was inconceivable that the Indians would go through the national park. Sherman's guide told them that the Indians had always avoided the area — afraid of the geysers was the oft-told explanation. Still, on August 23, the tourists decided they would head home the next day.

Deep into their last night in the park, the group reveled and reflected. After dressing as desperadoes, Frank Carpenter and Al Oldham traded their weapons for a guitar and a fiddle. Members of the group danced around the fire — fancy steps and high kicks, the pigeon wing, the double shuffle. Glowing in the night, "they made the woods ring with their nonsense and merriment for some time," Emma wrote. Even Myers, still nursing his severely burnt foot, "hobble[d] around with good grace," Carpenter wrote. Finally, toward midnight, everyone sang one last song together, a quiet, sentimental tune from the previous decade called "Flitting Away, or Nothing on Earth That Will Stay."

As they said their good nights, Frank Carpenter noticed that Emma appeared "uneasy" — the darkness, she admitted, often made her feel "somewhat timid." He asked his sister if anything was wrong. "Nothing," she said. But as he lay outside by the fire, she appeared in the door of the tent she was sharing with her husband and Ida. She gazed out at the woods, through the moonlight, into the blackness, then slowly retreated to sleep.

Yellow Wolf saw a tiny point of light in the darkness, a faint star fallen to earth — fire through the trees. It could only mean one thing, he figured: "soldiers or other white people." He considered ordering the horses unstaked and attacking immediately, but realized the ground all around him — a flat stretch near the lower geyser basin — was too muddy to cross safely in the night. Death would have to wait. "We will lie right here till morning," he said. "Then we are going to have a fight with them." He wrapped himself in a blanket and shut his eyes.

Earlier that day, August 23, Yellow Wolf had set out to ride alone, far ahead of the rest, but four young men were determined to come along. Since his bravery at the Big Hole, people had regarded him differently. Warriors wanted to follow him into battle. "You are supposed to be our leader," he remembered the young men telling him. For hours Yellow Wolf rode with his scouting party, from hills and meadow to swamp. After sunset, he determined that they would stop and set up camp. Handing his mount to one of the young men, Yellow Wolf turned and scanned the darkness. "Look that way!" he called.

The national park brought back memories of less troubled times. A year ago Yellow Wolf had been hunting in this very area, just as his people had done for generations. His grandfather had died on a buffalo hunt here. Yellow Wolf had visited the place where he was buried — "north of some hot springs, not over or beyond any big mountain, but . . . above where two rivers meet." "We knew that Park country, no difference what white people say!" Yellow Wolf insisted, "The hot smoking springs and the high-shooting water were nothing new to us."

But as the Nez Perce families fled from the army, the park appeared less than familiar. On their seasonal hunts they did not usually enter via

481

the Targhee Pass, nor were they seeking to leave the park by their normal route. Struggling to get their bearings, they also wondered what they should do when they encountered whites. The raid at the Camas Meadows had taken them back to a simpler and more certain kind of war. Some hoped the indiscriminate killing could stop. But the elation of that one moment had begun to ebb quickly, when they realized that most of the animals they had taken were mules, not the horses they prized. The army would keep following, they knew, and they would be crossing well-traveled land. The wounded and the dying remained among them. Nearly everyone was haunted by the husbands, wives, children, parents, brothers, and sisters whom they had buried and left behind at the Big Hole battle, their deaths largely un-avenged. Even so, the park cast them into a different place, with other paths to follow. When Yellow Wolf encountered a miner cooking a meal for himself, he did not think of killing the man; instead he found someone who could translate and asked if the man "knew the way . . . toward the Crow Indian lands about Elk Water," what the whites called the Yellowstone River.

At first light, Yellow Wolf and his men readied for battle and galloped until they reached the smoldering fire they had seen the night before. Six men were lying outside, and a small tent had been pitched nearby. Not soldiers, it was clear, "but all white people seemed our enemies," Yellow Wolf recalled. "We talked what to do with them. I said we would kill them." One of the young men, Heinmot Tosinlikt (Lightning Tied in a Bunch), born to a Snake Indian mother and a white father, who had married a Nez Perce woman and estab-

482

lished a reputation as a warrior, wondered if the whites would be more valuable as captives.

Yellow Wolf, Heinmot Tosinlikt, and one of the other young men rode toward the fire. The men jumped awake. They had weapons — rifles, a shotgun, hunting knives — but Yellow Wolf was unafraid. Heinmot Tosinlikt, who knew some English, introduced himself as Charley — what Indians often said when whites asked them their names. He pointed to Yellow Wolf and said, "There is our leader!" One of the men greeted Yellow Wolf with warmth. It was a lifesaving move. "Because I shook hands with him put me in mind not to kill him," the warrior would later say.

The man asked Yellow Wolf his tribe. On hearing they were Nez Perce, he wondered aloud, "Would you kill us?" Yellow Wolf tried to answer honestly — he would not, but others might. His people were "double-minded" about the settlers they met, the warrior said. After the Big Hole battle, they knew that any whites they befriended would soon enough join the soldiers against them.

"It was hard work, this talking to the white man," Yellow Wolf later said. "Not understanding many words of his language made hard work." Still, he sensed a wave of fear surge through the campsite. One of the white men began cooking breakfast, but no one seemed hungry. The white man who had spoken with Yellow Wolf, whom the warrior took to be their leader, began giving the Indians sugar, flour, and bacon. One of the other white men ducked inside the tent, and voices began softly humming inside. "Can we see the Chief Joseph?" the leader asked. "Will you take us to him?"

Yellow Wolf did not think it was a good idea. He

explained that while the chiefs had no interest in killing settlers, many of the warriors surrounding the main camp were "bad boys" seeking vengeance. The settlers heard Heinmot Tosinlikt translate, "Chief no kill you. No kill you, friends," but Yellow Wolf could not say what would happen to the settlers. "Don't know," the settlers heard, "maybe some Joseph's Injuns come up here, kill you, maybe want horses." Yellow Wolf wanted the white man to know how everything stood — "I wanted to be a friend to him," the warrior later said — but he hardly understood why himself.

Despite what Yellow Wolf thought was a clear warning, the one he regarded as "the leading white man" insisted on going to the chiefs. The other whites began to break camp, preparing a wagon, saddling up, while Yellow Wolf eyed their horses, counted them, and judged one roan to be especially good. He walked to the tent, opened the flap, and watched two women — one young, one about Yellow Wolf's age — run past him into the woods. A man walked from the tent to the brush and called to the women again and again. After a few minutes, the two emerged from the woods. The older one had been crying.

With the whites finally on their horses or in the wagon, the warriors mounted and led the way. They rode slowly for some time in pine woods, back through the marsh where the warriors had slept the previous night, then along the trails they had all taken from the Madison River to the geysers. Among the trees, in the quiet and shade, they made calm progress. Then, climbing one rise, they left the trees behind and found themselves under the morning sun. They could look back at geysers boiling behind them. But ahead, along a creek cutting east from the Firehole River, they saw the Nez Perce bands and their herd, a column maybe three miles long and ten or fifteen horses across. At a glance, it seemed a single continuous pushing mass, steadily advancing like a lava flow. On closer look they could see riders weaving in and out of line, the constant unsteady work of keeping the animals moving east.

Up on the ridge, the ground gradually began to tremble, and a low rumbling filled the air. It grew louder, closer, enveloping and disorienting Yellow Wolf and everyone riding with him; far from the geysers, it felt as if something were about to erupt. Within minutes they could see dozens of men on horseback rushing at the group. Yellow Wolf saw no chiefs among them — just warriors — and when they swept through, he lost control over his captives. "The warriors mixed us up," he said, taking the whites away and, to his regret, their horses, too, driving them toward the main column along the creek. The quiet returned. Yellow Wolf rode behind, out of sight, alone again in the park. Back in the woods, back along gentle water, it could have been another hunting expedition, another year. But then Yellow Wolf saw the wagon abandoned along the trail, cargo dumped and picked over, spokes hacked from the wheels.

Emma Cowan cried quietly as the warriors ransacked her trunk. Her possessions were not just disappearing — they were changing into entirely different objects before her eyes. Wheel spokes became whip handles. Yards of pink mosquito netting, so commonplace that it was barely meant to be seen, became a jaunty train tied to the tail of a Nez Perce horse. A strip of

485

swansdown, a souvenir of the journey from Radersburg to the national park, became a turban wrapped around an old man's head, which, she wrote, "did not please me either."

From tourist to captive, Emma's life was also transforming. The up and down of the trail, the pine woods surrounding her, the sublime sights and diversions of the park were no longer ennobling or diverting. She had become the latest heroine in a long series of stories of Indian peril, tales that even the night before she had regarded as remnants of a long gone, almost mythical past. She and everyone in her party knew how those stories ended. Emma's brother thought the warriors were taunting them, " 'whooping us up, plenty,' having lots of fun among themselves, seemingly at our expense." "The Indians watch us constantly like cats," he wrote. He was sure they were paying special attention to Emma and Ida, with "deviltry in their eyes," and wondered if he would have to shoot his sisters to spare them a worse fate.

But as Emma rode on toward the main column, still sidesaddle on her horse Bird, she began seeing a different story take shape. She was struck less by her captors' menace — the bright flashes of sun off the warriors' gun barrels — than by what she took to be a "light-hearted" mood. Her "first fright" began to subside, though she never stopped regarding the Indians as savages. On their faces even happiness appeared as an alien emotion. "The majority of the Nez Perces . . . seemed not to worry over the outcome of their campaign," she wrote. "Perhaps to worry is a prerogative of the white race."

Emma Cowan rode into the Nez Perce camp as

the column stopped for the midday meal. Lean Elk approached the group, introduced himself in English as Poker Joe, and shook their hands. One of the tourists, William Dingee, reminded him that they had met in Helena years before. Calm and friendly, the chief said everyone would be able to leave unharmed as soon as they traded their fresh horses for Nez Perce ponies — "old rackabone" mounts, Emma Cowan judged, no longer fit to ride. An Indian started leading Bird away with Cowan still in the saddle. She hopped to the ground and took a last look as her favorite horse faded into the herd.

Breaking camp and preparing to move again, Lean Elk urged the group to leave as quickly as they could and head straight into the woods before any warriors could follow. While the tourists surrendered their horses and mounted new ones — Emma Cowan kept her sidesaddle, and the others rode on blankets, if that — Dingee and A. J. Arnold ran into the brush and disappeared. The rest of the group made for timber. Ten yards, twenty yards, half a mile, they celebrated their good fortune — a felicitous revision to the old frontier stories.

But then Emma Cowan looked back and began crying again. Her husband's face paled. Indians were following quietly, gaining on them, soon telling them to turn around and return to the Nez Perce column. The group rode back through the site of the noon camp, now abandoned, and started to climb a steep wooded trail, up to much higher ground. The escort felt different from the morning — the Indians were no longer happy. "The silence seemed ominous," she wrote. "They seemed the same old dirty Indians familiar to all

Western people."

A crack in the woods broke the quiet — like a lightning strike, but it was a sunny day. Emma Cowan watched uncomprehending as her husband, riding right beside her, seemed to climb from his horse and then slide all the way down the hill, until he lay by a fallen pine. "In less time than it takes me to tell it," Cowan wrote, "I was off my horse and by my husband's side." She heard the warriors shouting, her sister screaming, then crouching close by her side. Another crack, and Al Oldham fell from his horse. Blood was spurting from George Cowan's leg, shot above the knee. He asked her for water, but she did not move. They looked uphill. Every warrior was aiming at them. "The holes in those gun barrels looked as big as saucers," she wrote. "Keep quiet," her husband whispered. "It won't last long."

Someone was tugging at Emma's shoulder. She looked back and saw a warrior with a pistol aiming at George's head. She broke out of his grip and lunged for her husband but was pulled away. She watched another warrior step forward, heard the shot, saw her husband fall backward, red pouring from his forehead, drenching his face. He was still wearing his hat. She was close enough to smell his blood. "The horror of it all," she wrote, "a faint remembrance of seeing rocks thrown at his head, my sister's screams, a sick faint feeling, and all was blank."

The white man shook Joseph's hand and introduced his sister. Ragged and pale, the woman could not stop crying. The chief said little but motioned for them to sit by the fire. They had all had a grueling ride, up a mountainside so thickly wooded that again and again packhorses got stuck between trees. The women tending to the horses spent much of the afternoon coaxing, pushing, and beating the animals to get them to back up. At the top, forest gave way to broad meadows. They stopped at sunset and built campfires, stretched canvas across branches and bushes for shelter, and spread blankets, buffalo robes, and deerskins for bedding.

The night was cold. The damp was spreading. It would be many days before the Nez Perce column could get through the park to the plains beyond the high mountains lining the horizon north and east. Joseph did not know this country. He did not know any of the ways out: north down the Yellowstone River, the usual route to buffalo country; east down Clark's Fork of the Yellowstone River, which cut deep and narrow canyons through the rock; and southeast to the Stinkingwater, named for its sulfurous smell, and Crow territory. Although Looking Glass had been certain that the Crow would give them sanctuary, help was far from assured — they had expected aid from the Flatheads in the Bitterroot Valley, only to be disappointed, then massacred at the Big Hole. While Joseph rode with the women and children, small bands of scouts were going out every day, probing in each direction, trying to determine what paths remained open to them.

Everyone around the fire — Joseph and his family, young and old — was eating, all except for the sobbing woman. She refused their offers of food. The chiefs — among them Lean Elk, White Bird, Joseph, and Looking Glass — had spoken against harming captives, but the young warriors were determined to follow their own conscience. Two weeks after the Big Hole, the Nez Perce families remained just as haunted by their losses as the woman seemed to be with hers. Any day now they faced the prospect of leaving another elder behind — a woman, too sick to go much farther. Many of the warriors insisted that anyone they encountered in the park could join the army or direct the soldiers, just as the Bitterroot settlers had done. Even the friendliest people might as well be killers. After the noon camp had broken and the tourists had ridden away, Lean Elk felt compelled to go after the warriors, reaching them in time to save the woman and her brother and sister. Now they lived under the chiefs' protection.

When a mother with her baby sat by the fire, the crying woman's brother reached for it. Trying to console his sister, he put the child on her lap. She finally looked up at the people around the fire. They smiled at her, but after a moment, she handed the baby back, relinquished any connection to them, and retreated once again into her grief. It rained in the night, but soon the sun was glinting off the polished brass kettles brewing coffee and willow bark tea in fires the women had fed before dawn. The captives' young sister was reunited with her siblings for the first time since the shootings the previous afternoon, their sobs breaking the quiet work of morning. After a quick breakfast — camas porridge, soda bread — Lean Elk rode to Joseph on his rounds. Today they would reach the other side of the rise they had climbed the previous day and descend to the Yellowstone River. It was time to break camp and get moving again, straight toward the rising sun.

The teamsters looked down through scattered

pines at the Yellowstone River. Since leaving Henry's Lake six days earlier on August 28, Howard's army had been following the enemy's trail. The early going was slow but sure. They had finally figured out how to cross rivers, fording the Madison five times on their first day in the park. Up the mountain, where the forest was thickest, a unit of paid civilian skilled laborers working under an infantry captain — the "skillets" for short — chopped a rough road. In the easy meadows at the top, soldiers could glimpse Yellowstone Lake shimmering in the distance. But at the eastern end of the plateau, the supply wagons stopped short. The teamsters gathered, "took a survey of the whole situation," one wrote, "and came to the conclusion that the only way to get down was to take a jump of some five hundred feet."

The slope was not a sheer fall, but more like the pitch of a roof. Rather than backtrack, the skillets proposed something else — they could construct what they called a beaver slide. Scuttling downhill, they cleared a path wide enough for the wagons. Then they tied a hundred-foot rope to the rear axle of one carriage and wrapped the other end twice around a thick tree. A driver climbed into his spring seat and gathered his reins. With several men anchoring the rope, then slowly letting it out, the wagon slid off the plateau.

It was a controlled plunge, the supply train hanging by an actual thread — the slightest slip would cascade into a speeding, tumbling wreck. All the way down the mountain, the wagon dropped inch by inch, the descent steep enough that the driver was practically standing straight up on his footrest. When there was no more rope, the driver tied the wagon fast to the nearby trees with a second coil of line. Skillets and teamsters slid their way down the slope, wrapped the long rope around another tree, and anchored the slide once again.

Howard's men entered the park rested and even relaxed, hailed by their general for their feats of endurance — marching 540 miles in a month, crossing and recrossing the Continental Divide, and surviving mountains, "where day brings the oppressive heat and dust of August, and night the ice and piercing winds of December." They had saved innumerable settlers and settlements, not to mention their comrades at the Big Hole. Many of them still lacked overcoats, proper shoes, and, in Howard's words, "underclothing sufficient to preserve health and cleanliness." But they had regained some of the morale lost in the Camas Meadows. Easily a week behind the Nez Perce — at least fifty miles away — they could sleep the night without fear of attack.

Spurred on by Sherman's telegrams, Howard urged his men to maintain their "disciplined spirit . . . in the sharp conflict of war to the death with a savage foe." But his officers joked about the remonstrances of distant generals, and the park's sublime attractions easily overshadowed the drudgeries of a stern-chase. Erskine Wood took out his sketchbook and started drawing the landscapes. The men caught trout and cooked them in geysers. They marveled at the variety of game — "beaver, deer, elk, moose, antelope, and even mountain sheep," by one captain's count — and cataloged the blooms that filled the meadows, "a flower paradise," he pronounced, "full of asters, lupine, white phlox and yellow columbine." Ordered to bathe and wash their union suits in a warm spring, the soldiers turned the chore into a rough frolic. "One of the sullen resentful dirtier troopers was sent cartwheeling into this mild cauldron by eager hands," the captain wrote. "This prude left his underwear on. The boys tore this off, claiming that the seam squirrels" — his body lice — "needed an airing."

The idyll began to darken on August 29 when the men found Al Oldham lying by the trail, nearly dead five days after being shot through the face, choking on his wounded, swollen tongue. As he struggled to communicate that all the other men in the Radersburg party had certainly been killed, the soldiers fixated on Emma Cowan and Ida Carpenter. "Too dreadful to think about," wrote Howard's chief of staff Edwin Mason. For the moment, the troops were no longer on a wilderness adventure. Their chase transformed into something entirely different, a crusade for the purity of white women. It was a story with roots in the oldest Puritan tales of Indian captivity. Two hundred years later, the narrative still tapped elemental fears of western settlers and was still shaping politics and lives across the country. After weeks of wondering why they were keeping after the Nez Perce bands, Mason found a new sense of urgency in avenging "the fate of the females." "I am perfectly willing to follow these fellows until the last one is disposed of," he wrote his wife and mother. "They should be killed as we kill any other vile thing."

The soldiers' sensation that they were living inside a dime novel only intensified the next day with reports that Emma Cowan and her sister and brother were safe. Although it had seemed a certainty that the Nez Perce bands would keep the women, the captives had been freed after just one night. The huzzahs of Howard's men had barely gone quiet when they marched into the Lower Geyser Basin and found scouts tending to George Cowan — shot in the head, leg, and hip, but after dragging himself through the brush for nearly a week, he was, Mason exulted, "alive!" The soldiers listened rapt to Cowan's tale of captivity and redemption: the shot glancing off his skull, knocking him unconscious, crusting his eyes over with blood; his last sight of Emma, trying in vain to protect him by covering his body with hers. The story was as exciting as it was ennobling, full of improbable twists, but also predictable and re-assuring in its portraits of manly endurance and womanly devotion. "The chapter was completed," Mason wrote. "The whole tale sounds like a ro-mance."

From the captives and his scouts, Howard was gaining a rough sense of where the Indians were headed: they would exit the park at its northeast corner, he predicted. Certain after his exchanges with Sherman that forces in Montana and Wyo-ming would mobilize ahead of the hostiles, Howard fired off dispatches directing cavalry companies under Colonel Samuel Sturgis to stake out positions by Clark's Fork, with other troops maneuvered to key points to the north so the Indians would have nowhere else to go. To his mind, there was little reason they would head for Crow country to the southeast. It was unlikely the Crow would risk everything to give sanctuary to the Nez Perce. While the Sioux and Cheyenne had suffered through a decade of war, the Crow had been careful to reject outright confrontation with the United States, and many were serving as

494

army scouts. With the exits from the park blocked, Howard's troops would come from behind, pulling the knot tight.

Just as Howard's spirits were swelling again, he received a dispiriting message. A lieutenant patrolling the park's northern boundary forwarded word from General Sherman: within days of expressing his unqualified support for Howard, he had decided to send an officer he had met in Helena to assume Howard's command. Lieutenant Colonel Charles C. Gilbert, Sherman wrote in a note to Howard, "has served long in this Territory, and is familiar with the Indians, and the country in which they have taken refuge." Sherman tried to soften the blow: turning over the command was "not an order but only advice." "You can with perfect propriety return to [Oregon]," Sherman wrote, "leaving the troops to continue till the Nez-Perces have been destroyed, or captured." But Howard felt deeply humiliated. At fifty-five Gilbert was, the general would write, "an officer much older than I, though of less rank."

With a newspaper reporter traveling with his column, eating with him and his staff every night, Howard saw how his days were being reduced into serial installments in a larger story — the story of his campaign, his worth as a general, and ultimately his life and career. Through months of hardship, Howard had drawn strength from the belief that everything would conclude in triumph. It was inconceivable that the story could go on without him, that he would be written out, reduced from a hero to a sorry footnote. Even as he bristled at Sherman's turn, Howard searched for ways to change the ending of his own story before it was committed to print.

Regardless of Sherman's wishes, Gilbert would still have to find Howard to replace him. Rather than wait to be shamed, Howard decided his best move was to continue deeper into the wilderness and redouble the pursuit. Reaching the Yellowstone River ahead of the pack train on September 2, Howard interviewed another escaped captive — a recently discharged soldier who had been touring the park. Heartening news: the hostiles were heading precisely where he had ordered Sturgis to go, through the canyons east of Yellowstone Lake toward Clark's Fork. Not following their usual paths through the park, the Indians appeared "uncertain of their exact whereabouts and rather bewildered," Howard learned. In the rough crossings from one long canyon to the next, east from the Yellowstone River up Pelican Creek to Cache and Miller Creeks, the Indians were leaving trails smeared with blood and littered with dead and dying animals. Buoyed at the thought that the Nez Perce were losing time, and confident of their eventual destination, Howard decided on a shortcut, north along the Yellowstone River and then east through the canyons to Clark's Fork. They might catch the enemy yet.

Howard waited for the wagons and pack train and then commanded his men to go quickly downriver. Even loyal supporters bristled at the general's manner. After Howard sought an additional "short march just long enough to make trouble," Mason complained that he "has very little idea how troops should be marched and manages so as to make double the trouble necessary. I could gain the same result with half the worry and labor to the troops but he commands and I don't." Along the way, Howard ordered all supplies packed onto mules and sent the wagons out of the park to Fort Ellis, just east of Bozeman. The troops would live on coffee, rice, flour, and salted beef. "Now one will not starve on beef and salt," Mason wrote, "still a civilized taste craves something more." Ordering long and late marches every day for a week, Howard insisted that the soldiers maintain their discipline. "A domineering officer," Captain Robert Pollock grumbled. "A dedicated army man, everything done by the book down to the last period."

Where the Yellowstone River met its east fork, Nez Perce scouts had burned a crude log bridge, but within three hours, Howard's army had patched it, and pack mules were being coaxed across the swinging span. Up the east fork to Soda Butte Creek, the horizon was impaled on soaring snowy peaks. By September 6, the soldiers were passing into a deep canyon, "the most magnificent . . . I have ever seen *from the bottom,*" Mason wrote, "mountains . . . on each side full 5000 ft high, worn by the rains of ages into all sorts of shapes." The nagging cold of morning began to stretch into the day. Their breath smoked in the air. Frost silvered their tents and tarps. The men told themselves that on the other side of the mountains, it was still summer. By September 8, they were out of the park, marching southeast along Clark's Fork. Where the canyon became impassably narrow, sheer walls plunging to the tightest of channels, they moved up to the bluffs above. Word came from Sturgis that he and his cavalry were posting some forty miles downriver at Heart Mountain, near where Clark's Fork turns sharply north. The Nez Perce bands were trapped somewhere in between.

On September 9, Howard and his command rode past the body of a Nez Perce man, wounded at the Big Hole and after a month of suffering too weak to keep going. One of the Bannock scouts riding ahead had shot him through the chest, and two others cut his scalp and stretched it to dry in a willow tree. When Howard reached them, the officer in charge distracted the general while a scout kicked the scalp into the tall rye grass. Howard was in high spirits. Sturgis was only twenty miles away. Under heavy guard the men tried to sleep. They would have a fight tomorrow.

At sunrise on the tenth, Howard's scouts raced up a steep hill toward Sturgis's position. The summit, a narrow pass, was a natural place for an ambush — "the boys are apprehensive that we will get a game there," the officer in charge wrote in his journal — but at the top the scouts found "no enemy in sight in any direction." They picked up the Indians' trail and found it cut to the southeast, toward the Stinkingwater and Crow country. For two miles the trail was clear, but then it seemed that the Nez Perce had run their herd in every direction. Milling their ponies — a common way to conceal a trail. The scouts scattered, trying to find it again. Finally, they picked it up. The Nez Perce families had turned north along a steep wooded slope — thick forest edging an abyss — and gone right back to Clark's Fork.

Ten miles away, with Heart Mountain straight ahead in plain sight, Howard ordered signalmen to "wave their flags furiously" to gauge how Sturgis was faring against the enemy. As much as they looked through their field glasses, they saw no reply. Gaining ground, Howard heard no sounds of battle — no echoes of gunfire, no bugle blasts, no rumble of horses, no whoops or cries.

Finally reaching Heart Mountain, they found the cavalry's camp abandoned — cold at least two days. No troops had been waiting to stop the Indians. "Where Sturgis is we have not the faintest idea," Mason fumed. When the Indians turned south, the colonel must have fallen for the ruse and ridden with his entire force to the Stinkingwater — right past the Indians, a distasteful bookend to Howard's detour across the Salmon River in Idaho back in July. "Disquieting to the extream," Mason wrote. The scouts tracked the Nez Perce column straight past Heart Mountain, through the canyon that everyone had figured was too narrow to thread. Along the river, where the canyon opened up, Howard's men found three bodies, dead a couple of days. Reading through letters strewn around the bodies, the soldiers figured the men for Norwegian or Danish, panning the riverbanks for new lives, new fortunes. Howard kept riding, up and over a divide, and looked out for miles at the rolling country. The hostiles had reached the plains.

CHAPTER 19
THROUGH THE VEIL

Galloping east along the Yellowstone River, the warriors saw the ranch quivering in the distance — a rough cabin and sheds, pasture in back studded with mounds of hay, a wagon hitched to horses out front. A woman, at least two men, and two dogs were running away from the buildings into a thicket of willows, the mouth of a creek, where the ranch ended and the wilderness began. The half-dozen Nez Perce riders fired at the sound of barking in the brush, but within minutes all was quiet. No one would be putting up a fight.

While a few warriors tore through the cabin for food — flour, sugar, coffee, meat — others set fire to the haystacks and hacked at a machine used to mow the field. The smells of late summer — dry grass mingling with the green along the river, sagebrush from the creek valley extending to the north — were overwhelmed by thick pillars of smoke. Black rising to blue sky, the smoke could be seen for miles, by other raiding parties fanned out over the area, the main Nez Perce column a mile or two up the creek, and whoever might be coming north in pursuit. When the cabin was cleared, it too was torched.

Along Clark's Fork, the land had smoothed into

rolling prairie, the east for once unbounded by great mountains. After months of steep climbs and slippery descents, the Nez Perce families had finally reached level ground, a place that invited them to stop, enjoy the leisure afforded by gentle terrain, and prepare for the coming winter. But they kept moving. Although they had reached the destination that Looking Glass had spoken of back in Idaho — Crow country — their arrival brought neither comfort nor relief. While crossing the national park, they had learned from Crow emissaries that the eastern prairies would be no sanctuary. Old alliances meant little in a changing world. Many among the Nez Perce families knew the territory they were traversing, but the progression of familiar landmarks only reinforced how everything had changed. They found no buffalo on the plains — just hundreds of skulls, bleached and scattered, remnants of richer years.

The path was straight north, from the national park sixty miles to the confluence of Clark's Fork and the Yellowstone River, up from the Yellowstone fifty miles to the Musselshell, a hundred miles more to the Missouri, and finally another hundred past the Milk River to an invisible boundary, the only one that mattered now: the Medicine Line, separating the United States from the British possessions. Sitting Bull and his people were living sixty miles north of the border. Until a peace council five years before, the Sioux had been hated enemies, a people called the Cut Throats in the Nez Perce language. Their battles had given Rainbow and Five Wounds, killed at the Big Hole, their renown as warriors. Now the Sioux were the only friends the Nez Perce people could hope for.

All along the Yellowstone below Clark's Fork, raiding parties took horses and supplies, burned buildings, and shot the few men they encountered. At the ranch, as the cabin and haystack flamed, warriors approached the wagon and held the horses still. It was not much, just a small covered platform with storage front and back, no springs to cushion the ride. It must have stopped moments before the raiders came into view, its driver and passengers fleeing before they had time to unload a mailbag and a small but heavy valise. The warriors recognized it exactly for what it was: a stagecoach.

The warriors — young men — may have been attacking the signs of settlement on their way to exile, yet they were not opposed to the world outside their bands, villages, and tribe. That world had always been a part of their lives. They had grown up trading with whites for horses, rifles, food, blankets, and cloth. They once claimed white friends alongside the enemies, people they had visited, eaten with, talked to. Just the year before, when Yellow Wolf wanted to travel from Nez Perce lands in Idaho to the Wallowa Valley, he had gone by stage.

The warriors could have destroyed the coach just as they had the rest of the ranch — cut the horses loose, set fire to the carriage, chopped wheels and spokes into splinters. Instead, they stopped for a moment, tied their horses to the back, and climbed aboard — in the driver's seat, in the coach, on the roof. A hard crack, and the horses took off running. The coach lurched into motion, turned north, and gathered speed. The warrior holding the reins had no trouble controlling it, horses front and back, men keeping their balance, cutting through the wind. From the ranch, the coach rolled to the dry creek, then up toward the herd and the women and children. The valise left behind by a passenger was opened, its contents scattered one by one: small metal instruments, not quite tools, not quite weapons. Then the mailbag — a wake of paper pluming from the stagecoach, each letter angry and awhirl before floating softly to the ground.

From the bluffs above the Yellowstone, a small group of army scouts watched the stagecoach weave along the creek bottom — Canyon Creek on their maps, a swath of sagebrush leading toward a narrow gorge bounded by imposing buttes. Horses at a trot, the coach was slowly gaining on the rest of the Indians, half a mile north. The scouts had not had breakfast the morning of September 13. Their clothes were still wet from fording the deep river. But at their vantage overlooking Canyon Creek, all discomforts were forgotten. They had followed the Nez Perce bands — tracked their phantom signs — for weeks. Finally, the enemy was all together before them, in their sights.

By this point the scouts had gone hundreds of miles, high and low, hot and cold, wet and dry. Little food, no tobacco — they were ripping the lining out of their jackets to smoke it. When their horses gave out, they cinched their saddles on pack mules. But the physical hardships paled in comparison to the emotional toll of tracking and locating the enemy, only to realize the army was too far away to strike. In the national park Stanton Gilbert Fisher, chief of the scouts, had to admit, "I . . . am becoming tired of trying to get the soldiers and the hostiles together. 'Uncle Sam's' boys are too slow for this business."

Now, after endless frustration, the scouts on the Yellowstone could exult in the knowledge that Sturgis's cavalry was just a few miles behind. When the Indians slipped the army's trap at Clark's Fork, Howard had ordered the 7th Cavalry's fresh horses to ride night and day after them. He sent his scouts and surgeon Jenkins FitzGerald ahead, along with a few others whose mounts remained healthy. The rest of the troops limped along, covering fifteen miles a day to Sturgis's fifty. At the same time, Howard dispatched a courier with a message for Colonel Nelson Miles, who led the army's newly created District of the Yellowstone at the Tongue River Cantonment, a cluster of rough log barracks 160 miles east. For much of the year following Custer's defeat, Miles had methodically destroyed Sioux and Northern Cheyenne resistance. When it became apparent earlier in the summer that the Nez Perce bands were headed to Montana, Miles recognized that even a small number of renegades could upset the order he was imposing upon the plains. He had supported Howard's campaign by sending his best companies under Sturgis to the national park. Now Howard was urging Miles to do what Sturgis had left undone, to ride northwest with his remaining force in order to head off the Indians before they reached Canada, "to make every effort in your power," the general wrote, "to prevent the escape of this hostile band, and at least to hold them in check until I can overtake them."

But as the scouts watched the Indians ride up Canyon Creek, it appeared that the war would be over before Howard's message even reached

Miles. One of the men turned and galloped for Sturgis's command. Viewed through their spyglasses, the stagecoach provided a moment of levity for the scouts — "a joy ride," one later described the scene, "driven in great style." But within minutes the coach was abandoned in the sagebrush. The warriors jumped on their horses and unhitched the animals pulling the wagon. The scouts had been spotted, and the Indians were rushing for the mouth of the canyon, still three miles away.

By the time Sturgis's force — some four hundred soldiers — reached Canyon Creek, the view from the ridge seemed entirely different. The surgeon FitzGerald saw the herd, the women and children, warriors outnumbered and plainly surprised. He had never shown much sympathy for the people he casually called savages, and his wife back in Lapwai echoed and amplified his antipathy, wishing that "all the Indians in the country were at the bottom of the Red Sea" and opining that "the country will have trouble until they are exterminated." But looking out at the Nez Perce families after three months of war — months of hardship, months away from his wife and children — the doctor felt a surge of unexpected emotion. "Poor Nez Percés!" he wrote. "I am actually beginning to admire their bravery and endurance in the face of so many well equipped enemies."

Colonel Sturgis scanned the Nez Perce column and saw something different still: the peril of following Indians into a canyon. A year after his 7th Cavalry had lost five of its twelve companies at the Little Bighorn — more than two hundred soldiers, including Sturgis's own son — the colonel sent 150 men to charge straight at the

505

enemy, while another hundred tried to race past and cut them off before they reached the canyon's mouth. But as soon as the initial charge encountered fire from the enemy, Sturgis ordered the men to dismount and form a battle line, all but guaranteeing failure. Just a few warriors were able to turn the soldiers' advance into an exhausting three-mile march across level ground broken by ravines. The remaining Nez Perce fighters rode for the bluffs guarding the canyon and were able to stop the remaining cavalry while the women, children, and herd escaped. By sunset, the warriors, too, had pulled back, leaving no dead on the field. With three of his own men killed and eleven wounded men howling with thirst, Sturgis felt it imprudent to follow the Indians in the dark.

The army scouts left the battlefield in disgust, knowing that Canyon Creek was, in one man's words, "where the war should have ended, but did not." Riding back to the Yellowstone, they found a deserted ranch. Log cabin, burned haystacks — they remembered seeing black smoke rising that morning as they crossed the river. They called out that the Indians were gone, and a man and woman emerged from the brush: Ed Forrest, who ran the stage station, and Fannie Clark, one of two passengers on the coach, a prostitute in her fifties who traveled a circuit of mining camps. The other passenger had fled downriver.

Forrest asked if the scouts were hungry. Glancing at his cabin, "looted of all its eatables," the men laughed, but Forrest said that in his time on the frontier he had always made a practice of hiding extra food. They dug up caches of flour, ham, coffee, and a pot, and Clark, dressed in men's breeches and a gray wool shirt, began "stacking up flapjacks as fast as we could eat them," a scout wrote, "hot cakes just like those that mother used to make."

As the "flapjack party" got under way, life began returning to normal. Clark recounted how she felt as if "the whole Nez Perce tribe" had been attacking them. With the Indians shooting at them, Forrest had killed Clark's dog — cut its throat — to stop it from barking. But as terrifying as their ordeal had been, the civilians had no fear they would ever experience anything like it again. Before the encounter, the settlers had consigned Indians to the distant past. And as the Indians moved north, they receded into memory and imagination once again. Their momentary presence would have no effect on the experience of daily life along the Yellowstone. Another stagecoach was sure to come. Fannie Clark would climb into the cab and continue to her destination. Ed Forrest would welcome the next set of travelers to his ranch — and entertain them with stories of his brush with Chief Joseph.

After a time, two men pulled up in an open wagon drawn by a single horse — a buckboard. They were familiar faces, blacksmiths employed by the stage line, on their usual rounds to check horseshoes and repair wagon hardware along the route. Learning of the Nez Perce raid, one of the men wandered off, tracing the stagecoach's errant path. As he walked in the sagebrush, he found the metal implements the warriors had discarded. Forceps, picks, tooth keys, sets of false teeth — the smith recognized them for what they were, what one scout referred to as the "tools of torture." The other passenger with Fannie Clark on the stagecoach must have been a dentist, but he was not coming back for his gear. The black-smith collected the instruments for himself. He gave no thought to who had scattered them, how they had wound up in the dirt, or why. Rather, he figured there were always people whose teeth were aching. With the right equipment, he could be a dentist, too.

Yellow Wolf walked alone on the plains, wrapped in a blanket against the cold. In the vast swell of treeless prairie, he was barely visible, the wind overwhelming the sounds of steady breath and footsteps on dry grass. At dawn he had left camp on horseback. After riding for hours, he came upon a pack of bighorn sheep, a joyful sight for a scout who could not count on eating every day. But as he slipped his rifle from the leather sheath hanging off his saddle, good luck turned bad. He accidentally pulled the trigger, firing into his horse's hind leg, leaving a messy wound and a useless animal. Yellow Wolf took off his saddle and set it on the ground for the main Nez Perce column to find when they came through later in the day. He would keep scouting on foot.

After the skirmish at Canyon Creek, Yellow Wolf felt consumed with anger. The soldiers were so far behind that when warriors spoke of General Howard, they no longer called him Cut Arm; after months of lagging, he had become General Day-After-Tomorrow. But for five days as the Nez Perce column crossed the high plains toward the Musselshell River, Indians working with the army had stalked them, waiting in the distance until they broke camp, then stealing horses that strayed and picking off old people who had fallen behind.

Yellow Wolf saw how each day's march and each

night's rest were edged with terror. Instead of ranging widely, the warriors had to stay close to the herd. Curious to learn who these "strange Indians" were, Yellow Wolf rode at them with Ollokot, until he saw that Howard's Indians were not just Snake — the Nez Perce name for their traditional enemies, the Bannock and Shoshone. Yellow Wolf would always remember his shock at the sight: "*Eeh!* Crows!" There were dozens of them. The old friends of the Nez Perce people had not just refused to take them in, as the Flatheads had done. The Crow were actively fighting them. The young warrior felt a bullet nick his thigh. Another hit his saddle, piercing his horse's neck at the mane. "My heart was just like fire," he later said.

In the days that followed, when Indians approached from afar, Yellow Wolf stopped assuming they were friends and tribesmen. He trained his rifle on one rider, only to realize at the last moment that he was getting ready to shoot one of his cousins. Though the threat from other tribes disappeared as the Nez Perce column crossed the Musselshell and then threaded the gap between two mountain ranges to open plains, the warrior remained unsettled. The families traveled another five days without incident — prime buffalo country, but still no herds in sight. Lean Elk, still leading the group, pushed them to cover dozens of miles each day in long, hungry marches. On September 22, instead of riding in back with most of the other fighters, Yellow Wolf chose the lonelier job of lead scout.

Half a day north of the rest, Yellow Wolf walked until he saw a line of brush ahead. It was getting dark, but he could hear the soft murmur of water flowing: a creek's trickle. As he approached, another sound cut low, a rumbling outtake of breath, something he had heard every day of his life — a horse nickering. If he had still been riding, he would have stopped to let his animal drink. But he had left it behind to die hours before. He was not alone.

Four men stood in a clearing past the creek — "four white men," Yellow Wolf knew, but not dressed as soldiers or scouts. They were just settlers. For hours he had been scouting, wandering alone, thinking, and remembering. Now there was only this moment, and only one place to go. The warrior walked straight at the men. "All white men were spies," he described his state of mind. "Enemies to be killed." One called out — "I did not understand very well," Yellow Wolf would say, "but I knew he wanted me to stop." He kept walking, saw the men holding their rifles, and started to raise his when he heard the blasts. His left arm flashed with pain, but he did not drop his gun. He shouted with fury, then fired — one man killed. The other three sprinted away toward the brush. Yellow Wolf paused, aimed, and dropped a second man.

Instantly in silence again, just wind and creek, the warrior found four horses staked to the ground near a tent. He ate some of the men's food, then saddled one horse and put a packsaddle on another. After loading it with a sack and a half of flour, he led all the horses away. Deep in the night, he heard familiar calls on the prairie. "Now I am getting to my friends alive!" he remembered thinking. He woke up on a buffalo robe, covered with his blanket. At breakfast, his uncle spoke to him about the previous day's encounter.

Yellow Wolf remembered the older man asking, "Were you afraid?"

"No!" Yellow Wolf laughed. "The whites are just like those little flies. Sometimes they light on your hand. You can kill them!"

On September mornings, thick mists would rise from the Missouri, floating, drifting. From the cliffs above, it could be impossible to see the water — it was as if earth had been displaced by cloud. Deep down on the canyon floor, it was hard to see the other side. Three months earlier, Joseph's band had twisted down a narrow hillside path and crossed the Snake, away from their beloved Wallowa Valley. On September 23, the Nez Perce families and herd had reached the edge of another gentle plain, and where the land broke and plunged to canyon, they descended to another mighty river. They were seven hundred miles from their ancestral land and had traveled nearly twice that distance, searching for a new home. They had started their journey during spring. Now summer was yielding to autumn. But as they stepped through the Missouri's misty veil, the world they saw carried distinct echoes of the one they had left behind — a river thousands of feet across, a labyrinth of creeks and canyons, hills ahead like closed fists, ridges knuckling down to bottom.

The experienced buffalo hunters led the column to a ford where the river bent, threading through islands thick with rustling cottonwoods. They figured at least some soldiers would be guarding the far bank, but it was hard to tell through the willows. Although the area had multiple Nez Perce names — Indians had followed the buffalo herds here for thousands of years — many also knew what the settlers called it: Cow Island, for the past fifteen years the site of a boat landing, the farthest upriver a steamer could travel in the hot, dry months. The Missouri had been dropping all summer. September would be high season for the roustabouts unloading freight from ships to wagons bound for Helena, Missoula, and Fort Benton. The Nez Perce families and herds moved upriver, out of sight and earshot, and found the water shallow enough to cross without rafts.

By sunset, the women had prepared camp a couple of miles inside a gentle creek valley, but after dark they led dozens of packhorses back down to the steamboat landing. Gunshots popped and crackled in the night, a scattered sound like burning logs. Earlier, a small Nez Perce delegation had approached the landing and discovered twelve soldiers cowering behind a breastworks, the only guard for what looked like a mountain of food — thousands of sacks piled ten feet high. Someone who knew English professed his friendship to the soldiers — a rhetorical gesture from before the war — and asked for food, but when the sergeant in charge refused, young warriors began climbing the hills and peppering the barricade with fire. With Cow Island's token guard pinned down all night, the women took their pick of supplies: beans, rice, flour, sugar, coffee, bacon, tobacco, hardtack, pots and pans, cups and buckets.

Then, when everyone's packsaddles were groaning, five hundred sacks of bacon went up in flames. "We figured it was soldier supplies, so set fire to what we did not take," Peopeo Tholekt later explained. Night turned to day in the intense light produced by tons of burning fat, and the smell of

512

sizzling sow belly seeped through the canyons. The Nez Perce column littered their trail with sacks and wrappers. Crossing the Missouri had felt less a battle than a celebration. In Yellow Wolf's words, "it had been nearly like play."

Oliver Otis Howard prayed while he rode, careful to keep what he called his "earnest petition[s]" to himself, and not to let his desperation show. But silently, "in my heart," he wrote, he beseeched and bargained for "God's help" to accomplish what increasingly seemed like a miracle. "One chance in a million," one of the surgeons estimated the odds of catching the hostiles before they crossed the British line.

Every passing hour, Joseph was extending his distance. The army could always count on a wide path to follow, but smoke hazed the skies ahead. The prairie was burning, and the trail disappeared amid thousands of acres of charred stubble. Howard started feeling his officers' disgust for him like cold on a tooth worn raw. When his chief of staff Mason tried to speak encouraging words about their prospects for success, the general only heard "a slight despondency of tone" in the aide's voice. Any indication that his officers thought their errand hopeless, and Howard's spirits plummeted. At times frustration became rage, alienating the men all the more. In private, Mason branded the expedition a "perfect farce" but was careful to warn his wife, "This is not to be repeated. I must not be quoted as growling about the actions of my chief."

Howard vowed to keep on to the Missouri. Yet the prairies appeared to him an endless, dusty desert. Temperatures were dropping. Soon it would be snowing — it could be any day — and the horses would have no grass to eat. Rather than descend into the canyons of the Upper Missouri River Breaks, he fixed on a steamer landing just east, Fort Carroll. By the time his column reached the river — at fifteen or twenty miles a day, he estimated September 30 — the Indians would likely be in the British possessions. Howard's officers entertained fantasies of boarding a riverboat and steaming a thousand miles downriver to Omaha. From there the rails would get them home in a week.

Howard's uncertainty about the Indians' path caused agony to "press upon" him, he wrote. Just three years ago, his political enemies had been ruining him in Washington — people sneered at the mention of his name, and he worried about his wife and children starving. His weeks on the Montana prairie felt worse. When he looked back, he would write, "I know of no period of my life when I needed sympathy and encouragement more."

Howard's aides did their best to comfort him. At dinner, they rehashed the campaign, teasing points of light out of their grim situation. Erskine Wood and Howard's son Guy regaled the general's mess with the story they had heard about warriors driving a stagecoach "in wild sport" by Canyon Creek. The officers laughed about hapless Colonel Gilbert, whom Sherman had sent to replace Howard. The man never caught up with their column; in the national park, they learned, he had been just a day's ride to the north, but inexplicably cut west all the way back to Henry's Lake, only to loop east to follow directly in Howard's tracks, by which point he was eighty miles to the rear. He gave up when his horses wore out. The officers amassed a field library of "books of an exciting character." Howard found it a "safety-valve" from "the pressure of heavy care and constant bodily fatigue" to set aside his own adventure for novels, presumably with happier endings.

The 7th Cavalry officers who had joined his command outside the national park also provided welcome new company for Howard. Unlike the men who had been with him since June, they were neither jaded nor exasperated with the general. Drawing from their experience fighting on the plains as Custer's old regiment, they did not seem to view him a failure. Sturgis suggested that Howard's weakness was really a strength — the slower he went, the less effort the Indians would put into outrunning him. As a result, Nelson Miles's force, riding from the Tongue River Cantonment, would have a chance to cut them off. "We must not move too fast, lest we flush the game," the colonel said. Encouraged by Sturgis's words, Howard wrote Miles on September 20 that "the moment we check pursuit they stop thirty or forty miles ahead and rest till their scouts discover our forward movement." As a result, Howard wrote, "We shall not hasten the pursuit over much in order to give you time to get into position." Uplifting as Sturgis's words had been, the fact remained that the hostiles were just a hundred miles from the border. Miles was leading five hundred men three times that distance to catch them. With cavalry, artillery, infantry riding horses captured from the Sioux, civilian packers, and thirty Northern Cheyenne scouts — could Miles move quickly enough?

At one camp, one of Sturgis's company commanders, Lewis Merrill, unrolled a map and showed Howard how a miracle could happen. Tracing a diagonal path northwest from the Tongue River Cantonment, Merrill declared that Colonel Miles would catch Joseph below the international border. Pasty and stout, his weak chin muffed with whiskers, Merrill appreciated the general's situation as few people could. After graduating West Point a year behind Howard, Merrill had spent his life in the army fighting elusive foes — rebel bushwhackers in Missouri during the Civil War and in the decade following, the Ku Klux Klan in upcountry South Carolina and the White League on the Red River near Shreveport, Louisiana. For his trouble, he bore some of the same scars as Howard. Democratic newspapers had branded him "Dog Merrill," and Reconstruction's enemies in Washington permanently stalled his promotion from major to lieutenant colonel. Within his regiment, he had feuded with Custer, and Custer, in turn, had vilified him in congressional testimony with accusations of bribery — base slanders, Merrill protested. With Howard, Merrill grew "lively" and "inclined to be prophetic," the general thought, yet the major's prediction of victory was hard to dismiss, even after weeks when it had seemed inevitable that the Nez Perce would escape.

Howard had to agree with Merrill that Miles would goad his men ceaselessly to intercept Joseph. Earlier in the year, Miles had boasted to Howard "a more extensive knowledge of this remote frontier than any living man," and the general knew no one hungrier for recognition. Miles had been Howard's aide-de-camp sixteen years before, in the earliest days of the Civil War.

His first battle had been at Fair Oaks — he had held Howard's right arm as it was being amputated. Before volunteering, Miles had known nothing of military life. Outside of his hours as a crockery store clerk, he had educated himself by reading at the Boston public library and seeing William Lloyd Garrison, Wendell Phillips, and Charles Sumner lecture at Faneuil Hall. With no connections in the army officer corps or with politicians in Washington, Miles still managed to rise steadily through the ranks and finished the war as major general of volunteers. In 1866, he was commissioned a colonel in the regular army. Two years later he married Sherman's niece, and after battling Indians from Texas to the Dakotas, he was eager to resume his ascent up the ranks. Taking Joseph would be a rare plum, surely the difference between a colonel's eagle and a general's star. "Miles is ambitious," the general remembered Merrill telling him. "He will never allow such an opportunity for a brigadiership to escape him."

Merrill gave Howard something to pray for. As the army crossed the plains, messages from Miles started to arrive — "glad, hearty tidings," Howard thought, optimistic about his progress, promising to make every effort to overtake the enemy. "My spirits grew lighter," Howard would recall. Riding alongside his chief of staff, he turned and said to Mason, "I believe that we shall capture these Indians yet. . . . Mark my words, and see if I am not right!"

Dripping fat flamed off red-glowing fires. Wrapped in blankets, people reached for their first tastes of buffalo, char, flesh, and blood. A few carcasses, freshly killed, had been waiting for them in a creek valley where the prairie folded and dipped into ridges and coulees. Just a decade before, the animals had run so thick for miles that the earth seemed to swirl and flow as they moved. But it took until September 29 — three weeks and hundreds of miles in buffalo country — before scouts finally found remnants of the herd by Snake Creek and were able to shoot a few for everyone else following. Hands warmed by muscle and viscera, women opened, skinned, and butchered the beasts. In the sharp winter air, each cut of the knife would have steamed.

The yellowed valley had no tree cover, no wood for fires, but it was studded with buffalo chips from years past — easy fuel. Though it was only midday, Looking Glass said they would make camp here, at Tsanim Alikos Pah, the Place of Manure Fires. Sheltered by squat meandering bluffs, the families put down buffalo robes, stretched scraps of canvas to approximate lodges, and gathered chips on the east side of Snake Creek. On the west bank, the herd spread out on flat land that rose to a plateau. To the south, the Bear Paw Mountains stretched hazy in the distance, snow at the peaks. They had been easily skirted, nothing compared to the mountains in Oregon and Idaho that the Nez Perce bands passed through every season, let alone the ranges they had spent the summer crossing. The Medicine Line lay north out of sight, maybe fifty miles away.

Had the Nez Perce column maintained Lean Elk's schedule — moving from dawn to noon, then after lunch to dark — they would have been in Canada by now, approaching Sitting Bull's

518

camp. But after crossing the Missouri, Looking Glass insisted on taking back the leadership he had lost after the Big Hole massacre and slowing the pace. Ragged and exhausted after months of flight, the families were unprepared for winter. The supplies they had taken at Cow Island were running low. The horse herd, their main source of wealth — what would enable them to trade for food and build new lives in the north — was footsore. At each encampment they were leaving dozens of animals behind.

Lean Elk protested. "You can take command," Many Wounds remembered him saying, "but I think we will be caught and killed." Others, haunted by the losses of the previous three months, saw dreams come "as passing clouds of approaching danger," in the elder Wottolen's words, visions of streams running red, leaves and grass withering yellow to brown, their world shrouded in smoke — portents of imminent attack. Most, however, welcomed Looking Glass's attention to their material needs. Even after a week of ten-mile rides and daylight camps, they slept easy, knowing General Howard and the army were still hopelessly behind.

As the enemy receded into abstraction and buffalo came into sight, the bands turned their gaze from the horrors of the summer to the lives waiting for them in Canada. They could see themselves crossing the Medicine Line well stocked with meat and robes, ready for winter, bodies restored, days defined once more by familiar routines, the cycles of seasons, the herd and the hunt. After a rainy night, September 30 dawned clear, perfect for a long meal around their fires. Soon the women would start loading horses for the next move, but for now, children ran barefoot, packing and throwing balls of mud. Warriors rested and played cards. A dozen men were away to the south, hunting buffalo.

Yellow Wolf was staying with his uncle Chief Joseph and Joseph's wives and two daughters. As breakfast was ending, he watched two scouts gallop into camp from the south, gasping that they had seen buffalo stampeding. Perhaps the animals could sense something coming — did it mean that soldiers were near? Looking Glass rode through the camp, saying it was nothing, refusing to believe the army was anywhere close. Not every sign had to be viewed through the lens of ambush and massacre. "Plenty, plenty time," Yellow Wolf heard Looking Glass say. A week earlier, the entire camp would have erupted in panic. Now calm prevailed.

An hour passed, and one of the buffalo hunters galloped close. Instead of descending the bluffs, he pulled up and circled, waving a blanket. Yellow Wolf saw the signal and understood: "Enemies right on us! Soon the attack!" Later he would reflect, "Because of Chief Looking Glass, we were caught," but there was no time to think as the sounds of a leisurely morning shattered into screams. "Soldiers, soldiers, soldiers!" people started shouting. "Soldiers have come!" Everyone, it seemed, was running in a different direction, reaching for weapons, scrambling for cover. Parents told their children to run through the brush across the freezing creek, catch an animal from the herd, and ride north; they said what they thought would be their last good-byes. Peopeo Tholekt found a horse in camp belonging to another man. "He happened to see," the warrior remembered, "and said to me, 'Take this horse!

This is perhaps to be the last day! *You* will die, and *I* will die!' " Stripped for battle, Ollokot climbed the bluffs just to the east with many of the warriors. Crouching behind a rock, he waited for the cavalry to approach. Yellow Wolf held his rifle and a cartridge belt. If he wondered where to go, Joseph's voice, roaring above the chaos, guided him away from the bluffs. "Horses!" the chief called. "Save the horses!"

CHAPTER 20
WHERE THE SUN NOW STANDS

Yellow Wolf ran until he was too tired to run anymore. Behind him, he could hear a deep noise rising from the south. It was a familiar sound — like a buffalo stampede, many thought, a sound of the plains, a terrifying thunder, but one that could be avoided and overcome. The rumbling rose until it overwhelmed the screams inside the camp, the death songs warriors were singing, the shrill breaths of the war whistles they blew. Yellow Wolf reached high ground and looked back — a cloud of dust appeared on the horizon, then hundreds of galloping soldiers. The massive army column split and circled wide, east and west. Soldiers were surrounding the camp, some attacking it head-on while the others rode straight for the herd.

About seventy tribesmen were following Joseph across the creek. Dozens of women and children were already among the horses, trying to pack them. No bridles, no saddles — some tore blankets and looped them into lariats. Joseph gave his twelve-year-old daughter Sound of Running Feet a length of rope. Gunfire began to toll, and hundreds of panicked horses stampeded, eluding Nez Perce hands in a stomping, rearing whirl. Strange Indians in war bonnets swept in, chasing

Nez Perce riders who had managed to catch horses, grabbing their reins and shooting them — men, women — pointblank. Yellow Wolf thought they must be General Howard's Bannock scouts. The herd — the reason the Nez Perce families had been able to outrun the army for three and a half months, the reason they could imagine being able to sustain and rebuild their way of life — slipped away before their eyes. Joseph lost sight of his daughter.

Cracking, hissing, humming, "buzzing like summer flies," the bullets trapped the Nez Perce bands in what they compared to hail on the prairie, thick, relentless. When two brothers riding together on the back of a horse made it to open ground, the younger boy discovered that one of his braids had been shot off right at his ear. Fighting against Indians alongside soldiers unsettled the Nez Perce warriors, blurring their old history of tribal warfare with the new history of battling the army. "Our war was with the whites," Yellow Wolf would explain. "Their joining, it became not like war with whites alone. It can not seem right to me." The warriors did not even know what tribe they were fighting. Not Bannock, Peopeo Tholekt thought as he rode to meet them north of camp. Perhaps Sioux? Battling for their lives in close combat, warriors began signing to the Indians fighting on the soldiers' side, using a set of gestures that all tribes on the plains understood. Despite the deafening noise, they started having conversations. "You see the sun as it stands there?" Peopeo Tholekt signed to one of his enemies. "You shall die! Then, afterwards I shall die, as there are troops — all whites — too many for me. But you will not kill me! You shall die before I die!"

Yellow Wolf watched a Nez Perce warrior gesturing to a foe. "You have a red skin, red blood. You must be crazy!" the warrior signed. "You are fighting your friends. We are Indians. We are humans. Do not help the whites!" The man, Heyoom Iklakit (Grizzly Bear Lying Down) walked through the battle, then after a minute collapsed to the dirt, dropped by a bullet. Other warriors began falling around Yellow Wolf, one, then five, then ten, "swept," he would say, "as leaves before the storm."

Joseph caught a horse but knew the herd was lost. Soldiers had sliced between the herd and camp, separating him from his wives and baby daughter. Unarmed, he "resolved to go to them or die," he later said. Riding straight through battle lines, he felt enveloped by bullets, felt their heat and pull as they riddled and tore his clothes, felt his horse stagger with wounds. Near him on the north edge of camp, where low bluffs came to a point of red rock, Toohoolhoolzote and five other warriors lay dead, trapped without cover, then overwhelmed by the cavalry. Joseph reached the camp untouched. He headed straight to where he had slept the night before — canvas still stretched, fires smoldering, the remains of a different life. One of his wives handed him his rifle. "Here's your gun," she said. "Fight!"

Up the bluffs to the east, to the south, and to the southeast, the battle took another turn. Warriors had waited until the cavalry was almost upon them, then cut the air with lead, stopping the charge short, slaughtering officers and buglers, sending horses tumbling over the side. The battle settled into stalemate, lethal fire exchanged at fifty, seventy-five, a hundred yards, the bodies of horses, soldiers, and warriors strewn between the two sides. But Joseph reached the bluffs too late to fight alongside his brother. In the first fury of the cavalry's charge, Ollokot was shot dead. In the smoke and din of battle, Nez Perce warriors found it hard to distinguish friend from foe. Husi-shusis Kute, leader of the Palouse band, looked from his bluff and saw men gathering on a rise across a coulee. Thinking they were Indians scouting for the army, he shot three before realizing they were Nez Perce. Lean Elk, chief from the Big Hole to the Missouri, was killed by a Nez Perce bullet.

On the ridges and across the creek, the battlefield was small, half a mile north to south and east to west, with the families seeking shelter in ravines between the bluffs, the storm's eye. Early on, the army surrounded the entire area, turning the Nez Perce camp into what warriors called "the soldiers' corral." While much of the fighting, hand to hand or "bullet for bullet," as Yellow Wolf described it, held the army at bay, in the middle of the afternoon two dozen soldiers charged cheering and screaming along the creek from the south, killing three warriors as they ran straight into the center of camp. Joseph, in the bluffs to the east, called for warriors to turn and fire down, then drive the soldiers back. They shot at each other "not more than twenty steps apart," Joseph later said, as much a duel as a battle. Up close he could see soldiers breaking and dying, scrambling for cover, crawling back up the gullies. When they finally retreated, the warriors took guns and cartridges from the army dead.

At sunset, the gunfire stopped. Yellow Wolf, who

had spent the day fighting to the north, west, and south, walked back toward the camp, only to discover that soldiers, sitting in groups of two, had cordoned it off. Outside the siege line, he lay on the ground, waiting for darkness to quicken. For the first time since stripping for battle, he felt the freezing wind on his bare skin. He had had nothing to eat since morning. Soon a heavy snow was falling, the first of the season.

After several hours, Yellow Wolf crept past the sentries. Where dozens of fires had burned the previous night, the flat between the bluffs and creek was dark. The sounds of the Nez Perce camp guided him — men and women screaming death wails for everyone they had lost in the fighting, children crying from the cold, the quiet final breaths of a young man, near Yellow Wolf's age, lying on a buffalo robe. Beneath the staggered rhythms of suffering, Yellow Wolf heard more deliberate sounds — scratching and digging, dirt being dumped, huffs and groans of people at work. Some were burying the dead, but most were focused on survival. In the ravines, women with butcher knives and iron hooks for digging camas roots were gouging deep shelters into the soft earth. At the beginning of the war they had dug caches to preserve food and protect their treasured possessions. Now they were caching themselves. With no fires for cooking, pots and pans became buckets. Loads from the ravines were hauled up to the bluffs where the warriors were mounding dirt, rock, and saddles for cover and digging rifle pits with trowel bayonets they had taken from soldiers' bodies at the Big Hole. An older man, still strong, circulated through camp, collecting stories of what had happened that day. He announced the battle's notable events and spread word of who had died, who was wounded, and who was missing. Learning that his mother had fled in the morning and that nearly two dozen warriors had been killed, Yellow Wolf climbed the bluffs and spent the rest of the night digging trenches. A hundred yards away, the soldiers were digging, too.

With first daylight on October 1, muzzles began flashing through thick wind-blown snow. A cannon thundered and flamed, sending round after round of shells that exploded over the Indian camp. The air laced with smoke. The besieged warriors held one hope for relief — that the people who had escaped the camp would reach Sitting Bull, who in turn would send his fighters south of the Medicine Line to crush the soldiers as they had done to Custer. Every strange sound and sight — a buffalo herd rumbling nearby, an Indian riding in the distance — carried the possibility that they would all be saved. Looking Glass stood up on the bluffs, scanning the horizon for signs that he had not, in the end, doomed his people. He sank back into his rifle pit with a gaping hole scorched above his sightless eyes.

Yellow Wolf heard bullets whipping around him as he rose from his rifle pit. Unlike Looking Glass, he had few illusions of rescue by the Sioux. "No hope!" he would describe his thinking. "Only bondage or death!" Two and a half months earlier, at the battle above the Clearwater, the shock of so much thick fire overhead had rendered him almost insensible. But now, after traveling fourteen hundred miles and surviving the Big Hole only to be trapped by an enemy he could not see through the snow, his mind raced. For an instant he broke free from the battle. "Thoughts came of the Wallowa where I grew up. Of my own country when only Indians were there," he would say. "Of tepees along the bending river. Of the blue, clear lake, wide meadows with horse and cattle herds. . . . I felt as dreaming. Not my living self." He stood up to die, firing his rifle again and again at no particular target. At first, all he heard was gunfire — his own gun blasting, soldiers' rifles popping in response, the cannon concussing. Then voices started coming to him through the din — speaking in Nez Perce, calling him Heinmot, Thunder, his name before he had become Yellow Wolf. Despite freezing and starving and staying up all night, despite the ravages of fear, rage, and despair, he was not dreaming the voices. He realized his comrades, the other warriors, were calling out, urging him to come back to the trenches, pleading with him to stay alive.

A bitter wind burned Lovell Jerome's cheeks as his horse paced through the snow. Five inches covering the ground — on a day much like this one in 1872, he had ridden the white streets of New York in a sleigh pulled by three horses, calling on the city's most prominent families to wish them a happy new year, sipping a celebratory drink at each stop. It had been his duty as a Jerome, namesake of a park, race track, and avenue in the Bronx and the son of a Wall Street financier known, according to the *Times,* as "the most popular man on the Stock Exchange," described in a book of society sketches as "a wit, a story-teller and a bon-vivant . . . to be met everywhere, especially at theatres and dinner parties."

At West Point, Lovell Jerome's social standing had been so high that General Grant sent his son Frederick to the academy bearing a letter of introduction to the young man. But seven years of frontier duty had battered Jerome; his fondness for drink had become what he called "a terrible depravity," getting him arrested in February 1877 and nearly court-martialed. Still, according to a newspaper reporter out in Montana, the cavalry lieutenant remained "the most dashing and handsome of them all." Like his father, he had the "knack of giving any story" "twang" and "peculiar flavor."

Now, bone cold, sober by sworn oath and through "determined and violent effort," Jerome had gone out on the bluffs once already on October 1 to retrieve the bodies of two friends. As the initial charge on the camp met heavy fire, Captain Owen Hale and his lieutenant Jonathan Biddle had ordered their men to dismount and form a skirmish line. Biddle, kneeling to fire, had been one of the first soldiers to fall. Hale followed soon after as he reloaded his pistol and tried to rally his decimated company. Snow was turning the men's rigid forms to soft mounds indistinguishable from the natural landscape. Preserved by the cold, Hale's face remained recognizable, if ghastly, completely drained of blood. Jerome looked for a charm the captain wore — moments before the order was issued to attack, he had given Jerome the name of a woman to send it to if anything happened to him that morning. A bullet had shattered Hale's neck, but the necklace was still there.

High on the horse, Jerome made an easy target — broad-shouldered, barrel-chested, six feet tall without boots or slouch hat. While his commander, Colonel Nelson Miles, wore a bearskin into battle, in wet weather the lieutenant covered his velveteen jacket and buckskin pants with a yellow oil-soaked cotton slicker — not unlike what his father would have worn during a winter yacht race from Lower New York Bay across the Atlantic to the Isle of Wight. While the soldiers traded stories of Nez Perce marksmanship, Jerome rode without fear. After a morning of stalemate — no more soldiers killed, but no way to advance — Miles called a truce and sent out word in Chinook Jargon for Chief Joseph to meet with him, easy requests to make on such a small battlefield. Restless in an army camp with no fires, little food, and fifty suffering wounded men, Jerome went out on the bluffs to collect the dead, then got permission to venture even farther.

From ridge to ravine and straight into the Indian camp, Jerome rode under a white flag. Curious about what was happening inside the army's cordon, he hoped to return with stories of the Indians he met and with some sense of their rifle pits and shelters. He introduced himself and shook hands with one man, but within moments several others grabbed hold of his horse. Someone explained in English to Jerome that Miles had taken Joseph prisoner — now the lieutenant would be their captive. Jerome carried a rifle but, surrounded by warriors, he figured there was no point in using it.

Jerome left his horse in a protected hollow where several others were staked. He found his captors surprisingly cheerful — smiling and laughing with him even while saying that some of the men wanted him killed. He did not feel that they were seeing him as their enemy. At the same time, he looked around camp — bluffs and coulees, shelter pits below, rifle pits above — and tried to draw a map in his mind. He thought about what a final assault would look like and how he could help the artillery crew fire more accurately. The stories he would tell started coming together — stories designed to highlight his heroism, to keep him from getting into too much trouble for spoiling Miles's gambit. They would be entertaining, of course, but also useful to their audience and lethal to their subjects. If his life was in danger, he figured that at least he would not die of boredom.

As the ravines receded into shadow, he was led to a shelter pit. Inside, mothers, children, wounded warriors, and old men and women sat propped against the walls; Jerome counted fifteen in all. They watched him crawl in, a big man entering a small space, and the pit was covered over with canvas. The cold and damp intensified in the darkness — like a jail cell, like a grave. Sitting on a buffalo robe, wrapped in blankets, Jerome could not sleep for more than a few minutes at a time, nor could anyone else around him. He could feel his cold revolver, the sidearm the Indians had let him keep. He knew he was surrounded by hungry people. An army orderly had delivered him a meal — his captors told him they did not have enough food to feed him and let him write a note to Colonel Miles. He could taste water from a curved drinking vessel, a buffalo horn. Periodically he heard distant gunfire — army rifles — which left him, in his words, "alarmed and disgusted." Would he be killed by his own men? Had they already killed Joseph? Would Joseph's people kill him first?

He tried talking with the others in the pit, but they remained mostly silent. To find an audience, he would have to survive the night.

"Here is Joseph," the chief's interpreter said. Joseph entered Colonel Miles's tent and shook his hand. From September 30 into October 1, it had slowly dawned on the warriors that they were fighting fresh soldiers. "I am the man that commands the troop," the interpreter remembered Miles telling Joseph. "They are all under my command." Miles was the sixth army commander they had faced in battle over the course of the war. He was a big man about Joseph's age — appearing even bigger when wearing his fur cloak and hat — taller than the chief, with a broad forehead and thick mustache.

The colonel was quick to smile. Even though dead soldiers were lying under tarps nearby, he had assured the interpreter — Tom Hill, half Nez Perce and half Delaware, who had joined the nontreaty bands as part of Lean Elk's group in the Bitterroot Valley — "You need not be frightened; nobody will hurt you." He had his cook prepare a meal for Hill. He asked Joseph if he wanted to sit by a fire. The war was over, Miles said. There was no point in any more bloodshed.

Joseph understood that the colonel was asking him to surrender. Miles thought he was the war chief, but Joseph did not correct the mistake. Looking Glass, Lean Elk, Ollokot, and Toohoolhoolzote were all gone. White Bird lived but wanted nothing to do with white generals. After months of riding alongside the women, children, and elderly, Joseph was ready again to speak for his people. Throughout the war, he had deferred to Looking Glass and Lean Elk and others who had more experience in battle and who knew the territory they were crossing. But now he found himself on familiar ground. A surrender was not solely about ending a war. It was about beginning the peace. Everything depended on the terms. "I was very anxious about my people," Joseph recalled of this moment. He could negotiate for the best conditions possible.

Miles asked for Joseph to hand over all the warriors' rifles — bring them to the army camp and pile them on the ground. It was a harsh demand. The Nez Perce bands had already lost their horses. Take their guns away as well, and they faced a winter without being able to trade or hunt for food. "I shall give you half of my arms," Tom Hill remembered Joseph countering, "and I shall retain half of them to use to kill game for my family." The colonel promised Joseph that their weapons would be returned once they were resettled back on the Nez Perce reservation. Hill translated Miles's instructions and assurances: "Now, you go back across to your people and tell all your people to come over to me. . . . We will fight no more, but come over to me."

Joseph had only gone a few steps toward the Nez Perce camp when Miles called him back. The colonel had changed his mind: Tom Hill could walk down into the ravines to relay the terms of surrender, but Joseph would have to stay behind as his prisoner. Under a white flag, the chief had tried to bargain with the colonel. Compared to his position with Howard and the Nez Perce Commission a year before, he had asked Miles for the most modest of concessions. In return, he was cuffed. Miles did not see him as a negotiating partner. Rather, he was a bargaining chip. The colonel imagined the Nez Perce warriors would surely yield without their tactical mastermind. Joseph held no such illusions; there would be no surrender, and after months of hardship, a war he had never wanted to fight, he would be killed. He started talking, not to Miles but to Hill. The interpreter looked at the chief and saw that he was crying. "Now you are going to throw me away," Joseph said.

"You will not die alone," Hill answered. "If you die today, I shall die for you also." He left Joseph in Miles's tent and walked back into the ravines. When he saw warriors pulling a cavalry lieutenant from his horse, he started to run. Even though Miles had flouted the truce, Hill believed there were still rules that the colonel was bound to follow. "I knew the custom of such battles," the interpreter later said. "Whenever you capture a prisoner or opponent, never kill him." He sent word back to Miles — the lieutenant was theirs now and would be safe as long as Joseph was.

The next morning, after shouting across the battle lines and passing notes, two small delegations met halfway. A buffalo robe was laid on the ground. Lieutenant Jerome shook Joseph's hand and walked off with an escort of officers. Joseph returned to the Nez Perce camp. Warriors who for months had followed other leaders — or followed no one at all — listened to him. "Go back to your trenches," Hill heard the chief say. "We must fight more," Yellow Wolf heard. "The war is not quit!" Some heard Joseph say he had been handcuffed, or that he had been bound, then quartered with the pack mules. Yellow Wolf would later say that after tying his hands and hobbling his feet, the soldiers rolled him in a blanket, "like you roll a papoose on a cradle board." They all agreed that the soldiers' white flag was a lie. The day before, Joseph had been willing to risk his life to make peace. But after a night in the colonel's custody, he concluded, "We will all have to die; we will not surrender."

Erskine Wood watched the animal move — small but indomitable in the cold, rooting through the snow for grass, a miniature emblem of the plains. After the great slaughters of the past five years, an up-close encounter with a buffalo, even a young one, was a rare treat. The lieutenant savored the opportunity for the most authentic of western experiences. He raised his rifle, put the beast in his sights, and squeezed the trigger.

As the lieutenant skinned the buffalo and began carving warm muscle from bone, his glee was evident to General Howard — a souvenir for home, and a meal for their riding party. To reach Miles, they needed to regain their strength. It was a relief that they were well enough to eat meat. Four days earlier, on September 30, Howard had boarded a small steamer at Fort Carroll with a token force. The journey upriver to Cow Island normally lasted the morning, but it had taken them all day and all night, fifty excruciating miles of "grasshoppering" over sandbars — again and again the steamer would run aground, plunge two enormous wooden arms into the river bottom, and, with a steam-powered winch, lift itself up, allowing the sternwheel to nudge it forward. "We are *crawling* up this crooked muddy snuggy river," Mason reported to his wife and mother. Not that he minded. "It is so very comfortable on this boat

535

and we live so nicely as regards the table," he wrote. "I confess to a disinclination to gout and sleep on the ground again and . . . bacon and 'hard tack.' "

At the boat landing, a messenger from Miles was waiting for Howard: the colonel was nearing Joseph and hopeful of surprising the Indians. Leaving Mason behind to move the rest of the troops across the Missouri, the general rode north with his son Guy, Lieutenant Wood, Miles's messenger, and three volunteers who had come with them from Idaho: two Nez Perce scouts he called Captain John and George, as well as an interpreter who could speak Nez Perce and English — Ad Chapman, the Idaho rancher who had fired the first shot at White Bird Canyon.

One day beyond the Missouri River Breaks, Howard's party found only alkaline water to drink. Even if they had not been riding dozens of miles on horseback, the resulting nausea and diarrhea would have been agonizing in the winter wilderness — squatting in the cold over gopher holes, trying in vain to keep clean with moss, leaves, or rocks. But after a long morning of rest, the group started to rally. From the Indians' trail, they headed east, picked up Miles's route, and by October 4 had entered the plains just beyond the Bear Paw Mountains, where buffalo could still be seen and shot.

Wrapped in a borrowed overcoat, hood sewn to the collar, Howard was waiting for his aide-de-camp to finish butchering his kill when two men overtook the group, scouts on their way back to Miles after riding down to the Missouri River with updates for the troops. They carried news Howard had waited nearly four months to hear — "a battle, going on when we left," not more than fifteen miles away. Forming his men into a small column, the general made for Miles's position. Dashes like this — the churn of excitement and worry — had become familiar to Howard. Directing forces in Montana to head off Joseph while he brought up the rear, he had raced ahead hoping to join a battle three times — at the Big Hole, in the northeast corner of Yellowstone, and up Clark's Fork toward Canyon Creek. Twice he had found the troops suffering and defeated, and once he found nothing at all — the hostiles had simply discovered a way to disappear. The general knew he had reached the last of these rides. By the time he found Miles, the Indians would be captured or across the British line. He would emerge from this ordeal with his reputation salvaged, or would need to begin the next chapter of redemption.

Howard watched the winter sky, already bruised, go black. Nearing the place where the scouts said Miles had set up camp, the column urged their horses into a gallop. Fast through darkness, up and down swells, in a crucible of cold wind — it was close to flight, tethered to the world only by the proximity of other riders. With a sliver of moon in the sky, the path ahead was hard to discern. But at the top of one rise, Howard saw spots of light scattered across a mile or so, like stars gone to ground — army campfires. Closer, he could hear dull percussive snapping over the rushing air and beat of hoofs — "musketry," he thought. Closer still, and he wondered if the pickets guarding Miles's camp had taken them for Indians. Were they shooting at him?

After Joseph returned from his captivity in the

army camp, Nez Perce warriors debated whether to mount one final charge. "If we whipped them, we would be free," Yellow Wolf described the logic. "If we could not whip, we would all be killed, and no more trouble." But that would leave the women and children, the wounded and the elderly, at the mercy of the soldiers. Each night, the warriors and many of the women could have slipped through the siege, escaped into darkness, and struck out for the Medicine Line. The only reason they stayed was because of the people who would have to be abandoned, too young or old or hurt to make the journey. "We had never heard of a wounded Indian recovering while in the hands of white men," Joseph would later say.

The soldiers blasted at the Nez Perce camp, but the warriors' trenches were so secure that army bullets failed to find a single fighter. Yellow Wolf and his comrades stopped firing back. "We thought the soldiers would get tired, maybe freeze out and charge us," he recalled. "We wanted plenty of ammunition for them if they did." Joseph still wondered if the Sioux might ride to their aid. After days of siege, a shell landed in a ravine lined with shelter pits, burying six people. Four were pulled alive from the loam, but a twelve-year-old girl and her grandmother were left in the ground, their refuge now a grave. Days blurred to night. Through snow and heavy clouds, the Indians saw neither sunrise nor sunset.

On the sixth day, two men rode into camp waving a large white flag and calling out in Nez Perce, "All my brothers, I am glad to see you alive this sun!" Each wore a wide-brimmed hat, something a soldier might wear, but decked with long feathers. Captain John (whose Nez Perce name, Jokais, meant Worthless or Lazy) and George (Meopkowit, meaning Baby or Know Nothing) had come all the way from Lapwai as General Howard's scouts, but they were also searching for their married daughters among the fleeing families. Women and children emerged from the ravines to greet the visitors. Yellow Wolf and other warriors streamed down from the rifle pits. Weeping at the sight, the two army scouts greeted old friends, relatives, and their daughters. "I am glad today we are shaking hands," George said. "We are all not mad. We all think of Chief Joseph and these others as brothers." The scouts told their audience that they had nothing to fear from a surrender. There would be no trials, no one swinging from gallows. Miles and Howard, they reported, had agreed that everyone could go back to the Nez Perce reservation.

As the Nez Perce families weighed the possibility of surrender, White Bird declared everything the scouts had told them a lie. "General Miles and General Howard are mad," the chief said. "They will get us in their power, and give us heavy punishment. You can go! Be a slave if you wish! I am going to Sitting Bull! All who want to go with me can do so." People considered just how much they had lost over the course of the war. Four months earlier, they had been rich. Now they had nothing. "We should get something out of our destroyed property," argued Yellow Wolf's mother's brother, who had been shot in the stomach at White Bird Canyon and lost a son at the Big Hole. "Get pay for our homes and lands taken from us."

Joseph was inclined to accept their terms. "I could not bear to see my wounded men and women suffer any longer," he would say. "We had lost enough already. . . . My people needed rest — we wanted peace." The chief told the scouts he was ready to talk directly with Miles and Howard. Joined by several others, Joseph met the commanders on middle ground. Yellow Wolf, standing by, remembered Miles promising peace, "good water," and "plenty time for sleep." But the warrior was particularly struck by Howard's good cheer at the end of a hard campaign. "You have your life. I am living," Yellow Wolf heard the general tell Joseph. "Do not worry any more. . . . Do not worry about starving. It is plenty of food we have left from this war. Any one who needs a sack of flour, anything the people want, come get it. All is yours." Everyone shook hands, with the Indian chiefs pointing to "where the sun was then standing," Yellow Wolf recalled. "This said: 'No more battles! No more war!' "

Two hours later, from the top of a knoll, Erskine Wood followed a slow procession from the creek bottom toward the army camp, one man on horseback surrounded by several more on foot. The attendants had their hands on the rider's legs and the horse's flanks — to keep their solemn formation, Wood figured, or perhaps just to ease the uphill climb. It was midafternoon, bitter cold. While Wood and the small group of men around him stood patiently together to watch the Indians' approach, each saw something different. If Miles anticipated his triumph, and Howard his vindication, Wood watched with an artist's eye. Anything he could draw — of the battle he had arrived too late to see, and now this, its closing moments — the illustrated newspapers in the East would surely pay him to print.

As Joseph came into focus, Wood saw the chief was wearing a blanket. The lieutenant would not remember its color — decades later, he wrote, "I would say grey with a black stripe" — but he would meticulously render its classical drape from right shoulder to left arm. Joseph was dressed for the moment, wrapped against the winter wind, shirt and buckskin leggings underneath, weapon across his lap. Wood regarded a scene that struck him as timeless, immortal.

Reaching the hilltop, Joseph slid off his horse and approached Howard, who was flanked by Wood, his son Guy, and interpreter Ad Chapman. The chief extended his gun to the general — in Wood's opinion, an "impulsive gesture." It was a pedestrian weapon, a snub Winchester 1866 repeating carbine called a Yellow Boy because of the warm brass color of its metal frame, made by the thousands in the firearms factories of New Haven, favored by settlers across the West, used by Sitting Bull's warriors against Custer. Instead of reaching out for the carbine, Howard motioned toward Miles — Joseph should present it to him. Joseph moved toward the colonel, who took the chief's offering in his hands. Adjusting his blanket, Joseph reached to the sky and spoke briefly in Nez Perce. A few weeks later, Howard would remember Chapman's translation as "From where the sun stands, forever and ever, I will never fight again." In Joseph's own telling, he said, "From where the sun now stands I will fight no more," or, pointing to the sun, "I fight white man no more."

As the chief shook the officers' hands, Wood studied the man up close. For months, the lieutenant, following his commander's lead, had attributed everything the hostiles did — every battlefield maneuver, every strategic ploy — to Joseph's genius. Finally in his presence, Wood tried to take his own measure of the man. The chief's hair was tied back from his forehead with a strip of animal skin. Long braids framed his face right and left. His forehead had been nicked by a bullet. So had one of his wrists. In Wood's estimation, Joseph was maybe ten years his senior, tall and handsome, straight in the saddle even when his head was bowed. Later, Wood pictured Joseph with "a mouth and chin not unlike that of Napoleon I." But at the time, he noted a face defined by fatigue and anxious feeling. "Joseph has a gentle face, somewhat feminine in its beauty, but intensely strong and full of character," the lieutenant would soon write. "A photograph could not do him justice."

Joseph mounted his horse and rode into the army camp flanked by Miles and Howard. Watching the procession, Wood noted the time of surrender for a message to the rest of the general's troops, still a couple of days away. Soon the remaining Indians would start coming to surrender their guns. "Where a moment before, not a head was to be seen nor any sign of life, the ravines now swarmed with people," Wood wrote. The procession of hundreds would extend for hours, well into the night. The lieutenant watched the "irregular column," the brilliant colors of their clothes, however ragged, "wrinkled hags, decrepit old men, fat, saucy children, wild Arab-like boys, a medley of blankets, buffalo-robes . . . and wild humanity." The blind led the blind. Wounded men and women crawled up the hill. After dark, Wood listened for their groans. However long it would take, the war with the hostile Nez Perce Indians had ended, he wrote, on October 5, a Friday, at 2:20 p.m.

After Joseph surrendered his weapon, hundreds more followed. But White Bird, along with several dozen other men and women, waited until the darkest part of night, then slipped away on foot. While most of the people escaping belonged to White Bird's band, Ollokot's widow Wetatonmi joined them. "Nothing to stay for," she later said. They carried light blankets, scant protection from the wind and snow. Many of them were wounded. Others, too, had escaped the siege during the course of the battle, including Peopeo Tholekt and Joseph's elder wife Heyoom Yoyikt. Although they believed that liberty awaited them with Sitting Bull, their confidence was overwhelmed by the feeling of loss. From start to finish the war had required constant revision of what it meant to be free. If at first it meant the ability to live as they had always lived, on their land, with the seasons, now it meant living with nothing — far from their homes, families gone, possessions looted. "It was lonesome, the leaving," Wetatonmi said. "Husband dead, friends buried or held prisoners. I felt that I was leaving all that I had; but I did not cry." For the people following White Bird, it felt as if they had died, too. "Our going was with heavy hearts, broken spirits," she remembered. "All lost, we walked silently on into the wintery night."

Joseph woke before dawn on October 6. On the first full day after the surrender, he had reason for optimism. Along with food, water, and medical treatment, the two commanders had offered good terms. The families would stay the winter with Miles at the Tongue River Cantonment, and when it was possible to cross the mountains again, they would move back into Howard's department and onto the reservation in Idaho, strong again and ready to resume their lives. Joseph was unequivocally the leader of the people who remained. Their new situation would depend on working and negotiating with the US government, processes that required his experience and understanding.

Still, no one knew what this peace would look like in the sunlight. Before the day began, the chief turned to his nephew Yellow Wolf and, in one of his first acts after the surrender, asked him to break its terms and escape to the north. Joseph's daughter Sound of Running Feet, his elder wife Heyoom Yoyikt, and Yellow Wolf's mother were out there, wandering the plains. They could be lost, freezing, starving, threatened by enemies — they were passing through Gros Ventre and Assiniboine territory. Joseph wanted Yellow Wolf to find them.

The young warrior had not surrendered his rifle the night before. The barrel was short enough that he could slip it down a legging. He hid his cartridges under his shirt, then pulled a blanket close and walked out toward the line of sentries. The sky was showing the dawn. Seeing two guards in the distance, he resolved not to hide from them. "If they tried stopping me, that would be good," he figured. "I would kill them both." But as he walked, tall and deliberate, they made no effort to corral him. Soon the camp, the guards, and the bluffs shrank and disappeared. He kept going, feeling the snow burn through his worn moccasins. In a canyon he found a horse. All trails from the battlefield had been covered with snow. Yellow Wolf rode alone, pressing a new path toward the Medicine Line.

Erskine Wood sketched Joseph in profile, as if the chief were a face on a Roman coin: prominent nose, strong forehead, a warm and searching eye, hair tied back and decorated with a small cluster of feathers. He drew Joseph's baby girl, paying less attention to her face than to her elaborate swaddling. Spending hours in Joseph's company, he heard the chief's voice — "quiet, dignified," Wood thought — and listened to interpreters speak of his worry for his older daughter, his sorrow over the loss of his brother. Joseph lifted his shirt to show him a flesh wound on the small of his back.

As the army organized supplies for the Indians — a third of the survivors escaped to Canada, leaving about 450 in the camp — Wood was busy preparing the general's reports and dispatches. But he still found time to explore the bluffs and the crooked ravines below. He stood in the rifle pits and sketched what the warriors must have seen looking out toward the soldiers. The Indians' fortress became an attraction for the officers, the shelters declared marvels of defensive engineering, some five feet deep, linked by tunnels.

Everywhere Wood looked, he saw objects of fascination. Despite their ordeal — cold, filth, hunger, and death — the Indians had held onto countless beautiful things. A blanket, bright red, twisting with bouquets of blue, pink, green, and yellow beaded flowers. Their bags, striped with geometric designs. Even as General Miles promised to provide sustenance to the Indians, he took the bullet-pocked shirt Chief Joseph wore to the surrender. Lovell Jerome left the battlefield with a stiff cylindrical rawhide case, a parfleche, painted with red and green triangles and trailing long leather braids. Inside the flap, he inked his name, rank, and regiment and the name and date of the battle. Joseph also gave the onetime Nez Perce prisoner a brilliant red jacket, cut like a soldier's coat, studded with mirrors and fringed along the back and sleeves with white weasel tails. Wood traded saddles with the chief.

On October 7, after a few days of companionable conversation, Wood and Joseph said goodbye. Howard and his staff were riding south from Snake Creek to rendezvous with Mason and the rest of their column. Within a week they would be aboard the steamers they had all spent weeks dreaming about, straight to Omaha, then west to San Francisco. While a small force would stay behind in northern Montana, watching for incursions by Sitting Bull's Sioux, Joseph would go southeast with Miles to the Tongue River. The chief would ride at the head of a long column of soldiers and Nez Perce families, many of them on ponies from their captured herd, the wounded dragged on travois.

The reports Wood was drafting were careful to justify Howard's decisions throughout the campaign, emphasizing how their men met the incredible challenges of the chase and how the general's arrival at Snake Creek on October 4 played a pivotal role in bringing the conflict to a close. But by the time the lieutenant was steaming down the Missouri, he was also regarding someone else as the hero of the story. Joseph had made the same journey, but with women and children and the elderly and thousands of horses. Unlike Howard, he had endured every battle of the war, against successive forces sent to stop them. And every time, against the odds, Nez Perce warriors had either routed the army or fought to a stalemate. In the end, when he could have escaped, Joseph chose to stand by the people who could not defend themselves. As a soldier and as a man of feeling, the chief stood alone.

In the last week of October, Howard's soldiers stopped at Fort Abraham Lincoln, in Dakota Territory. There the general read the first reports of Joseph's surrender in the Chicago papers — all credit to Miles, with a detailed accounting of Howard's failures and a description of Joseph's respect for Miles alongside his pointed disdain for the feckless "Bible Chief." In Wood's description, Howard was "heart-broken and furious," convinced that Miles had doctored official reports to claim full credit for the victory. Leaving his men to steam down to Omaha, Howard took Wood with him on a small boat to Bismarck, where they could catch a train to Chicago and defend themselves to Sherman's right hand, Philip Sheridan. Wood would then go on to Washington, DC, and continue to press Howard'scase.

Before finding his way to the Northern Pacific Railway depot, the lieutenant stopped in at the local tri-weekly newspaper. Even though he was committed to working for Howard, the lieutenant presented the editor with what Wood said was a verbatim transcript, that he alone had written down, of a message Joseph had relayed through Howard's Nez Perce scouts on October 5:

Tell General Howard I know his heart. What he told me before I have in my heart. I am tired of fighting. Our chiefs are killed. Looking-Glass is dead. Ta-hool-hool-shoot is dead. The old men are all dead. It is the young men who say yes or no. He who leads the young men is dead. It is cold and we have no blankets. The little children are freezing to death. My people, some of them, have run away to the hills and have no blankets, no food; no one knows where they are — may be freezing to death. I want time to look for my children and see how many of them I can find. May be I shall find them among the dead. Hear me my chiefs: I am tired. My heart is sick and sad. From where the sun now stands I will fight no more forever.

Whether the speech consisted of the words the man uttered when asked to surrender, as the newspaper headline declared, or a compendium of what Wood had heard and thought about during the time he had spent with Joseph, the editor found it the "remarkably pathetic and suggestive communication" of a "great chief." Howard might not receive full credit for his conduct of the war, but the lieutenant would ensure that Joseph would get his due.

PART III

PREVIOUS PAGE: The view from Fort Spokane, where Chief Joseph's band stopped on their return from exile in 1885 before crossing the Columbia River to a new home on the Colville Indian Reservation.

CHAPTER 21
THE BEST INDIAN

Washington, DC,
January 14, 1879

William Tecumseh Sherman checked his coat while his daughters were ushered across the corridor to the State Dining Room. There they found maids stationed to help women unwrap their woolens and furs and perfect their hair and gowns. Although guests would stream in for two solid hours, the general could remember far less comfortable affairs. The first White House reception of the year would always attract crowds, but the suffocating scrums of the Grant and Lincoln years had given way to, in one description, an atmosphere of "grace, ease, and cordiality." A woman could walk without fear of anyone stepping on her train.

Reunited with Lizzie and Ellie, the general followed the tide of people through the Red Room and into the Blue, where large gilt mirrors reflected and multiplied the crystal chandeliers. Though a newspaper would describe the sparkling effect as "what one reads about in the Arabian nights," the Shermans were less inclined to awe after countless functions at the mansion. Through the reception line in the middle of the round parlor, past President Hayes and his rote pleasantries, the general and his daughters may have recognized the first lady's wine-colored silk and velvet gown. She had worn it repeatedly the previous winter. "Sensible woman," a journalist opined.

The Shermans moved on to the East Room and joined a whirl of people between the large flowered carpet and low-hanging chandeliers, conversing and promenading over airs and minuets played by the Marine Band. An unusual number of women were wearing white — silks and satins, brocades, cashmeres, shirred velvet, crepe — the better to show off their diamonds and pearls and pink topaz necklaces. Others wore black and lavender, garnet, ruby, gold, and blue — the colors of sunset, according to one reporter. It was like being inside a kaleidoscope, wrote another.

Although the commander of the army was a figure of awe and renown, Sherman blended into the room, just one of many powerful government officials in attendance. Gliding past the attorney general and secretary of the navy, past Interior Secretary Carl Schurz, there with his children, past Ottoman diplomats in red fezzes, the French and Brazilian ambassadors and their wives, delegations from China and Japan, congressmen from the North, South, and West, socialites and journalists and a few select guests described as having "unmistakable African descent," the Shermans gravitated toward the thickest gathering in the East Room, mostly women, almost a reception within the reception. Lizzie Sherman was twenty-four, Ellie nineteen, and their father wanted them to meet the people the *Washington Evening Star* labeled "by far the most important guests present." He soon worked his way to the center of the throng, where two large men wrapped in blankets and a slight man in a dark suit were standing. Sherman reached out to the most important of the most important guests: Chief Joseph.

During the war, Sherman had pictured Joseph swinging from the gallows. Now he shook the chief's hand. Joseph was no longer an enemy — he was the sensation of Washington society. He had arrived in town just the day before, traveling from the Quapaw Agency in the northeast corner of Indian Territory, just across the Kansas border. His people had been held there for nearly six months. And whether he knew it or not, he was in the capital because of Sherman. After Miles and Howard had assured the chief that his people would be able to return to Nez Perce country, Sherman immediately overruled his subordinates. Upon learning of the surrender, it was he who telegrammed Philip Sheridan that the prisoners should be taken not to the Tongue River Cantonment but instead to Fort Leavenworth in Kansas, and from there to Indian Territory, where eventually they could "make a crop . . . and will soon become self supporting." The civilian authorities quickly adopted Sherman's position. "Those captured at the Bear Paws Mountain are . . . lost to their tribe," the general wrote Howard in December 1877. "There should be extreme severity," he telegrammed Sheridan; "else other tribes alike situated" — Spokane, Umatilla, Flathead — "may imitate their example."

More than two hundred people had escaped to Canada, leaving about 450 to surrender. Corralled at Fort Leavenworth on bottomland between a lagoon and the Missouri River, the tribe was wracked with malarial fevers by the spring of 1878, and cholera was killing dozens of people.

"It would seem as if this spot had been selected for the express purpose of putting an end to Chief Joseph and his band," a visitor wrote. "The 400 miserable, helpless, emaciated specimens of humanity . . . presented a picture which brought to my mind the horrors of Andersonville."

The dying only accelerated when the families were moved two hundred miles south to the Quapaw reservation in July 1878. The mosquito-infested spring and summer gave way to a vicious winter, rife with tuberculosis, pneumonia, and other diseases that left them gasping for air. Women and children suffered the most — "worse to die there than to die fighting in the mountains," Joseph would say. No babies were surviving infancy. Arriving at Quapaw too late to prepare for winter properly, forbidden guns for hunting, and denied medicine and tons of meat rations by a vengeful and corrupt Indian agent, many of the Nez Perce captives retreated into despair. Testifying before a visiting congressional delegation in the fall of 1878, Joseph described the land that his people were calling the Eeikish Pah, the Hot Place, as "like a poor man; it amounts to nothing." A senator reported back to his colleagues that at least one-fifth of the captives had died in agony, predicting that soon "two will die to every one that is born among them. Exile, he said, was "a slow and deadly poison," a "cloud that hangs over them by day and by night." "Their tents were as silent as the tomb," he said, "save when a wail arose, which must have been for the dead."

Joseph had come to Washington to plead for his people with the president, interior secretary, commissioner of Indian affairs, volunteer advisers on the Board of Indian Commissioners — anyone in and out of government who would listen. But in the din of the East Room, it was nearly impossible to have a conversation. The small man standing beside Joseph, Ad Chapman, who had been serving as his interpreter since the final battle, was known to inform well-wishers, "He don't speak English — only a word or two." Neither did the other man at Joseph's side, Yellow Bull, a warrior from White Bird's band who had surrendered to Miles and assumed a leading role in exile. No matter — all of Washington knew Joseph's surrender statement, which had been printed and reprinted in newspapers and magazines across the country and given official recognition in General Howard's report on the Nez Perce conflict to the secretary of war. "I will fight no more forever" had entered the common parlance, a light way to ease tension and extend an olive branch, no matter how petty the spat.

Craning for a view, White House guests saw a figure who confirmed every noble sentiment they had gleaned from his speech — his intelligence and intensity of feeling, his selfless concern for suffering children. He was "a light shade of copper color," came one report, "tall, lithe, well-formed, clean-limbed, with thin, spirited nostrils, small hands, and dainty feet." He was judged to be thoughtful, graceful, "amiable and enlightened," "dignified and distingue," at ease in a crowd, and possessed with "an unrelenting, appealing vigilance." Bowing to Mrs. Hayes in the reception line, another wrote, he was a "model of courtly grace." In his bright blanket coat — at a stop in St. Louis, his wrap was described as "striped in the strongest contrast in red, white, and blue" — and adorned with shell earrings, thick strands of necklaces, and intricate beadwork on his clothes, the chief more resembled the evening's gowned and bejeweled socialites, dressed to fascinate, than the men, who favored, in one reporter's words, "the stereotype undertaker's garb of sombre black." To welcome Joseph, to celebrate him and recognize and appreciate his estimable qualities — to admire his bangs and braids — seemed to confirm the magnanimity of his hosts and the reach and greatness of the nation. He was "so interesting to the people who have abused him so," an observer noted. The thrill of seeing the chief, the feelings he inspired, had a way of establishing the onlookers' good intentions toward Indians, regardless of what had been done to him or was actually happening to the tribes in the West. It was entertainment, edification, and absolution.

Holding Joseph's hand, Sherman called out "an earnest greeting" to the chief through his interpreter and then presented his daughters and several of their friends. Other eminences crowded forward to meet Joseph. Secretary Schurz, who had approved the plan to exile the Nez Perce captives, pronounced himself "more impressed with Chief Joseph than any Indian he has before seen." His daughter Agathe, mistress of the Schurz house after her mother's death the year before, invited Joseph and Yellow Bull to call on them the next day. Soon guests were streaming from the East Room across the White House to the large glass conservatory that extended from the mansion's west side. After clustering around the chief, they scattered among other exotic imports that seemed to thrive in the glow of gas flames, palms and camellias and flowering vines, some haloed in light, others washed with deep shadow.

■ ■ ■ ■

Back in the corridors of his hotel, Joseph ran into
Nelson Miles, the last man who had promised to
do his best for the Nez Perce families. Recognizing each other immediately, they exchanged warm
greetings. Since the surrender, Miles had repeatedly protested Joseph's exile to Indian Territory
and had started advocating for tribes on reservations to be allowed to herd horses and cattle rather
than tend crops. "We have carried on a cruel,
relentless war of extermination against the Indian," "the great Indian fighter" had told a
reporter a month earlier. The cruelty was rooted,
he explained, in the way the federal government
administered tribal matters. Split among military
and civilian authorities, power was too diffuse,
and the direction of government was constantly
shifting course — a recipe for conflict. "It all rises
from a mistaken policy, or rather no policy at all.
With every change of administration comes a
change in the Indian policy," he said. "The Indian
commissioner is a new man, and his agents are
new. . . . When they begin to realize what is
required of them, they are removed. One agent
will tell [the Indians] one thing; the new one has
a different story to relate. The Indian is naturally
suspicious, and his mistrust is becoming rapidly a
standing disaffection." Miles bore few illusions
that anything would change; too many vested
interests, from political hacks to missionaries,
profited from the system. So did the military and
its suppliers. Still waiting for his promotion to
brigadier general, Miles himself was in town to
chair a board that was recommending that the

army outfit its cavalry soldiers with large revolvers that blasted heavy buckshot. Upon seeing Joseph in Washington, he told a reporter that the chief was "the best Indian he ever met."

Miles's view of the administration of American Indian policy mirrored Joseph's experience. But the fluidity that Miles saw as pathological also presented the chief with room to maneuver. By reaching the right set of officials, he hoped to change how the government treated his people. And while Miles saw the solution to the "Indian problem" in transferring authority over the tribes from the civilian bureaucracy to the military, Joseph had started to advocate for something different. "When I was small I understood that there were two departments in our government dealing with the Indians — soldiers and civilians," he told a visiting congressional committee in October 1878. "They . . . have about the same authority . . . Yet I think both of them could be set aside." When asked what he would put in their stead, he said, "We should have one law to govern us all and we should all live together." "One law for the Indians and all citizens of the United States?" asked a Minnesota representative. "All should be citizens of the United States," Joseph said, "to come and go when they please, and be governed all alike. . . . Liberty is good and great, when a person can come and go when he pleases. It is not good to keep us as you keep prisoners. . . . It is hard to make us live in that way."

The day after he saw Miles, Joseph visited the man who, on the Fourth of July in 1872, heard his first attempt to convince the government that his band had never relinquished its claim on the

Wallowa Valley. Alfred B. Meacham, who had overseen Indian affairs in Oregon, almost died in 1873, when he was ambushed and left for dead at peace talks with the Modoc tribe. Although he supported himself in part by giving lectures about his ordeal, showing audiences what he called the "Modoc bullets in my maimed hands and mutilated face," he had also moved to the capital and started a magazine called *The Council Fire,* which advocated for "a better understanding between white and red men" and for "a solution of this great Indian problem" that he believed would save — and more effectively civilize — the native tribes.

Taller than Joseph, frail, his beard gone white within the previous few years, Meacham had become a familiar face in exile, visiting the Nez Perce settlement several times in 1878 while investigating conditions in Indian Territory for Interior Secretary Schurz. In peddling his story of the Modoc War, Meacham spent two years traveling with a troupe of Modoc Indians and made a star of the woman he claimed had saved him from being scalped — by his account a modern-day Pocahontas who proved that Indians were fit to assimilate into white society. Meacham saw a similarly mythic resonance in Joseph and arranged for the chief's journey to Washington.

The evening after the White House reception, Joseph joined Meacham at the Interior Department for a late meeting with the Board of Indian Commissioners and the commissioner of Indian affairs. Joseph arrived while Meacham was promoting his magazine and describing a scene from the Modoc War. "A distinguished visitor is just coming in, and I wait for a moment," Meacham said. "But I want to finish the story."

559

Several of the officials had met Joseph in Indian Territory the previous year. Like everyone else crossing paths with the chief in Washington, they were quick with praise "for his great power of leadership." "I have seldom been more impressed than by some words of his," said the chairman of the Board of Indian Commissioners. "I hope Joseph will meet an audience in New York," said another volunteer commissioner. A third attested, "I traveled with Joseph . . . 200 miles in a wagon, and he ate at the same table and was entertained with us, and there was in all his behavior the utmost propriety and dignity. He would not have done any dishonor to any of our parlors."

Through his interpreter, Joseph spoke briefly to the group, his first words in Washington that were recorded. He used the occasion to look back on the years he had spent trying to change American policy. "I have met many of the representatives of the government," he said. "I once talked with [Meacham], and tried to impress upon him the necessity of keeping my country. I was small then; I was inexperienced, but I tried to express as well as I could what I wanted." So much had happened since then, but the intervening years had only sharpened Joseph's sense of the power he was pushing against. "I could not see then as far as I can to-day," he said, "but still I had pretty nearly the same ideas. I am a wiser man today than I was then, but I think I have the same right to my country that I had then."

Even after enduring a cascade of loss, death, and displacement, Joseph still looked to the Wallowa Valley, not only as his property but also as a root of rights, a setting for describing how the government had wronged his people and how it should be treating them. At the meeting the chairman of the volunteer commissioners told the group that in Indian Territory he had seen Joseph "in tears because he could not stay where his father had lived and died, which land he had never surrendered." But Joseph kept calm in Washington, expressing confidence that they would soon see the wisdom of his position. "I am growing both in body and experience every day," he said. "It is the same with all of you gentlemen here tonight. The more you see and the further you travel, the greater experience you have." The men applauded when Joseph finished, and within days the commissioner of Indian affairs would acknowledge that his band still had a claim on the valley, offering to clear title for six townships in the Indian Territory and $250,000. Joseph accepted the offer, but Congress never funded it.

Two nights later, a Friday, Meacham brought Joseph to Lincoln Hall, just north of the Mall, almost exactly halfway between the Capitol and the White House. For one night the ornate venue, site of popular lectures, minstrel shows, and concerts by touring violin virtuosi, would see fourteen Indians take its stage in an event designed to raise funds and drum up subscriptions for Meacham's magazine. More than eight hundred people bought tickets to see Joseph, the main attraction alongside visiting Ute, Choctaw, Chickasaw, Cherokee, and Creek chiefs. "The powwow . . . was quite picturesque," one journalist wrote, "a semi-circle of beaded, bedecked, and blanketed Indians on the stage, and one by one they came forward, and in solemn tones told their tales of wrong, cruelty, oppression and dishonesty."

With Ad Chapman translating, Joseph spoke for more than an hour. To make his argument was to tell the history of his people among the whites. Much of his talk he had given countless times before the war — his tribe's long friendship with the United States, the injustice of the 1863 treaty, the pledge he made his father never to abandon the Wallowa Valley. But it was the most recent chapters of his story that transformed him and his audience. According to one reporter, as his account of the war unfolded, his voice — at first "sonorous," if "pitched in a high key" and "monotonous" — "developed its flexibility," and Joseph began gesturing and miming, "which for grace and appropriateness would have done credit to a Frenchman." Listeners gasped as he remembered the war, laughed when he described the raid on the army mule train in the Camas Meadows, wept as he told of the broken promises of the surrender.

The audience then heard a message that had fallen out of favor with the end of Reconstruction — an appeal for a new commitment to the basic values of liberty and equality. "If the white man wants to live in peace with the Indian, he can live in peace," Joseph said. "There need be no trouble. Treat all men alike. Give them all the same law. Give them all an even chance to live and grow." He called for an equal citizenship defined by broad fundamental liberties. "Let me be a free man," he said, "free to travel, free to stop, free to work, free to trade where I choose, free to choose my own teachers, free to follow the religion of my fathers, free to think and talk and act for myself — and I will obey every law, or submit to the penalty." When he finished with the simple declaration "This is my story and here I am," the theater roared with emotion.

One journalist was left wondering whether Joseph's message could change government policy, or if his audience would simply congratulate themselves for finding him so moving. "Theoretically it was a good, a fine and a noble thing when an oppressed and captive savage could speak out in this free and open way," he wrote, "but where is the good that will ever come of it? His whole tribe may die off from the strange and unhealthy climate in which they have been assigned a camping place, and there will be no help for them." Perhaps the only person who would benefit from the speech was Joseph himself, turned by the love of white crowds into a celebrity, a tragedian producing catharsis at twenty-five cents per ticket, "a fat, healthy savage in the prime of his life, in natural spirits, and in the grave, taciturn way of his race, enjoying the civilized show that he was the chief figure of."

Regardless, audience members felt that they had witnessed something momentous. On stage at Lincoln Hall, one of the founders of *The Council Fire* read a tribute in verse to Chief Joseph. A few days later, the *Washington Evening Star* ran another poem about Joseph, inspired by his speech. "Aye, lies, lies, lies, unblushing shameless lies, / Most coward lies, deceived and then betrayed," railed the poet, a Government Printing Office compositor named John Henry Boner. "Robbed of your birthright, treated as a slave, / Your kith and kin most mercilessly slayed." Within a few months, the Lincoln Hall speech had been adapted as an article in the widely read *North American Review,* and soon after that, the magazine piece was turned into a booklength poem by a Unitarian hymn writer in Somerville, Massachusetts, with a strong interest in Indian affairs: "They say that justice shall be done; / But Words will never give us back our dead; / Words, empty words, will never pay / For all our goods you took away."

The audience may have lost some of the nuances of Joseph's message in its righteous response, but at least one point was crystal clear. With many at Lincoln Hall shedding "quick quivering tears," in John Henry Boner's words, others "pressed clenched teeth to keep sharp curses in unspoken sheath." Many of the curses were for one man. The poem's epigram from King Lear alluded to his initials — "O! O! 'Tis foul!" If the audience now gazed adoringly at Joseph, the villain of his story was unmistakably his pursuer, Oliver Otis Howard. Imperious and disrespectful, the general had insisted on taking the Wallowa Valley, insulted the nontreaty bands at an important council by jailing Toohoolhoolzote, and issued an impossible deadline for moving onto the reservation within thirty days. "If General Howard had given me plenty of time to gather up my stock, and treated Toohool hool-suit as a man should be treated, there would have been no war," Joseph told the crowd. And once the killing had begun, Howard's pursuit had been both inept and vicious. The needless death, the pointless destruction, the looting of so much wealth, the betrayals and broken promises, the agonies of exile — they were all on Howard's hands.

The General fervently rejected Joseph's narrative, although his words seemed to fall on less receptive ears. "The wonderfully abrupt advent of General Howard, with a fear of the laughter of white men in his heart, and a threat of violence on his tongue, is all a fiction," Howard wrote of Joseph's account shortly after it appeared in print. "This idea that General Howard caused the war is an afterthought." The Nez Perce War was long over, but again Chief Joseph was making headlines across the country. While many newspapers were hailing him as "a remarkable individual of an exceptional tribe," the *Army and Navy Journal,* universally read by the officer corps, had distilled his words into "accusations . . . brought against" Howard. The general felt compelled to speak out in his own defense. The chief's version of the war "has . . . the summary brevity of Shakespeare's history, but is not more accurate," the general insisted in an open letter that was published, like Joseph's speech, in the *North American Review.* The rejoinder was only the latest in a seemingly endless series of reports, letters, and articles justifying how he had handled the campaign.

In its immediate aftermath and for years to come, Howard could not stop writing about the war. When he returned to Portland, he felt the warm embrace of family and friends. But to congratulate him for a job well done was also to commiserate with him over the "poor, but devlish slurs," in one supporter's words, that "slip shod men of heart & brain have ceaselessly tried to cast upon you." The slights and aspersions had begun immediately. From the first, Howard had been convinced that Miles was trying to take all credit for the victory. When he and Wood initially went to the press to set the record straight, General Sheridan raked him for speaking out of turn.

Newspapers from New York to California described Howard as inept and hypocritical, a "Bible Chief" widely "reviled as a failure." The general felt "abused and maligned," he said in a teary interview a few weeks after the surrender. "My countrymen . . . seem to have put me up before the country as some sort of politician," he went on. "The only politics I have is to be loyal to my government." Few seemed moved by what one paper called his "boohooing." "The trouble with O. O. Howard" — rendered "Oh! Oh! Howard" in the headline — "is that he is an ass."

Howard took solace in creating his own versions of the war. He and Wood spent much of the remainder of 1877 composing fifty pages for the secretary of war's annual report. For most of the year that followed, the general filled hundreds of column inches in his brother Charles's Congregationalist newspaper with a serialized memoir of the campaign, the first draft of what he hoped would become a book. By his account, he had done everything he could to avoid a war, he wrote, but when Indian perfidy forced him to fight, he and his men performed heroic and selfless feats of endurance that directly enabled Miles to trap Joseph, all in accordance with Howard's orders and plans. Howard defended his conduct in letter after letter to Sherman and Sheridan as well as in increasingly hostile missives to Miles, who finally lost patience with his old mentor. "You virtually gave up the pursuit of the Nez Perces . . . turned back your cavalry, left the trail," he wrote Howard in June 1878. "You need not be surprised if I am not pleased with . . . representations made that there had been one (and of course only one) continuous and successful Indian campaign from the time you started until Colonel Miles stood by your side to receive the surrender."

The general found no redemption in his next Indian campaign, when he returned to north-central Idaho the summer after the Nez Perce War and quickly crushed a rebellion led by some of his former Bannock scouts. It was not enough anymore to be victorious on the battlefield. Steaming for home down the Columbia, Erskine Wood asleep in a deck chair beside him, Howard was "roughly accosted" by a "burly citizen." Egged on by a hostile crowd of settlers, the man criticized the general for being too soft on the "accursed Indians," Howard would remember, and "showing great anger . . . imputed unworthy motives to my officers and myself." Howard all but challenged him to a duel.

In the national press Howard remained yoked to Joseph. Responding to the chief's speech, Howard argued that he "earnestly desired peace," but that he, too, was stymied by the decentralized nature of American power, which he described as a "very unfair distribution of power and accountability." He had been "subject to the requisition of the Indian Department," ordered "to put bands of roaming and nomadic Indians on reservations," and forced "to restore peace where fiendish murders have already begun." "Is it not a strange idea," he wrote, "that [I] should be held accountable for . . . the quarrels between the citizens and Indians, for the dispositions of the Indian Department, and for the horrid murders that inaugurate[d] the war?" "If I had the power and the management entirely in my hands," he maintained, "I believe I could have . . . established peace and amity with Joseph's Indians."

567

Like Joseph, Howard found that promulgating his own versions of the war afforded him some control over what was happening to him. He could subsume Miles's triumph within his command, emphasize what he called the "unparalleled vigor and perseverance" of his men, and neutralize slanders such as the chestnut that every Sunday the "Bible Chief" would stop the chase to observe the Sabbath. He could hit Miles for his raw ambition — Howard, by contrast, claimed that he prayed for victory "even at the expense of another's receiving the credit" — and for failing to do more in the final clash than fight the Indians to a stalemate.

Yet some aspects of the story were beyond his control. Joseph's fame quickly took on a life of its own. Initially, it made sense for Howard to put Joseph forward as a heroic figure. The general emphasized the chief's battlefield brilliance because it excused the army's performance at White Bird Canyon, the Clearwater, the Big Hole, and the Camas Meadows. By describing Joseph's noble qualities — his intelligence, devotion to home and family, initial inclination towards peace, and kindness toward women prisoners — and including his surrender statement in his report to the secretary of war, Howard could suggest that Indians were capable of becoming civilized, Christian farmers. "Let them settle down, and keep quiet, in the Indian Territory," Howard wrote of Joseph's people, "and they will thrive as they do."

But when Joseph's words cast blame on Howard, the general found himself with little room for recourse. In a letter addressing military officers, he could write that "these savages were not saints, and it is not well to attempt to use their treacherous memories to falsify history." But speaking more broadly required him to tread carefully. He could not directly attack the toast of Washington, DC, a man whom thousands had visited at Leavenworth and in the Indian Territory and who, outside of the Northwest, was universally admired for his eloquence. So even as Howard disputed some of the particulars of Joseph's account, he continued to praise the man. Anything less, and the audience Howard hoped to reach would have dismissed him as a pathetic churl. "I was so pleased with Joseph's statement," Howard began his piece in the *North American Review,* "necessarily *ex parte* though it was, and naturally inspired by resentment toward me as a supposed enemy." The chief's article was in parts "beautiful and quite affecting," "graphic and true," Howard wrote. "I dislike to mar the effect of it."

Howard soon realized that the only way to defend himself was to contribute to Joseph's celebrity. If doing so required Howard to engage in some rhetorical delicacy, he understood that such contortions were worthwhile. After all, writing about Joseph was emerging as a lucrative industry — and who was better poised to cash in than the man who had chased him? While Howard's 1878 newspaper serial on the war ran under the headline "Nez Perces Campaign of 1877," the general started toying with more exciting titles as he turned the articles into what he hoped would be a "popular, valuable and saleable book" — he was looking for "anything that prima facie would start a stranger to read." He considered calling the book "The Howard & Joseph Imbroglio: General Howard's Account of It." But soon after Joseph's speech appeared in the *North American*

Review, Howard settled on something he knew would work better: *Nez Perce Joseph: An Account of His Ancestors, His Lands, His Confederates, His Enemies, His Murders, His War, His Pursuit and Capture.* He was not sure if the book would sell, but he thought the widely publicized "resentment of Joseph towards me . . . may help." Howard's story had become Joseph's.

When the book finally came out in 1881, Howard was 2,700 miles from the site of the war, newly installed as the superintendent of West Point. He was back in the East, but it was hardly the triumphant homecoming he had envisioned during his years in exile. He had been appointed to his new post over Sherman's objection and faced the persistent disrespect of the commandant of cadets, a classmate of Howard's at the academy. His successor to the command of the Department of the Columbia was Nelson Miles, newly promoted to brigadier general.

President Hayes had sent Howard to West Point because the military academy was making national headlines as it prepared to expel a cadet named Johnson Chestnut Whittaker. Born a slave in South Carolina, Whittaker had spent nearly four years at West Point isolated and hazed by his white classmates. Just before his last set of final exams in April 1880, he was found tied hand and foot, slashed with a razor. West Point's administrators accused him of faking the attack in order to get back at his enemies, avoid taking his exams, and bring shame to the academy. Sherman maintained that Howard was too partisan to oversee the case fairly. "If you go to West Point," the commanding general wrote Howard, "the inference will be that it has reference to this case, and to the Race question. I am willing to go as far as the farthest in this question, but I do not believe West Point is the place to try the Experiment of Social Equality."

Sherman overestimated Howard's appetite for bold action. By the time Howard returned east, it seemed there was no place amenable to such an experiment. The notion that equality would follow from emancipation — the great hope of Reconstruction — had been destroyed the moment federal troops left the South in the mid-1870s. Through murder, fraud, beatings, and threats, white southerners, often acting in military-style terror campaigns, stripped blacks of their voting rights and trapped many in sharecropping contracts with no escape from lives of drudgery, debt, and want. Even in the North, the promise of equality had given way to a consensus steeped in white supremacy and the need for racial separation. Throughout his time in the West, Howard received letters describing the increasingly brutal conditions of the South. In 1879 a former Freedmen's Bureau official wrote him to see whether freed-people would be better off moving to Washington Territory.

Given the political situation, Howard worked to dispose of the Whittaker case quietly. On his advice, the president composed a court-martial on neutral ground — New York City — with a majority of officers who had not gone to West Point, where, in Howard's words, "the social prejudice was strong against a negro candidate." Led by Nelson Miles, the court found against Whittaker and ordered him discharged. Howard later described being back at his old school as "the hardest office to fill that I had ever had." "There is a beautiful outside to the Military Academy," he wrote, "but I found at that time a social undercurrent that was not so pleasant." The process that Howard had engineered helped turn violent resistance to racial equality at West Point into a new, placid consensus. For the first time in a decade, the Academy was all white again, and, Howard wrote, "after a few weeks the ugly excitement that grew out of this event disappeared altogether."

Shortly before he left the Northwest for West Point, in the summer of 1880, a letter from Joseph arrived for Howard at Fort Vancouver. While his interpreter Ad Chapman had sent occasional notes since the surrender, even including photographs of Joseph and Yellow Bull, it was the first time the chief had written the general. Joseph's letter was composed in the hand of James Reuben, the Christian Nez Perce man from the Lapwai reservation who had been one of Howard's scouts during the war and had come to the Indian Territory to open a school for Nez Perce children. Although Joseph's fame had outstripped Howard's, the chief humbled himself before the general. "I remember the counsiles we had at Lapwai," he wrote. "I regret those days. I now see that you was talking to me right."

Desperate in the Indian Territory, Joseph told Howard what he thought the general wanted to hear. "I wants you to know now I am going to be Christian man," the chief wrote, appealing for the general to "feel for me and sympathize with me and my people." More than 150 Nez Perce captives had perished in exile, "living in a country where cliamet is very hot." "I and my people are dying in this country," he stated bluntly. He believed that he needed Howard's help to get his people back to the Northwest. "You know more than I do so you can tell me what is best for me to do," he wrote. "I would do as you tell me to." At the same time, Joseph pressed one of the key points of his Lincoln Hall speech — that the government had to honor its word. "You told me at the time of surrender that I could go back to my country (Idaho)," he told Howard. "So I say as you have disappointed me do something for me now. . . . I want your assistances."

Howard was not wholly unsympathetic. In private, Howard wondered if the "Indian troubles" would ever find a solution. Perhaps they would be "irremediable," he wrote his brother, "by anything short of citizenship or Divine Smashing: which we as a people so often richly deserve." In theory, "thro[ugh] citizenship, Indians, Negroes & Chinamen will find a remedy," Howard wrote, "but it is even there a tough one!" After Reconstruction's failure, the prospects for establishing equal citizenship among the races seemed dim. Just as the very notion of equality had become uncertain, with people such as Sherman distinguishing "political equality" from "social equality" — two categories with shifting boundaries — the idea of citizenship as a single set of rights and privileges had also fractured. Some citizens, it was obvious, could claim more than others. Some, as Joseph had suggested in his speech, could move, pursue trades, learn, worship, express themselves, and live as they pleased. But the general continued to believe that Indians could claim equal rights only after shedding their nomadic habits and old gods for

Christian civilization.

Writing back to Joseph, Howard assured the chief, "I am your friend and no longer your enemy. I have much compassion for you. I feel sorry that so many have sickened and died." But he denied promising to restore Joseph's people to the Northwest; at the surrender he simply relayed what he thought his orders had been. The best path ahead for the Nez Perce captives, he wrote, was to stop complaining and start thinking of the Indian Territory as home. "I know . . . like children the living ones desire to see the hills and mountains where they were born," he wrote. "Can you not make good farms and have good schools there in the Indian Territory?" To Howard's mind, everything Joseph was doing to restore the original surrender terms — his speeches and articles and newspaper interviews — was in the end a recalcitrant refusal to acknowledge the finality of the government's decision for his people. Rather than persist in questioning it, a good citizen would accept and make the best of his lot. "Get your people well to work," Howard urged Joseph, "and make a garden of the land to which the Government has assigned you." Howard had sympathy for Joseph's suffering but was not going to help him. "If you can say to the children, go to school, and grow up contented and happy and industrious," the general wrote, "you Joseph will show yourself a truly great man and your people can never be blotted out."

In the five years since the Nez Perce War, Wood had realized professional success and personal triumph. When Joseph surrendered, Howard elected to keep the lieutenant on as an aide, ending his days of routine regimental work. Having sold his Nez Perce War drawings to *Harper's* and the *New York Daily Graphic,* Wood published his first article in a San Francisco monthly magazine shortly before moving to West Point — an account of his father's heroism during the Mexican War.

In his home life, he had at last found peace and passion. On leave in the East immediately after the war, he confronted his one-time love, Nanny Moale Smith, who promptly ended her dalliances with other suitors and accepted a renewed marriage proposal. "Sweetheart, it all was like a beautiful dream," she wrote as he was traveling back across the country to Fort Vancouver, "and I cannot make myself realize that there is no fear of a dreadful awakening." "I am sure no one else in the world but you is meant for me," Wood would write. "I have loved you ever since I knew you." At Christmas at the Howards' house, the general's family laughed with him about baby rattles in his future. Celebrating his twenty-sixth birthday in February, he supped on a pudding Nanny had posted across the country. "Why did you put so much camphor in it," he asked, "is that to make it keep, or to preserve it from moths?" The following autumn, on leave following the Bannock War, Wood returned east and married Nanny at her grandmother's house in Baltimore on November 26, 1878. By the time they reached San Francisco in January, she was pregnant.

As at the start of his western service years before, Wood remained vexed about what he called the "horrid horrid harsh facts of my money affairs." Even with a month's advance pay, he went broke while home for the wedding. "It is very trying to be East with as little money — none in fact for my capital was exhausted long ago," he wrote as he and Nanny began making their way westward. Nanny's once-doting stepfather provided little support. Much to her dismay, he had recently married one of her good friends — one of the reasons Nanny had been so eager to accept Wood's proposal in the first place. The newlyweds could not afford to buy food on the train and survived two days on anchovy paste they had packed in Baltimore.

But upon arriving in the West, Nanny found she could keep her station even in reduced circumstances. She had impeccable social connections: she was cousin to the San Francisco banking titan Louis McLane and a niece of Colonel John Gibbon, who had led the attack on the Nez Perce families at the Big Hole. She wore beautiful dresses; her pleated silk taffeta wedding gown had been made in Paris by the venerable House of Worth. And with the help of a Chinese cook, she knew how to give a memorable dinner in the French fashion, her table heavy with oysters, trout, terrapin, frog's legs, grouse, venison, lamb, artichokes, chestnuts, jellies and creams, cherries macerating in cognac, decanters of Madeira, champagne on ice. Together, Nanny and Erskine Wood became the envy of other strivers.

The demands of the army, the whirl of society, and, after the birth of son Erskine in September 1879, the routines of fatherhood gave the lieutenant's life a structure and substance that he had once longed for. Success, however, discomfited Wood. With every milestone achieved, it was as if he had climbed to the top of a ridge, only to see an entirely new landscape unfolding ahead. As Howard's aide during the war, Wood had felt charged with purpose. But the days he spent with Chief Joseph in the war's aftermath, followed by months of fighting Howard's battles with Nelson Miles, prompted the lieutenant to question the army's mission. Crushing Joseph's people did not seem like a victory. The war became less a reflection of what had actually happened on the battlefield than a function of which officer had sharper political skills and better contacts in the press. Wood became increasingly aware of how government Indian agents profited by their service and how, whether or not it benefited the Indians, keeping the tribes on reservations had become a lucrative industry. By the time he was serving as Howard's adjutant at West Point, he no longer found his responsibilities exciting. "I hate the work," he wrote his wife. "It is very confining and leaves me no leisure and is the merest mechanical routine which teaches me nothing. I am becoming very discontented and *will* not do this work for four years or more."

As contented as Wood professed to be with his family life — "without you now it would be impossible for my life to taste one bit of true happiness," he wrote Nanny — he grew increasingly aware of a world beyond it. Soon after the birth of his daughter Nan in July 1881, he was given leave by General Howard to study law and political science at Columbia. The lieutenant went alone to New York and found lodging near Washington Square Park in Greenwich Village, different from anywhere he had ever lived before. He befriended a circle of painters, sculptors, and illustrators his age and, at their studios, through games of whist, over glasses of Scotch, exulted in their freedom. He took his breakfasts at a nearby French restaurant, composing letters to his wife by firelight, watching the people around him. "François is serving . . . a very pretty actress who looks so demure that one might think she never flirted," he wrote home, "yet I am sure she is more than ready."

One of Wood's new friends, George de Forest Brush, was busy painting scenes of Indian life after an extended trip to Montana and Wyoming. "It is not necessary that an Indian learn to spell and make changes," Brush would soon write, "before we see that his long locks are beautiful as he rides against the prairie winds." Eager to develop his own literary talent, Wood began drafting new essays for publication. The first recounted his travels among the Tlingit people in Alaska. The second was a tribute to Chief Joseph, who, Wood wrote, "fought for that which the white man calls patriotism when it has been crowned with success."

As he advanced at Columbia Law School from the fall of 1881 to the spring of 1883, studying law gave Wood the strange feeling of being pulled in different directions. "Time drags now with me," he wrote, "though I am so busy that every minute is occupied." His legal education would undoubtedly help him as an officer, and he started pondering the opportunities the law opened beyond the army. But alongside the promise of a new career — and, conceivably, the end of his money troubles — came a nagging sense that the ideas and institutions of law were mortal creations, constructed out of politics, economic imperative, and social prejudice. Instead of cementing his commitment to a system of rules, law school prompted Wood

578

to wonder if other systems — different codes, alternate moralities — could be more just.

CHAPTER 22
RED MOON

Nanny Wood was unaccustomed to being ignored at her own parties. Normally she spent her days in constant conversation. "She could . . . keep up the liveliest interchange with the vegetable man," a friend would recall, "bandy witticisms with an ambassador, be amused and amusable, startle men callers by whisking them into the basement to help her track a rat that had been disturbing the peace." But Joseph, Mrs. Wood would say, "like all Indians . . . had no use for women." Around her dining room table, the chief and his companions talked right past her. She did not understand a word of their animated conversation.

Nanny felt jarred by the liberties the Indians were taking in her house, "a bit taken aback," she recalled decades later, "to go down to my parlor and see them lounging about on my divan and pillows." On the way into the dining room, one of them had bumped the sideboard, sending cups and saucers crashing. Watching them use their fingers to swirl sugar in their coffee, she finally interrupted with a question for the small sallow man in the dark suit, the chief's interpreter Ad Chapman — what was everybody saying? Chapman turned to her and explained. "They were reminiscing," she was told, "about their boyhood days and their hunting trips" — days of perfect freedom, now long past.

If the occasion was a burden for Mrs. Wood — "much to my consternation," she would say, "I did not know what to give them to eat" — her husband relished the notion that he would be entertaining Chief Joseph. As an additional guest, he invited Olin Warner, a sculptor visiting Portland from New York — one of Wood's boon companions in his Greenwich Village days, now commissioned to immortalize the occasion with a medallion of Joseph to be cast in bronze. After the older children spread the word that Chief Joseph would be coming for a luncheon, neighbors were hanging out of their windows on a cold and cloudless mid-November morning to glimpse the great man. Joseph, Chapman, and several other Indian men walked up the hill on Twenty-Third Avenue until they reached the Woods' rambling yellow home at the corner of Flanders Street, a quiet journey turned into an impromptu parade.

Twelve years after meeting on the battlefield, Joseph and Wood could look at each other as old friends but changed men. Almost fifty, Joseph appeared vital but visibly aged, heavier, his face starting to wrinkle and sag. His hair remained dark, braided long down his shoulders and combed high from his forehead. Wood was now the same age Joseph had been during the war, his large green eyes beginning to crease at the edges. The trimmed mustache he had worn as a lieutenant now flowed to a soft beard, thick and curling like the hair on his head; in the bust that Olin Warner had sculpted of him, Wood resembled a

Greek god groomed for a dinner party. "He was always being compared to Jove," one admirer would recall.

Both men had been back in the Northwest for several years. In May 1885, after multiple assurances by Nelson Miles, a steady drumbeat of articles and books advocating the Nez Perce cause, including an 1884 article in the *Century* by Wood, and thousands of signatures on petitions to Congress, the Nez Perce captives — now numbering 268 men, women, and children — were sent through mud and rain and swollen creeks from their land on the Ponca reservation in Indian Territory to the railroad station in Arkansas City, Kansas, for a five-day journey homeward. A few stayed behind, having married into local tribes. Hundreds more lay in graves.

Joseph's younger daughter was buried in Indian Territory. Born at Tepahlewam just as the war began, she had survived months of fighting — riding nearly fifteen hundred miles on her mother's back, saved by Yellow Wolf after the Clearwater battle, cradled by Joseph at the Big Hole, kept warm and fed during the final siege. But the ravages of Indian Territory were too much.

The survivors were weakened by malaria, diphtheria, dysentery, malnutrition, and the shock and melancholy that came from pain and loss. At least eight captives had killed themselves during their exile. The train rolled through Kansas, Colorado, Wyoming, and Utah before reaching Idaho Territory, where officials from the Department of the Interior worried that lynch mobs would be waiting. Idaho courts issued criminal indictments, holding Joseph and several others responsible for the killings of 1877, but the train sped for

Washington Territory at forty miles an hour.

Upon arriving at Wallula, the survivors were divided into two groups. One hundred eighteen — mostly people who had converted to Christianity in exile — were continuing east to Lapwai. Joseph's people were splitting, and his family had come apart. His younger wife Springtime had separated from him in Indian Territory after their baby daughter's death. His elder wife Heyoom Yoyikt had never joined him in exile. She and their daughter Sound of Running Feet had escaped to Canada. They returned in 1878 and settled in Lapwai. Sound of Running Feet attended the agency school, took the name Sarah, and married a reservation Indian. After a few years, before her father could see her again, she got sick and died, leaving no children.

The chief's journey was not over. Forbidden to settle on Nez Perce land, he and the rest of his people continued 150 miles north to Fort Spokane and the Colville Indian Reservation. Far up the Columbia River almost to the British line, the Colville agency had been created in 1872 as a catchall for bands that had never entered into treaties with the United States — Nespelem, San Poil, Okanagan, Methow, Lake, Colville, Kalispel, Spokane, Coeur d'Alene. The Columbia Indian leader called Moses, a longtime ally of Joseph's, had moved onto the reservation with his band in 1884. While Joseph agreed to join Moses there, he continued to insist to his people and to the Indian affairs officials coordinating the move that he had never ceded his claim to the Wallowa Valley.

At Colville life was far from easy. Moved onto lands too late to plant a crop, Joseph's people had to survive on rations from the nearby army garrison when the Indian agent refused to help. After two years of near starvation, they settled by Nespelem Creek, began the slow work of building a horse herd, and rediscovered what life could be like surrounded by mountains, canyons, and rivers — "wild game aplenty," said Yellow Wolf, who had returned from Canada a year after the final battle, endured exile in the Indian Territory, and ultimately chosen to stay with his uncle. "Fish, berries, and all kinds of roots. . . . It was better than Idaho, where all Christian Nez Perces and whites were against us."

If local bureaucrats were malicious or inept, Joseph soon found an important ally in the newly appointed commander of the Department of the Columbia: John Gibbon, now a brigadier general, the same officer who had led the attack on the Nez Perce families at the Big Hole. A couple of months before Joseph's Portland visit, the chief sought out Gibbon while the general was touring Lake Chelan. For hours they talked about the battle and the war — "most affecting," wrote one of Gibbon's traveling companions. Joseph then steered the conversation to "a woful story of the manner in which he and his Indians have been treated by the government." He asked for more services — someone to operate the sawmill that had been built on his land and then left idle. After hearing Joseph, Gibbon hoped to introduce the chief to the senator with the most power over Indian affairs, Henry L. Dawes of Massachusetts, who had supported the redemption of Joseph's people from the Indian Territory and would soon be visiting the Northwest to promote a new policy to break up tribal lands into individually owned allotments. The general also provided the chief a

584

letter that would enable him to travel more freely, declaring Joseph "a man of integrity and honesty . . . free from treachery and perfectly reliable . . . his friend."

Gibbon was also a patron to the Woods; Nanny was his niece. The arrival of "Uncle Gibbon" at Fort Vancouver in 1885 was just another bit of serendipity as the family rose in the world. While Lieutenant Wood had been studying law in New York, General Howard left West Point to assume command of the Department of the Platte. Although Wood initially expected to join Howard in Omaha, the general soon informed him that he would only be keeping two aides: his longtime assistant Joseph Sladen and his son Guy. "I feel that I owe you more than thanks for constant & faithful service," Howard wrote Wood, wishing him "some desirable turn of fortune in the future."

Ordered to Fort Boise in the spring of 1883, Wood found the routine work of a company lieutenant "very pleasant as military duty," but he told General Howard of "a desire to quit soldiering altogether and take to the law." "I will do so," he wrote, "if I can balance the chances of success against my duty to my family." Moving Nanny and their two children to Portland — she was pregnant with a third — Wood began taking steps to ease himself out of the army. Complaining of gastritis, bronchitis, and conjunctivitis, he convinced his post surgeon to send him to Fort Canby on the Oregon coast to recover — an easy distance from his family — and then applied for a transfer to Fort Vancouver. Nelson Miles, then commander of the Department of the Columbia and still stinging over Wood's attempts to give Howard credit for capturing Joseph, took a personal interest in the lieutenant's case, suggesting that he wanted leave and a transfer "to enter upon active business in the city of Portland." Wood drafted Miles a long, indignant, and sarcastic letter that years later he was sure had been more insulting than it was. He sought the leave and transfer "to build up shattered health that I might be in better condition *afterward* to engage in the practice of the law," he wrote, but "if [Miles] means that under <u>cover</u> of a sick leave I intended to practice law he is worse than misinformed, he has been told an absolute falsehood." It was a fine distinction, perhaps best appreciated by an attorney or someone about to become one. Wood resigned his commission and opened his law office in early 1884.

Well trained at Columbia and already a favorite of Portland society, Wood quickly developed a paying practice. Within months, the city's exacting federal judge, Matthew Deady, had declared that Wood's briefs "show[ed] a good deal of original thought and much care, research and taste." The presidents of Portland's two biggest banks, both personal friends, started sending him work. A leading Jewish attorney helped him get established as an admiralty lawyer — a coveted practice in a city built on shipping — and set him up in partnership with someone bound to attract business, a former Oregon chief justice and senator who had served as Grant's attorney general. He was invited to join elite clubs, led efforts to build a public library and an art museum, and because of his connections with New York artists was entrusted to find a sculptor for the imposing Skidmore Fountain in downtown Portland; he chose Olin Warner. From a humble three-room house

— Nanny bathed the children in the dining room — the Woods kept moving to bigger quarters on finer streets. When Nelson Miles turned the Department of the Columbia over to Gibbon, the new commander gave his niece and her family an officer's home at Fort Canby for a summer cottage on the shore. In the army Wood had never advanced beyond the rank of lieutenant. Within two years of arriving in Portland, he could answer to "Colonel," his rank in the Oregon Militia.

By the time Wood invited Joseph to his home, he had already landed the client of a lifetime: the San Francisco branch of the international banking house Lazard Frères, which several years earlier had bought 860,000 acres of Oregon land, originally a federal grant for a wagon road that was never built. Wood initially had to defend the bank's interest from the federal government, which was suing to get the land back because the terms of the grant had not been met. If he could perfect the bank's title to the property, much of it virgin forest, he could then oversee its sale for decades to come, with commissions that would amount to a fortune. Wood soon convinced the courts that the bank, having bought the land unaware of the government's terms, was entitled to keep it under rules that protected innocent purchasers. He traveled to San Francisco with a bill for fifty thousand dollars. In Wood's telling, the branch president, an Alsatian Jew named Marc Eugene Meyer, spent three days trying to convince him to accept thirty-five thousand but ultimately cut him a check for the full fee, wondering in the end, "Voodt, haff you got any Chew blood in you?"

Wood and his wife spent their money freely. After a decade of marriage, they had five children

— three boys, two girls, the oldest ten and the youngest a year and a half. They served food that was, in the words of a frequent visitor, Barbara Bartlett Hartwell, "fit for kings . . . kings with catholic tastes in oil and garlic, familiar with truffles and galantines; hams stuffed with honey; canvasbacks . . . lying in a bed of cress, served with wild rice and spiced huckleberry . . . haunch[es] of venison . . . ortolans and larks' tongues." They sat in dark rooms filled with art, fine oils on the walls, many of them by Wood's New York friends, and, Hartwell wrote, "rarities in glass, porcelain and metal gleam[ing] through a kind of rich smelling gloom." Bookshelves were lined with leather-bound editions, "smooth to the cheek," she recalled, "magnificent 'unexpurgated' books" that made youngsters blush while calling out to them to do some "extremely surreptitious reading." Wood brought home no end of curios and jewels — antique snuff bottles, carved and lacquered Japanese cases, opals and sapphires and jade. He made large donations to civic projects and invested in an inn at Mount Hood. When the family ran out of cash, Wood always had something he could sell from his teeming collections.

Some nights, the Woods' cook and "man of all work," a young Chinese immigrant named Guy, would sit by the children's beds and tell them stories until they fell asleep. Other nights, their father would read them Uncle Remus tales, luxuriating in the dialect and assuring the children that growing up at Rosewood Glen had given him "a perfect understanding of the Negro character and language." When he tired of Uncle Remus, he made up his own stories. A favorite was called "The Magic Pearl," whose possessor "could make himself invisible at will," his oldest son would recall, "could cross the oceans in the wink of an eye . . . fought savages or wild beasts. He rescued beautiful princesses, made himself a king, thwarted the plans of evil magicians." Wood stretched the story for weeks, imagining a world without limits, where the humblest people could do the most extraordinary things, where anything was possible. Some days it could seem as if he might own such a pearl, set in one of his watch fobs or tie pins or a bright yellow gold ring he had picked up in Chinatown.

Lunch with Chief Joseph was a simple affair — no multicourse feast, no dazzling repartee, just a chance for Wood and his guests to catch up. Wood had learned a few phrases in Chinook Jargon, and his oldest boy Erskine could speak some, too. Joseph watched the children play. He had been staying at Fort Vancouver and could pass along greetings from General Gibbon.

The day after the luncheon, the chief was the general's guest at a viewing of Portland's Gettysburg cyclorama, a massive painting of the battle — nine thousand square feet of canvas, weighing six tons — stretched around a cavernous room that took up much of a downtown block. Surrounded by the vast tableau of slaughter, Gibbon could point himself out on the canvas, twenty-six years younger, riding a horse, waving his sword, rallying his troops to counter Pickett's charge. He gestured to other generals and officers — perhaps showed the chief where Oliver Otis Howard had fought. Joseph listened to Gibbon talk and asked occasional questions. He lingered over a scene of hand-to-hand fighting, a fury of bayonets and rifle butts, all on a scale far beyond anything his people had experienced in 1877.

A great battle can leave the land gouged and torn, leave scars that people carry with them on their bodies. It can become scenes that participants replay in their minds, talk over with other veterans, or reveal to family and friends. And in time, its legacy expands into another set of stories, created for and sold to the public at large, sometimes by people who were there, but often by people who were not even close. Once the smoke clears and the bodies are limed and buried and the pools of blood have dried into the earth, what remains is myth and memory, tribute and desecration and art. Through Chapman, Joseph said that the cyclorama "proved to him what his father had told him, that when the white men got mad and fought among themselves they . . . kept it up until they made a lake of blood."

Over the course of his visit, Joseph kept returning to the Woods — not to their house on Flanders Street, but a short walk south, to a large parcel of land, half a city block, that they had bought in the hills west of downtown Portland. As Erskine and Nanny contemplated a truly grand home on what they called "the lots," they had already started planting hedges of holly and pink La France roses, quince trees and flowering cherries. Nanny's passion was her garden — "none of your casual kinds," her eldest son would write.

Olin Warner had spent much of his Portland visit at the lots sculpting various people — members of the Wood family, other local nabobs — taking over a shack that Erskine had erected as a makeshift studio for his watercolors. Now

Warner turned to the most famous of his Portland subjects. For several days, Joseph sat for him from morning to night. Bringing lunch from the house at noon, Nanny Wood watched Joseph posing "like a stone image . . . without blinking an eye" — silent and completely still, while the sculptor wrung meaning and emotion from every wrinkle and fold in Joseph's face, his strong gaze and set jaw. Warner, soft, sallow, and heavy, with dark cropped hair and a trim beard — "not prepossessing looking," Nanny Wood judged — had rendered other iconic images before, busts of Christopher Columbus and Benjamin Franklin, Shakespeare and Beethoven. He gave his subjects a timeless quality, favoring a classical style, like the sculptures he had studied at the Louvre while honing his craft in Paris during the days of the commune. The object Warner created from Joseph's likeness would inspire viewers to imagine Joseph's anger, sorrow, and resolve.

Since 1872, Joseph had spoken for his band countless times, with soldiers, settlers, and bureaucrats, with journalists and politicians, in cabins and concert halls, defining the rights he had never given up and the promises the government had made and broken. Even now, while in Portland, he continued to press General Gibbon for better conditions at the Colville reservation. His oratory could sway the powerful and make ordinary men and women weep. But from the beginning, people were moved not just by what they heard but by what they saw. His mere presence suggested a seemingly infinite range of aspirations and emotions. Even when he was silent, the rest of the world heaped meaning upon him. Seventeen years as a symbol and celebrity:

591

the weight of so much sentiment and expectation, prejudice and preconception, could be crushing. After each day that he posed for Warner, he returned to the garrison at Fort Vancouver too exhausted to do anything but go straight to sleep.

At first the boy thought the feast had been called in his honor. He had just arrived at the Colville Indian Reservation, and while two women were setting up his canvas pup tent, Chief Joseph took him under a thatched arbor extending from his teepee. Some twenty men from Joseph's band sat around blankets that ran the arbor's length, covered with pots of food. Sitting at Joseph's right hand, the boy studied the dishes — venison, trout, rice with raisins, boiled camas and cous root, pumpkins, potatoes, huckleberries, bread. Some were familiar — tins of preserved peaches, purchased from a trading post. Others were not — most notably "soup made of deer's leg," he remembered not long afterward, "with quite a respectable amount of the hair left on. This hair of course coming off in the boiling, floated around and I must confess bewildered me."

The boy could not understand a word anyone was saying. The celebration seemed joyous enough, the men laughing as they ate. But when he turned to Joseph, he felt a shadow fall. In what the boy would describe as a "somewhat deep and magnetic voice," the chief said in Chinook Jargon that "his heart was sick." Beneath the spirited conversations around the blankets, the boy could hear something else. It seemed to be coming from inside all the surrounding teepees — the sound of women crying. The more he focused on the sound, the more intense it seemed. They were "weeping and wailing and lamenting in a very frenzy of grief," he remembered. He asked Joseph what was happening. The chief explained that his nephew, a young man, had just died. The feast was not a grand welcome for the boy but a gathering of mourners.

Joseph had not been expecting the boy when the Indian agent had come to the camp on routine business, trying, perhaps, to convince the Indians to move from their teepees into houses, eschew their blankets for the "full suits" and "excellent supply of clothing" that the government had distributed, or give up their dangerous fondness for gambling with playing cards. Only after the agent had discussed his primary business did he introduce Joseph to young Erskine Wood, "the son of his old friend Lieut Wood," visiting now supposedly to make good on a promise the father had made two years before when Joseph had visited the Woods in Portland. Joseph initially appeared uncomprehending. Although Nanny Wood would believe that Joseph had said during their lunch that he wanted young Erskine to see the reservation, the boy was sure it had been his father who asked the chief "whether at some time in the future I could come visit him." Only after the boy pulled a photograph of Charles Erskine Scott Wood from his pocket did the chief greet young Erskine and express pleasure at the prospect of caring for a twelve-year-old boy.

Erskine had come at a fragile moment for Joseph and the families at the Colville agency, now known as Joseph's band. The chief's children were dead, and his wives had not come with him to his new home in far northern Washington. Everyone around him had lost people in the war and in exile. The vast majority of their kin were hundreds of miles away. People were improvising new connections, remarrying, adopting orphans, and taking in elders. After the loss of nearly every baby born in the Indian Territory, infants' cries were beginning to be heard again. Still, the bonds were uncertain. Each death, from tuberculosis or influenza or old age, dealt a blow.

New federal policy designed to force Indians to assimilate into the larger society posed an equally serious threat. Under Senator Henry Dawes's General Allotment Act of 1887, reservations were being taken from tribes, carved up into small plots, and allotted to individual Indians. Whatever property was left over would be sold to whites. With half of the Colville lands opening up to white settlers, the Nez Perce families there had been offered allotments down at Lapwai. Visiting Lapwai in the spring of 1890, Joseph met with the allotting agent for the Nez Perce reservation, Alice Fletcher, an ethnologist who had trained at Harvard's Peabody Museum and conducted extensive research among the Sioux and Omaha. A small woman about Joseph's age who favored heavy black dresses — the resemblance to Queen Victoria was so striking that her companion out west, the photographer Jane Gay, referred to her in letters as "Her Majesty" — Fletcher had been a driving force behind the new policy, personally convincing Senator Dawes of the progressive, civilizing effect of individual over tribal land ownership and then tirelessly lobbying for passage of his resulting bill. Now she was trying to put her theories to work in the field.

Although Joseph refused all entreaties to accept an allotment, he spent time with Fletcher during his visit to Lapwai, talking and posing for photographs. In her he likely saw yet another new bureaucrat to sway, someone with singular connections to powerful people in Congress and Indian Affairs. When asked, the chief again insisted the only land he would ever claim was his ancestral land. "He will have none but the Wallowa valley, from which he was driven," Gay wrote. "He will remain landless and homeless if he cannot have his own again." Gay thought "it was good to see an unsubjugated Indian. One could not help respecting the man who still stood firmly for his rights." In a letter to Dawes's wife, Fletcher pronounced Joseph "a most interesting blending of the old and the new — all of which I greatly enjoyed . . . a hero in many ways." But Joseph's commitment — even if heroic — came at a cost few could bear. In 1891 Yellow Bull, a leader during the exile who had accompanied Joseph to Washington, accepted his Idaho allotment and moved away.

Although his troubles were on a much smaller scale, young Erskine Wood had also come to the Colville reservation at a difficult time for his family. With his four brothers and sisters and the five boys from next door, he had grown up in a pack. Together they spent their days stampeding across Oriental rugs and bearskins, spilling out onto the porch and into the yard, playing with their terrier, Pants, and riding their pony, Punch, or pedaling bicycles, in Nanny's words, "there and everywhere all over town." Erskine had a loving mother, and a father who took enormous pride in his eldest son. But in May 1891, Nanny Wood gave birth to her sixth child, a girl, the first one who was not strong and healthy. Baby Katherine died that September, and the family was never the same. Weak and devastated, Nanny went to recover at Colorado Springs that winter with the children in tow. But being alone with them only further exhausted her. By the summer of 1892, the four youngest children were sent to stay with friends who ran a hotel and hot springs in the faded mining town of Ketchum, Idaho. Young Erskine returned to Portland with his father, who, preparing to try his big case for Lazard Frères, bought the boy a membership in a swim club and left him to his own devices. As the heat set in and wild strawberries ripened at the lots, the idea of sending the boy to Chief Joseph began to seem like a better plan, and Nanny was too far away to stop it.

Erskine prepared hurriedly for his journey. Rummaging for his tent at the family lots, young Erskine found a fringed buckskin hunting shirt; "it just fits me," he wrote his mother. He packed it, along with his rifle, some fishing flies, and a journal. Two days before the Fourth of July fireworks — Erskine was sure that it would rain, as it always seemed to do — he took a train bound for Spokane. The next day, just shy of the city, he caught a Sunday freight train thirty miles east to Davenport and then rode a stagecoach twenty miles north to Fort Spokane. After spending Independence Day with the Indian agent and his wife across the Spokane River from the garrison, he headed into the hills for Joseph's camp at Nespelem, a cluster of teepees in a small valley surrounded by gentle ridges, rising and folding. "Be careful about guns and streams," his father wrote him when he had been gone a week. "Keep clean and have a good time."

Up to this point, Erskine had experienced only

596

the rugged pursuits of a little gentleman. When he was ten, just a few months after meeting Chief Joseph in his home, he had gone hunting near Mount Hood with friends of the family and shot a bear. His father paid Portland's best furrier to tan and line the skin for the boy's bedroom and made sure that Theodore Roosevelt, then a friend from his New York days whose books on rugged western living had found a large readership, heard of the exploit. Roosevelt inscribed to the boy a copy of his latest, *Ranch Life and the Hunting Trail,* celebrating "the advent of so keen a hunter to the fields of sport." When Erskine was eleven, he went on a trout fishing expedition to Lake Coeur d'Alene with his father, Uncle Gibbon, and a few of Gibbon's staff officers. They borrowed a friend's private rail car and traveled with a chef who prepared what they caught "au meuniere," Erskine would remember, with "everything that properly goes with them." Every time supper was served, the general would say, "No damned crowned head of Europe ever sat down to a meal like this."

Accustomed to experiencing nature surrounded by luxury and adoring adults, Erskine struggled to adjust to a new way of living outdoors in his first weeks with Joseph. He recoiled at the food. "They put the fish in the water to boil without . . . tak[ing] the entrails out or anything," he wrote his father. "They eat the guts of a dear with the *doung* streaming out of them." Almost immediately his head was crawling with lice — caught from the Indians, who he believed were too dirty to live with. His tent, near Joseph's teepee, was surrounded by a ditch to keep the rain out. His rifle lost a screw in transit and would not shoot. His relationships with his hosts were at first mostly transactional. In early letters to his parents, most of the conversations he described with the chief's family revolved around negotiating for moccasins and hair ropes, the types of things the Indians had sold to visitors during their exile, when they were desperate to raise money — $2.50 for beaded shoes, he informed his father, but only a dollar if he could supply the beads himself.

Back in Portland, the elder Wood urged his son to move in with Joseph and live a Nez Perce life. All of the family's friends back home, he warned, were expecting to hear stories of "many wonderful things" and would be disappointed if Erskine kept to himself all summer. Authentic experience among "the original natives of this country who are now nearly gone" was more valuable than souvenirs. "All the disgusting features to us are nevertheless a part of savage life and you should leave out nothing, good or bad," Wood advised his boy. "You ought to find out if possible their legends, their ideas of where they (the Indians) first came from, how they got fire, water. What is their idea of God. Heaven. Hell. Spirits. Their fairy tales, etc. How they educate their boys. Write up their horse races, funerals." After contributing essays about Tlingit life in Alaska and Chief Joseph to the *Century,* Wood predicted, "There is not a paper in the U.S. that would not be glad to get an article from you telling of these strange people."

By the end of July, Erskine had taken his father's advice. He had conquered his lice and stopped trying to keep his distance from Joseph. He soon learned that the chief lived with two new wives, both war widows; a teenage boy orphaned as a baby in the war, whom Erskine called Nicky Mowitz; and another woman — pregnant — and her husband, named Looking Down, whose bandaged ankle had been oozing since 1877. Dressed head-to-toe in buckskin, sleeping in his tent next to the teepee with one of the chief's dogs for warmth, Erskine added himself to the new family Joseph was working to create.

Eventually, the boy took his meals at Joseph's side, listening to conversations that he did not understand. The chief's teepee was a large room, maybe thirty feet across, woven mat floors entirely covered in canvas and blankets except for the fire pit in the middle and a narrow path to the doorway. Traditional Nez Perce living, Erskine soon discovered, also integrated what he would call "many of the accessories of civilization — cooking utensils, knives, axes, saddles . . . etc." The air was clean inside, smoke noticeable only when one stood tall. But Erskine found he had little reason to stand. The teepee was as comfortable as a room in his own house, an inviting place to sit or lie down, to read and write, eat and sleep.

Each day that passed, Joseph cut a notch into a stick. With Nicky Mowitz, Erskine would fish for trout; they bit, he wrote his father, at flies that he tied with gray wings and bright colors. The two boys would hunt prairie chickens, ducks, grouse, and pheasants, Erskine shooting at first with arrows that he made himself but finding more success with a borrowed shotgun. Joseph's wives, among others, taught the boy to make moccasins, apply beads to buckskin, and braid rawhide ropes. He tried talking with as many people as he could. Soon his Chinook Jargon was "as good as anybody," and he started picking up what he called

"Nes Percy." "Whenever I learn a Nes Percy word I write it down," he wrote his mother, "and they think that is . . . lots of fun."

The rhythms of life at Nespelem felt natural. Every other day, Joseph would send Erskine out into the hills with Nicky Mowitz to drive the chief's small herd — maybe fifty horses — to a watering hole. Galloping bareback with his friend and lassoing fresh ponies to bring back to camp hardly felt like a chore. The boy watched people thresh grain and tend to gardens. In time he would see Joseph break a wild horse — choking him with a rope, pulling at him until his mouth bled and his body slicked with sweat, tying his legs and beating him until he would wear a saddle. Erskine went with men to slaughter and butcher government steers, corralled nearby for the benefit of the Nez Perce families. Occasionally the boy would accompany the chief to meet with the Indian agent, or they would row a canoe across the Columbia on an errand to a nearby store.

Every Sunday, Joseph put a dot on his calendar stick. On those days he shared a big breakfast with several other leading men, hunters and warriors and elders, figures of awe for Erskine — men like Two Moons, whom the boy later described as "a small old Indian with serpent eyes but always jolly and laughing." Nicky Mowitz and Erskine would ride several miles from camp to a stretch of open prairie where crowds gathered for weekly horse races. Stripped to breechcloths, the contestants were on the cusp of adulthood, eighteen, nineteen, twenty years old. Riding bareback and holding bridles made from hair rope, they disappeared in a cloud of dust, tearing down a long stretch, around, and back at the crowd. While the men rode, everyone else placed bets — blankets, rifles, horses, saddles. Some would arrange themselves along the final stretch of the racecourse, trying to whip their favorite horses to the finish. Erskine joined these spectators once, "just riding down to be with the crowd and the racers," he would remember. "For a joke they arranged themselves alongside me and whipped me in ahead of everybody. I didn't count, of course, but that was it. They love a joke."

As at home, Erskine wrestled and played with other boys his age. They threw spears through small rolling hoops and spun smooth rocks with a horse crop until they were whirling like tops. With Looking Down, who lived in Joseph's teepee, Erskine played war, soldiers against Indians, the boy always standing in for the army. The man had a wound that would not heal, yet in the warmth of summer, surrounded by friends, able to live a life that gestured toward what they had known in the Wallowa Valley, he could laugh at even the worst thing that had ever happened to him. "We used to have the fiercest battles," the boy recalled.

Summer became autumn. Erskine turned thirteen at Joseph's camp. He bid farewell to one of the chief's wives, who left to earn money picking hops in the Yakima Valley, and was there to welcome her back a month later. He saw Looking Down's wife go into seclusion in a small shelter a hundred yards away, then return with the baby. Despite his father's advice to keep his hair short, Erskine let it grow in waves, "as soft as Southdown fleece," he joked in verse to his mother. "Oh it shines and smells like Eden / When I slick her down with grease." The boy took early-morning sweats with Joseph in a small frame lodge covered

601

in hides, enduring the steam raised by water poured on hot rocks, then plunging into a cold creek nearby — small boy and large man enveloped by the heat, leaning against each other, feeling and smelling each other's sweat, breathing together and apart. Joseph's wives started cleaning the trout Erskine caught — just the way he liked it — and prepared a grouse stew thickened with flour that the boy devoured. He ate so much that his face grew full and round. Joseph's family joked that he needed a Nez Perce name. At first they called him White Boy, then Buckskin Shirt. But finally they seized on a phrase that fit him to a tee, especially when he was laughing: Red Moon.

Erskine was staying longer than anticipated. Even though his school back in Portland had begun, Erskine's father told him, "You can stay with the Indians as long as you like if you really live with them, and go into the mountains on their fall hunt." In the chill of autumn, the boy gladly went with Joseph and others north through the mountains almost to the British line. After sleeping in his pup tent for most of the summer, he moved into the hunting party's long lodge, which consisted of the teepees of several families combined, with multiple fires burning and hundreds of pounds of venison drying on racks. But by mid-October, Erskine resolved to head home. The hunt was not turning out to be much of an adventure for him because Joseph would not let him hunt alone. For the sake of the boy's father, or perhaps for his own peace of mind, the chief would not take the risk. "Joseph was afraid to let me go hunting for fear that I would get lost," he wrote his mother.

Joseph's concern — the concern of a parent —

reminded Erskine that there were other people who loved him. "I am getting a kind of a longing to see some of the family," he finally wrote his mother, "and then there is school." Although the boy went on the band's seasonal hunt at the end of October, this time without Joseph, he soon asked Nicky Mowitz to guide him out of the mountains and back to Nespelem. Erskine stayed with the chief another four days, then crossed the Columbia with the Indian agent, and the next day caught an overnight train to Portland. Before he left, he told Joseph that he would return the next summer.

Reaching Portland on November 6, the boy found his father waiting for him at the station. Erskine's hair, his moccasins, and his round face caused the senior Wood to pronounce, "He would do for a circus side show." Wood whisked his son out to dinner, where, he wrote, "about 17 people all asked him questions at once . . . all about archery and Indian doctors, customs, etc." The boy dutifully answered everyone, was "really very entertaining," Wood wrote, but seemed quiet and had no appetite. Wood brought him back to the small bungalow where he was staying while the rest of the family was away. The boy hosed himself down, unpacked, and collapsed into bed. For a time his father sat at his side, watching him sleep. With his long wavy locks spread over the pillow, the boy looked like no one so much as his mother. Reflecting on Erskine's experience with Chief Joseph, Wood imagined his son was "just now at Plymouth Rock in the Universal History of the United States," representing an ideal of pure encounter and exchange, as if the depredations of the nearly three hundred years that followed had never taken place. He resolved to get a photograph taken before the boy cut his hair short.

After a few days, the two Erskine Woods, father and son, traveled thirteen hundred miles to Colorado Springs. There they found Nanny being attended to by eleven-year-old Nan and, in her husband's words, "an army of doctors." She still had "the most wonderful brown eyes that keep as young as the stars themselves," Wood thought, "but she is an invalid now." The three youngest children — eight, almost seven, and five — were still in Ketchum, Idaho. For Thanksgiving dinner, father, mother, and Erskine and Nan feasted on oysters on the half shell, cream of celery soup, Lake Superior whitefish, prairie chicken, and, in a nod to tradition, pumpkin pie for dessert.

The reunion was both joyful and bittersweet. After sipping champagne with his wife, Wood swirled a blood-red Clos de Vougeot and said to his wife, "Our home is broken up. You are ill. Yet who knows we may yet look back to this very night and say, " 'How happy we were.' " The four then started talking about their earliest days together in Portland, before their place in the world had been assured, when, Wood said, "the dinner we have just eaten would have seemed a crime . . . when to walk or take a street car was a debateable economy." Wood was amazed at how much Nan and Erskine remembered, how they "brightened into remarkable reminiscence." They talked about their servant Guy, who had made tops and kites for Erskine, and about the time Nanny sewed up one sleeve of Nan's nightgown so she would stop sucking her thumb, only to be outwitted when the girl switched to the other one. The children began laughing, and soon Wood had the rare sight of seeing Nanny laugh, too. If Wood tended to brood — thinking "what a strange unknowable and . . . ever elusive thing is this Happiness" — it was not so complicated for his family. Near the end of the meal, Nanny walked over and gave him a kiss, asking, "Were we *ever* unhappy when we were together?"

CHAPTER 23
A GLORIOUS ERA

The stairway was narrow and steep, almost a ladder, daunting for a one-armed man. As Oliver Otis Howard climbed, the tropical air weighed him down, smothering and wet. The *Vixen* bobbed long and low in Santiago harbor, and there was little hope of catching an ocean breeze. To make it to the upper deck, Howard found himself focusing on his companion — the climb had to be worse for him. After weeks of fighting in Cuba, General William Shafter looked like a wrung-out rag, his usual cheery bloom grayed by fever, gout, and failure. A month earlier, a bold attack might have smashed the Spanish lines at Santiago de Cuba, but he had been obliged to settle instead for weeks of siege. Having finally captured the Spanish garrison, he told Howard he had "lost forty pounds of flesh" during the campaign. Even so, Howard estimated Shafter remained nearly twice his size — just a few inches taller, but a mountainous 270 pounds. It was remarkable that he could keep his wind.

In their sixties, the two men struggled upward, Shafter insisting that only the best vantage would do for a distinguished visitor. From the upper deck, he could show Howard what he had seen at first landing, from the beach at Aguadores north and east up to San Juan Hill, then west along the towering ridges behind the city toward El Cobre. As Shafter narrated recent events — the Spaniards' lethal Mauser fire, the treacherous crisscross of barbed wire at San Juan, the slowly tightening cordon of American forces — Howard looked out upon the city of Santiago. He saw past the chaos of docks that were "heaped," he wrote, "with every conceivable article of merchandise and government stores thrown together in reckless confusion." Instead, his eyes were drawn to the domes and steeples beyond, "Spanish towers," flamboyantly colored villas, palm groves and lush canopies of trees he could not name. Santiago rose along the foothills, terrace upon terrace, to the mountains beyond. It reminded him of Seattle, which he knew well from his days in the Department of the Columbia, or Naples, which he had visited the previous decade when he took seven months' leave from the army to tour Europe, Egypt, and Constantinople. But as much as Santiago inspired fond memories of the past, Howard was convinced he was seeing his nation's future.

Four years earlier, upon reaching the mandatory age of retirement for officers, Howard left his final command, the Department of the East at Governors Island, New York, with little fanfare. He and Lizzie moved to a rented house in Burlington, Vermont, near where his son Guy, rising in the officer ranks, had been posted with his wife and children. He traveled widely, lectured coast to coast, raised money for Howard University, and founded a second college near the Cumberland Gap in eastern Tennessee, Lincoln Memorial

University, for educating what he called "the youth of the mountains" — "a decided labor of love," he wrote.

Despite a busy and profitable life, as soon as Congress declared war on Spain in April 1898, Howard wanted back on the active list. "I have asked for a command six times," he told the *New York Tribune*. "I am hale and hearty and intend to get one before the war is over." Howard had reason to be optimistic. Freed by retirement to stump for political candidates, he had given scores of speeches throughout the country for William McKinley in 1896. At the Ohio Republican's inaugural parade, Howard had been chosen to lead the army veterans' contingent in the march from the Capitol to the White House. His partner on the stump, Russell Alger, became the new president's secretary of war. Howard could claim more influence in Washington than he had had since the 1870s. But the army, it seemed, had little use for a sixty-seven-year-old retiree, never mind his checkered combat record or frosty relationship with the commanding general, Nelson Miles.

Instead, Howard threw himself into a different struggle, what he called "Christian warfare." Wherever the military was training its forces or sending men on leave, a coalition of religious societies called the Army and Navy Christian Commission sought to steer them away from saloons, brothels, and gambling dens. The commission set up large tents and rented buildings where soldiers and sailors might write letters home, enjoy a cup of ice water while reading the latest newspaper, study the Bible and a range of religious tracts, and gather in fellowship to pray. By June, Howard was traveling to some of the

608

largest camps to assist in the commission's endeavors, inspire the men, and evangelize.

To season the troops for the coming fight, the army had established camps across the south. At Chickamauga, Mobile, and Tampa and even on the slow, stifling trains from one camp to the next, Howard preached to hundreds of young men who were days away from going to Cuba. At open-air meetings in fading sunlight and by flickering torch, he related Christ's sacrifice to the sacrifice of men in battle; a refrain of his sermons was "He died for me." At Chickamauga, near his first battles commanding the Army of the Tennessee, he experienced vivid memories of all the men, officers and soldiers, whom he saw die up close, right at his side. "I always felt that they died for me," he wrote. At Tampa, he saw even further back into the past. He had come to the very place where, forty-one years earlier, the path to God had opened up for him — where "my sins were blotted out," he wrote, and "I realized . . . that I had a wonderful and all-sufficient Savior." He shared his story with the men, knowing that such personal testimony could be "the most effective weapon in Christian warfare." Before they went off to fight and die, he wanted them to know "how simple it is to become a Christian. . . . The Lord will never fail to do his part."

By early July, Howard was marveling at news of stunning victories in Cuba, Puerto Rico, and the Philippines, where Commodore George Dewey had led a naval squadron that destroyed the Spanish Pacific fleet in six hours. The war seemed to be an act of Providence, and Howard saw other effects on the nation as equally heaven-sent. As he traveled and preached, he experienced something he had never felt during his career in the army and the Freedmen's Bureau: unqualified respect and esteem. The kindness made him very happy, but he took it to mean something more than that.

Through much of his life, he had come to represent, in his words, "the very incarnation of Yankee hostility." But the war on Spain "indicated a revolution in public sentiment," Howard wrote. The entire city of Mobile seemed decked in the Stars and Stripes, a sight he had never thought he would see. Wherever he went, the children and grandchildren of rebels greeted him with joy, even reached out to touch him. One of his most ardent audiences was an Alabama regiment, which gave him three cheers and then three more "for the old flag." On one leg of his travels, he was invited to ride in the private rail car of Joseph Wheeler, who had once commanded rebel cavalry against his men but now was leading a volunteer force to Cuba. Proudly wearing a blue uniform, Howard's former foe said with genuine warmth, "How glad I am to meet you again." Howard paid little mind to the fact that the southern regiments were all white, that the trains he rode separated white and black passengers, that just out of sight lynch mobs were murdering black men and women every few days. What he saw instead, for the first time in decades, was one unified nation. "Thank God," he said at one stop, "all the old hostility is gone. Forever gone!"

If Howard appreciated the irony "that it required another war to so reunite us," it was all the more joyous to him because the country seemed to be coming together for a particular cause: unshackling millions of people from Spanish oppression and governing them in ways that would foster happy, healthy, productive, and Christian lives. Finally, Howard thought, the nation was coalescing around principles he had championed in his work with the freedpeople and the Indians, principles the country had never before seemed ready to embrace. The South, the West, Cuba, Puerto Rico, and the Philippines — they all embodied the same cause, reconstructing the government into a force for kindness and benevolence, a government that was not "a mere machine," Howard wrote, but rather had heart and soul and would "give forth sympathy and aid to the destitute. . . . At last we have a Nation which cares for its children." As an old man no longer in uniform, his hair and beard completely white now, Howard was finding the redemption that he had spent earlier decades craving — for himself and his reputation and for a vision of American government that he considered the cause of his life. "With Porto Rico and the Philippines as our own, and with Cuba looking to us for protection, and the benefits of modern statecraft," he told an audience that winter, "we have entered upon a new and, to my mind, a glorious era."

From Tampa, Howard took a boat to Key West and accompanied the steamer *Niagara* as it carried Christian Commission materials to Guantánamo. At night off the southern coast of Cuba, the American fleet appeared to Howard as "a vast illuminated city." On July 27, he moved from the *Niagara* to the *Vixen,* a yacht that the navy had bought a few months earlier as it assembled its invasion fleet. Taking in Santiago from the upper deck, he thought about how the city's new military governor, the Boston-trained physician and Rough Rider commander Leonard Wood, was "working

611

grandly to root out" poverty and disease. "He cleans the city," Howard wrote, "introduces a system of drainage, and handsomely relieves impoverishment by employing able-bodied Cubans."

As he prepared to leave Santiago harbor on another boat, he was paid a call by a second dignitary stationed in the city: Clara Barton, in Cuba to run relief efforts by the Red Cross. In her late seventies and, in Howard's opinion, "evidently worn by the heat" if still showing "a calm sweet face, lighted with pleasant smiles," Barton needed to find a seat. Listening to her discuss the new military governor's efforts to distribute food, provide work, secure a safe water supply, and clean the city, Howard thought, "The world will rejoice."

But if Howard was seeing a promised land, he resisted the urge to set foot upon it. He had a busy schedule ahead of him — more preaching to troops back on the mainland, plus several paid lectures — and he did not want to risk a lengthy quarantine in Florida for malaria and yellow fever. Even though he never landed in Cuba, quarantine doctors kept Howard in Key West harbor for ten days. He gasped for air as his ship was fumigated. His valise was baked and treated with chemicals that scarred the leather and rusted the metal clasps. Although the ship's engineer lent Howard some netting, an assistant traveling with him had none. In one night, "abundant swarms" of mosquitoes — in Howard's words, "millions of . . . little savages" — rendered the man unrecognizable and just clinging to his sanity. Eyes swollen shut, "he had lost his philosophy," Howard wrote; "he had lost his quiet ways."

Despite the ordeal, Howard's belief in the wisdom and necessity — the blessing — of the Spanish-American War remained undimmed. Nor was his faith in the enterprise shaken when he traveled from Key West in a boat loaded with a thousand soldiers who were trembling and delirious with malaria. Though he had initially hoped the army would support and cooperate with Filipino patriots who had been fighting Spanish rule, Howard supported President McKinley's decision to annex the islands, a move at odds with the country's prior support for Cuban independence. And when Filipinos turned on American forces rather than submit to new colonial masters, Howard applauded the ensuing war of conquest. By the summer of 1899, Howard's oldest son Guy was fighting across the Pacific. As chief quartermaster for an army division, the meticulous, clean-shaven colonel was tasked with supplying food, medical supplies, guns, ammunition, and pack mules to soldiers fighting north of Manila. As Howard knew from his own experience in the West, officers in Guy's position laid the foundation of any army's success, all the more so with soldiers on unimaginably foreign terrain and supply lines spanning oceans. "The equipment and welfare of the corps," he wrote, "depends upon the ability of this staff officer." Guy, in his father's opinion, had reached the pinnacle of his profession. "I do not think I have ever met with an officer abler to plan a campaign or more thoroughly to execute one planned by another than he," Howard would write. Proud of his son's success, he felt no need to question the conflict.

Howard's unadulterated sense of triumph was short-lived. In late October 1899, two weeks before his sixty-ninth birthday, a telegram from the Philippines arrived in Burlington, Vermont, conveying news of Guy's death. He had been in the bow of a steam launch pulling barges up the Rio Grande de Pampanga, part of an effort to establish supply depots deep in the interior of Luzon Island. Insurgents hiding in the trees along the riverbanks opened fire. In the first volley, Guy was shot through his right lung, dying within moments.

"This is the heaviest blow that our family has had," Howard wrote. Unlike just about everyone they knew, Otis and Lizzie Howard had until then never experienced the loss of a child; all seven of theirs had reached adulthood. Guy left behind a widow and three children. Though the death forced Howard to stop and reflect, he never doubted the wisdom of battling Filipino insurgents in jungles eight thousand miles away. Instead, he took his son's last words to heart. Before dying, Guy had uttered one sentence: "Whatever happens keep the launch going." While President McKinley's opponents had begun to criticize the Philippines campaign as an un-American dalliance with empire, Howard dismissed "this talk about imperialism" as "nonsense." Even when his son's body was returned to the United States aboard a steamer called the *Belgian King* — a reference to Leopold II, whose brutal dominion over the Congo Free State was just coming to light — Howard refused to consider any parallel between the Philippines and the vast swathes of Asia and Africa being claimed by European powers. A caring administration that extended the reach of an elected president and Congress could never be an empire. "None of us want a king or an emperor," he said.

With McKinley running for reelection in 1900, Howard took to the stump once again, arguing in speeches from New York to Nebraska that the Philippines "should remain part and parcel of our domain." Long after the vote, he would say that with respect to the Filipinos the nation was bound to fulfill "what Providence has intended us to do, namely, Christianize them." In the years following Guy's death, Howard let his grief guide him. Just as the freedpeople on Edisto Island and Chief Joseph in the Wallowa Valley had refused to surrender the places where their fathers had died, now Howard felt an unshakeable commitment to the Philippines through his son. On podiums draped with flags, staring out at seas of men in identical straw boaters, he explained that the United States should never leave land where "some of our best men have shed their blood and lost their lives." It was an appeal that by one account could bring "unsentimental businessmen . . . almost to tears." While applause crescendoed into shouts of approval, Howard asked, "Shall that blood have been shed in vain? Shall the flag be pulled down? Shall all those heroes' deeds have gone for naught?"

Although hundreds of people had packed the local armory hall, their applause for the tall bearded man onstage was a shade shy of polite. There was little to do on a Saturday night in Baker City, a tiny county seat just below the Grande Ronde Valley on the west side of the Wallowa Mountains. A visiting orator who had come three hundred miles from Portland was bound to attract an audience. But even as Charles Erskine Scott Wood urged

615

the crowd to support William Jennings Bryan in the presidential election, people started taking bets that the county would go for McKinley instead. Four years earlier, in 1896, the area had been a Democratic Party stronghold. Allegiances began to sour, however, when the United States went to war with Spain. No one, it seemed, wanted to listen to a speech blasting American "imperialism."

The annexation of the Philippines raised more questions than answers for Wood. Initially a supporter of the war, he balked when the United States signed a treaty in December 1898 paying Spain $20 million for what the president called "the rights of sovereignty" over the Pacific islands, and McKinley proclaimed a policy of "benevolent assimilation." Defenders of "expansion" noted that the congressional resolution declaring war on Spain might have affirmed Cuba's independence and promised "to leave the government and control of the island to its people," but it had been silent on the question of the Philippines. Yet Wood declared it inconceivable that "this unselfish war for humanity was founded in hair splitting." After voting for McKinley in 1896, he felt that his basic sense of American democracy and freedom was being swept away by events. He spent much of the fall of 1900 crisscrossing Oregon for the Democrats.

"By what rule of war or morals have we been compelled . . . to assume sovereignty over the Filipinos against their will?" Wood asked in one speech. "If it was a war . . . to end Spanish oppression and misrule, and to establish a free and independent government in Cuba, what law . . . turns the same war into one of conquest and enforced government in Luzon?" Wood expressed particular indignation that shortly after the Battle of Manila Bay in 1898, the navy had all but promised Filipino independence, inviting and then transporting the exiled insurgency leader, Emilio Aguinaldo, back to the islands to lead native forces against the Spanish. To Wood, reneging on this promise required a belief that the Filipinos were unworthy of fair treatment. "Can we have a code of morals for A.," he wrote, "and a different code of morals for B.? . . . Where would you say . . . that a man stood who had in the matter of clearing land been treated as the Filipinos have been? Encouraged to go on, in the belief he was to own it."

Although Wood knew his position was unpopular, he was determined to challenge the direction of American power. He was confident he could be heard by virtue of who he was and what he had become. Recognized as one of Portland's leading lawyers, he had clients among the city's richest families. He continued to administer Lazard Frères's vast Oregon landholdings, had argued cases before the Supreme Court, and was about to serve as president of the Oregon Bar Association. He gave popular lectures with titles such as "How Success Is Won." The mansion and gardens that Nanny and he had built on their lots at Ford and Main Streets were described by one frequent visitor as "an enchantment . . . Bohemia without shabbiness." A team of servants kept the house running. The family had been shocked when their Chinese servant Guy, after working for them fifteen years, ran away with the Swedish second maid. Although Wood's finances remained slapdash — in 1897, he had to sell the fine Grolier

Club folios that lined his shelves to send young Erskine to Harvard — he was a fixture of elite clubs and civic boards. In Portland society he had assumed a particular and rarified station. "Men . . . who agree with him, men who disagree with him, men who know him only at a distance, unite in the assertion that C. E. S. Wood . . . is the most brilliant after-dinner speaker they have ever listened to, bar none," a journalist wrote. "They assert his scintillations revivify the broiled live lobsters at the feast and cause the electric lights to grow dim with envy."

Nearing fifty and seemingly at the peak of his influence, Wood continued to question the world in which he had brilliantly succeeded. He started to dress differently from everyone else in his social circle. His curls grew long and loose. He became indifferent to the wrinkles in the tweed suits he wore to work. And at formal gatherings, he traded the usual shirt fronts, "the stiff starched things that men wore in those days," in young Erskine's words, for shirts "of the finest handkerchief linen, with soft collars and bosoms of loose flowing pleats." His studs and cufflinks remained fine Tiffany opals, but the frills stood out in any room. At a dinner in New York in 1902, a journalist wrote that he "looked like some rare human exotic," someone who "might have taken the grand prize at a nineteenth century fashion show." "Had he not spoken," the account went, "his striking personality might have been remembered with an impression that he was probably a French poet or an Oriental prince traveling incognito."

At the same time, Wood began to regard his marriage as another social convention that he could shed. He loved his children and said he loved Nanny for the way she devoted herself to them. But he began imagining different possibilities with the women he worked and socialized with, his flirtatious manner taking on a hint of something more. Some of his lovers were social equals or better. Helen Ladd Corbett had been a client, a society matron about Wood's age, widowed young, who had inherited shares of two great Portland fortunes. Some were more vulnerable. His assistant, Kitty Seaman Beck, dark with sad eyes, was decades his junior, barely out of her teens, just divorced from a wealthy husband. "I am sure my mother knew of them," young Erskine would write of his father's affairs, "but she bore them, as ladies of her time often did, with resignation."

When Wood began speaking out against imperialism, he confronted the first serious personal criticism he had endured since Nelson Miles accused him of shirking his lieutenant's duties. When he stumped for Bryan, he was no longer a man of distinction. The *Oregonian,* which had never skimped on praise for his speeches and lectures, started calling him an "Anti," a "pretentious" "tangle-haired orator," and a "warm advocate of the 'scuttle' policy in the Philippines" who had a loose grip on the facts. Nevertheless, from Portland to Baker City and back to the Dalles, Wood kept going through the election season and beyond. He became a champion of the Democratic Party and one of its most visible members. In 1902, Oregon's Democrats put him forward as their candidate for the Senate. Blasted by the *Salem Statesman* as "a vote against retention of the Philippines" that would be "suicidal to the

619

interests of the State," Wood was soundly defeated. But he kept asking questions and searching for answers, drifting ever farther from the consensus view. Addressing a Democratic Party Club in Manhattan that year, he went so far as to confess, "As for myself, I do not know whether I am a Democrat or not." By 1906, Wood was publicly proclaiming himself an anarchist who believed in "peace and right without a ruler." When the widely feared anarchist Emma Goldman came to Portland to give a speech in 1908, Wood hosted her, putting her up in his mistress Kitty Seaman Beck's apartment. Goldman praised his "passionate yearning for a new and free arrangement of life," a "brilliancy of . . . mind" and "deep humanity" that could not help but "exert an influence even on the most conservative." But the *Oregonian* was immune to Wood's charms, deriding the way he professed "anarchy, socialism, [and] free love" while remaining a darling of high society, basking "in all the beauty and glory and social advantages of elegant life."

On the stump in 1900, Wood tried many different arguments against empire. He warned, as many southern Democrats were doing, of the dangers of absorbing "an Asiatic population of mixed blood," millions of "yellow, naked mongrels" and coolie laborers. Yet as Wood tried to stoke white fear, he also maintained that everyone regardless of race had equal rights that the American government was bound to respect. "Is it time, or is it not time . . . that men have a right to life, liberty and happiness; to pursue their own life in their own way, and to have some voice in the law to which they yield obedience?" he asked. "If it be true, then the savage has an unalienable

620

right to live in a palm-thatched hut and eat raw fish if he finds there greater happiness, rather than be well housed and fed in the rice fields of the tax gatherer."

If the outrages in the Philippines had any parallel in Wood's experience, it was the Nez Perce War, in which, he wrote in 1895, "Joseph cannot accuse the Government of the United States of one single act of justice." Early on he dismissed the analogy, writing, "Though the Indian has been a plundered being from the beginning, still our actual conflicts with him have been brought on by his own bloody outrages calling for repression and revenge." But he came to see the continuity from one conquest to the next. He started writing at length about Indians for the first time in years. From 1898 to 1901, he put together a collection of folktales that he had heard over the course of his army service, including two Nez Perce stories that his interpreters told him during the long chase. And when he was asked in 1900 to comment on Joseph, his answer could have easily been about the Philippines. The treaties with the tribe had been rigged, he wrote, and the surrender agreement violated on an indefensible technicality "the firm expectation of *everyone* . . . that Joseph and his people were to be sent back to the Department of the Columbia." "What constitutes Justice and good faith is nowadays matter of opinion," he wrote. "If you consider . . . Indians bound by rules and customs they never heard of and repudiate as soon as stated then this was 'just.' "

On the campaign trail, President McKinley's running mate Theodore Roosevelt justified the conquest of the Philippines on the grounds that the Nez Perce War constituted a far worse injustice

621

and that the Filipino rebel leader Aguinaldo "stands infinitely below Chief Joseph." But Wood refused to accept his friend's logic, that the events of 1877 provided moral cover for turning the republic into an empire. Drawing the opposite lesson, Wood continued to recite Joseph's surrender speech, and in a way it forged new paths for him. In the closing line to a speech he called "Imperialism vs. Democracy," he inverted the chief's promise "from where the sun now stands" to "fight no more forever." "Were I a Filipino," Wood said, "and . . . I watched coming from the East across the sea, the strong, Young Giant of the West, the bitterness to find he came with hammer and sword, not to strike off my shackles but to rivet them faster, . . . I would fight, fight, fight till the sun was blotted from my eyes."

Even on the loveliest days in June, the road into the Wallowa Valley was vicious, a narrow snaking mountain trail that for mile after mile held its riders on death's edge. It was almost too much for the two horses and light buggy that US Indian Inspector James McLaughlin had hired to convey Chief Joseph back to his old home. Despite thirty years of rugged field experience — joining the Standing Rock Sioux on their last great buffalo hunt in 1882, ordering the arrests that led to the shooting of Sitting Bull in 1890 — McLaughlin found the journey "frightful," "wearisome," and "wretchedly bad." But the twenty-mile mountain crossing must have been deeply familiar to Joseph.

At McLaughlin's side, the chief started remembering the first days of summer in 1877, almost exactly twenty-three years earlier. He spoke of the killings along the Salmon River, the cavalry's approach at White Bird Canyon. "He warmed to his story," McLaughlin would write. "The chief was very near to fighting his battles over again that day." Already well briefed on Nez Perce claims to the Wallowa Valley, the inspector listened intently to the chief's own version of the history, fully aware that hearing an account directly from Joseph's mouth presented a precious opportunity — something worth committing to writing, something people would pay to read.

The two men had left the Colville reservation together five days earlier, on June 11, 1900. Joseph and McLaughlin were both about sixty years old. The Indian inspector was almost as tall as the chief. Their suits had a similar cut. While McLaughlin wore a tie, Joseph tucked his braids into a dark kerchief knotted around his neck. Both wore their hair sweeping up from their foreheads — McLaughlin's curly and white, matching the soft arc of his grand mustache, Joseph's straight and still black. It had taken a day to reach Spokane and another to reach Lapwai, where they expanded their traveling party by three. Edward Raboin, a longtime interpreter for the Nez Perce agency, was also almost sixty, short, round, and balding, darker than the inspector but lighter than the chief; his mother was Nez Perce, his father white. Two younger men, both allies of Joseph's on the Idaho reservation, joined the group. Peopeo Tholekt had settled near Lapwai after returning from exile in Canada. A young man during the war, he had reached his midforties, thick-browed and strong, braids draped from shoulder to chest and tied together over his heart. Phillip Andrews had been a boy during the war, maybe fourteen years old. His left eye was covered with a large black patch.

Lapwai to the Wallowa Valley was the shortest leg of the journey, only about ninety miles, but the trip took two full days. As the men struggled along the mountain trail, another wagon going the opposite direction blocked their path. With no room to pass, Joseph's party did what some of the very first settlers had done as they crossed over from the Grande Ronde Valley: on the side of the trail, by a sheer drop, they dismantled their buggy, let the other wagon pass, and then put it back together again.

Riding into the valley on the morning of June 16, McLaughlin could not imagine that Joseph recognized the place. He had always pictured the Wallowa country in its natural state as a desert. None of his reading had disabused him of the notion, which fit the Indian Bureau's drive to turn nomadic tribes into farmers. Now, McLaughlin saw, the valley "blooms as the rose," with every acre seemingly fenced and furrowed, streams diverted for irrigation, apple and plum orchards extending in orderly rows. "Towns and villages stood," the inspector would write, "where the pony-herds of the Nez Perces were wont to graze on the scant grass."

As Joseph well knew, the valley had never been a desert. To McLaughlin's surprise, the chief seemed unfazed by the signs of settlement. He had come in hopes of claiming some property and moving back. The land's appearance might have changed, but it still called to him. Although McLaughlin had wondered why Joseph was so adamant about that one valley — was it a play to maintain his leadership position as he aged? —

the inspector could see that "the man had in him a strong love for the soil." Joseph was determined to press on with his errand.

For more than twenty years, Joseph had maintained that the valley belonged to his people and that he could change the government's policies by doing more or less what he had done before the war: cultivating allies near and far, arguing his case whenever the opportunity presented itself. He had no reason to think otherwise. During his years in the Indian Territory, now called Oklahoma, a succession of bureaucrats had vowed that the Nez Perce captives would be exiled forever; even General Howard had urged Joseph to stop dreaming of home and make the best of his new life. But still he tried to reopen the issue, using his celebrity to stay in the national limelight and align thousands of voices in his favor. Forever, it turned out, would only last eight years. Joseph and his people found their way homeward, and it became widely assumed among officials in Washington that Nez Perce title to the Wallowa Valley had never been properly extinguished. At the Colville reservation, he had worked for better terms for his people and was soon getting regular permission to travel throughout the Northwest. If some of the Indian agents were hostile, others proved friendly, and General Miles's and General Gibbon's support gave Joseph leverage against the civilian bureaucrats.

Five years after refusing to accept an allotment on the Idaho reservation, Joseph traveled east to the capital in April 1897 to petition the acting commissioner of Indian affairs for land in the Wallowa Valley. Although the petition met with a quick denial, Joseph took heart from the commissioner's refusal to "say positively that there were no vacant lands available." In the meantime, he continued to search for other sources of authority. He sought out Alice Fletcher, now a research scientist at the Smithsonian Institution after her work allotting the Nez Perce lands. During their interview, she asked the chief and his retinue to sing into an Edison recording machine, funneling Joseph's voice onto beeswax cylinders. He chose to perform war songs. He continued on to New York, where he sat in a place of honor at Buffalo Bill Cody's Wild West Show at Madison Square Garden, rode in the grand marshal's honor guard during the daylong dedication of Grant's Tomb, and held court "in full Indian toggery," one newspaper reported, on the plush sofas of the luxurious Republican redoubt, the Fifth Avenue Hotel, where Party kingmakers Mark Hanna and Thomas Platt and members of President McKinley's cabinet visited him. There, he was reunited with Lovell Jerome, the lieutenant and onetime hostage who had been exchanged for him during the final battle. Now a customs inspector, Jerome promptly wrote the *New York Tribune* with the exhortation that "twenty long years of banishment . . . have certainly atoned for what Chief Joseph did in simply protecting his own home. Send the Nez Perces home at once. Repair the wrongs the Government did in not protecting them." Some of his other callers, Joseph would recall, pledged to "ask the Government" or "ask Washington to let me go back to my old home." Nelson Miles encouraged him to keep making his claim. Even "Buffalo Bill said I could go to Wallowa to live," Joseph wrote, "and no one would care."

A couple of years later, in the summer of 1899, Joseph decided to see if Cody was right. He made a first trip back to the Wallowa Valley and found Anderson Corden Smith, who had built the toll road from the Grande Ronde Valley in 1872 and had invited Joseph to La Grande to lodge his protest that Fourth of July. The onetime mountain man now practiced law in the Wallowa County seat, a town called Enterprise. Joseph asked Smith to assemble a gathering of local citizens — the kind of invitation he used to make to the settlers a generation before.

In a crowded hall, the chief said through his interpreter, according to one account, "that this country was always considered as belonging to his people and he would like to know who sold this country to the whites." He then told the crowd that he had been to Washington "and laid the matter before the officials there," claiming that "they told him to come back here and pick out the section he wanted, then notify them and steps would be taken to secure it for him and his tribe." For two decades, valley residents had celebrated their connection to Chief Joseph. Much of their civic identity drew from their encounters with the man. One of the newspapers they read was called the *Chieftain.* Near Wallowa Lake was the town of Joseph. And they constantly told stories of visits and conversations with the chief. But the *Chieftain* reported that when he actually stood before them and made what seemed to him like a modest request — the place of his birth in the Imnaha River canyons, the area where his father was buried, and the land around the lake — "considerable sport was made of the old man."

Undaunted by the rebuff, Joseph returned to

Washington in March 1900 and once again petitioned the commissioner of Indian affairs to relocate his band to the Wallowa Valley. Less formally, Joseph visited General Miles at the War Department and prevailed upon him, the *Washington Times* reported, "to use his influence to secure the removal of their tribe . . . back to their old home in the highlands of Oregon." Miles took time out from overseeing the conquest of the Philippines to write the Office of Indian Affairs in favor of Joseph's request. When it seemed the petition would be denied, Joseph asked for another meeting and convinced the office to send an inspector with Joseph to the valley "for the purpose of ascertaining whether land sufficient and suitable could be found therein for making allotments to him and his band." The government, it seemed, fully acknowledged the legitimacy of Joseph's claim.

By the time McLaughlin and Joseph reached the Wallowa County seat at noon on June 16, 1900, the Indian inspector had largely made up his mind. The beauty of the verdant, blooming valley made a conclusive argument for keeping it in white hands. After the obvious expense of so much labor, it was only fair that the settlers would get the land. "There is grave doubt whether the title to the land ever passed out of the hands of Joseph and his people by any binding treaty," McLaughlin would write, but "it is enough that the white man has turned the desert into a garden, that he should enjoy the profit of his enterprise."

In the town of Enterprise, the inspector examined deeds and land sales, calculating that property for Joseph's band would cost the government hundreds of thousands of dollars. He talked to locals about the effect of so much agriculture on traditional hunting and fishing areas, reporting that "the game ha[d] almost entirely disappeared," while irrigation ditches had disrupted and destroyed the salmon spawns in local rivers. He rode with the chief down to Wallowa Lake, noting that it had become a popular summer resort.

At nearby Joseph, the chief greeted the town's mayor and said "that he was ready to return to Wallowa Valley with his people." Joseph's friend Phillip Andrews remembered the mayor responding, "This is your land, but I can make you no promise as to your return. We will both have to depend on the Government for that." Despite the courtesy the inspector felt they had been given everywhere they stopped, valley residents had started circulating petitions against the return of Joseph's band. "It is preposterous to even dream of turning the results of so much labor over to a band of lazy, shiftless Indians," one newspaper in Enterprise opined. In quiet conversation with McLaughlin, some citizens passed along ominous predictions: "Should the Indians be returned to the Wallowa Valley to remain permanently, Joseph would be assassinated within a year."

Resting in Lewiston after the arduous journey out of the mountains, Joseph told McLaughlin that even through the war, he had always believed he would be able to negotiate for the Wallowa Valley. "If I could remain safe at a distance and talk straight to the men that would be sent by the Great Father, I could get back the Wallowa Valley and return in peace," the inspector remembered the chief saying. "That is why I did not allow my young men to kill and destroy the white settlers after I began to fight. I wanted to leave a clean trail, and if there were dead soldiers in that trail I could not be held to blame."

Despite the chief's faith in his perpetual ability to negotiate with the government, upon parting ways with Joseph, McLaughlin immediately began preparing the report rejecting the chief's petition once and for all. With a population of six thousand, the valley had no room for Joseph's band of 150, the inspector wrote. Much of his band had never known the Wallowa country and seemed to consider the Colville reservation home. But ultimately, the inspector feared that if Joseph were allowed to live "anywhere in northeastern Oregon," an entire skein of government policy would come unraveled. Indians would be "constantly visiting there," McLaughlin wrote, "especially the renegade and loafer element." Joseph represented a type that McLaughlin called "a non-progressive Indian, who will not work, and . . . the advancement of his people is greatly retarded by his attitude and influence which does not encourage industrial pursuits." The Indian agents of earlier generations had constantly warned that no one would ever settle into a Christian farming life as long as nomadic Dreamers presented any kind of alternative. Nothing, in McLaughlin's view, had changed. He worried that Joseph's return to the Wallowa country risked "creating a feeling of discontent" that would induce otherwise happy Nez Perce farmers on the Idaho reservation to give up their allotments and join the chief.

Shortly after being informed of the decision, Joseph dictated a letter expressing bafflement with McLaughlin's conclusions. "There are many white people there now," he said, "but I told the inspector I would be satisfied with some land on one side of the river where there were only a few whites, and where creeks and mountains afforded good pasturage. I would be happy with very little." Back at Nespelem, Joseph continued to hold out hope. But he felt old. He was easily winded. His dreams started to shrink. He wanted less Wallowa land but also knew he had little time to enjoy it. In the end, what had always mattered most about the valley was the bones buried beneath it.

After visiting the town named for him, Joseph had led McLaughlin north and west along the Wallowa River to his father's burial site. In the late spring of 1877, as Joseph's band frantically prepared to depart the valley, the chief had asked the settler who claimed the area to promise to keep the site safe. The settler gave him his word but before long dug up the skull of Tuekakas and offered it to his brother-in-law for display in his dentist's office in nearby Baker City. But in the warm sunshine of June 1900, Joseph only saw that the grave remained marked and fenced, respected and apparently undisturbed. It was the place he had pledged to keep. It signified everything he had lost. "The heart of Joseph . . . was melted," McLaughlin wrote, "and he wept." The experience marked Joseph in the months that followed. "When I die," Joseph said shortly afterward, "I want to be buried there."

CHAPTER 24
SWING LOW

For a generation, survivors of the Nez Perce War hesitated to talk about their experiences. Fearing reprisals from reservation authorities, local settlers, and "treaty" Nez Perce Indians who had stayed loyal to the United States throughout the summer of 1877, they lived with their secrets. Remnants of old struggles, rifles and war shirts and clubs and whistles, were hidden away. Dozens of people who converted to Christianity in the Indian Territory took new names and wiped their pasts clean before settling on the Lapwai reservation. Few people knew and no one revealed that one of the former exiles, John Minthorn, had once been called Wetyetmas Wahyakt, or Swan Necklace, and that he had been among the first to draw blood along the Salmon River, with Wahlitits and Sarpsis Ilppilp — and was the only one of the three to survive what followed.

Chief Joseph, by contrast, felt compelled to speak about the past. The crime of the 1863 treaty that ceded the Wallowa Valley, the injustice of Howard's ultimatum in the spring of 1877, the good faith of the Nez Perce families trying to outrun the army, the brutality of the pursuing soldiers, the broken promises of surrender, and the ordeal of exile: Joseph's command of his people's history enabled him to connect with white audiences and press the levers of power. He was laying a foundation not just for rights to a particular piece of land but for a broader claim to fair and equal treatment by the government and to freedoms that all Americans could expect to enjoy.

In spite of these efforts, Joseph and his band were constantly being consigned to the distant past and to anecdotes of quaint encounters, even by people who appeared sympathetic to their cause. In the summer of 1901, a tall, wiry man with a close gray-flecked beard visited Joseph at Nespelem. The journey had taken Edmond Meany several days, from sleeper train to branch line to horse-drawn carriage. With meals, gifts for Joseph and several Colville agency officials, and a liberal supply of cigars for himself, it cost him more than $33.50. But the expense was worth it for Meany, and Joseph was delighted to see him. Though countless people had sought the chief out since 1877, Meany was the first who claimed to be a historian.

Before embracing the scholar's life, Meany had been a Washington state representative and tireless civic booster, promoting the state's ambitious pavilion at the 1893 Columbian Exposition in Chicago as a means of attracting newcomers to the Northwest. A driving force in the legislature for expanding and modernizing the University of Washington, he envisioned an institution that could rival the great public universities of the Midwest. His faith in his state's limitless prospects sparked a fascination with its pioneers, particularly the missionary Marcus Whitman, betrayed by what Meany called "miserable Cayuse fiends," and Isaac Stevens, the territorial governor whose ten treaties with Indian tribes in the 1850s established the first reservations in the region. Meany amassed a library of scholarly works and historical documents and in 1896 began to teach "The Development of the Northwest" at the university and to lecture throughout Washington. Meanwhile, he spent summers at the University of Wisconsin, learning the methods and practice of history from some of the leading minds of the day. For a course on the history of the American West with Frederick Jackson Turner, he elected to write his master's thesis on Chief Joseph, "to examine all possible evidence that this product of American savagery may be more fairly judged."

In many ways what Meany was learning at Wisconsin confirmed what he already believed. He often described history as an inevitable progression from what he called "the stages of savagery into barbarism and through the stages of barbarism into civilization." Professor Turner had become famous for defining the American experience in terms of the nation's cycles from frontier to settlement, as "the buffalo trail became the Indian trail, and this became the trader's 'trace;' the trails widened into roads, and the roads into turnpikes, and these in turn were transformed into railroads." This grand narrative of continuous progress fit Meany's sense of the Northwest, and looking out at the rest of the world, he saw the same processes at work. As he left Seattle for Madison, many of his students were leaving to fight in Cuba and the Philippines, a struggle that Meany believed showed an "Anglo-Saxon" resolve to bring enlightenment to the benighted places of the globe, echoing the wars of conquest over the Indians of the Northwest in the 1850s.

But as much as Meany's graduate education felt familiar, his professors also advocated less comfortable and less systematic modes of engaging with the past. Turner wanted his students to "discard [their] conception that there are standard ultimate histories," opting instead for a broader look at "all the spheres of man's activity . . . history as politics, history as art, history as economics, history as religion." History did not solely concern society's winners, Turner insisted. "Wherever there remains a chipped flint, a spear-head, a piece of pottery, a pyramid, a picture, a poem, a coloseum, or a coin, there is history," he wrote. In producing these new, more open accounts of the American past, another professor of Meany's, Wisconsin Historical Society director Reuben Gold Thwaites, modeled a hands-on approach that demanded extensive fieldwork. Thwaites visited with Indians on reservations and during seasonal hunts. He canoed down rivers, flavored his narratives with his own observations, and, Turner would write, "saw his characters, not as lay figures, but vividly and dramatically as real people." In deciding to write about Chief Joseph and visit him at the Colville reservation, Meany was trying to follow the ideas and methods his professors had been modeling.

After crossing the Columbia River on a cable ferry, Meany rode through the Colville reservation with a schoolteacher who had transcribed Joseph's letters and a subagent who could interpret for him in Chinook Jargon. The reservation seemed fragile to the historian. After the allotments of the early 1890s, the federal government had sold off the northern half to whites, but the tribes had never been paid for their land. Now, in the southern hills, he saw "a constant stream of prospectors." Just two miles from Nespelem, he visited a mining camp, its dull dynamite blasts followed by panicked cries from the Nez Perce pony herds.

If threats to the reservation abounded, the graceful stretch of land where Joseph's band had settled felt to Meany like a sanctuary. Welcomed into the chief's teepee, the historian was impressed by its "model appearance of neatness," which matched Joseph's "quiet and unassuming dignity which compels the respect of all who come in contact with him." As Joseph's wives were busy doing "all the work about the home," Meany wrote, the chief began talking about routine concerns — government cattle rations "not so good as used to be," neighboring tribes stealing from his herds. He was telling Meany what he might have told anyone else visiting him on the reservation. "Always wanted to go to Wallowa so he could be by himself with his own people," Meany jotted in a small notebook. "Wants to go back to Wallowa so as to die where his father and mother died for he is now getting old."

Meany pressed Joseph on subjects the chief usually reserved for his journeys far from home. As he went about his routine chores and errands — saddling a pony, unharnessing a team, taking an iron tool for digging camas to be recut into spikes for picketing horses — Joseph reminisced about the war. He mimed how one woman who lived nearby at Nespelem had been shot through the legs at the Big Hole massacre but still managed to climb a horse and shoot back at the soldiers. In the dirt floor of the blacksmith's shop, he scratched a map of the final battle. Twenty-four years later, he claimed to know exactly where his brother Ollokot, Looking Glass, and Toohoolhoolzote had died, "where his men and women were and where he and Miles met to shake hands," Meany wrote. The historian tried to copy the map onto a piece of paper.

Over the course of a couple of days, Meany transcribed the names of "the principal ones in Joseph's band" but talked to very few of them. One exception, the Palouse leader Husishusis Kute, recalled at length people who had escaped from the final battle, others who had been killed — "a friend whose wife was blind could not see where to run shot 8 times died two days from wounds," Meany scrawled — and the mules he had stolen from General Howard at the Camas Meadows. But the historian spent no time with Two Moons, now nearing seventy, nor did he find the man he listed as " 'Yellow Wolf' 40 yrs <in war>." He learned the names of Joseph's wives, who both survived the war, but nothing of their experiences. Joseph suggested he talk to one woman, but she just happened to be away, down at the Lapwai reservation. A year earlier, the Indian inspector McLaughlin had suspected the chief was trying to steer him to people who favored moving to the Wallowa Valley. So too with Meany, Joseph seemed to be curating the historian's experiences on the reservation, or shielding his people from an outsider with unclear motives.

Sensing the value of their meeting, Meany asked for the chief's autograph and had his interpreters sign the page as witnesses. But the historian left

Nespelem with little material that deviated from the standard accounts of the war that he had already consulted, including General Howard's book and the essays that Erskine Wood published in the *Century*. He still thought of Joseph as a military mastermind. And if he was convinced that "the methods employed by the Government to take away those lands would puzzle a wiser head than Joseph's," the primary lesson he drew from the chief's miming of the Big Hole battle was that "soldiers could not be blamed" for killing women and children.

Meany knew that the chief was thinking about the future. He kept his band together, taking the lead at festivals, funerals, and parades. The teacher at the Nez Perce school reported that Joseph cared deeply about the next generation. "He often visits the school, at which times the Indian children would remain almost motionless," Meany wrote. "On several occasions he administered light punishment to some of the little ones, who were not progressing to suit him."

But the experience of sitting at Joseph's side did nothing to shake Meany's long-held conviction that Indians belonged only to the past. As much as Joseph commanded his respect, the chief struck him as a dying breed, of a piece with the buffalo robes that Joseph's wives rolled into huge bundles each morning and pushed to the edge of the teepee. "Now quite scarce among the Indians," Meany wrote, the robes had to be decades old. As the historian admired them, Joseph reached into one and pulled out a small leather trunk. Inside were letters and photographs, an eagle-feather headdress, a bright red blanket appliquéd with little mirrors and two otter skins sewed nose to nose. Joseph lived surrounded by mementoes and keepsakes.

Joseph showed the historian a portrait of his brother, taken in Walla Walla after meeting with General Howard in the spring of 1877. He told Meany, "Considers his father greatest Indian Chief he knew. Next to him was Ollicutt." Joseph took out a picture of himself with Buffalo Bill, and another of James Reuben, Howard's Nez Perce scout who followed the captives to the Indian Territory and worked as their teacher. According to Meany, "he knew each face and seemed glad to call up memories of his friends and relatives." Most precious of all was a tintype of his daughter Sound of Running Feet. "He seems especially fond of her memory," the historian wrote, "and tells what a good girl she was while showing her picture." It had been taken after she had settled on the Lapwai reservation and been baptized, educated, and married. On the back, she had written three lines, an inscription her father could not read: "For Chief Joseph / from his loving Daughter / Mrs. Sarah Moses."

Despite Meany's impression that Joseph was leading a "quiet life" as a "ward of the Government," the chief continued to travel throughout the country to advocate the return of his people to the Wallowa Valley. In 1903 and 1904, he petitioned the interior secretary, the commissioner of Indian affairs, and members of Congress, and he met Theodore Roosevelt twice in the White House, seeking a personal intervention on his behalf. "The President greeted the chief cordially," a Washington newspaper reported, "said he had read of Chief Joseph's campaigns, and knew he was a great soldier, and that he would do what he could for him." His "determined persistency" reminded one newspaper in Nez Perce country of his efforts thirty years earlier to secure President Grant's 1873 executive order reserving part of the Wallowa Valley for his people. Countering the histories told by people like Meany, Joseph had never stopped pushing the government toward something resembling justice for his people.

The chief's celebrity was also undimmed. Twenty-four years after the sensation of his first White House reception, he remained the star attraction during his visit to Washington. Nelson Miles threw a luncheon in Joseph's honor at his home. The head of the Smithsonian's Bureau of Ethnology asked the chief to sit for a life cast. He was brought to New York to headline Cummins' Indian Congress at Madison Square Garden, the causes and concerns of his life distilled into "twenty thrilling . . . military and gymnastic feats," the *Times* reported, climaxing in a crowd-pleasing stagecoach robbery. Meany invited him to Seattle in November 1903. When the two men stood puffing cigars on the sidelines of a University of Washington football game, players left the muddy field midgame to shake Joseph's hand amid deafening cheers for the chief. Through it all, though, Joseph persisted in speaking of the Wallowa Valley. To Meany's students, he said, "I have made frequent visits to Washington and have met many persons high in official life. They have all promised to render their assistance, but it has been, wait, wait, wait."

Oliver Otis Howard was having trouble seeing, but he felt the bitter air. The early months of 1904 had been so busy that friends and family worried the seventy-three-year-old retired general would not be able to endure all the train travel. After Iowa and Chicago in January, he was lining up meetings and lectures in New York, Washington, DC, and Northampton. But first, he stopped in Carlisle, Pennsylvania, at the urging of a friend and admirer, a recently retired army colonel named Richard Henry Pratt. Finally off the train, in need of a bath, a meal, and a nap, Howard thought it so cold that he could have been home in Vermont.

Pratt had served in the army forty years but for the last twenty-five had worked as superintendent of a boarding school for Indian children at the old barracks in Carlisle. He had founded the school in the fervent belief that removed from the influences of their tribes, Indian children would gain, in his words, "a full fair chance to become assimilated with our people and our industries." Taken from their reservations, students at the Indian Industrial School were given new names, forced to speak English, pressured to embrace Christianity, and trained to be seamstresses, smiths, carpenters, and harness makers. "All the Indian there is in the race should be dead," he famously said in an 1892 speech. "Kill the Indian in him, and save the man." Through constant drills and chores and with military-style discipline, Pratt believed, his charges could "be made to feel all the advantages of a civilized life." Although the school educated girls as well as boys, he wrote that his students would experience "the manhood of supporting [themselves] and of standing out alone and battling for life as an American citizen."

Howard supported what Pratt called his "common-sense method" to assimilate Indians into citizenship by "compelling participation in our affairs." "It does not seem to be difficult to teach Indian boys and girls of every tribe our code of morals," Howard would write. "The most pronounced success in moral and Christian teaching is where the children are separated from the degrading influences of their rough life." Shortly before the general left the Department of the Columbia for West Point, he had encouraged his longtime aide and fellow evangelist Melville Wilkinson to lead a similar effort, the Forest Grove Indian Training School, just west of Portland.

For more than twenty years, the general and the colonel worked together on various matters relating to missionary efforts with Indians. Even in his old age, Howard had maintained his national profile as a champion of the Republican Party and its current policies but also the embodiment of a noble past. President Roosevelt described him as "*that living veteran* of the Civil War whom this country *most* delights to honor." On his deathbed, General Sherman chose Howard to organize his funeral services. Pratt told Howard that he could not imagine a better speaker on the occasion of his school's twenty-fifth anniversary. "It . . . ought to be an especially memorable one to us all," he wrote. "Your coming will very greatly help to make it so." Old soldiers in the area were sure to come see Howard, and Pratt wrote that he would be inviting "our best townspeople" to a special reception in the general's honor.

Arriving in Carlisle a couple of days early, Howard was pleased to learn that more than a thousand children were being educated at Pratt's institution, its forty-three graduates the largest senior class in the school's history. An enormous crowd — several thousand by one estimate — thronged the school grounds for the event. Pratt had tried to give Howard some advance notice of other dignitaries who would share the dais with him. John P. S. Gobin, Pennsylvania's former lieutenant governor, may have been a familiar face. A former Union Army general, he was active in the same veterans groups — the Grand Army of the Republic, the Military Order of the Loyal Legion — that claimed much of Howard's time. Sheldon Jackson, too, was undoubtedly known to Howard from his days in the Department of the Columbia onward. A Presbyterian minister and the government's general agent in charge of educating native children in Alaska, Jackson was making a special trip to the school he viewed as a model for his own efforts "to train up English speaking American citizens."

But Howard was preoccupied, unsettled even, by the final distinguished guest. Chief Joseph had interrupted his visit to Washington, DC, to attend the commencement exercises at Carlisle. The general had briefly encountered him seven years before during the dedication of Grant's Tomb. Howard had come to New York with his youngest son Harry to lead the Civil War veterans marching in the parade. When he heard that Joseph would be attending Buffalo Bill's Wild West Show, Howard had gone to Madison Square Garden and approached him, "but paused almost in the act of holding out his hand," the *New York Times* reported, "as if he were in doubt whether his presence might not cause pain to the chief." The general said, "I am glad to see you, Joseph; glad to see you!" Harry Howard remembered that Joseph stood, "but did not smile or shake hands with General Howard. . . . My father appeared a little disappointed at Joseph's old-time stolidity without showing cordiality."

At Carlisle, the two old foes sat side by side. Before the graduation, they shared a meal. Joseph looked tired, his eyelids sagging, wrinkles cutting deep. While he wore bright blankets and intricate beadwork on his official visits in the capital, for the commencement exercises he was dressed like the general: in a dark suit, white collared shirt beneath it. His hair was still combed up from his head, but it had thinned. It ran down to his chest without feathers, unwrapped by hides or ribbons. His ears were unadorned.

Colonel Pratt handed out the diplomas and, in what would be his final speech to a graduating class, pitched his remarks broadly, advocating the eradication of all tribes so that the Indians could better assimilate into the American family. When Howard stood to speak, his eyes, which he described as "uncertain," may not have been able to take in the graduates, their classmates, or the mass of onlookers. No matter — when his reedy voice sounded, it was as if he had an audience of one. His emotion was palpable as he "feelingly referred to old Chief Joseph," a newspaper reported. Howard quickly justified removing Joseph's people from the Wallowa Valley but attributed the Indian resistance to a lack of assimilation to American democratic values — the innocent ignorance that, in his mind, institutions like the Indian Industrial School were meant to correct. "A majority" of Nez Perce bands "had agreed to leave" by signing the 1863 treaty, he asserted. "But Joseph and White Bird and Looking Glass . . . did not agree to the treaty because they did not understand that a majority rules."

Howard's words grew more personal as he went on. In simple terms he sought a kind of absolution from Joseph. "The Indians rebelled and I was sent to carry out the government's instructions," he said. "I could not do otherwise. . . . I would have done anything to avoid the war, even to giving my life. But the time had come when we had to fight." He tried to find some transcendence in the conflict. "There come times," he continued, "when a fight is a mighty good thing and when it is over let's lay down all our feelings and look up to God and see if we cannot get a better basis on which to live and work together." And ultimately, he wanted something more. After decades of denying that he had any reason to feel guilt over his role in the Nez Perce War, he came as close as he ever would to admitting that the experience had haunted him. He called on Congress to pay reparations to Joseph's band. "Nothing is ever settled," he said, "until justice is done."

When Howard took his seat, Colonel Pratt turned to Joseph. Even in Western clothes, the chief seemed to be an emblem of what Pratt had devoted his career to eradicating, those Indians who valued tradition and autonomy over progress and assimilation. "Joseph would not go on his reservation," the colonel told the crowd. "He really never did go there." When the chief and his people had been captives at Fort Leavenworth, Pratt tried to have dozens of Nez Perce children sent to the Hampton Institute, where blacks and Indians both were being educated for citizenship and absorption. But "he had fixed his mind against it," Pratt recalled. "Joseph said he would not let the children go anywhere until he knew what the Government was going to do with him." Even so, Pratt admitted, "I always regarded Chief Joseph as one of our great Indians." "I . . . am glad he came here," the colonel said. "We have much sympathy for him. He has been a great heroic man in his way and has been through great trouble."

Joseph rose and looked out at the crowd. The children in front of him had marched in formation wearing dark blue uniforms with red trim. The boys' hair had been cut short. Many had not spoken their tribal languages in months or even years. They played football. They slept in army barracks. The school was not simply turning them into white people — by every appearance it seemed to be turning them into soldiers. From the dais Howard was watching the chief.

The chief began speaking through his interpreter. For once, an Indian at Carlisle was not punished for speaking in his native tongue. "Friends, I meet here my friend, Gen. Howard," he said. "I used to be so anxious to meet him. I wanted to kill him in war. To-day I am glad . . . to be friends with Gen. Howard. We are both old men, still we live and I am glad." At last, in a moment that the general found deeply moving, Joseph gave Howard unconditional forgiveness. Despite a lifetime of loss — "many friends and many men, women, and children," the chief told his audience — Joseph proclaimed that he had "no grievance against any of the white people, Gen. Howard or any one. If Gen. Howard dies first, of course I will be sorry."

Although he stood facing a tableau of harsh order, Joseph had only kind words to say about the Indian Industrial School. "I understand and I know that learning of books is a nice thing, . . . and I am thankful to know there are some of my children here struggling to learn the white man's ways and his books," he said. "I wish my children would learn more and more every day, so they can mingle with the white people and do business with them as well as anybody else."

Afterward, Pratt exulted at the remark. As the Indian Industrial School's newspaper, the *Red Man and Helper,* observed, "not always has Chief Joseph been of this mind." School officials saw a triumph of their vision. "Time has taught Chief Joseph to bow to the inevitable," the *Red Man and Helper* wrote, describing the chief's call for education as "the only way of salvation left for the Indians who are to follow — and a very straight and narrow way at that."

Yet if Joseph's words suggested a capitulation — another surrender speech — if, to a fault, he had always taken pains to assure white audiences of his friendship and good faith, the chief also knew the value of connecting with the influential men on the dais with him. The remarks, though freely given, succeeded in extracting certain concessions on his behalf as well. Joseph left Carlisle holding letters addressed to key congressmen and President Roosevelt — a proposal in Howard's crabbed hand that Congress add $35,000 to the annual Indian appropriations bill for Joseph and his band, representing a payment of five dollars an acre for seven thousand acres of the Wallowa Valley. At the general's insistence, Pratt was busy writing his own set of endorsements, too.

Back in Washington, the chief presented one of Howard's letters to an influential senator. While

Orville H. Platt of Connecticut might have ignored Joseph's request in due course — he cared far more about matters relating to Cuba — he felt compelled to contact the general. Twenty-seven years after the Nez Perce families had fled through the mountains, memories were fading. "I have an indistinct recollection about Chief Joseph's war, and its final adjustment, and also a vague impression that at the close of it, he was thought to have rendered some service to the government," the lawmaker wrote. "To secure anything for him in the way of an appropriation by the government, certainly requires that all the facts be brought out." It was becoming clear that the continued vitality of Joseph's claims depended on how the history of the summer of 1877 would be written and remembered. It was this narrative that Joseph ardently tended, keeping the story of the Nez Perce War alive, not for historians or nostalgic settlers but for succeeding generations of his people.

After his eastern journey, Joseph spent two months as an attraction at the St. Louis World's Fair alongside celebrated chiefs such as Geronimo and Red Cloud, returning home in time to lead the Fourth of July parade at Nespelem. To accommodate his travel schedule, his people postponed the festivities to July 5. Through the rest of the summer, he appeared diminished and melancholy, "a bent form, in a listless life," according to the resident physician at the Colville reservation. Reflecting on a routine visit from Joseph, the Indian agent wrote that "he looked thin, broken in spirit, and complained of feeling tired." When many in his band, including one of his wives, went south to the Yakima Valley to pick hops, Joseph stayed behind. As the sun was beginning to set on September 21, he died suddenly, alone in his teepee.

Although the chief had hoped to be buried in the Wallowa Valley, his band decided to keep him close, in the graveyard at Nespelem, which lay up a small rise from their teepees. Lavish, sentimental newspaper tributes to "the Napoleon of Indians" and "the Washington of his People" painted a picture of the kind of man who only exists in fiction, what one obituary called "a composite of all the virtues of an ideal Indian chief of the Fenimore Cooper type." His people focused not on supposed feats of battlefield derring-do but on his real and enduring place in their lives as their advocate. At the dedication of a tall white stone monument the following June, Yellow Bull, visiting from the Lapwai reservation, said, "Joseph is dead, but his words are not dead; his words will live forever." The photographer Edward Curtis, who had made portraits of Joseph the previous year in Seattle, was there taking pictures. "Perhaps he was not quite what we in our minds had pictured him," he wrote, "but still I think he was one of the greatest men that has ever lived."

From his home in Burlington, Vermont, and on his many travels, Oliver Otis Howard registered the public's fascination with the dying generation of Indians who resisted the final conquest of the West. Within a few years of Joseph's passing, he published two long books, one for children and one for adults, on his "personal observations, adventures, and campaigns among the Indians of the Great West." They were equal parts memoir, travelogue, biography, and catalog of Indian "habits, traits, religion, ceremonies, dress, savage instincts, and customs in peace and war," and Howard devoted multiple chapters to one of the biggest draws to his books, the man he called "the Great War Chief Joseph."

But in Howard's two-volume autobiography, published in 1908, Joseph appeared in just one short paragraph out of twelve hundred pages. The chapter on commanding the Department of the Columbia went into far more detail about the general's temperance work in Portland and even his family's 1875 Alaska vacation. His two sentences on the "Nez Perces campaign" focused solely on how he had "succeeded in detaining the Indians till General Nelson A. Miles overtook and had a battle with them" and then "through my own interpreters succeeded in persuading Chief Joseph to abandon further hostile effort." Howard felt compelled to justify his conduct of the war and settle scores with Miles, yet he did not want to be defined by his encounter with Joseph.

As he neared eighty years of life, the general reflected on how his "earliest knowledge of Indians greatly prejudiced me against them." As a child, he had listened to the stories of his grandfather, whom he described as "a man of the olden time when Indians were very troublesome . . . Their war-paint, their depredations, their knives, their tomahawks, bows and arrows, and wild life were the themes of common conversation." In contrast, among the many conversions in his life was coming to recognize the humanity of native peoples, and that there was no need to "exterminate them, in order that savagery might give place to civilization." Distanced from Joseph by death, decades, and thousands of miles, Howard in the end limited his recognition of Indians' humanity only so far as "a portion of them," he wrote, "might be . . . made respectable citizens . . . to attain unto the blessings of a civilized and Christian life." Similarly, he could reduce the Nez Perce War to one episode within "a slow process," he wrote, "to get entirely rid of the old savagery and all that goes with it . . . the development is not rapid even among the best." The war had been natural. It had been necessary. And whatever his immediate failures, he could be proud of what he was sure would be an ultimate success.

Two weeks shy of his seventy-ninth birthday, in October 1909, Howard attended a concert at his church by a quartet of singers visiting from the Tuskegee Institute in Alabama. At his request, they sang his favorite song, "Swing Low, Sweet Chariot." The next morning, he traveled five hundred miles from Burlington for a weekend in London, Ontario. Thirty-five years after riding circuit around the Department of the Columbia, he was still giving Saturday evening lectures on the Battle of Gettysburg, followed by a Sunday sermon at the YMCA. He returned home on Monday, October 25. He had lived in Burlington fifteen years, the last twelve in a handsome three-story brick colonial on Summit Street that he and his wife Lizzie had built. It was the longest he had ever lived anywhere. They had simple, New England tastes, though the house also had room for the Indian artifacts the general had collected over the course of his career.

Lizzie had been bedridden and tended to by a nurse for three years, though still cheerful with visitors, the local paper would report. Her health had been declining since Guy's death in the

Philippines a decade earlier in 1899. While the general maintained a busy schedule of lectures, veterans' parades, campaign events for Roosevelt and then Taft, and fund-raisers for Lincoln Memorial University, Lizzie needed constant attention. Their youngest son Harry, now forty years old, his wife Sue, a physician, and their twin baby girls lived with them. While their other children lived throughout the country, from Oregon to Delaware — and Jamie was an army lieutenant serving multiple tours in the Philippines — Harry had always been with them, from Washington to Portland to West Point to Omaha to New York. When the general retired from the army, Harry quit his job as a bank teller to serve as his father's secretary — a permanent aide-de-camp, watching over his parents' health and affairs with some time off to attend the University of Vermont and law school at New York University.

On Tuesday, October 26, Howard and his son walked to their office in town. The weather had cooled, and the dark clouds and occasional rain were reminiscent of autumn in the Northwest. Around midday, while dictating an article that reviewed the evolution of methods of warfare over the previous fifty years, the general felt sharp chest pains and took a horse cab to the doctor. He told the doctor to "get him well quickly," Harry later wrote, "because he had several important engagements and lectures which he must fulfill." Harry took him home to rest, walking him up to a bed on the third floor and helping him undress. Sue read him a new story by the English author Jerome K. Jerome about a mysterious stranger who moves into an apartment house and uplifts and redeems his nasty, venal neighbors by awakening them to their "Better Selves." After hours of nausea and discomfort, the general drifted off to sleep.

Around seven o'clock, Sue brought up some broth for supper. Finding the general sitting on the side of the bed, she put a cape around him to keep him warm and held the cup of soup while he took a few spoonfuls. His hand was shaking. As Sue set the cup on a bureau by the bed, Howard lurched back and collapsed on top of her. She felt for his wrist and could not find a pulse. Harry ran into the room and found Howard dead, his eyes still open. He kissed his father, walked his mother up to see him, and watched her stand silently at his side.

EPILOGUE:
ACTS OF REMEMBERING

San Francisco,
1942

It was early spring, the hills a brilliant green, when Charles Erskine Scott Wood endured the long drive from his estate north into San Francisco. Just inside the city limits, miles short of the fashionable districts he had once frequented, his car climbed through a humble neighborhood with streets wishfully named for great universities: Princeton, Oxford, Harvard. Between Yale and Cambridge Streets, he stopped at a complex that resembled a sort of church or school. As a young man, he might have sketched the three connected buildings — light brick and terra-cotta, arched windows, towers with red tile pyramid roofs — or the views of Twin Peaks to the northwest, San Francisco Bay to the east. But at age ninety, he could barely see.

Etched above the main entrance were the words "Salvation Army Training College," but no one there was trying to save souls anymore. During the Great Depression, the cash-strapped charity had been forced to sell the buildings, which now housed the local headquarters of the Immigration and Naturalization Service. In recent months, since the attack on Pearl Harbor, the INS had been working closely with agents of the Federal Bureau of Investigation to round up people classified as "enemy aliens," citizens of Japan, Italy, and Germany deemed threats to the war effort on the West Coast. The buildings, on eighteen acres, had always felt sprawling and empty. Now they were packed with prisoners. Wood had come to save one of them.

Identifying himself as "the oldest living graduate of West Point," Wood was ushered into an office. He did not catch the name of the man in charge but heard a southern twang in his voice. Wood's suit was out of fashion. His head was swaddled in a shock of white — thick wavy hair almost down to his shoulders, blending into a prophet's beard. There was no courtroom, no judge or jury, but Wood expected that the bureaucrat who ran this remote outpost of the federal government could give him the relief that he sought. Although he had been retired from the practice of law for decades, he began to argue one last case.

That day, Wood was hoping to free Takezo Shiota, a friend of nearly forty years. Back before the 1906 earthquake, while on business in San Francisco, Wood had ducked into Shiota's gallery on Grant Avenue during a ramble through Chinatown. At the time the proprietor was only thirty, but after eleven years in the United States he had established himself as a leading importer of what he called "Oriental objets d'art." He was "an Authority in his field," Wood wrote, "called to the great Museums of the East and to Paris and London to decide whether certain objects under dispute were or were not genuine antiques." Finding Shiota to be singularly "absorbed in the pursuit of Art," Wood took an immediate liking to the man. Over the decades of friendship that ensued, Shiota consulted him on legal matters. Wood, in turn, whiled away lazy hours at the gallery, "discussing Art," he wrote, "and examining [Shiota's] beautifully illustrated books on . . . Oriental sculpture, painting, pottery, bronzes etc."

On March 26, 1942, after forty-three years in business, Shiota posted a typewritten letter in his storefront window. He bid "au revoir" from a "loyal American" to his friends and clients, closing with "the words of beloved Shakespeare, 'PARTING IS SUCH SWEET SORROW.' " He was taken into INS custody as a citizen of Japan who had regularly visited his homeland to restock his gallery. Nearly seventy years old, he was separated from his wife and children, who as American citizens fell within the jurisdiction of two other bureaucracies, the Wartime Civil Control Administration and the Wartime Relocation Authority. Based on the suspicion that the 120,000 people of Japanese descent who lived on the West Coast would form a dangerous fifth column, those agencies had been empowered by President Roosevelt, Congress, and the military to deport them all to internment camps hundreds and even thousands of miles inland.

At INS headquarters, knowing his friend was languishing in a holding pen just steps away, Wood tried to vouch for Shiota's character by establishing his own bona fides as a loyal American: his father's heroic naval career, his education at the military academy, and, finally, his service as "aide-de-camp to General Howard, serving in all the Indian wars." It was a well-practiced speech, but the INS official insisted that the old man answer one question. Federal immigration law had never allowed people born in Japan to become citizens; the first Congress had restricted naturalization to "free white" people, expanding eligibility during Reconstruction only to "persons of African descent." But in the decades before a new federal agency was given sole charge of naturalization in 1906, local courts had near-complete discretion to administer the oath of citizenship. Many people born in Japan had been able to attain legal status as Americans. Shiota had lived in California since well before 1906. Why hadn't he tried to become a citizen back then?

Wood paused. The new order of things — the exigencies of wartime and the endless patchwork of government agencies — had cast his friend's freedom into the shadows of law. Everything seemed to hinge on how a low-level bureaucrat would exercise his discretion in an informal meeting after learning why decades earlier Shiota had not strayed, as so many others had, from the letter of the naturalization statutes. Wood earnestly considered why Shiota would not have sought citizenship when he had the chance. Offering what he called a "fairly accurate guess," Wood attributed his friend's inaction to his artistic calling, a singular focus that "kept him in a world remote from many practical considerations except as they impinged on his business." "Like many artists I have known," Wood said, "he was oblivious of matters beyond his special field. I think he was oblivious of his own advantage in becoming a citizen and of the importance of taking the necessary steps to do so."

Wood understood how strange his answer must have sounded to an INS official in 1942, that someone would care so little about citizenship. So he tried to explain it as something more than a function of his friend's eccentricity, or as the government seemed bound to conclude, disloyalty. "The era in which citizenship was still open to Mr. Shiota was not one which placed emphasis on the importance of it," Wood said. Speaking from his own experience, Wood said that in his younger days, he himself had never given the matter of citizenship any thought.

On one level, Wood's position seemed absurd considering how much of his early life was defined by military service, but there was truth in what he told the INS official. He had come of age as Reconstruction was ending, and with it the idea that the national government could confer a fundamental set of rights upon the freedpeople or, for that matter, anyone else — liberty and equality and what the Fourteenth Amendment called "the privileges or immunities of citizens of the United States." Instead, the promise of citizenship had given way to something entirely different. In the decades following the Civil War, what most people could expect from life, what they owed their communities, had little to do with some formal status of being American. There was no one definition of citizenship. It was a fluid abstraction that ebbed and flowed with race, region, gender, wealth or poverty, power and political allegiance.

If citizenship signified little to Wood as a young man, he had spent much of his adult life trying to give the concept substance. After beginning the twentieth century opposing American imperialism in the Philippines, he joined or tried to help just about every left-leaning cause that followed. In the final years of his law practice he devoted more and more of his time to anarchists, socialists, and labor unions, including the radical Industrial Workers of the World. Wood began contributing poems and articles to his fellow Portlander John Reed's magazine *The Masses* and scandalized Portland's high-society families by giving them gift subscriptions. After protesting America's entry into World War I, Wood defended the free speech of a Portland IWW activist who was imprisoned for publicly lamenting that "fellow workers" were being "pulled into the army against their wills, and were placed in the trenches to fight their own brothers and relatives."

When his son Erskine, a Harvard graduate who had joined his father's law practice, complained to Wood that his causes were alienating their paying clients, it was one of the few times the old man lost his temper. In the 1920s he railed against Prohibition, which, he wrote, succeeded in turning "a very temperate country where all are free" into "one great perfect penitentiary." He came to see the paramount importance of racial equality, resigning from the Oregon Bar Association after it refused to admit a black attorney and lending his support to a national movement seeking justice and a fair trial for the Scottsboro Boys, nine black Alabama teenagers wrongfully accused of raping two young white women in 1931. In 1936, at age eighty-four, he looked beyond national boundaries to join the American Committee for the Defense of Leon Trotsky, protesting the show trials of Stalin's rivals in Moscow. When the House of Representatives began investigating "un-American activities" in the mid-1930s, Wood was among the first targets.

Citizenship for Wood conferred a series of

protections from a government that he saw too often as an instrument of the powerful, "throttl[ing] . . . freedom and peace." Citizenship meant the right to speak and associate and organize. Despite its shortcomings in practice, it carried an ideal of equality, what he described as "equal freedom of opinion and equal rights and equal privileges — which is to say that there are no privileges, as with our Indian tribes."

But citizenship was more than political liberation. For Wood, it also gave Americans a right to personal liberation. He advocated for birth control, defending Margaret Sanger in police court when she was arrested during a speech in Portland in 1916. He imagined the possibilities of free love, although its emotional toll, as he found out, could prove excruciating in practice. By age seventy, he had been able to sell the bulk of the Lazard Frères landholdings that he had secured in his first days as a lawyer. The commissions were staggering. For the first time in his life, he had more money than he could ever spend. He handed over his practice to his son and created generous trusts for his wife, children, and onetime mistress Kitty Seaman Beck. Then he told Nanny that he was leaving her for Sara Bard Field, a suffrage activist and aspiring poet thirty years his junior with whom he had fallen in love after being introduced by his fellow IWW advocate Clarence Darrow. Nanny stayed behind in the house they had built together, filled with art that her husband had collected over decades. He wanted none of it. "Things — things — things — are nothing to me," he wrote his son Erskine, "nothing — *nothing at all.*" The Woods never divorced, and in the years before her death in 1933, her mind failing, Nanny

660

was convinced that he lived with her still.

Wood left Portland for San Francisco in 1918, and after several years in the city, he and Field built an estate sixty miles south, tucked in the hills above Los Gatos. They called it "The Cats." For two decades, Wood and Field devoted themselves to poetry and politics and turned The Cats into a salon for artists and radical activists. Lincoln Steffens, Ansel Adams, John Steinbeck, Charlie Chaplin, and many more crossed the gate flanked by large feline sculptures. Together they gazed across the Santa Clara Valley, watching the slow swirl of tall grass in the wind. They walked the terraced hillsides, the olive grove, and the vineyard and admired the mahogany paneling in the main house, imported from the Philippines, and the statues and mosaics and bronze reliefs, all tributes to peace and love and art.

Wood often delighted his friends with rollicking tales from a lifetime of collecting novel experiences. He dictated his reminiscences onto wax cylinders and scrawled long letters that were often accompanied by fragrant clippings of desert sagebrush. Throughout the odyssey of his long life, he never stopped talking about Chief Joseph. Wood "was practically the greatest story-teller I ever heard," recalled a young visitor to The Cats in the early 1940s. "He was unbelievable. He would tell stories about the days when he was pursuing Chief Joseph."

It made sense that sixty-five years after the Nez Perce War, Wood kept returning to his first experience in battle to compel an audience's awe and attention. It was Joseph, after all, who had awakened his political sensibility. "In my youth, as an army officer," Wood wrote in the 1920s, "I chased and killed Indians driven to revolt by the oppressions of that vague thing called, 'The Government.' . . . I saw that 'Nationalism', and 'Patriotism' were used to narrow the human sympathy, inflame the hate — and blind the vision of the people." Indeed, the lessons of the war and the critical lens it had given him followed him throughout his life. "I left the Army and entered law and found that the law was not the servant of justice and the protector of liberty, but was the protector of property and that there was one law for the rich, another for the poor," he wrote. His encounter with Joseph set him on a path that led directly to his commitment to making citizenship meaningful, to "abolishing poverty and increasing individual liberty and leisure" and restoring the promise of a government that served every American and not just "powerful capitalists and 'captains of industry.' "

In time, as Wood articulated his critique of what America was and honed an alternative vision for what it could be, he came to understand the shortcomings of the state as profoundly human imperfections. "I saw that the political organization known as 'The Government' was but a lot of politicians; good bad and indifferent," he wrote. "I grew to see that the courts were but men: generally good men — but unconsciously influenced by prejudice — partisanship and fear." During his military service, he, too, had been one of those men, a single consciousness armored by American power. And just as Joseph had reached him and so many others with words and deeds, Wood remained convinced that he could speak reason to the government and compel it to listen and change its course, no matter how long it had functioned as what Wood had called "the tools of property and industrialism," facilitating "the gradual collection of all the valuable parts of the earth into the hands of a shrewd, earlier-born few."

At the INS headquarters in San Francisco, Wood appealed to a government official's common sense. In his telling, Takezo Shiota was an extraordinary and energetic businessman with a large American-born family to support. "I wish Mr. Shiota <u>had</u> taken out citizenship papers," Wood said, "but knowing his temperament and interests, and judging by my own tendency to overlook the importance of matters beyond my daily interests, . . . Mr. Shiota's failure to do so does not in itself . . . constitute evidence of disloyalty to this country." The bureaucrat was a cordial listener and took voluminous notes — "most respectful," Wood later wrote, describing the man as "delightful." But ultimately, he was unmoved. He had no authority to free an enemy alien on anyone's, let alone Wood's, say-so. When Wood left the building, his friend remained in his cell. It was a temporary arrangement, before Shiota could be sent to Camp Livingston in sweltering central Louisiana. The rest of his family would be deported to the Poston internment camp fifteen hundred miles away in southwestern Arizona. Back at The Cats, Wood considered the situation and did what he thought he had to do. In time, he identified another federal official from an agency that overlapped and competed with the INS — the United States attorney in Los Angeles — took out his typewriter, and wrote a letter to demand a rehearing.

From a distance the Yakima Valley hop yards were a picture of order. With hills and mountains ringing the horizon, the long rows of vines trained around six-foot poles recalled, to one visitor, "the perfect symmetry of old Greek architecture." But up close, orderly fields gave way to something wilder. By August the vines grew lush, overwhelming the poles with thickets of large dark green leaves festooned with soft light green cones — the hops flowers, ready to pick just as they started to dry.

Yellow Wolf spent the second half of his life watching summer turn to fall in the hop yards, one of thousands of Indians recruited for the annual harvest. Entire families worked together in the fields, adults picking high, children picking low, fingers growing sticky and bitter, sweat mingling with the tarnished-pine perfume of the crop. While white families took trains from Seattle for the harvest — an "escape from the irksomeness of their daily duties" that helped "pale seamstresses and nervous housewives grow strong and rugged in the outdoor air and life," wrote one hopeful observer — most of the pickers came from dozens of northwestern tribes, coast and plateau. Chief Joseph's band started making the journey to the Yakima Valley within a few years of arriving at the Colville reservation. Joseph himself had gone at least once, in 1897, just months after riding in the parade to dedicate Grant's Tomb. In the years following Joseph's death, Yellow Wolf was one of the leaders of the hops-picking contingent.

By the biggest hop yards, Indian villages rose on

empty fields, a hodgepodge of tribal architectures, from cedar shake cabins to teepees covered in hides and woven mats, drab canvas and bright patterned cloth. Many in Joseph's band relished spending months away from the reservation, closer to the Wallowa Valley and alongside kin and friends on the Yakama and Umatilla reservations who had known them before the war. The harvest brought back memories of summer gatherings when Nez Perce bands came together to pick and prepare mountains of camas root, and early-fall salmon catches when Nez Perce families joined Yakama, Umatilla, and others along the Columbia River near the Dalles.

Well past the late sunsets, the hops pickers' villages pulsed with sounds of play — taunts, laughter, drumbeats, and song, the joys and agonies of stick and bone games that Indians had wagered over for generations. Much of their way of life had managed to survive war, exile, and reservation life. Many of the Indians still wore traditional blankets. The air was thick with salmon drying on large outdoor racks, the same smells that visitors to Nez Perce camps had noted fifty years earlier. On Sundays, the largest congregations were the ones that gathered for weekly horse races.

Yet the feeling that the world had remained the same could never last. Instead of gathering and preparing food that would sustain their families through the winter, the hops pickers earned a dollar a box. Come early October, the pickers held one final days-long celebration featuring, according to one account, "Indian pony races of all sorts and descriptions, Indian war dances, Indian wrestling matches, Indian barbecue and numerous other Indian doings." When it ended, Chief Joseph's band returned to the Colville reservation, poor and isolated and ravaged by tuberculosis, where more people died each year than were born. Yellow Wolf would mourn a daughter who died at birth and a son who did not reach adulthood. The land he had been allotted had no water. The challenges his people faced were hardly unique. The Idaho reservation was similarly plagued by disease, and there were fifteen whites for every Indian after most of the territory had been opened to sale and settlement. Compounding their problems, the Indian agent at Lapwai convinced many of the residents to deposit their earnings in a bank that failed. At Colville, government officials pressed year after year for Joseph's band to till fields, live in houses, wear Western clothes, go to church, and send their children to schools on and off the reservation.

By the early twentieth century, Indians had become essential farm workers, ensuring the success of the agricultural economy that had displaced them. Although Indian agents at Colville complained that Joseph's band left the reservation too often, they could not stand in the way of a money-making activity. Yakima Valley growers regularly sent recruiters out to the reservations. As employees, Chief Joseph's band finally could be trusted to live near white people, at least during the picking season. Local merchants set up shops at the Indian pickers' camps to deal supplies, and farmers brought wagons of peaches, plums, and apricots to sell. White curiosity seekers thronged the end-of-harvest jubilees. But even in the relative freedom of the pickers' village, local and federal authorities remained ever vigilant for "hard cases" among the Indians, the Yakama reservation agent reported. "It is necessary to keep police constantly on duty to protect life and property," he wrote.

At the end of the 1907 growing season, Yellow Wolf went home by riding east through the Yakima Valley. Before crossing out of the valley and turning toward Nespelem, he stopped at a vast cattle and sheep ranch on the southern slope of Rattlesnake Mountain and, in broken English, asked the owner if he would take care of a horse who had been cut by barbed wire and was too weak to continue the journey — a quick exchange of words at sunset. Though Yellow Wolf retreated into the shadows without revealing his name, he had probably sought out Lucullus Virgil McWhorter on purpose, knowing that the Yakama Indians regarded him as a worthy friend, someone who was spending his spare time writing letters in opposition to efforts by Congress and the secretary of the interior to distribute most of the tribe's land and water to whites. On his way to the hop yards the following August, Yellow Wolf returned to the ranch at Rattlesnake Mountain, and McWhorter gave him his horse, nursed back to health.

As the 1908 season closed, the rancher invited Yellow Wolf, his family, and the rest of their band to set up camp on his ranch for a few days among the prairie grass and sagebrush, away from the prying eyes of hops growers and the government. Indians were always camping on McWhorter's land, which lay on the trail between the Yakama reservation and the biggest town in the valley, North Yakima. It was exactly what McWhorter, pale and owlish with a lank mustache, had hoped for in his western life. He and his wife Annie had

667

sold their Ohio farm and most of their possessions in 1903 in large part because they wanted to be near Indians. After the families traveling with Yellow Wolf set up their teepees, the McWhorters took photographs of the camp. While Annie held the camera, Lucullus, in suit and tie, sat cross-legged and posed beside his new friend.

The sight of Yellow Wolf stirred romantic notions about Indians that McWhorter had nurtured since his West Virginia boyhood, exploring the forests and hills and poring over novels by James Fenimore Cooper. At age fifty — just a couple of years older than McWhorter — Yellow Wolf had maintained a "strikingly strong physique," the rancher would write, tall enough to pick hops from the very top of the posts, "quick and accurate in movement," and brilliant on a horse. But the power he projected was coupled, in McWhorter's mind, with total powerlessness. Just as many of Chief Joseph's admirers described him as the exemplar of a noble but dying race, McWhorter looked at Yellow Wolf and saw "tragedy . . . written in every lineament of his face; his laughter was infrequent, and was never more than a soft, scarcely audible chuckle."

McWhorter could have let his own imagination fill in Yellow Wolf's silences. Instead, he tried talking to his guests and, despite the language barrier, learned that they were Chief Joseph's band and that Yellow Wolf had fought during the summer of 1877. McWhorter then asked if Yellow Wolf would describe his experiences in the war.

No one had ever asked Yellow Wolf to tell his story before. He had never told his children — his older son Billy and fragile younger boy Jasper — about what he called his "war-day fighting." Even

668

thirty years after the final battle, it was not a subject that survivors routinely discussed. Some of them still tried to hide their involvement, fearing reprisals for killing settlers and defying the government. But Yellow Wolf had kept the repeating rifle he carried through the summer of 1877 — which his parents had traded a horse for, and his mother had saved during the attack on Looking Glass's village in the early weeks of the struggle. It no longer worked, but he never threw it away. Yellow Wolf also had his war whistle, made from a crane's wingbone, as well as his war club.

It was not an easy decision to start talking about the war after decades of silence. At the very least, it would delay his plans to strike camp, head north to the reservation, and begin provisioning for winter. But Yellow Wolf trusted McWhorter and realized, above all, that he wanted to talk. His sons did not know his story, but perhaps they should.

Yellow Wolf tried to find someone who could speak English. The most fluent among his people was a boy who presumably had had some instruction at a reservation school, but he did not have the vocabulary to interpret Yellow Wolf's story. Yellow Wolf rode off to look for someone else — there were still other hops pickers in the area — and returned with a younger Nez Perce man in a wide brim hat: Thomas Hart, who had fought in the Philippines as a cavalry private and spoke good English. To Hart, Yellow Wolf expressed the urgency of his task. "I am going to say things, and I need you! I need you!" Yellow Wolf told Hart. "I will tell of my war story; of facts that I have seen. . . . It is hard work for me — this talking. Like the heaviest lifting, it buzzes in my head!"

With Hart's assistance, Yellow Wolf attempted his first account of the war. Even filtered through the interpreter, the power of his testimony stunned McWhorter. After Yellow Wolf and his family left for Nespelem days later, the rancher was gripped by the need to gather more material, enough to create a story of the war from the point of view of the Nez Perce participants. Soon, he found his way to Peopeo Tholekt at Lapwai, who continued to advocate for restoring Chief Joseph's band to the Wallowa Valley. McWhorter interviewed the elderly warrior Wot-to-len, who had fought alongside Yellow Wolf in the bluffs above the Clearwater River, and started working closely with Wot-to-len's son Many Wounds. In the years to come, he tracked down and extensively questioned scores of participants, Nez Perce and white, from Ollokot's widow Wetatonmi to Charles Erskine Scott Wood.

To create the time and space for ever more conversations, McWhorter began organizing Wild West shows at fairs and rodeos from Astoria, Oregon, to Walla Walla, staffing them almost exclusively with aging Nez Perce warriors. Even as they reenacted a version of their history for the thrills of a paying audience, in their downtime they reflected on the events of 1877, and McWhorter took notes. From the 1910s into the 1920s, he kept the conversations going by organizing his informants to make feather headdresses. McWhorter supplied the feathers, and every shipment provided an opportunity to ask more questions. He brokered the completed goods to theater companies, film studios, and collectors. Indian characters in some of the first Westerns on film likely wore war bonnets that had been constructed by Yellow Wolf and Peopeo Tholekt.

Outraged at the distortions in the official accounts of the war and Oliver Otis Howard's books, McWhorter felt compelled to research the Nez Perce War until his death in 1944. His wife took in boarders to help fund the work. Through it all, he was guided by Yellow Wolf's story, told in installments, by letter and in person, for nearly thirty years, until shortly before Yellow Wolf died in 1935. McWhorter finished a book about the war from Yellow Wolf's perspective in 1940, and a larger "field history" of the war that drew on his thousands of pages of notes and interviews was published posthumously in 1952.

The act of remembering changed Yellow Wolf's life. Alongside the new daily routines brought about by Wild West shows and orders for headdresses, there were more profound changes. Between 1927 and 1930, Yellow Wolf drove to every major battle site with McWhorter, Peopeo Tholekt, and Many Wounds, among the first of many visitors to trace parts of what would become known as the Nez Perce Trail. At the site of the final struggle on Snake Creek beyond the Bear Paw Mountains, they placed stakes at sites of interest: where Ollokot died, where Toohoolhoolzote fell, where Joseph surrendered. Traces of the battle — attempts at fortifications, bullet-scarred rocks — were still obvious fifty years later. At White Bird Canyon, Yellow Wolf narrated the fight step by step while McWhorter diagrammed and mapped the field. Above the Clearwater, Yellow Wolf crouched in the rifle pits where he had sought cover as a young man.

Visiting the Big Hole, Yellow Wolf stood silently for long stretches of time. "It all comes back like a picture," he said, "what I saw, what I did, so many snows ago." He pointed out scenes of the slaughter, telling in a calm, even voice one story after another that McWhorter could only describe as "ghastly." He and his party scratched diagrams in the sand and reenacted scenes of some of his kills. He only grew emotional when McWhorter mentioned the ways in which his story diverged from John Gibbon's justification of the massacre, "as if comprehending that his story would be discredited," McWhorter wrote.

Over time, the impact of sharing his story became fully apparent to Yellow Wolf. He saw how the summer of 1877 had been remembered — primarily by white settlers and government officials — and connected it to real consequences in the present. "Nobody to help us tell our side — the whites told only one side," he said to McWhorter. "Told it to please themselves. Told much that it not true. Only his own best deeds, only the worst deeds of the Indians, has the white man told." The result, he said in 1931, was that "white people, aided by Government, are smothering my Indian rights." Thin in his final years, his right shoulder slumping after a horse he had been riding fell and rolled over him, he knew his words, his truth, had continuing power. "If people do not like it, I would tell it anyway," he said to McWhorter, one old man to another. "I am telling my story that all may know why the war we did not want. War is made to take something not your own."

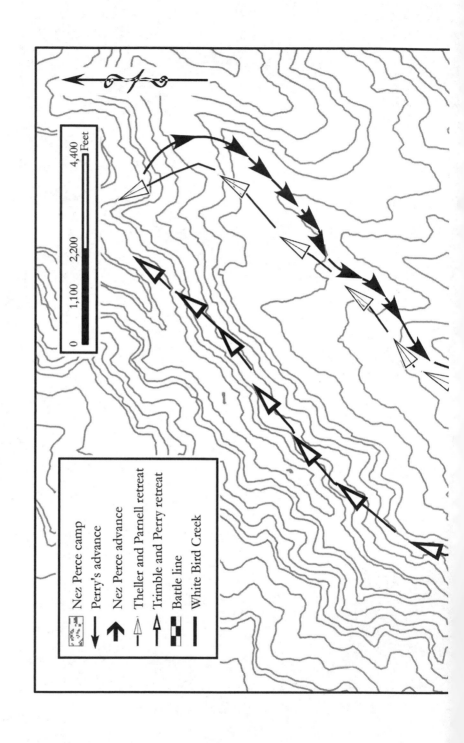

Nez Perce camp

↓ Perry's advance

⬆ Nez Perce advance

↑ Theller and Parnell retreat

↑ Trimble and Perry retreat

▧ Battle line

| White Bird Creek

0   1,100   2,200   4,400
⬛ Feet

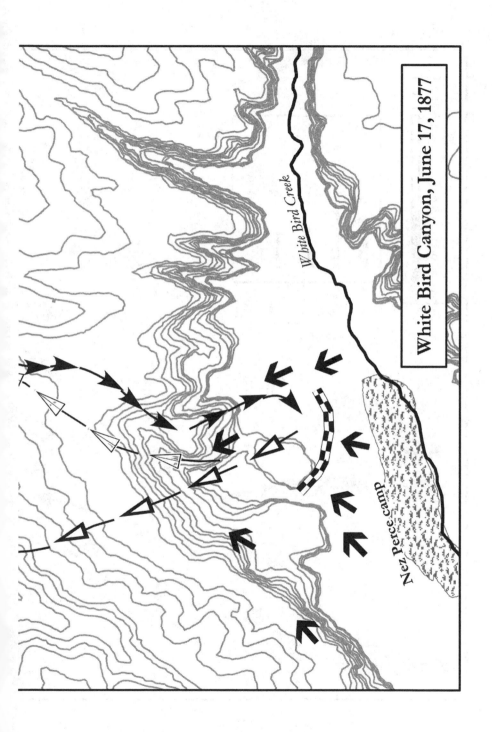

White Bird Creek

White Bird Canyon, June 17, 1877

Nez Perce camp

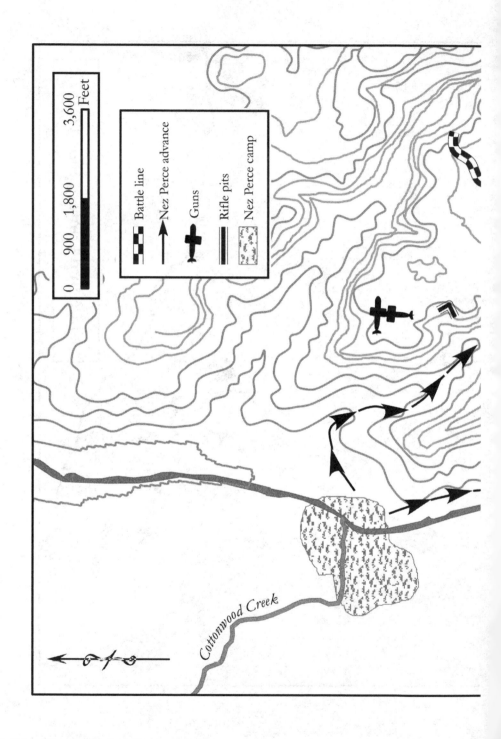

Cottonwood Creek

Battle line
Nez Perce advance
Guns
Rifle pits
Nez Perce camp

0   900   1,800   3,600
Feet

Army
Headquarters

South Fork Clearwater River

Clearwater, July 11-12, 1877

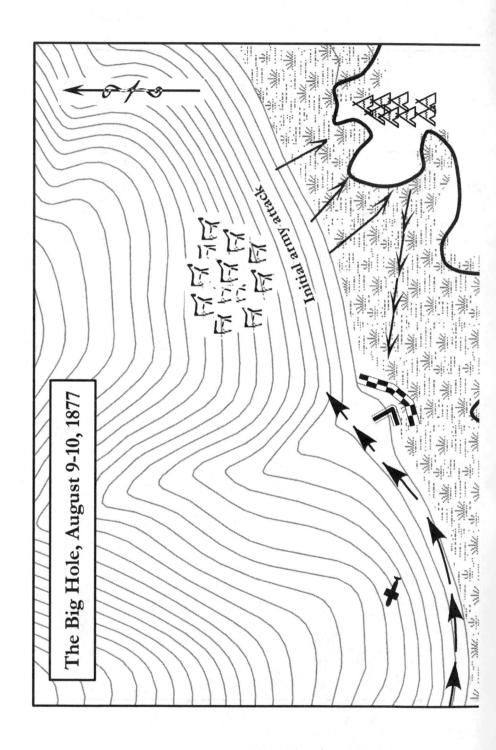

The Big Hole, August 9-10, 1877

Initial army attack

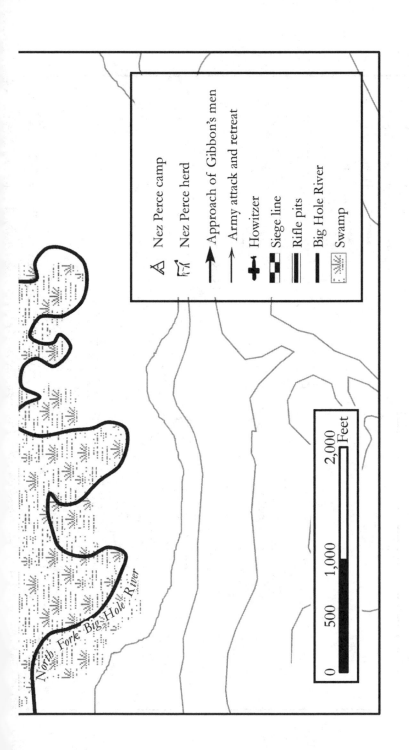

North Fork Big Hole River

Nez Perce camp
Nez Perce herd
Approach of Gibbon's men
Army attack and retreat
Howitzer
Siege line
Rifle pits
Big Hole River
Swamp

0   500   1,000   2,000
Feet

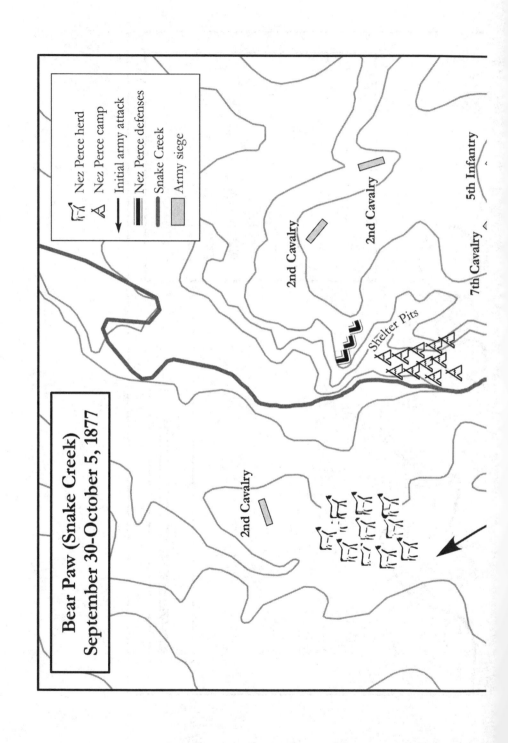

Bear Paw (Snake Creek)
September 30–October 5, 1877

Nez Perce herd
Nez Perce camp
Initial army attack
Nez Perce defenses
Snake Creek
Army siege

2nd Cavalry

2nd Cavalry

2nd Cavalry

5th Infantry

7th Cavalry

Shelter Pits

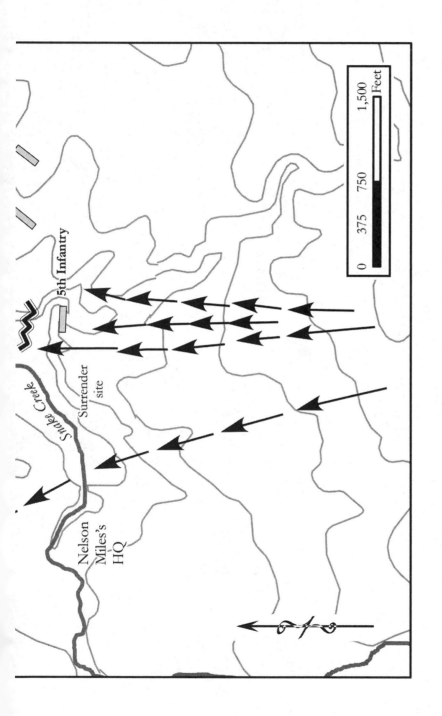

ACKNOWLEDGMENTS

Throughout the process of writing this book, I relied on the generosity and kindness of countless people and many institutions. A fellowship from the John Simon Guggenheim Memorial Foundation in 2013–14 enabled me to begin researching this project in earnest. Conversations with Edward Hirsch, André Bernard, and others inspired me to broaden my thinking and make the most of the fellowship year and beyond. I am deeply grateful to my dean at Vanderbilt University Law School, Chris Guthrie, who provided material and moral support that at key moments enabled me to research, write, and finish this project. The Chancellor Faculty Fellowship Program at Vanderbilt afforded me a crucial semester of leave at the end of the project, and I thank Susan Wente, John Geer, Nick Zeppos, and a delightful cohort of colleagues for making Vanderbilt such an exciting community of thinkers. While working on the book, I spent two years as a fellow at Vanderbilt's Robert Penn Warren Center for the Humanities; my sincere thanks go to Mona Frederick, Joy Ramirez, Terry Tripp, and Allison Thompson for making the Vaughn Home my intellectual home away from my intellectual home. My initial research was aided immeasurably by an Alphonse Fletcher Sr. Fellowship in 2011–12, and I am grateful to the Fletcher Foundation, the selection committee, and Abby Wolf.

As I wrote the book, workshops and symposia with colleagues across the country helped me sharpen my thinking and sent me in new and important directions. I thank the Harvard Legal History Colloquium, Tomiko Brown-Nagin, Ken Mack, and the students who wrote terrific response papers; Jack Schlegel and Mark Fenster, who organized an unforgettable conference on "Opportunities for Law's Intellectual History" at the Baldy Center for Law and Social Policy at SUNY Buffalo Law School; the Boston College Legal History Roundtable, Jim Rogers, Mary Bilder, and Hugh Ault, who shared stories of his father Nelson's important work with the Lucullus McWhorter Papers; the University of Minnesota Legal History Workshop, Susanna Blumenthal, Barbara Welke, and an amazing group of graduate students; and the 2014–15 Americanist Seminar in the Vanderbilt History Department, convened by Paul Kramer and Michell Chresfield. I presented chapters twice to Robert Penn Warren Center faculty seminars and received valuable feedback from Jane Landers, Richard Blackett, Teresa Goddu, Catherine Molineux, Herbert Marbury, Celso Castilho, Caree Banton, Emily August, Nihad Farooq, Joel Harrington, Holly Tucker, Ifeoma Nwankwo, Marshall Eakin, Paul Stob, Aimi Hamraie, and Laura Stein Pardo. My gratitude also goes to Lisa Szefel, for conversations before and after the Kniep Lecture at Pacific University, and to Jill Fraley, for conversations around the Hendricks Lecture at Washington &

Lee University. I also thank Bill Nelson, Bob Gordon, Lawrence Friedman, John Witt, Nick Parrillo, Brad Snyder, Michael Willrich, and Mary Dudziak, for advice about and advocacy for the project.

People have been writing books about the Nez Perce War almost from the moment it ended in 1877. This book would not have been possible without their work, and without the extraordinary record of the war that wound up in a number of archives. I owe special thanks to Elliott West, Jerome Greene, Alvin Josephy, and Lucullus Virgil McWhorter, none of whom I have met but whose visionary work has taught me more than I can say. McWhorter's archive at Manuscripts, Archives & Special Collections in the Washington State University Library, which includes the remembrances of dozens of Nez Perce participants in the war, is a national treasure. I thank Trevor James Bond, Cheryl Gunselman, Greg Matthews, and Marianne Kinkel for making my time in Pullman so fruitful and enjoyable. Greene's archive at the Nez Perce National Historical Park in Spalding, Idaho, is an incredible gift for historians and was an enormous help to me. I thank Beth Erdey, Bob Chenoweth, and Kevin Peters for their help with the NPNHP's vast archival and physical collections and for their conversation during my visit to Spalding. Oliver Otis Howard came alive in his letters, diaries, articles, and speeches that are collected in the George J. Mitchell Department of Special Collections & Archives at the Bowdoin College Library. Richard Lindemann, Kat Stefko, Caroline Moseley, and Sophie Mendoza deserve my heartfelt thanks. While I was researching at Bowdoin, Richard was kind enough to introduce me to Russell Howard, a direct descendant of Charles Henry Howard, and his wife Rosalie Howard, who have spent years painstakingly transcribing Howard family letters and were very generous with me. The papers of Charles Erskine Scott Wood and his family are split among the Huntington Library, Special Collections & Archives at Lewis & Clark, the Bancroft Library at UC Berkeley, and the Oregon Historical Society, and archivists and librarians at all four institutions were incredibly helpful, with special thanks to Zach Selley at Lewis & Clark. I am also grateful to archivists and librarians at the Montana Historical Society, National Archives, Library of Congress, University of Washington, University of Oregon, Washington State Historical Society, Brigham Young University, Denver Public Library, and Lincoln Memorial University. Kim Allen Scott at Montana State University was a pleasure to work with. Guy Moura in the history department of the Confederated Tribes of the Colville Indian Reservation facilitated an illuminating visit to Nespelem. Jim Simard at the Alaska State Library in Juneau and Jacqueline Fernandez at the Sheldon Jackson Museum in Sitka were of invaluable assistance. I am especially grateful to Jackie for connecting me with Barth Hamberg, Laura Kaltenstein, and Brenda Reynolds, who together were responsible for the single greatest hike of my life, on glorious trails through Kruzof Island and up Mount Edgecumbe.

The dazzling wealth of archival material relating to the Nez Perce War — official reports, journals and diaries, letters, eyewitness journalistic accounts, sketches drawn by officers, and remembrances — made this narrative possible. But I would not have been able to picture the events properly without extensive travel to the Northwest. After I learned that I am not, in fact, allergic to horses, Anastasia Curwood directed me to one of the best teachers I have ever had: Paula Brown, a riding instructor who inspired me with her knowledge, skill, patience, good humor, common sense, and deep love of everything equine.

In September 2013, after driving the length of the Nez Perce Trail, I spent five days on a horse in the Yellowstone backcountry, in a part of the park that the nontreaty bands crossed to evade Howard and Sturgis's troops. I am grateful that Yellowstone National Park historian Lee Whittlesey connected me with Yellowstone Wilderness Outfitters and Jett Hitt, a brilliant guide who, along with the equally terrific Hannah Lipomi and Shannon Forshee, stayed calm and clearheaded as late-fall sunshine turned to days of rain, sleet, snow, and freezing rain.

My travels would not have been possible without Cheryl Wilfong's extraordinary book, *Following the Nez Perce Trail: A Guide to the Nee-Me-Poo National Historic Trail with Eyewitness Accounts.* As I made multiple trips through Oregon, Idaho, Montana, and Wyoming, I benefited from the wisdom, guidance, and hospitality of many people I met along the way. Particular thanks go to Dennis Sullivan and Frances Conklin in Cottonwood, Idaho, Bob and Robin Berry in Cody, Wyoming, and Jason and Kristene Gillmer in Spokane.

So much travel made me appreciate all the more the importance of home. The friendship, support, and brilliant work of my colleagues and students in law and history at Vanderbilt were an endless inspiration. In addition to the many I have already named, special thanks go to Kevin Stack, Chris Serkin, Lisa Bressman, Mark Brandon, Ed Cheng, Ed Rubin, Ganesh Sitaraman, Randall Thomas, Terry Maroney, Alistair Newbern, Spring Miller, Tracey George, Yesha Yadav, Mike Vandenbergh, Sarah Igo, Ole Molvig, Gary Gerstle, Dennis Dickerson, Dan Usner, and Jason Bates. I have been energized by conversations with Vanderbilt alumni and am especially grateful to Bailey Spaulding for taking me to look at her hop vines at Jackalope Brewery's plot at Glen Leven Farm. Vanderbilt's librarians and library staff devoted years to collecting books, articles, manuscripts, and microfilm for this project. I could always rely on their patience, skill, dogged effort, and deep intelligence. I thank LaRentina Gray, Susan Grider, Michael Jackson, Sara Saddler, Catherine Deane, Larry Reeves, Bill Walker, and especially Mary Miles Prince. Kate Gilchrist, Drew Austria, and Shalom Rottman-Yang were superb student research assistants. For excellent administrative assistance, I thank Susan Button, Renee Hawkins, Erin Parr, and Sue Ann Scott. Scott Nelsen and Dane Vick's able technical support kept me sane and working. And it is no exaggeration to say that this book would not have been published in this decade but for the assistance of Frances Kolb, a postdoctoral researcher who cataloged thousands of pages of manuscripts, transcribed hundreds of letters, steered me to sources, read drafts, and helped me wrangle more than two thousand endnotes. She is an extraordinary historian, and I am thrilled for her colleagues and students as she begins her career at Western Kentucky University. When the manuscript was nearly complete, Michael Willrich, Conevery Bolton Valencius, Jona Hansen, Seth Rockman, and Steve Biel came to Nashville and, as they have been doing for more than a decade, read my work closely and drew me into an hours-long conversation that pushed and challenged me to finish. Jeff Gonda also read the entire manuscript with a sharp set of eyes and a degree of care that touched and humbled me.

Wendy Strothman and Lauren MacLeod at the Strothman Agency championed this project, and I will always be grateful. At Norton, John Glusman and Alexa Pugh have been unfailingly thoughtful, exceedingly patient, and inspiringly ambitious for the project. I owe them, my copy editor India Cooper, and Rebecca Homiski and Norton's extraordinary production staff so much.

Most of all, I am thankful for my family. My parents Steven and Margaret, my mother-in-law Mary, my brother Josh and Yngvild, my sister Sarah and Jay, Erika and Mike, and Sam, Isak, Sydney, Nate, Jack, Katherine, and James — their love sustains me, even when we are all together for the holidays. My father-in-law Curt Mikkelsen, who grew up in Waitsburg and Spokane, took a special interest in this book. He died too soon, and there are many days when I imagine the conversations we could have had.

When I first started thinking about this project, my sons Saul and Abe were four and one. In the six years since, I have had the indescribable joy of watching them grow up. One of the first books I ever read, when I was six years old, was a biography called *Chief Joseph: Guardian of His People*. I read it to Saul just as I started researching *Thunder in the Mountains*. As I neared the end, he was reading *Yellow Wolf's Own Story,* bringing it to school each day. I am so proud of the boy he has become — I love his kindness, sharp wit, keen sense of justice, and enthusiasm for nature and numbers and a good story. Abe has the amazing ability to make me smile. He has a way with words, a rhyme for everything, and the sweetest hugs. I am awed by his intelligence, exuberance, and soul.

My wife Ann Mikkelsen is my first and best reader, my most trusted counsel, and my best friend. For more than half my life, she has made my life complete. Ann, Saul, and Abe — this book is dedicated to you.

NOTES

Abbreviations

CESW Charles Erskine Scott Wood

CESWP Charles Erskine Scott Wood Papers, Huntington Library, San Marino, California

CHH Charles Henry Howard

CHHP Charles Henry Howard Papers, Bowdoin College, Brunswick, Maine

ESMP Edmond S. Meany Papers, University of Washington, Seattle

EW Erskine Wood

JAGP Jerome A. Greene Papers, Nez Perce National Historic Site, Spalding, Idaho

JTGP James Taylor Gray Papers, University of Oregon, Eugene

LVM Lucullus V. McWhorter

LVMP Lucullus V. McWhorter Papers, Washington State University, Pullman

MHS Montana Historical Society, Helena

NARA National Archives and Records Administration, Washington, DC

NMS Nanny Moale Smith

NMW Nanny Moale Wood

NPJ Oliver Otis Howard, *Nez Perce Joseph: An Account of His Ancestors, His Lands, His Confederates, His Enemies, His Murders, His War, His*

Pursuit and Capture (Boston: Lee & Shepard, 1881).

OHS Oregon Historical Society

OOH Oliver Otis Howard

OOHP Oliver Otis Howard Papers, Bowdoin College, Brunswick, Maine

OOHP-LMU Oliver Otis Howard Papers, Lincoln Memorial University, Harrogate, Tennessee

RBH Rowland Bailey Howard

RBHP Rowland Bailey Howard Papers, Bowdoin College, Brunswick, Maine

RG Record Group (NARA)

WMCP-BYU Walter M. Camp Papers, Brigham Young University

WMCP-DPL Walter M. Camp Papers, Denver Public Library

WP Charles Erskine Scott Wood and Erskine Wood Family Papers, Lewis & Clark College, Portland, Oregon

Author's Note

In many ways: A vast and important literature examines this transformation from a myriad of perspectives. See, e.g., Amy Dru Stanley, *From Bondage to Contract: Wage Labor, Marriage, and the Market in the Age of Slave Emancipation* (Cambridge: Cambridge University Press, 1998); William Forbath, *Law and the Shaping of the American Labor Movement* (Cambridge, MA: Harvard University Press, 1991); Barbara Young Welke, *Recasting American Liberty: Gender, Race, Law, and the Railroad Revolution, 1865–1920* (Cambridge: Cambridge University Press, 2001); Barbara Young Welke, *Law and the Borders of Belonging in the Long Nineteenth Century United States* (Cambridge: Cambridge

University Press, 2010); Lucy Salyer, *Laws Harsh as Tigers: Chinese Immigrants and the Shaping of Modern Immigration Law* (Chapel Hill: University of North Carolina Press, 1995); Mae M. Ngai, *Impossible Subjects: Illegal Aliens and the Making of Modern America* (Princeton, NJ: Princeton University Press, 2004); Richard White, *Railroaded: The Transcontinentals and the Making of Modern America* (New York: Norton, 2011); Sarah Barringer Gordon, *The Mormon Question: Polygamy and Constitutional Conflict in Nineteenth-Century America* (Chapel Hill: University of North Carolina Press, 2002); Michael Willrich, *Pox: An American History* (New York: Penguin, 2012).

Vast corporations: See Eric Foner, *Reconstruction: America's Unfinished Revolution, 1863–1877* (New York: Harper & Row, 1988), 512–34.

Reach of the federal government: See Steven Hahn, "Epilogue: The Widest Implications of Disorienting the Civil War Era," in *Civil War Wests: Testing the Limits of the United States,* ed. Adam Arenson and Andrew R. Graybill (Oakland: University of California Press, 2015), 270–71; Steven Hahn, "Slave Emancipation, Indian Peoples, and the Projects of a New American Nation-State," *Journal of the Civil War Era* 3, no. 3 (2013): 307–30; Elliott West, "Reconstructing Race," in *The Essential West: Collected Essays* (Norman: University of Oklahoma Press, 2012), 119 ("Always the Greater Reconstruction was as much about control as liberation, as much about unity and power as about equality.").

Through the West: Heather Cox Richardson, *West from Appomattox: The Reconstruction of America After the Civil War* (New Haven: Yale University Press, 2007); C. Joseph Genetin-Pilawa, *Crooked Paths to Allotment: The Fight over Federal Indian Policy After the Civil War* (Chapel Hill: University of North Carolina Press, 2012); Gregory P. Downs and Kate Masur, "Echoes of War: Rethinking Post–Civil War Governance and Politics," in *The World the Civil War Made,* ed. Gregory P. Downs and Kate Masur (Chapel Hill: University of North Carolina Press, 2015).

For the bloodshed: See Ari Kelman, *A Misplaced Massacre: Struggling over the Memory of Sand Creek* (Cambridge, MA: Harvard University Press, 2013); Brendan C. Lindsay, *Murder State: California's Native American Genocide, 1846–1873* (Lincoln: University of Nebraska Press, 2015); Benjamin Madley, *An American Genocide: The United States and the California Indian Catastrophe* (New Haven: Yale University Press, 2016).

Prologue

Roaring for battle: OOH, *Autobiography of Oliver Otis Howard,* 2 vols. (New York: Baker & Taylor, 1908), 1:245–46. Howard's "unimpressive voice" was "taken as a confirmation of his sincerity." William S. McFeely, *Yankee Stepfather: General O. O. Howard and the Freedmen* (New Haven: Yale University Press, 1968), 11–12. For enrollment in the regiments under Howard's command, see *The Union Army: A History of Military Affairs in the Loyal States, 1861–*

694

65, 8 vols. (Madison, WI: Federal, 1908), 2:95, 98.

Waiting rebel line: Ibid., 246.

"General, you shall not": Ibid.

Tiny shards of bone: Ibid., 247.

"Wounded wanderers": Ibid., 249.

Over felled trees: Ibid., 247–49; G. Grant, "Battle of Fair Oaks," June 5, 1862, box 1, folder 53, CHHP.

Head, chest, or face: Grant, "Battle of Fair Oaks."

Six hours to wait: OOH, *Autobiography* 1:249; Edward D. Neill, "Incidents of Fair Oaks and Malvern Hill Battles," *Macalester College Contributions,* 2nd ser. (St. Paul, MN: Pioneer Press, 1892), 208.

"I lifted my soul": OOH, *Autobiography* 1:154.

Relieved of his right arm: Ibid., 154, 249; Neill, "Incidents of Fair Oaks," 208.

Leeds, Maine: John A. Carpenter, *Sword and Olive Branch: Oliver Otis Howard* (Pittsburgh, PA: University of Pittsburgh Press, 1964), 2.

Commission to West Point: Ibid., 3, 6.

"The coarse & profane": OOH to Eliza Gilmore, Sept. 8, 1850, box 1, folder 19, OOHP; OOH to Eliza Gilmore, Aug. 28, 1850, box 1, folder 18, OOHP; OOH to RBH, Sept. 19, 1850, box 1, folder 14, RBHP.

Fourth out of forty-six: Carpenter, *Sword and Olive Branch,* 7–9.

"Tugging & burning": OOH to Lizzie Howard, May 31, 1857, box 1, folder 93, OOHP.

"A new well spring": OOH to Lizzie Howard, June 3, 1857, box 1, folder 94, OOHP.

"Pluck[ed] my feet": OOH to Lizzie Howard, June 9, 1857, box 1, folder 94, OOHP.

"While, I am humiliated": Ibid.

Ten Commandments: OOH, *Autobiography* 1:113, 127.

"The tone and manner": Abner R. Small as quoted in Carpenter, *Sword and Olive Branch,* 26.

Facing the enemy: Ibid., 24.

"Slave property": CHH to Eliza Gilmore, Aug. 12, 1861, box 1, folder 8, CHHP. Many of Howard's letters are collected in David K. Thomson, ed., *We Are in His Hands Whether We Live or Die: The Letters of Brevet Brigadier General Charles Henry Howard* (Knoxville: University of Tennessee Press, 2013).

"Her babe & a boy": Ibid.

"The slave woman": Ibid.

"Oh! my child": OOH, *Autobiography* 2:166.

"Unqualified abolitionists": Ibid., 166–67.

"He did not wish": CHH to Eliza Gilmore, Aug. 12, 1861, box 1, folder 8, CHHP.

"Exasperated & talked": Ibid.

"I had reluctantly complied": OOH, *Autobiography* 2:166.

"Arm & train the negroes": OOH to Lizzie Howard, May 17, 1862, box 2, folder 41, OOHP.

"To humble, disenthral": OOH to Eliza Gilmore, Dec. 7, 1862, box 2, folder 50, OOHP.

Not steady himself: OOH, *Autobiography* 1:254 (describing a fall after his amputation).

Miles had been nicked in the heel: Robert Wooster, *Nelson A. Miles and the Twilight of the Frontier Army* (Lincoln: University of Nebraska Press, 1993), 3, 5, 9–10; Peter R. DeMontravel, *A Hero to His Fighting Men: Nelson A. Miles,*

1839–1925 (Kent, OH: Kent State University Press, 1998), 8.

Even a hundred bodies: G. Grant, "Battle of Fair Oaks," box 1, folder 53, CHHP.

"Poor fellows": OOH, *Autobiography* 1:250.

Sent Howard into darkness: Ibid.; Miles to Howard, Sept. 26, 1887, OOHP.

"The tables groaned": A. B. Meacham, *Wigwam and War-path; or, The Royal Chief in Chains,* 2nd and rev. ed. (Boston: J. P. Dale, 1875), 49–50.

O.K. Grocery: *An Illustrated History of Union and Wallowa Counties* (Spokane, WA: Western Historical Publishing, 1902), 224.

"To make glorious": "Fourth of July," *Mountain Sentinel* (La Grande, OR), July 6, 1872.

"Solid rather than brilliant": Elwood Evans, *History of the Pacific Northwest: Oregon and Washington,* 2 vols. (Portland, OR: North Pacific, 1889), 2:561.

Superintendent of Indian affairs in Oregon: See Thomas Augustus Bland, *Life of Alfred B. Meacham* (Washington: T. A. & M. C. Bland, 1883), 5.

"The man of the mountains": "The Innocents Abroad: What We Know About the Wallowa Valley," *Mountain Sentinel,* July 6, 1872.

"Cut off a grouse's": "A Great Hunter," *Mountain Sentinel,* July 6, 1872; "The Innocents Abroad"; T. T. Geer, *Fifty Years in Oregon* (New York: Neale, 1912), 294; Grace Bartlett, *The Wallowa Country, 1867–1877* (Fairfield, WA: Ye Galleon Press, 1984), 13.

Mountains to the east: "Interesting Wow Wow," *Mountain Sentinel* (La Grande, OR), July 6, 1872.

"He thought it was": Bartlett, *The Wallowa Country,* 22n5.

Dig for camas roots: Caroline James, *Nez Perce Women in Transition, 1877–1990* (Moscow: University of Idaho Press, 1996), 11–17. Nez Perce women dug for Camas roots usually from June to September. For more on Nez Perce women as traditional food gatherers, see ibid., 11–21.

"Did not contemplate": "Interesting Wow Wow."

New farms in the Wallowa Valley: Ibid.; Bartlett, *The Wallowa Country,* 19, 22.

"One of the grandest": "The Innocents Abroad."

"As soon as I came": J. F. Johnson as quoted in Bartlett, *The Wallowa Country,* 17.

Coarse wandering lines: Jennifer Williams and Erin Melville, *The History of Grazing in Wallowa County,* Sept. 2005, 12 (collected in online compilation by Oregon State University Extension Service–Wallowa County, http://extension .oregonstate.edu/wallowa/sites/default/files/ _in_Wallowa_County_Compilation_edited_4_ 2009.pdf); "The Innocents Abroad"; Bartlett, *The Wallowa Country,* 17, 21; "A. C. Smith," *Enterprise Business Directory 1902,* reprinted at http://www.oregongenealogy.com/wallowa/ reavis/a_c_smith.htm.

"Prayed with his heart": Samuel Parker, *Journal of an Exploring Tour Beyond the Rocky Mountains* (Ithaca, NY: published by the author, 1838), 279 (describing the opinion of Parker's Indian interpreter Kentuc). "If there is one among this multitude, who it may be hoped, has been everlastingly benefited by the gospel," Reverend Parker wrote, "I should believe it is this man." See also Alvin M. Josephy Jr., *The Nez Perce Indians and the Opening of the Northwest* (New Haven: Yale University Press, 1965), 142.

"The bosom of the visible": *The Diaries and Letters of Henry Harmon Spaulding and Asa Bowen Smith relating to the Nez Perce Mission, 1838–1842* (Glendale, CA: Arthur H. Clark, 1958), 280 (journal entry describing Joseph's baptism on Nov. 17, 1839).

"Back to Egypt": Kate C. McBeth, *The Nez Perces Since Lewis and Clark* (New York: Fleming H. Revell, 1908), 63; Young Joseph, "An Indian's View of Indian Affairs," *North American Review* 128 (April 1879): 416.

"My father was the first": Young Joseph, "An Indian's View," 416.

"You ask me": Robert H. Ruby and John A. Brown, *Dreamer-Prophets of the Columbia Plateau: Smohalla and Skolaskin* (Norman: University of Oklahoma Press, 1989), 31–32 (quoting Smohalla); Elliott West, *The Last Indian War: The Nez Perce Story* (New York: Oxford University Press, 2009), 81–84.

Chinook Jargon: Josephy, *The Nez Perce,* 453; J. H. Horner and Grace Butterfield, "Chief Joseph: He Met White Men Half Way," *Oregonian,* Jan. 26, 1947.

They were trespassing: Josephy, *The Nez Perce,* 453.

Eleven townships: Ibid., 447.

Federal office in La Grande: Lafayette Grover

to Columbus Delano, July 21, 1873, reprinted in *Report of Governor Grover to General Schofield on the Modoc War* (Mart V. Brown, 1874), 61, 64.

Rights that were being violated: Josephy, *The Nez Perce,* 453; Colin G. Calloway, *Pen and Ink Witchcraft: Treaties and Treaty Making in American Indian History* (New York: Oxford University Press, 2013), 227.

"Until the authorities": "Interesting Wow Wow."

Agents of the federal government: Ibid.

"We will never": Young Joseph, "An Indian's View," 412, 416–18.

Follow their conscience: West, *The Last Indian War,* 12.

"Speak for his people": Young Joseph, "An Indian's View," 418. See Frederick E. Hoxie, *This Indian Country: American Indian Political Activists and the Place They Made* (New York: Penguin, 2012) for a discussion of Native American leaders who "were born within the boundaries of the United States, rose to positions of community leadership, and decided to enter the nation's political arena" (4).

"Some of you": Young Joseph, "An Indian's View," 415.

Chapter 1: A Willing Exile

Pennsylvania Avenue: "Pennsylvania Avenue, Washington, D.C.," *Engineering News,* Aug. 22, 1878.

Grip for the night: "Personal" and "The Washington Grove Camp Meeting," *Washington Evening Star,* Aug. 7, 1874; "The Weather," *Washington Evening Star,* Aug. 6, 1874.

Washington to Springfield, Illinois: "The New

Depot Topped Out," *National Republican,* July 17, 1874; Dian Olson Belanger, "The Railroad in the Park: Washington's Baltimore & Potomac Station, 1872–1907," *Washington History* 2 (1990): 4–27.

"Apparently constructed": "Gen. O. O. Howard," *Elevator,* Sept. 19, 1874, 2.

Vassar in September: Grace Howard to Elizabeth Howard, Aug. 9, 1874, box 12, folder 74, OOHP.

Chicago would be in sight: Belanger, "The Railroad in the Park," 13–15.

Extension of the other: Wolfgang Schivelbusch, *The Railway Journey: The Industrialization of Time and Space in the 19th Century* (Berkeley: University of California Press, 1986), 35–38, 55, 64–68.

Farewell supper a couple of nights earlier: "General O. O. Howard," *National Republican,* Aug. 4, 1874.

Howard University: Rayford W. Logan, *Howard University: The First Hundred Years, 1867–1967* (New York: New York University Press, 1968), 13–15, 59–63; Everett O. Alldredge, *Centennial History of First Congregational United Church of Christ, Washington, D.C., 1865–1965* (Pikesville, MD: Port City Press, 1965), 6–9, 21–23, 26; John A. Carpenter, *Sword and Olive Branch: Oliver Otis Howard* (Pittsburgh, PA: University of Pittsburgh Press, 1964), 236; "This Evening's Dispatches," *San Francisco Daily Evening Bulletin,* Aug. 4, 1874.

Washington, they took it: On the social and political situation in Washington, DC, as Reconstruction was ending, see Kate Masur, *An Example for All the Land: Emancipation and* *the Struggle over Equality in Washington, D.C.* (Chapel Hill: University of North Carolina Press, 2010); Daniel J. Sharfstein, *The Invisible Line: Three American Families and the Secret Journey from Black to White* (New York: Penguin, 2011), 181–214.

"Exile": Francis H. Smith to OOH, Aug. 7, 1874, box 12, folder 74, OOHP.

On the train: N. Guilford to W. H. Freudenthal, July 25, 1874, box 12, folder 73, OOHP (The B&O Railroad's "present rate on one Horse from Washington to San Francisco is $65. Two horses $113.75 at an agreed valuation of not more than $100 for each horse. Man in charge to water and take care of the same, will have to pay full fare.")

"There is plenty to do": OOH to CHH, July 11, 1874, Letterbooks, roll 7, OOHP.

It was for the best: Ibid.; Francis H. Smith to OOH, Aug. 7, 1874, box 12, folder 74, OOHP ("On the whole I am glad that you have gone. That, to me, is about the strongest test of friendship I can think of, when I remember what is before us without your assistance in the church, Young Men's Association, and University.").

"Tedium and wearisomeness": Henry T. Williams, *The Pacific Tourist* (New York: H. T. Williams, 1876), 9; Schivelbusch, *Railway Journey,* 54.

"This is the place": The young man wound up becoming one of Chicago's greatest architects. Louis Sullivan, *The Autobiography of an Idea* (New York: Press of the American Institute of Architects, 1924), 244.

Newspaper in 1872: David K. Thomson, ed., *We*

Are in His Hands Whether We Live or Die: The Letters of Brevet Brigadier General Charles Henry Howard (Knoxville: University of Tennessee Press, 2013), 201; *Memorials of Deceased Companions of the Commandery of the State of Illinois* (Chicago, 1912), 2:476–78.

"Supreme indiscretion": CHH to Eliza Gilmore, n.d., CHHP.

While the Howards were visiting: "Beecher-Tilton," *Chicago Tribune,* Aug. 10, 1874. For more on the scandal, see Richard Wightman Fox, *Trials of Intimacy: Love and Loss in the Beecher-Tilton Scandal* (Chicago: University of Chicago Press, 1999), or the felicitously titled *The Great Brooklyn Romance: All the Documents in the Beecher-Tilton Case, Unabridged* (New York: J. H. Paxon, 1874).

Photographs to remember them: Grace Howard to Elizabeth Howard, Aug. 9, 1874, box 12, folder 74, OOHP; R. H. Gilmore to OOH, July 24, 1874, box 12, folder 72, OOHP.

Floating below: Deborah Morse-Kahn and Joe Trnka, *Clinton, Iowa: Railroad Town* (Des Moines: Iowa Department of Transportation, 2003).

"20 minutes at the depot": "Northwestern News," *Milwaukee Daily Sentinel,* Aug. 17, 1874 (describing events of Aug. 11).

"Mechanical wonder": Williams, *The Pacific Tourist,* 18.

Real travels could begin: Ibid., 13, 18.

"Here the phases": "Across the Continent," *Frank Leslie's Illustrated Newspaper,* Aug. 18, 1877.

Hint of what was to come: Ibid.; W. F. Rae, "A Barbecue near Elko," in August Mencken, *The*

Railroad Passenger Car (Baltimore: Johns Hopkins University Press, 2000), 151; see also Mencken, *Railway Passenger Car,* 22.

"Quite complete possession": OOH, *Autobiography of Oliver Otis Howard,* 2 vols. (New York: Baker & Taylor, 1908), 2:461.

Journey began like any other train's: Ibid.; Williams, *Pacific Tourist,* 19; John H. White Jr., *The American Railroad Passenger Car* (Baltimore: Johns Hopkins University Press, 1978), 266–67.

"The bell rings": Williams, *Pacific Tourist,* 19.

Hundreds of thousands: William G. Thomas, *The Iron Way: Railroads, the Civil War, and the Making of Modern America* (New Haven: Yale University Press, 2011), 206–7, 209.

Consumers in the East: Barbara Young Welke, *Recasting American Liberty: Gender, Race, Law, and the Railroad Revolution, 1865–1920* (New York: Cambridge University Press, 2001): 18–19, 139, 263, 269; Richard White, *Railroaded: The Transcontinentals and the Making of Modern America* (New York: Norton, 2011), 23–24; Thérèse Yelverton, *Teresina in America,* 2 vols. (London: Richard Bentley and Sons, 1875), 2:5.

Tompkins Square Park in New York: White, *Railroaded,* 63–66; Scott Reynolds Nelson, *A Nation of Deadbeats: An Uncommon History of America's Financial Disasters* (New York: Knopf, 2012); Heather Cox Richardson, *West from Appomattox: The Reconstruction of America After the Civil War* (New Haven: Yale University Press, 2007), 136–39; Eric Foner, *Reconstruction: America's Unfinished Revolution, 1863–1877* (New York: Harper & Row, 1988), 512–14.

Bad loans on the books: Jonathan Levy, *Freaks of Fortune: The Emerging World of Capitalism and Risk in America* (Cambridge, MA: Harvard University Press, 2012), 107, 144–46; Foner, *Reconstruction,* 527–28.

Seven thousand dollars from a friend: OOH, *Autobiography* 2:460–61.

Funding for education: McFeely, *Yankee Stepfather,* 302, 327–28.

Went missing on Howard's watch: Carpenter, *Sword and Olive Branch,* 203–8, 220–23.

"Did his whole duty": "The Finding of the Court of Inquiry," July 2, 1874, as quoted in OOH, *Autobiography* 2:452.

"Crippled & broken": OOH to CHH, July 11, 1874, Letterbooks, roll 7, OOHP.

Haunted by the recent past: Ibid.; Carpenter, *Sword and Olive Branch,* 230–33; OOH to RBH, Feb. 19, 1874, Letterbooks, roll 7, OOHP; OOH to CHH, July 11, 1874, Letterbooks, roll 7, OOHP.

"I risk everything": OOH to CHH, July 11, 1874, Letterbooks, roll 7, OOHP.

"Now that the Chapter": Francis H. Smith to OOH, Aug. 7, 1874, box 12, folder 74, OOHP.

The other, the freedpeople: Richardson, *West from Appomattox,* 139; Carpenter, *Sword and Olive Branch,* 203; Mark Twain and Charles Dudley Warner, *The Gilded Age: A Tale of Today* (Hartford, CT: American, 1874).

Seldom noticed the general: OOH, *Autobiography* 2:461; White, *American Railroad Passenger Car,* 267–70.

"People would come along": OOH, *Autobiography* 2:461.

"Still sweating from": Robert Louis Stevenson, "Across the Plains," in *Across the Plains: With Other Memories and Essays* (New York: Charles Scribner's Sons, 1905), 46.

"Like a cue": Ibid., 42.

Caused by rail sparks: Williams, *Pacific Tourist,* 21.

"No brushing, no shaking": Susan Coolidge [Sarah Chauncy Woolsey], "A Few Hints on the California Journey," *Scribner's Monthly,* May 1873.

Could be hypnotic: Stevenson, "Across the Plains," 43.

"No depression sticks": OOH to RBH, Feb. 19, 1874, Letterbooks, roll 7, OOHP.

"Not always done right": Ibid.

"The control of all subjects": An Act to Establish a Bureau for the Relief of Freedmen and Refugees, 13 Stat. 507-09 (Mar. 3, 1865).

A more conservative course: OOH to RBH, Feb. 19, 1874, Letterbooks, roll 7, OOHP.

"Had I been more rigid": An Act to Establish a Bureau for the Relief of Freedmen and Refugees, 13 Stat. 507-09 (Mar. 3, 1865); OOH to RBH, Feb. 19, 1874, Letterbooks, roll 7, OOHP.

Continuing on to Raleigh: RBH to Ella Howard, Oct. 9, 13, 1865, RBHP; Sidney Andrews, *The South Since the War* (Boston: Ticknor & Fields, 1866), 201.

"Let no man come": Andrews, *The South Since the War,* 201.

"Mere boy": RBH to Ella Howard, Oct. 7, 1865, RBHP.

Coughing all night: OOH, *Autobiography* 1:552, 2:36 ("[Stinson] never saw a well day again till the time of his death soon after the close of the war."); RBH to Ella Howard, Oct. 7, Nov. 7, 1865. Howard Stinson died in Tallahassee on February 22, 1866. *American Annual Cyclopaedia and Register of Important Events of the Year 1866* (New York: D. Appleton, 1867), 558.

"Working men of the North": On the rise and fall of the Freedman's Bank, see Levy, *Freaks of Fortune,* 104–46.

"Hot country": RBH to Ella Howard, Oct. 9, 1865, RBHP.

Run on overcoats: Ibid.; Harry M. Stinson to CHH, Oct. 5, 1865, transcription courtesy of Russell and Rosalie Howard (on file with author).

"A hard faced 'rich-looking' ": RBH to Ella Howard, Oct. 7, 1865, RBHP.

Hoped and presumed: See Foner, *Reconstruction,* 159, 190; Michael Perman, *Reunion Without Compromise: The South and Reconstruction, 1865–1868* (Cambridge: Cambridge University Press, 1973).

"Arch Rebel": RBH to Ella Howard, Oct. 7, 1865, RBHP.

"Sir" and "Would you have asked": Ibid.; "Washington News," *New York Times,* Oct. 7, 1865.

The upper hand in Washington: On Howard's submission to the new order in Washington, see McFeely, *Yankee Stepfather,* 120, 125, 136.

"Hercules' task": OOH, *Autobiography* 2:208–10.

Work on the ground: Brian Balogh, *A Government out of Sight: The Mystery of National Authority in Nineteenth-Century America* (Cambridge: Cambridge University Press,

2009), 2–4; Jerry L. Mashaw, *Creating the Administrative Constitution: The Lost One Hundred Years of American Administrative Law* (New Haven: Yale University Press, 2012); William J. Novak, *The People's Welfare: Law and Regulation in Nineteenth-Century America* (Chapel Hill: University of North Carolina Press, 1996).

As much abandoned land as possible: McFeely, *Yankee Stepfather,* 103–8.

International demand for cash crops: Ibid., 107–29.

"Otis is the hardest worked": RBH to Ella Howard, Oct. 7, 1865, RBHP.

As quickly as possible: Willie Lee Rose, *Rehearsal for Reconstruction: The Port Royal Experiment* (New York: Oxford University Press, 1976); Special Field Orders, No. 15, Jan. 16, 1865.

"Passed happily": "General Howard at the Orleans Theater," *New Orleans Tribune,* Nov. 6, 1865.

Rooted in the land: Steven Hahn, *A Nation Under Our Feet: Black Political Struggles in the Rural South from Slavery to the Great Migration* (Cambridge, MA: Belknap Press, 2003), 127–46.

"Endeavor to effect": OOH, *Autobiography* 2:237.

Hold onto their land: Hahn, *A Nation Under Our Feet,* 146–52.

"The President sends him": RBH to Ella Howard, Oct. 7, 1865, RBHP.

"Sad" and "chagrined": OOH, *Autobiography* 2:237.

"He dreads it": RBH to Ella Howard, Oct. 7, 1865, RBHP.

"Why did I": OOH, *Autobiography* 2:237–38.

"Whipped, but . . . proud": RBH to Ella Howard, Oct. 13, 1865, RBHP.

"Well-dressed ladies": RBH to Ella Howard, Nov. 13, 1865, RBHP.

"Dead & cold": RBH to Ella Howard, Oct. 13, 1865.

"To put the foot": CHH to RBH, Oct. 8, 1865, RBHP.

Like Maine in June: RBH to Ella Howard, Oct. 24, 1865, RBHP.

Out to Edisto Island: OOH, *Autobiography* 2:238; McFeely, *Yankee Stepfather,* 138; CHH to RBH, Oct. 8, 1865, RBHP.

Union blockade: McFeely, *Yankee Stepfather,* 142. Howard had met him earlier in the year when Sherman's army had gone through Charleston.

William Whaley, the planters' lawyer: Ibid., 141. Edisto was on Howard's itinerary because Whaley's direct appeals to President Johnson had resulted in an order to hand back the land on the island. In July 1865, Whaley had been instrumental in convincing President Johnson to appoint a provisional governor for South Carolina who would restore all Confederate incumbents to the positions they had held during the war. A man who had met the South Carolina delegation to Washington that included Whaley described the group as being "as Secesh as ever and have the least respect for National Supremacy as any man that I have heard from the South since the close of the war." Perman, *Reunion Without Compromise,* 63–64n16 (quoting a June 29, 1865, letter from Taliaferro P. Shaffner, who had met the South

Carolina delegation at their Washington hotel, to President Johnson's personal secretary Reuben D. Mussey).

Episcopal church: Julie Saville, *The Work of Reconstruction: From Slave to Wage Laborer in South Carolina, 1860–1870* (New York: Cambridge University Press, 1994), 90.

"With gladness": "Edisto Island — The Freedmen — Gen. Howard's Recent Visit," *Liberator,* Dec. 1, 1865.

"Noise and confusion": OOH, *Autobiography* 2:238.

"Kindly and gently": Mary Ames, *From a New England Woman's Diary in Dixie in 1865* (Springfield, MA: Plimpton, 1906), 95–97.

"They did not hiss": OOH, *Autobiography* 2:238.

"Did not weep": RBH to Ella Howard, Oct. 20, 1865, RBHP (describing Alvord's account).

"Very black . . . thick set": OOH, *Autobiography* 2:238–39.

"He had lived": Ames, *From a New England Woman's Diary,* 98.

"Neck would [not]": "Edisto Island — The Freedmen."

"None, or almost none": As quoted in *Congressional Globe,* 39th Cong., 1st sess., pt. 1, 517.

"I am ashamed": "Edisto Island — The Freedmen."

"The old Masters": RBH to Ella Howard, Oct. 20, 1865, RBHP; RBH to Eliza Gilmore, Oct. 20, 1865, RBHP.

Eventually purchase the land: McFeely, *Yankee Stepfather,* 142–43.

"How many would trust": As quoted in *Con-*

gressional Globe, 39th Cong., 1st sess., pt. 1, 517.

"What troubles them most": Ibid.

"We wish to have": Henry Bram et al. to the President of these United States, Oct. 28, 1865, B-53 1865 and P-27 1865, Letters Received (ser. 15), Washington Headquarters, BRFAL, NARA, in Ira Berlin et al., "The Terrain of Freedom: The Struggle over the Meaning of Free Labor in the U.S. South," *History Workshop* 22 (Autumn 1986): 129.

"*You* only lost": Ibid.

"Cheerful & well": CHH to Eliza Gilmore, Oct. 23, 1865, CHHP.

"Noted for his amiability": Edwin R. Sweeney, ed., *Making Peace with Cochise: The 1872 Journal of Captain Joseph Alton Sladen* (Norman: University of Oklahoma Press, 1997), 48.

"Hardihood" and "Unfailing cheerfulness": Ambrose Bierce, "On General O. O. Howard," in *Phantoms of a Blood-Stained Period: The Complete Civil War Writings of Ambrose Bierce,* ed. Russell Duncan and David J. Klooster (Amherst: University of Massachusetts Press, 2002), 230–31.

"A downright hypocrite": General Hooker on General Howard, *Historical Magazine,* 3rd ser. 253 (Oct. 1873): 2. Hooker was asked to comment on his experience with Howard during the Civil War while Howard was being investigated for corruption in the Freedmen's Bureau.

"Very little time": CHH to Eliza Gilmore, Oct. 26, 1865, CHHP.

"Five Negro minstrels": RBH to Ella Howard, Oct. 30, Nov. 8, 1865, RBHP.

Brick buildings: RBH to Ella Howard, Nov. 13, 1865, RBHP.

"You couldn't help": RBH to Ella Howard, Nov. 8, 1865, RBHP.

"Talk, talk, talk": RBH to Ella Howard, Nov. 5, 1865, RBHP. See also Reginald Horsman, *Josiah Nott of Mobile: Southerner, Physician, and Racial Theorist* (Baton Rouge: Louisiana State University Press, 1987); RBH to Ella Howard, Nov. 13, 1865, RBHP.

"Necessary to define": "Gen. Howard at the Orleans Theater," *New Orleans Tribune,* Nov. 6, 1865.

"To be considered before": Edisto Committee as quoted in Hahn, *A Nation Under Our Feet,* 143–44.

"We sung patriotic": RBH to Ella Howard, Nov. 18, 1865, RBHP.

Great Salt Lake: John H. White Jr., *Wet Britches and Muddy Boots: A History of Travel in Victorian America* (Bloomington: Indiana University Press, 2013), 464.

"Met with *no silver*": Yelverton, *Teresina in America* 2:4.

Panning for gold: Ibid.; White, *Wet Britches,* 465. See also Robert Hamburger, *Two Rooms: The Life of Charles Erskine Scott Wood* (Lincoln: University of Nebraska Press, 1998), 67, which describes a prospector living outside a train station who shocked a rail traveler with the story of his roommate, who walked into the wilderness and simply disappeared — eaten by coyotes, the frontiersman reckoned. Patricia Limerick argues that individuals in the West, whether panning for gold, farming, or trapping, were aware of the risks they were taking and that those risks might prove profitable in the end; Limerick, *The Legacy of Conquest: The Unbroken Past of the American West* (New York: Norton, 1987), 41–42.

Their drivers scalped: "The Indians," *Chicago Tribune,* Aug. 7, 1874.

"Ready for war": "The Indians," *Chicago Tribune,* Aug. 11, 1874.

"Old haunts": Ibid.

"Beautiful beyond description": *Chicago Tribune,* Aug. 10, 1874. For a recent study of the Sioux, see Jeffrey Ostler, *The Plains Sioux and U.S. Colonialism from Lewis and Clark to Wounded Knee* (New York: Cambridge University Press, 2004).

Sixty cents to the dollar: OOH, *Autobiography* 2:461; Williams, *Pacific Tourist,* 259–62; Charles Eugene Banks and Opie Read, *The History of the San Francisco Disaster and Mount Vesuvius Horror* (N.p., 1906), 172.

Chapter 2: New Beginnings

Gave way to blunt requests: Mrs. E. J. Thomas to OOH, Aug. 19, 1874, box 12, folder 75, OOHP; Walter T. Burr to OOH, Aug. 10, 1874, box 12, folder 74, OOHP; S. J. Hollensworth to OOH, Aug. 11, 1874, box 12, folder 75, OOHP.

"& now General": Mrs. E. J. Thomas to OOH, Aug. 19, 1874, box 12, folder 75, OOHP.

Orderly on his staff: J. G. Scott to OOH, July 8, 1874, box 12, folder 69, OOHP.

San Francisco Mint: Mrs. E. J. Thomas to OOH, Aug. 19, 1874, box 12, folder 75, OOHP.

"Anything honorable": Ed Sands to OOH, July 13, 1874, box 12, folder 70, OOHP.

"Now in some ordinary": Thomas S. Malcolm to OOH, Aug. 3, 1874, box 12, folder 74, OOHP.

"The climate has caused": C. H. Van Wyck to OOH, July 13, 1874, box 12, folder 70, OOHP.

"Getting worse every day": George W. Trueheart to OOH, Aug. 15, 1874, box 12, folder 75, OOHP.

"Aid given the freedmen": OOH, *Autobiography of Oliver Otis Howard,* 2 vols. (New York: Baker & Taylor, 1908), 2:311, 368.

Slavery in all but name: Ibid.; "Gen. Howard at the Orleans Theater," *New Orleans Tribune,* Nov. 6, 1865; William S. McFeely, *Yankee Stepfather: General O. O. Howard and the Freedmen* (New Haven: Yale University Press, 1968), 110; "The Freedmen," *New York Times,* Aug. 20, 1865. Howard's beliefs were prevalent at the time. See, e.g., Amy Dru Stanley, *From Bondage to Contract: Wage Labor, Marriage, and the Market in the Age of Slave Emancipation* (Cambridge: Cambridge University Press, 1998); Karen Sawislak, *Smoldering City: Chicagoans and the Great Fire, 1871–1874* (Chicago: University of Chicago Press, 1996).

Great commonplace of Reconstruction: See Eric Foner, *Reconstruction: America's Unfinished Revolution, 1863–1877* (New York: Harper & Row, 1988), 152–53. For a differently nuanced perspective, see Stanley, *From Bondage to Contract,* 130n61.

A few dollars: Many others crowded soup kitchens and poorhouses. Philanthropists and social reformers fixated on the "problem of dependency" during the depression of the 1870s. Rather than question the fundamental assumptions of self-reliance, free labor, and liberty of contract, they often supported measures that criminalized vagrancy. See Stanley, *From Bondage to Contract,* 100–102.

For his move west: To make matters worse, Howard's modest government salary was paid out in greenbacks, which were worth a fraction of face value in Portland. He worried that he would never be able to save enough to pay down his debt. OOH, *Autobiography* 2:473.

New York during the Civil War: *Hildreth v. State of New York,* Documents of the Assembly of the State of New York, 103d sess. (1880), 1:101–8.

"Insane [leaving] a": OOH to John T. Hildreth, Sept. 30, 1874, Letterbooks, roll 7, OOHP.

"The light sometimes": Ibid.

"The human soul": "How to Show Sympathy," n.d., box 40, folder 1, OOHP.

Pale and despairing: OOH, *Autobiography* 2:465–67.

"Cudlipp, look at me": Ibid.

"Juvenile but audacious": Wallis Nash, *Two Years in Oregon* (New York: D. Appleton, 1882), 256.

With classical symmetry: See *Samuel's Directory of Portland and East Portland* (Portland, OR: L. Samuel, 1874).

Sold stoves and metals: Ibid.; see also Leveridge, Wadhams & Co. Letterhead, Record No. AD/1215, Subject Files — Loose Materials, Archives and Records Div., City Auditor's Office, Portland, OR.

Bowed to money and trade: On the primacy of commerce in Portland, see E. Kimbark Mac-Coll, *Merchants, Money, and Power: The Portland Establishment, 1843–1913* (Portland, OR: Georgian Press, 1988), 163–77.

Price of entry for nearly everyone: Ibid., 122–24; Dorothy O. Johansen, "The Oregon Steam Navigation Company: An Example of Capitalism on the Frontier," *Pacific Historical Review* 10, no. 2 (1941): 179–88. See also P. W. Gillette, "A Brief History of the Oregon Steam Navigation Company," *Quarterly of the Oregon Historical Society* 5, no. 2 (1904): 120, 126 ("So enormous were the charges for freight and passage, I am credibly informed, that the steamer Okanogan paid the entire cost of herself on her first trip. . . . The Oregon Steam Navigation Company had become a millionaire-making machine.").

Liverpool, England: "Oregon," "Too Soon," and "Deep Plowing for Crops," *Oregonian*, Aug. 25, 1874.

Tax the government: MacColl, *Merchants, Money and Power*, 124 (on OSN's "lucrative government mail and army supply contracts"); see also Gillette, "Brief History," 123 ("The Government bought a quantity of hay at San Francisco for the military post at Fort Dalles. By the time it reached its destination it had cost 'Uncle Sam' $77 per ton.").

Stayed largely in Portland: Company investors and other wealthy Portlanders did go on occasional shopping sprees in Europe, paying top dollar for "scores of second-rate Munich oils of tediously sentimental themes and dull brownish tones." Dorothy O. Johansen and Charles

M. Gates, *Empire of the Columbia: A History of the Pacific Northwest* (New York: Harper & Row, 1957), 351, as quoted in MacColl, *Merchants, Money and Power,* 186. Assessing one OSN investor's collection, Johansen and Gates wrote, "The art works have perhaps fortunately disappeared" (352).

Pennies on the dollar: MacColl, *Merchants, Money and Power,* 207–9.

"Surpassed in few respects": Henry Villard, *The Early History of Transportation in Oregon* (New York: Arno Press, 1944), 43–44. Written in 1900, Villard's memoir of his first decade in Oregon (1874–83) was first published serially in the *Oregonian* in 1926.

New Hampshire, among other places: MacColl, *Merchants, Money and Power,* 1, 34–35, 37–38.

Upstate New York: Helen Weeks Wadhams Stevens, *Wadhams Genealogy* (New York: Frank Allaben Genealogical Company, 1913): 403–4.

German Jews: William Toll, *The Making of an Ethnic Middle Class: Portland Jewry over Four Generations* (Albany: State University of New York Press, 1982), 94; "Goldsmith & Loewenberg," ser. 57, Oregon Jewish Businesses Collection, Oregon Jewish Museum, Portland. See also Ellen Eisenberg, Ava F. Kahn, and William Toll, *Jews of the Pacific Coast: Reinventing Community on America's Edge* (Seattle: University of Washington Press, 2009).

Another German Jew: MacColl, *Merchants, Money and Power,* 168; Toll, *The Making of an Ethnic Middle Class,* 10, 80–83.

"Good sense": Howard, *Autobiography* 2:462–63.

Stumps and swirling dust: In the 1850s, when settlers reported that there were "more stumps than houses," Portland became known as Stumptown. MacColl, *Merchants, Money and Power,* 18 (quoting OSN investor John C. Ainsworth). It would not outgrow its nickname for decades. One resident remembered Portland in the late 1860s as "out this way, stumps; out that way, stumps, stumps." Earl Morse Wilbur, *A History of the First Unitarian Church of Portland, Oregon, 1867–1892* (Portland: First Unitarian Church, 1893), 57. For Howard's comments on the dust, see also OOH, *Autobiography* 2:462.

Reeking with manure: The *Oregonian* devoted part of a regular column ("Local Brevities") to warnings when the streets and crosswalks were "muddy" (Sept. 10, 1874); "terribly muddy" (Dec. 23, 1874; Feb. 22, 1875 ["terrible muddy"]); or "in a chaotic condition" (Oct. 17, 1874. See also Mar. 2, 1875 ("Muddy streets and crossings. Promenading with trailing skirts isn't popular among the ladies now."); Jan. 17, 1874 ("Several streets not a dozen blocks from this office, are as muddy as it is possible to imagine; and it is the dirtiest, blackest mud we ever gazed upon.").

Every hundred residents: In 1871, the *New Northwest* reported that Portland had thirteen liquor wholesalers, ninety-seven saloons, and thirty-nine bottle stores — "One hundred and forty-nine liquor dealers in Portland! Only think of it!" — one for every sixty residents. "Temperance and Woman's Rights," *New North-*

west, Aug. 18, 1871; see also Ruth Barnes Moynihan, *Rebel for Rights: Abigail Scott Duniway* (New Haven: Yale University Press, 1983), 141 ("Six out of nine members of the Democratically controlled city council were saloon keepers."). Yamhill Street, in the heart of the saloon district, was known as the "Court of Death." See MacColl, *Merchants, Money and Power,* 191–92 (estimating one saloon for every two hundred residents in 1876).

Obstacles along the way: OOH, *Autobiography* 2:469. The *Oregonian* often reported on the spectacle of drunkards "raising thunder" on the streets. See, e.g., "City: A Sleeping Beauty," Aug. 27, 1874 ("Yesterday a confirmed old 'bum' was observed stretched out at full length on the sidewalk near the corner of B and First streets, locked in the strong embraces of drunken slumber."); "City: An Inebriate Asylum," Nov. 26, 1873 ("[A] low miserable old 'bum' . . . utterly limp and helpless . . . wallowed about in the gutters until he presented a repulsive mass of filth and mud."); "City: Street Speaking," Apr. 1, 1870 ("An old settler . . . got an overdose of noisy whisky, which caused him to 'demonstrate' in front of one of the popular hotels.").

Drop of strong drink: "Notable People of the Day," *Phrenological Journal,* July 1890.

Womanish, and even sinister: See John A. Carpenter, *Sword and Olive Branch: Oliver Otis Howard* (Pittsburgh, PA: University of Pittsburgh Press, 1964), 24–25. General Joseph Hooker told the *San Francisco Chronicle* in 1872 that Howard "was always a woman among troops." "If he was not born in petticoats," Hooker said, "he ought to have been, and ought to wear them. He was always taken up with Sunday Schools and the temperance cause. . . . He would command a prayer meeting with a good deal more ability than he would an army." *San Francisco Chronicle,* May 23, 1872.

Soldiers serving under him: OOH, *Autobiography* 1:28 (describing a college roommate's entreaty: "Howard, you are ambitious, you would like to make something of yourself in the future; you do not expect to do it without ever taking a glass of liquor, do you?"). When Howard took command of the 11th Corps, his soldiers — largely German immigrants — mocked his order to forswear drinking. See Margaret S. Creighton, *The Colors of Courage: Gettysburg's Forgotten History* (New York: Basic Books, 2005), 19. In his memoirs, Howard also recalled being teased in May 1864 for his "oddities and exclusiveness" by General Thomas John Wood, one of Howard's division commanders: "What's the use, Howard, of your being so singular? Come along and have a good time with the rest of us. Why not?" General Sherman hushed Wood: "Let Howard alone! I want one officer who don't drink!" OOH, *Autobiography* 1:537.

"The only beverage": OOH, *Autobiography* 1:128.

Intoxicating spirits: Howard's agents found the temperance efforts to be laughable. Carpenter, *Sword and Olive Branch,* 238; Lee Willis, *Southern Prohibition: Race, Reform, and Public Life in Middle Florida, 1821–1920* (Athens: University of Georgia Press, 2011), 91.

New start in life: See McFeely, *Yankee Step-father,* 87 (describing Howard's unified conception of his civil rights and temperance work).

Sailor on shore leave: "City: Troops," *Oregonian,* Aug. 27, 1874 (describing a shipload of soldiers from Sitka purposely kept anchored offshore before transfer to a steamer to San Francisco: "This is to prevent the soldiers from coming ashore, which, if allowed, would occasion the officers no little trouble and vexation.").

"At least partial intoxication": OOH to H. Clay Wood, Sept. 28, 1874, Letterbooks, roll 7, OOHP; OOH to J. M. Schofield, Oct. 2, 1874, Letterbooks, roll 7, OOHP.

"The cavalry of the Church": Congregational Association of Oregon, *Minutes of the Annual Meeting of the Congregational Association of Oregon* (Portland, OR: Congregational Association, 1876), 7.

"Pray, sing, read": F. F. Victor, *The Women's War with Whisky; or, Crusading in Portland* (Portland, OR: Geo. H. Himes, 1874), 59; "The War Progresses," *New Northwest,* Apr. 17, 1874.

"Rivalled Pandemonium": Victor, *Women's War with Whisky,* 11–12, 22.

"Death to the fiend": Ibid., 4.

"God bless them women": OOH, *Autobiography* 2:471.

"Of wealth, of position": "The War Progresses"; Moynihan, *Rebel for Rights,* 138.

"Much wickedness": OOH to RBH, Sept. 30, 1874, Letterbooks, roll 7, OOHP.

"Slatternly dressed": OOH, *Autobiography* 2:470.

Men he had saved: Ibid., 468–69.

"The veins in his": "Gen. O. O. Howard," *Elevator,* Sept. 19, 1874.

Conversations with him: OOH, *Autobiography* 2:469.

"I am ashamed": Ibid.

Surrounded by lush gardens: MacColl, *Merchants, Money and Power,* 185.

Living in a simple cottage: OOH, *Autobiography* 2:463.

Sixteen-year-old boy: Carpenter, *Sword and Olive Branch,* 5.

"Whooping cough minus": OOH to R. H. Gilmore, Nov. 3, 1874, Letterbooks, roll 7, OOHP.

"Plain decent people": Matthew Deady, *Pharisee Among Philistines: The Diary of Judge Matthew P. Deady, 1871–1892,* 2 vols. (Portland, OR: Oregon Historical Society, 1975), 1:166.

"Give us the slip": OOH, *Autobiography* 2:469–70.

A good Chinese cook: In his less radical days, Portland's John Reed opined in a college essay on how "the old-time Chinese of Oregon and California had the *knack* of fine cooking, I believe, more than the Virginia darky of antesecession days, perhaps even more than the French." Fred DeWolfe, "Portlander John Reed Remembers Lee Sing, His Family's Chinese Servant," *Oregon Historical Quarterly* 97 (1996): 356, 364.

"Very dignified": OOH, *Autobiography* 2:478.

His parents were dead: Luke S. Fetters, "The Church of the United Brethren of Christ Support of the Community Education Work of Moy Ling Among the Chinese in Portland, Oregon, 1882–1931: Implications for a Missiological Understanding of Partnership" (Ed.D. dissertation, Ball State University, Sept. 2005); D. K. Flickinger, *Our Missionary Work from 1853 to 1889* (Dayton, OH: United Brethren Publishing House, 1889), 214. Most Chinese immigrants at the time came from the same region as Moy. See Marie Rose Wong, *Sweet Cakes, Long Journey: The Chinatowns of Portland, Oregon* (Seattle: University of Washington Press, 2004), 16–18.

Place for the newcomers: See generally Nancy D'Inzillo, lead ed., *Dreams of the West: A History of the Chinese in Oregon, 1850–1950* (Portland, OR: Ooligan Press, 2007); Nelson Chia-Chi Ho, *Portland's Chinatown: The History of an Urban Ethnic District* (Portland, OR: Bureau of Planning, 1978); Wong, *Sweet Cakes, Long Journey.*

Arrived in Portland: MacColl, *Merchants, Money and Power,* 175; Deady, *Pharisee Among Philistines* 1:132.

"Wicked anti-Chinese fanatics": Deady, *Pharisee Among Philistines* 1:132.

"Dirt, filth, stench": "The Chinese Nuisance," *Oregonian,* May 22, 1873 (reprinting an item from the *San Francisco Chronicle*).

Treaty obligations with China: MacColl, *Merchants, Money and Power,* 167–68; Toll, *The Making of an Ethnic Middle Class,* 83. For a recent discussion of the limits placed on Chinese immigrants in the West, see also Joshua Paddison, "Race, Religion, and Naturalization: How the West Shaped Citizenship Debates in the Reconstruction Congress," in Adam Arenson and Andrew R. Graybill, eds.,

723

Civil War Wests: Testing the Limits of the United States, ed. Adam Arenson and Andrew R. Graybill (Berkeley: University of California Press, 2015), 181–201.

Discrimination disgusted General Howard: OOH, *Autobiography* 2:479.

"A light . . . dawned": Flickinger, *Our Missionary Work,* 214; OOH, *Autobiography* 2:478.

Second chances and starting over: See generally Fetters, "The Church of the United Brethren of Christ Support."

"A larger, more intelligent": "Battle of Gettysburg," *Oregonian,* Nov. 25, 1874.

"Mortified and": OOH, "Campaign and Battle of Gettysburg, June and July, 1863," *Atlantic Monthly,* July 1876, 48, 59.

"Uh Oh Howard": Creighton, *The Colors of Courage,* 178.

"One who mingled": See Carpenter, *Sword and Olive Branch,* 69.

"Consummate master": See Ambrose Bierce, "On General O. O. Howard," in *Phantoms of a Blood-Stained Period: The Complete Civil War Writings of Ambrose Bierce,* ed. Russell Duncan and David J. Klooster (Amherst: University of Massachusetts Press, 2002), 230.

"An emotion never": "Battle of Gettysburg," *Oregonian,* Nov. 25, 1874.

"A sheet of fire": OOH, "Campaign and Battle of Gettysburg," 65–66.

"Men fell while eating": Ibid., 67; "Battle of Gettysburg."

"Very interesting and": Deady, *Pharisee Among Philistines* 1:172.

"Marriages happy ones": Ibid., 173; *New North-*

west, Dec. 4, 1874.

"All the late": *New Northwest,* Oct. 2, 1874.

Passed for society: MacColl, *Merchants, Money and Power,* 188.

Turn down invitations: "City: Declined to Lecture," *Oregonian,* Dec. 2, 1874.

"Let it all go": OOH to RBH, Sept. 30, 1874, Letterbooks, roll 7, OOHP.

The Freedmen's Bureau: See, e.g., Communication from Second Auditor of Treasury Dep't, Aug. 19, 1874, box 12, OOHP.

Crushed his toenail: OOH, *Autobiography* 1:128.

"Moral integrity and": "Complimentary Serenade to Gen. Howard," *Oregonian,* Sept. 26, 1874.

"Conscientious, brave and": "Battle of Gettysburg."

Boarded a steamer: W. B. Cudlipp for OOH to John H. Cook, Sept. 14, 1874, Letterbooks, roll 7, OOHP.

Spring-wagon, and horseback: On Howard's many travels, see his *Famous Indian Chiefs I Have Known* (New York: Century, 1908) and *My Life and Experiences Among Our Hostile Indians* (Hartford, CT: A. D. Worthington, 1907).

"You will never": OOH to R. H. Gilmore, Nov. 3, 1874, Letterbooks, roll 7, OOHP.

"Roaring frightfully": OOH, *Famous Indian Chiefs,* 349.

Through tavern walls: Ibid., 267.

"Wild and frightful": Ibid., 269.

"Half-starved": Ibid., 329.

"Miserable" and "queer words": Ibid., 324.

"Squaw men": Ibid., 330–31; OOH, "Men Tied to Squaws: General Howard Explains Why

They Cannot Be Happy," Dec. 30, 1890, newspaper clipping in OOHP.

Cut Arm: OOH, *Famous Indian Chiefs,* 205, 332. For a discussion of the organization of reservations, see Stephen J. Rockwell, *Indian Affairs and the Administrative State in the Nineteenth Century* (New York: Cambridge University Press, 2010), 275–302.

Never revealed themselves: OOH, *Autobiography* 1:84–86; OOH, *My Life,* 89–91.

They were unarmed: OOH, *Famous Indian Chiefs,* 112–36; OOH, *My Life,* 177–225.

Coffee and bacon: See generally OOH, *My Life;* Sweeney, *Making Peace with Cochise.*

Freedpeople in the South: See Norman J. Bender, *"New Hope for the Indians": The Grant Peace Policy and the Navajos in the 1870s* (Albuquerque: University of New Mexico Press, 1989), 27–29; Rockwell, *Indian Affairs and the Administrative State,* 253–54; C. Joseph Genetin-Pilawa, *Crooked Paths to Allotment: The Fight over Federal Indian Policy After the Civil War* (Chapel Hill: University of North Carolina Press, 2012): 94-111; Pekka Hämäläinen, *Comanche Empire* (New Haven: Yale University Press, 2008), 325–29; Francis Paul Prucha, *The Great Father* (Lincoln: University of Nebraska Press, 1984), 481–83, 501–33; Robert M. Utley, *The Indian Frontier of the American West, 1846–1890* (Albuquerque: University of New Mexico Press, 1984), 129–56.

"Just the right way": OOH, *Famous Indian Chiefs,* 264.

Show that it could work: OOH to CHH, July

11, 1874, Letterbooks, roll 7, OOHP; OOH to RBH, Feb. 19, 1874, Letterbooks, roll 7, OOHP; see also Stephen Kantrowitz, " 'Not Quite Constitutionalized': The Meaning of 'Civilization' and the Limits of Native American Citizenship,' " in *The World the Civil War Made,* ed. Gregory P. Downs and Kate Masur (Chapel Hill: University of North Carolina Press, 2015), 76.

"The low moaning of the wind": OOH, *My Life,* 219.

Another war on Americans: Ibid.; see also Sweeney, *Making Peace with Cochise,* 60.

"On the Reservation": S. W. Fountain to OOH, Aug. 15, 1874, box 12, folder 75, OOHP.

Their lives and property: "Death of Cochise," *New York Times,* Oct. 29, 1874.

"Corn, potatoes, squashes": OOH, *Famous Indian Chiefs,* 264–65.

"Restless roamers": Ibid., 343.

"Great contrition": "Indian Chief in Trouble," *Oregonian,* Nov. 4, 1874.

Bordering Kansas and Missouri: See generally Arthur Quinn, *Hell with the Fire Out: A History of the Modoc War* (Boston: Faber & Faber, 1997); Boyd Cothran, *Remembering the Modoc War: Redemptive Violence and the Making of American Innocence* (Chapel Hill: University of North Carolina Press, 2014), 48–58.

"Obedient and well disposed": OOH, *Autobiography* 2:463–64. On the lessons various parties drew from the war, see Cothran, *Remembering the Modoc War.*

"My work is not": OOH to Grace Howard, Oct. 6, 1874, Letterbooks, roll 7, OOHP.

Chapter 3: Quite Good Friends

"Good coffee": OOH, *NPJ,* 37 (describing his April 1877 journey, based on his reminiscences of multiple trips east).

Quinine and sulfur: OOH to Grace Howard, Mar. 18, 1875, box 1, JTGP.

"Unfailing good company": OOH, *NPJ,* 37–38.

"Quick eye": Ibid., 38–39.

"More sudden": Ibid.

"Its sweetness": Ibid., 44.

"The filthiest place": "Filthy Streets," *Walla Walla Statesman,* Apr. 24, 1875.

"To see the country": "For Grande Ronde Agency," *Willamette Farmer,* Mar. 19, 1875.

"Deep & sticky": OOH to Grace Howard, Mar. 18, 1875, box 1, JTGP.

"Great 'Christian soldier' ": "The 'Christian Soldier,' " *Oregon City Enterprise,* Mar. 26, 1875. The paper deemed Howard's demands as "worse than taking funds from niggers."

Gettysburg in Walla Walla: "Department Commander," *Walla Walla Statesman,* Apr. 24, 1875.

Earth to grow wheat: Robert H. Ruby and John Arthur Brown, *The Cayuse Indians: Imperial Tribesmen of Old Oregon* (Norman: University of Oklahoma Press, 1972), 278–79.

"Singular little man": OOH to Grace Howard, Mar. 18, 1875, box 1, JTGP.

"Sprightly Frenchman": OOH, *NPJ,* 28.

Canadians in the fur trade: Sworn Statement by N. A. Cornoyer, Oct. 20, 1873, in Petition and Papers of Toussaint Mesplie, Misc. Doc. No. 97, 43rd Cong., 1st sess. (1874), 3–4.

"Open for settlement": as quoted in Elliott

West, *The Last Indian War: The Nez Perce Story* (New York: Oxford University Press, 2009), 70.

Burned his body: Ibid.; Alvin M. Josephy Jr., *The Nez Perce Indians and the Opening of the Northwest* (New Haven: Yale University Press, 1965), 345.

Flesh as trophies: William Parsons, *An Illustrated History of Umatilla County* (Spokane, WA: W. H. Lever, 1902), 92–96; West, *The Last Indian War*, 70–71; Hubert Howe Bancroft, *History of Washington, Idaho, and Montana, 1845–1889* (San Francisco: History Company Publishers, 1890), 141n; Josephy, *The Nez Perce*, 359; Clarence L. Andrews, "Warfield's Story of Peo-Peo-Mox-Mox," *Washington Historical Quarterly* 25 (1934): 182–84 ("I lifted old Mox-Mox's hair." "I have heard that his scalp is in Salem in the Oregon Archives. Is that true?" "No. So many came to see it that I got tired of it and I buried it between my barn and a neighbor's house, about halfway between. That is where it is still.").

Oregon's Catholic bishop: John Y. Simon, ed., *Papers of Ulysses S. Grant,* vol. 24, *1873* (Carbondale: Southern Illinois University Press), 418.

Conversation with Howard: OOH, *My Life and Experiences Among Our Hostile Indians* (Hartford, CT: A. D. Worthington, 1908), 238.

"I was royally": Ibid., 238.

"Embrac[ing] a large body": *Annual Report of the Commissioner of Indian Affairs to the Secretary of the Interior for the Year 1875* (Washington: Government Printing Office, 1875), 353.

"The dress of the whites": *Annual Report of the Commissioner of Indian Affairs to the Secretary of the Interior for the Year 1874* (Washington: Government Printing Office, 1874), 322–23.

"Well-marked religious": *Annual Report of the Commissioner of Indian Affairs . . . 1875, 354.*

"It is now": *Annual Report of the Commissioner of Indian Affairs . . . 1874, 322.*

"A good many": Ibid., 323.

"Morally and intellectually": *Annual Report of the Commissioner of Indian Affairs to the Secretary of the Interior for the Year 1876* (Washington: Government Printing Office, 1876), 125. For a discussion of the context of the Whitman Massacre, see Patricia Limerick, *The Legacy of Conquest: The Unbroken Past of the American West* (New York: Norton, 1987), 36-41.

"A few worthless": As quoted in Ruby and Brown, *The Cayuse Indians, 279.*

"Persons of a worthless": *Annual Report of the Commissioner of Indian Affairs . . . 1874, 322.*

"Universal and ardent": *Annual Report of the Commissioner of Indian Affairs . . . 1875, 354.* On the centrality of treaties in the nineteenth century, see Colin G. Calloway, *Pen and Ink Witchcraft: Treaties and Treaty Making in American Indian History* (New York: Oxford University Press, 2013).

They had rights: Stephen Kantrowitz, " 'Not Quite Constitutionalized': The Meaning of 'Civilization' and the Limits of Native American Citizenship,' " in *The World the Civil War Made,* ed. Gregory P. Downs and Kate Masur (Chapel Hill: University of North Carolina

Press, 2015), 75.

"Rapacious": *Annual Report of the Commissioner of Indian Affairs . . . 1875,* 353.

"All believe[d] in": *Annual Report of the Commissioner of Indian Affairs . . . 1874,* 323; see also Robert H. Ruby and John A. Brown, *Dreamer-Prophets of the Columbia Plateau: Smohalla and Skolaskin* (Norman: University of Oklahoma Press, 1989).

A vast distance: *Annual Report of the Commissioner of Indian Affairs . . . 1874,* 323.

Beaten they had been: Ruby and Brown, *Dreamer-Prophets,* 4, 9–11 (describing the followers' desperation to turn "despair to delight").

"H[e]ld a control": *Annual Report of the Commissioner of Indian Affairs . . . 1874,* 323.

"Could pass at any time": Parsons, *An Illustrated History of Umatilla County,* 56, 90.

New army commander: OOH, *NPJ,* 28.

Eighteen degrees below zero: *An Illustrated History of Union and Wallowa Counties* (Spokane, WA: Western Historical Publishing, 1902), 153–54.

Snow fell in one day: Grace Bartlett, *The Wallowa Country, 1867–1877* (Fairfield, WA: Ye Galleon Press, 1984), 52.

"Noticeably tall and stout": OOH, *NPJ,* 28; OOH, *My Life,* 233.

"Quite carefully dressed": OOH, *NPJ,* 28.

"Most solemn": Ibid., 29.

"An audacious stare": Ibid.

In a deep voice: Josephy, *The Nez Perce,* 668n49.

"I heard that Washington": OOH, *NPJ,* 29.

Never been interrupted: Ibid.

"An Indian is usually": Ibid.

Silvered the rolling country: *The American Ephemeris and Nautical Almanac for the Year 1875* (Washington: Bureau of Navigation, 1872), 67.

Riders could easily ford: "Lost His Way," *Walla Walla Statesman,* April 24, 1875.

Reach the destination: Ibid.

Scotsman about Howard's Age: 1880 US Census, Umatilla County, OR.

"Not one cent": "Lost His Way."

Chapter 4: Winding Waters

Younger brother Ollokot: Interview with Yellow Bull, Feb. 13, 1915, WMCP-BYU. On the disjuncture between native and non-Indian perspectives on a chief, see Lisa Blee, *Framing Chief Leschi: Narratives and the Politics of Historical Justice* (Chapel Hill: University of North Carolina Press, 2014), 17, 82–84.

"T-under (thunder)": Alvin M. Josephy Jr., *The Nez Perce Indians and the Opening of the Northwest* (New Haven: Yale University Press, 1965), 669 (describing Frances G. Hamblen's reminiscence of Chief Joseph's 1893 visit to her home).

Gospel to the Nez Perce: Ibid., 190.

Horse and cattle herds: Ibid., 191.

"The miners, packers": *An Illustrated History of Union and Wallowa Counties* (Spokane, WA: Western Historical Publishing, 1902), 148.

Democratic and Republican: Ibid., 148–50, 152–53.

Rich high country: Young Joseph, "An Indian's View of Indian Affairs," *North American Review* 128 (April 1879): 419.

Streams, prairies, and the lake: LVM, *Yellow*

Wolf: His Own Story (Caldwell, ID: Caxton Printers, 1940), 265.

"That beautiful valley": Young Joseph, "An Indian's View," 419.

From the Pacific: Caroline James, *Nez Perce Women in Transition, 1877–1990* (Moscow: University of Idaho Press, 1996), 26–28.

Entirely in molars: Ibid., 40–58.

Bread for the coming year: David Lavender, *Let Me Be Free: The Nez Perce Tragedy* (New York: HarperCollins, 1992), 15.

World for thousands of years: Alvin M. Josephy Jr., *Nez Perce Country* (Lincoln: University of Nebraska Press, 2007), 5.

Appeared before his nephew: LVM, *Yellow Wolf,* 295–300.

"You may think": Ibid., 27.

Returned with another: Ibid., 295–300.

Umatilla, and Walla Walla: Elliott West, *The Last Indian War: The Nez Perce Story* (New York: Oxford University Press, 2009), 12–13.

Shriveled and dry: LVM, *Hear Me, My Chiefs! Nez Perce History and Legend,* ed. Ruth Bordin (Caldwell, ID: Caxton, 2001), 557, 562, 576.

"Over the eyebrows": Ibid., 38.

Holding on to a boy: Josephy, *The Nez Perce,* 447, 449; West, *The Last Indian War,* 106; Young Joseph, "An Indian's View," 419.

"My body is returning": Young Joseph, "An Indian's View," 419.

White man stole it: Josephy, *The Nez Perce,* 449.

Wandering the bunchgrass: Ibid., 449–52; West, *The Last Indian War,* 106–7.

One of their own: West, *The Last Indian War,* 21; LVM, *Hear Me,* 17–18.

"These are the people": LVM, *Hear Me,* 17.

Chief on the Clearwater: West, *The Last Indian War,* 20–23. For a discussion of Indians of the Northwest before the expedition of Lewis and Clark, see Colin G. Calloway, *One Vast Winter Count: The Native American West Before Lewis and Clark* (Lincoln: University of Nebraska Press, 2003), 294–304.

"Our fathers gave": Young Joseph, "An Indian's View," 415.

Old ways of living: West, *The Last Indian War,* 25–28, 41, 43.

Government and the bands: Ibid., 29–32.

Through the enemy's cordon: LVM, *Yellow Wolf,* 25.

Amounted to theft: Young Joseph, "An Indian's View," 419–20; Colin G. Calloway, *Pen and Ink Witchcraft: Treaties and Treaty Making in American Indian History* (New York: Oxford University Press, 2013), 227.

Several other bands: West, *The Last Indian War,* 89, 93–94.

"In order," Joseph wrote: Young Joseph, "An Indian's View," 418.

"Inside is the home": Ibid.

"Always remember that": Ibid., 419–20.

"I pressed my Father's": Ibid.

Chapter 5: The Wilderness of American Power

"105 miles distant": John B. Monteith to F. A. Walker, Aug. 27, 1872, Lapwai Reservation Letterbooks, Nez Perce National Historical Park, Spalding, Idaho.

Ready to see him: Ibid.

"Appointment of some person": "Interesting Wow Wow," *Mountain Sentinel* (La Grande, OR), July 6, 1872.

Slight as to be imperceptible: Grace Bartlett, *The Wallowa Country, 1867–1877* (Fairfield, WA: Ye Galleon Press, 1984), 22.

"It is in the nature": "Interesting Wow Wow."

Answered to President Grant: On reservation bureaucracy, see Stephen J. Rockwell, *Indian Affairs and the Administrative State in the Nineteenth Century* (New York: Cambridge University Press, 2010), 246–74, esp. 254; Robert M. Kvasnicka and Herman J. Viola, eds., *The Commissioners of Indian Affairs, 1824–1977* (Lincoln: University of Nebraska Press, 1979), 135–66 (documenting the lives and tenures of the four commissioners who served from 1872 to 1877).

Authority to inspect reservations: Norman J. Bender, *"New Hope for the Indians": The Grant Peace Policy and the Navajos in the 1870s* (Albuquerque: University of New Mexico Press, 1989), 6–7.

Improvised every day: At the same time, without the interference of state and local governments, federal power on the frontier could be more direct and immediate. See Brian Balogh, *A Government out of Sight: The Mystery of National Authority in Nineteenth-Century America* (Cambridge: Cambridge University Press, 2009), 154, 205–11.

"Fix up matters": Monteith to F. A. Walker, Aug. 27, 1872, Lapwai Reservation Letterbooks, Nez Perce National Historical Park, Spalding, Idaho.

Nez Perce claim on the valley: Ibid.; Alvin M. Josephy Jr., *The Nez Perce Indians and the Opening of the Northwest* (New Haven: Yale University Press, 1965), 454; Bartlett, *The Wal-*

Iowa Country, 23.

"In their finery": Monteith to F. A. Walker, Aug. 27, 1872, Lapwai Reservation Letterbooks, Nez Perce National Historical Park, Spalding, Idaho.

Made sense to wait: Ibid.

"Painted up &c.": Ibid.

"The Country was sold": Ibid.

" 'It was a lie' ": Ibid.

"With force enough": Ibid.

"Do anything that would": Ibid.

"Those who term": Monteith to Thomas K. Cree, Aug. 27, 1872, as quoted in Allen P. Slickpoo and Deward E. Walker, *Noon Nee-Me-Poo: We, the Nez Perces* (Lapwai, ID: Nez Perce Tribe of Idaho, 1973), 172. For a recent discussion of the meaning of "civilization" and "citizenship" as they related to the plight of Native Americans during Reconstruction, see also Stephen Kantrowitz, " 'Not Quite Constitutionalized': The Meaning of 'Civilization' and the Limits of Native American Citizenship,' " in *The World the Civil War Made,* ed. Gregory P. Downs and Kate Masur (Chapel Hill: University of North Carolina Press, 2015), 75–105; David Wallace Adams, *Education for Extinction: American Indians and the Boarding School Experience, 1875–1928* (Lawrence: University of Kansas Press, 1995), 12–21.

"Wild habits" and "civilization": Monteith to F. A. Walker, Aug. 27, 1872, Lapwai Reservation Letterbooks, Nez Perce National Historical Park, Spalding, Idaho.

Time they spent together in the 1830s: Ibid.

As any American citizen: Native American

leaders advocated for the rights of citizenship during the years of Reconstruction. See Kantrowitz, " 'Not Quite Constitutionalized,' " 75.

"Keep away from": Monteith to F. A. Walker, Aug. 27, 1872, Lapwai Reservation Letterbooks, Nez Perce National Historical Park, Spalding, Idaho.

"It is a great pity": Ibid. For more on Walker, see Francis Paul Prucha, *The Great Father* (Lincoln: University of Nebraska Press, 1984), 535.

Smith Mountain: "Important Letter from A. C. Smith," *Mountain Sentinel,* Mar. 8, 1873.

"I had no fears": As quoted in Bartlett, *The Wallowa Country,* 30.

Signed away the Wallowa Valley: Calloway, *Pen and Ink Witchcraft,* 227.

"If any respect": As quoted in F. L. M., "The Nez Perce War," *Galaxy,* Dec. 24, 1877, 817, 823; see also H. Clay Wood, *The Status of Young Joseph and His Band of Nez-Perce Indians Under the Treaties Between the United States and the Nez-Perce Tribe of Indians, and the Indian Title to Land* (Portland, OR: Assistant Adjutant General's Office, Department of the Columbia, 1876), 32.

"The laws and customs": Young Joseph, "An Indian's View," 419–20.

"To remain in said valley": Wood, *Status of Young Joseph,* 32.

"The claims and improvements": Advertisement, *Oregonian,* May 29, 1873.

For better and worse: See generally Elliott West, *The Last Indian War: The Nez Perce Story* (New York: Oxford University Press, 2009); Heather Cox Richardson, *West from Appomattox: The*

Reconstruction of America After the Civil War (New Haven: Yale University Press, 2007).

Bureaucracy should interpret it: Cf. James Q. Wilson, *Bureaucracy: What Government Agencies Do and Why They Do It* (New York: Basic Books, 2000), 299–300 ("Policy making in the United States is more like a barroom brawl: Anybody can join in, the combatants fight all comers and sometimes change sides, no referee is in charge, and the fight lasts not for a fixed number of rounds but indefinitely or until everybody drops from exhaustion. To repeat former Secretary of State George Shultz's remark, 'it's never over.' "); Hendrik Hartog, "Pigs and Positivism," 1985 *Wisc. L. Rev.* 899. I thank Nick Parrillo for directing me to the reflection by Wilson.

"Renegade Indians": "Indian Affairs: Public Meeting at La Grande," *Oregonian,* Apr. 28, 1873.

"The sub-chief of": James K. Kelly and Joseph G. Wilson to E. P. Smith, May 28, 1873, as quoted in "The Wallowa," *Oregonian,* June 26, 1873.

"Extensive tracts": Ibid.

"Will of the majority": Ibid.

"Reservation for the roaming": As quoted in Josephy, *The Nez Perce,* 456

Remained open to settlement: Ibid., 456–57; West, *The Last Indian War,* 107.

"Robbing the settlers": "The Awful Outrage," "Read White Men!" and "Wallowa Valley News," *Mountain Sentinel,* May 31, 1873.

"Citizens of the Wallowa": "Read White Men!"

"The other day": "Letter from Wallowa," *Mountain Sentinel,* May 31, 1873.

"Stinks in the nostrils": "The Awful Outrage."

Never paid the settlers: "Oregon," *Oregonian,* July 3, 1873; see also Josephy, *The Nez Perce,* 458.

The 1874 elections: Bartlett, *The Wallowa Country,* 44–45, 51.

Summer buffalo hunt: *Annual Report of the Commissioner of Indian Affairs to the Secretary of the Interior for the Year 1873* (Washington: Government Printing Office, 1873), 245.

"The only thing": Monteith to E. P. Smith, April 28, 1874, as quoted in Bartlett, *The Wallowa Country,* 47.

"Forked tongue": Monteith to F. A. Walker, Nov. 22, 1873, as quoted in Josephy, *The Nez Perce,* 462.

"At first I let": Monteith to F. A. Walker, Nov. 22, 1873, as quoted in Bartlett, *The Wallowa Country,* 45.

"Nothing more would be": Kelly to James H. Slater, May 18, 1874, as quoted in *An Illustrated History of Union and Wallowa Counties* (Spokane, WA: Western Historical Publishing, 1902), 480–81.

"And . . . the former": "Oregon," *Oregonian,* June 8, 1874.

"He done this": As quoted in Bartlett, *The Wallowa Country,* 46, 48–49; "Oregon," *Oregonian,* July 20, 1874.

Claim to the valley: Josephy, *The Nez Perce,* 463–65.

Humboldt County: Robert Wooster, *The American Military Frontiers: The United States Army in the West, 1783–1900* (Albuquerque: University of New Mexico Press, 2009), 175; Richard H.

Orton, *Records of California Men in the War of the Rebellion, 1861 to 1867* (Sacramento: J. D. Young, 1890), 826–31; "Letter from Humboldt County," *Sacramento Daily Union,* June 24, 1865.

"Heavy chastisements": "Letter from Humboldt County."

"Giving no intentional": Whipple to Adj. General Dept. of the Columbia, Sept. 5, 1874, as quoted in Bartlett, *The Wallowa Country,* 49.

"Perfect" and "perfect good will": As quoted in ibid., 54.

"Henry rifles, carbines": Ibid., 54–55.

Crackled in the fire: Ibid.; Josephy, *The Nez Perce,* 467.

"A feeling of": As quoted in Bartlett, *The Wallowa Country,* 54–55.

"Was inclined to be": John B. Monteith to E. P. Smith, Sept. 6, 1875, reprinted in *Annual Report of the Commissioner of Indian Affairs to the Secretary of the Interior for the Year 1875* (Washington: Government Printing Office, 1875), 260–61.

Across Nez Perce country: Josephy, *The Nez Perce,* 467.

Death to the Sioux: LVM, *Hear Me,* 183, 572–74. On battles at that time between the Crow and the Sioux, see Frederick E. Hoxie, *Parading Through History: The Making of the Crow Nation in America, 1805–1935* (New York: Cambridge University Press, 1995), 107.

Distinguished in battle himself: LVM, *Hear Me,* 181.

He was angry: Ibid., 183–84.

Proud of their crimes: Ibid., 181.

"Heavy, guttural voice": OOH, *NPJ,* 58.

"He who lives above": LVM, *Hear Me,* 163.

"Tired and sore": Whipple, Aug. 18, 1875, as quoted in Bartlett, *The Wallowa Country,* 53.

"He hoped I could tell": Ibid.

"Did not make": Ibid., 54.

Competing for the same pastureland: Jennifer Williams and Erin Melville, "The History of Grazing in Wallowa County," Sept. 2005, 12 (Oregon State University Extension Service–Wallowa County) http://extension.oregonstate .edu/wallowa/sites/default/files/_in_Wallowa_ County_Compilation_edited_4_2009.pdf.

Definition of citizenship: See Kantrowitz, " 'Not Quite Constitutionalized,' " esp. 76–77, 98–99; C. Joseph Genetin-Pilawa, *Crooked Paths to Allotment: The Fight over Federal Indian Policy After the Civil War* (Chapel Hill: University of North Carolina Press, 2012), 108–11; for the way concepts of assimilation shaped the Indian Service, see Cathleen D. Cahill, *Federal Fathers and Mothers: A Social History of the United States Indian Service, 1869–1933* (Chapel Hill: University of North Carolina Press, 2011).

"The two races": as quoted in *Report of the Secretary of War, 1875,* H. Exec. Doc. 1, pt. 2, vol. 1, 44th Cong., 1st sess., Serial Set 1674 (Washington: Government Printing Office, 1875), 128.

"The stories of the hostile": "Letter from Wallowa," *Oregonian,* Sept. 2, 1875.

"This band of Indians": *Report of the Secretary of War, 1875,* 128.

"Separate and independent": Ibid.

"I think it a great": Ibid., 126.

Chapter 6: Adonis in Blue

Summer months ahead: "The Weather," *Oregonian,* Jan. 24, 1876; "The City," *Oregonian,* Jan. 25, 1876; "Brief Notes," *Oregonian,* Jan. 26, 1876.

"Appropriated it": CESW Diary, July 10, 1928, box 29(4), CESWP.

Awaited an opening: Ibid.

"I'm going to obey": CESW Reminiscence, box 6(9), folder 28, CESWP.

Started taking on water: CESW Diary, July 10, 1928, box 29(4), CESWP.

"The agony for air": CESW Autobiographical Notes, box 6(1), CESWP.

As it slipped under: CESW Diary, July 10, 1928, box 29(4), CESWP.

General Oliver Otis Howard: Ibid.

Winter lecture series: "City: The Lecture," *Oregonian,* Jan. 26, 1876.

Flirtation Walk back at West Point: NMS to CESW, Apr. 8, 1875, box 1, item 1.17, WP.

Paws, he said: CESW to NMS, Jan. 3, 1873, box 1, item 1.8, WP.

Public and private receptions: "Hail to the Chief," *Oregonian,* Sept. 1, 1875; "Private Reception," *Oregonian,* Sept. 2, 1875.

Waltz with Lieutenant Wood: CESW to NMS, Sept. 12, 1875, box 1, item 1.31, WP. For a broader picture of these Indian wars, see Francis Paul Prucha, *The Great Father* (Lincoln: University of Nebraska Press, 1984), 533–41.

Anything in the world: CESW Autobiographical Notes, box 6(9), CESWP.

Glass of mulled ale: Ibid.

Program at Vassar: Philip W. Leon, *Nanny Wood: From Washington Belle to Portland's Grande Dame* (Bowie, MD: Heritage Books, 2003), 74.

Howard family's guest: CESW to NMS, Jan. 4, 1876, box 243(12), CESWP.

"Many difficulties": "City: The Lecture," *Oregonian,* Jan. 26, 1876.

"Too many initials": Matthew Deady, *Pharisee Among Philistines: The Diary of Judge Matthew P. Deady, 1871–1892,* 2 vols. (Portland: Oregon Historical Society, 1975), 2:451.

Andrew Jackson at the White House: CESW Autobiographical Notes, box 6(7), CESWP.

Diarrhea, and the "shakes": K. Jack Bauer, *Zachary Taylor: Soldier, Planter, Statesman of the Old Southwest* (Baton Rouge: Louisiana State University Press, 1985), 269.

Navy's Pacific Squadron: William Maxwell Wood, *Wandering Sketches of People and Things* (Philadelphia: Carey & Hart, 1849).

His father's valor: CESW, "An Unknown Turning-Point in the Destiny of the Republic," *Californian* 2 (Dec. 1880): 539–43; Robert Hamburger, *Two Rooms: The Life of Charles Erskine Scott Wood* (Lincoln: University of Nebraska Press, 998), 68.

From an old marine: CESW Autobiographical Notes, box 6(1) CESWP.

"Fine remorseless Naval discipline": Ibid.

Mahogany sideboard: CESW Autobiographical Notes, boxes 6(7) and 6(10), CESWP.

Topic was "Children": "City: The Lecture."

"Grand romp": CESW to NMS, Dec. 29, 1875, box 243(11), CESWP.

"Was replete with": "City: The Lecture."

"He had been in every": CESW Autobiographical Notes, box 6(9), CESWP.

"A fine American": CESW Autobiographical Notes, box 6(1), CESWP.

"The Constitution, the Union": "Reception and Speech at Buffalo," *New York Times,* Feb. 18, 1861.

Lost on the boy: Ibid.; CESW Autobiographical Notes, box 6(7), CESWP.

"As if the sky": CESW Autobiographical Notes, box 6(7), CESWP.

Naval blockade of Norfolk: Ibid.

March 1862: Ibid.; Hamburger, *Two Rooms,* 17.

Gettysburg the following year: CESW Autobiographical Notes, boxes 6(7) and 6(9), CESWP.

"For keeps": CESW Autobiographical Notes, box 6(1a), CESWP.

Naked in the Chesapeake: CESW Autobiographical Notes, box 6(7), CESWP.

Kept their home dark: Ibid.

"I am sure we knew": Ibid.

"Picturesque, jingling": Ibid.

An easy ride away: Ibid.

World was changing: See Barbara Fields, *Slavery and Freedom on the Middle Ground: Maryland During the Nineteenth Century* (New Haven: Yale University Press, 1985).

"Was continually trying": CESW Autobiographical Notes, box 6(9), CESWP.

Light a new one: Ibid.

"Plumes, sash, gold": CESW to Eliza Bryson Wood Smith, Dec. 14, 1933, box 237(6), CESWP.

Mother of pearl: Ibid.; CESW Autobiographical Notes, box 6(9), CESWP.

For his next guest: CESW Autobiographical

Notes, box 6(9), CESWP.

"Beautiful Minnie Buckmaster": NMS to CESW, Apr. 8, 1875, box 1, item 1.17, WP; CESW, Autobiographical Notes, box 6(8), CESWP.

Denied his request: CESW Autobiographical Notes, box 6(9), CESWP.

"It rises and falls": CESW to NMS, Sept. 12, 1875, box 1, item 1.31, WP.

"*That* Mr. Wood": Ibid.

Silver-buttoned livery: CESW Autobiographical Notes, box 6(9), CESWP.

Burning from gunpowder: CESW Autobiographical Notes, box 6(7), CESWP.

"Diamond cut diamond": CESW to NMS, May 25, 1875, box 1, item 1.19, WP.

Reams of passionate declarations: CESW to NMS, Dec. 24, 1874, box 1, item 1.12, WP; CESW to NMS, Jan. 4, 1876, box 243(12), CESWP.

"Your loving lover": CESW to NMS, Jan. 4, 1876, box 243(12), CESWP.

"Things that you probably": CESW to NMS, Dec. 24, 1874, box 1, item 1.12, WP.

"Slapped me on the back": CESW Autobiographical Notes, box 6(9), CESWP.

"You say 'I hate 'em' ": CESW to NMS, May 25, 1875, box 1, item 1.19, WP.

"Those poor devils": CESW to NMS, June 10, 1875, box 1, item 1.22, WP.

"What could be": CESW Autobiographical Notes, box 6(9), CESWP.

"Don't want em": CESW to NMS, June 9, 1875, box 1, item 1.21, WP.

"Tremendously beautiful, breathtaking": CESW Autobiographical Notes, box 6(9),

CESWP.

"Tedious, hot dusty trip": CESW to NMS, Sept. 12, 1875, box 1, item 1.31, WP.

Collections of birds' eggs: Mark V. Barrow Jr., *A Passion for Birds: American Ornithology After Audubon* (Princeton: Princeton University Press, 1998), 29, 41.

"Wonderful blue birds": CESW Autobiographical Notes, box 6(9), CESWP.

"Impudent and disobedient": CESW to NMS, Sept. 12, 1875, box 1, item 1.31, WP.

Piles of paper: Ibid.

Mail from his love: CESW to NMS, Dec. 29, 1875, Box 243(11), CESWP.

"I spend nothing": CESW to NMS, Oct. 1875, box 1, item 1.32, WP.

"They really look": CESW to NMS, June 10, 1875, box 1, item 1.22, WP.

"Then I will": CESW to NMS, June 16, 1875, box 1, item 1.24, WP.

"I won't ever": NMS to CESW, Apr. 8, 1875, box 1, item 1.17, WP.

"I would honestly": NMS to CESW Apr. 4, 1875, box 1, item 1.16, WP.

"I look . . . just": CESW to NMS, Apr. 24, 1875, box 1, item 1.18, WP.

Greens, blues, and browns: Elizabeth Howard to Grace Howard, Dec. 4, 1874, box 2, JTGP.

"Chatty": CESW to Grace Howard, June 22, 1878, box 2, JTGP.

"One among many": CESW to James T. Gray, June 5, 1879, box 2, JTGP.

"How I hated": CESW Autobiographical Notes, box 6(1a), CESWP.

"Tortured" and "A bare and bitter": CESW to NMS, Oct. 1875, WP.

"Moody, and changeable": CESW to NMS, Feb. 8, 1878, box 243(14), CESWP.

His previous twenty: Grace Howard Diary, box 2, JTGP.

"He has such": CESW to NMS, Feb. 8, 1878, box 243(14), CESWP.

Civil War experiences: Grace Howard Diary, box 2, JTGP.

"Sketches of our": OOH, *Autobiography of Oliver Otis Howard,* 2 vols. (New York: Baker & Taylor, 1908), 2:473.

Make some notes: Grace Howard Diary, box 2, JTGP.

"Blue room": CESW to NMS, Oct. 1875, box 1, item 1.32, WP.

Chapter 7: Wind Blowing

Fired already: Much of the account that follows is drawn from "Findley's Story," in LVM, *Hear Me, My Chiefs! Nez Perce History and Legend,* ed. Ruth Bordin (Caldwell, ID: Caxton, 2001), appendix X, 612–13; Elliott West, *The Last Indian War: The Nez Perce Story* (New York: Oxford University Press, 2009), 110; Alvin M. Josephy Jr., *The Nez Perce Indians and the Opening of the Northwest* (New Haven: Yale University Press, 1965), 470–71; J. H. Horner and Grace Butterfield, "The Nez Perce-Findley Affair," *Oregon Historical Quarterly* 40 (1939): 41–42.

"Wiry": *Mountain Sentinel,* July 1, 1876.

Spirits to Joseph's band: Grace Bartlett, *The Wallowa Country, 1867–1877* (Fairfield, WA: Ye Galleon Press, 1984), 23, 61–62.

Raise his weapon: Statement of A. B. Findley in Union County Court, Sept. 23, 1876, reprinted in ibid., 107–8.

For them to keep: J. H. Horner and Grace Butterfield, "Chief Joseph: He Met White Men Half Way," *Oregonian,* Jan. 26, 1947; Ovid McWhorter to LVM, Oct. 10, 1929, box 6, folder 32, LVMP ("The Younger Findley says that he now has trinkets, earrings etc. that Chief Joseph gave them as children when he visited his father's place on different occasions.").

"God damn": H. R. Findley to LVM, Feb. 18, 1935, box 6, folder 32, LVMP.

"Bad" and "quarrelsome": H. Clay Wood to OOH, "Copy of Major H. Clay Wood's Suplimentary [*sic*] to his Report on the Status of Young Chief Joseph, and Indian Claims to Lands," Aug. 1, 1876, typescript in box 12, folder 83, LVMP.

"A parley ensued": *Mountain Sentinel,* July 1, 1876.

"Resolved not to shoot": Findley as quoted in Bartlett, *The Wallowa Country,* 107–8.

Department of Columbia's headquarters: *Mountain Sentinel,* July 1, 1876; Horner and Butterfield, "The Nez Perce-Findley Affair," 43.

Live together: At least one newspaper regarded the killing as a ploy to dispossess Joseph's band, opining that "the civil authorities of Oregon should take the Wallowa question in hand, and convince the parties concerned that even an Indian has some rights that should be respected." "Wallowa Valley," *Walla Walla Statesman,* July 1, 1876.

Civil War battles: "The First Regiment of Infantry," in Theodore F. Rodenbough and William L. Haskin, eds., *The Army of the United States: Historical Sketches of Staff and Line with Portraits of Generals-in-Chief* (New York: Maynard, Merrill, 1896), 407.

System of Nez Perce bands: West, *The Last Indian War,* 109; Josephy, *The Nez Perce,* 473; Mark H. Brown, *The Flight of the Nez Perce* (Lincoln: University of Nebraska Press, 1967), 68–69.

"The non-treaty Nez-Perces": H. Clay Wood, *The Status of Young Joseph and His Band of Nez-Perce Indians Under the Treaties Between the United States and the Nez-Perce Tribe of Indians and the Indian Title to Land* (Portland, OR: Asst. Adjutant General's Office, Department of the Columbia, 1876), 41.

"The Nez-Perces are distinguished": Ibid., 20.

"A strong desire": Wood, "Copy of Major H. Clay Wood's Suplimentary to his Report on the Status of Young Chief Joseph," 1.

"Unjustifiable killing": Ibid., 1–2.

Sacred Black Hills: T. J. Stiles, *Custer's Trials: A Life on the Frontier of a New America* (New York: Knopf, 2015), 411–12.

Overwhelmed and slaughtered: For a discussion of the Treaty of Medicine Lodge and Cheyenne resistance to its terms, see Colin G. Calloway, *Pen and Ink Witchcraft: Treaties and Treaty Making in American Indian History* (New York: Oxford University Press, 2013), 182–225, and on Little Bighorn, ibid., 233–34.

A bloody endgame: For a discussion of the shift away from treaties to the Peace Policy and the death of the Peace Policy, see ibid., 226–34; Cathleen D. Cahill, *Federal Fathers and Moth-*

ers: *A Social History of the United States Indian Service, 1869–1933* (Chapel Hill: University of North Carolina Press, 2011), 17–20; Francis Paul Prucha, *American Indian Treaties: The History of a Political Anomaly* (Berkeley: University of California Press, 1994), 287–358; Robert M. Utley, *The Indian Frontier of the American West, 1846–1890* (Albuquerque: University of New Mexico Press, 1984), 203–26; Francis Paul Prucha, *The Great Father* (Lincoln: University of Nebraska Press, 1984), 541 ("The Sioux war had accomplished what the peace policy had been unable to; it had forced the Indians to abandon their hunting grounds and accept government control on the reservations.").

Their world — differently: See Stephen Kantrowitz, " 'Not Quite Constitutionalized': The Meaning of 'Civilization' and the Limits of Native American Citizenship,' " in *The World the Civil War Made,* ed. Gregory P. Downs and Kate Masur (Chapel Hill: University of North Carolina Press, 2015), 76 ("Although the laws and amendments establishing national citizenship spoke only of nativity and allegiance, the framers of that language understood citizenship to require a good deal more. They wanted Native Americans — like freedpeople, non-Protestant immigrants, 'beggars.' And 'tramps' — to demonstrate their fitness by embracing a matrix of values and behaviors: the principles of private property and contract; habits of fixed settlement, market orientation, and patriarchal household organization; and particular modes of dress, speech, and worship.").

"The ordinary covering": Wood, "Copy of

Major H. Clay Wood's Suplimentary to his Report on the Status of Young Chief Joseph," 17–18.

Not the adjutant's: Ibid.; John D. McDermott, *Forlorn Hope: The Battle of White Bird Canyon and the Beginning of the Nez Perce War* (Boise: Idaho State Historical Society, 1978), 57–58, 64–66; Elizabeth F. Hiestand, preface to Emily McCorkle FitzGerald, *An Army Doctor's Wife on the Frontier: Letters from Alaska and the Far West, 1874–1878,* ed. Abe Laufe (Pittsburgh, PA: University of Pittsburgh Press, 1962), xiii–xiv; LVM, *Hear Me,* 135–37 (excerpting a July 31, 1876, letter from Monteith to the commissioner of Indian affairs); Josephy, *The Nez Perce,* 477.

"A period of silence" and "The writer of the": Wood, "Copy of Major H. Clay Wood's Suplimentary to his Report on the Status of Young Chief Joseph," 3.

"Wanted to know how": Ibid., 10.

"Concerning the recent": Ibid., 3.

"Quiet, peaceable, well-disposed": Ibid., 4.

"Tried for their crime": Ibid., 5.

"Among the Indians": Ibid., 4.

A split-rail fence: Gregory P. Downs and Kate Masur reflect upon this reality in "Introduction: Echoes of War: Rethinking Post–Civil War Governance and Politics," in *The World the Civil War Made,* ed. Gregory P. Downs and Kate Masur (Chapel Hill: University of North Carolina Press, 2015), 6–11.

"Among the whites": Wood, "Copy of Major H. Clay Wood's Suplimentary to his Report on the Status of Young Chief Joseph," 6.

"I want you": Ibid., 14.

"That he was not": Ibid.

"The settlers and local": Ibid., 6–7.

"His face, manners": Ibid., 17–18.

"Crude but quite accurate": Ibid., 9; LVM, *Hear Me,* 157–58; W. R. Parnell, "The Battle of White Bird Cañon," in *Northwestern Fights and Fighters,* ed. Cyrus Townsend Brady (New York: Doubleday, Page, 1910), 96–97.

"Nothing further to speak of": Wood, "Copy of Major H. Clay Wood's Suplimentary to his Report on the Status of Young Chief Joseph," 16.

"In strong language": Ibid., 17.

"One having wisdom": Ibid., 16–17.

Chapter 8: A Sharp-Sighted Heart

"War that might": "More Trouble with the Indians: A Threatened War That Might Exceed in Magnitude the War with the Sioux," *Sun,* Sept. 21, 1876; "The Indian Trouble in Oregon," *Evening Star,* Sept. 21, 1876 ("The difficulty with the Nez Perces Indians . . . threatens to result in a general Indian war on that frontier.").

Howard had come: "The Indian Trouble in Oregon."

He would press: Howard had devised this plan before the disaster at Little Bighorn, endorsing the suggestion of a Presbyterian minister in Portland that a government commission be formed to negotiate with the nontreaty Nez Perce bands "for the relinquishment of all their land-claims by fair purchase" and to "persuade them to enter within the reservation in a reasonable time." *Report of the Secretary of War, 1876,* H. Exec. Doc. 1, pt. 2, vol. 1, 44th

Cong., 2nd sess., Serial Set 1742 (Washington: Government Printing Office, 1876), 92.

J. Donald Cameron: "More Trouble with the Indians" ("At Cheyenne, [Howard] had an interview with Secretary Cameron and Gen. Sherman, who recognized the importance of the prompt intervention of a peace commission.").

Suited to the task: "The Indian Trouble in Oregon."

Newly favored status: OOH, *Autobiography of Oliver Otis Howard,* 2 vols. (New York: Baker & Taylor, 1908), 2:475–76.

"Though so brief": "Letter from Washington," *Congregationalist,* Oct. 25, 1876.

"Gradually the work": OOH, "Chattanooga," *Atlantic Monthly,* Aug. 1876, 203, 218–19.

Washington on the train west: *Eighth Annual Report of the Board of Indian Commissioners for the Year 1876* (Washington: Government Printing Office, 1877), 43.

Members of Howard's commission: Ibid.

Docked in Portland: "City: Passenger List," *Oregonian,* Oct. 30, 1876.

"The school was a busy": "Chinese School," *Oregonian,* Nov. 1, 1876.

"Urg[ing] upon them": Ibid.

"As large a number": Ibid.

Fifteen miles to Lapwai: *Eighth Annual Report of the Board of Indian Commissioners . . . 1876,* 43.

"No reliable tidings": Ibid., 44.

His triumph, galling: Ibid., 44.

Late summer and fall: *Eighth Annual Report of the Board of Indian Commissioners . . . 1876,* 51.

Findley stayed clear: Grace Bartlett, *The Wallowa Country, 1867–1877* (Fairfield, WA: Ye Galleon Press, 1984), 64.

"The Wallowa was their": Henry Rhinehart, Sept. 12, 1876, in ibid., 93–94.

"When I saw": *Eighth Annual Report of the Board of Indian Commissioners . . . 1876,* 63.

"As it was": Henry Rhinehart, Sept. 12, 1876, in Bartlett, *The Wallowa Country,* 93–94.

Waited for the end: Ibid.

Away soon after: Alvin M. Josephy Jr., *The Nez Perce Indians and the Opening of the Northwest* (New Haven: Yale University Press, 1965), 479–80.

Forty armed men: Henry Rhinehart, letter to the *Union County Review* (Summerville, OR), Sept. 12, 1876, excerpted in Bartlett, *The Wallowa Country,* 93–94; Albert G. Forse to Judge Brainard, Sept. 9, 1876, Forse Papers, Collection N-6, Order of Indian Wars, Manuscript Division, US Army Military History Institute, copy in box 10, folder 16, JAGP; Forse to H. Clay Wood, Sept. 11, 1876, Forse Papers, copy in box 10, folder 16, JAGP.

"The Indians of late": Forse to Wood, Sept. 11, 1876, Forse/JAGP; Jerome A. Greene, *Nez Perce Summer, 1877: The U.S. Army and the Nee-Me-Poo Crisis* (Helena: Montana Historical Society, 2000), 15, 381n30; Elliott West, *The Last Indian War: The Nez Perce Story* (New York: Oxford University Press, 2009), 110-11; Josephy, *The Nez Perce,* 479–83.

Breechcloths for battle: Forse to Wood, Sept. 11, 1876, Forse/JAGP.

Trust his word: Ibid.; LVM, *Hear Me, My Chiefs!*

Nez Perce Legend and History (Caldwell, ID: Caxton Press, 2001), 618–19.

"I feel satisfied": Forse to Wood, Sept. 11, 1876, Forse/JAGP.

"I earnestly recommend": Ibid.

"Seemed to give him": Forse to Wood, Sept. 25, 1876, in Bartlett, *The Wallowa Country,* 97–98.

Only plausible option: *Eighth Annual Report of the Board of Indian Commissioners . . . 1876,* 51.

"Intelligence, sagacity": Ibid., 39, 51.

"A father and": Ibid., 54.

"In all dealings": Ibid., 56.

Rights every day: Cathleen D. Cahill, *Federal Fathers and Mothers: A Social History of the United States Indian Service, 1869–1933* (Chapel Hill: University of North Carolina Press, 2011), 628.

"We know something": *Eighth Annual Report of the Board of Indian Commissioners . . . 1876,* 54.

Modern American state: On the difference between policy and its enforcement, see Gregory P. Downs and Kate Masur, "Introduction: Echoes of War: Rethinking Post–Civil War Governance and Politics," in *The World the Civil War Made,* ed. Gregory P. Downs and Kate Masur (Chapel Hill: University of North Carolina Press, 2015), 3–11.

"We are poor": *Eighth Annual Report of the Board of Indian Commissioners . . . 1876,* 55–56.

"Full and warm": Ibid., 39.

Had familiar settings: Ibid.

"entirely receptive": Ibid.

"Earnest, serious": Ibid.

Was similarly blessed: Ibid.

"He had come": Ibid., 44.

"Amassed itself in front": "That New Treaty," *Lewiston* (ID) *Teller,* Nov. 18, 1876.

"Will teach us": *Annual Report of the Commissioner of Indian Affairs to the Secretary of the Interior for the Year 1873* (Washington: Government Printing Office, 1874), 159.

"Prominent non-treaty": *Eighth Annual Report of the Board of Indian Commissioners . . . 1876,* 44.

"The President had": Ibid., 57.

"The President understands": Ibid., 58.

"Mr. Jerome informed": Ibid.

"My heart is": Ibid.

"Do you think": Ibid., 58, 59.

"The country was": Ibid., 59.

"My mind it": Ibid., 44, 59.

"Propositions" and "we" and "tillable and pasture": Ibid., 59.

"If he had anything": Ibid., 59–60.

"When we heard": Ibid., 60.

"The right to the land": Ibid.

"Have accused me": Ibid.

"Here in the interest": Ibid., 61.

"Tak[e] Joseph's advice": Ibid., 62.

"When did I": Ibid.

"What did you": Ibid.

"Is there any": Ibid., 62–63.

"All I have": Ibid., 63.

"Suppose several thousand": Ibid.

"Caused [him] to feel": Ibid.

"Joseph speaks well": Ibid., 64.

"The commission wants": Ibid.

"This one place": Ibid.

Whites and blacks together: See Stephen Kantrowitz, " 'Not Quite Constitutionalized': The Meaning of 'Civilization' and the Limits of Native American Citizenship,' " in *The World the Civil War Made,* ed. Gregory P. Downs and Kate Masur (Chapel Hill: University of North Carolina Press, 2015), 76, 98–99.

"The Government has to": *Eighth Annual Report of the Board of Indian Commissioners . . . 1876,* 62.

"I have been here": Ibid., 64.

"Explained to them": Ibid.

"Why do you persist": Ibid.

"With no favorable": Ibid., 65.

"Their coming was": "The Commission," *Lewiston* (ID) *Teller,* Dec. 2, 1876.

"As for the Wallowa": *Eighth Annual Report of the Board of Indian Commissioners . . . 1876,* 64.

Chapter 9: Aloft

The baseball season was about to begin: "Local Brevities," *Oregonian,* April 5, 6, 1877.

Rise or fall: "Urges C. H. Taylor to Climb," *Chicago Tribune,* Oct. 7, 1904.

"Pursue the eagle": Personal, *Chicago Tribune,* Oct. 5, 1875.

"Child's play": "Pacific Coast Items," *Sacramento Daily Union,* May 11, 1877.

"At least there is": "City," *Oregonian,* Apr. 10, 1877.

"All the necessary instruments": Ibid.

"Well provided": "Pacific Coast Items," *Sacramento Daily Union,* May 10, 1877.

"If you would like to go": OOH to CESW, Apr. 5, 1877, WP.

North from west: Personal, *Vancouver Indepen-*

dent, Apr. 6, 1877; George Venn, *Soldier to Advocate: C. E. S. Wood's 1877 Legacy* (La Grande, OR: Wordcraft of Oregon, 2006), 11.

"Equal to the Bay of Naples": William Gouverneur Morris, "The Customs District, Public Service, and Resources of Alaska Territory" (1878), in *Seal and Salmon Fisheries and General Resources in Alaska,* 4 vols. (Washington: Government Printing Office, 1898), 4:85.

"The sharp peak": CESW, "Among the Thlinkits," *Century Magazine* 24, no. 3 (July 1882): 323.

They had been granted: "The Territory of Alaska," *New York Times,* Jan. 15, 1876.

"Singular embarrassment": Morris, "The Customs District, Public Service, and Resources of Alaska Territory," 122.

Classified as Indians: H. Clay Wood to OOH, Dec. 16, 1875, reprinted in *Jurisdiction of the War Department over the Territory of Alaska,* H. Ex. Doc. 135, 44th Cong., 1st sess. (Washington: Government Printing Office, 1876), 49–56.

"Indians, Russians": CESW, "Among the Thlinkits," 324.

"Drunkenness, squalor": CESW, "Among the Thlinkits," 323; CESW Diary, May 1877, box 26(1), CESWP; Venn, *Soldier to Advocate,* 25.

Normally the lieutenant's: *Sitka Post,* Apr. 20, 1877, 1.

The heart of town: CESW, "Among the Thlinkits," 324.

Phillipson's trading post: Ibid.

"They was the most": CESW Diary, May 1877, CESWP.

"A group of loungers": CESW, "Among the Thlinkits," 324.

Broken off for firewood: Morris, "The Customs District, Public Service, and Resources of Alaska Territory," 83.

"The store was full of Indians": Emily FitzGerald, Jan. 13, 1875, in *An Army Doctor's Wife on the Frontier: Letters from Alaska and the Far West, 1874–1878,* ed. Abe Laufe (Pittsburgh, PA: University of Pittsburgh Press, 1962), 85.

Russian sable: Emily FitzGerald, Sept. 6, 1874, in ibid., 46; "Local Matters," *Alaska Bulletin* (Sitka, AK), Mar. 5, 1875, available at http://alaskaweb.org/itn/bulletin/18750305.html; "Alaska Items," *Daily Alta California,* July 17, 1875; William Healey Dall Diary, May 20, 24, 1874, Smithsonian Institution Archives, transcription available at https://transcription.si.edu/pdf_files/8074.pdf.

To the mountain: CESW, "Among the Thlinkits," 324.

The local Tlingit: CESW to OOH, May 16, 1877, box 13, folder 68, OOHP.

A reasonable price: CESW, "Among the Thlinkits," 324–25.

Slaves, he imagined: Ibid.

"This slavery does not seem": CESW to Lute Pease, Feb. 22, 1928, box 235(57), CESWP. In 1886, a federal judge declared that Tlingit slavery was covered and outlawed by the Thirteenth Amendment. *In re Sah Quah,* 31 F. 327 (D. Alaska 1886).

"Grasping, shrewd": CESW, "Among the Thlinkits," 324–25.

"Russian half-breed": CESW to Lute Pease, Feb. 22, 1928, box 235(57), CESWP.

Coast above Sitka: CESW to OOH, May 16, 1877, box 13, folder 68, OOHP, quotation; CESW, "Among the Thlinkits," 324–25.

Wives and daughters: On the social dynamics in Sitka just before Wood's arrival, see Sergei Kan, *Memory Eternal: Tlingit Culture and Russian Orthodox Christianity Through Two Centuries* (Seattle: University of Washington Press, 1999), 180.

"A late hour": "Local Matters," *Sitka Post,* May 5, 1877.

Frigid water: CESW, "Among the Thlinkits," 324, 326.

Dried cedar bark: CESW to OOH, May 16, 1877, box 13, folder 68, OOHP.

Into a blank beyond: CESW, Sketch of Sitka Interpreter "Our Sam," May 1877, box 293(1), CESWP.

Just beyond Yakutat Bay: CESW to OOH, May 16, 1877, box 13, folder 68, OOHP; Wood, "Among the Thlinkits," 331–32.

"One mountain": CES Wood to OOH, May 16, 1877, box 13, folder 68, OOHP.

"They are pushing the sea": Aurel Krause, *The Tlingit Indians: Observations of an Indigenous People of Southeast Alaska* (1881), trans. Erna Gunther (Kenmore, WA: Epicenter, 2013), 153.

The crew as absurd: Ibid. ("In spite of the skill with which the Tlingit handle their canoes they did not like to risk the open sea in stormy weather.").

"The Indians made a stand": CESW to OOH, May 16, 1877, box 13, folder 68, OOHP

"Threats and bribes": CESW, "Among the Thlinkits," 332.

Back to Portland: CESW to OOH, May 16, 1877, box 13, folder 68, OOHP.

"Weary, disappointed": "Local Items," *Sitka Post,* June 5, 1877.

"Owing to our": CESW to OOH, May 16, 1877, box 13, folder 68, OOHP.

"Were quite willing": *Sitka Post,* June 5, 1877.

Yukon River: CESW to OOH, May 16, 1877, box 13, folder 68, OOHP; CESW to Department of the Interior, Oct. 22, 1941, box 238(17), CESWP; CESW to Lute Pease, Feb. 22, 1928, box 235(57), CESWP.

"I would like": CESW to OOH, May 16, 1877, box 13, folder 68, OOHP.

Wanted to forget: For a discussion of Wood's memories and writings of his encounters with the Thlinkits, see Sherry L. Smith, *Reimagining Indians: Native Americans Through Anglo Eyes, 1880–1940* (New York: Oxford University Press, 2000), 25–26.

Forbidden to whites: CESW to OOH, May 16, 1877, box 13, folder 68, OOHP.

Tyrannical rule: Ibid; CESW, "Among the Thlinkits," 328–29; Eliza Ruhamah Scidmore, "The Northwest Passes to the Yukon," *National Geographic* 9, no. 4 (Apr. 1898): 108, 110.

"Wanted his country": CESW to OOH, May 16, 1877, box 13, folder 68, OOHP.

"Barbarian Chilcat": Ibid.

"One-eyed": CESW, "Among the Thlinkits," 325.

"Old pock marked": CESW to Lute Pease, Feb. 22, 1928, box 235(57), CESWP.

Almost sixty degrees: "Sitka, Weather Record for 1877," *Sitka Post,* June 5, 1877.

Land and water were divided: Thomas F.

Thornton, *Being and Place Among the Tlingit* (Seattle: University of Washington Press, 2008), 44.

Forbidding distances: Ibid.; CESW, "Among the Thlinkits," 331–32.

Grew in small plots: CESW, "Among the Thlinkits," 333–34; George Emmons, *The Tlingit Indians,* ed. Frederica de Laguna (Seattle: University of Washington Press, 1991), 141–52; Frederica de Laguna, *Under Mount St. Elias: The History and Culture of the Yakutat Tlingit,* pt. 1 (Washington: Smithsonian Institution Press, 1972), 391–410.

Religious belief: CESW, "Among the Thlinkits," 336–39.

"Were greatly frightened": Ibid., 337.

"The buckskin": Ibid., 333.

"Of a wonderland": Ibid., 338.

Clan-based Tlingit society: Ibid., 337.

"Foam[ed] magically": CESW to Lute Pease, Feb. 22, 1928, box 235(57), CESWP.

"Disinterested kindness": CESW, "Among the Thlinkits," 338.

Sleep in her house: CESW Autobiographical Notes, box 6(7), CESWP.

"Fit for": CESW Diary, May 1877, CESWP.

"Young, plump": CESW to Lute Pease, Feb. 22, 1928, box 235(57), CESWP.

"Her lover": Ibid.

"Bashful Scotch": CESW Autobiographical Notes, box 6(1a), CESWP.

"Locked the door": Ibid.

"Sexual advances": Ibid.

"I'm not sure": CESW to Lute Pease, Feb. 22, 1928, box 235(57), CESWP.

"Proposed that": Ibid.

The same distance: Ibid.

"Return to her": Ibid.

"The town of Sitka": *Sitka Post,* June 5, 1877.

"Wretched": CESW Diary, June 12–13, 1877, CESWP.

"The leave taking": Ibid., June 14, 1877.

"Sudden and unexpected": CESW to Lute Pease, Feb. 22, 1928, box 235(57), CESWP.

"Excellent, not too long": OOH to CESW, May 25, 1877, Letterbooks, roll 8, OOHP.

"Attack and murder": CESW Diary, June 12–13, 1877, CESWP.

"Tearful group": Ibid., June 14, 1877.

"Rumors of war": Ibid., June 19, 1877.

"The telegram": Ibid., June 20, 1877.

Chapter 10: Split Rocks

Familiar, quick work: Wetatonmi in LVM, *Hear Me, My Chiefs! Nez Perce History and Legend,* ed. Ruth Bordin (Caldwell, ID: Caxton, 2001), 195.

Camas roots: Ibid., 176.

World around them: Ibid., 197; Caroline James, *Nez Perce Women in Transition, 1877–1990* (Moscow: University of Idaho Press, 1996), 36, 72–73.

Ancestral lands: OOH, *NPJ,* 35.

"The same being": John B. Monteith to J. Q. Smith, March 19, 1877, enclosure in Monteith to OOH, March 19, 1877, OOHP.

"I told Ollicut": Ibid.

At Umatilla that March was chilling: OOH, *NPJ,* 35–37; OOH to J. C. Kelton, Apr. 24, 1877, in Record of Field Orders and Official Letters Published and Written in the Matter of Chief Joseph Difficulty, RG 393, pt. 1, entry

721, NARA; LVM, *Hear Me,* 152–54.

"Very curtly": Harry Painter to LVM, Aug. 3, 1941, box 13, folder 93, LVMP.

"Had never shed": LVM, *Hear Me,* 152–54; Painter to LVM, n.d., box 13, folder 93, LVMP.

"I think": Monteith to OOH, March 19, 1877, OOHP.

April 1877: OOH, *NPJ,* 36; LVM, *Hear Me,* 155.

"Alli-cott": "The Pow-Wow, or Council," *Walla Walla Statesman,* Apr. 28, 1877.

"The Indians would be": *Report of the Secretary of War, 1877,* H. Ex. Doc. 1, pt. 2, vol. 1, 45th Cong., 2nd sess., Serial Set 1794 (Washington: Government Printing Office, 1877), 590.

See with new eyes: Ibid.

"Indians and white men": Painter to LVM, n.d., box 13, folder 93, LVMP.

"The observed": "Joseph," *Walla Walla Statesman,* Apr. 28, 1877.

Photographer's studio: Painter to LVM, July 21, Aug. 3, 1941, Seattle, box 13, folder 93, LVMP.

Dark lines underneath: Ibid. This portrait was probably the only one Ollokot ever sat for. On photography and photographers' studios at this time, see Robert Taft, *Photography and the American Scene: A Social History, 1839–1889* (New York: Macmillan, 1942), 347–48, 353; Miles Orvell, *The Real Thing: Imitation and Authenticity in American Culture, 1880–1940* (Chapel Hill: University of North Carolina Press, 1989), 90–91. On the process and cultural significance of photographing Native Americans in the late nineteenth century, see Riku Hämäläinen, "Mató-Tópe's Knife and Crazy Horse's Shield: Use of Ethnographic

Objects as Cultural Documents," in *The Challenges of Native American Studies: Essays in Celebration of the Twenty-Fifth American Indian Workshop,* ed. Barbara Saunders and Lea Zuyderhoudt (Leuven: Leuven University Press, 2004), 275; Joanna Cohan Scherer, "The Public Faces of Sarah Winnemucca," in ibid., 239–40. On the first photographs of Chief Joseph, see James S. Brust, "Photojournalism, 1877: John H. Fouch, Fort Keogh's First Post Photographer," *Montana: The Magazine of Western History* 50 (Winter 2000): 32–39; James S. Brust, "John H. Fouch: First Photographer at Fort Keogh," ibid. 44 (Spring 1994): 2–17.

"Government wants": LVM, *Yellow Wolf: His Own Story* (Caldwell, ID: Caxton Printers, 1940), 37.

Out of the mountains: Ibid.; OOH, *NPJ,* 57.

Watching from the windows: LVM, *Yellow Wolf,* 37; OOH, *NPJ,* 57–58.

"A soldier": LVM, *Yellow Wolf,* 37.

"I am here to listen": OOH, *NPJ,* 53.

"We want to talk": Ibid., 53–55.

"You may as well know": *Report of the Secretary of War, 1877,* 593; OOH, *NPJ,* 53–55.

What the law required: Cathleen D. Cahill, *Federal Fathers and Mothers: A Social History of the United States Indian Service, 1869–1933* (Chapel Hill: University of North Carolina Press, 2011), 26–28.

"This hurt the Indians": LVM, *Yellow Wolf,* 38.

"Louder and stronger": OOH, *NPJ,* 57.

"I belong to the land": Ibid., 59.

"Caus[ed] the abundant grasses": Ibid., 57–60.

Their religious beliefs: Ibid., 63–64.

"The usual words": Ibid., 64.

"The law is": Ibid.

"*Wasn't true law* at all": Ibid., 64–65.

"I am the man": Ibid., 65.

"Strong mad": LVM, *Yellow Wolf,* 39–40.

"You are trifling": OOH, *NPJ,* 66.

"Joseph and White Bird": Ibid.

Sitting outside the tent: Ibid., 66–67; LVM, *Yellow Wolf,* 40.

"Restlessness": Wottolen in LVM, *Hear Me,* 168.

"In peace councils": LVM, *Yellow Wolf,* 41.

"The question is": OOH, *NPJ,* 66.

Territories for the reservation: Ibid., 68–69.

"None of the chiefs": Peopeo Tholekt in LVM, *Hear Me,* 167.

Grande Ronde: LVM, *Hear Me,* 175–77.

Floodwaters: *Report of the Secretary of War, 1877,* 596; the occupying force described the nearby Grande Ronde as "wide, full, and torrent-like, with water very cold."

Currents and disappear downstream: Alvin M. Josephy Jr., *Nez Perce Country* (Lincoln: University of Nebraska Press, 2007), 106–7; Alvin M. Josephy Jr., *The Nez Perce Indians and the Opening of the Northwest* (New Haven: Yale University Press, 1965), 510–11; LVM, *Hear Me,* 176–77.

"A torrent": OOH, *NPJ,* 109.

The old ways: LVM, *Yellow Wolf,* 41–43.

There would be war: Wetatonmi and Two Moons in LVM, *Hear Me,* 195-196 and 202-3.

Packhorses: Wetatonmi in LVM, *Hear Me,* 196; James, *Nez Perce Women in Transition,* 97.

"Do nothing": LVM, *Hear Me,* 122.

Lose everything: Ibid., 189–91 ("Reason I didn't want to kill the murderer of my father, because some of my tribesmen are wealthy with stock and I don't like to see them get robbed.").

He told the assembly: Ibid., 190.

With impunity: Ibid., 191–92.

Barely walk: Ibid., 191–92; LVM, *Yellow Wolf,* 44–45, 45fn11.

Deserved to die: War Singer in LVM, *Hear Me,* 192.

1862 gold rush: *An Illustrated History of North Idaho* (N.p.: Western Historical Publishing, 1903), 451.

"He should not be": LVM, *Hear Me,* 211–12.

Whipping two Indians: Ibid., 192; OOH, *Nez Perce Joseph,* 100–102.

Sound of gunshots: LVM, *Hear Me,* 192.

Reaching home: Ibid., 210–13; Howard, *NPJ,* 101–2.

The day's exploits: Josephy, *The Nez Perce,* 514.

"You poor people": LVM, *Hear Me,* 202.

Salmon River settlements: Josephy, *The Nez Perce,* 515–16.

"Let us stay": Wetatonmi in LVM, *Hear Me,* 195–96.

"They were watched": Ibid.

New world: Josephy, *The Nez Perce,* 515–16.

Joseph's men tried to engage them: LVM, *Yellow Wolf,* 46–47.

"We must pack and go": Ibid.

Two wagons: Ibid., 47.

Pursuing them: LVM, *Hear Me,* 15; Haruo Aoki, *Nez Perce Dictionary* (Berkeley and Los Angeles: University of California Press, 1994), 960.

Rode out to the prairie: LVM, *Yellow Wolf,* 47–48.

Chapter 11: Fait Accompli

"Awfully queer": Emily FitzGerald, May 5, 1877, in *An Army Doctor's Wife on the Frontier: Letters from Alaska and the Far West, 1874–1878,* ed. Abe Laufe (Pittsburgh, PA: University of Pittsburgh Press, 1962), 249.

"What next is yet to appear": OOH to Grace Howard, May 2, 1877, box 1, JTGP.

"Spoke pleasantly": Ibid.

"Fait accompli": OOH, *NPJ,* 74–75.

Release Toohoolhoolzote: Ibid., 67, 72.

"In dealing with Indians": Ibid., *NPJ,* 67.

West down the Columbia: He reached Portland on May 22. "Brief Notes," *Oregonian,* May 18, 1877.

"With the feeling": OOH, *NPJ,* 74.

"Settlers in the Wallowa": "Settlement with the Indians," *Oregonian,* May 21, 1877.

Two pounds for a quarter: "Brief Notes," *Oregonian,* May 30, 1877.

"A button-hole bouquet": Ibid., May 15, 1877.

"Bade adieu": OOH, *NPJ,* 77.

"Simply miraculous": Ibid.

"Remarkably contented": Ibid., 78.

"To catch": Ibid., 79.

"Gladdened the hearts of the Yakimas": Ibid., 82–83.

Catch up on his sleep: Ibid., 83–85.

Next day's deadline: Ibid., 87–88.

"The Indians are all right": Ibid., 88.

The sun was warm: Michael McCarthy Diary, June 13, 1877, Michael McCarthy Papers,

Library of Congress, copy in box 4, folder 15, JAGP.

"Spirited and handsome": OOH, *NPJ,* 90.

"Altogether sunshiny": OOH's description of Perry, *NPJ,* 88. John D. McDermott's *Forlorn Hope: The Battle of White Bird Canyon and the Beginning of the Nez Perce War* (Boise: Idaho State Historical Society, 1978), 55–68, includes terrific individual biographies of the officers and aggregate sketches of the enlisted men in the companies based at Fort Lapwai.

Leader Captain Jack: Howard, *NPJ,* 89; Will J. Trimble, "A Soldier of the Oregon Frontier," *Quarterly of the Oregon Historical Society* 8 (1907): 43; Boyd Cothran, *Remembering the Modoc War: Redemptive Violence and the Making of American Innocence* (Chapel Hill: University of North Carolina Press, 2014), 63–64.

Next to the fort: W. D. Boyle to OOH, May 24, 1876, OOHP; OOH, *NPJ,* 90.

The Crimea: See Lawrence W. Crider, *In Search of the Light Brigade* (Barnham, West Sussex: Eurocommunica, 2004), 201.

"Claimed a high degree": Quoted in McDermott, *Forlorn Hope,* 66.

Light Brigade's few survivors: "Taps Sound for Hero of Balaklava," *San Francisco Call,* Aug. 21, 1910.

"Monotony": McCarthy Diary, June 13–14, 1877.

"Joseph ha[d] put": Ibid., June 12, 1877.

Across the country: Elizabeth Howard to Grace Howard, May 1877, box 2, JTGP ("Papa has accomplished a great deal for the country, will soon tell you all about it").

"A chorus of them": McCarthy Diary, June 13–

14, 1877.

Tepahlewam: OOH, *NPJ,* 90–91.

"I do not feel": Ibid., 90. See also Perry, Court of Inquiry Testimony, in McDermott, *Forlorn Hope,* 196.

To warn the army: Nat Webb in LVM, *Hear Me, My Chiefs! Nez Perce History and Legend,* ed. Ruth Bordin (Caldwell, ID: Caxton, 2001), 231.

"Insist[ing] that Joseph": Howard, *NPJ,* 93.

"Grand looking Indian": McCarthy Diary, June 12, 1877.

"It is dreadful": Emily FitzGerald to Mamma, June 13, 1877, in *An Army Doctor's Wife on the Frontier,* 259.

"The most intense feeling": OOH, *NPJ,* 95.

"Killed and left in the road": L. P. Brown to Commanding Officer at Fort Lapwai, June 15, 1877, in OOH, *NPJ,* 95.

Bitten off: Elliott West, *The Last Indian War: The Nez Perce Story* (New York: Oxford University Press, 2009), 128–29.

"Don't delay": L. P. Brown to Commanding Officer at Fort Lapwai, June 15, 1877, in OOH, *NPJ,* 95.

"Help shall be prompt": OOH to L. P. Brown, June 15, 1877, in ibid., 97.

"Boots and Saddles": McCarthy Diary, June 16, 1877.

Five mules: "The Nez Perce War," CESW to C. J. Brosnan, Jan. 7, 1918, C. J. Brosnan Collection, University of Idaho Library, copy in box 5, folder 5, JAGP.

Little more: Perry, Court of Inquiry Testimony, in McDermott, *Forlorn Hope,* 53–54.

"Constant motion": OOH, *NPJ,* 93.

Stop fighting: LVM, *Hear Me,* 243n17; Statement of Abraham Brooks, in *Claims of Nez Perce Indians,* Sen. Doc. 257, 56th Cong., 1st sess., Serial Set 3867 (Washington: Government Printing Office, 1900), 84.

"Think we will make": OOH to McDowell, June 16, 1877, in *Claims of Nez Perce Indians,* 10.

"To remain behind": OOH, *NPJ,* 99.

Paced back and forth, for hours: Ibid.

Chapter 12: A Perfect Panic

Tangle of brush: W. R. Parnell, "The Battle of White Bird Cañon," in *Northwestern Fights and Fighters,* ed. Cyrus Townsend Brady (New York: Doubleday, Page, 1910), 99.

"Reverses in business": John D. McDermott, *Forlorn Hope: The Battle of White Bird Canyon and the Beginning of the Nez Perce War* (Boise: Idaho State Historical Society, 1978), 61.

No place to go: Ibid., 71; OOH, *NPJ,* 109–10.

"Looked so homelike": Michael McCarthy Diary, June 16, 1877, Michael McCarthy Papers, Library of Congress, copy in box 4, folder 15, JAGP.

Back in their saddles: Ibid.

Bodies were gone: Ibid.

"Even if there were Indians": Ibid.

"Ghastly gossip": Ibid.

"Be comparatively safe": Perry, Court of Inquiry Testimony, in McDermott, *Forlorn Hope,* 197.

To hear out the settlers: Parnell, "The Battle of White Bird Cañon," 100.

"In the same house": LVM, *Yellow Wolf: His Own Story* (Caldwell, ID: Caxton Printers,

1940), 55.

Crossing the Salmon River: Perry, Court of Inquiry Testimony, in McDermott, *Forlorn Hope,* 197.

Ammunition and long coats: McCarthy Diary, June 16, 1877.

"Was the best": Perry, Court of Inquiry Testimony, in McDermott, *Forlorn Hope,* 197.

"Mount without noise": McCarthy Diary, June 16, 1877.

Into darkness: William Coram Interview, Feb. 12, 1915, WMCP-DPL.

"A long howling": Parnell, "The Battle of White Bird Cañon," 100.

"Not quite natural": McCarthy Diary, June 16, 1877.

"Enough to make": John P. Shorr in LVM, *Hear Me, My Chiefs! Nez Perce History and Legend,* ed. Ruth Bordin (Caldwell, ID: Caxton, 2001), 235; Alvin M. Josephy Jr., *The Nez Perce Indians and the Opening of the Northwest* (New Haven: Yale University Press, 1965), 524.

Many times before: Caroline James, *Nez Perce Women in Transition, 1877–1990* (Moscow: University of Idaho Press, 1996), 32–35.

Victims were whites: Patricia Limerick, *The Legacy of Conquest: The Unbroken Past of the American West* (New York: Norton, 1987), 42–44 ("Misfortune has usually caused white Westerners to cast themselves in the role of the innocent victim. . . . The basic plot played itself out with a thousand variations.").

Fighting age: Josephy, *The Nez Perce,* 524–25; LVM, *Hear Me,* 241.

"Big bunch": LVM, *Yellow Wolf,* 51.

Time to fight: LVM, *Hear Me,* 245.

"An old-time": Roaring Eagle in ibid., 251n29

Earlier generations: LVM, *Yellow Wolf,* 50–51.

Not fire the first shot: LVM, *Hear Me,* 243–44.

"Something seemed moving": LVM, *Yellow Wolf,* 50–51.

"My God!": Coram Interview, Feb. 12, 1915, WMCP-DPL.

Passing into the canyon all night: Ibid.; Schorr to LVM, May 20, 1926, box 9, folder 55, LVMP; McCarthy Diary, June 16, 1877.

"Indian deviltry": Parnell, "The Battle of White Bird Cañon," 101.

Deeper into the canyon: McCarthy Diary, June 16, 1877.

Loaded their rifles: McDermott, *Forlorn Hope,* 80.

"Dressed more like": LVM, *Yellow Wolf,* 55.

Began to play: Ibid., 55–56; LVM, *Hear Me,* 243–44; Elliott West, *The Last Indian War: The Nez Perce Story* (New York: Oxford University Press, 2009), 134.

"Calling orders": Two Moons in LVM, *Hear Me,* 246.

"A Cavalry command": Court of Inquiry in McDermott, *Forlorn Hope,* 198.

High ground, Perry thought: F. A. Fenn to Camp, Sept. 19, 1915, WMCP-BYU; Court of Inquiry in McDermott, *Forlorn Hope,* 197–98.

After about five minutes: Coram Interview, Feb. 12, 1915, WMCP-DPL.

"Hardly saw them": Two Moons in LVM, *Hear Me,* 247.

" 'Stop, stop' ": Swarts Interview, Feb. 15, 1915, WMCP-DPL.

"Those three warriors": Two Moons in LVM, *Hear Me,* 247.

In just as many minutes: West, *The Last Indian War,* 134–35.

"Receiving [them]": Wounded Head in LVM, *Hear Me,* 239.

Abandon the fight: Ibid., 239–40; LVM, *Yellow Wolf,* 57–61.

"Be careful": LVM, *Hear Me,* 254.

Blend into the rock: McCarthy Diary, June 17, 1877; McDermott, *Forlorn Hope,* 107.

Ammunition belt: LVM, *Yellow Wolf,* 58–59.

"An old-time pistol": Wounded Head in LVM, *Hear Me,* 239–40.

"A perfect panic": Perry, Court of Inquiry Testimony, in McDermott, *Forlorn Hope,* 198.

"Die right here": Trimble, Court of Inquiry Testimony, in ibid., 168.

"It was impossible": Perry, Court of Inquiry Testimony, in ibid., 199.

"From knoll to knoll": Parnell, "The Battle of White Bird Cañon," 108.

Never hit anyone: Ibid.; Frank L. Powers to W. W. Camp, Nov. 24, 1913, WMCP-DPL.

"Scolded, swore, and abjured": McCarthy Diary, "The Battle of White Bird."

Wait out the Indians: Ibid.

"Somewhat confused": Parnell, Court of Inquiry Testimony, in McDermott, *Forlorn Hope,* 178.

"He seemed to have lost": Ibid., 179.

"Did not seem to know": Perry, Court of Inquiry Testimony, in ibid., 200.

Old wagon road: Fenn to Camp, Sept. 19, 1915, WMCP-BYU.

Chapter 13: Death in Ghastly Forms

"Arms and cheeks gone": CESW Diary, June

27, 1877, box 26(1), CESWP.

"Changed into awful shapes": H. L. Bailey, "An Infantry Second Lieutenant in the Nez Perce War of 1877," box 14, folder 101, LVMP.

"The most sickening": Frederick Mayer, June 29, 1877, in "Nez Perce War Diary — 1877 of Private Frederick Mayer," *Idaho State Historical Society, Seventeenth Biennial Report, 1939–1940* (Boise: State Historical Society, 1940), 28.

"We had to run": Bailey, "An Infantry Second Lieutenant."

Unearth the remains: Ibid.; CESW Diary, June 27, 1877, CESWP; Mayer, June 29, 1877, in "Nez Perce War Diary."

"It is easier to go into a battle": OOH, *NPJ,* 118.

"No tears": Robert Pollock to wife, June 27, 1877, in Robert W. Pollock, *Grandfather, Chief Joseph and Psychodynamics* (Caldwell, ID: Caxton, 1964), 44.

"Oh, my poor": Emily FitzGerald, July 12, 1877, *An Army Doctor's Wife on the Frontier: Letters from Alaska and the Far West, 1874–1878,* ed. Abe Laufe (Pittsburgh, PA: University of Pittsburgh Press, 1962), 274.

"As if she were": Emily FitzGerald, June 25, 1877, in ibid., 265.

Legs of his drawers: Michael McCarthy Diary, June 17, 1877, Michael McCarthy Papers, Library of Congress, copy in box 4, folder 15, JAGP.

"Instructed her to escape": Wounded Head in LVM, *Hear Me,* 240.

"She refused to believe": Pollock to wife, June 27, 1877, in *Psychodynamics,* 44.

"Gentlemanly officers": CESW Diary, June 27,

1877, CESWP.

"Go in and kill 'em": Ibid., June 20, 1877.

"Say howdy": Ibid., June 20–21, 1877.

"Men all over the superstructure": Pollock to wife, June 18, 1877, in *Psychodynamics,* 34.

"Party of damsels": CESW Diary, June 21, 1877, CESWP.

"Don't believe it": Ibid., June 22, 1877.

"Peculiar nervous feeling": Ibid., June 23, 1877.

Outfitters in Lewiston: Ibid., June 24–25, 1877; OOH, *NPJ,* 130.

"An irregular body": OOH, *NPJ,* 130.

"Fresh from garrison": Peter S. Bomus to Asher Robbins Eddy, Dec. 20, 1877, FD 291, Fort Dalles Papers, Huntington Library.

"Pouring rain": CESW Diary, June 26, 1877, CESWP.

Indians and fired: Ibid., June 27, 1877; Bailey, "An Infantry Second Lieutenant."

"We were actually surrounded": Bailey, "An Infantry Second Lieutenant."

Joseph's dark genius: Stephen Perry Jocelyn, *Mostly Alkali* (Caldwell, ID: Caxton, 1953), 223, 227–29; "The Idaho Indian War," *Oregonian,* June 28, 1877; [Thomas A.] Sutherland, "Latest from the Front," *Portland Daily Standard,* July 5, 1877, box 4, folder 3, JAGP; Edwin C. Mason to wife and mother, June 28, July 1, 1877, Edwin C. Mason Scrapbooks, 1877–78, MF 80, MHS.

"Joseph had managed": OOH, *NPJ,* 113.

"Keen-eyed": Ibid.,145.

"The Non-Treaty": Emily FitzGerald, June 19, 1877, in *An Army Doctor's Wife,* 261.

"They tell me": Pollock to wife, June 23, 1877,

in *Psychodynamics,* 39.

As they had the others: Bailey, "An Infantry Second Lieutenant"; Howard, *NPJ,* 144.

"Mud till": Pollock to wife, June 27, 1877, in *Psychodynamics,* 44.

"Mutilated corpses": CESW Diary, June 27, 1877, CESWP.

Next day: Field Order 18, June 27, 1877, and Field Order 19, June 28, 1877, Camp Theller White Bird Creek, NARA.

"Singing story telling": CESW Diary, June 27, 1877, CESWP.

"Everybody seems very cheerful": Pollock to wife, June 27, 1877, in *Psychodynamics,* 44.

"For fear of": CESW Diary, June 27, 1877, CESWP.

Hundred local volunteers: Eugene T. Wilson, "Nez Perce Campaign," box 6, folder 32, LVMP.

Nez Perce attacks on settlers: OOH, *NPJ,* 135.

"In a combat": Ibid., 136–37.

Committing his troops: Elliott West, *The Last Indian War: The Nez Perce Story* (New York: Oxford University Press, 2009), 145–46.

And seize the chief: OOH, *NPJ,* 148–49.

"Indians speckling": CESW Diary, June 28, 1877, CESWP.

"Little silvery thread": Howard, *NPJ,* 147–48.

"Vicious": Pollock to wife, July 6, 1877, in *Psychodynamics,* 57.

Boats from Lewiston: CESW Diary, June 28, 1877, CESWP; PeoPeo Tholekt Narrative, box 6, folder 31, LVMP.

"Whirled over": Bailey, "An Infantry Second Lieutenant."

Thousands of horses and cattle: Alvin M. Josephy Jr., *The Nez Perce Indians and the Opening of the Northwest* (New Haven: Yale University Press, 1965), 534.

"As broad as": Michael McCarthy, "Journal of M. McCarthy," 13, McCarthy Papers, Library of Congress, copy in box 4, folder 15, JAGP.

"*Horse* beef": Jocelyn, *Mostly Alkali,* 229.

"Misery": CESW Diary, July 2, 1877, CESWP.

Large pine campfires: "Latest from the Front," *Portland Daily Standard,* July 16, 1877, box 5, folder 6, JAGP.

"Dead Mule Trail": CESW Diary, July 2, 1877, CESWP.

"No doubt breaking": Bailey, "An Infantry Second Lieutenant."

"Overboard!": W. R. Parnell, "The Salmon River Expedition," in *Northwestern Fights and Fighters,* ed. Cyrus Townsend Brady (New York: Doubleday, Page, 1910), 128.

"Trusting that Providence": Eugene T. Wilson, "Nez Perce Campaign," box 6, folder 32, LVMP.

"Escape and join": Jocelyn, *Mostly Alkali,* 228–29.

"The most beautiful": Pollock to wife, July 6, 1877, in *Psychodynamics,* 57.

"Literally covered": "From the Front," *Idaho Tri-Weekly Statesman,* July 14, 1877, box 11, folder 10, JAGP.

"Sweat bath": Parnell, "The Salmon River Expedition," 129.

A little more than a hundred men: OOH, *NPJ,* 150.

Let them pass: Mason, Dispatch to Officers at Cottonwood and Ft. Lapwai, July 6, 1877, RG 393, entry 897, Part III, 1877, box 1, NARA, copy in box 4, folder 8, JAGP.

Miles downstream: CESW Diary, July 5–6, 1877, CESWP.

"Long weary": Ibid., July 7, 1877.

Made it across: Howard, *NPJ,* 154–55.

"The smell from half-buried": McCarthy, "Journal," 15.

"No food": CESW Diary, July 9, 1877, CESWP.

"To get [Joseph] quick": Pollock to wife, July 6, 1877, in *Psychodynamics,* 57.

Finally turned for the better: Greene, *Nez Perce Summer,* 60.

White Bird Canyon: McDermott, *Forlorn Hope,* 74–75; George Venn, *Soldier to Advocate: C. E. S. Wood's 1877 Legacy* (La Grande, OR: Wordcraft of Oregon, 2006), 41n58.

Kill at will: West, *The Last Indian War,* 143–45.

Farms, fields, and fences: Greene, *Nez Perce Summer,* 73.

To find them: Ibid., 74–75; LVM, *Hear Me,* 294–97. Patricia Limerick emphasizes the sense of victimization among Westerners; Limerick, *The Legacy of Conquest: The Unbroken Past of the American West* (New York: Norton, 1987), 44 ("Blaming nature or blaming human beings, those looking for a scapegoat had a third, increasingly popular target: the federal government. Since it was the government's responsibility to control the Indians . . . Westerners found it easy to shift the direction of their resentment.").

Cross a river on a bridge: CESW Diary, July 10, 1877, CESWP.

During the previous week: Luther P. Wilmot, "Misery Hill" (c. 1922), NP Campaign — 1877, Luther P. Wilmot Papers, University of

Idaho, copy in box 5, folder 4, JAGP; Thomas Sutherland, "Latest from the Front," *Portland Daily Standard,* July 12, 1877, box 4, folder 1, JAGP.

Straight to the Clearwater: OOH, *NPJ,* 155–58.

"So as to": McCarthy, "Journal," 15.

Bitterroot Mountains to Montana: Greene, *Nez Perce Summer,* 400n17; "The Indian War," *Idaho Tri-Weekly Statesman,* July 14, 1877, box 4, folder 10, JAGP; see also "Military Movements," *Oregonian,* July 14, 1877 (describing July 5 report of the *Helena Herald* warning that the Nez Perce would cross the Bitterroots).

"Taking the enemy in reverse": OOH, Aug. 27, 1877, in *Report of the Secretary of War, 1877,* H. Ex. Doc. 1, pt. 2, vol. 1, 45th Cong., 2nd sess., Serial Set 1794 (Washington: Government Printing Office, 1877), 604.

"Now not worthy the name": As quoted in Greene, *Nez Perce Summer,* 78.

"Blind man's bluff": Bailey, "An Infantry Second Lieutenant."

Stands of trees: Josephy, *The Nez Perce,* 546.

Signs of Indians: LVM, *Hear Me,* 299–300; Greene, *Nez Perce Summer,* 77.

"We were . . . hoping": Bailey, "An Infantry Second Lieutenant."

"I rode to the bluff": OOH, Aug. 27, 1877, in *Report of the Secretary of War, 1877,* 604.

Down to the river: Ibid.

Began firing: Ibid.

Chapter 14: Bullets Singing Like Bees

Burned at their death: Caroline James, *Nez Perce Women in Transition, 1877–1990*

(Moscow: University of Idaho Press, 1996), 54.

And sharpened blades: Ibid., 20, 23–35, 58–63.

Long exhale: Ibid., 81; Wetatonmi in LVM, *Hear Me, My Chiefs! Nez Perce History and Legend,* ed. Ruth Bordin (Caldwell, ID: Caxton, 2001), 298.

Some of the corpses: LVM, *Hear Me,* 256–57; see also Horse Blanket, "Nez Perce Women Accompanying War Parties," 1926, box 8, folder 41, LVMP; Wetatonmi in LVM, *Hear Me,* 256.

"I heard bullets": Wetatonmi in LVM, *Hear Me,* 288.

Regarded as a friend: LVM, *Yellow Wolf: His Own Story* (Caldwell, ID: Caxton Printers, 1940), 76–77.

With their guns: Two Moons in ibid., 42–43, 42n7.

"That he got his power": Ibid., 42–43.

On the far side: Ibid., 69.

Reservation boundaries: Elliott West, *The Last Indian War: The Nez Perce Story* (New York: Oxford University Press, 2009), 141–42.

"Does not want war": Peopeo Tholekt in LVM, *Hear Me,* 266.

" 'Now I am to die' ": Ibid., 265–67.

"Everything looked yellow": Ibid., 269.

Two in the saddle: Ibid., 265–69.

"Tired, tired": Ibid., 270.

"Of course that settled it": Ibid., 267.

Along the river: LVM, *Yellow Wolf,* 85.

Waist deep: Wetatonmi in LVM, *Hear Me,* 298.

"We are under": Ibid., 298.

Extended for miles: Ibid.

"Washed his face": LVM, *Yellow Wolf,* 73, 85–87.

"We had to stop": Ibid., 87.

Keep him safe: Ibid., 87–88; "War Singer's Explanation of Wy-akin," box 14, folder 104, LVMP; Questionnaires, Sam Lott, box 6, folder 26, LVMP; Alvin M. Josephy Jr., "Origins of the Nez Perce Indians," *Idaho Yesterdays* 6 (Spring 1962): 12–13; "Yellow Wolf on Wy-akin," box 13, folder 88, LVMP.

"Calling, 'Come on!' ": LVM, *Yellow Wolf,* 72.

Sweep of the battlefield: PeoPeo Tholekt Narrative, box 6, folder 31, LVMP; CESW, "Chief Joseph, the Nez-Percé," *Century* 28 (May 1884): 137.

"I did not look": Ibid.

"The Indian way": Roaring Eagle in LVM, *Hear Me,* 304.

River to the rifle pits: Josephy, *The Nez Perce,* 549; Narrative of E-lah-we-mah, box 6, folder 28, LVMP.

"Bullets came thicker": LVM, *Yellow Wolf,* 88.

Companion in war and peace: On the significance of horses in Nez Perce culture, see West, *The Last Indian War,* 16–18; Amelia-Roisin Seifert, "An Introduction to Contemporary Native American Horse Culture: Notes from the Northwest Plateau," in *The Meaning of Horses: Biosocial Encounters,* ed. Dona Lee Davis and Anita Maurstad (New York: Routledge, 2016), 151–52.

"I grew hot with mad": LVM, *Yellow Wolf,* 88.

"Warrior power": Ibid, 28.

"From the fowls that fly": Ibid., 301–2.

"To kill as it strikes": Ibid, 28. Another name that Yellow Wolf used was Heinmot Hihhih (White Thunder). Ibid., 302.

"Good prayer": Ibid., 302.

Sixteen shots: Ibid., 78.

"If we die": Ibid., 89.

"Grass on fire": LVM, *Hear Me,* 317.

"Seeing nothing": LVM, *Yellow Wolf,* 90.

"Zee-zipping": CESW to Edgerton, July 20, 1877, WP.

Pierce and turn quickly: CESW, "Chief Joseph, the Nez-Percé," 137.

Scalp, and head: Ibid.; West, *Last Indian War,* 158; Greene, *Nez Perce Summer,* 402n38, appendix A ("U.S. Army Casualties, Nez Perce War, 1877"), 359–71.

"In less time": Michael McCarthy Diary, July 11, 1877, Michael McCarthy Papers, Library of Congress, copy in box 4, folder 15, JAGP.

"One continual peal": Ibid.

"Red devils": CESW to Edgerton, July 20, 1877, box 1, item 1.39, WP.

Behind the soldiers: McCarthy Diary, July 11, 1877.

Coming from Lapwai: OOH, *NPJ,* 159.

"A ticklish business": H. L. Bailey, "An Infantry Second Lieutenant in the Nez Perce War of 1877," box 14, folder 101, LVMP.

Nowhere to run: Ibid.; McCarthy Diary, July 11, 1877.

Resemble soldiers: Ibid.; Bailey, "An Infantry Second Lieutenant"; Bailey in LVM, *Hear Me,* 307.

Fight above the Clearwater: "Interesting Letters: From Our Special War Correspondent," *Portland Daily Standard,* July 23, 1877, box 4, folder 10, JAGP.

"Manifested extraordinary": OOH, *NPJ,* 161.

"Creep and crawl": Melville C. Wilkinson letter, July 17, 1877, reprinted in "Indian Affairs,"

Army and Navy Journal, Aug. 18, 1877, 22.

"Savage demonstrations": OOH, *NPJ,* 161.

"Get up and go": Thomas Sutherland, *New York Herald,* Sept. 10, 1877.

"Anxious times": CESW Diary, July 11, 1877, CESWP.

"Haranguing": McCarthy Diary, July 11, 1877; Melville C. Wilkinson letter.

Water to the men: Ibid.; OOH, *NPJ,* 162.

"That we were in a bad fix": McCarthy Diary, July 11, 1877.

Dashed back to the lines: Greene, *Nez Perce Summer,* 88.

"We kn[e]w how things stood": McCarthy Diary, July 11, 1877.

War while it raged above them: LVM, *Yellow Wolf,* 92, 89; LVM, *Hear Me,* 313.

Wanted him to be alone: LVM, *Yellow Wolf,* 29.

"I paid attention": Ibid., 95.

Yellow Wolf kept firing: Ibid., 96.

"Make it the last fight": Ibid., 100; Wottolen in LVM, *Hear Me,* 315–16n35.

"Why all this war": LVM, *Yellow Wolf,* 100.

Only invite death: While Howard estimated that fifteen warriors had fallen in the battle, Yellow Wolf maintained that only four died. Ibid., 98–99.

"Everybody was running": PeoPeo Tholekt Narrative, box 6, folder 31, LVMP.

"The cannon boomed": Ibid.

Blasting rock into gravel: LVM, *Hear Me,* 316–18; CESW, "Chief Joseph, the Nez-Percé," 138.

Abandon her daughter: LVM, *Yellow Wolf,* 96–97.

"I am troubled": Ibid., 97.

Horses would run: Ibid., 96–97.

Behind the field hospital: Stephen Perry Jocelyn, *Mostly Alkali* (Caldwell, ID: Caxton, 1953), 237; Trimble as quoted in ibid., 233–34; Greene, *Nez Perce Summer,* 406n86.

Gaping holes on exit: Pat Leonard, "The Bullet That Changed History," Disunion series, *New York Times,* Aug. 31, 2012, http://opinionator .blogs.nytimes.com/2012/08/31/the-bullet-that-changed-history/?_r=0.

Leaking urine: Edwin C. Mason to wife and mother, July 14, 1877, Edwin C. Mason Scrapbooks, 1877–78, MF 80, MHS; Wood Diary, July 12, 1877, CESWP: Appendix A, "U.S. Army Casualties," in Greene, *Nez Perce Summer,* 359–71; George M. Sternberg to E. J. Bailey, July 15, 1877, RG 94, entry 64, box 1, NARA, copy in box 4, folder 8, JAGP; George M. Sternberg to Surgeon General, July 22, 1877, RG 94, entry 624, box 1, NARA, copy in box 4, folder 8, JAGP; Sternberg, "Wounds and Injuries Received in Action on the 11th and 12th day of July 1877 at Battle of Clearwater," RG 94, entry 624, box 1, NARA, copy in box 4, folder 9, JAGP.

"The Indian camp": Bailey, "An Infantry Second Lieutenant."

"Many had evidently": CESW to C. J. Brosnan, Jan. 7, 1918, C. J. Brosnan Collection, University of Idaho, copy in box 5, folder 5, JAGP.

"We got flour": McCarthy Diary, July 12, 1877.

Commerce with whites: James, *Nez Perce Women in Transition,* 31–32.

"Judged dated": Bailey, "An Infantry Second Lieutenant."

"Putting on style rigged out": McCarthy Diary, July 12, 1877.

Beaded sheaths, and leggings: Bailey, "An Infantry Second Lieutenant"; Emily FitzGerald to mother, Aug. 6, 1877, in *An Army Doctor's Wife on the Frontier: Letters from Alaska and the Far West, 1874–1878,* ed. Abe Laufe (Pittsburgh, PA: University of Pittsburgh Press, 1962) 290.

"They are made of beautifully": Emily FitzGerald to mother, Aug. 6, 1877, in *An Army Doctor's Wife,* 290.

Buffalo horn and pocketed it: CESW to C. J. Brosnan, Jan. 7, 1918, C. J. Brosnan Collection, University of Idaho, copy in box 5, folder 5, JAGP; Emily FitzGerald to mother, Aug. 6, 1877, in *An Army Doctor's Wife,* 290.

Collection of Indian artifacts: In 2011, eleven items from Howard's personal collection were sold at auction. A searchable archive of the auction lots is available at http://www.cowanauctions.com.

"Doctor Sternberg": Emily FitzGerald to mother, Aug. 6, 1877, in *An Army Doctor's Wife,* 290.

Chapter 15: Heart of the Monster

"Real houses": *Report of the Secretary of War, 1877,* H. Ex. Doc. 1, pt. 2, vol. 1, 45th Cong., 2nd sess., Serial Set 1794 (Washington: Government Printing Office, 1877), 595.

Fenced and cultivated: Ibid.

"Well dressed and well behaved": Ibid.

Skill and sympathy: Ibid.

Now turned to stone: Horse Blanket, "Corrections for Coyote's Combat with the Mighty Kamiah Monster, as Told by Yellow Wolf" (1926), box 45, folder 438, LVMP; see also

Herbert J. Spinden, "Myths of the Nez Percé Indians," *Journal of American Folklore* 21 (Jan.–Mar. 1908): 13–23; Archie Phinney, *Nez Perce Texts* (New York: Columbia University Press, 1934), 18–29; Haruo Aoki, *Nez Perce Texts* (Berkeley: University of California Press, 1979), 28–29.

"We laughed at those soldiers": LVM, *Yellow Wolf: His Own Story* (Caldwell, ID: Caxton Printers, 1940), 103.

Another river to cross: Ibid.; PeoPeo Tholekt Narrative, box 6, folder 31, LVMP.

Nontreaty bands pitched camp: LVM, *Yellow Wolf,* 103–4.

Camas bread and soup: William Clark, journal entry, Sept. 20, 1805, http://lewisandclark journals.unl.edu/read/?_xmlsrc=1805-09-01 .xml&_xslsrc=LCstyles.xsl.

Baby granddaughter: Many Wounds, "Lament of Wot-to-len," 1920, box 9, folder 53, LVMP; LVM, *Hear Me, My Chiefs! Nez Perce History and Legend,* ed. Ruth Bordin (Caldwell, ID: Caxton, 2001), 498–99.

Long journey ahead: Cheryl Wilfong, *Following the Nez Perce Trail: A Guide to the Nee-Me-Poo National Historic Trail with Eyewitness Accounts,* 2nd ed. (Corvallis: Oregon State University Press, 2006), 164.

"A farewell": LVM, *Yellow Wolf,* 104–5.

Advocated by Looking Glass: LVM, *Hear Me,* 334; Elliott West, *The Last Indian War: The Nez Perce Story* (New York: Oxford University Press, 2009), 165–66.

Far side of the mountains: Edwin C. Mason to

wife and mother, July 14, 1877, Edwin C. Mason Scrapbooks, 1877–78, MF 80, MHS; Camille Williams to LVM, Apr. 5, 1938, box 7, folder 34, LVMP; LVM, *Hear Me,* 334.

Less than a week: Henry Buck, "The Story of the Nez Perce Indian Campaign during the Summer of 1877 as Told by Henry Buck, a Citizen who Participated in the Chase with Gen. O. O. Howard," SC 492, MHS.

Through the mountains: PeoPeo Tholekt Narrative, box 6, folder 31, LVMP.

There was no escape: John Martens Journal, July 23, 1877, MHS.

"While they were talking": Ibid.

Begun killing settlers: Ibid., July 24, 1877.

In the area from an Indian: *Progressive Men of the State of Montana* (Chicago: A. W. Bowen, 1902), 1391.

"Pies, great piles of them": Will Sutherlin, as quoted in Robert J. Bigart, *Getting Good Crops: Economic and Diplomatic Survival Strategies of the Montana Bitterroot Salish Indians, 1870–1891* (Norman: University of Oklahoma Press, 2010), 137.

"Fortefy ourself": Martens Journal, July 23–25, 1877.

Rancher in the area: Bigart, *Getting Good Crops,* 146–47.

A generation earlier: Martens Journal, July 26, 1877.

Relatives in Philadelphia: Buck, "Story of the Ncz Perce Campaign." See also "Major Owen's Lolos," http://www.lewis-clark.org/article/3150.

"Exitement prevailed": Martens Journal, July 28, 1877.

Block the invaders' path: Ibid., July 26–28, 1877; Wilson Harlan in Gilbert Drake Harlan, ed., "The Diary of Wilson Barber Harlan — Farming in the Bitterroot and the Fiasco at 'Fort Fizzle,' " *Journal of the West* 4, no. 3 (Oct. 1964): 506.

Fight for his life: *Progressive Men,* 1391.

"Seat of War": Martens Journal, July 25, 1877.

"Everything was live": Ibid., July 27, 1877.

"Disarm and dismount": Charles C. Rawn to Levi F. Burnett, July 27, 1877, Fort Missoula Letterbook, July 1, 1877–Dec. 25, 1877, Mansfield Library, University of Montana, copy in box 5, folder 10, JAGP.

Through their lines: Ibid.; Rawn to Adjutant General, Aug. 1, 1877, Fort Missoula Letterbook.

"Another 'Custer massacre' ": Harlan, "The Diary of Wilson Barber Harlan," 504–5.

"Clear and bright": Martens Journal, July 28, 1877.

"Shoot low": Harlan, "The Diary of Wilson Barber Harlan," 505.

Thunder of their horses: Ibid.

"He replied that": Ibid.

"The Indians . . . like": Martens Journal, July 28, 1877.

Normalcy once again: Buck, "Story of the Nez Perce Indian Campaign."

"Don't shoot": Duncan McDonald, "The Nez Perces War of 1877," *New North-west* (Deer Lodge, MT), Jan. 17, 1879.

Open for business: Buck, "Story of the Nez Perce Indian Campaign." For peddlers trading with Nez Perce, see also, Harlan, "The Diary of Wilson Barber Harlan"; Amos Buck, "Review of the Battle of the Big Hole," *Historical Society of Montana* 7 (1910): 117–30.

Michigan in the 1860s: Michael A. Leeson, ed., *History of Montana, 1739–1885* (Chicago: Warner, Beers, 1885), 1300; *Progressive Men,* 1011–13; Joaquin Miller, *An Illustrated History of the State of Montana* (Chicago: Lewis, 1894), 211, 221, 733.

Back to the store: Buck, "Story of the Nez Perce Indian Campaign."

Calico by the yard: John Fahey, *The Flathead Indians* (Norman: University of Oklahoma Press, 1974), 196–97.

"We held a consultation": Buck, "Story of the Nez Perce Indian Campaign."

Gold dust, silver: Jerome A. Greene, *Nez Perce Summer, 1877: The U.S. Army and the Nee-Me-Poo Crisis* (Helena: Montana Historical Society, 2000), 122; Fahey, *The Flathead Indians,* 197.

Discounts for cash purchases: In the decades following the Nez Perce War, the *Ravalli Republican* of Stevensville, Montana, often ran advertisements promising "special inducements to cash customers." See, for example, the front page of the Apr. 28, 1897, issue.

Horrors of the previous months: For Nez Perce women conducting trade, see Caroline James, *Nez Perce Women in Transition, 1877–1990* (Moscow: University of Idaho Press, 1996), 100–106.

Finally had their audience: Buck, "Story of the Nez Perce Indian Campaign."

"A number of Indians": Martens Journal, July 30, 1877.

Warriors back to camp: Ibid.; McDonald, "The Nez Perces War of 1877," Jan. 17.

"Trade widt them": Martens Journal, July 25, 1877.

"People somewhat pusled": Ibid., July 30, 1877.

"The Nes Perces": Ibid., Aug. 2, 1877.

Continental Divide: Rawn to Adjutant General, Aug. 1, 1877, Fort Missoula Letterbook, box 5, folder 10, JAGP.

"No more fighting": LVM, *Yellow Wolf,* 108. For a discussion of the Crow during this era, see Hoxie, *Parading Through History,* pt. 1, 9–166.

Flathead territory: Yellow Bull Interview, Feb. 13, 1915, MS 57, box 2, folder 115, WMCP-BYU; "The Story of Pe-Naw-We-Non-Mi, Charley White Interpreter," July 1925, box 8, folder 43, LVMP.

State and local authorities: On this issue my thinking has been informed by Gregory Ablavsky, "Species of Sovereignty: Native Claims Making and the Early American State," unpublished conference paper, Oct. 2014 (on file with author).

"They were a band of fools": Duncan McDonald, "The Nez Perces War of 1877," *New North-west* (Deer Lodge, MT), Jan. 10, 1879.

"Why should I": Greene, *Nez Perce Summer, 1877,* 416n7; McDonald, "The Nez Perces War of 1877," Jan. 17.

From a position of strength: On Looking Glass's choice of route, see McDonald, "The Nez Perces War of 1877," Jan. 10.

"A feeling some of us": LVM, *Yellow Wolf,* 108.

"My shaking heart": Ibid., 109; Lone Bird in

LVM, *Hear Me,* 364.

"By the way": Duncan McDonald, "The Nez Prces [*sic*] War of 1877," Jan. 24.

"Who is going to trouble us": Ibid.

Joyous summer migration: Greene, *Nez Perce Summer,* 122–23; Rawn to Adjutant General, Aug. 1, 1877, Missoula Letterbook.

Mouth of the Canyon: LVM, *Yellow Wolf,* 110.

"Everybody with good feeling": Ibid.

"No nothin' now": CESW Diary, July 18–19, 1877, CESWP.

"We had to dump our packs": CESW to Edgerton, July 20, 1877, WP.

"We are living like": Mason to wife and mother, July 9, 1877 [this is misdated, more likely July 19], Edwin C. Mason Scrapbooks, 1877–78, MF 80, MHS.

"Rest for the weary": CESW to Edgerton, July 20, 1877, WP.

"Trout, ease": CESW Diary, July 20–21, 1877, CESWP.

Prisoners of war: LVM, *Yellow Wolf,* 104–5.

"Woes and troubles": CESW Diary, July 17–18, 18–19, 1877, CESWP.

To Fort Vancouver: LVM, *Hear Me,* 332–33 and n18; LHVM, *Yellow Wolf,* 310–12.

Changed Wood's life: CESW Diary, July 22, 1877, CESWP; H. L. Bailey to mother, July 26, 1877, box 14, folder 101, LVMP.

"I hardly have": Mason to wife and mother, July 14, Edwin C. Mason Scrapbooks, 1877–78, MF 80, MHS.

"Burst[ing] forth": CESW to James T. Gray, Aug. 24, 1877, MHS.

"I like Wood": Mason to wife and mother, Aug. 5, 1877, Edwin C. Mason Scrapbooks, 1877–

78, MF 80, MHS.

Silver spoons: Mason to wife and mother, Sept. 3, 1877, Edwin C. Mason Scrapbooks, 1877–78, MF 80, MHS.

General and his son: OOH, *NPJ,* 177.

Burning at Lewiston: "The Idaho Indian War," *Daily Oregonian,* July 16, 1877; Mason to wife and mother, July 22, 1877, Edwin C. Mason Scrapbooks, 1877–78, MF 80, MHS; Gerstein and Binnard to OOH, July 26, 1877, RG 393, entry 107, Part III, Department of the Columbia, Nez Perce Indian Campaign, 1877, box 2, NARA, copy in box 4, folder 8, JAGP.

"The advisability of superseding": H. Clay Wood to the President, July 14, 1877, RG 393, entry 107, Part III, Department of the Columbia, Nez Perce Indian Campaign, 1877, box 2, NARA, copy in box 4, folder 8, JAGP.

"The most unjust": Mason to wife and mother, July 22, 1877, Edwin C. Mason Scrapbooks, 1877–78, MF 80, MHS.

"Nothing can surpass": H. Clay Wood to the President, July 14, 1877, NARA/JAGP.

Would surely begin: West, *The Last Indian War,* 165–66.

"A perfect sea": Mason to wife and mother, July 2, 1877, Edwin C. Mason Scrapbooks, 1877–78, MF 80, MHS.

Prepare carefully: E. C. Watkins to J. Q. Smith, July 20, 1877, Nez Perce War, 1877, "Special Files" of Headquarters, Division of the Missouri, Relating to Military Operations and Administration, 1863–1885, RG 393, Microfilm Publication M1495, roll 5, NARA; Mason to wife and mother, July 9, 1877 [this is misdated, more likely July 19], Edwin C.

Mason Scrapbooks, 1877–78, MF 80, MHS.

March to Montana: Mason to wife and mother, July 22, 1877, Edwin C. Mason Scrapbooks, 1877–78, MF 80, MHS; Peter S. Bomus to Asher Robbins Eddy, Dec. 20, 1877, FD 291, Fort Dalles Papers, Huntington Library; OOH, *NPJ,* 171–72.

Close in and trap them: West, *The Last Indian War,* 95–96, 177–81.

"Over take Joseph": Mason to wife and mother, July 25, 1877, Edwin C. Mason Scrapbooks, 1877–78, MF 80, MHS.

"What Shall the Harvest Be?": Mason to wife and mother, July 22, 1877, Edwin C. Mason Scrapbooks, 1877–78, MF 80, MHS.

"Sown in the darkness": Wilbur Fisk Crafts, *Song Victories of "The Bliss and Sankey Hymns"* (Boston: D. Lothrop, 1877), 39.

Chapter 16: Lightning All Around

"Built as a Catholic Mission": James Bradley, "Fort Owen," *Contributions to the Historical Society of Montana* 8 (1917): 136.

Story that could be told: Bradley to wife, Aug. 1, 3, 1877, James H. Bradley Papers, MHS.

"By the rude hearth": James Bradley, "Sketch of the Fur Trade of the Upper Missouri," *Contributions to the Historical Society of Montana* 8 (1917): 178–79.

"All obtainable books": Bradley to Sanders, Aug. 6, 1876, James H. Bradley Papers, MHS.

"Writer of ability": "The Sioux Campaign," *Bozeman Times,* Mar. 15, 1877, box 5, folder 13, JAGP.

"Even the Indian character": Bradley, "Sketch of the Fur Trade," 179.

"Strong, brave, hardy": Ibid.

"A white slouch hat": James Bradley, "Affairs at Fort Benton," in *Contributions to Montana Historical Society* 3 (1900): 206, 232, 271.

"Severe colic" and "as if infatuated": Ibid., 271, 232, 217 (infected wounds), 228 (ambushed and left "weltering in his gore"), 230 (in a rage of whiskey), 231, 236 (point-blank shots to the head), 246 (scurvy), 254 (swallowed by mud and quicksand), 265 (cholera), 268 (suicide).

"Hundreds of decaying forms": Bradley, "Affairs at Fort Benton," 225.

"Thousands of robes": Ibid., 227.

"That were but are not": James Bradley, "Account of the Attempts to Build a Town at the Mouth of the Musselshell River," in *Contributions to the Montana Historical Society* 2 (1896): 305.

"Our Centennial Indian War": "Announcement," *Benton* (MT) *Record,* Mar. 2, 1877; James Bradley, "Journal of James H. Bradley: The Sioux Campaign of 1876 Under the Command of General John Gibbon," *Contributions to the Montana Historical Society* 2 (1896): 218.

"The corpses of Custer's men": James Bradley, "Custer's Death," *Montana Weekly Herald,* July 27, 1876.

"With thanks for the hearty": James Bradley, "The Sioux Campaign," *Bozeman Times,* April 5, 1877, box 5, folder 13, JAGP.

Battle after all: Bradley to wife, Aug. 1, 1877, James H. Bradley Papers, MHS.

Hatred for the Indians: John Martens Journal, Aug. 6, 1877, MHS.

"There was too much": Amos Buck, "Review

of the Battle of the Big Hole," *Historical Society of Montana* 7 (1910): 117–30.

"That bunch of ponies": Bunch Sherrill Reminiscence, transcribed by A. J. Noyes (1916), SC 739, MHS.

"I was nothing but a boy": Tom Sherrill, "The Battle of the Big Hole as I Saw It," SC 739, MHS.

"We would take": Bunch Sherrill Reminiscence.

Sundown on August 8: Elliott West, *The Last Indian War: The Nez Perce Story* (New York: Oxford University Press, 2009), 183–84; T. Sherrill, "The Battle of the Big Hole as I Saw It"; Bunch Sherrill Reminiscence; C. A. Woodruff, "Battle of the Big Hole," in *Contributions to the Montana Historical Society* 7 (1910): 107–8.

Devised his attack: T. Sherrill, "The Battle of the Big Hole as I Saw It"; Bunch Sherrill Reminiscence; J. B. Catlin, "The Battle of the Big Hole," MHS.

"None of us understood": Bunch Sherrill Reminiscence.

Call and response with coyotes: Jerome A. Greene, *Nez Perce Summer, 1877: The U.S. Army and the Nee-Me-Poo Crisis* (Helena: Montana Historical Society, 2000), 128–29.

Three volleys: Ibid., 130.

"Reveille of blood": Woodruff, "Battle of the Big Hole," 108.

"Few men go rejoicing": Ibid.

Into the teepees: Narrative of Ho-sus-pa-ow-yein [Shot in the Head], box 6, folder 28, LVMP; PeoPeo Tholekt Narrative, box 6, folder 31, LVMP.

"Go in and strike": Woodruff, "Battle of the Big

Hole," 109.

"To charge through the camp": T. Sherrill, "The Battle of the Big Hole as I Saw It."

Welter of gore: Bradley, "Affairs at Fort Benton," 228.

"Silent rifles began to speak": James Bradley, "Yellowstone Expedition of 1874," *Contributions to the Montana Historical Society* 8 (1917): 114.

"Wild commotion": Bradley, "Affairs at Fort Benton," 237.

"Like that of a swarm": Bradley, "Yellowstone Expedition of 1874," 124.

"Now we shall see": Bradley, "Affairs at Fort Benton," 216.

Bullet to the face: Catlin, "The Battle of the Big Hole," MHS; Fisk to Mrs. Bradley, Aug. 14, 1877, Bradley Correspondence, MHS; West, *The Last Indian War,* 190.

From the inside: Archie Phinney, *Nez Perce Texts* (New York: Columbia University Press, 1934), 183.

"Oh, he just": Ibid., 226.

She-Bear's ear: Ibid., 266. When Raccoon Boy eats all of the bear without sharing, his grandmother crushes him to death in her mighty jaws (267).

Pick his bones clean: Ibid., 203–4.

"It was like spurts": LVM, *Yellow Wolf: His Own Story* (Caldwell, ID: Caxton Printers, 1940), 141.

"Raining lead": Two Moons in LVM, *Hear Me, My Chiefs! Nez Perce History and Legend,* ed. Ruth Bordin (Caldwell, ID: Caxton, 2001), 385.

"Swinging one arm": Penahwenonmi in LVM,

Yellow Wolf, 136.

"You better not stay here": Kowtoliks in ibid., 144.

"Killed under my arm": Penahwenonmi in ibid., 136; "Mrs. Shot in Head at Big Hole Fight," box 7, folder 38, LVMP.

See through it: LVM, *Yellow Wolf,* 140.

"Nearly half-grown": Wetatonmi in ibid., 138.

Filled the air: PeoPeo Tholekt Narrative, box 6, folder 31, LVMP; Alvin M. Josephy Jr., *The Nez Perce Indians and the Opening of the Northwest* (New Haven: Yale University Press, 1965), 581.

Choke and burn: Ibid.; Owyeen in LVM, *Yellow Wolf,* 137.

Tied to lodgepoles: Two Moons in LVM, *Hear Me,* 384.

Across her husband: Wetatonmi in LVM, *Yellow Wolf,* 138; "The Story of Pe-Naw-We-Non-Mi," box 8, folder 43, LVMP.

"I can . . . walk": Two Moons in LVM, *Hear Me,* 386; "Owhi's Story of the Nez Perce War," box 7, folder 38, LVMP.

"I have no gun": LVM, *Hear Me,* 385.

"My brothers!": LVM, *Yellow Wolf,* 118.

"Now is our time": LVM, *Hear Me,* 383; Duncan McDonald, "The Nez Prces [*sic*] War of 1877," *New North-west* (Deer Lodge, MT), Jan. 24, 1879.

"Crawling like a drunken": LVM, *Yellow Wolf,* 117–18, 120.

Who needed one: Ibid., 120.

Far from the soldiers: West, *The Last Indian War,* 199–200; Greene, *Nez Perce Summer,* 134; LVM to Black Eagle, questionnaire, May 31, 1939, box 13, folder 97, LVMP.

Floating in the water: Narrative of Ho-sus-pa-ow-yein [Shot in the Head], box 6, folder 28, LVMP; Catlin, "The Battle of the Big Hole," MHS.

An army knife: LVM, *Yellow Wolf,* 117.

hardtack and bacon: Ibid., 129; Bunch Sherrill Reminiscence, MHS.

Down a steep drop: PeoPeo Tholekt Narrative, box 6, folder 31, LVMP.

"They had to see": Wetatonmi in LVM, *Yellow Wolf,* 138.

Both dead: LVM, *Yellow Wolf,* 132 and n7; West, *The Last Indian War,* 189.

Children were screaming: LVM, *Yellow Wolf,* 129.

"The air was": Ibid., 129.

"Look around": Ibid, 130–31.

"Cried over his friend": Ibid., 138; PeoPeo Tholekt in LVM, *Hear Me,* 392.

"This sun, this time": Ibid., 138. PeoPeo Tholekt in LVM, *Hear Me,* 392.

Watched him fall: PeoPeo Tholekt Narrative, box 6, folder 31, LVMP; Two Moons, box 6, folder 28, LVMP.

Still wearing red: LVM, *Hear Me,* 392.

Lives that awaited them: Wetatonmi in LVM, *Yellow Wolf,* 138; Narrative of Ho-sus-pa-ow-yein [Shot in the Head], box 6, folder 28, LVMP; Tom Sherrill, "The Battle of the Big Hole as I Saw It," MHS; PeoPeo Tholekt Narrative, box 6, folder 31, LVMP; Caroline James, *Nez Perce Women in Transition, 1877–1990* (Moscow: University of Idaho Press, 1996), 97.

Chapter 17: Fury

"I was astonished": John FitzGerald to Emily FitzGerald, July 29, 1877, in *An Army Doctor's Wife on the Frontier: Letters from Alaska and the Far West, 1874–1878,* ed. Abe Laufe (Pittsburgh, PA: University of Pittsburgh Press, 1962), 283–84.

Matter of perspective: For a description of life in Kamiah in 1877, see *Annual Report of the Commissioner of Indian Affairs to the Secretary of the Interior for the Year 1877* (Washington: Government Printing Office, 1877), 80–81.

"Slip, slip": OOH, *NPJ,* 174.

A beef dinner: John FitzGerald to Emily FitzGerald, Aug. 7, 1877, in *An Army Doctor's Wife,* 297; Edwin C. Mason to wife and mother, Aug. 5, 1877, Edwin C. Mason Scrapbooks, 1877–78, MF 80, MHS; H. L. Bailey to Home, Aug. 4, 1877, in "Running Extracts from Lt. Bailey's Letters During the Nez Perce War of 1877," box 14, folder 101, LVMP.

"Poor things": John FitzGerald to Emily FitzGerald, Aug. 1, 1877, in *An Army Doctor's Wife,* 291–92.

"Cheery, hearty, happy": OOH, *NPJ,* 178.

"Presto, everybody is changed": John FitzGerald to Emily FitzGerald, Aug. 1, 1877, in *An Army Doctor's Wife,* 291–92.

"Was in a sad state": Mason to wife and mother, Aug. 5, 1877, Edwin C. Mason Scrapbooks, 1877–78, MF 80, MHS.

Rendered idle: "The Railway Strike," *Oregonian,* July 26, 1877. On the strikes of 1877, see David O. Stowell, ed., *The Great Strikes of 1877* (Urbana: University of Illinois Press, 2008); David O. Stowell, *Streets, Railroads, and the*

Great Strike of 1877 (Chicago: University of Chicago Press, 1999).

Officers' morale: Mason to wife and mother, July 1877, Edwin C. Mason Scrapbooks, 1877–78, MF 80, MHS; Stephen Perry Jocelyn, *Mostly Alkali* (Caldwell, ID: Caxton, 1953), 240–41; H. L. Bailey, Aug. 4, 1877, box 14, folder 101, LVMP.

"The dreadful riots": Mason to wife and mother, July 1877, Edwin C. Mason Scrapbooks, 1877–78, MF 80, MHS.

For their children: Mason to wife and mother, Aug. 5, 1877, Edwin C. Mason Scrapbooks, 1877–78, MF 80, MHS; John FitzGerald to Emily FitzGerald, Aug. 1, 1877, in *An Army Doctor's Wife,* 292.

"Our mountain climbing": John FitzGerald to Emily FitzGerald, Aug. 1, 1877, in *An Army Doctor's Wife,* 292.

"If the Indians": Mason to wife and mother, Aug. 7, 1877, Edwin C. Mason Scrapbooks, 1877–78, MF 80, MHS.

"Feeling very anxious": OOH in *Report of the Secretary of War, 1877,* 127.

Big Hole the next morning: OOH, *NPJ,* 196–97.

Set the woods ablaze: Jerome A. Greene, *Nez Perce Summer, 1877: The U.S. Army and the Nee-Me-Poo Crisis* (Helena: Montana Historical Society, 2000), 137.

"Every once in a while": Tom Sherrill, "The Battle of the Big Hole as I Saw It," MHS.

"Cheerful and confident": *Report of the Secretary of War, 1877,* 609; CESW, "Journal of Expedition Against Hostile Nez Percé Indians, from Lewiston I. T. to Henry Lake I. T., Aug.

11, 1877," box 26(2), CESWP.

"The Indians gave us": Bunch Sherrill Reminiscence, MHS.

Little Bighorn after all: Charles M. Loynes to LVM, Jan. 18, 1928, box 10, folder 61, LVMP; Bunch Sherrill Reminiscence, MHS.

Joltingly present: Bunch Sherrill Reminiscence, MHS; OOH, *NPJ,* 210–11.

"You could not help": Loynes to LVM, Jan. 14, 1943, box 10, folder 61, LVMP.

"I . . . think I recognized": John FitzGerald to Emily FitzGerald, [c. Aug. 14, 1877], in *An Army Doctor's Wife,* 304.

"Who used to come": Henry Buck, "The Story of the Nez Perce Indian Campaign during the Summer of 1877 as Told by Henry Buck, a Citizen who Participated in the Chase with Gen. O. O. Howard" (1922), SC 492, MHS.

"Why should I shoot": T. Sherrill, "The Battle of the Big Hole as I Saw It," MHS.

"Dreadful sight": Mason to wife and mother, Aug. 13, 1877, Edwin C. Mason Scrapbooks, 1877–78, MF 80, MHS.

"I heard Gen. Howard remark": Loynes to LVM, June 6, 1926, box 10, folder 61 LVMP.

"Poor, harmless forms": OOH, *NPJ,* 210–11.

Just about every battle: Ibid., 209–10; Mason to wife and mother, July 22, Aug. 23, 1877, Edwin C. Mason Scrapbooks, 1877–78, MF 80, MHS.

"Heroic devotion to duty": Howard, *NPJ,* 209–10.

Progress and civilization: Ibid., 211.

"It is the same with": Ibid.

"Ferocious": Ibid., 211–12.

"If antelope acted": LVM, *Yellow Wolf: His Own*

Story (Caldwell, ID: Caxton Printers, 1940), 163.

To die alone: J. W. Redington, "Scouting in Montana in the 1870s," *Frontier,* Nov. 1933, 55–68, box 5, folder 13, JAGP; Narrative of Ho-sus-pa-ow-yein [Shot in the Head], box 6, folder 28, LVMP; LVM, *Hear Me, My Chiefs! Nez Perce History and Legend,* ed. Ruth Bordin (Caldwell, ID: Caxton, 2001), 405.

Stay out of the army's reach: Wottolen in LVM, *Hear Me,* 406.

Torn into bandages: Ibid., 408; LVM, *Yellow Wolf,* 161; H. L. Bailey, "An Infantry Second Lieutenant in the Nez Perce War of 1877," box 14, folder 101, LVMP.

Like beggars' hands: LVM, *Hear Me,* 407–8.

Inconsolable fear, he laughed: Alexander Cruickshanks, "The Birch Creek Massacre," SC 584, MHS; LVM, *Yellow Wolf,* 163–64; J. P. Clough, "Recollections of the Nez Perce Indian War of 1877, and Their Entrance into Lemhi Valley," March 1935, Idaho State Historical Society, copy in box 6, folder 2, JAGP.

Burning behind them: LVM, *Yellow Wolf,* 164–65; Greene, *Nez Perce Summer,* 144–45.

Feared would be coming: PeoPeo Tholekt in LVM, *Hear Me,* 414.

"Not far": Ibid.

"Go hurry!": Ibid, 414–15.

Cold air: Redington, "Scouting in Montana," 56.

Edge of the Camas Meadows: Mason to wife, Aug. 16, 19, 1877, Edwin C. Mason Scrapbooks, 1877–78, MF 80, MHS.

"Harass enemy": OOH in *Report of the Secretary of War, 1877,* H. Ex. Doc. 1, pt. 2, vol. 1, 45th Cong., 2nd sess., Serial Set 1794

(Washington: Government Printing Office, 1877), 128–29.

Following the Indians' trail: Ibid.

"A stern-chase": Ibid., 610.

At the stage junction: H. J. Davis, "The Battle of Camas Meadows," in *Northwestern Fights and Fighters,* ed. Cyrus Townsend Brady (New York: Doubleday, Page, 1910), 192.

"Leg-weary": Redington, "Scouting in Montana," 57.

"Deficient . . . overcoats": *Report of the Secretary of War, 1877,* 617.

They always fled, Howard complained: OOH to Sherman, Aug. 24, 1877, in ibid., 13.

Department of the Platte: Mason to wife and mother, Aug. 16, 19, 1877, Edwin C. Mason Scrapbooks, 1877–78, MF 80, MHS.

"Surely he might have": OOH to J. C. Kelton, Aug. 14, 1877, in *Claims of Nez Perce Indians,* Sen. Doc. 257, 56th Cong., 1st sess., Serial Set 3867 (Washington: Government Printing Office, 1900), 60–61.

Agonies of the march: John FitzGerald to Emily FitzGerald, Aug. 1877, in *An Army Doctor's Wife,* 302–5; Mason to wife and mother, Aug. 16, 19, 1877, Edwin C. Mason Scrapbooks, 1877–78, MF 80, MHS; Stephen Perry Jocelyn, *Mostly Alkali* (Caldwell, ID: Caxton Press, 1953), 243–44, 250–51.

"To follow them up": Sherman to McDowell, July 29, 1877, in *Claims of Nez Perce Indians,* 53.

"Is it worth while for me": OOH to J. C. Kelton, Aug. 14, 1877, in ibid., 60–61.

"The division commander": J. C. Kelton to Howard, Aug. 17, 1877, in ibid., 61.

He doubted he could win: *Report of the Secretary of War, 1877,* 129.

Straying too far: CESW, Journal of Expedition, Aug. 19, 1877, box 26(1), CESWP.

"Have driven the hostile Indians": OOH to J. C. Kelton, Aug. 19, 1877, in *Claims of Nez Perce Indians,* 64.

Enemy land: PeoPeo Tholekt Narrative, box 6, folder 31, LVMP.

Cover of darkness: Wottolen in LVM, *Hear Me,* 418.

Stampede the herd: Ibid.

"An Indian does not": Ibid.

Time to move: Ibid.

"Who are you there": LVM, *Yellow Wolf,* 167.

Inch past the guard: PeoPeo Tholekt Narrative, box 6, folder 31, LVMP; LVM, *Yellow Wolf,* 164–67.

Howard's army, it seemed: PeoPeo Tholekt Narrative, box 6, folder 31, LVMP.

"I laughed to myself": PeoPeo Tholekt in LVM, *Hear Me,* 420.

"Who in hell": Wottolen in LVM, *Hear Me,* 419; LVM, *Yellow Wolf,* 167n5.

"Firing like crazy": Ibid.

"Skipped away": Peopeo Tholekt in LVM, *Hear Me,* 420.

They were crying: LVM, *Yellow Wolf,* 167.

"I heard them cry": Ibid.

"Blowing a gale": Mason to wife and mother, Aug. 23, 1877, Edwin C. Mason Scrapbooks, 1877–78, MF 80, MHS.

Weeks of grime: Mason to wife and mother, Aug. 24, 26, 1877, Edwin C. Mason Scrapbooks, 1877–78, MF 80, MHS.

"Whoppers": Robert Pollock to wife, Aug. 25,

1877, in Robert W. Pollock, *Grandfather, Chief Joseph and Psychodynamics* (Caldwell, ID: Caxton, 1964), 83–84.

Ten thousand feet: OOH, *NPJ,* 229.

Cautious pace: Pollock to wife, Aug. 25, 1877, in *Psychodynamics,* 83.

"They were to be": Ibid.

Not see their families for months: Mason to wife and mother, Aug. 24, 26, 1877, Edwin C. Mason Scrapbooks, 1877–78, MF 80, MHS.

"I want to go home": John FitzGerald to Emily FitzGerald, Aug. 23, 1877, in *An Army Doctor's Wife,* 307; Pollock to wife, Aug. 25, 1877, in *Psychodynamics,* 83.

"The Hostiles . . . are traveling": Mason to wife and mother, Aug. 24, 1877, Edwin C. Mason Scrapbooks, 1877–78, MF 80, MHS.

"The General is disappointed": Mason to wife and mother, Aug. 23, 1877, Edwin C. Mason Scrapbooks, 1877–78, MF 80, MHS.

"The craving after newspaper": Mason to wife and mother, Aug. 24, 1877, Edwin C. Mason Scrapbooks, 1877–78, MF 80, MHS.

"Poor man": John FitzGerald to Emily FitzGerald, Aug. 23, 1877, in *An Army Doctor's Wife,* 307.

"Some 'flesh pot' ": CESW to Gray, Aug. 24, 1877, Edwin C. Mason Scrapbooks, 1877–78, MF 80, MHS.

"One minute he is a happy": Pollock to wife, Sept. 16, 1877, in *Psychodynamics,* 100.

"Quite wrathy": Mason to wife and mother, Aug. 23, 1877, Edwin C. Mason Scrapbooks, 1877–78, MF 80, MHS.

"Telegraph me some account": Sherman to OOH, Aug. 21, 1877, in *Report of the Secretary* *of War, 1877,* 12.

"An eastern force": OOH to Sherman, Aug. 24, 1877, in *Report of the Secretary of War, 1877,* 12–13.

"That force of yours": Sherman to OOH, Aug. 24, 1877, in *Report of the Secretary of War, 1877,* 13.

To camp on August 25: Mason to wife and mother, Aug. 27, 1877, Edwin C. Mason Scrapbooks, 1877–78, MF 80, MHS.

"You misunderstood me": Howard to Sherman, Aug. 27, 1877, in *Report of the Secretary of War, 1877,* 13.

Chapter 18: A World of Our Own

Made perfect brigands: Mrs. George F. Cowan, "Reminiscences of Pioneer Life," *Contributions to the Historical Society of Montana* 4 (1903): 165.

Separate wagon for baggage: Ibid., 160–61.

"Rough and uncultured": Ibid., 157–58.

Landscape of boundless dreams: Ibid., 156–58.

"Fragrant pine boughs": Ibid., 162.

Steaks for supper: Ibid.

"Indians coming": Ibid., 163–64.

Vision of an empty West: See Karl Jacoby, *Crimes Against Nature: Squatters, Poachers, Thieves, and the Hidden History of Conservation* (Berkeley: University of California Press, 2001), 87.

Made the country strong: See Mark David Spence, *Dispossessing the Wilderness: Indian Removal and the Making of the National Parks* (New York: Oxford University Press, 1999), 27, 55–56.

Left his people behind: Cowan, "Reminiscences of Pioneer Life," 161.

"An old time Indian scare": Ibid.

"The poetry of nature": Frank Carpenter, "The Wonders of Geyser Land," in *Adventures in Geyserland,* ed. Heister Dean Guie and Lucullus Virgil McWhorter (Caldwell, ID: Caxton Printers, 1935), 46.

Arrived in Wonderland: Cowan, "Reminiscences of Pioneer Life," 164.

"Simply wild with the eagerness": Ibid., 164.

"We salute[d] it with": Carpenter, "The Wonders of Geyser Land," 52.

"A somewhat creepy": Cowan, "Reminiscences of Pioneer Life," 165.

"One involuntarily reverts": Carpenter, "The Wonders of Geyser Land," 52.

"As nice and clean": Ibid., 64.

"The skin and flesh": Ibid., 55.

"Received the very unpleasant": Cowan, "Reminiscences of Pioneer Life," 166.

"In true Indian": Carpenter, "The Wonders of Geyser Land," 87–88.

The oft-told explanation: Spence, *Dispossessing the Wilderness,* 55.

Head home the next day: "The Radersburg Party," *Idaho Statesman,* Sept. 18, 1877, box 6, folder 14, JAGP; Cowan, "Reminiscences of Pioneer Life," 165.

"They made the woods ring": Cowan, "Reminiscences of Pioneer Life," 165.

"Hobble[d] around with good grace": Carpenter, "The Wonders of Geyser Land," 88.

"Uneasy": Cowan, "Reminiscences of Pioneer Life," 161.

Retreated to sleep: Carpenter, "The Wonders of

Geyser Land," 89.

"Soldiers or other white people": LVM, *Yellow Wolf: His Own Story* (Caldwell, ID: Caxton Printers, 1940), 172.

"You are supposed": Ibid., 170–72.

"Look that way": Ibid., 172.

"North of some hot springs": Ibid., 26.

"We knew that Park country": Ibid., 26, 30.

"Knew the way . . . toward": Ibid., 171.

Whites called the Yellowstone River: Ibid.

"But all white people": Ibid., 173.

More valuable as captives: Ibid.

Asked them their names: Carpenter, "The Wonders of Geyser Land," 92; McGuie and McWhorter, *Adventures in Geyser Land,* 253–54n8.

"There is our leader": LVM, *Yellow Wolf,* 173–74.

"Would you kill us": Ibid., 174.

"Will you take us": Ibid.

"Bad boys": Carpenter, "The Wonders of Geyser Land," 93.

"I wanted to be a friend": LVM, *Yellow Wolf,* 174.

"The leading white man": Ibid., 175.

Older one had been crying: Carpenter, "The Wonders of Geyser Land," 92; LVM, *Yellow Wolf,* 175.

Animals moving east: Carpenter, "The Wonders of Geyser Land," 97.

"The warriors mixed us up": LVM, *Yellow Wolf,* 175.

Hacked from the wheels: "Reminiscences of Pioneer Life," 168.

An old man's head: Ibid.

"Did not please": Ibid.

" 'Whooping us up' ": Carpenter, "The Wonders of Geyser Land," 95, 97, 98, 100.

"light-hearted": Cowan, "Reminiscences of Pioneer Life," 168–69.

Helena years before: William Dingee in "In the National Park," *Helena Weekly Herald,* Sept. 6, 1877.

Faded into the herd: Cowan, "Reminiscences of Pioneer Life," 169.

Old frontier stories: Ibid., 170; Robert Pollock to wife, Aug. 27, 1877, Robert W. Pollock, *Grandfather, Chief Joseph and Psychodynamics* (Caldwell, ID: Caxton, 1964), 92–96; "The Radersburg Party."

"The silence seemed": Cowan, "Reminiscences of Pioneer Life," 170.

"In less time than": Ibid., 171.

"All was blank": Ibid,

Deerskins for bedding: Ibid., 162–63.

Paths remained open to them: Thomas A. Sutherland, "Letter from the Front," *Portland Daily Standard,* Sept. 20, 1877, box 6, folder 14, JAGP.

To go much farther: S. G. Fisher, "Journal of S. G. Fisher," *Contributions to the Historical Society of Montana* 2 (1896): 273.

Under the chiefs' protection: LVM, *Yellow Wolf,* 177–78.

Toward the rising sun: Cowan, "Reminiscences of Pioneer Life," 172–75.

"Took a survey of": Henry Buck, "The Story of the Nez Perce Indian Campaign during the Summer of 1877 as Told by Henry Buck, a Citizen who Participated in the Chase with Gen. O. O. Howard" (1922), SC 492, MHS.

Slid off the plateau: Ibid.

Slide once again: Ibid.

"Where day brings": *Report of the Secretary of War, 1877,* H. Ex. Doc. 1, pt. 2, vol. 1, 45th Cong., 2nd sess., Serial Set 1794 (Washington: Government Printing Office, 1877), 619.

"Disciplined spirit": Ibid.

Drawing the landscapes: Edwin C. Mason to wife and mother, Sept. 2, 1877, Edwin C. Mason Scrapbooks, 1877–78, MF 80, MHS.

"Beaver, deer, elk": Pollock to wife, Sept. 2, 1877, in *Psychodynamics,* 97.

"Too dreadful to think about": Mason to wife and mother, Aug. 29, 1877, Edwin C. Mason Scrapbooks, 1877–78, MF 80, MHS.

"Alive": Mason to wife and mother, Aug. 30, 1877, Edwin C. Mason Scrapbooks, 1877–78, MF 80, MHS.

Crow country to the southeast: OOH to S. D. Sturgis, Sept. 8, 1877, RG 393, Part III, entry 107, Department of the Columbia, Nez Perce Campaign, 1877, box 1, NARA.

Serving as army scouts: Frederick E. Hoxie, *Parading Through History: The Making of the Crow Nation in America, 1805–1935* (New York: Cambridge University Press, 1995), 9, 21, 109.

"Has served long": Sherman to OOH, Aug. 29, 1877, Nez Perce War, 1877, "Special Files" of Headquarters, Division of the Missouri, Relating to Military Operations and Administration, 1863–1885, RG 393, Microfilm Publication M1495, roll 5, NARA; Jerome A. Greene, *Nez Perce Summer, 1877: The U.S. Army and the Nee-Me-Poo Crisis* (Helena: Montana Historical Society, 2000), 167–68. See also Sherman to Sheridan, Aug. 29, 1877, NARA as above.

"An officer much older": OOH, *My Life and*

Experiences Among Our Hostile Indians (Hartford, CT: A. D. Worthington, 1907), 295.

"Uncertain of their exact": OOH in *Report of the Secretary of War, 1877,* 620.

Dead and dying animals: Fisher, "Journal," 275. On the routes taken by the Nez Perce families through Yellowstone, see William L. Lang, "Where Did the Nez Perces Go in Yellowstone in 1877?" *Montana: The Magazine of Western History* 40 (Winter 1990): 14–29; Lee Whittlesey, "The Nez Perces in Yellowstone in 1877: A Comparison of Attempts to Deduce Their Route," ibid. 57 (Spring 2007): 48–55, 94–95.

Catch the enemy yet: OOH, *NPJ,* 243.

"Short march just long enough": Mason to wife and mother, Sept. 3, 1877, Edwin C. Mason Scrapbooks, 1877–78, MF 80, MHS.

Just east of Bozeman: Buck, "Story of the Nez Perce Indian Campaign."

"Now one will not starve": Mason to wife and mother, Sept. 12, 1877, Edwin C. Mason Scrapbooks, 1877–78, MF 80, MHS.

"A domineering officer": Pollock to wife, Sept. 16, 1877, in *Psychodynamics,* 100.

"The most magnificent": Mason to wife and mother, Sept. 7, 1877, Edwin C. Mason Scrapbooks, 1877–78, MF 80, MHS.

Somewhere in between: Mason to wife and mother, Sept. 8, 1877, Edwin C. Mason Scrapbooks, 1877–78, MF 80, MHS.

Tall rye grass: Fisher, "Journal," 276–77.

"The boys are apprehensive": Fisher, "Journal," 277.

Back to Clark's Fork: Fisher, "Journal," 95; CESW, "Chief Joseph, the Nez-Percé," *Century*

28 (May 1884): 140.

"Wave their flags": Howard, *NPJ,* 254–55.

"Where Sturgis is": Mason to wife and mother, Sept. 12, 1877, Edwin C. Mason Scrapbooks, 1877–78, MF 80, MHS.

New lives, new fortunes: Fisher, "Journal," 277; Mason to wife and mother, Sept. 12, 1877, Edwin C. Mason Scrapbooks, 1877–78, MF 80, MHS.

Chapter 19: Through the Veil

Putting up a fight: J. W. Redington, "Stolen Stage Coach," box 10, folder 69, LVMP; LVM, *Hear Me, My Chiefs! Nez Perce History and Legend,* ed. Ruth Bordin (Caldwell, ID: Caxton, 2001), 456–57.

It too was torched: Ibid.

Remnants of richer years: Stephen Perry Jocelyn, *Mostly Alkalai* (Caldwell, ID: Caxton, 1953), 254; Frederick E. Hoxie, *Parading Through History: The Making of the Crow Nation in America, 1805–1935* (New York: Cambridge University Press, 1995), 21.

British possessions: On the significance of the Canadian border in late nineteenth-century Native American life, see Beth LaDow, *The Medicine Line: Life and Death on a North American Borderland* (New York: Routledge, 2001).

Nez Perce language: Haruo Aoki, *Nez Perce Dictionary* (Berkeley and Los Angeles: University of California Press, 1994), 597.

What it was: a stage coach: LVM, *Hear Me,* 456–57; Jocelyn, Sept. 16, 1877, in *Mostly Alkali,* 257; Jocelyn, Sept. 1877, in ibid., 257–59.

Gone by stage: LVM, *Yellow Wolf: His Own Story* (Caldwell, ID: Caxton Printers, 1940), 30.

Floating softly to the ground: Redington, "Stolen Stage Coach."

Half a mile north: Ibid.

Fording the deep river: S. G. Fisher, "Journal of S. G. Fisher," *Contributions to the Historical Society of Montana* 2 (1896): 278.

Before them, in their sights: Fisher, "Journal," 96.

Too far away to strike: Ibid.

"I . . . am becoming tired": Ibid., 1877, 92.

Before they reached Canada: Jerome A. Greene, *Nez Perce Summer, 1877: The U.S. Army and the Nee-Me-Poo Crisis* (Helena: Montana Historical Society, 2000), 247.

"To make every effort": OOH in *Report of the Secretary of War, 1877,* H. Ex. Doc. 1, pt. 2, vol. 1, 45th Cong., 2nd sess., Serial Set 1794 (Washington: Government Printing Office, 1877), 514.

"A joy ride": Redington, "Stolen Stage Coach."

Still three miles away: Ibid.; Peopeo Tholekt to LVM, Oct. 1, 1929, box 6, folder 27, LVMP.

"All the Indians in the country": Emily FitzGerald to Aunt Annie, June 25, 1877, in *An Army Doctor's Wife on the Frontier: Letters from Alaska and the Far West, 1874–1878,* ed. Abe Laufe (Pittsburgh, PA: University of Pittsburgh Press, 1962), 266.

"Poor Nez Percés": Jenkins FitzGerald to Emily FitzGerald, Sept. 16, 1877, in ibid., 312.

Indians in the dark: Fisher, "Journal," 96, 99.

"Where the war should have": Redington, "Stolen Stage Coach."

Passenger had fled downriver: Ibid.; Redington described Clark as a "popular entertainer" and Thomas Sutherland of the *Daily Standard* called her "a well known public character in Portland in other days" in "Special Correspondence," *Portland Daily Standard,* Oct. 5, 1877, box 7, folder 11, JAGP. The 1870 US census listed Clark as a prostitute in Deer Lodge. See also Anne M. Butler, *Daughters of Joy, Sisters of Misery: Prostitutes in the American West, 1865–90* (Urbana: University of Illinois Press, 1985), 62.

"Looted of all its eatables": Redington, "Stolen Stage Coach."

"Flapjack party": Jack McGoey, "Letter from the Front," *Rocky Mountain Husbandman,* Sept. 27, 1877.

Stop it from barking: Redington, "Stolen Stage Coach."

Be a dentist, too: "Indian Attack Caused Smith to Become Dentist," *Rocky Mountain Husbandman* (Great Falls, MT), May 17, 1928, box 49, folder 490, LVMP.

Keep scouting on foot: LVM, *Yellow Wolf,* 195–96.

Who had fallen behind: Ibid., 191–94.

"Strange Indians": Ibid., 187.

He later said: Ibid.

Job of lead scout: Ibid., 195.

He was not alone: Ibid., 196.

"Four white men": Ibid., 196–97.

Dropped a second man: Ibid., 196.

"Now I am getting": Ibid., 196–97.

Cross without rafts: LVM, *Hear Me,* 469.

Pots and pans, cups and buckets: LVM, *Yellow Wolf,* 199; PeoPeo Tholekt Narrative, box 6, folder 31, LVMP.

"We figured it": PeoPeo Tholekt Narrative, box 6, folder 31, LVMP.

Seeped through the canyons: Greene, *Nez Perce Summer,* 237.

"It had been nearly": LVM, *Yellow Wolf,* 199.

"Earnest petition[s]": OOH, *NPJ,* 263.

"One chance in a million": Alexander in OOH, *NPJ,* 264.

"A slight despondency": Ibid.

"Perfect farce": Edwin C. Mason to wife and mother, Sept. 15, 1877, Edwin C. Mason Scrapbooks, 1877–78, MF 80, MHS.

Home in a week: Mason to wife and mother, Sept. 24, 1877, Edwin C. Mason Scrapbooks, 1877–78, MF 80, MHS; Jocelyn, Sept. 13, 1877, in *Mostly Alkali,* 254–55.

"Press upon": OOH, *NPJ,* 262.

Horses wore out: Mason to wife and mother, Sept. 12, 1877, Edwin C. Mason Scrapbooks, 1877–78, MF 80, MHS; OOH, *NPJ,* 260–61.

"Books of an exciting character": OOH, *NPJ,* 261.

"We must not move": Ibid., 263.

"The moment we check": OOH to Miles, Sept. 20, 1877, RG 393, Part III, entry 107, Letters and Telegrams Received by D. Yellowstone HQ, Sept. 1877–April 1878, box 3, NARA, copy in box 7, folder 11, JAGP.

Red River near Shreveport, Louisiana: Ted Tunnell, *Crucible of Reconstruction: War, Radicalism, and Race in Louisiana, 1862–1877* (Baton Rouge: Louisiana State University Press, 1984), 202–3; Lou Falkner Williams, *The Great South Carolina Ku Klux Klan Trials, 1871–1872* (Athens: University of Georgia Press, 1996), 38, 45, 56.

Slanders, Merrill protested: Ted Tunnell, *Edge of the Sword: The Ordeal of Carpet-bagger*

Marshall H. Twitchell in the Civil War and Reconstruction (Baton Rouge: Louisiana State University Press, 2001), 220; T. J. Stiles, *Custer's Trials: A Life on the Frontier of a New America* (New York: Knopf, 2015), 435; James Donovan, *A Terrible Glory: Custer and the Little Bighorn — the Last Great Battle of the American West* (New York: Little, Brown, 2008), 99.

"Lively": OOH, *NPJ,* 262.

"A more extensive knowledge": Miles to OOH, Sept. 26, 1887, OOHP.

As it was being amputated: Robert Wooster, *Nelson A. Miles and the Twilight of the Frontier Army* (Lincoln: University of Nebraska Press, 1993), 3–4, 11.

Lecture at Faneuil Hall: Nelson A. Miles, *Serving the Republic: Memoirs of the Civil and Military Life of Nelson A. Miles* (New York: Harper, 1911), 11; Wooster, *Nelson A. Miles,* 3–4.

A general's star: When Miles used family money to raise and outfit a volunteer company, the Massachusetts governor refused to commission him captain. Wooster, *Nelson A. Miles,* 5; Miles, *Serving the Republic,* 25–26.

"Miles is ambitious": OOH, *NPJ,* 262.

"Glad, hearty tidings": Ibid., 264.

Knife would have steamed: LVM, *Yellow Wolf,* 204; Yellow Bull Interview, Feb. 13, 1915, MS 57, box 2, folder 115, WMCP-BYU; PeoPeo Tholekt Narrative, box 6, folder 31, LVMP.

Maybe fifty miles away: LVM, *Yellow Wolf,* 204–5; PeoPeo Tholekt Narrative, box 6, folder 31, LVMP.

Dozens of animals behind: Many Wounds in LVM, *Hear Me,* 473–74.

"You can take command": Ibid.

"As passing clouds": "The Last Battle: Prophetic Dreams of Wot-to-len," box 9, folder 56, LVMP.

Still hopelessly behind: LVM, *Hear Me,* 474; Yellow Bull Interview, Feb. 13, 1915, MS 57, box 2, folder 115, WMCP-BYU.

South, hunting buffalo: LVM, *Hear Me,* 478; White Bird II in ibid., 479; "Black Eagle's Statement Concerning Horses Ready Packed When Attacked by Colonel Miles," box 9, folder 56, LVMP; Narrative of Ho-sus-pa-ow-yein [Shot in the Head], box 6, folder 28, LVMP.

Mean that soldiers were near: LVM, *Yellow Wolf,* 205; PeoPeo Tholekt Narrative, box 6, folder 31, LVMP; Narrative of Ho-sus-pa-ow-yein [Shot in the Head], box 6, folder 28, LVMP.

"Plenty, plenty time": LVM, *Yellow Wolf,* 205.

Now calm prevailed: Ibid.

"Enemies right on us": Ibid.

"Soldiers, soldiers, soldiers": Shot in Head in LVM, *Hear Me,* 482.

Away from the bluffs: LVM, *Yellow Wolf,* 205; PeoPeo Tholekt Narrative, box 6, folder 31, LVMP; Narrative of Ho-sus-pa-ow-yein [Shot in the Head], box 6, folder 28, LVMP.

"Horses!": LVM, *Yellow Wolf,* 205.

Chapter 20: Where The Sun Now Stands

Straight for the herd: LVM, *Yellow Wolf: His Own Story* (Caldwell, ID: Caxton Printers, 1940), 205–6.

Lost sight of his daughter: Young Joseph, "An Indian's View of Indian Affairs," *North American Review* 128 (April 1879): 428; "The Story of

Pe-Naw-We-Non-Mi," box 8, folder 43, LVMP.

"Buzzing like summer flies": Shot in Head in LVM, *Hear Me, My Chiefs! Nez Perce History and Legend,* ed. Ruth Bordin (Caldwell, ID: Caxton, 2001), 385; LVM, *Yellow Wolf,* 208.

"You see the sun": PeoPeo Tholekt Narrative, box 6, folder 31, LVMP.

"You have a red skin": LVM, *Yellow Wolf,* 207, 211.

Handed him his rifle: Young Joseph, "An Indian's View," 428.

"Here's your gun": Ibid.

Air with lead: Narrative of Ho-sus-pa-ow-yein [Shot in the Head], box 6, folder 28, LVMP; LVM, *Hear Me, My Chiefs! Nez Perce History and Legend,* ed. Ruth Bordin (Caldwell, ID: Caxton, 2001), 483.

Nez Perce bullet: LVM, *Yellow Wolf,* 209–11; Mrs. Ollicot's Narrative [Wetatonmi], box 6, folder 28, LVMP.

"Bullet for bullet": LVM, *Yellow Wolf,* 207.

"Not more than twenty": Young Joseph, "An Indian's View," 428.

First of the season: LVM, *Yellow Wolf,* 209; Narrative of Ho-sus-pa-ow-yein [Shot in the Head], box 6, folder 28, LVMP; LVM, *Hear Me,* 483.

Soldiers were digging, too: LVM, *Yellow Wolf,* 11; Wotolen, "Chief Joseph Captured," box 10, folder 62, LVMP; Mrs. Ollicot's Narrative [Wetatonmi], box 6, folder 28, LVMP.

His sightless eyes: LVM, *Yellow Wolf,* 214; LVM, *Hear Me,* 495; Mrs. Ollicot's Narrative [Wetatonmi], box 6, folder 28, LVMP.

"No hope": LVM, *Yellow Wolf,* 212.

Pleading with him to stay alive: Ibid.

Wall Street financier: "L. H. Jerome Dead," *New York Times,* Jan. 18, 1935; Stephen Fiske, *Off-Hand Portraits of Prominent New Yorkers* (New York: Lockwood & Son, 1884), 198. Lovell Jerome's uncle Leonard, who was even more successful on Wall Street until the Panic of 1873, owned the racetrack. He endowed an annual prize at Princeton "for the student who best displayed the characteristics of an American gentleman." Fiske, *Off-Hand Portraits,* 201.

"The most popular man": Fiske, *Off-Hand Portraits,* 198.

Nearly court-martialed: Barry C. Johnson, "Solved: The 'Mystery' of Lt. Lovell Jerome," *Montana* 19 (1969): 90–91.

"The most dashing": "Brave Jerome: A Dashing Lieutenant's Experience in Chief Joseph's Trenches," *New York Herald,* Oct. 30, 1877.

Necklace was still there: Ibid.; Myles Moylan to E. A. Garlington, Aug. 16, 1878, University of Idaho Library, copy in box 8, folder 10, JAGP.

Without boots or slouch hat: "Life in New York," *Nashville American,* June 23, 1901.

Cotton slicker: LVM, *Yellow Wolf,* 215.

Isle of Wight: Charles A. Peverelly, *The Book of American Pastimes* (New York: published by the author, 1866), 68–71.

Venture even farther: Tom Hill in *Memorial of the Nez Perce Indians Residing in the State of Idaho to the Congress of the United States, Together with Affidavits, and Also Copies of Various Treaties Between the United States and the Nez Perce Indians* (Washington: Government Printing Office, 1911), 32.

Shook hands with one man: Edward S. Curtis,

The North American Indian, vol. 8 (Norwood, MA: Plimpton Press, 1911), 171.

No point in using it: Tom Hill in *Memorial of the Nez Perce Indians,* 32; "Brave Jerome"; "Indian Battle Retold," *Winners of the West,* Apr. 30, 1935, box 9, folder 1, JAGP.

Fire more accurately: "Brave Jerome."

Die of boredom: Ibid.

"Alarmed and disgusted": Ibid.; LVM, *Yellow Wolf,* 215.

Survive the night: "Brave Jerome."

"Here is Joseph": Tom Hill in *Memorial of the Nez Perce Indians,* 32.

"You need not be frightened": Curtis, *The North American Indian* 8:171.

Any more bloodshed: Young Joseph, "An Indian's View," 428.

"I was very anxious": Ibid., 429.

"I shall give you": Tom Hill in *Memorial of the Nez Perce Indians,* 32.

"Now you are going to": Ibid.

"You will not": Ibid.

"Go back to your trenches": Ibid.

"We must fight more": LVM, *Yellow Wolf,* 217–18.

"We will all have to die": Tom Hill in *Memorial of the Nez Perce Indians,* 32.

Emblem of the plains: Sebastian Braun, *Buffalo Inc.: American Indians and Economic Development* (Norman: University of Oklahoma Press, 2008), 49.

A rare treat: Elliott West, *The Last Indian War: The Nez Perce Story* (New York: Oxford University Press, 2009), 258–63; Richard White, *Railroaded: The Transcontinentals and the Mak-*

ing of Modern America (New York: Norton, 2011), 462–66.

Squeezed the trigger: OOH, *NPJ,* 266.

Evident to General Howard: Ibid.

"We are *crawling*": Edwin C. Mason to wife and mother, Oct. 2, 1877, Edwin C. Mason Scrapbooks, 1877–78, MF 80, MHS.

White Bird Canyon: Ibid.; OOH, *NPJ,* 265; CESW, "Chief Joseph, the Nez-Percé," *Century* 28 (May 1884): 141.

Still be seen and shot: OOH, *NPJ,* 266–68.

"A battle, going on": Ibid.

Next chapter of redemption: Ibid.

Shooting at him: Ibid., 268–69.

"If we whipped": LVM, *Yellow Wolf,* 219.

"We had never heard": Young Joseph, "An Indian's View," 429.

"We wanted plenty of ammunition": LVM, *Yellow Wolf,* 221.

Ride to their aid: Young Joseph, "An Indian's View," 429.

Refuge now a grave: LVM, *Yellow Wolf,* 220.

"All my brothers": Ibid., 221.

And their daughters: Tom Hill in *Memorial of the Nez Perce Indians,* 34; CESW, "Chief Joseph, the Nez-Percé," 141.

"I am glad today": LVM, *Yellow Wolf,* 222.

Back to the Nez Perce reservation: Ibid., 222–23.

"General Miles and General Howard": Mrs. Ollicot's Narrative [Wetatonmi], box 6, folder 28, LVMP.

"We should get something": LVM, *Yellow Wolf,* 223.

"I could not bear": Young Joseph, "An Indian's View," 429.

"Good water": LVM, *Yellow Wolf,* 224–25.

Pay him to print: CESW to LVM, Sept. 1, 1935, box 9, folder 56, LVMP; "The Surrender of Joseph," *Harper's Weekly,* Nov. 17, 1877, 905–6; *New York Daily Graphic,* Nov. 3, 1877.

"I would say grey": CESW to LVM, Jan. 31, 1936, box 13, folder 92, LVMP.

"Impulsive gesture": CESW, "Chief Joseph, the Nez-Percé," 142.

"From where the sun stands": *Chicago Times,* Oct. 26 1877, as quoted in Jerome A. Greene, *Nez Perce Summer, 1877: The U.S. Army and the Nee-Me-Poo Crisis* (Helena: Montana Historical Society, 2397), 312.

"From where the sun now stands": Chief Joseph, "An Indian's View," 429.

His head was bowed: CESW, "The Surrender of Joseph," 906; CESW, "Chief Joseph, the Nez-Percé," 142.

"A mouth and chin": CESW, "Chief Joseph, the Nez-Percé," 142.

"Joseph has a gentle face": "The Surrender of Joseph," 906.

"Where a moment before": CESW, "Chief Joseph, the Nez-Percé," 142.

"Irregular column": "The Pursuit and Battle: Semi-Official Report of a Staff Officer," *Chicago Tribune,* Oct. 25, 1877.

A Friday, at 2:20 p.m.: CESW to Edwin C. Mason, Oct. 6, 1877, RG 393, Part III, entry 897, box 1, NARA, copy in box 8, folder 6, JAGP.

"Nothing to stay for": Mrs. Ollicot's Narrative [Wetatonmi], box 6, folder 28, LVMP.

Many of them were wounded: LVM, *Hear Me,* 551n4 (citing a letter from Catholic priest with the Milk River Métis who tended to White Bird's group).

"It was lonesome": Mrs. Ollicot's Narrative [Wetatonmi], box 6, folder 28, LVMP; LVM, *Hear Me,* 511.

Yellow Wolf to find them: LVM, *Yellow Wolf,* 229–30.

"If they tried": Ibid., 230.

Toward the Medicine Line: Ibid., 229–31.

"Quiet, dignified": "The Pursuit and Battle."

Small of his back: For a discussion of C. E. S. Wood and the documenting and imagining of Indians, including the Nez Perce, see Sherry L. Smith, *Reimagining Indians: Native Americans Through Anglo Eyes, 1880–1940* (New York: Oxford University Press, 2000), 21–44.

Linked by tunnels: Greene, *Nez Perce Summer,* 314–15.

Date of the battle: John W. Painter, *American Indian Artifacts: The John Painter Collection* (Cincinnati: George Tassian Org., Inc., 1992), 94, 96.

White weasel tails: "Chief Joseph's Coat," Nez Perce National Historical Park, http://www.nps.gov/museum/exhibits/nepe/exb/contact_change/1877War/BIHO1256(2)_Chief-Joseph-Ja.html.

Saddles with the chief: George Venn, *Soldier to Advocate: C. E. S. Wood's 1877 Legacy* (La Grande, OR: Wordcraft of Oregon, 2006), 64.

Dragged on travois: Mason to wife and mother, Oct. 8, 11, 13, 1877, Edwin C. Mason Scrapbooks, 1877–78, MF 80, MHS.

"Bible Chief": "Joseph," *Chicago Tribune,* Oct. 19, 1877.

Press Howard's case: CESW, "History by One

Who Aided in Making It: To Whom Belongs the Credit for the Capture of Chief Joseph? Here Are the Facts," *Spectator,* July 11, 1925, JAGP. Wood insisted that the speech was Joseph's own words, unaltered when he transcribed them; Smith, *Reimagining Indians,* 26–27.

"Tell General Howard": "Joseph," *Bismarck Tri-Weekly Tribune,* Oct. 26, 1877.

"Remarkably pathetic": Ibid.

Chapter 21: The Best Indian

Far less comfortable affairs: "Society," *Washington Evening Star,* Jan. 15, 1879.

"Grace, ease": "Washington Gossip," *St. Louis Globe-Democrat,* Jan. 19, 1879.

"What one reads": "Washington Society," *Chicago Daily Tribune,* Jan. 22, 1879.

"Sensible woman": "Washington Gossip."

Kaleidoscope, wrote another: Ibid.; "Society."

"Unmistakable African descent": "Washington Society."

"By far the most important": "Society."

Chief Joseph: "Washington Gossip"; "Society"; "Washington Society."

Swinging from the gallows: Sherman to Sheridan, Aug. 31, 1877, Nez Perce War, 1877, "Special Files" of Headquarters, Division of the Missouri, Relating to Military Operations and Administration, 1863–1885, RG 393, Microfilm Publication M1495, roll 5, NARA.

From there to Indian Territory: West, *The Last Indian War,* 293.

"Make a crop": Sherman to Sheridan, Oct. 10, 1877, Nez Perce War, 1877, "Special Files" of Headquarters, Division of the Missouri, Relating to Military Operations and Administration, 1863–1885, RG 393, Microfilm Publication M1495, roll 5, NARA.

"Those captured at the Bear Paws Mountain": Sherman to OOH, Dec. 12, 1877, box 13, folder 83, OOHP.

"There should be extreme": Sherman to Sheridan, Aug. 31, 1877, NARA.

"It would seem as": "Exiled Nez Perces," *Council Fire* 1 (August 1878), 125; LVM, *Hear Me*, 529–30.

"Worse to die": Young Joseph, "An Indian's View," 430.

"Like a poor man": Chief Joseph in *Testimony Taken by the Joint Committee Appointed to Take into Consideration the Expediency of Transferring the Indian Bureau to the War Department*, Sen. Misc. Doc. 53, 45th Cong., 3rd sess., Serial Set 1835 (Washington: Government Printing Office, 1879), 77.

"Two will die": Speech of Sen. McCreery, 8 *Cong. Rec.* 1155, 45th Cong., 3rd sess., pt. 2, Feb. 10, 1879; J. Diane Pearson, *The Nez Perces in the Indian Territory: Nimiipuu Survival* (Norman: University of Oklahoma Press, 2008), 117–26.

"He don't speak": "Joseph and His Friends," *St. Louis Globe-Democrat*, Jan. 11, 1879.

How petty the spat: See, e.g., *Wheeling Daily Intelligencer*, Feb. 7, 1878.

"A light shade": "Chief Joseph," *Milwaukee Daily Sentinel*, Feb. 4, 1879 (reporting Schurz's impression).

"Amiable and enlightened": "Washington Gossip," *St. Louis Globe-Democrat*, Jan. 26, 1879.

"Dignified and distingue": Ibid.

"An unrelenting, appealing": "Chief Joseph," *Milwaukee Daily Sentinel,* Feb. 2, 1879.

"Model of courtly grace": "Washington Gossip," *St. Louis Globe-Democrat,* Jan. 19, 1879.

"Striped in the strongest": "Joseph and His Friend," *St. Louis Globe-Democrat,* Jan. 11, 1879.

"The stereotype undertaker's": "Washington Society."

"So interesting to the": "Washington Gossip."

Tribes in the West: "The Man from Kentuck": *Milwaukee Daily Sentinel,* Feb. 14, 1897; "Mr. Hayes' Reception," *Washington Post,* Jan. 15, 1879; "Washington Society," *Chicago Daily Tribune,* Jan. 22, 1879; "Washington Gossip," *St. Louis Globe-Democrat,* Jan. 19, 26, 1879.

"An earnest greeting": "Washington Gossip," *St. Louis Globe-Democrat,* Jan. 19, 26, 1879.

"More impressed with": "Chief Joseph," *Milwaukee Daily Sentinel,* Feb. 2, 1879.

Exchanged warm greetings: "Chief Joseph," *Concord Independent Journal,* Jan. 16, 1879.

"We have carried on": "Gen. Nelson A. Miles," *St. Paul Daily Globe,* Dec. 4, 1878.

Blasted heavy buckshot: *Wellington* (OH) *Enterprise,* Jan. 16, 1879.

"The best Indian": "Chief Joseph," *Concord Independent Journal,* Jan. 16, 1879.

"When I was small": Chief Joseph in *Testimony Taken by the Joint Committee,* 78.

"Modoc bullets in": Alfred B. Meacham, "The Tragedy of the Lava Beds" (1874), in Thomas Augustus Bland, *Life of Alfred B. Meacham* (Washington: Bland, 1883) 6.

The native tribes: Ibid.; *Tenth Annual Report of*

the Board of Indian Commissioners for the Year 1878 (Washington: Government Printing Office, 1879), 125; see also Boyd Cothran, *Remembering the Modoc War: Redemptive Violence and the Making of American Innocence* (Chapel Hill: University of North Carolina Press, 2014), 83–93.

White society: Cothran, *Remembering the Modoc War,* 82–83.

"A distinguished visitor": *Tenth Annual Report of the Board of Indian Commissioners . . . 1878,* 126.

"For his great power": Ibid.

"I have met many": Ibid.

"In tears because": Ibid.

Indian Territory and $250,000: "Meeting of Indian Commissioners," *Washington Post,* Jan. 16, 1879; "Buying Land of the Indians," *New York Times,* Feb. 2, 1879.

Touring violin virtuosi: See, e.g., *Washington Evening Star,* Oct. 14, Dec. 6, 18, 1878.

Subscriptions for Meacham's magazine: Pearson, *The Nez Perces in the Indian Territory,* 154–55.

"The pow-wow": "Washington Gossip," *St. Louis Globe-Democrat,* Jan. 26, 1879.

"Sonorous": "Broken Pledges," *Washington Post,* Jan. 18, 1879.

"If the white man": Young Joseph, "An Indian's View of Indian Affairs," *North American Review* 128 (April 1879): 432–33.

"Theoretically it was a good": "Washington Gossip," *St. Louis Globe-Democrat,* Jan. 26, 1879.

"A fat, healthy": Ibid., Jan. 19, 1879.

"Aye, lies, lies": John Henry Boner, "Chief Joseph, the Nez Perce," *Washington Evening Star,* Jan. 20, 1879.

"They say that justice": Martha Perry Lowe, *The Story of Chief Joseph* (Boston: D. Lothrop, 1881), 35–36.

"Quick quivering tears": Boner, "Chief Joseph, the Nez Perce."

"If General Howard had given me plenty": Young Joseph, "An Indian's View," 425.

"The wonderfully abrupt advent": "An Aboriginal Review Article," *Vermont Phoenix,* Apr. 4, 1879.

"Accusations . . . brought against": "Chief Joseph's Own Story," *Army and Navy Journal,* Mar. 22, 1879, 586–87.

"Has . . . the summary": OOH, "The True Story of the Wallowa Campaign," *North American Review* 129 (July 1879): 56.

How he had handled the campaign: Ibid., 53–64; OOH to William H. Hare, April 12, 1879, Letterbooks, roll 9, OOHP; OOH to Editor, *North American Review,* Apr. 15, 1879, Letterbooks, roll 9, OOHP.

"Poor, but devlish": A. J. Carrier to OOH, Oct. 26, 1877, box 13, folder 75, OOHP.

Howard as inept and hypocritical: "Not for Joseph," *New York Herald,* Sept. 15, 1877; "The Nez Perces," *New York Herald,* Oct. 23, 1877; "General Howard Viewed from Various Standpoints," *Helena* (MT) *Independent Record,* Sept. 8, 1877.

"Reviled as a failure": "Not for Joseph," *New York Herald,* Sept. 15, 1877.

"My countrymen . . . seem": OOH Interview, *Chicago Times* as quoted in *Boston Daily Adver-*

tiser, Oct. 29, 1877.

"Boohooing": Quoted in Peter R. DeMontravel, *A Hero to his Fighting Men: Nelson A. Miles, 1839–1925* (Kent, OH: Kent State University Press, 1998), 133.

"You virtually gave up": Miles to OOH, June 8, 1878, box 14, folder 28, OOHP.

"Roughly accosted": OOH, *My Life and Experiences Among Our Hostile Indians* (Hartford, CT: A. D. Worthington, 1907), 416–17.

"Earnestly desired peace": OOH, "The True Story of the Wallowa Campaign," 53–54.

"Unparalleled vigor and perseverance": OOH, *NPJ,* 264, 272.

Fight the Indians to a stalemate: CESW to C. J. Brosnan, Jan. 7, 1918, C. J. Brosnan Collection, University of Idaho, copy in box 5, folder 5, JAGP.

"Let them settle down": OOH, "The True Story of the Wallowa Campaign," 64.

"These savages were not saints": OOH, Letter to the Editor, Apr. 3, 1879, in *Army and Navy Journal,* May 3, 1879, 698.

"I was so pleased": Howard, "The True Story of the Wallowa Campaign," 53, 55, 56.

"Popular, valuable and saleable": OOH to Charles Howard, Jan. 6, 1879, Letterbooks, roll 9, OOHP.

"Resentment of Joseph": OOH to CHH, May 9, 1879, Letterbooks, roll 9, OOHP.

Bring shame to the academy: See John F. Marszalek, *Assault at West Point: The Court-Martial of Johnson Whittaker* (New York: Maxwell Macmillan International/ Collier, 1994).

"If you go to West Point": Sherman to OOH, Dec. 7, 1880, box 15, folder 28, OOHP.

Drudgery, debt, and want: Steven Hahn, *A Nation Under Our Feet: Black Political Struggles in the Rural South from Slavery to the Great Migration* (Cambridge, MA: Harvard University Press, 2003), 319–28; Gregory P. Downs, *After Appomattox: Military Occupation and the Ends of War* (Cambridge, MA: Harvard University Press, 2015), 239–40.

Moving to Washington Territory: O. S. B. Wall to OOH, Sept. 13, 1878, box 14, folder 35, OOHP; Daniel J. Sharfstein, *The Invisible Line: Three American Families and the Secret Journey from Black to White* (New York: Penguin, 2011), 203–4.

"The social prejudice": OOH, *Autobiography of Oliver Otis Howard,* 2 vols. (New York: Baker & Taylor, 1908), 2:487.

All white again: Marszalek, *Assault at West Point,* 277.

"After a few weeks": OOH, *Autobiography* 2:486.

Joseph and Yellow Bull: OOH to A. I. Chapman, Jan. 6, 1880, Letterbooks, roll 9, OOHP.

"I remember the counsiles": Chief Joseph to OOH, Oakland Agency I.T., June 30, 1880, box 15, folder 11, Howard Papers.

"I wants you to know": Chief Joseph to OOH, June 30, 1880, box 15, folder 11, Howard Papers.

"Indian troubles": OOH to CHH, May 9, 1879, Letterbooks, roll 9, OOHP.

"Political equality": This distinction was not new. See, for example, Eric Foner, *Free Soil, Free Labor, Free Men: The Ideology of the Republican Party Before the Civil War* (New York: Oxford University Press, 1995), 292.

For Christian civilization: Stephen Kantrowitz, " 'Not Quite Constitutionalized': The Meaning of 'Civilization' and the Limits of Native American Citizenship,' " in *The World the Civil War Made,* ed. Gregory P. Downs and Kate Masur (Chapel Hill: University of North Carolina Press, 2015), 76, 98–99.

"I am your friend": OOH to Joseph, July 20, 1880, Letterbooks, roll 9, Howard Papers.

During the Mexican War: CESW, "An Unknown Turning-Point in the Destiny of the Republic," *Californian* 2 (Dec. 1880): 539–43. Wood's sketches of the end of the Nez Perce War were published in *New York Daily Graphic,* Nov. 3, 1877, 20; *Harper's Weekly,* Nov. 17, 1877, 905.

"Sweetheart, it all was": NMS to CES, Dec. 3, 1877, WP.

"I am sure no one": CESW to NMS, Mar. 5, 1878, box 243(15), CESWP.

Baby rattles in his future: CESW to NMS, Dec. 27, 1877, box 243(13), CESWP.

"Why did you": CESW to NMS, Mar. 5, 1878, box 243(15), CESWP.

She was pregnant: Philip W. Leon, *Nanny Wood: From Washington Belle to Portland's Grande Dame* (Bowie, MD: Heritage Books, 2003), 72.

"Horrid horrid harsh": CESW to NMS, Mar. 5, 1878, box 243(15), CESWP.

"It is very trying": CESW to Grace Howard, Dec. 25, 1878, box 2, JTGP.

Proposal in the first place: Leon, *Nanny Wood,* 53.

Packed in Baltimore: Ibid., 67–68; Robert Hamburger, *Two Rooms: The Life of Charles Er-*

skine Scott Wood* (Lincoln: University of Nebraska Press, 1998), 68.

House of Worth: Leon, *Nanny Wood,* 59; "Worth Gown Up Close," blog post, *Tweed Librarian,* June 9, 2012, available at https://tweedlibrarian .wordpress.com/2012/06/09/worth-gown-up-close/.

Madeira, champagne on ice: Leon, *Nanny Wood,* 78, 91.

Envy of other strivers: Ibid., 72–73; Hamburger, *Two Rooms,* 68.

A lucrative industry: CESW Autobiographical Notes, box 6, folder 3, CESWP.

"I hate the work": CESW to NMW, Feb. 24, 1881, box 243(20), CESWP.

"Without you now": CESW to NMW, Jan. 12, 1883, box 243(21), CESWP.

Exulted in their freedom: CESW to Mark Twain as quoted in Leon, *Nanny Wood,* 92–93.

"François is serving": CESW to NMW, Jan. 12, 1883, box 243(21), CESWP.

Montana and Wyoming: Nancy K. Anderson, *George de Forest Brush: The Indian Paintings* (Washington: National Gallery of Art, 2008), 1–2, 12–13.

"It is not necessary": George De Forest Brush, "An Artist Among the Indians," *Century* 30 (May 1885): 57.

"Fought for that": CESW, "Chief Joseph, the Nez-Percé," *Century* 28 (May 1884): 135.

"Time drags now": CESW to NMW, Jan. 12, 1883, box 243(21), CESWP.

Chapter 22: Red Moon

"She could . . . keep up": Barbara Bartlett Hartwell, "The Wood Household," OHS.

"Like all Indians": NMW, "Personal Recollections of Nanny Moale Wood, Dictated to Deane Fischer, Her Nurse and Companion" (1932), 37, HM 80474, Huntington Library.

"A bit taken aback": Ibid.

"They were reminiscing": Ibid.

"Much to my consternation": Ibid.

Entertaining Chief Joseph: "Personal Notes," *Oregonian,* Nov. 17, 1889.

An impromptu parade: Ibid.; NMW, "Personal Recollections," 37–38; Philip W. Leon, *Nanny Wood: From Washington Belle to Portland's Grande Dame* (Bowie, MD: Heritage Books, 2003), 107–8.

"He was always being compared": Hartwell, "The Wood Household."

Lay in graves: CESW, "Chief Joseph, the Nez-Percé," *Century* 28 (May 1884): 135-42; see J. Diane Pearson, *The Nez Perces in the Indian Territory: Nimiipuu Survival* (Norman: University of Oklahoma Press, 2008), 266–94. Near the start of captivity, the government counted 431 men, women, and children. John Pope to Assistant Adjutant Gen., Div. Missouri, Dec. 4, 1877, Nez Perce War, 1877, "Special Files" of Headquarters, Division of the Missouri, Relating to Military Operations and Administration, 1863–1885, RG 393, Microfilm Publication M1495, roll 5, NARA.

During their exile: Pearson, *The Nez Perces in the Indian Territory,* 178.

Lynch mobs would be waiting: Ibid., 287.

Forty miles an hour: Robert H. Ruby, "Return of the Nez Perce," *Idaho Yesterdays* 15 (Spring 1968): 12; Pearson, *The Nez Perces in the Indian Territory,* 286–88.

Leaving no children: Many Wounds Questionnaire, box 9, folder 48, LVMP; Camille Williams, "Story of the Big Hole Battle" and notes,
box 8, folder 43, LVMP; LVM, *Yellow Wolf: His
Own Story* (Caldwell, ID: Caxton Printers,
1940), 287n.

Claim to the Wallowa Valley: Pearson, *The Nez
Perces in the Indian Territory,* 277–78.

"Wild game aplenty": LVM, *Yellow Wolf,* 290.

Gibbon's traveling companions: "Famed Lake
Chelan," *Seattle Post-Intelligencer,* Oct. 4,
1889.

"A woful story": Ibid.

Promote a new policy: "Faithless Chief Joseph,"
Seattle Post-Intelligencer, Nov. 8, 1889.

"A man of integrity": *Lewiston* (ID) *Teller,* June
19, 1890.

"I feel that I owe you": OOH to CESW, Mar.
15, 1883, box 153(18), CESWP.

"Very pleasant as military duty": CESW to
OOH, June 13, 1883, box 17, folder 42, OOHP.

"To enter upon active business": CESW to
Nelson A. Miles, Dec. 11, 1883, box 235(7),
CESWP.

"To build up shattered": Ibid.

"Show[ed] a good deal": Matthew Deady, *Pharisee Among Philistines: The Diary of Judge Matthew P. Deady, 1871–1892,* 2 vols. (Portland,
OR: Oregon Historical Society, 1975), 451.

Rank in the Oregon Militia: Robert Ham-
burger, *Two Rooms: The Life of Charles Erskine
Scott Wood* (Lincoln: University of Nebraska
Press, 1998), 74, 85.

Check for the full fee: EW, "Lazard Freres: My
Father's $50,000 Fee, as Told by Charles Er-
skine Scott Wood" (privately printed by Er-

skine Wood, 1969), 1–10, OHS; EW, *Life of Charles Erskine Scott Wood* (Vancouver, WA: Rose Wind Press, 1991), 87.

"Voodt, haff you": EW, "Lazard Freres," 10.

"Fit for kings": Hartwell, "The Wood Household."

Opals and sapphires and jade: EW, *Life of Charles Erskine Scott Wood,* 52–53.

"Character and language": Ibid., 100.

"Could make himself invisible": Hamburger, *Two Rooms,* 99.

Greetings from General Gibbon: NMW, "Personal Recollections," 37–38.

Pickett's charge: Jeffrey Uecker, "Portland's Gettysburg Cyclorama: A Story of Art, Entertainment, and Memory," *Oregon Historical Quarterly* 36 (2012): 113; Chris Brenneman and Sue Boardman, *The Gettysburg Cyclorama: The Turning Point of the Civil War on Canvas* (El Dorado Hills, CA: Savas Beatie, 2015).

"Proved to him what": "Chief Joseph Here," *Oregonian,* Nov. 16, 1889.

"None of your": EW, *Life of Charles Erskine Scott Wood,* 124.

"Like a stone image": NMW, "Personal Recollections," 38.

"Not prepossessing looking": Ibid., 39.

Anger, sorrow, and resolve: CESW, "Work of Olin Warner," *Oregonian,* Nov. 17, 1901.

Straight to sleep: NMW, "Personal Recollections," 39; "Chief Joseph the Nez Perce," *Oregonian,* Nov. 12, 1889; "Chief Joseph Here," *Oregonian,* Nov. 16, 1889.

Purchased from a trading post: EW to CESW, July 27, 1892, box 2, item 89, WP; EW, Original journal and transcript, EW's notes to "Madge" relating to 1892 visit, box B, item B5, WP.

"Soup made of": EW, Original journal.

"Somewhat deep and magnetic voice": EW, "Remarks of Erskine Wood at Dedication of Chief Joseph Dam," June 12, 1956, WP.

"Heart was sick": EW, Original journal.

Gathering of mourners: Ibid.; CESW to NMW, July 10, 1892, WP. On funeral rites, see Caroline James, *Nez Perce Women in Transition, 1877–1990* (Moscow: University of Idaho Press, 1996), 92.

"Full suits": *Sixty-first Annual Report of the Commissioner of Indian Affairs to the Secretary of the Interior, 1892* (Washington: Government Printing Office, 1892), 487–88.

"The son of his old": EW, *Life of Charles Erskine Scott Wood,* 106.

Twelve-year-old boy: EW, Original journal; Sherry L. Smith, *Reimagining Indians: Native Americans Through Anglo Eyes, 1880–1940* (New York: Oxford University Press, 2000), 29 ("C.E.S. Wood, then, sent *his* son not to West Point but to the Nez Perce, his former enemy, to be trained, not in army regimentation, but in Nature's rhythms. In this way, Wood was able to bridge the gap between army and Indian, between a life of monotony and freedom, shallowness and substance, methodical route and limitless imagination, modernity and antimodernity.").

bonds were uncertain: Pearson, *The Nez Perces in the Indian Territory,* 291, 295–96.

Allotted to individual Indians: For a discussion of the policy shift by reformers toward assimilation during the late 1870s and the 1880s, see Frederick E. Hoxie, *A Final Promise: The Campaign to Assimilate the Indians, 1880–1920* (Lincoln: University of Nebraska Press, 2001), 1–39; David Wallace Adams, *Education for Extinction: American Indians and the Boarding School Experience, 1875–1928* (Lawrence: University Press of Kansas, 1995), 3–94.

Passage of his resulting bill: Joan T. Mark, *A Stranger in Her Native Land: Alice Fletcher and the American Indians* (Lincoln: University of Nebraska Press, 1988), 116–18; C. Joseph Genetin-Pilawa, *Crooked Paths to Allotment: The Fight over Federal Indian Policy After the Civil War* (Chapel Hill: University of North Carolina Press, 2012), 134–55; Nicole Tonkovich, *The Allotment Plot: Alice C. Fletcher, E. Jane Gay, and Nez Perce Survivance* (Lincoln: University of Nebraska Press, 2012); Hoxie, *Final Promise,* 24–28. On the reformers themselves, see Adams, *Education for Extinction,* 12. Cathleen D. Cahill, *Federal Fathers and Mothers: A Social History of the United States Indian Service, 1869–1933* (Chapel Hill: University of North Carolina Press, 2011), 20–33, places this policy in an era of reform and highlights the role of women in that era.

"He will have none": E. Jane Gay, *With the Nez Perces: Alice Fletcher in the Field, 1889-92,* ed. Frederick E. Hoxie and Joan T. Mark (Lincoln: University of Nebraska Press, 1981), 90.

"It was good": Ibid., 90.

"A most interesting": E. Jane Gay as quoted in Tonkovich, *Allotment Plot,* 3–4.

Allotment and moved away: Pearson, *The Nez Perces in the Indian Territory,* 296. Hoxie and

Mark, introduction to Gay, *With the Nez Perces,* xxix; Hoxie, *Final Promise,* 24–28.

"There and everywhere": NMW, "Personal Recollections," 32.

Ketchum, Idaho: EW, *Fishing* (privately printed, 1968), 15, WP; CESW to EW, July 26, 1892, box 2, item 2.88a, WP; EW, "My Journeys to Chief Joseph's Camp at Nespelem," OHS Annual Meeting, Nov. 10, 1977.

Away to stop it: EW to NMW, June 13, 1892, box 2, item 2.80, WP.

"It just fits me": EW to NMW, July 1, 1892, box 2, item 2.82, WP.

Rising and folding: EW to CESW, July 3, 1892, box 2, item 2.83, WP; EW to NMW, July 5, 1892, box 2, item 2.84, WP.

"Be careful about": CESW to EW, July 11, 1892, box 2, item 2.86, WP.

Heard of the exploit: EW, "A Wee Dash of Heliotrope," *Oregon Historical Quarterly* 75, no. 2 (June 1974): 101–3.

"The advent of": EW, *Life of Charles Erskine Scott Wood,* 102.

"Au meuniere": EW, *Fishing,* 8.

"They put the fish": EW to CESW, July 27, 1892, box 2, item 2.89, WP.

Would not shoot: EW to NMW, July 10, 1892, box 2, item 2.85, WP; EW to CESW, July 16, 1892, box 2, item 2.87, WP; EW to NMW, July 20, 1892, box 2, item 2.88, WP.

Supply the beads himself: EW to NMW, Nespelem, July 10, 1892; EW to CESW, July 16, 1892; EW to NMW, July 20, 1892.

"Many wonderful things": CESW to EW, July 11, 1892, box 2, item 2.86, WP.

Kept to himself all summer: Ibid.

"The original natives": CESW to EW, n.d. [likely about July 30, 1892], box 2, item 2.91, WP.

Nicky Mowitz: In government documents, he was known as Willie Andrews, or Nick-e-wous. "Message from the President of the United States, transmitting a communication from the Secretary of the Interior, submitting an agreement with the Indians of the Colville Reservation for the cession of a part of their lands," 52nd Cong., 1st sess., Sen. Ex. Doc. 15, Serial Set 2892 (Jan. 6, 1892), 16, 23.

Another woman — pregnant: EW, "My Journeys to Chief Joseph's Camp at Nespelem."

Oozing since 1877: EW, Original journal.

Head-to-toe in buckskin: EW to CESW, Aug. 6, 1892, box 2, item 2.94, WP.

Next to the teepee: EW to CESW, Sept. 10, 1892, box 2, item 2.99, WP.

"Many of the accessories": Erskine Wood, "Diary of a Fourteen Year Old Boy's Days with Chief Joseph," *Oregon Historical Quarterly* 51, no. 2 (June 1950): 73.

Read and write, eat and sleep: EW, "A Boy's Visit to Chief Joseph," *St. Nicholas* 20 (Sept. 1893): 815–19; EW, Original journal; EW, "My Journeys."

Gray wings and bright colors: EW to CESW, July 16, 27, 1892, box 2, items 2.87, 2.89, WP.

Borrowed shotgun: Ibid.; EW, "A Boy's Visit to Chief Joseph."

Braid rawhide ropes: EW to CESW, Aug. 20, 1892, box 2, item 2.97, WP.

"As good as anybody": EW to CESW, Aug. 10, 1892, box 2, item 2.95, WP.

"Whenever I learn": EW to NMW, July 30,

1892, box 2, item 2.90, WP.

Errand to a nearby store: EW, "A Boy's Visit to Chief Joseph"; EW to CESW, Aug. 20, 1892, box 2, item 2.97, WP; EW to NMW, Aug. 20, 1892, WP; EW, "My Journeys."

"A small old Indian": EW, Original journal.

Favorite horses to the finish: Ibid.; EW, "A Boy's Visit to Chief Joseph."

"Just riding down to be": EW, Original journal.

Had ever happened to him: EW, "A Boy's Visit to Chief Joseph."

"We used to have": EW, Original journal.

Welcome her back a month later: EW to CESW, Aug. 10, 1892, box 2, item 2.95, WP. For more on hops picking, see Paige Raibmon, *Authentic Indians: Episodes of Encounter from the Late-Nineteenth-Century Northwest Coast* (Durham: Duke University Press, 2005), 74–97.

Return with the baby: EW, "My Journeys."

"As soft as": EW to NMW, Oct. 15, 1892, box 3, item 3.2, WP.

Breathing together and apart: EW, "My Journeys."

Red Moon: Ibid. Erskine Wood wrote that his Nez Perce names were "Suyapoo Hatswul" (in his translation, "the White Boy") and "Wellim Sumka" ("Buckskin Shirt"). His father told Nanny that Erskine was also given the name "the red moon." EW to CESW, Sept. 20, 1892, box 3, item 3.1, WP; CESW to NMW, Nov. 6, 1892, box 3, item 3.3, WP.

"You can stay": CESW to EW, Sept. 7, 1892, box 2, item 2.98, WP.

"Joseph was afraid": EW to NMW, Oct. 15, 1892, box 3, item 3.2, WP.

"I am getting": Ibid.

Return the next summer: EW to NMW, Nov. 7, 1892, box 3, item 3.4, WP.

"He would do for": CESW to NMW, Nov. 6, 1892, box 3, item 3.3, WP.

So much as his mother: Ibid.

"Just now at Plymouth Rock": CESW, Thanksgiving reminiscence, Nov. 1892, box 3, item 3.5, WP.

Cut his hair short: CESW to NMW, Nov. 6, 1892, box 3, item 3.3, WP.

"An army of doctors": CESW, Thanksgiving reminiscence, Nov. 1892, box 3, item 3.5, WP.

Pumpkin pie for dessert: Ibid.

Chapter 23: A Glorious Era

Keep his wind: OOH, *Fighting for Humanity* (New York: F. T. Neely, 1886), 202–10.

"Heaped": Ibid., 210.

His nation's future: Ibid.

"The youth of the mountains": OOH, *Autobiography of Oliver Otis Howard,* 2 vols. (New York: Baker & Taylor, 1908), 2:568–69.

"I have asked": "Mission of General Howard," *New York Tribune,* May 13, 1898.

Capitol to the White House: OOH, *Autobiography* 2:574.

"Christian warfare": Howard, *Fighting for Humanity,* 8.

Inspire the men, and evangelize: Ibid., 46.

"He died for me": Ibid., 27.

"My sins were blotted": Ibid., 45.

"The most effective weapon": Ibid., 46.

"The very incarnation": Ibid., 28.

"For the old flag": Ibid., 29.

"How glad I am": Ibid., 37.

Men and women every few days: Edward L. Ayers, *The Promise of the New South: Life After Reconstruction* (New York: Oxford University Press, 1992), 156–59; see also David S. Cecelski and Timothy B. Tyson, eds., *Democracy Betrayed: The Wilmington Race Riot of 1898 and Its Legacy* (Chapel Hill: UNC Press, 1998).

"Thank God": OOH, *Fighting for Humanity,* 29; see also David W. Blight, *Race and Reunion: The Civil War in American Memory* (Cambridge, MA: Harvard University Press, 2001), 352–53.

"That it required": OOH, *Fighting for Humanity,* 28.

"A mere machine": OOH, *Autobiography,* 2:203.

"With Porto Rico": "Die Cast," *Cincinnati Enquirer,* Dec. 18, 1898.

"A vast illuminated": OOH, *Fighting for Humanity,* 75–76.

Invasion fleet: Ibid.

"Working grandly to root out": Ibid., 83.

"Cleans the city": Ibid., 96–101.

"Evidently worn": Ibid., 96.

"World will rejoice": Ibid., 101.

"Abundant swarms": Ibid., 140–41.

Fighting north of Manila: See Michael E. Shay, ed., *A Civilian in Lawton's 1899 Philippine Campaign: The Letters of Robert D. Carter* (Columbia: University of Missouri Press, 2013). Howard's fourth son John served three tours in the Philippines.

"The equipment and welfare": OOH, *Fighting for Humanity,* 185.

"I do not think": OOH, *Autobiography* 2:574.

Dying within moments: "General Howard's

Son Killed," *New York Tribune,* Oct. 29, 1899.

"This is the heaviest": OOH, *Autobiography* 2:573.

Son's last words to heart: "Lieut.-Colonel Guy Howard," *Vermonter* 5 (Jan. 1900): 8, 10; "General Howard's Son Killed."

"Whatever happens keep": "General Howard's Son Killed."

"This talk about": "Gen. Howard for the War," *New York Trib*une, Aug. 22, 1900.

The *Belgian King:* "General Howard's Son," *Cincinnati Enquirer,* Nov. 24, 1899; "Funeral of Captain Howard," *San Francisco Chronicle,* Oct. 26, 1899.

"None of us": "Gen. Howard for the War."

"Should remain part": "Merchants to the Front," *New York Tribune,* Sept. 14, 1900.

"What Providence has": "Mission of the United States Is to Christianize Philippines, Says General Howard," *Cincinnati Enquirer,* Mar. 26, 1906.

"Some of our best": "Gen. Howard Moves Men," *Chicago Tribune,* Sept. 21, 1900.

"Shall that blood": "Merchants to the Front," *New York Tribune,* Sept. 14, 1900.

Blasting American "imperialism": "Bryan Speech at Baker City," *Spokane Spokesman-Review,* Oct. 7, 1900.

Answers for Wood: See also Walter L. Williams, "United States Indian Policy and the Debate over Philippine Annexation: Implications for the Origins of American Imperialism," *Journal of American History* 66 (Mar. 1980): 810–31.

"The rights of sovereignty": William McKinley, Executive Order, Dec. 21, 1898, in *A Compilation of the Messages and Papers of the*

Presidents, new ser. (New York: Bureau of National Literature, 1909), 14:6581–83.

"To leave the government": 30 Stat. 738-9 (Apr. 20, 1898).

Oregon for the Democrats: CESW, "Imperialism vs. Democracy. An Address Delivered at the Jefferson Birthday Dinner," April 13, 1899, in *Pacific Monthly* 2 (1899): 63.

"By what rule": Ibid., 62–63.

"Can we have": "Perplexities of Antis," *Oregonian,* July 16, 1900.

"How Success Is Won": "How Success Is Won," *Oregonian,* Apr. 7, 1899.

"An enchantment": Barbara Bartlett Hartwell, "The Wood Household," OHS.

Swedish second maid: NMW, "Personal Recollections of Nanny Moale Wood, Dictated to Deane Fischer, Her Nurse and Companion" (1932), 30, HM 80474, Huntington Library.

"Men . . . who agree": Frances A. Groff, "Western Personalities," *Sunset* 28 (1912): 234.

"The stiff starched": EW, *Life of Charles Erskine Scott Wood* (Vancouver, WA: Rose Wind Press, 1991), 53.

"Looked like some": CESW, "Democratic Democracy," March 1, 1902 in *Public,* March 8, 1902.

He could shed: When his son Erskine went to Harvard in 1897, Wood sent him twenty-seven typed pages of advice, including a lengthy discourse on love and marriage that urged him to adhere to conventional morality and "keep your sexual desire down by good, hard work and study," while acknowledging that other paths existed besides "sexual restraint enforced by what I may call artificial morals," starting with "the life of nature" led by "man and woman in savage life." CESW to EW, April 24, 1897, box 7, Charles E. S. Wood Papers, Bancroft Library, University of California, Berkeley. See also Sherry L. Smith, *Reimagining Indians: Native Americans Through Anglo Eyes, 1880–1940* (Oxford: Oxford University Press, 2000), 37.

"I am sure": EW, *Life of Charles Erskine Scott Wood,* 122.

His speeches and lectures: E.g., "How Success Is Won," *Oregonian,* Apr. 7, 1899 ("Judicious"); "Trained Nurses," *Oregonian,* Nov. 7, 1893 (describing Wood's address as "an eloquent effort, full of good thoughts, sound common sense and friendly advice"); "Eloquent Address," *Oregonian,* June 4, 1893 (praising the "brilliancy and originality" of Wood's speech, delivered on Memorial Day).

"Anti" and "pretentious": "They Oppose Expansion," *Oregonian,* Dec. 10, 1899.

"Tangle-haired orator": "Note of Discord," *Oregonian,* Jan. 10, 1904.

"Warm advocate": "Hits His Own Party," *Oregonian,* May 28, 1902.

Loose grip on the facts: "Some Inaccuracies," *Oregonian,* Apr. 26, 1899.

"A vote against retention": "Work to Do," *Oregonian,* May 15, 1902.

"As for myself": CESW, "Democratic Democracy."

"Peace and right without": "Warm Debate in Socialist Hall," *Oregonian,* Nov. 26, 1906; "Says Anarchism Means Freedom," *Oregonian,* May 24, 1908; "Wood Denounces Y.M.C.A.

Directors," *Oregonian,* May 25, 1908.

Kitty Seaman Beck's apartment: "Says Anarchism Means Freedom," *Oregonian,* May 24, 1908.

"Passionate yearning": Emma Goldman, "On the Trail," *Mother Earth* 9 (1914): 227–28, microfilm, roll 8, Emma Goldman Papers, University of California, Berkeley.

"Anarchy, socialism": "Petronius Arbiter," *Oregonian,* Nov. 27, 1906.

"An Asiatic population": CESW, "Imperialism vs. Democracy," 57.

"Is it time": Ibid., 66.

"Joseph cannot accuse": CESW to Moorfield Storey, May 27, 1895, in *Oregon Inn-Side News* 1, no. 6 (Nov.–Dec. 1947), CESWP.

"Though the Indian": CESW, "Some Phases of Our National Life," *Pacific Monthly* 1 (March 1899): 238.

During the long chase: Smith, *Reimagining Indians,* 34.

"The firm expectation": CESW to Edmond S. Meany, July 23, 1900, box 18, folder 4, ESMP.

"Stands infinitely below": "Gov. Roosevelt Given an Ovation in Chicago," *Seattle Post-Intelligencer,* Oct. 7, 1900; "The Progress of the Campaign," *Harper's Weekly,* Oct. 20, 1900.

"Imperialism vs. Democracy": CESW, "Imperialism vs. Democracy," 67.

"Frightful," "wearisome": James McLaughlin, *My Friend the Indian* (Boston: Houghton Mifflin, 1910), 350, 361.

"Wretchedly bad": McLaughlin to Secretary of the Interior, June 23, 1900, box 18, folder 2, ESMP.

Deeply familiar to Joseph: Ibid.; McLaughlin,

My Friend the Indian, 350–51, 361.

"He warmed to": McLaughlin, *My Friend the Indian,* 351.

Large black patch: Phillip Andrews in *Memorial of the Nez Perce Indians Residing in the State of Idaho to the Congress of the United States, Together with Affidavits, and Also Copies of Various Treaties Between the United States and the Nez Perce Indians* (Washington: Government Printing Office, 1911), 105.

Back together again: McLaughlin, *My Friend the Indian,* 350.

"Blooms as the rose": Ibid., 346, 366.

"The man had": Ibid., 345.

Land in the Wallowa Valley: "Nez Perces Appeal for Land," *Washington Post,* Apr. 17, 1897.

"Say positively that": "No Lands for Chief Joseph and His Band," *San Francisco Chronicle,* Apr. 18, 1897.

War songs: Loran Olsen, *Guide to the Nez Perce Music Archive: An Annotated Listing of Songs and Musical Selections Spanning the Period 1897–1974* (Pullman: Washington State University School of Music and Theatre Arts, 1989), 8.

"In full Indian toggery": "Chief Joseph's Drink," *Hartford Courant,* Apr. 30, 1897.

"Twenty long years": "Letters to the Editor: Justice to Chief Joseph," *New York Tribune,* May 5, 1897.

"Ask the government": Joseph to Edmond S. Meany, June 23, 1901, box 9, folder 18, ESMP.

Settlers a generation before: "Wants His Hunting Ground," *Enterprise Chieftain* in *Oregonian,* Aug. 14, 1899; J. H. Horner to LVM, Feb. 7, 1943, box 13, folder 93, LVMP.

"That this country": "Wants His Hunting Ground."

"Considerable sport": Ibid.

"To use his influence": "Indians See General Miles," *Washington Times,* Apr. 6, 1900.

"For the purpose of": *Annual Reports of the Department of the Interior for the Fiscal Year Ended June 30, 1900: Indian Affairs* (Washington: Government Printing Office, 1900), 176–77.

"There is grave": McLaughlin, *My Friend the Indian,* 346.

"The game ha[d] almost": McLaughlin to Secretary of the Interior, June 23, 1900, box 18, folder 2, ESMP.

"That he was ready": Andrews in *Memorial of the Nez Perce Indians,* 105.

"It is preposterous": "Joseph Not Wanted," *Enterprise Bulletin,* in *Lewiston* (ID) *Teller,* June 25, 1900.

"Should the Indians": McLaughlin to Secretary of the Interior, June 23, 1900, box 18, folder 2, ESMP.

"If I could remain": McLaughlin, *My Friend the Indian,* 362.

"Anywhere in northeastern": McLaughlin to Secretary of the Interior, June 23, 1900, box 18, folder 2, ESMP.

"There are many white": Joseph to Edmond S. Meany, Aug. 24, 1900, box 9, folder 18, ESMP.

Nearby Baker City: Grace Butterfield, "Old Chief Joseph's Grave, *Oregon Historical Quarterly* 46, no. 1 (Mar. 1945): 70–73; Alvin M. Josephy Jr., *The Nez Perce Indians and the Opening of the Northwest* (New Haven: Yale

University Press, 1965), 449n4; J. H. Horner to LVM, Jan. 2, 1927, box 10, folder 58, LVMP.

"The heart of Joseph": McLaughlin, *My Friend the Indian,* 366.

"When I die": Joseph to Edmond S. Meany, Aug. 24, 1900, box 9, folder 18, ESMP.

Chapter 24: Swing Low

To survive what followed: John D. McDermott, *Forlorn Hope: The Battle of White Bird Canyon and the Beginning of the Nez Perce War* (Boise: Idaho State Historical Society, 1978), 162.

More than $33.50: Meany Notebook, box 85, folder 6, ESMP.

"Miserable Cayuse fiends": George Frykman, *Seattle's Historian and Promoter: The Life of Edmond Stephen Meany* (Pullman: Washington State University, 1998), 78.

Leading minds of the day: Ibid., 89. For example, Reuben Gold Thwaites, political economist Richard T. Ely, Charles Homer Haskins, and Jesse Macy.

"To examine all": Edmond Stephen Meany, "Chief Joseph, the Nez Perce" (master's thesis, University of Wisconsin, 1901), ii.

"The stages of savagery": Frykman, *Seattle's Historian and Promoter* 90 (quoting "The Liberty and Free Soil Parties," a term paper Meany wrote at the University of Wisconsin in the summer of 1899); Robert R. McCoy, *Chief Joseph, Yellow Wolf, and the Creation of Nez Perce History in the Pacific Northwest* (New York: Routledge, 2004), 61–68, 153–54.

"The buffalo trail": Frederick Jackson Turner, "The Significance of the Frontier in American History" (1893) in *The Frontier in American His-*

tory (New York: Henry Holt, 1921), 14. See also Ellen Fitzpatrick, *History's Memory: Writing America's Past, 1880–1980* (Cambridge, MA: Harvard University Press, 2002).

Northwest in the 1850s: Frykman, *Seattle's Historian and Promoter,* 82–84.

"Discard [their] conception": Frederick Jackson Turner, "The Significance of History," *Wisconsin Journal of Education* 21 (1891): 230, 233. See also Fitzpatrick, *History's Memory,* 48–50.

"Wherever there remains": Turner, "The Significance of History," 234.

"Saw his characters": Frederick Jackson Turner, *Reuben Gold Thwaites: A Memorial Address* (Madison: State Historical Society of Wisconsin, 1914), 30–31, 39, 41.

"A constant stream of prospectors": Meany, "Chief Joseph, the Nez Perce," 45.

Nez Perce pony herds: Ibid., 45.

"Model appearance of neatness": Ibid., iii, 48.

"All the work": Ibid., 50.

"Always wanted to go": Meany Notebook, box 85, folder 6, ESMP.

"Where his men and women": Ibid.

Piece of paper: Ibid.

"The principal ones": Ibid.

"A friend whose wife": Ibid.

Outsider with unclear motives: Ibid.

"The methods employed": Meany, "Chief Joseph, the Nez Perce," 8.

Killing women and children: Ibid., 31–32.

"He often visits": Ibid., 48–49.

"Now quite scarce": Ibid., 48.

Mementoes and keepsakes: Ibid., 48–49.

"Considers his father": Meany Notebook, box

85, folder 6, ESMP.

"He knew each face": Meany, "Chief Joseph, the Nez Perce," 48–49.

"He seems especially": Ibid., 51.

"For Chief Joseph": Meany Notebook, box 85, folder 6, ESMP.

"Quiet life": Meany, "Chief Joseph, the Nez Perce," iii, 51.

Members of Congress: "Chief Joseph in the City," *Evening Star,* Jan. 29, 1904.

"The President greeted": "President Greeted Joseph of Nez Perces," *Washington Times,* Feb. 26, 1904.

"Determined persistency": "Chief Joseph Still Hopes to Return to Willowa," *Lewiston* (ID) *Teller,* Jan. 6, 1904.

Wallowa Valley for his people: Ibid.

Luncheon in Joseph's honor: "Gen. Miles Entertains Chief Joseph," *New York Times,* Feb. 22, 1903.

Sit for a life cast: "Indians in Full Dress," *Washington Post,* Feb. 15, 1903.

"Twenty thrilling": "Productions for This Week," *New York Times,* Sept. 20, 1903.

Cheers for the chief: "Shadow Catcher," *Seattle Post-Intelligencer,* Nov. 21, 1903.

"I have made": "Speech of Chief Joseph," enclosed in Henry M. Steele to Edmond S. Meany, Jan. 10, 1904, box 85, folder 1, ESMP.

Home in Vermont: OOH to H. S. Howard, Feb. 16, 1904, box 38, folder 34 OOHP; L. Clark Seelye to OOH, Feb. 16, 1904, box 38, folder 34, OOHP.

"A full fair": R. H. Pratt, *Battlefield and Classroom* (New Haven: Yale University Press, 1964), 214. See also David Wallace Adams,

Education for Extinction: American Indians and the Boarding School Experience, 1875–1928 (Lawrence: University Press of Kansas, 1995), 62–64, 97–103, 168–69, 321–26.

Carpenters, and harness makers: For an extensive study of education as part of the policy of assimilation, see Adams, *Education for Extinction,* and for the specific aims of education, see 21–24, 108–9, 137, 149, 170–71. For discussions of student experiences and resistance, see also K. Tsianina Lomawaima, *They Called It Prairie Light: The Story of Chilocco Indian School* (Lincoln: University of Nebraska Press, 1994); Brenda Child, *Boarding School Seasons: American Indian Families, 1900–1940* (Lincoln: University of Nebraska Press, 1999); Matthew Gilbert, *Education Beyond the Mesas: Hopi Students at Sherman Institute, 1902–1929* (Lincoln: University of Nebraska Press, 2010).

"All the Indian": R. H. Pratt, "The Advantages of Mingling Indians with Whites," *Proceedings of the National Conference of Charities and Correction* 19 (Boston: Geo. H. Ellis, 1892), 46.

"Be made to feel": Pratt, *Battlefield and Classroom,* 266.

"Common-sense method": Ibid., 268.

"It does not seem": OOH, *My Life and Experiences Among Our Hostile Indians* (Hartford, CT: A. D. Worthington, 1907), 569.

Just west of Portland: On Wilkinson and Pratt cooperating, see Pratt, *Battlefield and Classroom,* 285. Wilkinson eventually rejoined the active duty military and at age sixty-five, in October 1898, was killed fighting Pillager Ojibwes by Leech Lake, Minnesota, in what became known as the Battle of Sugar Point. "Bacon's Men at Bay," *St. Paul Globe,* Oct. 7, 1898; "Crack of Guns Could Still Be Heard," *Cincinnati Enquirer,* Oct. 7, 1898.

Missionary efforts with Indians: *Twenty-Fifth Annual Report of the American Missionary Association* (New York: AMA, 1871), 10.

"That living veteran": Theodore Roosevelt to Powell Clayton, Feb. 19, 1904, enclosure in OOH to Porfirio Díaz, Feb. 18, 1904, box 38, folder 34, OOHP.

Organize his funeral services: OOH, *Autobiography of Oliver Otis Howard,* 2 vols. (New York: Baker & Taylor, 1908), 2:553.

"It . . . ought to be": Pratt to OOH, Jan. 19, Feb. 9, 1904, box 38, folder 34, OOHP.

Department of the Columbia onward: Both, for example, participated in the Lake Mohonk Conference of Friends of the Indian. See Isabel C. Barrows, ed., *Proceedings of the Thirteenth Annual Meeting of the Lake Mohonk Conference, 1895* (N.p.: Lake Mohonk Conference, 1896), 70–72.

"To train up English": Richard Dauenhauer, "Two Missions to Alaska," *Pacific Historian* 26 (1982): 29–41.

"But paused almost": "Joseph Meets Old Foes," *New York Times,* Apr. 27, 1897.

"But did not smile": H. S. Howard to LVM, Aug. 25, 1933, box 6, folder 29, LVMP.

They shared a meal: "A Meeting of Former Foes," *Red Man and Helper,* Mar. 18, 1904.

American family: "Commencement at Carlisle," *Washington Post,* Feb. 19, 1904.

"Uncertain" and "feelingly referred": Ibid.

"A majority": "A Meeting of Former Foes."

"The Indians rebelled": Ibid.

"Nothing is ever": "Commencement at Carlisle," *Washington Post,* Feb. 19, 1904.

"Joseph would not": "A Meeting of Former Foes."

Citizenship and absorption: See Adams, *Education for Extinction.*

"He had fixed": *Red Man and Helper,* Feb. 26, Mar. 4, 1904.

"I always regarded": "A Meeting of Former Foes."

"I . . . am glad": *Red Man and Helper,* Feb. 26, Mar. 4, 1904.

"Friends, I meet here": "A Meeting of Former Foes."

"I understand and I know": Ibid. For a comparison of Joseph's remarks to those of other Native American leaders at Carlisle, see Adams, *Education for Extinction,* 248–49.

"Not always has Chief Joseph": "A Meeting of Former Foes."

Seven thousand acres of the Wallowa Valley: Copied at the bottom of OOH to OOH Jr., Feb. 18, 1904, box 38, folder 34, OOHP.

Set of endorsements, too: R. H. Pratt to OOH, Feb. 22, 1904, box 38, folder 34, OOHP.

"I have an indistinct recollection": Orville H. Platt to OOH, Feb. 29, 1904, box 38, folder 34, OOHP.

Geronimo and Red Cloud: "Chief Joseph Here," *St. Paul Globe,* Apr. 30, 1904; "Miss Roosevelt Calls" and "God of Thunder Angry at Fair," *St. Louis Republic,* June 4, 1904.

"A bent form": As quoted in M. Gidley, *Kopet: A Documentary Narrative of Chief Joseph's Last Years* (Seattle: University of Washington Press,

1981), 67.

"He looked thin": *Annual Reports of the Department of the Interior for the Fiscal Year Ended June 30, 1904: Indian Affairs* (Washington: Government Printing Office, 1904), 123.

Alone in his teepee: Henry M. Steele to Edmond S. Meany, Sept. 26, 1904, in Gidley, *Kopet,* 64.

"The Napoleon of Indians": "Chief Joseph, the Noblest Indian of Them All, the Washington of His People," *New York Times,* Sept. 25, 1904; "Chief Joseph Dead," *New York Times,* Sept. 24, 1904,

"A composite of all": "Chief Joseph's 1500-Mile Fight with Four Generals," *San Francisco Chronicle,* Oct. 30, 1904.

"Joseph is dead": Yellow Bull, Speech, box 85, folder 1, ESMP.

"Perhaps he was not": Quoted in Gidley, *Kopet,* 69.

"Personal observations": OOH, *My Life and Experiences Among Our Hostile Indians* (Hartford, CT: A. D. Worthington, 1907).

"The Great War Chief Joseph": OOH, *Famous Indian Chiefs I Have Known* (New York: Century, 1908), 184.

"Nez Perces campaign": OOH, *Autobiography of Oliver Otis Howard,* 2 vols. (New York: Baker & Taylor, 1908), 2:474–75.

"Earliest knowledge of Indians": OOH, *My Life,* 567–68.

"Exterminate them": Ibid., 568, 570.

"A slow process": Ibid., 570.

Sermon at the YMCA: Harry S. Howard, "Last Days of General O. O. Howard," Oct. 13, 1950, OOHP-LMU.

Had ever lived anywhere: "Another Dormitory," *Burlington Weekly Free Press,* May 25, 1911.

Indian artifacts: Several pieces that Howard collected were auctioned in 2011. See http://www.cowanauctions.com.

A decade earlier in 1899: "Mrs. O. O. Howard," *Burlington Weekly Free Press,* Aug. 3, 1911.

Autumn in the Northwest: "Gen. Howard Died Without Warning," *Burlington Weekly Free Press,* Oct. 28, 1909.

"Get him well": Howard, "Last Days of General O. O. Howard."

Awakening them to their "Better Selves": Sue E. Howard to R. L. Kincaid, Oct. 14, 1950, OOHP-LMU.

Silently at his side: John A. Carpenter, *Sword and Olive Branch: Oliver Otis Howard* (Pittsburgh, PA: University of Pittsburgh Press, 1964), 298–99; "Gen. Howard Died Without Warning"; Sue E. Howard to R. L. Kincaid, Oct. 14, 1950, OOHP-LMU; Howard, "Last Days of General O. O. Howard."

Epilogue

He could barely see: CESW to Leo V. Silverstein, Jan. 22, 1943, box 37(7), CESWP; Richard Docter, "The West's First College for Officer Training," *New Frontier* 28, no. 11 (June 13, 2010), http://www.usw.salvationarmy.org/usw/www_newfrontierpub.nsf/a602303c3fd52b9888256e3f007b7de6/a2a6e0611e7bdc1288257743006f1afc?OpenDocument; Susan Dinkelspiel Cerny, *An Architectural Guidebook to San Francisco and the Bay Area* (Layton, UT: Gibbs Smith, 2007), 92.

"The oldest living": CESW to Leo V. Silverstein, Jan. 22, 1943, box 37(7), CESWP.

Argue one last case: Ibid.

"Oriental objets d'art": Ibid.

"Au revoir": T. Z. Shiota to San Franciscans and Friend Customers, March 26, 1942, as captured in the photograph by Dorothea Lange, "San Francisco, California. Farewell Letter Posted in Show Window of T. Z. Shiota" (April 1942).

"Aide-de-camp to General Howard": CESW to Leo V. Silverstein, Jan. 22, 1943, box 37(7), CESWP.

Status as Americans: Hiroshi Motomura, *Americans in Waiting: The Lost Story of Immigration and Citizenship in the United States* (New York: Oxford University Press, 2006), 145.

Citizen back then: CESW to Leo V. Silverstein, Jan. 22, 1943, box 37(7), CESWP.

"Fairly accurate guess": Ibid.

"The era in which": Ibid.

Publicly lamenting: Robert Hamburger, *Two Rooms: The Life of Charles Erskine Scott Wood* (Lincoln: University of Nebraska Press, 1998), 196–97, 207.

"Fellow workers": *Equi v. United States,* 261 F. 53, 54 (9th Cir. 1919).

"A very temperate": CESW, *Too Much Government* (New York: Vanguard Press, 1931), 10.

Among the first targets: Hamburger, *Two Rooms,* 328.

"Throttl[ing] . . . freedom": CESW, *Too Much Government,* 6.

"Equal freedom": Ibid., 14.

"Things — things — things": EW, *Life of*

Charles Erskine Scott Wood (Vancouver, WA: Rose Wind Press, 1991), 131.

Lived with her still: Ibid., 132.

Love and art: Hamburger, *Two Rooms,* 301–5.

Talking about Chief Joseph: For a discussion of Wood's long engagement with Chief Joseph, see Sherry L. Smith, *Reimagining Indians: Native Americans Through Anglo Eyes, 1880–1940* (New York: Oxford University Press, 2000), 30–44.

"Was practically the greatest": Joseph Esherick, "An Architectural Practice in the San Francisco Bay Area, 1938–1996," an oral history conducted in 1994–96 by Suzanne B. Riess, Regional Oral History Office, Bancroft Library, University of California, Berkeley, 1996, 95.

"In my youth": CESW Autobiographical Notes Prepared for Max Hayek, box 6(2), CESWP.

"I wish Mr. Shiota": CESW to Leo V. Silverstein, Jan. 22, 1943, box 37(7), CESWP.

Demand a rehearing: Ibid. T. Z. Shiota died while in custody on Jan. 12, 1944; see "Poston Camp Updates: Preservation Project," Poston Restoration Project, Lafayette, CA, http:// postonupdates.blogspot.com/2011/11/issei -paroled-from-nm-doj-camps-to.html.

"The perfect symmetry": Susan Lord Currier, "Some Aspects of Washington Hop-Fields," *Overland Monthly and Out West Magazine* 32 (Dec. 1898): 541.

Seattle for the harvest: "Hops Pickers in Demand," *Seattle Post-Intelligencer,* Sept. 17, 1895.

"Escape from the irksomeness": Currier,

"Some Aspects of Washington Hop-Fields," 543.

Grant's Tomb: "Judge Reuben Visits," *Pullman Herald,* Nov. 27, 1897.

Near the Dalles: Charles F. Luce and William Johnson, "The Beginning of Modern Tribal Governance and Enacting Sovereignty," in *Wiyaxayxt/Wiyaakaa'awn/As Days Go By: Our History, Our Land, Our People — The Cayuse, Umatilla, and Walla Walla,* ed. Jennifer Karson (Seattle: University of Washington Press, 2015).

"Indian pony races": "Wayside Gleanings," *Dalles Daily Chronicle,* Sept. 21, 1897.

Ravaged by tuberculosis: See, e.g., Statement of Dr. J. A. Murphy, Medical Supervisor, Indian Bureau, in *Indian Appropriation Bill: Hearings Before a Subcommittee of the Committee on Indian Affairs, 1913* (Washington: Government Printing Office, 1914), 105 (estimating one-third of the total population of the Colville reservation was suffering from tuberculosis).

Than were born: Steven Ross Evans, *Voice of the Old Wolf: Lucullus Virgil McWhorter and the Nez Perce Indians* (Pullman: Washington State University Press, 1996).

Did not reach adulthood: Ibid., 145.

Had no water: LVM, *Yellow Wolf,* 14.

Sale and settlement: Evans, *Voice of the Old Wolf,* 22–23.

Bank that failed: Ibid., 39.

Reservation too often: See, e.g., *Annual Reports of the Department of the Interior for the Fiscal Year Ended June 30, 1898: Indian Affairs* (Washington: Government Printing Office, 1898), 298.

Apricots to sell: Currier, "Some Aspects of

Washington Hop-Fields," 544.

"Hard cases": "Report of Agent for Yakima Agency," in *Annual Reports of the Department of the Interior for the Fiscal Year Ended June 30, 1901: Indian Affairs* (Washington: Government Printing Office, 1902), 395.

Water to whites: Evans, *Voice of the Old Wolf,* 2–3.

To be near Indians: Ibid.,7.

"Strikingly strong": LVM, *Yellow Wolf: His Own Story* (Caldwell, ID: Caxton Printers, 1940), 13–14.

"Tragedy . . . written": Ibid., 14.

"War-day fighting": Ibid., 290.

Never threw it away: Yellow Wolf to LVM, June 9, 1909, box 6, folder 26, LVMP.

Perhaps they should: LVM, *Yellow Wolf,* 290.

"I am going": Ibid., 20–21.

McWhorter took notes: Ibid., 52–53.

Film studios, and collectors: Evans, *Voice of the Old Wolf,* 76–77.

Fund the work: Ibid., 112.

"It all comes back": LVM, *Yellow Wolf,* 112.

"Ghastly": Ibid., 131.

"As if comprehending": Ibid., 122.

"Nobody to help": Ibid., 291.

"White people, aided": Ibid., 18.

"If people do not": Ibid.

ILLUSTRATION CREDITS

Part-Opener Images

p. 43: Wallowa Valley, 2013, photograph by Daniel J. Sharfstein.

p. 255: Yellowstone backcountry, 2013, photograph by Daniel J. Sharfstein.

p. 549: The view from Fort Spokane, 2014, photograph by Daniel J. Sharfstein.

ABOUT THE AUTHOR

Daniel J. Sharfstein is a professor of law and history at Vanderbilt University and a 2013 Guggenheim Fellow. His first book, *The Invisible Line: A Secret History of Race in America*, received the J. Anthony Lukas Prize. He lives in Nashville.

The employees of Thorndike Press hope you have enjoyed this Large Print book. All our Thorndike, Wheeler, and Kennebec Large Print titles are designed for easy reading, and all our books are made to last. Other Thorndike Press Large Print books are available at your library, through selected bookstores, or directly from us.

For information about titles, please call:
(800) 223-1244

or visit our website at:
gale.com/thorndike

To share your comments, please write:
Publisher
Thorndike Press
10 Water St., Suite 310
Waterville, ME 04901